# Economics

## of the

# Public Sector

SARA CONNOLLY

ALISTAIR MUNRO

**FT** Prentice Hall
FINANCIAL TIMES

*An imprint of* **Pearson Education**

Harlow, England • London • New York • Boston • San Francisco • Toronto
Sydney • Tokyo • Singapore • Hong Kong • Seoul • Taipei • New Delhi
Cape Town • Madrid • Mexico City • Amsterdam • Munich • Paris • Milan

**Pearson Education Limited**
Edinburgh Gate
Harlow
Essex CM20 2JE
England

and Associated Companies throughout the world

*Visit us on the World Wide Web at:*
http://www.pearsoneduc.com

First published 1999 by
Prentice Hall Europe

Typeset in 9½/12 pt Merdian
by Dorwyn Ltd, Rowlands Castle, Hants

Printed and bound in Great Britain by
Ashford Colour Press Ltd, Gosport, Hampshire

Library of Congress Cataloging-in-Publication Data

Available from the publisher

British Library Cataloguing in Publication Data

A catalogue record for this book is available from
the British Library

ISBN: 0-13-096641-X

10  9  8  7  6  5  4
07  06  05  04  03

To our parents

# Contents

# Preface

In most academic texts, the preface is the place where the authors explain why they were driven to write the book (despite little chance of enrichment), say a little about its target audience and how teachers might use it and then thank all the people who have aided its genesis. Our preface does not deviate from this pattern. Like most tyro authors we wrote a textbook because of our dissatisfaction with the available options. In our case, we wished for a book that was up-to-date in scope and in its treatment of public policy issues, but at the same time firmly grounded in microeconomic theory. Also on our wish list was a text which covered all aspects of government activity: expenditure as well as taxation, regulation in addition to redistribution; private goods as well as public. This book is the result.

Our main constituency is likely to be undergraduates who, having done a unit in principles of microeconomics, wish to see how these principles can be applied to understanding the actions of governments. As such, the book presumes some familiarity with most of the basic instruments of the microeconomist's toolkit. There is calculus in a small number of places where its use is most valuable, yet students with an interest in the economics of public policy, but with backgrounds other than honours economics should also be able to navigate much of the text. Pedagogically, the book is designed to be a stepping stone between the student-friendly texts of introductory and intermediate economic theory and more specialist sources of enlightenment. It has definitions in the margin, review questions, summaries etc., but since it covers such a wide range of issues it is not designed to be self-contained. Rather we envision readers using the text to understand the core information on each topic, so that they can then delve more successfully into the specialist reading given at the end of each chapter.

Although we have endeavoured to cover each of the main aspects of the subject, we have not tried to be comprehensive, preferring instead to provide more detail on linked issues (such as poverty and social policy) rather than skimming over everything. The choice of topics is partly motivated by personal inclination and partly by what we believe to be important and topical. We have therefore included areas such as the environment, healthcare and pensions, but like most textbooks post-Musgrave, there is little macroeconomics. We have also largely omitted urban and regional issues, such as housing, crime, transport and industrial policy. Some ancillary material, including self-assessed multiple choice quizzes and updates can be found at the website for the book, the address for which is given below.

The book has been divided into five sections, partly to emphasise links between chapters, but also to aid the lecturer in tailoring its use to the preferred course design.

These divisions are not hard and fast; we cover environmental issues (Part Five), for instance, in the same section of our course as cost-benefit analysis and externalities (Part One) and use regulation and privatization to illustrate the conflict between public choice and public interest models of government. There are a number of ways the book can be used. In our one semester unit in Public Sector Economics we begin with most of the core chapters on market failure and public choice, then teach selected topics drawn from each of the other three sections of the book. Alternatively, a traditional public finance course could begin in the same fashion, with Chapters One to Seven, before covering the tax chapters in detail with the possible addition of Chapters Eighteen (on pensions) and Twenty-four (which looks at multi-jurisdictional issues). A more modern variant of the same might substitute in the chapters on regulation and privatization. A Social Policy course, on the other hand, would focus on Part 3, perhaps enhanced with the material on labour taxation in Chapter Thirteen.

Draft versions of the book have been used at the University of East Anglia for two years. We would like to thank our guinea pigs, students on the Public Sector Economics unit, especially those who pointed out errors, ambiguities and infelicities in the manuscript. Special mention in this regard should go to Ben Botolo and Amy Mearing. Chris Gerry and Claire Leaver also taught on the course and provided valuable feedback as well as doing a careful job compiling our indices. We are extremely grateful to Jan Northway, Economics Secretary at UEA, who fought with the print room and its uncertain technologies to make draft versions available on time. Thanks are also due to Nick Bardsley who provided useful references on experimental evidence on public good games and to Kevin Denny of UCD, Brendan Kennelly of Galway and Sue Rice of the DSS for drawing our attention to errors in the original print run.

Applied textbooks such as this one depend heavily on access to a wide range of statistical material. Acknowledgement to specific copyright holders is given below, but a general vote of thanks is due to our sources, especially those who, bucking a trend which threatens the future viability of applied texts, did not charge for the reproduction of material. Thanks are also due to the anonymous reviewers at Prentice Hall whose comments improved the text enormously and to our editors at Prentice Hall – Tony Johnston and Derek Moseley who saw the project's inception and to Catherine Newman and Ian Stoneham who saw it to completion.

Sara would also like to thank Hussein Kassim for reading through draft versions of chapters and for love, support and encouragement.

We would both like to thank David Beckham for enabling us to devote more attention to the book in June 1998 than we had anticipated, thus ensuring its timely completion and Alistair would like to thank Sara for her Banoffee pie, another necessary ingredient.

Sara Connolly & Alistair Munro
University of East Anglia

Website: http://www.uea.ac.uk/soc/econ/pubecon.htm

# Acknowledgements

The authors would like to express their gratitude to the original sources for permission to reprint the following items. The material used in Table 7.3, Figure 14.8 and Table 21.1, reprinted with the permission of the Cambridge University Press; Tables 7.4, 13.3, 23.3 and 23.4, reprinted by the permission of Oxford University Press and the authors; the material in Tables 1.2, 15.3–4, 17.2, 17.9–12, Figures 1.2, 14.11–12, and the expenditure data in Figure 19.4, reprinted with permission from the Office for National Statistics © Crown Copyright; the data in Figures 1.1, 1.3–1.5, 10.1, and 19.1–2, Tables 1.3, 10.4–5, 10.7 columns 4 and 5, 12.2, 16.7, 18.4, 18.6, 19.1, 19.3–4, 20.2, 20.4, 20.6 and 23.2 reprinted with the permission of the Organisation for Economic Cooperation and Development, copyright OECD; Table 14.6, reprinted with the permission of the American Economic Association; Tables 15.6 and 15.7 reprinted with the permission of *Benefits*, School of Sociology and Social Policy, University of Nottingham; the material in Figures 17.3 and 17.4 and Tables 13.2, 15.5, 16.5, 17.1, 17.2, 17.3, and 17.4, Crown copyright, reprinted with the permission of the Controller of Her Majesty's Stationery Office; the data in Figure 15.2, Tables 16.1, 24.1 and 24.3, copyright European Communities, reprinted with permission; Tables 15.2 and 16.3, reprinted with the permission of the *Review of Income and Wealth*; Tables 10.3, 10.6, Table 10.7 (columns 2 and 3), Table 10.8, Box 10.7, Tables 12.3, 13.1, 14.1, 14.4, 16.6, 16.9, 17.8, 18.1, 18.5, 20.1 and 23.6 and Figures 14.9–10 reprinted with the permission of the Institute for Fiscal Studies; Figure 15.4 reprinted with the permission of the Joseph Rowntree Foundation; the material in Box 17.1 and Tables 21.2, 21.3, and 21.5 reprinted by permission of Addison Wesley Longman Ltd; the material in Table 23.5 reprinted with permission from the Institute for International Economics, Washington, DC; the material in Tables 21.4, and 22.1–3 reprinted with the permission of the MIT Press; Table 16.2 reprinted with the permission of Blackwell Publisher Ltd; the material in Table 16.8, reprinted with the permission of Macmillan Press Ltd; Table 17.5 reprinted with the permission of Frank Cass and Company; Figure 18.2 reprinted by permission of Age Concern; material in Table 18.7 reprinted with the permission of the Population Council; Table 19.6 reprinted by permission of Duke University Press; waiting list data in Figure 19.4 reprinted with the permission of the Office of Health Economics; Table 20.3 reprinted with the permission of Routledge Ltd.

# Introduction

## Key concepts

| | | |
|---|---|---|
| normative economics | positive economics | public interest |
| ideologies | minimal value judgements | public economics |
| Wagner's Law | regulation | incentives |
| public choice | government budget | Baumol Effect |

## 1.1 Introduction

When you woke up this morning, perhaps you took a shower in water the quality of which is set by the European Union. Probably you made a cup of tea or coffee using electricity from a company that used to be in the public sector, but has recently been privatised. You travelled to the university on a bus owned by the local municipality, or cycled along roads constructed by the same organisation. At the university, built, owned and regulated by the government, you bought some cigarettes, taxed by the state, and maybe later on, after some encouragement from your mum, you will ring your grandma who has just been discharged from a government-run hospital and is receiving some nursing at home, provided by the local authority. Afterwards, friends will call round and you will go to the cinema and pay VAT on your ticket. In between you catch up on your studies, partly financed by the government, although as a result you will probably pay more income tax later on in life. Everything you do is affected by the decisions made by governments and has been for the whole of your life. For the vast majority of citizens in the mixed economies of the richer countries of the world, the same is true: all our lives are influenced and shaped by the actions of the state.

This book is about the economics of the public sector. Our aim is to show how microeconomic theory can be extended and adapted to shed light on what governments do. Now, despite the great complexity of the world we live in, at heart governments carry out only three categories of economic activity:

● *Regulation:* they regulate and enact laws to create and amend property rights;

- *Price setting:* they set prices directly or through taxes and subsidies; and
- *Production:* they produce goods of all kinds, from law and order to education and defence.

These three types of action have two important consequences: they alter incomes and they change incentives (see Table 1.1). When a government raises taxes on cigarettes it reduces the purchasing power of smokers, and possibly the owners of cigarette-producing firms and the people who work for them. Simultaneously, it creates substitution effects which alter the incentive to smoke or to own tobacco company shares. The consequences of the tax will permeate the rest of the economy, changing the demand for healthcare, raising demand for tobacco substitutes and providing a boost to the income of anyone who benefits from the revenue raised.

The state is not limited to purely economic actions – a campaign to raise AIDS awareness provides a counter-example, but because every decision it makes affects the allocation of resources, all government activities have economic implications and that is why our remit is so large. In fact it is far larger than appears from the contents of this book. We have omitted many important areas of activity, from macroeconomic policy to crime and punishment, from housing to the transport system, from agriculture to defence. Our aim, in being selective, is to concentrate on the principles underlying the economics of the public sector, illustrated by a suitably wide range of examples.

## Public sector economics

Public sector economics has a number of elements, all of which you will encounter in this book. At a basic but very necessary level, the subject involves the description of what it is the government does: how it raises its money, where it spends it, the

**Table 1.1** Classifying some of the effects of government policies

|  | Income and wealth effects | Incentive effects |
|---|---|---|
| Increased cigarette taxes | Reduced spending power for smokers; reduced dividend income for tobacco company shareholders; increased incomes for the beneficiaries of the tax revenue raised | Reduced number of smokers; more investment in non-tobacco companies |
| A lower limit on sulphur dioxide emissions from power stations | Reduced incomes of electricity company shareholders and employees | Switch to cleaner fuels; switch away from energy-intensive activities |
| A rise in education spending on nurseries | Higher incomes for nursery school teachers; lower incomes for private sector nurseries; higher incomes for parents with pre-school children, who can now work | More people attracted into nursery school teaching |

mechanisms by which it decides how to allocate resources and the institutions of the State. For instance, government income and expenditure has a number of components:

Income = Taxes and Charges
    + Asset Income
    + Asset Sales
    + Borrowing

Expenditure = Transfers
    + Government Consumption
    + Subsidies
    + Interest Paid
    + Capital Expenditure

As can be seen from Figure 1.1, the bulk of expenditure in the UK is on transfers (e.g. pensions and other social security benefits) and on consumption expenditure (e.g. salaries of state employees such as doctors and university lecturers). The next largest item is the interest paid on outstanding loans. Relatively little is spent on capital goods (e.g. building new roads) and still less is classified as subsidies (e.g. payments to farmers).[1]

For the UK, the budget, in which the government sets tax rates for the following year, takes place in March of each year. Expenditure plans are set annually (although the Labour government is moving towards a three-year planning horizon) after negotiations between the spending ministries (such as Health or Defence) and the Treasury. Both expenditure and tax plans are made on the basis of forecasts of the shape of the economy over the next year. Expenditure plans for most items are made in cash terms, so that any deviations from anticipated inflation are reflected in the real level of expenditure, but not in its nominal level. Recipients of the expenditure therefore bear all the risk from inflation. However, with few exceptions, the total budget for transfers is not set instead the cash amounts of benefits such as Income Support (see Chapter 17) are set for the year, but there is no upper or lower limit on

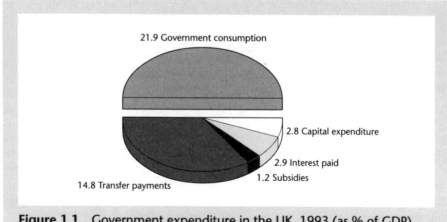

**Figure 1.1** Government expenditure in the UK, 1993 (as % of GDP) (Source: OECD Historical Statistics, 1996, Table 7.9)

---

[1] See Figure 1.3 for comparative data from other OECD countries.

the number of claims. As with benefits, for taxes it is *rates* rather than *revenue* which is set for the year and so any unforeseen shortfall or windfall is reflected in the amount the government borrows for the year. The level of borrowing is therefore a residual item and must always adjust so that government income and expenditure are equal.

Table 1.2 shows the functional breakdown of UK Government expenditure and income for 1996.

**Table 1.2**  Income and expenditure for the UK government, 1996

| Expenditure | £million | % total | Income | £million | % total |
|---|---|---|---|---|---|
| General public services | 13,223 | 4.3 | Taxes on income | 94,685 | 30.9 |
| Defence | 23,018 | 7.5 | Taxes on expenditure | 108,484 | 35.4 |
| Public order and safety | 15,458 | 5.0 | Social security contributions | 46,270 | 15.1 |
| Education | 39,133 | 12.8 | Council Tax | 9,906 | 3.2 |
| Health | 43,199 | 14.1 | Gross trading surplus | 681 | 0.2 |
| Social security | 106,958 | 34.9 | Rent, etc. | 5,757 | 1.9 |
| Housing and community amenities | 4,580 | 1.5 | Interest and dividends etc. | 5,339 | 1.7 |
| Recreational and cultural affairs | 4,579 | 1.5 | Miscellaneous current transfers | 632 | 0.2 |
| Fuel and energy | −2,978 | −1.0 | Consumption of capital (imputed charge) | 3,653 | 1.2 |
| Agriculture, forestry and fishing | 5,395 | 1.8 | Taxes on capital | 3,228 | 1.1 |
| Mining and mineral resources | 679 | 0.2 | | | |
| Transport and communications | 8,386 | 2.7 | | | |
| Other economic affairs | 6,285 | 2.1 | | | |
| Other | 33,369 | 10.9 | Income before financial transactions | 278,635 | 91.0 |
| | | | Financial transactions* | 26,751 | 8.7 |
| | | | Balancing item | 831 | 0.3 |
| Total | 306,217 | 100 | Total | 306,217 | 100 |

Source: National Income Accounts, Tables 9.1, 9.4 and 9.6, 1997.

* Net financial transactions, less privatisation proceeds plus net lending by government.

In this table, general public services includes the cost of running the Civil Service and the Foreign and Commonwealth Office, as well as tax collection. That recorded expenditure can be negative, as is the case for the fuel and energy item, is due to the previous government's peculiar treatment of the receipts from privatisation as negative expenditure rather than as income (see Box 1.1 for more on this). The size of the 'Other' item towards the base of the table is largely accounted for by interest paid (£27.1bn) on debts accumulated in previous years of government. Meanwhile, public order and safety includes the Fire Service as well as the Police, and the legal and prison systems.

Five functions (social security, health, education, defence and public order) account for almost three-quarters of total expenditure. Social security alone takes up more than one-third of the budget. Figure 1.2 shows how the importance of the various functions in the UK has altered over the last thirty years: real expenditure (i.e. measured at 1985 prices) has almost quadrupled on public order and social security, tripled on health, but halved on housing. For many of the functions, the years 1976–7 are critical, the point at which the then Labour government, struggling to contain public expenditure, ran into a balance of payments crisis swiftly followed by a crash in the value of the pound and a bail out from the International Monetary Fund (IMF).

On the income side there has been a slow trend towards taxes on expenditure and away from taxes on income (see Chapter 10 for a more detailed discussion). Social security (National Insurance) contributions and borrowing make up the major sources of income for the government, with the latter sensitive to the state of the economy.

We have given examples of the descriptive role of public sector economics, but the discipline is also analytical: it is about trying to understand what impact the actions

**BOX 1.1**

## Government accounting and borrowing

The gap between expenditure and income, the amount the Government needs to borrow, is known as the Public Sector Borrowing Requirement (PSBR). As a measure of fiscal stance this has deficiencies: it swings wildly from month to month because the pattern of tax receipts and expenditure over the fiscal year is not smooth. Government spending, for instance, tends to peak in March when departments use up any unspent portion of their annual budgets. Perhaps more worryingly, the accounts mix up capital and revenue items. When an asset is sold, for instance during privatisation, the income is credited to the account, but not the loss of the asset, unlike in a private company. Similarly, student loans are treated as expenditure, without any compensating increase in the assets owned by the state. The new Public Sector Net Borrowing (PSNB) measure updates the accounting procedures for the UK and brings them into line with other European Union countries. It omits financial transactions such as asset sales or loans and measures the country's fiscal stance using the method of *accrual* accounting, which means, for instance, registering income from VAT when consumers buy the goods rather than when companies hand over the tax. This will smooth out the accounts over the year and will also make it easier to implement the government's intention to obey the so-called 'Golden Rule' – borrowing only for capital expenditure and not to finance revenue shortfalls. A record of the day-to-day borrowing position will still be required; this will now be known as the Public Sector Net Cash Requirement (PSNCR).

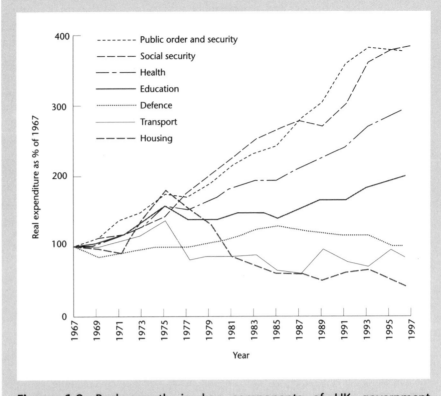

**Figure 1.2** Real growth in key components of UK government expenditure
(Source: National Accounts, Table 9.4, SO)

of the government have on the economy and the outside world and why the state makes the decisions it does. The aim is not simply to understand what has happened in the past, but also to clarify the economic implications of choosing, say, to introduce a carbon tax, or to legalise soft drugs such as cannabis. Finally, it is prescriptive, making statements of the kind 'if these are the goals of the government, then those are the measures it should take' and even judging some of the goals of the state against more fundamental criteria of desirability, such as efficiency. Public sector economics therefore involves both normative and positive aspects of economics.[2]

## 1.2  What is the state?

We have reached this point without asking such an awkward question and we cannot provide a definitive answer, partly because, like many beasts, the state is easier to

---

[2] Recall that positive theories concern themselves with what *actually* exists, normative theories with what *should* happen. When examining normative issues, we start with what are viewed by most economists as minimal value judgements. This means that each individual is usually the best judge of his or her own welfare and that a policy change is desirable for society if it benefits one individual (according to that individual's own viewpoint), while not reducing the welfare of others (see Chapters 2 and 3).

recognise than it is to define, in part at least because the nature of the state varies from country to country and is in a process of continuous change. Leaving that aside, there are at least three important features of the state in a democratic society:

- *Compulsion:* The state is the most powerful single institution in a society and has a monopoly over certain types of activity, among them law-making, maintaining an army and waging war with other countries. This power of compulsion is vital to an understanding of the state's potential role in the supply of public goods, explored in Chapter 4.

- *Accountability:* Although it can be claimed that the state has a monopoly on power, in practice it is hemmed in by constraints, from the actions of other states to the actions of its earlier self, in the form of the constitution (written or unwritten) and its laws, which do not constrain the government from writing new legislation, but do limit the other components of the state, the judiciary, the Civil Service and public sector organisations, such as schools. The constraint which makes the democratic state distinct is that the members of its government face the test of elections from time to time – they are accountable to all the voters of their country.

- *Motivation:* A third and much disputed feature of the state concerns the motives of the people who work for the state and the expectation that other people have about such motives. State employees and, more generally, anyone within the public arena, are expected to serve the 'public interest' and, to a greater extent, compared to employees of profit-maximising organisations, tend to be motivated by desire to serve their country and its citizens.[3] There are many who deny this. For instance, Buchanan, arguing that the motives of public and private sector workers are exactly the same, writes that,

> man must be assumed to shift his psychological and moral gears when he moves from the realm of organized market activity . . . [One must demonstrate that there is] something in the nature of the market organization, as such, that brings out the selfish motives in man and something in the political organization, as such, which in turn suppresses these motives and brings out the more 'noble' ones . . .

One such 'something' is the expectations of others and the punishments meted out to those who do not serve the public interest, forces which (i) will tend to reward and encourage public-spirited behaviour within the state, and (ii) will also tend to attract the public-spirited to careers serving society through the state, rather than to jobs in the private sector.

Of course, these features are present to some degree in many other kinds of organisation. Other institutions, such as firms and charities, also face democratic constraints on their activities, via shareholder or membership meetings, but the constraint of having to seek election is probably far more significant to a government than it is to the board of a company faced with the more immediate constraint of competition. Non-selfish motives can also be found throughout the economy (just as selfish

---

[3] Surveying the evidence on the motives of civil servants in the USA, Steven Kelman (1987) writes, 'In a 1984 survey of senior civil servants managers in the Federal government, respondents were asked "To what extent are the following reasons to continue working for the government?" Only 18 percent said that their salary was a strong reason for staying (or more of a reason to stay than leave) . . . Seventy-six percent, however, responded that the "opportunity to have an impact on public affairs" was a reason to stay. A study by Edward Lawler III, a professor of management, comparing the importance of pay for different kinds of managers concluded that "managers in industrial organizations place the most importance on pay; people who work in government agencies place less emphasis on pay; and people who work in hospitals and social service organizations place the least emphasis on pay." ' (p. 90)

motives are common within people who work for the state) and are of prime importance in families and many charities. The lesson is that it is probably dangerous to look for a unique property which is possessed by all democratic states, but not by other institutions. In practice, it seems to be a cluster of attributes and their strength which makes the state unique.

A further dimension to the question, What is the state? is provided by the observation that, like most large organisations, the state is not a monolith; it operates at many levels. National or federal governments may control defence and foreign policy, while local or provincial governments deal with matters such as health and education, and waste collection and street lighting are dealt with at an even lower level. This separation of activities partly represents a managerial decision (it would be a foolish waste of a Prime Minister's time if the Cabinet had to decide on whether to adjust the opening hours of a local park in Cleethorpes, for example). In most countries of the Organisation for Economic Cooperation and Development (OECD) there are also constitutional limits which separate out the powers of local and federal governments. And, in western Europe, an increasing proportion of power now lies beyond national governments in the organs of the European Union.

## 1.3 The changing nature of the public sector and its economics

One of the exciting aspects of public sector economics, apart from its relevance, is the rate of change of the subject, partly because of the changing world around us, but also because of developments within the fields of economic theory and data analysis.

### New theory – public economics, public choice

The last twenty-five years have seen two major revolutions in the foundations of public sector economics, both of which have been reflected in recent Nobel Prizes for Economics. The presentation of the award to James Mirrlees and William Vickrey in 1996 was for their work in developing the field of public economics, a branch of theory which deals rigorously with the issue of incentives in welfare economics. In other words, it is concerned with optimal policy when there is asymmetric information. For instance, if governments are to provide efficient levels of services, then they need to know individual preferences, but if individuals face the wrong incentives, they may opt to misrepresent the value they place on publicly provided goods (see Chapter 4). One research line in public economics has therefore been concerned with discovering mechanisms for determining preferences where it is optimal to be honest. Another line considers the problem of designing tax systems which minimise the burden of taxes (for optimal taxation see Chapter 11) and much recent work has been done on the issue of regulating privatised firms. In all these cases the analysis moves beyond the utopian but fictional world where government knows everything which there is to know about its citizens and its firms before it embarks on public policy.

In recent years, Nobel Prize winners have also included Gary Becker, James Buchanan and George Stigler, all of whom have been key figures in the rise of public choice theory, often called the 'economics of politics', and meaning the application of economic analysis to political institutions and the actions of individuals within those institutions. Previously, economists had tended to picture government as a black box,

**Public interest model**

A model which depicts government as benevolent

out of which benevolent policies sprung wholesale. The public choice view challenged this **public interest** model in that it questioned the relevance of welfare economics for understanding what is done in government, as opposed to what should be done. Public choice theorists argue that individuals are essentially self-interested in or out of the public arena and therefore it models the policy-making process as the result of trade between selfish agents, such as politicians granting policies in exchange for votes and campaign contributions (see Chapters 8 and 9). It is doubtful that this model is entirely true; specific public choice models, such as the rational voter model, have a poor record in explaining actual outcomes, but the public choice approach has brought with it a profound shift in economists' conceptual view of government, which has resonated far outside the profession. It has also laid down a challenge to the public interest view to explain how a public interest outcome comes about.

It should be stressed that the public interest and public choice views of government are not always contradictory. Consider a situation where everyone is better off with policy x rather than policy y. Accordingly, the public interest model predicts that the benevolent government will enact policy x. Meanwhile, public choice predicts that self-interested humans will vote in favour of x rather than y. Thus, even if individuals are purely selfish, simple public interest models will often be a good predictor of actual government behaviour. However, we have already noted that human beings are not always selfish or unsympathetic to society beyond the garden gate. Thus in our view, the public interest view is not simply a normative theory, but also an important component in positive theories of public sector activity.

## New data

A less prominent development in the subject, but in many ways equally profound, has been the increasing availability of large data sets and their increasing comparability across countries. Data sets are the raw ingredients of applied economics. If it is said that high taxation or social security lowers the incentive to work, then we need to know whether this is true. Data sets, such as the UK's Family Expenditure Survey (FES), provide the material required to examine the impact of changing taxes and prices on individual and household behaviour. Meanwhile, social experiments such as the New Jersey Negative Income Tax experiment in the USA provide more detailed evidence of changes in labour supply following a controlled tax reform. Along with the rise of microeconometrics (the application of econometric techniques to these large data sets, to investigate microeconomic questions), the last two decades have seen a sharp increase in the quality of comparative data. This is chiefly due to the work of the OECD, with its detailed studies of the organisation of healthcare, education, pensions and so on within its member countries, and the Luxembourg Income Study, which focuses on the difficult task of comparing income and wealth distributions across countries (see Box 1.2).

**Ideology**

A system of core beliefs and values (which shapes an individual's attitude to policy)

## New ideologies, new controversies

It cannot escape the attention of any student of the public sector that the last two decades have seen an enormous shift in political attitudes, a break-up of consensus attitudes to the role of the state and the emergence of new **ideologies**, often labelled the 'New Right', marked by a belief in the corrupting role of the state on moral values and incentives and a strong faith in the power of markets. Whatever the reasons for its rise, the strength of the New Right view has left its mark in Western economies,

BOX 1.2

## Cross-country comparisons

In this book we have tried to introduce data and empirical work from a wide variety of countries. We discuss healthcare reforms in the UK and the Netherlands, social insurance systems in Singapore and Germany, examine the determinants of government spending in Switzerland and the Swedish variety of Eurosclerosis. We have not attempted to be comprehensive in our coverage, nor could we be. The aim is to illustrate underlying economic principles, to compare cases of common and divergent experience, and to offer examples of the innovatory or bizarre. Most of the economies we sample have certain things in common: the democratic process (of some kind) and, relative to the majority of the world's population, a high level of economic development. Even within such a narrowly defined group of countries (basically the OECD), cross-country comparisons should be made with caution.

One important reason for this caution lies in the variations in the data produced across nations. Carrying out comparative analysis has become much easier following the pioneering work of international bodies such as the OECD and the Luxembourg Income Study, but it remains the case that all data transported internationally should carry a health warning, not because some countries are meticulous in collecting data and some are downright sloppy, but because definitions and collation methods vary (sometimes dramatically) between countries. Often the devil is in the footnotes. For instance, figures produced by the OECD for expenditure on social security transfers in 1994 show a sharp rise over 1993: the OECD average increases from 15.5% of GDP to 18.9%, the largest one-year growth rate on record. In fact the jump arises because when the OECD collated its statistics and computed the average, some countries were unable to supply 1994 figures and so were left out. Since these tended to be the member states which spent a low proportion of GDP on social security, the average shot up!

with most governments keener now on tax cuts and limiting expenditure than they have been in the entire post-war period. This has shifted the focus of much of public sector economics, with questions about the burden of taxation and the comparative performance of private and public sector enterprises moved to the centre of the stage. Two other ideological developments are also worth noting. The impact of feminism on public policy has been far subtler (i.e. weaker) than that of the New Right, and the same is true of its impact on public sector economics. Nevertheless, it is rarer nowadays for the interests of women and men to be treated by economists as always coincidental and there is increasing interest in 'women's' issues as the proper subject of study. So the feminisation of poverty, for example, receives a deal of research attention, while almost all studies of the impact of incentives on work effort now differentiate between the genders. The other rising ideology at the end of the twentieth century is environmentalism, signalled by the increasing share of the Green vote in many European countries and the upward momentum of environmental issues on the political agenda. What sets environmentalism apart from traditional utilitarian approaches to public sector economics, is a concern for the non-human world and a belief that growth and prosperity are not necessarily desirable goals, because of the costs they impose on the non-human environment.

The chart-topping ideologies of the last two decades have sometimes preceded and sometimes pursued changes in the focus of public policy. A glance at a newspaper (broadsheet rather than tabloid) suggests that the issues which have moved up the agenda include the role of Europe, the effect of the Welfare State on growth, the increasing feminisation of poverty, the implications of a greying population, the causes and consequences of greater drug use, the role of the family, the quality of the urban and world environment and the desirability of government involvement in the production of goods such as electricity and telecommunications. Public sector economics has to address all these problems.

## 1.4 The size of government

Having listed some of the conceptual components of public sector economics, we illustrate them in the context of the debate over the changing size of the public sector. Table 1.3 lists government expenditure as a proportion of GDP for a number of OECD countries over the period 1960–98. In each case, the figure for 1998 is higher than that for thirty-eight years earlier, but though the trend is broadly upward, the average figure at the base of each column hides a great deal of variation. For instance, there are countries such as the USA, where there is no discernible trend over the period; there are others, such as Ireland, where, after a

**Table 1.3**  Total government expenditure as a percentage of GDP

| | 1960 | 1968 | 1974 | 1979 | 1984 | 1986 | 1988 | 1990 | 1992 | 1994 | 1996 | 1998 |
|---|---|---|---|---|---|---|---|---|---|---|---|---|
| Australia | 22.1 | 25.1 | 30.4 | 33.2 | 35.4 | 37.5 | 33.7 | 34.8 | 37.5 | 36.7 | 35.8 | 34.6 |
| Canada | 28.9 | 33.0 | 37.4 | 39.8 | 45.3 | 45.4 | 43.4 | 46.7 | 51.1 | 47.5 | 44.7 | 41.6 |
| Denmark | 24.8 | 36.3 | 39.4 | 53.2 | 60.3 | 55.7 | 55.3 | 54.5 | 56.6 | 59.3 | 55.9 | 52.5 |
| Finland | 26.7 | 33.4 | 32.9 | 38.5 | 42.0 | 44.7 | 44.0 | 45.4 | 59.1 | 59.3 | 57.3 | 51.7 |
| France | 34.6 | 40.3 | 43.5 | 45.5 | 51.9 | 51.3 | 50.0 | 49.8 | 52.3 | 54.5 | 58.8 | 53.9 |
| Germany | 32.5 | 39.2 | 44.7 | 47.7 | 47.4 | 46.4 | 46.3 | 45.1 | 48.5 | 48.9 | 48.9 | 47.4 |
| Ireland | 28.0 | 35.2 | 43.0 | 49.8 | 50.1 | 50.7 | 45.2 | 39.0 | 40.7 | 40.4 | 37.4 | 34.5 |
| Italy | 30.1 | 34.7 | 37.9 | 45.2 | 49.8 | 51.0 | 50.5 | 53.6 | 53.8 | 54.9 | 52.7 | 49.5 |
| Japan | 18.3 | 19.3 | 24.4 | 32.0 | 32.3 | 31.9 | 31.3 | 31.3 | 31.7 | 34.4 | 35.9 | 35.6 |
| Netherlands | 33.7 | 43.9 | 51.5 | 58.0 | 58.7 | 57.0 | 56.7 | 54.1 | 55.1 | 52.8 | 49.6 | 47.5 |
| New Zealand | | | | | 38.5 | 57.2 | 54.5 | 57.5 | 54.3 | 47.3 | 46.1 | 45.5 |
| Norway | 29.9 | 37.9 | 44.6 | 50.9 | 42.1 | 45.4 | 49.5 | 49.7 | 52.0 | 49.9 | 45.5 | 45.3 |
| Sweden | 31.1 | 42.8 | 48.1 | 61.1 | 62.0 | 61.6 | 58.1 | 59.1 | 67.2 | 68.3 | 64.2 | 59.6 |
| United Kingdom | 32.6 | 39.6 | 45.2 | 43.4 | 45.2 | 42.4 | 38.0 | 39.9 | 43.1 | 43.2 | 41.9 | 39.2 |
| United States | 27.6 | 31.3 | 33.0 | 32.9 | 32.3 | 33.1 | 32.1 | 32.8 | 34.4 | 32.8 | 32.7 | 31.6 |
| OECD mean | 28.3 | 32.3 | 35.2 | 38.7 | 38.5 | 38.8 | 37.7 | 38.4 | 40.3 | 40.5 | 40 | 39 |

Source: OECD, Table 6.5, 1996. Note: Figures for 1998 are predicted

significant early increase, there is a sustained drop in government expenditure as a proportion of GDP.

There are differences not just in the level and growth of government expenditure, but also in the components of that expenditure. Figure 1.3 shows the breakdown of expenditure for many of the countries of the OECD, ranked according to the proportion of GDP spent by the government. In some countries such as Italy, a large proportion of that expenditure goes to service the debts incurred by previous governments. Meanwhile in others, notably Japan, a relatively high proportion of expenditure is capital rather than current.

Despite these differences, there is enough commonality in the experiences of the richer nations of the world for a set of stylised facts about public expenditure to be advanced:

● Over the last century, the time trend of government expenditure as a percentage of GDP has been upwards in all developed nations – in the 1920s, for instance, government expenditure was only 20.6% of UK GDP;

● Superimposed on any time trend is a cyclical element – G/GDP tends to rise during recessions and fall during booms, though not all of its components move in the same direction;

● For most countries the trend continued up until the late 1970s/early 1980s;

● Since then, for many countries, there is no discernible trend, while for many others the upward trend is much weaker and for some the trend is downwards;

● There are significant differences between the level and rate of growth of G/GDP across developed nations and no tendency towards convergence;

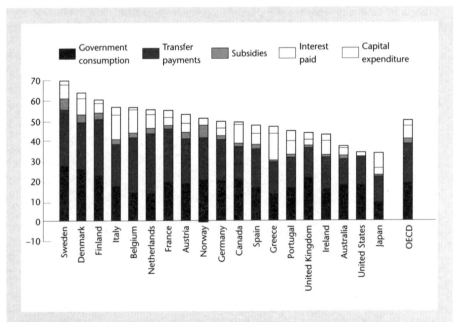

**Figure 1.3** The components of government spending in OECD countries, 1993
(Source: OECD Historical Statistics, 1996, Table 7.9)

- Government consumption has risen much more slowly than government expenditure as a whole and, as a proportion of GDP, has been broadly flat in many countries for nearly thirty years (see Figures 1.2 and 1.4);

- However, the social security budget has shown a much sharper upward trend in most countries, including many of those, such as Japan and USA, where expenditure as a whole has traditionally been a much smaller percentage of GDP than the OECD average (see Figure 1.5).

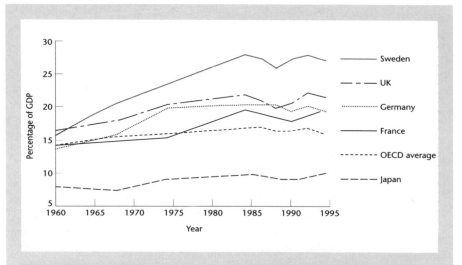

**Figure 1.4** Government consumption, % GDP in five OECD countries (Source: OECD, 1996, Table 6.3)

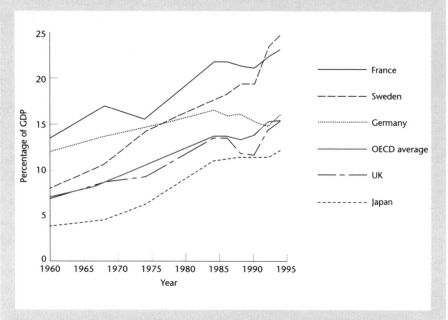

**Figure 1.5** Social security spending, % GDP in five OECD countries (Source: OECD, 1996, Table 6.3)

**Wagner's Law**

The tendency for government expenditure to grow faster than GDP

**Fiscal illusion**

The failure by voters to understand the implications for taxes of changes in public expenditure

**Baumol Effect**

The rise in the share of GDP taken up by labour-intensive services as a result of innovations in other sectors

The first of these stylised facts is known as **Wagner's Law**, stated more formally as the tendency of government expenditure to rise more quickly than GDP. The debate between the public interest and public choice approaches to public sector economics is nowhere so clearly illustrated as in the dispute over the factors which lie behind Wagner's Law.

Most theories tend to fall into one of three categories: those which seek to offer an explanation of the growth of transfers, those which predict rises in expenditure on goods and services, and those which expound stories covering all aspects of government expenditure. Included in the last category, for instance, would be theories based on **fiscal illusion**, the idea that voters are unable to comprehend the full implications for taxation of expenditure rises and so vote for high-spending governments. Associated with this is the idea that governments manipulate the complexity of tax systems, so as to hide their real costs. Other theories stress the power of interest groups, associations such as unions and defence manufacturers, but also groups internal to the state such as teachers and doctors. Both the fiscal illusion and interest group theories struggle to explain why G/GDP rises, but as we shall see in Chapter 9, some authors, notably Mancur Olson (1982), argue that the power of interest groups tends to grow over time and hence can explain not just the level of public expenditure, but also its growth.

Amongst theories largely directed at explaining growth in government expenditure, perhaps the simplest is that which suggests that goods and services such as healthcare are luxury goods, demand for which, by definition, rises faster than income. In countries such as the USA, where healthcare is largely privately financed, its production has outstripped the rate of GDP growth, so it is perhaps not surprising that the same is also true for countries where healthcare expenditure is largely set by the government. Other theories point to *urbanisation and growth* itself as a source of the rise in G/GDP. Urbanisation increases the demand for public goods[4] and reduces their cost of provision. Meanwhile, both urbanisation and economic growth tend to raise pollution and congestion. A third important theory in this category is the **Baumol Effect**, the tendency of the relative price of labour-intensive services to rise, compared to manufactured goods, because of the stronger rate of technological progress in the latter. Thus, as long as demand for services is inelastic, their share in national output will tend to rise. State sectors, such as health or education, come into this category and their take of GDP has risen (see Figure 1.2).

A key weakness shared by all members of this category of theories is that modern increases in G/GDP have been largely fuelled by the explosion in transfers rather than by expenditure on goods and services (see Figures 1.4 and 1.5). The third group of explanations is therefore concerned with redistributive policies in general and transfers in particular. Many authors aiming to explain mushrooming transfers point to *changing suffrage* over the course of the last 150 years. Before the 1832 Reform Act, less than 1.8% of the UK population had the right to vote. With this Act the proportion rose to 2.7%; with the 1867 Universal Suffrage Act all male householders were enfranchised, pushing the proportion to 6.4%. By 1919 all men over 21 and women over 30 had the vote (20 million) and in 1928 women over 21 joined the franchise, making 29 million potential voters in all. Similar trends can be observed in other countries. With each extension, the average age and the average income of voters fell;

---

[4] For instance, crime is associated with urbanisation, so the movement of the population to cities would be expected to increase the demand for public safety services.

according to many public choice theories, the power of groups favouring redistribution from rich to poor would rise and with it taxes and transfers. However, changes in the franchise have been discrete, whereas the growth of government has not been (except for the surges in expenditure during the First and Second World Wars). Moreover, the last extension of the franchise was in 1970, when 18–21 year olds gained the right to vote and G/GDP has continued to climb since. Other theories stress demographic changes, such as the ageing of the population or changes in inequality and poverty, as the primary force behind the trend.

Some of these theories cross the borders between categories: an ageing population, for instance, may increase demand both for pensions (a transfer) and healthcare (consumption expenditure). Meanwhile, as we stressed in section 1.1, all government policies have some redistributive impact and some government programmes, particularly healthcare and education in the UK, have a significant impact on the income distribution.[5] We shall encounter a number of these theories in more detail in the separate chapters of this book. Nevertheless, at this stage we can already see that it appears that one explanation or even one category of explanation is insufficient to account for all the complexities of government expenditure, an interpretation suggested by the wide variation in trends for the individual components of public expenditure seen earlier in the chapter in Figures 1.2, 1.4 and 1.5.[6] It is also worth pointing out that theories drawn only from public interest perspectives or only from public choice angles have limited success in explaining the data of government expenditure. Borcherding (1985), for instance, in a survey of US evidence found that variables compatible with the public interest approach struggled to explain more than half of the growth, but that public choice theories did no better. Moreover, looking at Table 1.3, it is not clear that Wagner's Law applies any more. In this book therefore, we draw back from searching for one encompassing model for the public sector. Rather, the emphasis is on developing general tools which can be applied to understanding particular aspects of government activity.

## 1.5 Conclusion

In this chapter we have laid out some of the background to the economics of the public sector and introduced the two main theoretical approaches to the subject. Despite the bewildering variety of economic problems involving the state, there are therefore certain analytical essentials for the successful student of the public sector, among them a firm understanding of welfare economics and public choice theory. The next few chapters are therefore devoted to understanding these two approaches.

Armed with these skills, improved and extended in the theory chapters of the first half of the book, you can then go on to understand how they are applied. The aim in the remaining chapters is not to be comprehensive, but to show you how basic principles can be employed to understand the complex world we live in.

---

[5] Though this raises a deeper question: why do governments use transfers in-kind, such as health and housing, as instruments of redistribution, when cash transfers are available?

[6] For instance, in a survey of the issue, Mueller (1989) concludes: '*at best*, the Baumol effect seems capable of explaining about a quarter of the increase in final consumption expenditure for the average OECD country' (p. 326), emphasis added.

## Summary

- There are three types of economic action undertaken by governments: production, price setting and regulation.

- All government actions have income and incentive effects on individuals and firms.

- Government expenditure has grown over the last century in all OECD countries, both in absolute terms and also as a proportion of national income.

- More recently the growth has been concentrated in transfers rather than final consumption. Moreover, the growth in the overall G/GDP has tailed off and possibly reversed itself in some countries.

- Within public sector economics, there are two main, complementary approaches. The first, the public interest approach, treats the government as a benevolent welfare maximiser. The second, the public choice approach, assumes that all individuals are selfish in all spheres.

## Questions

1. Identify the income and incentive effects of the following changes of government policy:

   a rise in income tax rates
   the building of a major new underground line
   the selling of government-owned housing stock
   a cull of dairy cattle in the wake of a BSE scare
   the deregulation of bar and pub opening hours.

2. Go through the list of activities in the opening paragraph of this chapter. Which of them are the tasks of local government, which are national government and which are supra-national? (Note: some may cross boundaries.)

3. Examine the list of explanations of G/GDP growth. Which of them are public interest, which are public choice and which could be either?

## Further reading

Up-to-date data on government expenditure in the UK can usually be found in the 'Blue Book', Office of National Statistics (1997). For comparative data, the OECD (1996) is the standard source, with their *Historical Statistics* volume providing data going back thirty years or so. The book of readings edited by Baker and Elliot (1990) has a number of perspectives on the subject of public sector economics. The book by Mueller (1989) contains a good summary of the voluminous literature on the growth of government. Cullis and Jones (1987) is also a good source, and particularly strong on the difference between the size of government as measured in national accounts and its actual impact. Borcherding (1985) is a formal attempt to compare different theoretical explanations for the USA, updated in Holsey and Borcherding (1997), while North (1985) is an historian's perspective on the same issue. International comparisons can be found in Abizadeh and Grey (1985), and from a more sceptical perspective, Solano (1983).

## Public sector texts

You may find it useful to consult other public sector texts with different perspectives on the subject. For convenience we list some of them below.

Atkinson, A.B. and Stiglitz, J.E. (1980) *Lectures on Public Economics*, London: McGraw-Hill.

Bailey, S. (1995) *Public Sector Economics*, London: Macmillan.

Barr, N. (1994) *The Economics of the Welfare State*, 2nd edn, Oxford: Oxford University Press.

Brown, C.V. and Jackson, P. (1991) *Public Sector Economics*, Oxford: Blackwell.

Cullis, J.G. and Jones P.R. (1998) *Public Finance, Public Choice*, 2nd edn, Oxford: Oxford University Press.

Musgrave, R. and Musgrave, P. (1989) *Public Finance in Theory and Practice*, New York: McGraw-Hill.

Myles, G. (1996) *Public Economics*, Cambridge: Cambridge University Press.

Stiglitz, J.E. (1988) *Economics of the Public Sector*, London: Norton.

## References

Abizadeh, S. and Grey, J. (1985) 'Wagner's Law: a pooled time-series, cross section comparison', *National Tax Journal* 38, 209–18.

Baker, S.H. and Elliot, C.S. (1990) *Readings in Public Sector Economics*, Lexington: D C Heath.

Borcherding, T.E. (1985) 'The causes of government expenditure growth: a survey of the US evidence', *Journal of Public Economics* 28, 359–82.

Cullis, J.G. and Jones, P.R. (1987) *Microeconomics and the Public Economy*, Oxford: Basil Blackwell.

Holsey, C.M. and Borcherding T.E. (1997) 'Why does government's share of national income grow: an assessment of the recent literature on the US experience', in D.C. Mueller (ed.), Ch. 25, *Perspectives on Public Choice*, Cambridge: Cambridge University Press, 562–90.

Kelman, S. (1987) 'Public choice and public spirit', *The Public Interest* Spring, 80–94.

Mueller, D.C. (1989) *Public Choice*, Cambridge: Cambridge University Press.

Mueller, D.C. (ed.) (1997) *Perspectives on Public Choice*, Cambridge: Cambridge University Press.

North, D.C. (1985) 'The growth of government in the USA: an economic historian's perspective', *Journal of Public Economics* 28, 359–82.

Office of National Statistics (1997) *National Income Accounts*, London: The Stationery Office.

Organisation for Economic Cooperation and Development (1996) *Historical Statistics*, Paris: OECD.

Solano, P.L. (1983) 'Institutional explanations of public expenditures among high income democracies', *Public Finance/Finance Publiques* 38, 440–57.

# Market Failure

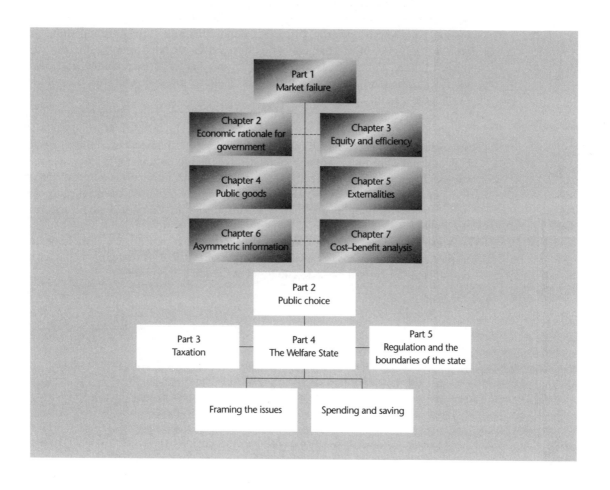

The first part of this book is primarily concerned with the efficiency arguments for government intervention in a market economy. It may seem perverse to answer the question, When should a government intervene?, by starting with a model (the Walrasian competitive model), in which there is **no** efficiency role for government. However, this is exactly what we do and it means that, having established the link between competition and efficiency, we can then go on to investigate the issue of market failure systematically. Chapter 2 builds this link between competition and efficiency, then each of Chapters 4–6 is devoted to considering a specific aspect of market failure. Public goods are introduced in Chapter 4; externalities and asymmetric information follow (the fourth market failure, increasing returns, is examined in Chapters 21 and 22).

Of course, efficiency is only one of the rationales for government activity. For instance, many people believe that the government should also be responsible for moderating the inequalities thrown up by the market. Chapter 3 examines the issue of equity and some of its various aspects. Unlike the promotion of efficiency, where in theory all can gain from government intervention, with most forms of redistribution some must lose. This gives rise to the efficiency–equity trade-off, a central concept in public sector economics, one which is introduced in Chapter 3 and then runs throughout the course of the book, particularly Parts 3 and 4.

While market failures are conceptually simple, it is not always clear how they translate into the practical. Finishing this part of the book is therefore a chapter on cost–benefit analysis, a basic decision tool of the applied economist.

# CHAPTER 2

# Economic Rationales for the State

## Key concepts

| | | |
|---|---|---|
| general equilibrium analysis | Pareto value judgements | Pareto improvements |
| Pareto optimal | Edgeworth box | efficiency in consumption |
| efficiency in production | top-level efficiency | fundamental theorums |
| market failure | equity | |

## 2.1 Introduction

In modern economies, most decisions regarding production and the appropriate use of the factors of production are taken by the private sector. Even in countries which had planned economies, such as eastern Europe, and the former Soviet Union, the state is relinquishing its responsibility. There is a widespread belief that reducing the role of the state is desirable and that production by the private sector is more efficient.

The centrepiece of the chapter and the keystones of public sector economics are the two Fundamental theorems of welfare economics, which provide a formal answer to the question, In what sense is a competitive market system efficient? In the first part of the chapter we review the Walrasian model of general competitive equilibrium (GCE).[1] We then examine the conditions under which an economy can be said to be efficient. Having done that, we bring the two separate concepts of competition and efficiency together for the theorems. The final part of the chapter is devoted to putting the theorems in context and showing how they relate to the economic rationale for government.

---

[1] You may find it useful to refresh your memory about GCE by referring to a text such as Katz and Rosen (1998) or Varian (1996).

## 2.2 Competitive equilibrium

**General competitive equilibrium**

Exists when agents are price takers and prices have adjusted to eliminate all excess demands and supply, so all markets clear

A **general competitive equilibrium** (GCE) has two main properties. First, behaviour is competitive; that is, firms and individuals take prices as given when making their decisions. Second, prices have adjusted to eliminate any excess demand or supply, so that there is equilibrium in all markets.

This can be illustrated in a two-person (Ann, Bill) and two-good (X, Y) exchange economy. For the moment we will assume that there is no production, but subsequently we examine the competitive outcome when X and Y are produced goods. The set of possible allocations of the two goods is represented in an Edgeworth box (see Figure 2.1), the dimensions of which are determined by the total amount of X and Y available in the economy. In this figure, $O_A$ represents an allocation where Bill has all the goods and Ann has nothing. Ann's consumption $(X_A, Y_A)$ is therefore measured away from her origin. Meanwhile, Bill's consumption is measured from his origin, $O_B$, which is the other extreme and the allocation where Ann has all the goods and Bill has nothing. The endowment point in this example is E, where Ann is endowed with $(X_A^E, Y_A^E)$ and Bill has $(X_B^E, Y_B^E)$. At this point Ann has the largest portion of Y and Bill has most of X.

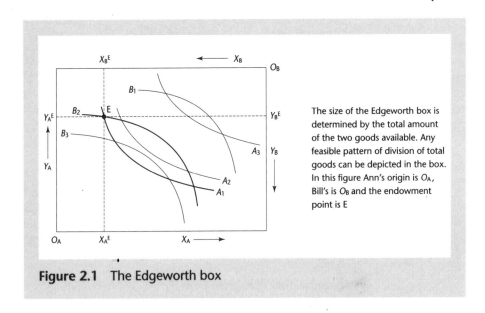

The size of the Edgeworth box is determined by the total amount of the two goods available. Any feasible pattern of division of total goods can be depicted in the box. In this figure Ann's origin is $O_A$, Bill's is $O_B$ and the endowment point is E

**Figure 2.1   The Edgeworth box**

Within the box in Figure 2.1, illustrative indifference curves are shown for Ann $(A_1, A_2$ and $A_3)$ and for Bill $(B_1, B_2$ and $B_3)$.[2] Recall that at any point on an indifference curve, the marginal rate of substitution $(MRS_{XY})$ is the maximum amount of Y the individual is willing to sacrifice in order to gain one more unit of X. $MRS_{XY}$ is therefore the same as the negative of the slope of the indifference curve.

Figure 2.2 concentrates on Ann's choice problem, showing three budget constraints, $PR_1$, $PR_2$ and $PR_3$ and her endowment point E. Since Ann can always refuse to trade, the endowment point is always on her budget constraint, the slope of which is $-P_Y/P_X$, where $P_X$ and $P_Y$ are the prices of X and Y respectively. As the price of Y

---

[2] Except where indicated, in this book we assume that preferences are well-behaved.

rises relative to $P_X$, the constraint becomes shallower, swivelling around E. If the constraint is $PR_1$, for instance, Ann's preferred bundle is at A, where $\text{MRS}_{XY}{}^A = P_X/P_Y$. To reach this point from E, she must sell some of her endowment of Y, $\Delta Y$, exchanging it for units of X $\Delta X$. Thus, the curve joining up all her preferred bundles is known as the **price offer curve** since it shows how much she offers to trade at different prices. We could sketch a similar price offer curve for Bill and, given the initial endowments shown, we would expect B to sell good X in order to buy good Y (though this does not have to be the case).

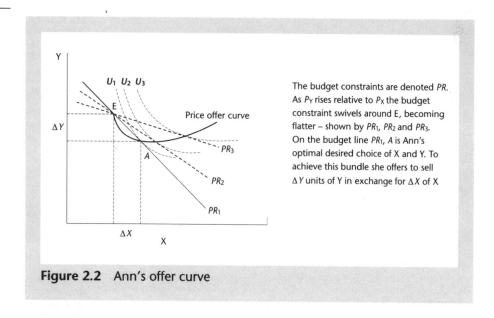

The budget constraints are denoted *PR*. As $P_Y$ rises relative to $P_X$ the budget constraint swivels around E, becoming flatter – shown by $PR_1$, $PR_2$ and $PR_3$. On the budget line $PR_1$, A is Ann's optimal desired choice of X and Y. To achieve this bundle she offers to sell $\Delta Y$ units of Y in exchange for $\Delta X$ of X

**Figure 2.2** Ann's offer curve

At a GCE, prices are such that all markets clear and all individuals are maximising utility. So, in our two-person/two-good model, a general equilibrium occurs when what Ann wants to buy is what Bill wants to sell and what Ann wants to sell is what Bill wants to buy. This is where the price offer curves cross, shown in the Edgeworth box in Figure 2.3. At this point, the price line, $PR^*$ (whose slope is given by the ratio of market clearing prices), is tangential to $IC_A$ and also tangential to $IC_B$. It follows that at the GCE the indifference curves of A and B are also tangential, a fact we will use later on. In short, at a competitive equilibrium:

$$\text{MRS}_{XY}{}^A = \frac{P_X}{P_Y} = \text{MRS}_{XY}{}^B \qquad \qquad \textit{Consumer optimisation}$$

## An economy with production

We can add production to the competitive economy model by supposing that the two goods are produced using two factors, labour, $L$, and capital, $K$, which are available in fixed amounts, $L^E$ and $K^E$. $K_X$ and $L_X$ are employed to produce good X and $K_Y$ and $L_Y$ to produce good Y, under diminishing or constant returns to scale. Once produced by profit-maximising firms, the goods are sold to the two consumers. To complete the circle, it is the consumers who own the factors which they supply to firms, producing the income required to buy goods.

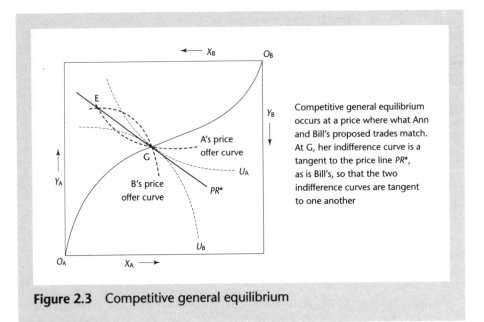

Competitive general equilibrium occurs at a price where what Ann and Bill's proposed trades match. At G, her indifference curve is a tangent to the price line $PR^*$, as is Bill's, so that the two indifference curves are tangent to one another

**Figure 2.3** Competitive general equilibrium

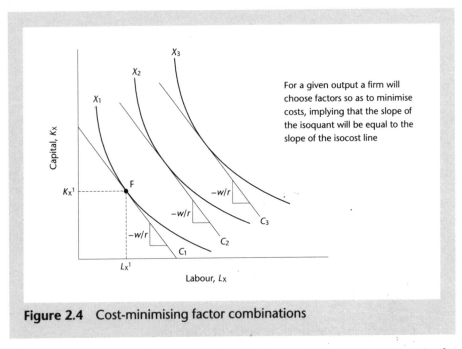

For a given output a firm will choose factors so as to minimise costs, implying that the slope of the isoquant will be equal to the slope of the isocost line

**Figure 2.4** Cost-minimising factor combinations

Since firms are profit maximising, they also have to be cost minimising, in the sense that, for any given output level, each firm will wish to use the combination of inputs which minimises the cost of production. Figure 2.4 shows isoquants (combinations of inputs which produce the same output level) $X_1$, $X_2$ and $X_3$ and three isocost lines (combinations of inputs which cost the same to the firm) $C_1$, $C_2$, $C_3$. Along an isoquant, the marginal rate of technical substitution, $\mathrm{MRTS}_{KL}{}^X$ is the increase in $K$ required to keep output constant if one less unit of $L$ is used in the production of X. Meanwhile, $-w/r$ is the slope of the isocost line. For a given output level, cost minimisation occurs when the slope of the isocost line is equal to the slope of the isoquant since $\text{MRTS}_{KL}$ is the negative of the slope of the isoquant, this means that $\text{MRTS}_{KL}{}^X = w/r$. At a point F, for instance, if the firm uses one less unit of $L$ then to maintain the same output, it must increase its use of capital by $\text{MRTS}_{KL}{}^X$. By doing so, it saves $w$, but the extra use of capital costs it $r.\text{MRTS}_{KL}{}^X$. If costs are minimised, then these two items cancel, so that:

$$\text{MRTS}_{KL}{}^X = \frac{w}{r} \qquad \textit{Cost minimisation (for X) condition}$$

Similarly, inputs for the production of Y will be such that:

$$\text{MRTS}_{KL}{}^Y = \frac{w}{r} \qquad \textit{Cost minimisation (for X) condition}$$

These cost minimisation conditions define the optimal use of factors for given levels of X and Y, but what about output? Under perfect competition, firms are price takers and so, to maximise profits, each will set output at the point where price is equal to marginal cost, MC, that is:

$$\text{MC}_X = P_X; \qquad \text{MC}_Y = P_Y \qquad \textit{Profit maximisation condition}$$

This determines the supply of the two goods.

In summary, a GCE is a set of prices for the factors and goods, where all agents are price takers and all markets clear. So it is characterised by demand equalling supply:

$$K^E = K_X + K_Y \text{ and } L^E = L_X + L_Y \qquad \textit{factor markets clear}$$

and

$$X = X_A + X_B \text{ and } Y = Y_A + Y_B \qquad \textit{product markets clear}$$

and by the conditions for cost minimisation, profit maximisation and consumer optimisation.[3]

In this section we have revised the basic framework of the general competitive equilibrium model. To illustrate the argument we have used a simple two-good, two-factor, two-agent model, but before moving on, it is worth noting that there are no conceptual barriers to extending the analysis to a world of $n$ goods and $H$ households supplying $m$ factors. The same is true of the next section.

## 2.3 Efficiency

**Pareto improvement**

Occurs when it is possible to make at least one person better off without making anyone else worse off

An economy is efficient if it provides the maximum amount of the goods that people want, given the resources available. The standard notion of efficiency used within economics is called Pareto efficiency or Pareto optimality. Within this framework, a **Pareto improvement** occurs when it is possible to make at least one person better off without making anyone else worse off. A Pareto optimum is then defined as a situation where it is no longer possible to make any Pareto improvements. In other words, society has reached a Pareto optimum when it is impossible to make one person better off without making someone else worse off.

---

[3] It is worth noting that the profit maximisation conditions imply cost minimisation; we have set them out separately to stress the fact that a profit maximiser will need to minimise its costs.

In order to identify the conditions for **Pareto efficiency**, we pose the following question: Under what circumstances are no further Pareto improvements possible? We answer this in three steps.

## Efficiency in consumption

Consider the Edgeworth box shown in Figure 2.5 where, as with Figure 2.1, initial endowments are represented by E. This allocation of goods is clearly not Pareto optimal, because, for instance, both Bill and Ann would be better off if they were at Z. Z can be reached if Ann passes some of her endowment of Y to Bill and he gives some of his allocation of X to her. In fact any reallocation of the goods which leaves the consumers inside the shaded area is a Pareto improvement over E.

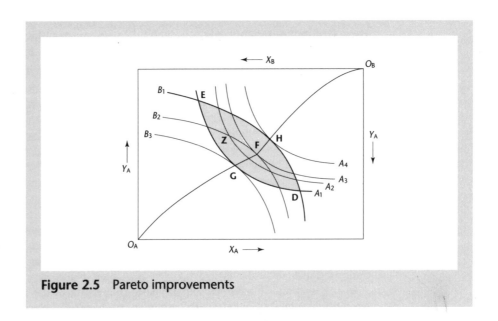

**Figure 2.5** Pareto improvements

Points on the edge of the shaded area also represent allocations that increase the utility of one consumer without diminishing the utility of the other. Along $A_1$ there is a set of possible reallocations which leave Ann's utility unchanged, but increase Bill's utility. This is a Pareto improvement. Meanwhile, changes along $B_1$, up to D, are clearly also Pareto improvements. However, at the point of tangency between $A_1$ and $B_3$ there are no further Pareto improvements, since any reallocation from this point would place either Ann or Bill (or both) on a lower indifference curve, so this point is Pareto optimal. Similarly, F and H are also Pareto optimal. In fact, there is a continuum of Pareto optimal consumption bundles, representing the set of all points of mutual tangency between A and B's indifference curves and shown as a curve running between $O_A$ and $O_B$. This is known as the **contract curve** or the locus of exchange efficient distributions. The contract curve is often translated into utility space to give the **utility possibility frontier** (UPF) as in Figure 2.6. The UPF identifies the maximum utility that A can attain, given B's utility. Points on the UPF, such as F', are therefore Pareto efficient, whereas Pareto improvements are still available at E'.

Each point on the utility possibility frontier (*UPF*) such as *F'* corresponds to a point on the contract curve (*F*). Any point inside the box that is not on the contract curve (e.g. *E*) will lie below the *UPF*, (*E'*). Thus, points on the utility possibility frontier are Pareto efficient and points below the utility possibility frontier are Pareto suboptimal. It follows that from *E'*, there is room for a Pareto improvement. From *S'*, however, no Pareto improvement is possible, A's welfare can only be improved at the expense of B and *vice versa*. At *O$_A$'*, B has all of the resources in the economy; meanwhile at At *O$_B$'*, all consumption is A's. So the *UPF* can also be employed to summarise equity issues.

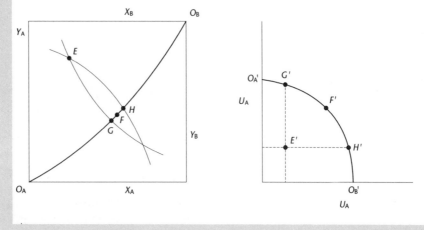

**Figure 2.6** The utility possibility frontier

As just stated, at all points on the contract curve we have tangency between Ann and Bill's indifference curves. It follows that Pareto efficiency requires that the marginal rates of substitution of all consumers be equal. This requirement for Pareto efficiency is called *exchange efficiency*, and the condition for it is therefore summarised as:

$$\mathrm{MRS}_{XY}{}^{A} = \mathrm{MRS}_{XY}{}^{B} \qquad\qquad \textit{exchange efficiency}$$

### Efficiency in production

Now let us consider the question of what would characterise a Pareto optimal use of the factors. This exercise is almost identical to that already described. The endowments of the factors of production determine the size of the production Edgeworth box, shown in Figure 2.7, which also depicts isoquants for the two goods. At $O_X$, for instance, all available factors are employed in the production of Y; at $O_Y$ all inputs are used to produce X. From a point such as Z, if labour is diverted into production of X, while capital is moved into production of Y, more of both goods can be produced. This extra would then be available for consumption, so that Z cannot be part of a Pareto optimum, since it is wasteful of resources. At points such as F, meanwhile, where isoquants form mutual tangents, reallocating factors so as to produce more of one of the goods must be the detriment of production of the other.

It follows that Pareto efficiency requires tangency between the isoquants. We saw in the previous section that the slope of an isoquant is the negative of the marginal

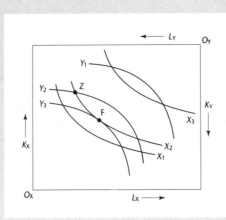

From Z, if less labour is used in production of Y and more in production of X and less capital is used in production of X and more in the production of Y, it is possible to produce more of both goods. At a point of tangency between the isoquants, such as F, no further gains can be made. It is only possible to increase production of one good by reducing production of the other.

**Figure 2.7**  The production Edgeworth box

rate of technical substitution. Thus, for Pareto efficiency, we also require production is efficient or that:

$$\mathrm{MRTS}_{LK}{}^{X} = \mathrm{MRTS}_{LK}{}^{Y} \qquad \qquad production\ efficiency$$

**Production possibility frontier**

The maximum level of good Y that can be produced given the level of production of X. Along the PPF production is making the best use of the factors

Just as the UPF summarised the opportunities for efficient exchange, so the **production possibility frontier** (see Figure 2.8) summarises efficient production opportunities. More formally, it shows the maximum amount of Y which can be produced for any given level of X, with fixed endowments $L^E$ and $K^E$. For example, point $Y_{max}$ on the PPF is where all of the factors are used in the production of Y and relates to $O_X$ on the contract curve, similarly, $X_{max}$ on the PPF is where all of the factors are used to produce X and relates to $O_Y$ on the contract curve. Note that the PPF is concave to the origin this is because of our earlier assumption that returns to scale were non-increasing.

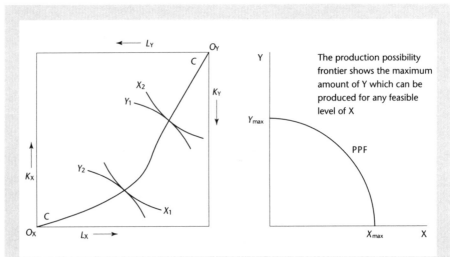

The production possibility frontier shows the maximum amount of Y which can be produced for any feasible level of X

**Figure 2.8**  The production possibility frontier

The slope of the PPF shows how much extra Y is feasible if production of X is changed by one unit, hence the negative of the slope is called the **marginal rate of transformation** between X and Y, $MRT_{XY}$. Now one less unit of X saves $MC_X$ (where, recall, $MC_X$ is the marginal cost of X). If $MC_X$ is saved, then $MC_X/MC_Y$ more of Y can be produced. So the slope of the PPF is also the negative of the ratio of marginal costs.

**Marginal rate of transformation**

The technical possibilities for transforming production of good X into production of good Y at the margin, by reallocating the factor inputs

### Efficient allocation of resources

Neither exchange efficiency nor production efficiency ensures that the right combination of goods is produced. If X is fish, for instance, and Y is chips, and all factors are used in the production of fish, both consumers might prefer some resources to be switched into output of Y for a more balanced diet. The final condition therefore brings together the consumption and production activities in our economy and ensures that what is produced is what people want. It is often referred to as the top-level condition. Formally, the condition required is that:

$$MRS_{XY}{}^A = MRT_{XY}; \qquad MRS_{XY}{}^B = MRT_{XY} \qquad \textit{allocative efficiency}$$

Intuitively, we can think about this in the following way:

$MRS_{XY}$ – The rate of trade-off for consumers between X and Y, how much extra of Y consumers need to be given to compensate them for marginally less of X.

$MRT_{XY}$ – The rate of trade-off between production of X and Y, how much more of Y can be produced if firms produce marginally less of X.

Suppose that the condition fails to hold:

$MRS_{XY}{}^A = 1$

$MRT_{XY} = 2$ (society can produce 2Y by giving up 1X)

If Ann loses one unit of X because one less unit is produced, then the minimum compensation she requires is one extra unit of Y. But in this example two extra units of Y can be produced, so Ann can be more than compensated. It is clear therefore that Ann's welfare can be improved by producing less X and more Y (and Bill is unaffected by the change in production). Therefore, it is only when $MRS_{XY} = MRT_{XY}$ that all of the options for Pareto improvement are exhausted.

This top-level condition is illustrated in Figure 2.9, which uses the numbers of the previous paragraph. At any point along the production possibility frontier (such as G) firms are producing the amounts of X and Y that are available for consumption, ($X^G$, $Y^G$). As G is on the PPF, we know that it is production efficient. Given this level of production, we can sketch in a consumption Edgeworth box which represents the consumption opportunities. If production is at G and consumption is at H, the separate conditions for efficiency in consumption and production are satisfied. However, a Pareto gain is still possible: if one less unit of X is produced, 2 more of Y are available. But Ann's $MRS_{XY}{}^A$ is 1, so she gains if it is her that loses the one unit of X, but gains 2 of Y. Bill meanwhile faces no change in consumption, so he does not lose. It follows that along with the other two conditions, allocative efficiency condition must be satisfied for Pareto efficiency.

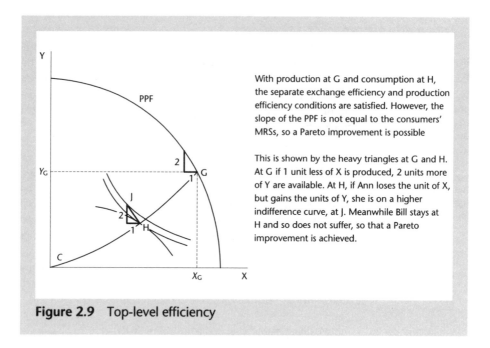

**Figure 2.9** Top-level efficiency

## Second-order conditions

We have assumed that our economy was characterised by the diminishing or constant returns to scale, which would result in a concave production possibility frontier. The assumption is necessary for the conditions we have stated to characterise Pareto efficiency. To show this, we examine the simplified case of a single consumer, faced with a convex PPF as a result of increasing returns to scale. In this case, the top-level condition would not yield Pareto efficiency. In Figure 2.10 we can see that a point of tangency would occur between the PPF and $U_1$, but that utility would be higher on $U_2$. Utility would be highest when the economy specialised in the production of Y.

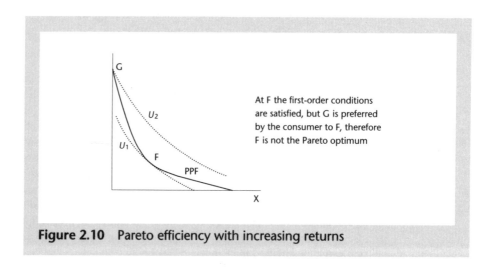

**Figure 2.10** Pareto efficiency with increasing returns

## 2.4  Pareto efficiency and the market

Having outlined the conditions for Pareto efficiency, we now consider the market structures under which the conditions hold. The crucial link between the GCE in section 2.2 and the conditions for Pareto efficiency in the previous section is provided by the two propositions called the Fundamental Theorems of Welfare Economics. In this section we outline the theorems and then provide interpretation of their significance and underlying assumptions in the remainder of the chapter.

### First Fundamental Theorem

*A general competitive equilibrium is Pareto efficient*

We have already proved this in outline. Recall that Pareto efficiency requires the conditions for exchange efficiency, production efficiency and allocative efficiency to hold. Meanwhile, in section 2.2 we saw that a competitive equilibrium required consumer optimisation, cost minimisation and profit maximisation. Table 2.1 summarises the close relationship between these conditions. Consumer optimisation implies exchange efficiency, cost minimisation implies production efficiency and these conditions together with profit maximisation imply top-level efficiency. Hence, the equilibrium of a perfectly competitive market system satisfies all three of the Pareto efficiency conditions.[4]

---

**Table 2.1**  The First Fundamental Theorem

| | | |
|---|---|---|
| General competitive equilibrium | implies . . . | Pareto efficiency |
| Consumer optimisation $$MRS_{XY}{}^A = \frac{P_X}{P_Y}$$ $$MRS_{XY}{}^B = \frac{P_X}{P_Y}$$ | implies . . . | Exchange efficiency $$MRS_{XY}{}^B = MRS_{XY}{}^A$$ |
| Cost minimisation $$MRTS_{LK}{}^X = \frac{w}{r}$$ $$MRTS_{LK}{}^Y = \frac{w}{r}$$ | implies . . . | Production efficiency $$MRTS_{LK}{}^X = MRTS_{LK}{}^Y$$ |
| Profit maximising $$P_X = MC_X$$ $$P_Y = MC_Y$$ | implies . . . | Top-level efficiency $$MRT_{XY} \equiv \frac{MC_X}{MC_Y} = \frac{P_X}{P_Y} = MRS_{XY}{}^i$$ $$i = A, B$$ |

---

[4] The arguments summarised by Table 2.1 only constitute the outline of a proper proof if the PPF is concave. When it is not, a GCE may not exist, but if it does the equilibrium is still Pareto efficient. See Varian (1996) for a general proof.

### Second Fundamental Theorem

*If preferences and technology are convex, any Pareto efficient outcome is a competitive equilibrium for some pattern of initial endowments.*

Again, we have already done all the groundwork for this theorem. To show that the theorem is true we take the conditions for Pareto efficiency shown in the final column of Table 2.1. We use them to *define* our prices. For instance $P_X/P_Y$ will be defined as $MRS_{XY}$ etc. We then allocate ownership of the factors, so that, given the value of their endowment and the newly created prices, Ann and Bill wish to buy the amounts of X and Y which are assigned to them in the Pareto-efficient outcome. The result is illustrated in Figure 2.11, where the common tangencies at H and G define the relative price of X and Y in the competitive economy.

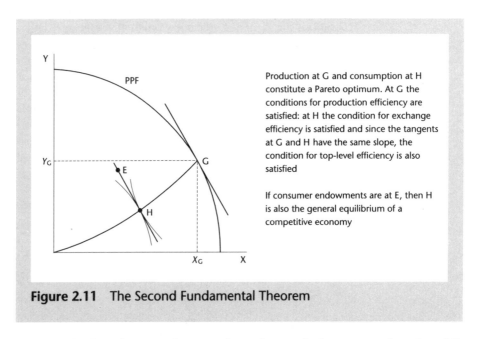

Production at G and consumption at H constitute a Pareto optimum. At G the conditions for production efficiency are satisfied: at H the condition for exchange efficiency is satisfied and since the tangents at G and H have the same slope, the condition for top-level efficiency is also satisfied

If consumer endowments are at E, then H is also the general equilibrium of a competitive economy

**Figure 2.11   The Second Fundamental Theorem**

Unlike the first theorem, the Second Fundamental Theorem requires the additional convexity assumptions which imply that, among other things, there are no increasing returns and hence that the PPF is concave. If the PPF is not concave, then price-taking producers will not wish to produce a mix of goods, which is what consumers usually prefer. As a result, the Pareto-efficient outcome may not be sustainable via competitive behaviour.

## 2.5   Interpretations

Having set out the theory in its barest form, we now provide some context.

### Interpreting Pareto efficiency

Underlying the concept of efficiency we have employed are the Paretian value judgements which assume that:

1. There is no 'society' above and beyond individuals. So, in making value judgements, we should only be interested in the welfare of individuals and nothing else;

2. Individuals are the best judges of their own welfare and choose what is best for themselves;

3. Social welfare can be said to have increased if at least one person's welfare has increased and no-one else's has fallen.

In general, economists prefer to make claims which are value free. Where this is not possible they aim to use minimal value judgements, those based on values which have wide acceptance. Much of modern welfare economics is based on these Paretian value judgements, but are they really minimal assumptions?

Some might take issue with the first assumption and contend that we should not just be concerned with the welfare of individuals, but also with the well-being of larger social entities, such as families or class, and wider concerns such as heritage, the natural world and national identity. These concerns might be partly *instrumental*, in the sense that we might consider nature conservation important not for itself, but because it enables future individuals to thrive, yet they need not be. For instance 'deep Green' ecologists value the natural world for itself and not for any of the benefits it delivers to human beings, whether unborn or not.

We might have concerns about the second postulate on at least two grounds. First, many individuals (not only small children) do not necessarily know what is best for themselves in all circumstances. Few, for instance, could diagnose their own illnesses as accurately as a trained doctor. As a result, individuals are not always the best judges of their own welfare. Second, even if we know what is best for us, we might suffer from a weakness of the will and choose suboptimally, like addicts who know they should stop taking drugs, but nevertheless continue.

The weakness of the third assumption is not that it is minimal, but that it reveals how little Pareto optimality can say about the 'right' allocation of resources. Formally it provides a *partial ordering* of allocations, rather than a full ordering. If Ann has all of X and all of Y while Bill dies from starvation then, provided both are selfish, the outcome is Pareto efficient. So too is the situation where Ann has nothing and Bill consumes everything. The Pareto criterion therefore does not say anything about equity. Unfortunately, many of the outcomes we wish to compare are precisely ones where one individual or group of people is better off with one solution and another individual or group of individuals is better off with another outcome. Many of the fiercest political debates are for instance over the level of redistributive taxation or public expenditure. Yet such comparisons cannot usually be made using the Pareto criterion. Similarly saying which of two options is best when both are Pareto improvements is impossible with the Pareto criterion.

However, if we were to define an alternative notion of efficiency, it is likely we would produce something very similar to the Paretian definition with similar defects. Moreover, as Barr (1994) points out, the Liberal who believes in some redistribution, the Socialist who believes in equality of well-being and the Libertarian who believes in the acceptability of only voluntary actions can all accept the Paretian criterion, by and large. So that, although this section has shown that the Paretian approach does involve significant value judgements and cannot rank all options, we shall continue to work with it in this book, while recognising its limitations.

### Interpreting the Fundamental theorems

These theorems are called 'Fundamental' so they must be important, but what exactly is their role in welfare economics?

The simplest view is that the assumptions underlying the theorems are true, so that the world is characterised by perfect competition and so on. If that is the case, then the first theorem says that there is no efficiency role for government, because the competitive market yields an efficient outcome. Governments therefore only ought to intervene in the market for other reasons, such as redistribution.

Meanwhile, the second theorem tells us that the government can achieve an equitable outcome without necessarily sacrificing efficiency. Any point on the UPF can be attained by a reallocation of resources. We know from the First Fundamental Theorem that for a given set of endowments the competitive equilibrium will be Pareto efficient. Let us say this occurs at a point on the UPF, say F in Figure 2.12. Although this outcome may be Pareto efficient, it may be unequal. We may prefer another point on the UPF, such as F', which is both efficient and more equal.

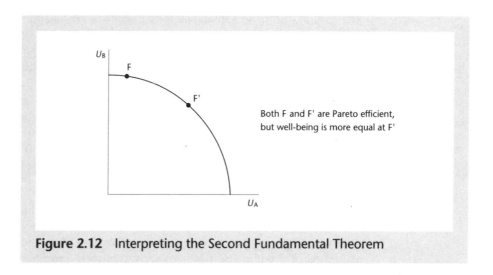

**Figure 2.12**  Interpreting the Second Fundamental Theorem

The Second Fundamental Theorem therefore shows that if a point such as F' is desired, then it is not necessary to abandon the market system; government intervention may be needed to reallocate the initial endowments, but then the market can be relied upon to ensure Pareto efficiency.

There are problems with this interpretation of the theorems. If the first theorem is to hold we must be at a competitive equilibrium. Yet even Walras, the inventor of GCE, was sceptical, believing instead that the market is 'like a lake stirred by the wind, in which the water continually seeks its equilibrium without achieving it' (Kirman A. (1998) p. 1186). Many economists, particularly of a Keynesian persuasion, even doubt that there is a tendency for a competitive economy to seek its equilibrium. The theorem also requires the full complement of markets, which means a full set of futures markets (markets for goods to be supplied in the future), and also markets to cover all possible contingencies. In practice, markets for the supply of umbrellas to be delivered in three years' time, provided it rains, are notable by their absence from the world.

The second theorem is also not without its critics, among them Hayek. He pointed out that in order to pick its desired Pareto-efficient allocation, the government would have to know the preferences of all individuals (so that their marginal rates of substitution could be predicted) and the available technology, so that marginal costs and rates of transformation could be computed. In practice this information is only available via the market, leaving the government which wishes to apply the second theorem in a 'Catch-22' situation: it needs the information *before* setting endowments and unleashing the competitive process, but it is only *after* markets have opened and trades executed that the information becomes available.

An alternative interpretation accepts that the real world is very different from the assumptions of the theorems. Consider a doctor faced with a patient covered in large, purple spots. The doctor knows that the patient is ill, because the doctor has a model of what a healthy person looks like. For the welfare economist, the Fundamental theorems provide a model of the healthy economy, a world where intervention by government on efficiency grounds is unjustified. The source of inefficiencies can then be diagnosed by comparing the real world to the ideal model.

## Market failure

**Market failure**

When market outcomes are not Pareto efficient

The major efficiency 'illnesses' of the market are summarised in Table 2.2.[5] Collectively they are known as **market failures** and they are discussed in detail in subsequent chapters.

In the case of public goods for instance, the market fails because of the properties which characterise a public good: non-rivalry and non-excludability. Non-rivalry

**Table 2.2** The main market failures – a summary

| Problem | Definition | Example | Possible intervention | See also: |
|---|---|---|---|---|
| Public goods | Goods which are *non-rival* and *non-excludable* | Defence, street lighting | Public provision | Chapter 4 |
| Externalities | Actions of individuals or firms affect others, but the cost or benefit of this is not reflected in the value of their transactions | Pollution, road congestion | Taxes or subsidies to equate private and social costs and benefits | Chapter 5 |
| Asymmetric information | Transactions where the parties (e.g. buyer and seller) have different sets of information | Healthcare, second-hand cars | Regulation of quality; compulsory pooling of insurance | Chapter 6 |
| Increasing returns | Average cost decreases as output increases | Natural monopolies, e.g. water supply; electricity transmission | Social ownership; regulation of private monopoly | Chapters 21 and 22 |

[5] Often *missing markets* and *imperfect competition* are added to this list, although it can be argued that these extra items arise either as a result of government policy or as a consequence of other, more fundamental market failures.

implies that one unit of the good can be consumed simultaneously by all consumers and non-excludability means that it is impossible to prevent consumers consuming the good when they have not paid for it. As a consequence, the market may supply too little of the good or fail to supply the good completely. With the other cases, the market also fails in ways which we shall examine in the chapters which follow.

While market failure is often used to justify a role for government in the economy, it should not be assumed that public intervention always raises efficiency. For example, it may be costly to establish a public corporation or agency to supply a good or service and these costs may exceed those associated with the market failure. Therefore, just as markets may fail, so might government, an argument aired in more detail in Chapters 8 and 9.

### Second best

The efficiency conditions that we have outlined in this chapter are referred to as the First Best conditions. If the conditions fail to hold in one sector of the economy, it seems natural to assume that efficiency requires that the First Best conditions should hold wherever possible. However, this need not be the case. Consider a monopolist which produces an unregulated pollutant as a by-product. Breaking up the firm into smaller companies may 'cure' the monopoly problem, but the extra output produced in a competitive industry will exacerbate the damage caused by the pollutant.

This issue is known as the problem of the Second Best (Lipsey and Lancaster, 1956). In such cases it may be more efficient to abandon the First Best conditions completely. For instance, as a result of capital market imperfections, firms may need a degree of market power in order to develop and to grow. So, there may be a conflict between perfect competition which yields the best use of resources at any moment in time, and some monopoly power which results in the best use of resources over time.

## 2.6 Further rationales

The Pareto criteria are clearly valuable when making judgements over efficiency, but they are not always central in the justifications offered for the role of government in society, even amongst economists.

### Merit goods

Sometimes the Paretian assumption that individuals are the best judges of their own welfare is violated. Merit goods is the term used for those goods where it can no longer be assumed that the individual knows best. Examples often put forward include healthcare and education (see Chapters 19 and 20). With merit goods, it may be desirable for the government to amend or control consumption. There are a number of ways in which this can be done. The government may act as a supplier, offer subsidies, or as is the case with compulsory education, legislate so that all citizens must consume at least a certain minimum. It is also possible to identify dis-merit goods; examples include tobacco, alcohol and certain drugs. In these cases governments may pass legislation to prevent or tax the goods with the aim of reducing consumption.

### Redistribution

As we have already stressed, Pareto efficiency has little to say about inequality and yet many of the fiercest advocates of government intervention do so because they believe that markets produce an unfair allocation of resources. It is likely therefore that many, perhaps most, individuals will regard certain points upon the contract curves, where the distribution is unequal, as unacceptable. Exactly what is deemed unacceptable may vary over time and across countries, but one potential role for government is then to redistribute resources and so reduce inequality. These issues are discussed in Chapter 3.

### Stabilisation

We have already mentioned that an economy may not be at equilibrium and that some economists (and many non-economists) believe that there is no automatic reason why the economy will tend towards general equilibrium. If this is the case, then there may be a case for a government intervening in order to stabilise the economy. For instance, there may be a role for government in maintaining high levels of employment, for example, by intervening to limit the effects of a downturn in the economic cycle. Similarly there may also be a role for the economy in ensuring the stability of the monetary system. We shall not address these issues in detail, but they will be of relevance in later chapters.

## 2.7  Conclusion

Market failure and concerns of inequality and poverty provide the main justifications usually offered for state involvement in the economy. In this chapter, we have examined how we define economic efficiency and the link between economic efficiency and the free market. We have also seen that the criteria by which we judge efficiency fail to take account of concepts such as fairness and justice. In the next chapter we look at these issues in more detail.

## Summary

- General competitive equilibrium occurs when price-taking producers and consumers are optimising and when prices are such that all markets clear.
- Economic efficiency is identified using the Pareto criteria, which state that an outcome can only be improved if change leads to an improvement for at least one person without making anyone else worse off.
- Pareto efficiency requires efficiency in consumption and production as well as top-level or allocative efficiency.

- The First Fundamental Theorem states that every competitive equilibrium is Pareto efficient.
- The Second Fundamental Theorem states that, provided all preferences and technology are convex, then every Pareto-efficient allocation is a competitive equilibrium for some initial allocation of resources.
- The two Fundamental Theorems of Welfare Economics establish a link between the competitive market and Pareto efficiency.
- Market failure describes a situation where the unregulated market fails to provide a Pareto-efficient outcome. It provides one justification for a role for government in the economy.
- Government may also have a redistributive and a stabilisation role.

## Questions

1. How acceptable are the value judgements embedded in Paretian welfare economics?
2. What are the implications for the conditions for efficiency in consumption of non-convex preferences?
3. Why are Pareto improvements possible if producers' current use of factors is not on the production contract curve?
4. Why is it that an efficient outcome might also be unfair?
5. To what extent does Paretian welfare economics help to legitimate a free-market system?

## Further reading

Much of this material is covered in intermediate microeconomics texts, you may find it useful to refer to Katz and Rosen (1998) or Varian (1996). A more technical treatment is given by Myles (1995) or Ng (1983). The first five chapters of Hahn (1984) put GCE and the fundamental theorems in context. Useful discussions on the applications of this material can be found in Barr (1994) or Helm (1986).

## References

Barr, N. (1994) *The Economics of the Welfare State*, 2nd edn, Oxford: Oxford University Press.

Hahn, F. (1984) *Equilibrium and Macroeconomics*, Oxford: Blackwell.

Helm, D. (1986) 'The economic borders of the state', *Oxford Review of Economic Policy* vol. 2, no. 2.

Katz, M.L. and Rosen, H.S. (1998) *Microeconomics*, 3rd edn, London: McGraw-Hill.

Kirman, A. (1998) Book review in *Economic Journal*, July 1998, vol. 108, pp 1184–6.

Lipsey, R.G. and Lancaster K. (1956) 'The general theory of the second best', *Review of Economic Studies* 24, 11–32.

Myles, G. (1996) *Public Economics*, Cambridge: Cambridge University Press.

Ng, Y.-K. (1983) *Welfare Economics*, Basingstoke: Macmillan.

Rowley, C.K. and Peacock, A.T. (1975) *Welfare Economics: A Liberal Restatement*, London: Robertson.

Varian, H.R. (1996) *Intermediate Microeconomics*, 4th edn, London: Norton.

# CHAPTER 3

# Equity and Efficiency

## Key concepts

| | | |
|---|---|---|
| social welfare function | marginal cost of public funds | equity–efficiency trade-off |
| utility possibility frontier | Pareto principle | inequality aversion |
| consequentialism | utilitarianism | horizontal equity |
| | Impossibility Theorem | |

## 3.1 Introduction

Should governments do something about poverty? Should they transfer income to less-developed nations? Should they limit the wealth of their richest citizens? How should the tax burden be shared? The answers to these questions depend directly on value judgements about what is good for society and for individuals. Most arguments about economic policy involve such views, judgements which seem to lie outside the scope of economic analysis. Nevertheless, economics can still bring something to the debate. If the choice is between pursuing the goal of increased equality in society or maximising efficiency, we can identify the trade-off between the two and point out the options. We can also trace the inconsistencies between ethical beliefs and draw out the links between different kinds of beliefs and the policy options which follow from them. The point of this chapter is not to arbitrate between different sets of beliefs. Instead, the aim is to make clear how ethical views differ and why the differences matter for public sector economics.

**Equity–efficiency trade-off**

The tendency for the pursuit of redistribution by government to create efficiency losses

The Oxford English Dictionary defines equity as 'that which is fair and right'. Not surprisingly there are many alternative views on what is equitable, many different types of ethical belief and a large number of ways in which they can clash, but because it is at the heart of so many real-world debates, economists tend to concentrate on one particular issue, the clash between efficiency and the pursuit of greater equality; it is this which is usually labelled the **equity–efficiency trade-off**. Consider a country where the unfettered labour market throws up a division between rich and poor and where it is proposed that a safety net is introduced, financed by a lump-sum tax on the rich and involving a payment which means no-one has less than £100 per week to live on. Some people on very low incomes, with poor future prospects, who dislike their job, might prefer not to work at all, meaning that total output in the economy falls. Pursuing equity therefore leads to a drop in efficiency. Within economics, the standard way of evaluating this proposed safety net is to say that the policy should go ahead if the gain to society from reducing poverty out-weighs the cost of reduced output.[1] So, in order to state whether the safety net should proceed, we need two items of information: the cost in lost output of the proposal and the value to society of reducing poverty. The difficulty usually lies in finding agreement on the latter figure.

## 3.2  When more equality means more efficiency

It may come as a surprise, but there are several cases when raising the degree of equality can lead to a Pareto improvement. If this were true of the safety-net pro-posal, then there would be no equity–efficiency trade-off.

### Externalities (crime and altruism)

There are two main kinds of external effects which are important here. First, individuals may care about aspects of the welfare of other individuals. If their con-cern is specifically for the well-being of other people, then they are altruistic, e.g. they might have preferences of the form $U(x,V)$ where $x$ is goods consumed and $V$ is the well-being of some other member of society. If, though, their worry is over particular aspects of other peoples' consumption, such as their health or the amount of food available to them, the preferences are termed paternalistic (because the individual who cares would wish the subject to change their consumption behaviour). Other people may simply dislike inequality or relative poverty or have views on the just distribution of income which enter their utility function. Richer individuals may therefore gain from transferring some of their income to the poorer members of society. Figure 3.1 shows a utility possibility frontier. Unlike the similar curves of the previous chapter, each individual has some altruistic feeling towards the other agent. As a result, though for most of the curve an increase in the well-being of one person leads to a drop in the well-being of the other, from F to G, transfers from person 2 to person 1 lead to strict Pareto improvements; both individuals gain from some redistribution.

However, if they get pleasure from seeing the relief of poverty (and not from the act of giving itself), such transfers have something of the property of public goods; there is an incentive to free-ride on the giving of others (see Chapter 4). To illustrate this argument, consider Alison and Ben, each of whom is considering whether to make a donation of £1 to reduce poverty. A £1 reduction in poverty raises Alison's utility by the equivalent of £0.75; the same applies to Ben. Table 3.1 summarises their choices and payoffs.

In this table, Alison's payoffs are given first, Ben's are second. For instance, if they both give £1, then the total amount donated is £2, which yields a benefit of £1.50 for

---

[1] A second view is that the policy is wrong not because of the outcomes achieved, but because of the way it is achieved – through compulsory taxation. We come back to this alternative later in the chapter.

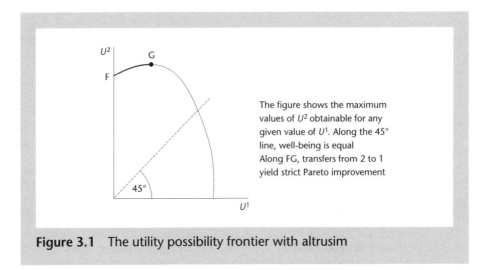

The figure shows the maximum values of $U^2$ obtainable for any given value of $U^1$. Along the 45° line, well-being is equal Along FG, transfers from 2 to 1 yield strict Pareto improvement

**Figure 3.1** The utility possibility frontier with altrusim

**Table 3.1** Free riding and voluntary giving

| | | Ben | | | |
|---|---|---|---|---|---|
| | | Give £1 | | Do Not Give | |
| Alison | Give £1 | 0.50, | 0.50 | −0.25, | 0.75 |
| | Do Not Give | 0.75, | −0.25 | 0, | 0 |

Alison, from which she must deduct the cost of her donation, £1, to give her net payoff of £0.50. Similarly, when she gives, but Ben does not, £1 is given in total, producing a benefit of £0.75 to her at a cost of £1. Alison's optimal strategy in this game does not depend on Ben's decision; she has a dominant strategy. If Ben gives £1 she can obtain a payoff of £0.75 by free riding on his contributions, compared to £0.50 if she also contributes. If Ben does not give, again she is better off not giving. Ben's optimal strategy is the same: Do Not Give, producing a Nash equilibrium outcome where neither gives.

In this situation, the outcome where both give £1 Pareto dominates the Nash equilibrium, meaning that if they were compelled to give, perhaps through an income tax system, then both could benefit. In short therefore, individuals who care about the well-being of others may gain from replacing voluntary contributions with compulsory redistributive taxation.

In addition to caring about the welfare or consumption of others, we may also be affected by their actions or the consequences of their actions. Crime, especially economic crime such as robbery, is linked to the degree of inequality and relative poverty in a society, as Figure 3.2 shows. This diagram takes data from two international sources and shows the close relationship between the incidence of robbery and the percentage of the population who are poor, as defined by a poverty line set at 50% of median incomes. Taken at face value, it suggests that robbery rates in the UK would nearly halve if the proportion of the population with incomes below 50% of the

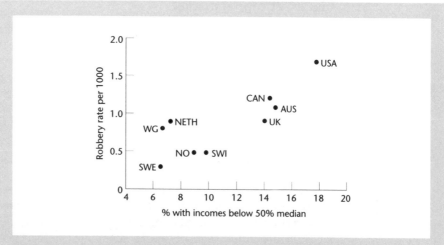

**Figure 3.2** The link between poverty and crime, nine OECD countries (Sources: income: LIS; crime: international crime survey)

median was cut in two.[2] Since many people suffer from robbery, many more live in fear of it and most citizens adjust their behaviour in some way to cope with its threat (e.g. by locking doors and buying car alarms). Reducing crime brings benefits and therefore reducing poverty might bring about some of these same benefits.

## Social insurance

Groups of people who do not know exactly their future circumstances may be willing to pool some of their future income in order to reduce the risks they face. For many risks we can reduce our exposure by taking out insurance against the associated loss of wealth. *Ex ante* (i.e. when the insurance is taken out) there is no redistribution, but *ex post* (when the true state of world is revealed) there is, because the net effect of insurance is to transfer wealth from those who do not suffer the loss to those who do. Insurance is widely provided, so for there to be an efficiency argument for intervention there has to be market failure, i.e. the market must be poor at insuring against some risks. It is notable that, for many major life risks such as the threat of disability, old age, unemployment, ill-health, divorce and so on, private insurance is very limited or just not available, which suggests that there are some market failures and suggests why social insurance is common in the OECD. We shall explore this issue in more detail in Chapter 16, but it is worth emphasising that some of the risks mentioned are associated with large drops in wealth, so that a significant degree of *ex post* redistribution can be associated with a Pareto improvement *ex ante*.

---

[2] There are a number of reasons for not taking the figure at face value, one of which is that levels of poverty and robbery rates might reflect common underlying forces, such as the degree of respect for the welfare of fellow citizens. It might be no coincidence that the three countries with the highest poverty/robbery figures are individualistic Anglo-Saxon cultures.

### Imperfect capital markets

All the examples given so far involve the correction of market failures. The final case where redistribution can be Pareto improving is no exception. For a variety of reasons (see Chapter 20 on education) access to capital markets may be inefficiently restrictive, in the sense that there may be borrowers who could pay back their loans at the prevailing rate of interest, but who are denied access to funds. Mostly, this rationing arises as a result of asymmetric information (see Chapter 6): banks do not know who will default and who will not, so they ask for collateral when forwarding large loans. People without collateral (i.e. those with low current wealth) therefore tend to have only limited access to investment funds. Government-backed loans or the direct provision of subsidised investment goods, such as education and training, provide a means for people lacking assets to invest in their future. Viewed at any point in time, this type of government action is not Pareto improving, but seen over the lifetime of the investment, it can be efficient, provided that the return on the investment exceeds the opportunity cost of capital. The immediate beneficiary of the investment gains directly, while the taxpayer who provided the funds gains through receiving a higher return than that available in the market, with the dividends paid back in the form of reduced future taxes or via improved public services.

To summarise, income redistribution has external benefits: it makes the altruistic donor happier, it reduces the propensity to engage in economic crime, it eases access to capital markets. Redistributing income can therefore help correct market failures, sometimes yielding Pareto improvements. Note, though, that transferring income to raise efficiency, either by overcoming the deficiencies of private insurance markets or to cure these externality problems, may lead to other distortions in the economy; for instance, the individual who relies on donations from the rich may cease to work. In this case, the problem is not one of an equity–efficiency trade-off, but a trade-off between two ingredients of efficiency.

## 3.3  Social choice

The previous section showed that sometimes redistribution is Pareto improving, but typically, if one Pareto improvement is possible, then so are a number of others. For instance, if A is a rich altruist and B and C are poor, a Pareto improvement is possible by transferring £1 from A to B or £1 from A to C. More usually, Pareto improvements are not available and one choice will be favoured by one group of people, while other choices will be preferred by other sections of society. Typically there will be winners as well as losers when departing from the status quo. What we need therefore is a **social choice** function, a way of ranking the choices open to society, just like a utility function summarises the preferences for an individual. There are two important issues we need to focus on. The first is the problem of coherence: is it actually possible to construct a social choice function, given that every individual in a society has different desires? Second, if we can construct one social choice function, then we might be able to construct any number of functions, but which is the right one?

To obtain answers, we need to be more precise about the questions. One way of constructing a social choice function would be to base it on the preferences of a single individual; for instance, 'if the Queen is better off, then society is better off', or 'l'état c'est moi' as Louis XIV put it. Similarly, we could make social choices on the number of vowels in the proposal, so that AAA Taxis would be more likely to qualify for a

**Social choice**

The problem of constructing a ranking of the options open to society

subsidy than XXX Cabs. The point is that only some principles may be ethically defensible and we want to restrict our social choice functions to those which obey these principles.

The first person to investigate this issue rigorously was Kenneth Arrow, who argued that any social choice function should be complete and transitive in its rankings of options and that it should obey at least four criteria:

P    Pareto principle: If at least one individual strictly prefers option $x$ to option $y$ and no-one strictly prefers $y$ to $x$ then society prefers $x$ to $y$.

U    Universal domain: The social choice function should work for any set of individual preferences.

D    Non-dictatorship: The social choice function should not depend solely on the rankings of one individual.

I    Independence of irrelevant alternatives: The social ranking of $x$ and $y$ should only depend on individual rankings of $x$ versus $y$ and not depend on the preferences of individuals over $x$ and $z$ or $y$ and $z$ (where $z$ is another option).

These are relatively weak requirements, but unfortunately Arrow was able to prove his famous Impossibility Theorem: that no social choice function satisfying P, U, D and I can exist. Some idea of why P, U, D and I are incompatible is given by Condorcet's paradox. The table shows three individuals (A, B and C) and their rankings of three alternative outcomes (x, y and z). For instance, x could be a hospital, y a school and z could be the status quo.

|   | x | y | z |
|---|---|---|---|
| A | 1 | 2 | 3 |
| B | 2 | 3 | 1 |
| C | 3 | 1 | 2 |

Suppose majority rule is offered as the social choice function. A and B both prefer x to y, so society must also prefer x to y. Likewise A and B both prefer y to z, meaning that society prefers y to z under majority rule. Finally, C and B prefer z over x, so that society must prefer z to x, but then the social preferences are not transitive, making coherent social choice impossible. We could imagine alternative rules to majority voting, but what Arrow showed is that no rule which satisfies his four requirements can be relied upon always to deliver a complete and transitive social choice function.

Can we escape the problem by using utility numbers rather than rankings? The answer is no, as shown below. In the revised version of the table, the rankings are unchanged, but now each option has a utility number.

|   | x | y | z |
|---|---|---|---|
| A | 15 | 10 | 5 |
| B | 8 | 6 | 10 |
| C | 3 | 20 | 17 |
| A+B+C | 26 | 36 | 32 |

It appears from the final row that the utilitarian rule (meaning, add up utilities and see which option has the highest total) provides a social choice function. Option y has the highest score so is preferred over z and then z is preferred to x. Recall, though, that in standard consumer theory utilities are ordinal, meaning that the utility numbers below represent the same preferences and so can also be employed to represent the ranking of the options.

|         | x  | y  | z  |
|---------|----|----|----|
| A       | 30 | 11 | 10 |
| B       | 4  | 3  | 5  |
| C       | 3  | 20 | 17 |
| A+B+C   | 37 | 34 | 32 |

Apparently, the best choice is now x since it has the highest score, according to the utilitarian rule, contradicting our previous result. The point is that the utility numbers used in the social choice function cannot be ordinal if we are to avoid the Impossibility Theorem. In fact they cannot be cardinal either (unique up to linear transformation, like temperature). For all individuals they must be measured on the same scale, up to a constant, so that, for instance, adding or subtracting 10 to all utilities would not change the ranking.

This conclusion means that to have a social choice function either we relax the assumptions of the Impossibility Theorem or we have some common scale for measuring well-being, which in turn means having **interpersonal comparisons** of well-being. The conditions U, P, I and D are mild, so relaxing some of them in order to be able to construct a social choice function seems undesirable. This leaves interpersonal comparisons. In the next section we discuss where these comparisons might come from, but before doing so, note that there is one other means of avoiding the impossibility result which is of interest. In the theorem, the social choice function must work for all types of preferences. It may be empirically true that not all types of preference actually occur, so that assumption U may be unnecessary. In fact, if all preferences have the property that they are *single peaked* then it is possible to construct social choice functions obeying P, I and D. One of these functions is majority rule (see Chapter 8).

**Interpersonal comparisons**

Judgements about the relative weight of individuals' well-being

## 3.4 Social welfare functions[3]

**Social welfare function**

A measure where the well-being of society as a whole is an increasing function of individual well-being

Once we allow interpersonal comparisons of well-being we can construct a **social welfare function** (SWF), a function which relates the welfare of society as a whole to the welfare of individuals. Let us write social welfare as $W = f(U^1, U^2 \ldots)$ where U means utility and the numbers refer to different individuals. Three properties are usually assumed for $f$:

P    Pareto principle: If $U^i$ rises then $W$ rises. Or, the partial derivative of $W$ with respect to $U^i$ is positive.

N    Individualism: Social welfare is only a function of individual well-being.

I    Inequality aversion: $f$ is concave, so that averages are preferred to extremes and therefore welfare is higher when inequality is lower.

---

[3] A social welfare function provides a ranking of all the options open to society against a common scale. A social choice function selects one of these options as the best, so a social welfare function can provide the basis for social choice.

The first assumption is non-controversial, as is the second amongst most economists, although many people might want to include the well-being of their pets or other animals, for instance, in a measure of social welfare, while others might believe that there are goals for a society which cannot be expressed in terms of the welfare of its members. The third assumption is more problematic; few people would argue that, other things being equal, more inequality is better than less, but most people will differ in their aversion to inequality and some may be completely indifferent.

### Inequality aversion and types of SWF

These different attitudes towards inequality can be summarised in the shape of the social welfare function, as the following examples show:

**Utilitariansim**

A belief that social welfare is the sum of individual well-being

1. **Utilitarian**    $W = U^1 + U^2 + \ldots$ or social welfare is the sum of individual well-being.

2. **Rawlsian**    $W = \min\{U^1, U^2, \ldots\}$ or social welfare is the welfare of the worst-off member of society.

3. **Isoelastic**    $W = \Sigma_i U^{i1-e}/(1 - e)$ or social welfare depends on the degree of inequality aversion, as measured by $e$. Higher $e$ means greater inequality aversion so that, if $e = 0$, then we have utilitarianism and if $e = \infty$, then we have the Rawlsian function and for $e$ between these two extremes we have intermediate levels of inequality aversion.

Figure 3.3 illustrates these three types of social welfare function, together with FF, a UPF. The points U, I and R show the optimum positions for the three different welfare functions and, as can be seen, as inequality aversion rises, so we move closer to the 45° line or absolute equality between the two individuals, a result which holds generally, provided the UPF is downward sloping as it crosses the 45° line.

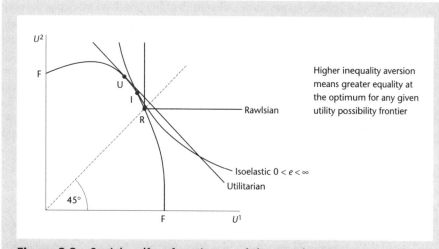

**Figure 3.3**    Social welfare functions and the social optimum

## Social justice and the correct social welfare function

In this discussion we have avoided some fundamental issues: what value of $e$ is correct and, going back to the original social choice problem, how do we make the interpersonal comparisons which enable us to fix numbers for well-being? There are two kinds of answers which are commonly given. The original utilitarian view of social welfare was based on the idea that we desire pleasure and wish to avoid pain, so that the U numbers are measures of the happiness of each individual. Is this acceptable from an ethical viewpoint? Compare a billionaire aesthete who obtains great pleasure from eating exotic foods to someone who is very poor and who gets no satisfaction from life. From a utilitarian perspective, it may be socially desirable to transfer £1 from the dull, poor individual to the billionaire so that the latter can purchase more caviare. This and similar examples suggest that basing social welfare purely on pleasure is not particularly defensible.[4]

Believers in social justice provide the second kind of answer, the principle that equality of some kind is a desirable feature of a society. A large number of authors have written on the subject of social justice. Some argue for equality of outcomes, while others for equality of opportunity. In most cases, though, there is a shared belief that an average distribution of resources is better than extremes, as in property I. Under these circumstances, the social welfare function can be understood as a simple device for summarising attitudes to redistribution. The question remains, what is the right value for $e$?

As an example of an answer, John Rawls (1971) effectively argues in favour of setting $e = \infty$ (hence the Rawlsian SWF described above). He asks us to imagine a 'veil of ignorance' preventing us from knowing what position, what tastes and what endowments we will actually have. We are asked to decide the ethical principles which should guide society when rational individuals draw up a contract in such a situation. Rawls argues that under these circumstances, we would be concerned to equalise political rights such as freedom of expression and the ability to vote and then to maximise the resources available to the worst off member of society, because this will limit how badly off we can be once the true state of the world and our position in it are revealed. These resources will be measured by a basket of primary goods, commodities such as clothing and food essential to survival. Many economists have taken this basket of goods and replaced it with income, on the grounds that income provides generalised purchasing power that can accommodate variations in tastes in a way that a fixed basket cannot.

The individuals drawing up the contract in Rawls' world are infinitely risk averse; they are unwilling to trade off the chance to be £1m richer, if that means the worst possible outcome leaves them £1 worse off. Others have therefore used the same 'veil of ignorance' device as Rawls, but obtained different views on social justice, by arguing in favour of less risk aversion.[5] For instance, Harsanyi (1955) favours the utilitarian-style social welfare function which reflects a positive, but less than

---

[4] Some economists such as Sen (1985) argue that we should abandon social welfare functions based on individual preferences altogether and move to more objective measures of well-being (see Chapter 15). He argues that well-being is a product of our 'functionings' (our achievable living conditions) and 'capabilities' (the ability to carry out these functions).

[5] Rawls has been criticised on other grounds, for instance, that individuals may wish to trade off political liberties for economic rewards and that, by removing all knowledge of individual circumstances from the agents negotiating behind the veil, some features of justice which are culture-related may be omitted.

infinite, degree of risk aversion. The point is that there is no agreement on the correct value of *e*, even amongst philosophers arguing from broadly similar positions.

## Horizontal equity

In addition, single measures of social welfare may fail to capture important aspects of social justice. Imagine two different societies. In one, half the men have a high income and half the women have the same high income. The remainder of the population have a low income. In the second society all the men have the high income and all the women have the low income. On the measures of social welfare employed above, the two societies rank equally, yet the second is profoundly less fair than the first. This is because social welfare functions are usually based on concerns about the distribution of income between rich and poor (**vertical equity**) and not with the distribution between sexes or races, the question of **horizontal equity**.

It is possible to build measures of horizontal equity, but in order to do so we have to have an idea of a world with zero horizontal inequity and this can be problematic because tastes differ. Consider a society where we observe that half the population eats pork and the other half does not. A society in which everyone has pork may seem more equitable, but if the reason one half of the population does not eat pork is because it is Jewish or Moslem, the picture is dramatically altered. This does not imply that horizontal equity has no meaning, but rather, as with concepts of vertical equity, we have to be careful about stating the ethical assumptions built into particular positions.

While it is usually argued that there is a vertical equity–efficiency trade-off, it is less clear that there is a trade-off between the pursuit of horizontal equity and efficiency. If workplace inequality between the sexes is largely due to discrimination, then a reduction in discrimination should lead to a rise in output (and possibly to a Pareto improvement), as women are used more productively. However, to the extent that some people gain from the act of discrimination, then their welfare may be reduced by a reduction in horizontal inequality, implying that there may well be a trade-off here too.[6]

Three main messages emerge from this debate over ethical principles. First, that welfare measures based on utilitarian notions of pleasure have only limited support and that therefore it is probably better to think of social welfare being a function of the distribution of resources rather than of happiness or pain. Second, the arguments do not tell us the correct value for *e*. Different people will have different views on the *e*, but what we can do is relate these different ethical principles to the social choice which should result. For instance, in Figure 3.3, the economist can advise the utilitarian that U is optimal or the Rawlsian that R is the best option, given their ethical beliefs. Third, there are many dimensions to the equality debate, such as horizontal equity, and it is not always possible to reduce them to arguments over the distribution of income. We explore this issue further in the next section.

---

**Vertical equity**

A belief in the desirability of reducing income and wealth inequality through redistribution

**Horizontal equity**

A belief in the desirability of equal treatment of equals

---

[6] The existence of a trade-off between Pareto efficiency and the pursuit of reduced discrimination, because sexists or racists feel worse off with equality, is another reminder of the unacceptability of the utilitarian approach to social welfare, which counts all emotions equally in the calculus of pleasure and pain, whatever their source.

## 3.5 The limits of consequentialism

Imagine a football match where a large crowd is booing a player because he is black. The members of the crowd gain from their act, the player suffers, but if we add up the pleasure created for the many it outweighs the pain suffered by the one, meaning if we are utilitarians that social welfare rises. Perhaps the pain is extreme, but if the crowd is large enough or the experience is shared by television viewers who are also racist, then with any social welfare function we can find an example of this kind, where the gains to society outweigh the benefits. The example reminds us that there are acts which are wrong even when their outcomes are such that benefits outweigh the costs and similarly, there are acts which are right even when costs exceed benefits. Social welfare functions perform poorly here because they are **consequentialist**, meaning that they are concerned only with outcomes, not with the process by which the outcomes are achieved.

**Consequentialism**

The belief that social choices should be evaluated by their outcomes and not by the processes by which they are reached

Another example illustrates the argument. A parent is deciding how to divide up £100 between two twins. The parent can either split the money equally, or give £70 to one child and £30 to the other. In the absence of other information, most people would suggest that £50 to each child is fairest. Now consider a professor who is allocating marks to two students, based on their performance over a term. Again two splits are possible: one where both get 50% and one which gives 70% to one student and 30% to the other. The same social welfare function which leads us to split the money equally between the children, also leads to the suggestion that the 50% to each rule is optimal for the professor. However, suppose that one student is hardworking, attends lectures and has written a good essay, while the other is a complete slacker with an appalling essay to their credit, and now most people will abandon a consequentialist view and argue that giving the better student 70% is fairer. The same kinds of argument dominate discussions of equity and redistribution, where there is a split between those advocating just outcomes and those in favour of just processes.

The most famous modern advocate of the anti-consequentialist viewpoint is Nozick (1974). He argues that transfers from the rich to the poor are unjust because they must be supported by taxation, which represents involuntary exchange. Nozick says 'Taxation of earnings from labour is on a par with forced labour.' According to Nozick, only processes are just, not outcomes, and just processes are those where exchange is voluntary. Thus a just society allows trade (including trading labour for a wage), bequests and gifts. Since injustices have occurred in the past, Nozick also allows that there ought to be some mechanism for righting past wrongs ('the principle of rectification'), but this would be too complicated, he argues. The issue of rectification is one serious problem with this viewpoint, but it is not the only one. The principles which make certain forms of processes acceptable are not common to all forms of voluntary behaviour. Usually we would say that one student deserves the higher mark because he or she has worked hard and this gives them the right to the 'fruits of their labour'. The same argument does not apply to children receiving inheritances.

Nevertheless many of the ideas underlying Nozick's approach are commonly expressed in debates about equity. Arguments for positive discrimination or for the land rights of native peoples in Australia and the USA, for instance, often embody some version of the principle of rectification. And, as with other interpretations of 'what is fair and right' there may be a trade-off between it and efficiency.

### Liberalism

Utilitarians, Rawlsians and anti-consequentialists such as Nozick all accept the Pareto principle (although for different reasons) and therefore the desirability of efficiency. Our final example is a reminder that, unfortunately, there are principles, widely viewed as desirable elements of the 'good' society, which are incompatible with the Pareto principle. The most famous example of this is liberalism, which, roughly speaking, is the belief that for any individual there should be spheres of their life where their own preferences are decisive, whatever other people think; if Ronnie wishes to put up orange or purple wallpaper in his house that is his business; if Susi wants to call her car 'Sonic' then she should be allowed to. Imagine Mr Tidy, whose back garden lives up to his name, living next door to Ms Sloth, whose own patch is a mass of weeds. Mr Tidy is appalled by the mess in his neighbour's garden, which he can see daily from his upstairs window and would be willing to tame it himself. Ms Sloth enjoys seeing others work and so is happy to agree. If garden maintenance is part of the sphere where individual preferences should count, then this proposed Pareto improvement clashes with the liberal principle.[7]

Essentially, liberalism denies the acceptability of some external effects (Mr Tidy's disgust at his neighbour's disorderly garden) when assessing welfare. As with Nozick's arguments, it asks to look beyond the consequences of actions and instead focuses on the processes by which those outcomes have been achieved. Such ideas about equity do not fit tidily into the framework of the social welfare function. However, they are often important components of debates over public policy.

## 3.6 Equity versus efficiency: the marginal cost of public funds

So far we have stated that there may be a trade-off between equity and efficiency, without suggesting exactly how it arises or how it can be measured. In this section we remedy the deficiency. As we will mainly do elsewhere in this book, we identify equity with the pursuit of equality, although the analysis can be applied to other interpretations of the word.

With lump-sum taxation, a £1 transfer from one person to another produces no changes in the incentives faced by either agent. Taxation rarely takes this form; it is usually *distortionary*. Figure 3.4 illustrates the problem, showing a consumer who divides her spending between pizzas, $x$, and all other goods, $y$. The price of pizzas is $p$, the price of $y$ is 1 and $m$ is her income. A lump-sum tax of $T$ moves her from $E^0$ to $E^1$, producing a new budget constraint, $m - T = px + y$. Alternatively, suppose that the revenue is raised by a distortionary tax on pizzas, pushing up their price from $p$ to $p + t$. The budget constraint is now $m = (p + t)x + y$ and if the two taxes raise the same revenue then $T = tx_2$, where $x_2$ is the equilibrium value of $x$ with the pizza tax. This means that $(p + t)x_2 + y_2 = m$ can be rearranged to yield $px_2 + y_2 = m - T$, which tells us that the new equilibrium bundle is also on the budget constraint for the lump-sum tax, at $E_2$. Clearly the consumer is worse off with the distortionary pizza tax than she is with the lump-sum tax. To compensate her (in the sense of putting her back on

---

[7] The original argument is by Sen (1970). Clearly it is possible to define liberalism in another way (e.g. 'anything is acceptable as long as it does not harm anyone else') consistent with the Pareto principle. Whether therefore Paretian liberal truly is impossible is still debated.

her old indifference curve), for the lump-sum tax of $T$, she would require an extra T of income or £1 for every £1 of revenue raised, but to compensate her for the pizza tax she would require $T$ plus AB (marked by the heavy line in Figure 3.4), or £$(T + AB)/T$ (> £1) per £1 of revenue raised.[8] AB is known as the **excess burden** of the distortionary tax, because it is the burden placed on the taxpayer over and above the cost of the tax itself. For small changes in government revenue, the ratio of the compensation required to the extra revenue raised $(T+AB)/T$ is called the **marginal cost of public funds** (MCPF). As we have seen, it provides a measure of the efficiency costs of raising tax revenue through distortionary means and is a fundamental concept for optimal policy.

There is a slightly different way of measuring the costs of distortionary taxation which you will also encounter. Instead of comparing taxes which raise the same revenue and asking what compensation must be given, we could ask 'what is the difference in revenue raised?' for taxes which place the consumer on the same indifference curve. Figure 3.5 illustrates this means of calculating the cost. The heavy black line connecting A and B shows the loss of revenue when distortionary rather than lump-sum taxes are employed.

The two distinct approaches arise because, when we compare the cost of tax A against tax B, we need to know that we are comparing like with like. It would be unsurprising if a tax which raised £10bn had a greater cost than one which raised £1bn, so one basis for comparison requires that the taxes raise the same revenue, meaning that public expenditure is the same in both cases as well. Alternatively, the yardstick could be the sacrifice of well-being incurred by the taxpayer, so taxes are

**Excess burden**

or deadweight loss. A measure of the efficiency cost of distortionary taxation

**MCPF**

The efficiency cost of raising an extra £1 of government revenue

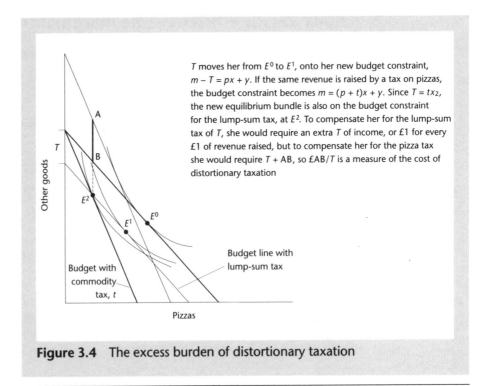

$T$ moves her from $E^0$ to $E^1$, onto her new budget constraint, $m - T = px + y$. If the same revenue is raised by a tax on pizzas, the budget constraint becomes $m = (p + t)x + y$. Since $T = tx_2$, the new equilibrium bundle is also on the budget constraint for the lump-sum tax, at $E^2$. To compensate her for the lump-sum tax of $T$, she would require an extra $T$ of income, or £1 for every £1 of revenue raised, but to compensate her for the pizza tax she would require $T + AB$, so £AB/$T$ is a measure of the cost of distortionary taxation

**Figure 3.4   The excess burden of distortionary taxation**

---

[8] This is the compensating variation of the tax change; see Katz and Rosen (1998), Chapter 4 or any other good intermediate microeconomics text for a reminder of this important concept.

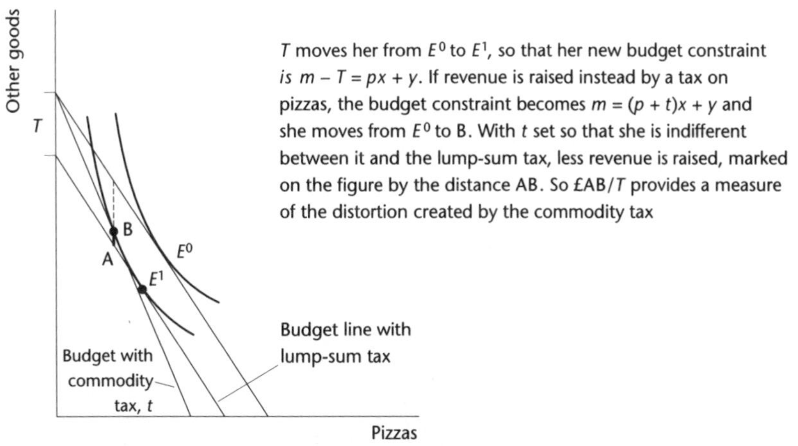
Other goods
T
B
A
$E^0$
$E^1$
Budget with commodity tax, t
Budget line with lump-sum tax
Pizzas
*T* moves her from $E^0$ to $E^1$, so that her new budget constraint is $m - T = px + y$. If revenue is raised instead by a tax on pizzas, the budget constraint becomes $m = (p + t)x + y$ and she moves from $E^0$ to B. With *t* set so that she is indifferent between it and the lump-sum tax, less revenue is raised, marked on the figure by the distance AB. So £AB/*T* provides a measure of the distortion created by the commodity tax

**Figure 3.5** The excess burden of distortionary taxation II

compared on the basis that the consumer ends on the same indifference curve.[9] For small changes in taxes, the two routes to calculating the costs produce almost identical answers in most cases.

How does the cost of distortionary taxation affect the equity–efficiency trade-off? Suppose society consists of two individuals, Rich and Poor; then optimal income distribution means choosing tax revenue, *T*, to maximise the sum of individual welfare, $W(R - T) + W(P + T)$, where *W* is the welfare of an individual, *R* and *P* are the respective original income levels. If there is no efficiency loss, £1 taken from Rich produces a marginal loss of welfare, $-MW^R$, and when transferred to Poor, creates a marginal rise in welfare, $MW^P$. So the optimal outcome is where $MW^R = MW^P$, in other words, where the marginal social welfare of income (MW) is equal for all individuals.

With distortionary taxation, the gain from transferring £1 to the Poor individual is still $MW^P$, but as we saw in Figure 3.4, for Rich there is an extra loss of social welfare from taking that income. For every £1 lost by Rich, welfare goes down by $MW^R$MCPF. The optimum is therefore now at the point where $MW^P = \text{MCPF} \cdot MW^R$. Figure 3.6 illustrates some calculations of the resulting trade-off, showing the optimal ratio between Rich's final income and Poor's, for different degrees of inequality aversion, based on the assumption that the individuals are identical, apart from their initial income. For the sake of the example, it is assumed that Rich's original income is five times that of Poor. Three things are clear from the figure: if there is no burden from distortionary taxation (MCPF = 1), then in this example perfect equality is optimal; as the degree of inequality aversion increases, the optimal gap between Rich and Poor narrows, whatever the MCPF, and for the Rawlsian, equality is always optimal; for non-Rawlsians the optimal degree of redistribution falls as the MCPF rises and there is a critical value of the MCPF above which no redistribution is desirable.

[9] One problem with this approach is that the level of government expenditure will be lower under the distortionary tax compared to the lump-sum tax, and this would normally affect the consumer's well-being.

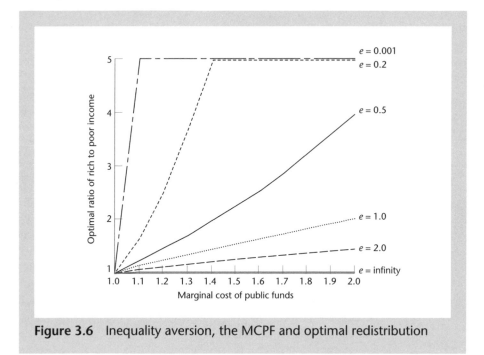

**Figure 3.6** Inequality aversion, the MCPF and optimal redistribution

Estimates of the actual value of the MCPF vary and we shall investigate this further in Chapters 11 and 13, but typically it lies well within the range depicted in the figure. In their study of Sweden, for instance, Ingemar Hansson and Charles Stuart (1984) produced figures varying from 1.05 to 1.29 for a marginal tax on labour of 40% and with the money raised being spent on transfers, but note that for other parameter values and uses of the taxes raised a value of between 0.67[10] and 4.51 was possible. Meanwhile, Don Fullerton (1991) surveyed estimates of the marginal excess burden of taxation for the USA which ranged from 1.07 to 1.21.

In summary, the concept of the marginal cost of public funds provides a means of calibrating the efficiency part of the equity–efficiency trade-off. The higher it is and the lower the degree of inequality aversion, then the lower will be the amount of redistribution which maximises social welfare.

## 3.7 Conclusion

David Miller (1976) argues that social justice consists of three often contradictory elements: rights, deserts and needs. Here, the concept of right means equality before the law or equal rights to participate in political activities such as voting; deserts includes the idea that individuals should receive the rewards of their labours; needs represents the notion that people need resources in order to fulfil themselves. Most consequentialist theories focus on the needs aspect of justice, while libertarians such as Nozick are concerned about rights and deserts. Of course, many individuals mix the three elements in their views of what is right for society.

---

[10] The MCPF can be below 1.0 if the funds are used to reduce distortions elsewhere in the economy.

Most ideas of what constitutes a better society subscribe to the Pareto principle, but there is wide disagreement over the virtues of equity. Understanding the trade-off between the pursuit of (Pareto) efficiency and equity dominates large sections of this book. You should not expect to be able to 'solve' the ethical dimensions of policy debates, but you should learn to identify the point at which views on equity enter the debate and to map out the common ground between different positions.

## Summary

- Most public policy issues involve alternative distributions of resources and welfare. A social welfare function is a means of representing the goodness of different options.

- Sometimes redistributing resources can produce a Pareto improvement, in which case there is no equity–efficiency trade-off. Altruism, other external effects (such as crime reduction) and insurance all provide Pareto-improving motives for increasing equity.

- Arrow's Impossibility Theorem shows that in general, to create a coherent social choice function requires interpersonal comparisons of well-being.

- As the example of the rich aesthete shows, pleasure-based measures of individual well-being do not provide ethically defensible foundations for social welfare functions.

- Anti-consequentialists argue that social justice does not lie in outcomes (such as the distribution of income), but in the processes by which those outcomes come about.

- The degree of aversion to inequality can be represented by the parameter $e$ in the isoelastic social welfare function, with larger values indicating greater willingness to put equity before efficiency in policy issues.

- The marginal cost of public funds measures the cost of raising revenues through distortionary taxation.

- Horizontal equity captures the belief that measures of income inequality do not reflect all important elements of social welfare, which should also include equal treatment of people with the same pertinent characteristics.

## Questions

1. What are the arguments for redistribution; what are the arguments against?
2. Why have compulsory redistributive taxation if people care about one another?
3. Explain the concept of inequality aversion.
4. Some people favour equality of opportunity rather than equality of outcomes. Suggest some ways of measuring 'opportunity'.
5. Is there a difference between horizontal and vertical equity?
6. We have seen that there is an excess burden for distortionary taxation. Explain why there is also a cost for distortionary *subsidies*.

# Further reading

The books by Robert Sugden (1981) or David Miller (1976) provide good overviews of modern theories of equity. One important theory only briefly mentioned here is that developed by Amartya Sen. A summary of his thinking can be found in Sen (1985). For more on the issue of social choice, consult Mueller (1990) or McLean (1987). A short discussion of the marginal cost of social funds is provided by Fullerton (1991), based on the original work of Browning (1976). Further reading on this topic is provided in Chapters 11 and 13.

# References

Browning, E. (1976) 'The marginal cost of public funds', *Journal of Political Economy* 84, 283–98.

Fullerton, D. (1991) 'Reconciling recent estimates of the marginal welfare cost of taxation', *American Economic Review* 81, 302–8.

Hansson, I. and Stuart, C. (1984) 'Tax revenue and the marginal cost of public funds in Sweden', *Journal of Public Economics* 27, 331–53.

Harsanyi, J.C. (1955), 'Cardinal welfare, individualistic ethics and interpersonal comparisons of utility', *Journal of Political Economy* 73, 309–21.

Katz, M. and Rosen, H.S. (1998) *Microeconomics*, 3rd edn, London: McGraw-Hill.

McLean, I. (1987) *Public Choice: An Introduction*, Oxford: Basil Blackwell.

Miller, D. (1976) *Theories of Social Justice*, Oxford: Oxford University Press.

Mueller, D. (1990) *Social Choice II*, Cambridge: Cambridge University Press.

Nozick, R. (1974) *Anarchy, Utopia and the State*, Oxford: Basil Blackwell.

Rawls, J. (1971) *A Theory of Justice*, Oxford: Oxford University Press.

Sen, A. (1970) 'The impossibility of a Paretian liberal', *Journal of Political Economy* 78, 152–7.

Sen, A. (1985) *The Standard of Living*, Cambridge: Cambridge University Press.

Sugden, R. (1981) *The Political Economy of Public Choice: An Introduction to Welfare Economics*, Oxford: Martin Robertson.

# CHAPTER 4

# Public Goods

## Key concepts

| | | |
|---|---|---|
| excludability | clubs | free riders |
| privately provided goods | efficiency | preference revelation |
| rivalry | tax solutions | |

## 4.1 Introduction

The most frequently cited examples of public goods are street lighting, law and order and defence. Public goods exhibit two key characteristics: first, they are non-excludable; second, they are non-rival in consumption. These features create difficulties both in finding a private supplier for the public good and in determining the efficient level of provision. As a consequence, public goods are typically provided by the state. We will find that the assumption of non-rivalry in consumption causes us to revise the efficiency conditions in the case of public goods. Finally, having identified a possible role for government, we need to consider how, in the absence of the usual market indicators of demand, the government determines the appropriate level of provision of public goods.

It is useful to clarify at the outset two common misunderstandings concerning public goods. First, it is a mistake to consider public goods to be any goods or services which are provided by the state. As we shall see, only some of the goods that are provided by government are public goods. Second, it is incorrect to assume that public goods are *only* provided by the state. Some public goods may be supplied by the private sector.

## 4.2 What is a public good?

In fact there are very few pure public goods, but many goods and services exhibit degrees of non-excludability or non-rivalry.

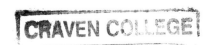

## Non-excludable

**Non-excludability**

A good is non-excludable if, once it is provided, it is either physically impossible or prohibitively expensive to prevent users consuming the good

When we say that a good or service is non-excludable, we mean that once the good is provided for one person it is either logistically impossible or extremely expensive to exclude people from consuming the good. For instance, once street lighting has been erected, anyone who walks along the lit street benefits from the light. Similarly once a nation has established a defence force, all citizens will be protected.

Further examples of goods which are non-excludable are a lighthouse on the coast or a display of flowers in a garden. The owner of the lighthouse will find that any ships sailing along the coast will benefit from the lighthouse, regardless of whether they have contributed towards its provision or upkeep. The only way to prevent non-paying ships from benefiting is to turn out the light as they sail past. However, this solution is only practical if the owner can be certain that no paying ships will also be passing by when the lighthouse is switched off. This would require that the owner gathers information on all sailing times and routes and monitors the movements of all ships, a costly and time-consuming exercise. Although it would be possible to prevent some other ships from benefiting from the lighthouse, it would be expensive to do so.

A gardener who spends hours planting and creating a display of flowers in a garden will find that it is difficult to prevent neighbours or passers-by from enjoying the display (we will ignore the possibility of anyone having allergies to flowers!). To exclude other people, the gardener must build high walls, which may affect the quality of the display by cutting out the light for the flowers and thereby reducing the gardener's own enjoyment.

## Non-rivalry

**Non-rivalry**

A good is non-rival if all users can consume the *same* unit

A good or service is **non-rival** if the consumption of one person does not affect the quantity available for consumption by others. Non-rivalry means that the marginal cost of supplying to an additional user, $MC_u$, is zero. We can illustrate this using the example of street lighting again. As one person walks down the street, they benefit from the lighting, but this does not change the benefit attained from the lighting or the quantity of lighting available to other pedestrians. Another example would be a radio broadcast, assuming that all who want to listen have a radio. Any number of people can listen to and enjoy the same broadcast. Once the good is provided for one person, it is available to all; the supplier incurs no additional cost, no matter how many more consumers benefit. In the case of street lighting, once the street is lit, there is no additional cost of lighting for each pedestrian who passes.

**$MC_u$**

The marginal cost of an extra user is zero for a non-rival good

In practice, we find that overcrowding may occur when many consumers attempt to use the same good at one time. This is the case with roads or the police. Once roads have been built they can be used by a large number of drivers. Since the road system covers the whole country, it is generally true that if one car is on the road this does not prevent other drivers from undertaking a journey. However, where certain stretches of roads are particularly heavily used, they become congested (see discussion of congestion externalities in Chapter 5). Once this has occurred, the presence of other cars on the road does affect the length of the same journey made by an additional driver. We can see a similar effect with policing. If one member of the public needs police attention then there are still many other officers to deal with other problems or enquiries. But if there is a crime wave, the consumption of police services becomes rival.

A pure public good has both characteristics, non-excludability and non-rivalry; a pure private good has neither. However, many goods and services exhibit elements of one or other of these characteristics (see Figure 4.1).

**A** *Pint of beer:* This is a private good: it is excludable because it is served in a glass to each customer and so customers may be prevented from consuming a pint of beer; and it is rival, because once one person has enjoyed the pint of beer, it is no longer available to others.

**B** *National park:* This is a public good: the size of the boundaries of a national park means that it is simply too expensive to exclude visitors, so it is non-excludable; and it is non-rival because even if there are a lot of visitors, the parks are so large that the presence of others does not diminish one's own enjoyment.

**C** *Theatre:* Once a play is being shown, many people can enjoy the same performance and so this has some elements of non-rivalry, but it is not a public good because it is necessary to buy a theatre ticket!

**D** *Beach on bank holiday:* Assuming that the length of the beach makes it difficult to effectively police the perimeter, a beach is essentially non-excludable. But, as the crowds gather, the beach itself becomes more crowded and the presence of one group of holiday makers does diminish the space and enjoyment available to others. There are few examples of goods which are non-excludable but also rival, another would be wild berries, which anyone can pick, but they are rival just like private goods.

In defining non-excludability, we assumed that it was either impossible or extremely costly to exclude people. In some cases, the degree of excludability is dependent upon technology. Taking the example of a TV broadcast, if the broadcast is made on terrestrial television, then one only needs a television with an aerial to pick up the transmission. With technological changes, broadcasts are now made on satellite and cable and to receive these one also needs a satellite dish or cable connection. In addition, technology is now available for television companies to offer pay-per-view broadcasts (used for sport and movies). Thus, as technological advances occur, goods which were previously considered non-excludable can in fact become excludable.

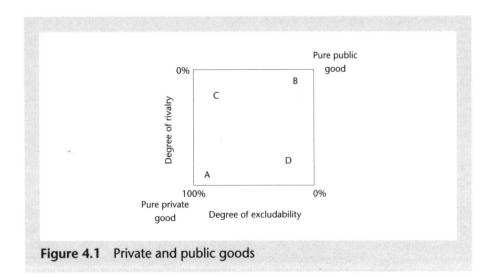

**Figure 4.1** Private and public goods

We have already noted that there is no necessary link between public goods and state provision. Many goods that are provided by the state are not public goods, for example education and health. Education is not a public good, because pupils can be excluded from classrooms and the teacher's attention is rival. Similar restrictions apply to health.[1]

## 4.3  Optimal provision

In Chapter 2, we saw that a competitive market will ensure a Pareto-efficient allocation of resources in the production of private goods. Here, we examine the appropriate efficiency conditions for a public good and find that unless we take account of non-rivalry, provision will not be optimal.

Private goods are rival in consumption. As more of the good is demanded, so more needs to be produced. The value that consumers place on a private good is given by the marginal benefit curves, the overall value of a private good is given by the horizontal sum of individual marginal benefit curves (see Figure 4.2).

Public goods are non-rival; all consumption is at the same quantity of the good or service. If the public good is provided, both A and B benefit. So, in the case of public goods, the aggregate value of the good is given by the vertical sum of individual marginal benefit curves, as in Figure 4.3.

In a partial equilibrium model, the efficient level of production of a private good is where the marginal benefit to the consumer equals the marginal cost to the producer.

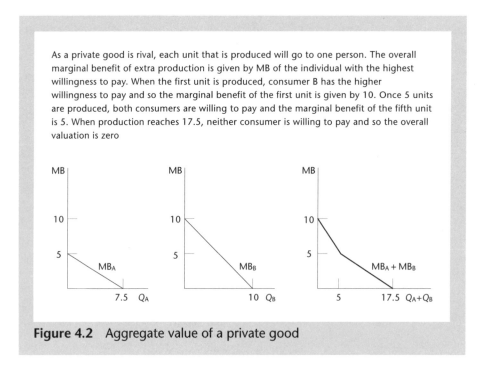

As a private good is rival, each unit that is produced will go to one person. The overall marginal benefit of extra production is given by MB of the individual with the highest willingness to pay. When the first unit is produced, consumer B has the higher willingness to pay and so the marginal benefit of the first unit is given by 10. Once 5 units are produced, both consumers are willing to pay and the marginal benefit of the fifth unit is 5. When production reaches 17.5, neither consumer is willing to pay and so the overall valuation is zero

**Figure 4.2**  Aggregate value of a private good

---

[1] See Chapters 19 and 20 for a discussion of the market failures which do apply to health and education.

As a public good is non-rival, each unit that is produced will go to both A and B. The overall marginal benefit of extra production is given by MB of both consumers. In this case, the marginal benefit of the first unit is 5 for consumer A and 10 for consumer B, so the total willingness to pay is 15. Once 7.5 units are produced, only consumer B is willing to pay and so the total willingness to pay is given by MB$_B$

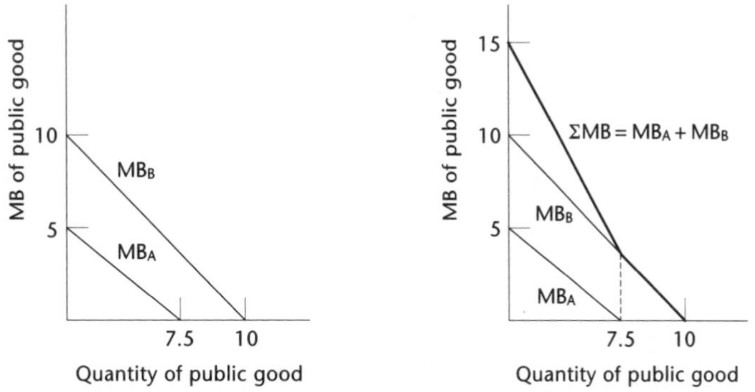

**Figure 4.3**   Aggregate value of a public good

But, a public good is non-rival in consumption, so in this case the aggregate value to society must equal the marginal cost. As we saw in Figure 4.3, the aggregate value to society or the overall willingness to pay is the vertical sum of the individual marginal benefits. Therefore, the optimal level of provision of a public good is $\Sigma MB = MC$ (see Figure 4.4). The general equilibrium condition is discussed in Box 4.1.

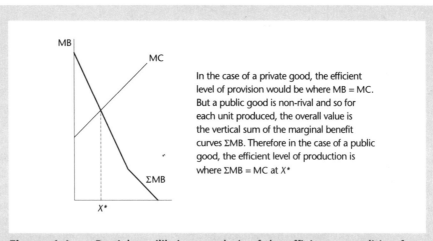

In the case of a private good, the efficient level of provision would be where $MB = MC$. But a public good is non-rival and so for each unit produced, the overall value is the vertical sum of the marginal benefit curves $\Sigma MB$. Therefore in the case of a public good, the efficient level of production is where $\Sigma MB = MC$ at $X^*$

**Figure 4.4**      Partial equilibrium analysis of the efficiency condition for a public good

---

**BOX 4.1**

## Top-level Pareto condition for public goods: a general equilibrium approach

Recall the top-level condition for Pareto efficiency that the value of the good to the consumer, MRS, equals the value to the producer, MRT, that is $MRS_{XY} = MRT_{XY}$.

$X_A$ and $X_B$ represent the private levels of consumption of consumers A and B, $R$ is the resources available for consumption and $c(G)$ is the cost of the supply of the public good.

A Pareto-efficient outcome is where consumer A is as well-off as possible, given B's level of utility subject to their total resource constraint.

Max $U_A(X_A, G)$ with respect to $X_A$, $X_B$ and $G$

subject to $U_B(X_B, G) = U^*$ and $X_A + X_B + c(G) = R$

This gives us a Lagrangrian:

$L = U_A(X_A, G) - \lambda(U_B(X_B, G) - U^*) - \mu(X_A + X_B + c(G) - R)$

Maximise $L$ with respect to $X_A$, $X_B$ and $G$ to get the First-Order Conditions:

$\partial L/\partial X_A = \partial U_A/\partial X_A - \mu = 0$           (1)

$\partial L/\partial X_B = -\lambda\partial U_B/\partial X_B - \mu = 0$        (2)

$\partial L/\partial G = \partial U_A/\partial G - \lambda\partial U_B/\partial G - \mu\partial c/\partial G = 0$    (3)

Solve (1) to find $\mu$               $\mu = \partial U_A/\partial X_A$

Solve (3) to find $(\mu/\lambda)$        $\mu/\lambda = \partial U_B/\partial X_B$

Divide (3) by $\mu$ and rearrange    $(1/\mu)\partial U_A/\partial G - (\lambda/\mu)\ \partial U_B/\partial G = \partial c/\partial G$

Now substitute in for $\mu$ and $(\mu/\lambda)$ in this:

$[\partial U_A/\partial G]/[\partial U_A/\partial X_A] + [\partial U_B/\partial G]/\partial U_B/\partial X_B = \partial c/\partial G = MRT$

Note that $[\partial U/\partial G]/[\partial U/\partial X] = MRS_{GX}$; therefore the Pareto-efficient outcome is where:

$MRS_{GX}{}^A + MRS_{GX}{}^B = MRT$

i.e. $\Sigma$ **MRS** = **MRT**

When a public good is financed by taxation which is distortionary, this condition becomes:

$\Sigma\ MRS = MRT \times MCPF$

where MCSF is the marginal cost of public funds discussed in Chapter 3.

---

## 4.4 Why does the market fail?

Given the nature of public goods, the cost of provision is often extremely high and when neither individual consumer places sufficient value on the good for it to be provided, complete market failure occurs. In Figure 4.5, if we consider A and B individually, we see that neither places a high enough value on the public good. As they would not be willing to pay for X, X will not be produced. This outcome is

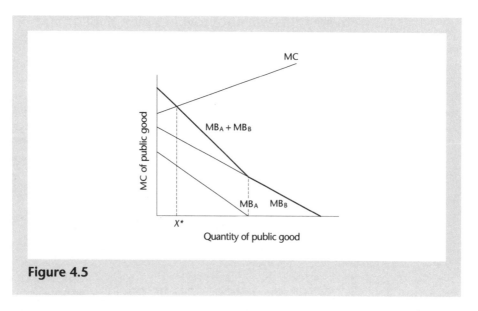

**Figure 4.5**

inefficient, because if we consider the value of X to both consumers, the value to society exceeds the cost.

### Free riding and non-payment: the problem of non-excludability

As soon as more than one consumer is involved in consuming a public good, each person has an incentive not to contribute towards the provision of the good in the hope of **free riding**. Let us assume that each individual believes that their contribution is small relative to the overall, so their decision whether to contribute or not will not affect the collective decision. There is no reason to contribute in the first place. The good may still be provided, if a sufficient number of other consumers choose to contribute. However, if all consumers rationalise in the same manner, none of them will contribute and so the good will not be provided. This is an example of the prisoner's dilemma, where each player's strategies are to contribute, C, or not to contribute, N. The payoffs are given in the matrix below. The benefit to each of the public good is 8 and the total cost is 10. If both A and B contribute, they share the costs of provision, and they each have a payoff of 3. If only one contributes, they bear the full cost of provision and the other free rides. The payoff to the person who contributes is now much lower, –2, because they pay the whole cost of provision, and the payoff to the person who free rides is much higher, 8. If neither contributes, then the good is not provided and the payoff to each is 0.

|  |  | **Player A** | |
|---|---|---|---|
|  |  | **C** | **N** |
| **Player B** | **C** | (3, 3) | (–2, 8) |
|  | **N** | (8, –2) | (0, 0) |

N is the dominant strategy for each player and so the public good will not be provided. As we can see from the payoff matrix, this leads to a collectively inferior outcome (the sum of payoffs is higher when both contribute).

**Free riding**

Consumption or use of a good without making a payment

### Private firms will not provide a pure public good: the problem of non-rivalry

A firm supplying a private good can exclude customers who are unwilling to pay the price that they set for the good, $P > 0$, and under conditions of perfect competition will set the price to achieve allocative efficiency, $P = MC$. So, in a market economy, firms will be prepared to supply efficient levels of a private good. In contrast, a firm supplying a public good will make a loss, because it cannot exclude consumers who do not pay $P > 0$. Consumers are able to free-ride if the good is provided. Even if firms can charge $P > 0$, it will be inefficient; this can be illustrated by the loss of consumer surplus in Figure 4.6.

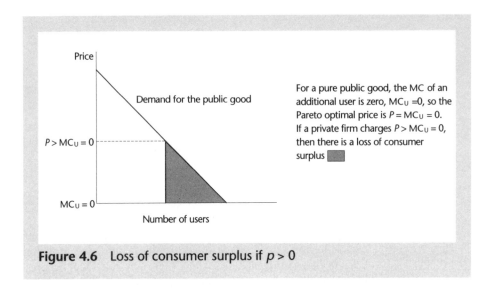

**Figure 4.6** Loss of consumer surplus if $p > 0$

## 4.5 Is government intervention always necessary?

As we have seen there are problems of market failure in the case of public goods, but does this mean that we can only ensure optimal provision through government provision? There are relatively few incentives for a private firm to supply a public good,[2] but there are special categories of public good in which private provision will occur.

### Private collective provision

It may be that our model of a rational individual who has the incentive to free-ride and does so is incorrect. In small communities, the problems of truthful revelation and free riding may be small, because when individuals can see that they are part of a community, they are more likely to behave honestly and do not attempt to free-ride. An example might be community schemes, such as a neighbourhood watch. Once a neighbourhood watch scheme is established, it benefits all homes in the area, so it is non-excludable and non-rival. Since these schemes cover relatively small areas, it is easy to identify those households who do not contribute, either financially or through

---

[2] Vanity, advertising, marketing reasons, shame of not supplying, or employee motivation.

active patrols. Householders may not be tempted to free-ride because they have some feeling of social responsibility; they do not want to let the other households down, or they would feel guilty if they did not help in some way; they do not want other householders to know that they are free riding. Moreover, experimental evidence suggests that, despite the fact free riding is a dominant strategy, consumers will often be influenced by considerations of fairness and will offer to share the cost to ensure that the public good is provided (see Box 4.2). Of course, the cost of provision of this type of community scheme is relatively low; it might be more difficult to persuade villagers to pay for their own traffic-calming scheme or by-pass.

**BOX 4.2**

## Is free riding always a problem? Some experimental evidence

Ledyard (1995) surveys recent experimental work on the levels of contribution towards public goods.

*What is an economics experiment?*
Much of the empirical work in economics uses data on the outcomes of economic activity. In the growing field of experimental economics, economic problems are simulated and data is collected on the decisions made. The advantages of the experimental approach are that researchers can examine the sensitivity and consistency of individual choices by slightly changing the parameters and repeating the problems that they set. The disadvantage is that experiments typically involve volunteers 'playing-out' the economic problems at a computer terminal and there is no guarantee that they are playing for real or that the choices that they make in the laboratory are the same as those which they would make in the marketplace.

*How is the public good problem modelled?*
A typical experiment involves a group of participants. Each is allocated a budget and a choice is made about whether to invest in a public good. The return to the investment in the public good depends on whether contributions are made by the other participants. Variations on this experiment include repeating the game, running the game in smaller groups, and repeatedly playing the game changing the members of the sub-groups at each round. These allow researchers to test whether participants learn over time and whether it matters if decisions are made by individuals within smaller groups, where the members are known or unknown to one another.

*What are the results?*
The main predictions of game theory appear to be rejected by the experimental evidence. Rather than opting not to contribute, participants make contributions of about 50% of the Pareto-efficient level. In repeated games without communication, contributions tend to fall over time, but where there is communication this is not the case.

*How do we interpret these results?*
In his introduction, Ledyard contrasts the way in which individual motivation in

terms of contribution towards a public good is modelled within social sciences. As we have seen, economists tend to assume that individuals are self-interested and will therefore free ride and fail to contribute. In sociology and political science, it is often argued that altruism and a belief in the collective is what motivates people to contribute.

A sceptic might argue that the experiments are flawed; however, given the consistency with which such results are found this is a difficult position to maintain. Alternatively, one might argue that the results are the consequence of errors being made on the part of the participants. This is disputed, but to test this it is necessary for participants to make higher and lower contributions than game theory would suggest. Therefore some experiments have been run where making a positive contribution is the dominant strategy. In these experiments participants only typically make higher contributions.

In the main, researchers have argued that these results show that the participants are motivated by altruism, social norms and group identity. The fact that individuals frequently choose to contribute is seen as evidence of altruism. That contributions are higher when participants make decisions within smaller groups, particularly when the group is known, is seen as evidence of social norms and group identity.

## Club solutions

**Club solution**

If users can be excluded from consuming a public good, private provision may occur through clubs which exclude non-members from using the good

A **Club solution** is another private solution to the problem of the optimal provision of public goods and is only possible when the good is excludable in some way. It is important that the good is excludable, so that it is possible to charge a price and there are no free-rider problems. In such cases, there is an incentive to set up clubs which provide the good; an obvious example is a sport facility. A golf course or a swimming pool are to a limited extent non-rival, because they can be shared by a number of users, but it is possible to exclude non-payers. Once the club is established, each member pays to join the club and use the golf course or the swimming pool. There is an incentive to encourage membership, since this will reduce the cost to each individual. However, as the club becomes larger, it becomes more difficult to enjoy the facilities because of overcrowding. Therefore, the size of the club will be optimised when the marginal cost (overcrowding) equals the marginal benefit (lower costs).

## Provision of complementary goods

A private firm may be willing to provide a public good when it is in joint supply or is complementary with a private good. The firm is able to charge a price for the good which is excludable and to cross-subsidise the good which is not. For example, a firm may jointly supply a beach with sun loungers. We know that the beach is non-excludable, but the sun loungers are not. The price that consumers pay for the sun loungers will contribute towards the cost of providing a clean and safe beach.

Many professional or representative bodies serve functions which are examples of public goods. For example, when the union negotiates wages or employment conditions, these are both non-rival and non-excludable, because they affect anyone working in that firm or industry, regardless of whether they are a paid-up union member or not. If everyone could benefit from the existence of the union, all workers would free ride by enjoying the benefits of the union without paying union subscriptions. In order to counter this, unions offer services that are excludable. These would include legal or financial advice. In this way, the full benefits of being a trade union member are only available if the subscriptions are paid.

## 4.6 Government provision of public goods

As we have seen, in some cases private provision does occur. However, this is not a solution for a national pure public good, such as law and order. Here government provision is necessary.

Governments confront the same problems as a private firm of financing the provision of a public good. But they do not have to rely on charging a price to cover the cost; they can instead raise taxes to pay for the provision of public goods. What remains is the question of determining a Pareto-efficient level of production. However, finding the overall valuation of a public good requires some kind of collective action, because of the problems of **preference revelation** and free riding.

**Preference revelation**

Giving details to the provider of the public good of one's own value of consumption of the good

### Contributions and preference revelation

It may be problematic for government to obtain truthful valuations of a public good. The nature of the difficulties reflects whether or not consumers believe that their payment for the public good will be determined by their stated valuations.

#### No link between payment and stated valuations

If customers face a fixed charge regardless of their valuations, they may use the opportunity to influence the outcome by over- or understating their valuations. For example, a consumer who passionately believes in the value of a public park has an incentive to exaggerate the value in the hope that this will ensure its provision. Alternatively, those opposed to the widening of an already busy motorway might understate the value, hoping that this will prevent the scheme from going ahead. In either case, the valuations are given in the knowledge that they will not be expected to pay an amount equal to their valuations and that there is no penalty for providing untruthful valuations.

#### Payment is determined by the stated valuation

This case is rather similar to the free-riding problem. Even those who place a high value on the provision of a public good will be tempted to understate the value of the good in order to reduce the amount that they have to contribute.

In both of these cases, the appropriate incentives for telling the truth are missing. The values that are given for a public good may therefore be false and result in an inefficient level of provision. Whether there is under- or overprovision will depend on whether most consumers are tempted to under- or to overstate their values. This is illustrated in Box 4.3.

| BOX 4.3 | **Example of the preference revelation problem** |

For each consumer $i$, let, $v_i$ = true value of the public good, $c_i$ = share of cost and $n_i = v_i - c_i$ = net value of the good.

Now let us consider a public good costing £600, shared by three consumers. A and B place the same low value on the public good, $v_A = v_B = 100$ and C places a much higher value, $v_C = 500$.

| Consumer | $v_I$ | $c_I$ fixed | $n_I = v_I - c_I$ | $c_I = v_I$ | $n_I = v_I - c_I$ |
|----------|-------|-------------|-------------------|-------------|-------------------|
| A | 100 | 200 | −100 | 100 | 0 |
| B | 100 | 200 | −100 | 100 | 0 |
| C | 500 | 200 | 300 | 500 | 0 |

*Fixed Cost*             $c_i = 200$

In this case, the net value to A and B is negative $n_A = n_B = -100$ and they are tempted to undervalue the good in order to prevent it from being produced. For example, if A and B both stated values of zero, then $\Sigma v_i = 500$, assuming that C tells the truth, which is less than the cost £600 and the public good would not be provided.

C also faces incentives to overvalue in order to ensure that $\Sigma v_i > 600$, particularly if C suspects that A and B will undervalue.

*Cost given by valuation*        $c_i = v_i$

Now all of the consumers face an incentive to undervalue. If they give a true valuation, then their net value is zero. If they undervalue, their net valuations will be positive as long as the public good is produced.

## Clarke tax

**Clarke tax** is a tax solution to the problem of consumers failing to reveal their true preferences. The intention is to make each consumer feel as though their behaviour is critical, so that they are not tempted to free-ride by failing to contribute or over/understate their valuations. This translates the problem from one of large groups to small groups. Each consumer is treated as a possible 'pivotal agent', where the revelation of their preferences could change the level of provision of the public good. The tax is designed to make revelation of true preferences the dominant strategy.

The consumer is asked to state their net value of the public good, $s_i$. The good is produced if $\Sigma s_i > 0$. A pivotal agent is a consumer who changes the decision from provision to non-provision or vice versa. The tax is designed to impose the full social cost of the decision of a pivotal agent upon that consumer, that is internalise the external cost. If the pivotal agent, $i$, changes the decision from provision to non-provision (other consumers, $j$, would like the public good provided, so $\Sigma s_j > 0$, $i \neq j$, but $\Sigma s_i \leq 0$), then the tax $t_i$ is the social cost to the other consumers, $t_i = \Sigma s_j$, $i \neq j$. If instead the decision is changed from non-provision to provision (other consumers, $j$, do not want the public good provided $\Sigma s_j \leq 0$, $i \neq j$, but $\Sigma s_i > 0$), then $t_i = -\Sigma s_j$, $i \neq j$. So the tax on the pivotal agent is the absolute value of the sum of the stated net values

**BOX 4.4**

# Example of a Clarke tax

Let us continue with the example in Box 4.3 and consider the incentives to individuals, assuming that the others tell the truth, $s_i = n_i$.

*Consumer A*   $\Sigma n_i$ for B and C is $-100 + 200 = 300 > 0$
If A gives a truthful valuation $s_i = n_i = -100$, she is not a pivotal agent; the good will still be produced, so $t_i = 0$. If A is tempted to understate her value, e.g. $s_i = -300$, she becomes a pivotal agent, because the good will no longer be produced. She will now face a tax equal to the cost to society, which is the sum of the net value of the good to B and C, $t_i = 300$. Consumer A is not worse off, although A no longer contributes towards the public good, so does not incur $n_i = -100$; she is now taxed and the net value becomes $-300$.

| | $c_i$ | $v_i$ | $n_i$ | $s_i$ True | $t_i$ | $s_i$ False | $t_i$ | $n_i$ after t |
|---|---|---|---|---|---|---|---|---|
| **A** | 200 | 100 | −100 | −100 | 0 | −300 | 300 | −300 |

*Consumer B*   B would reason in the same way as A, described above.

*Consumer C*   $\Sigma n_i$ for A and B is $-100 - 100 = -200 < 0$
If C gives a truthful valuation $s_i = n_i = 300$, she is a pivotal agent. This means that C faces a tax equal to the cost of her action to A and B, that is a tax of £200. Since C is a pivotal agent, she has no incentive to over- or undervalue the good. For example, if she were to overstate the value $s_i = 250$, she is still a pivotal agent and faces the same costs of her action, the tax of £100.

| | $c_i$ | $v_i$ | $n_i$ | $s_i$ True | $t_i$ | $s_i$ False | $t_i$ | $n_i$ after t |
|---|---|---|---|---|---|---|---|---|
| **C** | 200 | 500 | 300 | 300 | 200 | 400 | 200 | 100 |

A and B face identical payoffs. If $s_i = n_i = -100$ or if they overstate $s_i > n_i = -100$, they are not pivotal, the public good is still provided and $n_i = -100$.

C places a much higher value on the public good. If $s_i = n_i = 300$ or if she overstates $s_i > n_i = 300$, she is pivotal and faces a tax $t_i = 200$, so the net value after tax is 100.

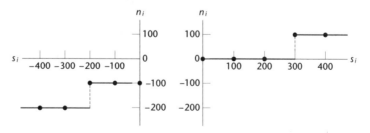

They become pivotal when they understate $s_i < -200$, so that the public good is no longer provided. They now face $t_i = 300$ and are worse off.

Were C to understate, $s_i < n_i = 300$, she would no longer be pivotal, the public good would no longer be provided, so the net value is zero.

of the good to the other consumers, $t_i = |\Sigma s_j|$, $i \neq j$. A simple example of a Clarke tax is given in Box 4.4.

Whilst we can see that the tax works well in the example in Box 4.4, when the number of consumers increases, it clearly will become more difficult and costly to administer the tax. Also, as the administration costs rise, the outcome becomes less efficient. This is because the taxes cannot be redistributed, as this may influence the incentives; they are simply imposed to penalise false preference revelations and so constitute a loss in consumption. A further problem may arise if consumers attempt to influence the outcome by forming coalitions with like-minded people. If coalitions are permitted, the pivotal agent can give false valuations and the Clarke tax is shared by the rest of the group. Finally, the Clarke tax will only necessarily work if the agent's valuations of the public good do not depend upon their income, i.e. preferences are quasi-linear. Other approaches to the provision of public goods through government include the Tiebout model of the provision by local government, discussed in Chapter 24, and government attempting to estimate the value using contingent valuation techniques, discussed in Chapter 7. Finally, when taxation occurs across large groups, preference revelation may cease to be a problem.

## 4.7 Conclusion

We have argued that market failure occurs in the case of public goods. The characteristic of non-rivalry changes our efficiency conditions for the level of production. We now have to consider the value of the public good to the whole set of potential consumers and in the absence of this sort of collective action, the outcome will be inefficient. The second characteristic of non-excludability means that it is possible to consume the good without paying for it, which makes it unattractive for private firms to supply the good. Correcting the market failure is not a simple matter. Although government provision of public goods would certainly address the problem of finding a supplier, without some method of correctly calculating overall valuation, the level of production will be inefficient. It will be necessary for the supplier to estimate the value to the consumers of the public goods. However, there are incentives for consumers to conceal their true preferences, such as the hope of reducing the contribution toward the public good or of influencing the outcome. It is only when we implement a mechanism such as the Clarke tax which penalises false valuations that there are incentives to reveal true preferences.

## Summary

- Public goods are non-excludable and non-rival. Examples include defence and street lighting.
- Since non-rivalry implies that all consumers consume the same amount, the necessary and sufficient condition for provision to be Pareto efficient is that the aggregation of marginal valuations exceed the marginal cost.
- Because a public good is non-excludable, there is an incentive to free-ride.

- There are no appropriate incentives for consumers to reveal their true marginal valuations, other than in very small communities.
- Private firms have few incentives to provide public goods. However, there are appropriate incentives to supply a public good if a private good exists which is a complement to the public good.
- Private provision may occur via clubs if the good is excludable.
- Tax mechanisms, such as the Clarke tax, can be used to overcome the problem of failure to reveal true preferences.

## Questions

1. Can the following be regarded as a public goods?

   Education    Clean beaches    Good roads    Income redistribution    The BBC
2. To what extent have technological advances reduced the problem of non-excludability?
3. How can policy makers assess the true demand for public goods?
4. Is free riding more of a problem in theory than in practice?
5. Under what circumstances will private firms provide an efficient level of a public good?

## Further reading

A more formal treatment of the problems associated with public goods can be found in Myles (1995) and Ng (1983). The problems of preference revelation and the Clarke tax are discussed in more detail by Barnett (1993). Recent experimental evidence on the levels of contribution towards public goods can be found in Ledyard (1995) or in Davis and Holt (1993).

## References

Barnett, R.R. (1993) 'Preference revelation and public goods', in P.M. Jackson (ed.) *Current Issues in Public Sector Economics*, pp. 94–131, London: Macmillan.

Davis, D.D. and Holt, C.A. (1993) *Experimental Economics*, Princeton: Princeton University Press.

Davis, R.J. and Hulett, J.R. (1977) *An Analysis of Market Failure*, Gainesville: University Presses of Florida.

Ledyard, J.O. (1995) 'Public goods: a survey of experimental research', in J.H. Kagel and A.E. Roth (eds) *The Handbook of Experimental Economics*, Princeton: Princeton University Press.

Myles, G. (1995) *Public Economics*, Cambridge: Cambridge University Press.

Ng, Y.-K. (1983) *Welfare Economics: Introduction and Development of Basic Concepts*, revised edn, London: Macmillan.

Peston, M.H. (1974) *Public Goods and the Public Sector*, London: Macmillan.

# CHAPTER 5

# Externalities

## Key concepts

| | | |
|---|---|---|
| externality | depletable | undepletable |
| missing markets | Coase Theorem | internalisation |
| transaction costs | bargaining | congestion externalities |
| global commons | marketable permits | Pigouvian taxation |
| non-convexities | | |

## 5.1 Introduction

**Externality**

An action by one agent which affects directly the well-being or production possibilities of other agents, but is chosen without regard to those consequences

**Non-depletable externality**

An externality which is non-rival, such as pollution

We choose how much food to eat or what CDs to buy, but when a smoker lights up a cigarette on the next table in a restaurant, or noise from a neighbour's hi-fi stops us from sleeping, our well-being is affected directly by choices made by other people. The noisy hi-fi and the unwelcome smoke are examples of **externalities**, goods which enter an agent's production or utility function, but which are chosen by others without regard to the affected person's welfare. The definition rules out cases, called *pecuniary externalities*, where the effects are via the price mechanism, e.g. through taxes. It also excludes situations where the damage (or gain) is deliberate or where one agent fully internalises the consequences of his or her actions. In both these cases, the chooser decides his or her actions having regard to the effect on the other person or persons involved. The examples of smoking and noise were both instances of *negative externality*, but externalities can be positive (e.g. waste water from a power station raises the rate of fish growth in an adjacent river) or reciprocal, such as in the well-known example of bees and orchards, where honey production benefits from adjacent nectar and fertilisation of the fruit trees is improved by a supply of bees. An externality is said to be *depletable* if the consumption of the externality by one agent means another does not. For instance, if a bee pollinates a tree in one orchard it cannot be pollinating another. Many of the most pressing environmental problems in the world are examples of **non-depletable externalities**: one person's consumption of the externality does not diminish another agent's ability to suffer from the externality. In other words, the externality is non-rival and will share some of the characteristics of a public good. Traffic congestion is of this kind, as is acid rain, many examples of pollution, depletion of the ozone layer and global warming. The latter is an example of an externality that may be positive for some agents (Canadians) and negative for others (Maldivians and Fenlanders).

As the examples suggest, externality is the market failure which gives rise to many of the problems of pollution faced by developing and developed nations alike. The problem in all cases is that there is no price for the good and therefore no opportunity for the affected parties to trade in it. Thus the theory in this chapter underpins Chapter 23, but external effects are not confined to the environment. Altruism, for example, is an externality where one person's well-being enters another's utility function; vaccination by one individual has benefits for others around them. So the theory of externalities also has implications for the understanding of redistribution and healthcare.

## 5.2 Externalities and market failure

**Social cost**

The private cost of an action plus the extra external cost to society

In choosing whether to smoke, an individual weighs up the private benefits to themselves against the private costs of the cigarette. Ignored in the calculation is the **social cost** to anyone else who inhales the smoke and it is this which gives rise to the central problem of externalities: competitive markets yield prices which do not reflect the social costs (and benefits), only the private costs. Now, in the absence of market failures such as external effects, social and private costs are equal and competitive markets yield a Pareto-efficient outcome. When private and social costs diverge the result is inefficiency. In fact, as we shall see, market failure is produced in two ways: via divergent incentives for the players in the market economy and through the creation of increasing returns to scale.

### Divergent incentives

The first problem caused by externalities can be considered using a simple example. Suppose there are two students: Ann, who likes smoking, and Bill, who does not, and who also suffers from the smoke created by Ann. Figure 5.1 illustrates the situation

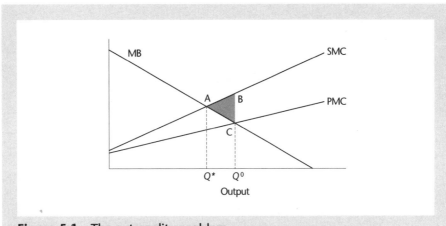

**Figure 5.1** The externality problem

**BOX 5.1**

## Surplus and welfare loss – a reminder

**Consumer surplus** is an approximate value for the gain an individual makes from consumption. The left-hand panel of Figure 5.2 depicts the demand curve for a single consumer. They would demand one unit of the good at a price of $P^1$, so if the actual market price for the good is $P^c$, they make a profit or *surplus* on that unit of $(P^1-P^c)$. For the second unit, the profit is the difference between the market price and the price the agent would pay for two units and so on, until $Q^0$ is reached. It follows that the area ABC is the total consumer surplus for this individual at the price $P^c$. Just as the consumer surplus is the difference between what a consumer is willing to pay and what they actually pay, so the **producer surplus** is the difference between the price a firm actually receives for a given output and the variable costs of producing it. Thus, in the right-hand panel of Figure 5.2, where the firms receive a price $P^s$, producer surplus is the shaded area DFG above the marginal cost curve. In this diagram a tax, $t$, has created a wedge between producer and consumer prices. If there was no tax then total surplus (consumer plus producer) would be AEG. With the tax, ABC is the consumer surplus while the tax raised, CFDB, is a transfer, leaving BED as the surplus lost as a result of the tax. This is the efficiency cost of the distortion. See Chapter 11 for a discussion of the relationship between this measure and exact measures of the efficiency cost.

### Consumer surplus

The difference between a consumer's willingness to pay (as measured by the area under the demand curve) and what they actually pay

### Producer surplus

The difference between what firms actually receive and the minimum compensation they require to supply the good, as measured by the area under the supply curve

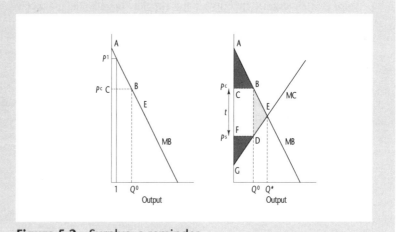

**Figure 5.2**  Surplus: a reminder

in a partial equilibrium setting. Ann is producing smoke up to the point at which her private marginal cost equals private marginal benefit. But the smoke creates costs for Bill as well, meaning that the social cost lies above the private cost (it would make no difference if we said that the social benefits lie below the private benefits, as long as both cost and benefit functions were not adjusted simultaneously). Ann ignores the extra costs, so the private optimum ($Q^0$) lies above the social optimum, $Q^*$, creating a welfare loss of ABC (see Box 5.1 for a reminder of the concepts of consumer and producer surplus). Note that, even at the optimum, there is some level of external effect and some social cost. It will rarely if ever be optimal to eliminate an externality entirely, because cutting back on the externality normally means sacrificing another good which is valued. We could eliminate air pollution by banning industrial processes such as electricity generation, steel and products such as cars, but the gains from having a little steel or power, for instance, will outweigh the benefits of eliminating the last few molecules of pollution.

It is instructive to see how the presence of externalities destroys the First Fundamental Theorem of Welfare Economics. Suppose we have the same two individuals and two goods, $x$ and $y$, with $x$ as cigarettes and $y$ representing 'other goods'. Utility functions are therefore:

$$U^A = U(x^A, y^A); \quad U^B = U(x^A, y^B) \tag{5.1}$$

Note how Bill's utility depends not only on his own consumption, but also on Ann's consumption of cigarettes, $x^A$. With the slope of the production possibility frontier given by MRT, Pareto efficiency requires:

$$\text{MRS}^A + \frac{\partial U^B / \partial y^B}{\partial U^B / \partial x^A} = \text{MRT} \tag{5.2}$$

The first term on the left-hand side of equation (5.2) is Ann's willingness to trade cigarettes for a marginal change in $x$. The second term reflects the external effect on Bill; it shows the amount of other goods he would accept in return for a marginal decrease in Ann's cigarette consumption and of course it is negative, because a rise in Ann's smoking ($x^A$) makes Bill worse off. The right-hand side shows the rate at which $x$ can be transformed into $y$, at the margin. As we saw in Chapter 2, in a competitive market, Ann sets her $\text{MRS}^A = p/q$, where $p$ is the price of $x$ and $q$ is the price of $y$, while profit-maximising firms set output at the point where $p/q = \text{MRT}$. Thus $\text{MRS}^A = \text{MRT}$. In short, equation (5.2) does not hold and the conditions for Pareto optimality are broken. Ann produces too much smoke relative to the social optimum, because the price she pays does not reflect the externality.

## Fundamental non-convexities

Even if prices reflect marginal social costs, the social optimum may not be achievable via a (modified) competitive equilibrium, because external effects create increasing returns to scale. The easiest way to show it is via an example. Suppose there are two firms: one upstream, producing titanium dioxide (a paint pigment) and one fish farm, downstream from the polluter pigment manufacturer. Suppose that both products require only labour to create an output and there are constant returns to scale. With the fish farm, 1 day of labour yields 4,000 fish ($f$), while in the pigment factory one day's work yields 50 tonnes of oxide ($x$). There are 1,200 days of labour available, so if all labour is used on the fish farm 4,800,000 fish can be harvested while, if only the factory is operating, 6,000 tonnes of pigment are produced. Giving up 1 tonne of pigment therefore effectively creates 80 fish. This creates the linear (PPF) of equation (5.3), depicted in Figure 5.3.

$$f = 4,800,000 - \frac{4,000x}{50} = 4,000 \left( 1,200 - \frac{x}{50} \right) \tag{5.3}$$

Suppose that producing the oxide also creates a pollutant which enters the river, reducing the productivity of the fish farm. Specifically, for every extra tonne of pigment, each unit of labour used at the fish farm produces ½ a fish less. For example, with 100 tonnes of pigment produced in the factory, only 3,950 fish can be produced per unit of labour and not the full 4,000. Note that as more units of pigment are produced the problem gets worse. With the externality, therefore, the equation of the PPF becomes:

$$f = \left( 1,200 - \frac{x}{50} \right) (4,000 - 0.5x) \qquad (5.4)$$

This means that the PPF is convex, as in Figure 5.3. In other words, the presence of the externality turns a situation of constant returns to scale into one of increasing returns. But we have seen in Chapter 3 that this means competitive markets cannot be employed to create a Pareto-efficient outcome.

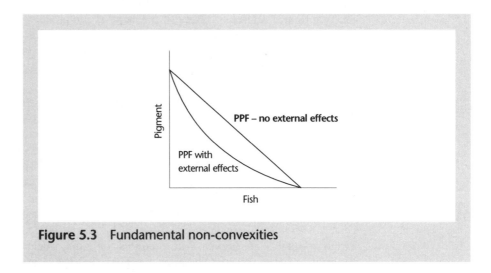

**Figure 5.3** Fundamental non-convexities

## 5.3 Solutions to the externality problem

### Bargaining to efficiency: the Coase Theorem

In the cigarette example, Ann could offer Bill money to let her smoke or Bill could demand compensation off Ann to allow her to light up. The situation is illustrated in Figure 5.4, which shows an Edgeworth box of the type encountered in Chapter 2, but now with cigarettes and other goods along the axes. What is clearly important here is the distribution of *property rights* in the student hall or house that they share. If Bill owns the property rights to clean air, then Ann will have to pay him for the smoke she creates, while if Ann owns the rights to the air, then Bill will have to bribe her to stop smoking. In other words, if Ann has the right to smoke, then the endowment point is at A, where she can smoke all her cigarettes; if Bill owns the rights to clean air, then the endowment is at B, where no cigarettes are smoked. The figure illustrates two fundamental points about externalities. First, the outcome is Pareto ineffi-cient in the absence of bargaining (or some other solution). That is, all parties can gain compared to the competitive outcome. This is completely general; it applies as

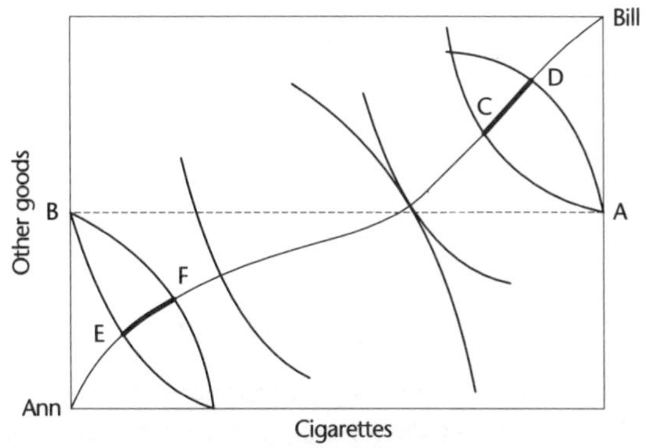

**Figure 5.4** Bargaining over externalities

much to acid rain or road congestion as it does to two students bargaining over smoking rights. Second, if the individuals involved do trade, they can continue to bargain until no Pareto improvement is possible. The outcome would be Pareto efficient, although who would gain more from the deal we cannot say. Bargaining brings the agents to the contract curve. If the endowment point is A, then CD is the locus of Pareto-efficient points which are Pareto superior to A, but if Bill owns the rights and B is the endowment point, then EF is the corresponding locus. Thus, in general, the efficient level of smoking which results from bargaining will depend on initial endowments. Only if their preferences are both quasi-linear will the final level of the externality (smoke) be independent of the initial distribution.

The idea that bargaining will lead to a Pareto-efficient outcome in the absence of bargaining or transaction costs is known as the **Coase Theorem** after its originator.[1] Yet fundamentally, transaction costs are like any other forms of cost and so should be included in any discussion of what is the efficient outcome. If, for instance, bargaining costs are 10 and the potential gains from Ann reducing smoke levels is only 8, then it will not be efficient to come to a deal which reduces her smoking. So, a more careful interpretation of the Coase Theorem is that bargaining will lead to an efficient outcome for a given institutional framework, provided property rights are well-defined, whether there are bargaining costs or not.

This is not the whole story. Different institutional frameworks (the rules under which bargaining occurs) may well alter the bargaining costs. So what is efficient under one set of rules may not be efficient by another. With undepletable externalities such as air pollution, for instance, bargaining costs are likely to be high for two reasons: first, the large number of people involved who must come to an agreement; second, the public good nature of the externality which gives individuals incentives to free-ride and misrepresent their preferences in the bargaining process. The outcome might therefore be a long way from the zero bargaining cost optimum (though see Box 5.2 for an alternative view).

**Coase Theorem**

States that bargaining over externalities will lead to Pareto efficiency, provided property rights are well defined

---

[1] Sometimes it is interpreted as meaning that the level of the externality will be independent of the distribution of property rights in the absence of bargaining costs. This depends on the preferences of all individuals being quasi-linear. Since profit functions are quasi-linear, then bargaining between firms should always lead to the same level of the externality.

To summarise, bargaining makes sense when there are only a few individuals involved and the externality is depletable. With undepletable externalities, where almost by definition the numbers involved are much higher, other mechanisms may produce a Pareto-superior result. Governments, for instance, may be more efficient institutions for dealing with undepletable externalities, but what mechanisms are available to them?

| BOX 5.2 | **Experimental tests of the Coase Theorem** |

A challenge to the view that bargaining over undepletable externalities will not produce efficiency comes from the experiments conducted by Elizabeth Hoffman and Matthew Spitzer (1982, 1986), using students to mimic behaviour in markets with externalities. Batches of subjects were split randomly into two subgroups, 'polluters' and 'pollutees', and given charts showing their potential payoffs. Each batch had to agree a number ('pollution') with one side of the market preferring higher numbers and one facing higher payoffs from lower numbers. Payoffs were set so that there was a clear joint-profit-maximising option which, if chosen with the appropriate side-payments (which were allowed), would Pareto dominate the next-best alternative by at least $1 per subject.

In an environment with externalities, one side of the market has the property rights to set externality levels without the agreement of the other side. In these experiments, these control rights were assigned through either (in early versions) the flip of a coin or (in later versions) through a preliminary 'game'. For some versions of the experiment, there were several subjects on either side of the market, all of whom had a veto on the level of the externality if control rights were assigned to their side. So if the 'polluters' held the rights and five wished to set the level at 4 (say), one dissenter could insist that the figure chosen was 6 (or any other number).

Altogether, 445 runs were made of the experiment, with player numbers in each batch ranging from 2 to 20, with and without full information on other players' payoffs. Out of this, 93% of the groups chose the profit-maximising outcome (i.e. the outcome predicted by the Coase Theorem for zero transaction costs), with little variation between the different forms of the experiment; limited information groups, for instance, achieved the Coasean outcome in 91% of occasions, compared to 94% for the full information groups. Surprisingly, large groups were more likely to reach the efficient solution, mainly, it seems, because they tended to delegate negotiations to small teams from each side.

These results therefore appear to support the applicability of the simple Coase Theorem for all types of externality. Nevertheless, two reservations are in order. First, even twenty, the maximum number of players in these experiments, is small compared to the millions and even billions of individuals affected by atmospheric pollution, for instance. Second, the technology of undepletable externalities does not match that described in the experiment. Typically, individual polluters choose their own emissions levels, not the pollution level common to all players. Similarly, the subjects were instructed to reach an agreement, with payoffs delayed until that point was reached, whereas in markets with pollution individuals can continue to receive payoffs in the absence of any agreed level of the externality. There is therefore less common interest on the polluter side of the equation and less interest in reaching an agreement in real life than was created in this experiment.

Perhaps these criticisms miss the point. As we have seen in previous chapters, part of the *raison d'être* of government is its ability to lower the transaction costs associated with determining the efficient level of public goods. The crucial institutional development which made the twenty-person experiment manageable was the delegation of negotiations. In effect, the players reduced transaction costs by creating a primitive form of representative government.

## Pigou and taxation

**Pigouvian taxation**

A tax on the production of an externality designed to bring social and private marginal costs into line

We have already seen that, when Ann decides on the smoke level, there is too much smoke compared to the social optimum. Perhaps if we taxed her smoking we could bring about the social optimum. Similarly a carbon tax might reduce global warming, taxing petrol could reduce road congestion and taxing polluters might reduce the level of pollution. These are examples of **Pigouvian taxes**, named after the economist A.C. Pigou, who first examined their use. Figure 5.5 repeats the partial equilibrium analysis of Figure 5.1. Suppose a tax of $t$ is levied on the polluter. This raises private marginal cost to PMC'. The firm cuts back output to $Q^*$, the social optimum. What are the distributional consequences of this action? It depends on what is done with the taxes raised. Note though that $Q^*$ represents a Pareto improvement on $Q^0$; in other words, with the right policy, everyone can gain from the imposition of the tax. However, if the money goes into general taxation or is given to the agents suffering from pollution, then the polluter will lose from the policy and may well wish to resist its imposition.

As an alternative, the government could subsidise a cutback in output, reducing the benefits to producers of expanding output. The optimal price to consumers would

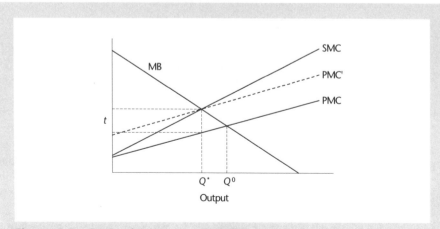

**Figure 5.5** Optimal taxes on externalities

be the same as under taxation,[2] but the distributional consequences may be different and the polluter may actually gain from the change. This kind of policy is often suggested as a means of dealing with nitrate and pesticide pollution by farmers, by subsidising reduced use of the offending substances rather than taxing increased use.

In the mathematical example what should the tax $t$ be? Rearranging equation (5.1) we can see that optimality requires:

$$MRS^A = -\frac{\partial U^B/\partial y^B}{\partial U^B/\partial x^A} + MRT \tag{5.5}$$

In a competitive system, Ann will set consumption so that $MRS^A = (p + t)/q$. Meanwhile, firms will set production at the point where $MRT = p/q$, which, for Pareto efficiency, means that:

$$\frac{p + t}{q} = -\frac{\partial U^B/\partial y^B}{\partial U^B/\partial x^A} + \frac{p}{q} \tag{5.6}$$

Thus, the tax which leads to efficiency is:

$$\frac{t}{q} = -\frac{\partial U^B/\partial y^B}{\partial U^B/\partial x^A} \tag{5.7}$$

In other words, the tax is set so that $t/q$ is equal to the amount of other goods Bill would accept in return for a marginal increase in Ann's smoking. Notice that this tax is specific to Ann; as long as different people pollute differently or suffer the effects of pollution in different ways, then taxes must be differentiated at the individual level for full optimality.

What happens if the PPF is non-convex, as in the fish/oxide example? De-centralised linear pricing (and therefore using linear taxes) cannot be employed to achieve the social optimum, as this would imply losses for the firms involved. In fact, unless the social optimum coincides with one of the corners, then producing at it will *minimise* total profits for the firms involved. It might be possible to employ non-linear prices to achieve the optimum, but, given their complications, some form of direct intervention might be easier. For instance, in this case we could ban oxide plants upstream of fish farms. At a stroke the problem would disappear. An alternative solution is internalisation.

## Internalisation

If a firm pollutes a lake from which fish are drawn for profit, then it creates an external effect that will damage the profits of the fishermen. Taxing the output of the firm is one way to remedy the problem, but another is for the fishery to take over the factory (or vice versa). This process is called *internalisation* and it means that the merged company is forced to take note of the externality if it wishes to maximise the profits of the joint operation. Common instances include the coke furnace, blast furnace and rolling mill of a steel mill, where heat is the positive externality. Bees and orchards are another case, but obviously when the externality producer is a firm and the affected agents are individual consumers, it is much harder for internalisa-tion to occur. Other forms of internalisation occur when we 'worry' about the

---

[2] This is true in the short run. In the long run, with entry to and exit from a competitive industry, the outcome will differ. Generally, in the long run, the subsidy will make the externality problem worse, since it attracts entrants into the industry. See Baumol and Oates (1988).

environment. If we were all highly responsible in our attitude to global warming for instance and internalised the potential damage, this would act as a personal tax on consumption habits.

## Direct controls

So far we have considered market-based instruments for curing externalities, using taxes to adjust the incentives faced by individuals or allowing bargaining to produce the optimum, but when smog threatens air quality, municipal authorities often close city centres to traffic rather than taxing vehicle use and when congestion clogs roads, governments often respond with bus lanes rather than road pricing. Meanwhile, setting limits on the emission of pollutants and using regulations on the allowable technology are alternatives widely used by governments in the real world of anti-pollution policy. In principle, these quantitative controls are just as efficient as taxation, the pollution control agency simply sets output at $Q^*$ in Figure 5.5, but in practice there are problems with direct controls.

## Differential costs

Direct controls are inferior to pricing when costs differ between firms and it is not feasible to set controls which differentiate between firms. Figure 5.6 illustrates the problem, showing two price-taking firms, one with a higher marginal cost (MC) than the other. The example assumes that the relationship between output and pollution is the same for both firms, so it is only the total quantity of output which matters for pollution, not who produces it.

Suppose first that a tax system is used to restrict output. The firms face the same price in equilibrium, $P^*$; the high-cost firm produces at $Q^H$, while the low-cost firm produces at $Q^L$, giving a total output of $Q = (Q^H + Q^L)$. Alternatively, suppose that quantity restrictions are employed instead and each firm is allowed to produce $Q/2$, half the total. As a result, the high-cost firm produces more under quantity restrictions, compared to the tax-based solution, while the output of the low-cost firm

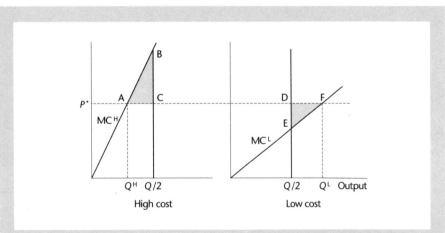

**Figure 5.6** The superiority of taxes over direct controls with differential costs

drops. The costs of the high-cost firm rise by the shaded area ABC, while the low cost firm sees a drop in costs of DEF. The net change is ABC − DEF, but since ABC > DEF, then total industry costs rise. In short, therefore, a switch to quantity controls transfers output to higher cost producers, thereby raising total costs for the industry.

## Uncertainty

If there is uncertainty over the position of the marginal benefit and cost curves, then issues are not so clear cut; direct controls might be superior to prices. The argument is due to Weitzmann (1974) and is summarised in Figure 5.7, which shows social marginal benefit and cost curves. The heavy lines represent the average positions of the marginal social benefit and costs curves, but the actual marginal costs could be either High or Low (shown in grey), implying that the efficient level of output could be B or G. An agency responsible for controlling pollution can either set a quantity level, or it can set a price level, but either way it must typically do so before the actual positions of the marginal cost curves are known. As long as the benefit or cost curves are not in their expected position, there will be a cost to society, in the sense that output will be wrong *ex post*. If the agency uses prices as the instrument, then it will set price = $p^*$. Consequently, output will be at the point where $p^* = $ MC, wherever the marginal cost curve happens to be. So if the cost curve is Low, and prices are used as the control, then output will be at J. However, if the marginal cost curve is Low, then the optimum point is G (not J), creating a welfare loss of GJK. Alternatively, if the marginal cost curve is High, then the optimum is B, whereas the actual output level is A, incurring a welfare loss of ACB. Meanwhile, if the agency uses output as the control variable, it will set it at $Q^*$, but this too will be wrong *ex post* and creates efficiency losses. The table below summarises the costs of getting it wrong for the two different instruments.

| Control | Actual marginal cost curve | Actual output | Optimum output | Welfare loss |
|---------|---------|---------|---------|---------|
| Prices | | | | |
| | Low | J | G | GJK |
| | High | A | B | ACB |
| Output | | | | |
| | Low | E | G | EGD |
| | High | E | B | FEB |

In this example, EGD and FEB (the welfare losses associated with quantity controls) are much smaller than GJK and ACB (losses from using price as the instrument), respectively, so if there is an equal chance of the MC curve being either Low or High, then fixing output is superior to fixing the price, since the expected welfare loss is smaller. More generally, the lessons are:

1. uncertainty about the position of the MB curve does not have consequences for the prices versus quantities decision;

2. uncertainty about the position of the MC curve raises the advantages of prices as the decision rule, provided that the absolute slope of the MC curve is greater than that of the MB curve;

3. uncertainty about the position of the MC curve raises the advantages of quantities as the decision rule, provided that the absolute slope of the MC curve is less than that of the MB curve (as it is in Figure 5.7).

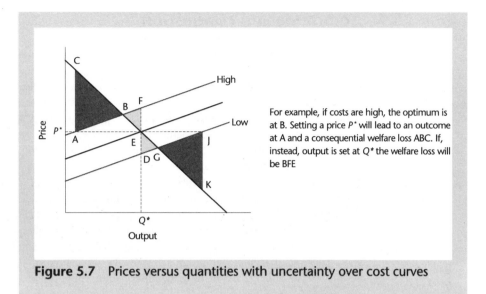

For example, if costs are high, the optimum is at B. Setting a price $P^*$ will lead to an outcome at A and a consequential welfare loss ABC. If, instead, output is set at $Q^*$ the welfare loss will be BFE

**Figure 5.7** Prices versus quantities with uncertainty over cost curves

The relative slopes of MC and MB curves will differ from example to example, but, for instance, if the industry is close to constant returns to scale (as in the diagram), then this will tend to favour the use of output as the instrument rather than prices.

## Choosing the best option

Typically, the optimal intervention will depend on the nature of the externality. It is difficult to give hard and fast rules, but this section offers some guidance. If the external effect is depletable or the bargaining costs are low, then it is probably best to use the Coase Theorem to find the optimum, in other words, defining property rights and allowing the affected parties to come to an agreement. If, on the other hand, the externality is non-rival and so is undepletable, then the size of bargaining costs suggests the need for more direct government intervention. Whether taxes or quantities should be the instrument used depends on the degree of uncertainty over the position of the marginal cost function, but there is one more problem which must be faced. In order to set the optimal output level or tax, the planner must know the position of the expected MC and MB curves, but this is not usually straightforward. In particular, benefits are hard to estimate. As a result, the level of pollution or the tax rate might have to be set arbitrarily. This does not mean that all notions of economic efficiency need be abandoned. The planning authority could try to iterate towards the optimum, using the information gleaned from one year's operations to plan its decisions in the following year. Alternatively, a policy could be instituted of issuing pollution permits up to the level of the allowed emission level and then allowing trade. This will encourage firms with high costs of cutting back on pollution to buy permits from firms with low costs, leading to a cost-minimising outcome, provided bargaining costs are low. This possibility is explored further in Chapter 23.

## 5.4  Commons and congestion

Often the producers of the externality are also the consumers; congestion on roads is the most common example. Each individual considers only the cost and benefit of their own use, ignoring the consequences for other individuals. The classic instance of this is described by Hardin (1968) as the **tragedy of the commons**, because the roads or other resource are common rather than private property and open access leads to overuse. Examples other than roads include fisheries (where overfishing is the result of everyone ignoring the social consequences of their actions), grazing lands, and deforestation, where individuals have no incentive to consider the consequences for soil erosion, for the climate and the local ecology of clearing a small plot of land.

| **Tragedy of the commons** |
| --- |
| The tendency of open-access resources to be over-exploited |

Figure 5.8 uses the example of a fishery to illustrate the problem. Suppose that $x$ is the number of fishing boats. The total benefits from a fleet of size $x$ are $B(x)$ and the marginal cost of adding another boat is $MC(x)$. The total benefits, $B(x)$, depend on the total numbers already fishing. As more people fish, output increases (at least in the short run), so marginal benefit MB is positive, but there are diminishing returns because of the effect of overfishing. Optimal fishing therefore occurs when the marginal benefits of another boat equal the marginal costs. That is, when, MB = MC. Yet, if there is free access to the fishing grounds, individuals will add boats to the fleet as long as the gains outweigh the benefits to them. Since the total benefit is $B$, the benefit per boat is $B/x$, so an individual will be prepared to add a boat to the fleet provided:

$$\frac{B(x)}{x} \geq MC(x) \tag{5.8}$$

And as we can see from equation (5.8) and Figure 5.8, this leads to overuse. In the figure, because the average benefit declines as the size of the fleet increases, then the marginal benefit curve must lie below the average benefit line $B/x$. As a result, the open-access equilibrium point, $x^o$, lies above the efficient point, $x^*$, where the MB of an extra boat equals its marginal cost. In the same way, cars will join a busy motorway when the average benefit to the driver exceeds their marginal cost. But this leads to overuse of the resource and the inefficiency of traffic jams.

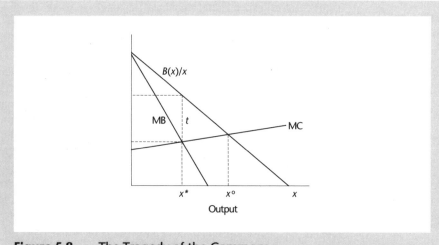

**Figure 5.8**    The Tragedy of the Commons

### Solving the congestion problem

As with standard externalities, a number of possible options are open.

#### Taxes

Putting a tax on the resource equal to the difference between average benefit and marginal cost will lead to the optimal level of use. In Figure 5.8, the optimal tax is $t$, which reduces the benefits of buying a boat to $B/x - t$, and lowers the numbers of boats in the open-access equilibrium to $x^*$.

#### Monopoly

If access to the resource can be policed (and this assumption is implicit in the tax option as well), transferring property rights to one individual removes the externality problem. The monopolist will maximise the net benefits from the resource, the gap between costs and the value of output. But this just produces the condition in equation (5.8). With a large-scale common resource, such as a motorway system or a fishery, the transfer of property rights to one individual may be seen as unacceptable on equity grounds, although it would often be possible for a government to auction off the property rights to the highest bidder. The monopolist still chooses the optimal output, but the profit is transferred to the community, enabling everyone to gain.

#### Cooperatives: collective monopolies

Collective ownership of the common resource represents an alternative which achieves similar ends: efficiency with equity. The cooperative owns the common, then charges members for access. The optimal price is just the tax rate $t$, since this makes users of the resource internalise the costs they impose on other members. Alternatively, the cooperative can just choose the total level of output, then auction permits for access to the common.

## 5.5 Conclusion

External effects create one of the classic market failures, leading to a gap between market prices and social values. In principle, the problem can be solved by defining property rights, but this assumes that transaction costs are sufficiently low for the market to provide the optimal solution. In practice, many of the most serious externalities have public good characteristics, which raises bargaining costs and calls for a more interventionist response (a point taken up in Chapter 23, on the environment). Once the government is involved, however, it needs to have estimates of marginal benefit and cost functions. Obtaining estimates is not easy, particularly those for benefits, as we shall see in Chapter 7.

## Summary

- An external effect occurs when the consequences of one agent's actions enter directly someone else's utility or production function.

- Externalities can be classified in a number of ways, but for policy purposes, the most important distinction is between depletable and undepletable externalities, the latter being non-rival.

- Externalities create two forms of market failure: a gap between social and private cost and non-convexities. It is not clear how important the second example is in real life.

- In the case of depletable externalities, the Coase Theorem demonstrates that efficiency is possible via trading, providing property rights are well defined.

- The transaction costs involved with bargaining over undepletable externalities usually rules out private contracting as a producer of efficiency.

- Whether taxes or regulations should be employed depends on the relative slopes of the marginal cost and benefit curves and the degree of uncertainty about their position.

- Optimal intervention requires knowledge of the shape of the benefit and cost functions, but often such knowledge is hard to come by.

- With congestion externalities, free access to the resource leads to its overuse.

- In the case of many living commons, such as grazing lands and fisheries, the dynamic costs of open access are severe, with the destruction of the resource as a possible outcome.

## Questions

1. Why are the following *not* externalities: (a) the noise of a car-revving from a neighbour who is trying to annoy you; (b) your radio-alarm waking you up after you have set it the night before; (c) a cut in a firm's profits following an increase in production by a competitor?

2. Why are bargaining costs likely to be higher with undepletable externalities?

3. Draw a diagram showing the long-run equilibrium in a competitive industry with a tax on an externality. How do the long and short run compare if instead firms are subsidised to cut back their production?

4. Why does uncertainty about the position of the marginal benefit curve have no implications for the prices versus quantities debate?

5. Do 'tragedy of the commons' problems always need external authority for an efficient solution to develop?

# Further reading

Ronald Coase's original 1960 article is probably the best introduction to his theorem, but Dahlman's (1979) interpretative essay and Ralph Turvey's (1963) survey of the issue are also useful sources. Dorfman and Dorfman (1994) collect many of the main articles on the subject into one sampler volume. Externalities are dealt with in most texts on environmental policy, but Baumol and Oates (1988) is one of the best and also has a thorough discussion of the prices versus quantities debate. More references on environmental issues can be found at the end of Chapter 23.

# References

Baumol, W. and Oates, W. (1988) *The Theory of Environmental Policy*, 2nd edn, Cambridge: Cambridge University Press.

Coase, R. (1960) 'The problem of social cost', *Journal of Law and Economics* 1, 1–44.

Dahlman, C.L. (1979) 'The problem of externality', *Journal of Law and Economics* 22, 141–63.

Dorfman, R. and Dorfman, N.C. (1994) *Economics of the Environment*, 3rd edn, London: Norton.

Hanley, N. and Spash, C. (1994) *Cost–Benefit Analysis and the Environment*, Aldershot: Edward Elgar.

Hardin, G. (1968) 'The tragedy of the commons', *Science* 162, 1243–8.

Hoffman, E. and Spitzer, M. (1982) 'The Coase Theorem: some experimental tests', *Journal of Law and Economics* 25, 73.

Hoffman, E. and Spitzer, M. (1986) 'Experimental tests of the Coase Theorem with large bargaining groups', *Journal of Legal Studies* 15, 149–71.

Turvey, R. (1963) 'On divergencies between social cost and private cost', *Economica*, August, 309–13.

Weitzmann, M. (1974) 'Prices versus quantities', *Review of Economic Studies* 41, 477–91.

# Asymmetric Information

## 6.1 Introduction

**Asymmetric information**

When two parties to a transaction hold different information

**Moral hazard**

When information about actions is hidden from one party to a transaction

**Adverse selection**

When knowledge about characteristics is hidden from one party to a transaction

**Asymmetric information** (AI) occurs when one individual or organisation knows something that another individual or organisation does not. For instance, the regulators of a utility company may have only a hazy notion of costs known with precision by the managers of the firm. This, the fourth form of market failure, is profoundly different from the previous three we have encountered and really should be called an *institutional* failure rather than a *market* failure, because it affects the actions, not only of markets, but also of governments and other non-market institutions. Hence, unlike externalities, public goods and increasing returns, it is not always clear what advantage the state has over the market for commodities afflicted by AI.

### Adverse selection and moral hazard

The two forms of AI are hidden action and hidden knowledge. Hidden action is called **moral hazard** and for instance occurs when an insurance company is unable to observe how many cigarettes a smoker buys. **Adverse selection** occurs when information is hidden from one party, for instance when a candidate vows to stick to the manifesto once elected, but only he or she knows if the promise will be kept.[1]

In this chapter we spell out how AI damages the efficient function of markets. Because asymmetric information, by definition, takes place in a context of uncertainty, we need first to review the basic model of behaviour under uncertainty, in order to understand the conditions for efficiency.[2]

---

[1] In many cases the distinction between the two categories of AI is not clear cut.
[2] Readers unfamiliar with the basic models of choice under uncertainty might find it helpful to consult an intermediate microeconomics textbook, e.g. Katz and Rosen (1998) Chapter 6.

## 6.2 The value of insurance

The demand for insurance arises because many individuals prefer security and certainty over uncertainty and risk. Consumers therefore favour a world in which their standard of living is certain over a world with the same wealth on average, but which is marked by uncertainty about the standard of living they will actually experience. Individuals who prefer the certain world over the uncertain are called **risk averse** and will be willing to sacrifice some of their wealth in order to avoid risks such as sudden drops in income.

**Risk averse**

Being willing to pay to reduce risk

Expected utility provides the most commonly employed theory of decision-making under uncertainty. In it, the value of a risky prospect is equal to the sum of the utility of the outcomes multiplied by their probabilities. Suppose an individual has wealth, $Y$, but faces a world in which two outcomes are possible. With probability $(1 - p)$, they face no loss of wealth, but in outcome 2, some calamity (ill-health, theft or unemployment for instance) means a loss of $L$. Expected utility is then:

$$EU = (1 - p)U(Y) + pU(Y - L) \qquad (6.1)$$

whereas expected income $EY = (1 - p)Y + p(Y - L)$.

Figure 6.1 represents this contrast for a risk-averse individual. The fact that the individual is risk averse means that the utility gained from expected income $(U(EY))$ lies above expected utility, $EU$, which means that $U(Y)$ must be concave. Since the individual prefers the expected income to the risky prospect, then they will be willing to sacrifice income in order to gain security. The *risk premium* (RP) in Figure 6.1 shows the maximum sacrifice they are willing to make; any more and they would prefer to take a chance on the risk of losing $L$.

While RP is the maximum this individual is willing to pay for a guaranteed income, in a competitive market the premium paid will be lower, leaving some net gain from the act of insurance for the consumer. To see this, suppose now that the consumer can buy units of insurance cover at a price of $\pi$ per unit, meaning that if they purchase $z$ units of cover, they pay a premium of $\pi z$ and receive a payout of $z$ in the event of suffering the loss $L$. For instance, if a consumer pays £100 for £10,000 cover then $z =$

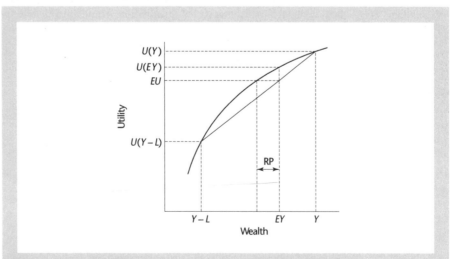

**Figure 6.1**   Risk premium for a risk-averse individual

10,000 and $\pi = £0.01$ The choice faced by the consumer is illustrated in Figure 6.2, a *state space* diagram in which the horizontal axis represents wealth in state of the world 1 (no loss) and the vertical axis shows wealth in state of the world 2 (loss). States of the world therefore represent different commodities and the consumer can use insurance to transfer consumption between different states. The expected utility is:

$$EU = (1-p)U(Y_1) + pU(Y_2) \tag{6.2}$$

where $Y_1 =$ income in the good state of the world $= Y - \pi z$ and $Y_2 =$ income in the bad state of the world $= Y - L - \pi z + z = Y - L + (1-\pi)z$.

In Figure 6.2, N is the endowment point, the position where no insurance is bought. The line NF represents the budget constraint up to the point F where the consumer is fully insured. Reducing the insurance purchased by one unit saves the consumer $\pi$ in the no-loss state of the world. They also save $\pi$ in state of the world 2 (since insurance premiums must be paid whether or not losses occur), but face a reduced payout of £1, giving a net reduction of $(1 - \pi)$. The slope of the budget constraint is therefore $-(1 - \pi)/\pi$. For the maximising consumer, the demand for insurance is given by the point at which the marginal rate of substitution (MRS) between the two states of the world is equal to the negative of the slope of the budget line. Using equation (6.2) to derive the MRS, the condition is therefore:

$$\text{MRS} = \frac{(1-p)U'(Y_1)}{pU'(Y_2)} = \frac{(1-\pi)}{\pi} \tag{6.3}$$

where $U'$ is the marginal utility of income, the first derivative of $U$

Without knowing the relationship between the price of a unit of insurance and the probability of a loss occurring, we cannot say much about the quantity of cover purchased. With a competitive insurance industry, expected profits will be zero. In the simplest possible model of the industry where the only costs are the payouts on losses, the zero expected profit condition is then:

$$Revenue - expected\ costs = \pi z - pz = 0 \tag{6.4}$$

So $\pi = p$ or, in other words, the probability of claiming for a loss equals the price for a unit of cover. This is exactly what intuition would lead us to expect. If there is a one

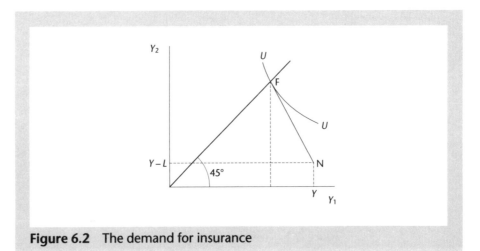

**Figure 6.2   The demand for insurance**

in ten chance of a major illness then to break even the insurance company should charge £1 for every £10 it will pay out in the event of the illness. When this relationship holds, the insurance premium is said to be **actuarially fair.** The consumer's insurance demand condition simplifies to:

**Actuarially fair insurance**

When the price of one unit of cover is equal to the probability of a claim

$$\frac{U'(Y_1)}{U'(Y_2)} = 1 \qquad\qquad (6.5)$$

This says that the marginal utility of income must be equal in the two states of the world. But the only way marginal utilities can be equal is for income to be equal in the two states of the world, meaning that, with actuarially fair insurance, the consumer is fully insured against the loss in equilibrium. In Figure 6.2, therefore, indifference curve UP is shown as a tangent to the budget line at F, a position of full insurance.

## 6.3 Asymmetric information

There is no market failure in this story, so it is important to understand what the conditions are for equation (6.5) to hold. First, insurance for the risk is available. Second, the insurance offered is actuarially fair. Third (and this is implicit in the second condition), consumer perceptions of the risk are accurate. Fourth, the insurance company also knows the chances of a loss with accuracy. Fifth, any actions taken to increase or mitigate risk should be observable. If any or all of these conditions fail, there is the possibility of market failure.

It is the fourth and fifth conditions for the absence of insurance market failure which are undermined by the existence of AI.[3] How carefully we drive, whether we lock all doors and windows upon leaving home, how hard we strive to keep a job, are all examples of actions which are difficult for insurance companies to monitor. Worse, insuring against car accidents, burglary or unemployment will lead to changes in behaviour (compared to a world without insurance), leading to a rise in the probabilities of claims occurring. Adverse selection, meanwhile, enters the frame when individuals know they have characteristics, which are unobservable by the insurer, but which affect their chances of being unemployed, or ill, for instance. If insurance premiums are based on risks for the 'average' member of the population, there will be a tendency for high risks to buy more cover than low risks, again leading to a rise in the chances of a claim compared to a world without insurance.

### Moral hazard

To see these problems in more detail, we modify the basic model of insurance demand outlined above, initially to focus on the issue of moral hazard. Recall that in moral hazard actions are hidden. Here, the care taken by the individual taking out insurance might be such a hidden variable. Suppose that the risk, $p$, is unemployment, but by increasing effort, $e$, the individual can reduce the chance of being made redundant, making $p$ a declining function of effort, $e$. Effort is costly for the individual, so that expected utility is now:

$$EU = (1 - p(e))U(Y_1) + p(e)U(Y_2) - c(e) \qquad\qquad (6.6)$$

---

[3] We will return to the first three conditions in Chapter 14, on social insurance.

where $c(e)$ is the cost of effort, increasing in $e$. Differentiating expected utility with respect to $e$ shows us the net gain to the consumer from putting in higher effort (' indicates a derivative):

$$\frac{dEU}{de} = -p'(e)[U(Y_1) - U(Y_2)] - c'(e) \tag{6.7}$$

Recall that, in the case of full insurance, the consumer has the same income in both states of the world and hence the same level of utility. This means that the terms in the square brackets are equal and therefore cancel. Removing this term, we are left with the expression $-c'$, which is obviously negative. It follows that if the consumer is fully insured, there is no gain in taking even the smallest amount of care; they are indifferent about the state of the world and so have no reason to care about the probability of unemployment or theft, etc. Compared to a world of no insurance, $e$ will be lower, meaning that the probability of unemployment (for instance) will be higher.

What implications does this have for insurance? If the moral hazard (the reduction in effort associated with insurance) is not anticipated by insurance companies, then claims will be more common than they expected and the competitive industry will face losses. Firms may then try to raise premiums, withdraw insurance cover or take measures which attempt to reduce the problem.

The key to any reduction in moral hazard is the effort level, $e$, so any solutions must involve incentives for the consumer to raise effort. One option is monitoring, either *ex ante*, which is often difficult, or *ex post*; for instance, by refusing to pay out on claims where individuals are sacked for negligence, or where workplace accidents occur and there is clear evidence of recklessness. Monitoring is often expensive or even infeasible, so a second kind of option accepts that $e$ cannot be observed directly, but instead offers the consumer incentives to keep the probability of a claim down. Equation (6.7) also tells us something about how this might be done. If the consumer is better off in the good state of the world, compared to the bad state, then the term in the square brackets is positive. The consumer will then have an incentive to avoid the bad state of the world and so will take more care, compared to the full insurance case. For instance, health policies may have an *excess* (or deductible), forcing the consumer to pay for the first £100, say, of any treatment, and this lowers $Y_2$ relative to $Y_1$.

## Adverse selection

In the 1911 debate on the introduction of National Insurance, Winston Churchill argued that 'voluntary schemes of unemployment insurance . . . have always failed because those men likely to be unemployed resorted to them, and, consequently, there was a preponderance of bad risks . . . which must be fatal to the success of the scheme'.[4] The problem he was referring to is adverse selection. Some of us are born into families with a history of heart disease; a lower educational level puts an individual at greater risk of divorce and unemployment; a past episode of poverty raises the chance of future want. Those most likely to suffer a loss are most likely to seek insurance and this fact that the chances of suffering from ill-health, marital breakdown or unemployment vary across the population leads to the problem known as adverse selection.

To show what happens in this case, we go back to the basic model of insurance, but now have two types of individuals: low risk and high risk. The accident probabilities are $p^L$, $p^H$ respectively (with the second one higher, of course); $p$ (with no

---

[4] Hansard, 1911, vol. 26, col 495, quoted in Atkinson (1995), p. 207.

superscript) is the population mean. We simplify the buying and selling of insurance. Firms offer contracts, with premiums of $\pi$ producing payouts of $C$ in the event of a loss. The initial wealth for individuals is $Y$, with final wealth of $Y_1$ in state of the world 1 (no loss) and $Y_2$ in state of the world 2. So, $Y_1 = Y - \pi$ and $Y_2 = Y - \pi + C - L$. Expected utility is $(1 - \pi^L)U(Y_1) + \pi^L U(Y_2)$ for low, similarly for high. Thus, the MRS for low is:

$$\text{MRS}^L = \frac{(1 - p^L)\ U'(Y_1)}{p^L\ U'(Y_2)} \tag{6.8}$$

This means that the low-risk agent has steeper indifference curves at any given value of $(Y_1, Y_2)$ and this is illustrated in Figure 6.3. In this diagram, the lines NE and NF represent the budget constraints for high and low risks, respectively, if faced with insurance terms which are actuarially fair for their own type. The line NG represents the average of NE and NF. Since the line NF represents actuarially fair insurance for the low risks, it must be the case that $\pi - p^L C = 0$ along it. But a firm's expected payoff from selling to a low consumer is $\pi - p^L C$, so along NF competitive firms make zero expected profits selling to low consumers. For points below NF, the consumer is worse off, so the firm must be better off. Hence, below NF the firm is making positive expected profits on its low-risk contracts. Similarly, if a contract is sold to a high-risk consumer at a point below NE, the firm makes positive expected profits and if a contract sold to all customers is at a point below NG to all consumers, then again the firm makes positive expected profits.

Now, if insurance companies could identify low and high risks, then they could offer different contracts to the two groups. The result, with actuarially fair insurance, would place the low risks at F in the diagram and the high risks at E. The apparent problem with adverse selection is that insurance companies may not know to which group an individual belongs. As the diagram shows, if the high risks could purchase the contract aimed at the low risks, they would, because they prefer F to E. So, in a

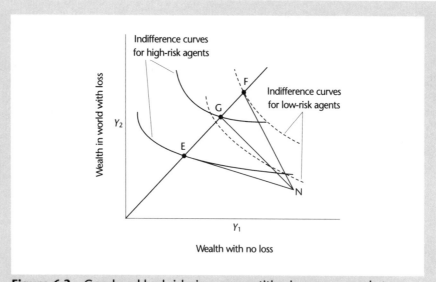

**Figure 6.3** Good and bad risks in a competitive insurance market

**Incentive compatible**

Behaviour which is optimal, given the incentives faced by the individual concerned

world where the types are not readily identifiable, the pair of contracts is not **incentive compatible**; in other words, the assumptions built into the contracts are not compatible with the actual behaviour which results. Only incentive-compatible outcomes represent potential equilibria. Two types of equilibrium are potentially incentive compatible: one where all individuals buy the same contract and one where different types buy different contracts, but each prefers their own contract to the alternative. The first class of equilibrium is called *pooling*, the second, *separating*. The problem with adverse selection is that neither form of equilibrium might exist, meaning that no competitive equilibrium exists at all.

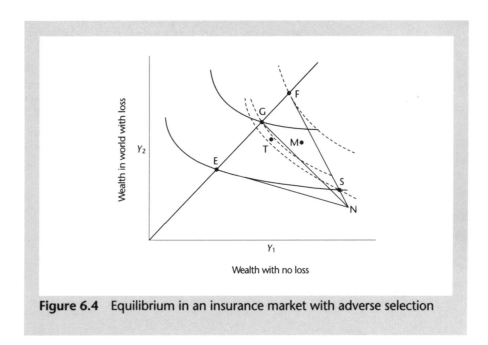

**Figure 6.4** Equilibrium in an insurance market with adverse selection

### Pooling

**Pooling equilibrium**

An outcome where agents in all risk categories choose the same option

Suppose we are at a competitive equilibrium which was a **pooling equilibrium**. All consumers buy the same contract and firms make zero expected profits, so the contract must lie on NG, at G say in Figure 6.4 (the exact point does not matter). Suppose that a firm enters the market and offers a new contract which would place consumers at M. If we look at the indifference curves for the two types which go through point G, we can see from Figure 6.4 that low-risk consumers prefer the new contract and so will buy it; high-risk consumers prefer the old contract, so will shun the new offer. Since the contract lies below the zero profit line for low-risk contracts and since only low-risk consumers purchase it, then the new firm makes positive profits from it. But this means that G could not have been an equilibrium after all, so that no pooling equilibrium can exist.

### Separating

We have just seen that a pooling equilibrium is vulnerable to the entry of a firm supplying a contract which attracts only safer prospects. This process is called

**Cream-skimming**

The tendency for insurers to offer terms only to low-risk customers

**Cream-skimming**. Unfortunately, a separating equilibrium may be vulnerable to the introduction of a contract which attracts both types of risk. In Figure 6.4, the separating equilibrium is defined by the pair of contracts represented by E and S. High risks prefer E to S and so choose the former; low risks prefer S to E and opt for it. The outcome is therefore incentive compatible, but a price is paid by the low risks for this separation. In order for the low-risk contract not to attract the high risks, it cannot be too desirable, meaning that the first best outcome is not attainable by the low risks. The result may still not be a competitive equilibrium. Consider the contract represented by the point T. High risks prefer T to E, low risks also prefer it to their outcome at S, so both types will opt for it, if it is introduced by a new firm. T is below the pooling equilibrium zero profit line, so it will yield expected profits for the newcomer. We are forced to conclude that S and E do not represent an equilibrium after all. But, of course, T itself cannot be an equilibrium, since we have already demonstrated that no pooling equilibrium exists.

What does all this mean? First, note that it is not automatic that the separating equilibrium fails to exist. In the diagram, the line NG has been carefully drawn so that it cuts the low-risk indifference curve passing through S. If this was not the case, then we could not find a pooling contract to undermine the separating outcome and the pair E, S would represent a competitive equilibrium. Since it is an average of the high-risk and low-risk budget lines, the position of NG is determined by the relative number of high and low risks. If there are many low risks, it lies close to the low-risk zero profit line. Conversely, if high risks dominate the market, it lies close to the high-risk budget line. Competitive equilibrium may therefore exist if the proportion of high risks is large enough.

However, the practical consequences of adverse selection have more to do with cream-skimming than the non-existence of competitive equilibrium. It seems that when private firms are asked to provide insurance in markets where adverse selection is a problem, high-risk groups tend not to get served. As one head of marketing for an American health insurer put it, 'let's face it competition in health care is all about making sure you don't have ill people on your books'.[5] The point is that insurance companies are not ignorant and powerless in the face of adverse selection. There are demographic variables, such as age and gender, or experience variables, such as past claims or education level, which provide pointers to the probability of a future claim. As a result, over time an insurance company can determine pretty well which risk class a claimant falls into. High risks then face high premiums or are refused insurance completely, while insurers compete for the profitable low risks. Fundamentally, therefore, adverse selection creates an equity problem, not an efficiency problem. Arguments for intervening in the face of adverse selection are based primarily upon the desirability of transferring wealth from low risks to high risks, rather than on propping up an inefficient market.

## 6.4 Principal and agent

**Agency**

When one person (the agent) acts on behalf of another (the principal)

An **agency** relationship exists whenever one person or organisation (the agent) acts on behalf of another (the principal). A doctor is a patient's agent, the chief executive is the shareholder's agent and the politician is the electorate's agent. There is a problem, in the sense of potential market failure, when the relationship is marked by three features: principal and agent have conflicting goals; the actions of the agent

---

[5] Quoted in Glennerster (1995), p. 23.

cannot be inferred directly from observable outcomes, such as profit or output, and costless monitoring of the agent is also not feasible. For example, when a firm's sales are low, it may be due to the inertia of its sales team or to an unfortunate drop in demand. The sales team presumably know, but their managers and the shareholders might not and it is this asymmetry of information between principal and agent which is at the heart of the problem.[6]

## An example

In this example, shareholders wish to hire a chief executive to run their company. Shareholders wish to maximise expected net profits, with net profits equal to the difference between gross profits (shown in Table 6.1) and the wages paid to the executive, but the shareholders can only observe gross profits, not their underlying causes. The 'state of world' – low, medium or high – represents all those factors which influence sales and costs, but which are essentially random, beyond the control of the managers. For the firm, this might include the state of overseas markets, the weather, or efforts of rivals. The 'effort' variable might also represent a variety of factors: not just how hard the executive works, but, in the case of civil servants, for instance, how easy they find it to serve the electorate rather than their own interests. As shown in Table 6.1, the level of gross profits depends on both the efforts of the executive and the state of the world, so if the shareholders observe a gross profit of £100, they cannot tell whether the state of the world is Low or the manager has been idle (effort = 0) and the state of the world is 'Medium'.

We will suppose that utility for the chief executive is given by $U = y^{1/2} - 4e$ where $y$ is his or her income and $e$ is effort, but not any wage will secure their services; expected utility must lie above 10, which represents the fallback level that the executive could achieve in another job.

If the manager is offered a flat salary, then he or she would be foolish to set any effort other than 0. Thus the best flat salary offered will be 100, since this yields a utility of 10, just enough to capture the manager's services. Expected gross profits are then £175 (= 1/4 × £100 + 1/2 × £100 + 1/4 × £400), giving expected net profits of just £75.

The shareholders can do better if they offer a bonus for high profits. This may tempt the manager to work harder, but notice that this effort comes at a cost: the manager is risk averse and so must be offered a higher average salary in order to compensate for the greater risk. If the average salary is too high, then it will not be in the interest of the shareholders to offer the bonus arrangement. Call the basic salary $S$ and let the bonus be $B$, then any agreement must tempt the manager to join the firm. Hence:

**Table 6.1** Gross profits in a principal–agent example

| State of the world | Low | Medium | High |
|---|---|---|---|
| Probability | 1/4 | 1/2 | 1/4 |
| Idling, effort = 0 | £100 | £100 | £400 |
| Working hard, effort = 1 | £100 | £400 | £400 |

[6] Agency problems may be depicted as problems either of moral hazard or of adverse selection. In this section, we take the former approach.

$$\frac{1}{4} S^{1/2} + \frac{3}{4} (S + B)^{1/2} - 4 \geq 10 \qquad (6.9)$$

**Participation constraint**

Means that the principal must offer a contract that leaves the agent as well-off as they could achieve elsewhere

In the formal language of the principal–agent literature, this is called the **participation constraint**. The contract must also be designed so that the shareholders get the effort level they intend. In this case, that means the executive must prefer to choose $e = 1$, rather than $e = 0$. That is:

$$U(\text{working hard}) \geq U(\text{being idle})$$

or,

$$\frac{1}{4} S^{1/2} + \frac{3}{4} (S + B)^{1/2} - 4 \geq \frac{3}{4} S^{1/2} + \frac{1}{4} (S + B)^{1/2} \qquad (6.10)$$

This second equation is the *incentive compatibility* constraint, so called because rationality requires that behaviour is compatible with the incentives on offer. Solving these two equations[7] gives $S = £64$ and $B = £192$, which means expected net profits of £117 for the shareholders. These are higher than those achievable from a flat salary, so offering the agent incentives to work harder pays off for the principal and does not reduce the well-being of the agent. A Pareto improvement is therefore possible from having the bonus system.

There are a number of important lessons to be learnt from this example. First, in order to reduce the AI problem, it is usually necessary to offer incentives, in the sense of tying rewards to observables such as profits, which are correlated with the underlying but unobservable variables, such as effort. Second, both parties can gain from this incentive scheme, compared to a system without incentives. Third, because in many important agency relationships, such as in healthcare, important parts of the service may not be measurable, tying rewards to observable variables may distort other aspects of the service. Thus formal incentive schemes, like the one shown here, may only be desirable in a limited range of circumstances. For instance, if a health visitor is rewarded for the number of visits to patients she or he makes in a day, this may reduce the quality of the unobservable care given to each patient.

## Market cures

In some cases, markets may provide their own remedies for AI, so that a formal incentive scheme may be unnecessary. Fama (1980) points out that over a number of years, good and bad luck will tend to even out, so that average output or gross profit will be an increasingly accurate guide to the efforts of the agent. Knowing this, the agent will choose to work hard even without a formal incentive system, because she or he realises that future earnings will depend on current performance. Similarly, in consumer markets, the tendency for firms to sell 'lemons', low-quality goods, will be undermined if consumers purchase on a regular basis (see Klein and Leffler 1981). Also, Nelson (1970) argues that advertising intensity will be a good guide to quality in such markets, because customers will only return to the same suppliers if they are satisfied and only if sales are repeated will the heavy costs of advertising be justified.

---

[7] One way of doing this starts by noting that the shareholders will want to keep $S$ and $B$ as low as possible, so both equations will be satisfied as equalities. Then collect all the terms in $S$ and $S + B$ onto the left-hand side of the equations, multiply both sides of the participation constraint by 2 and add the two equations. This eliminates terms in $S^{1/2}$ and means we can find $S + B$. It is then a simple matter to go back to the participation constraint and solve for $S$.

Firms can also offer warranties, which provide two forms of protection to the customer: *ex post* they reduce the costs to the consumer of product failure, but *ex ante* they provide a signal of the firms which are most likely to supply reliable products. In short, there are a number of methods by which the problems of AI can be ameliorated. Generally, these involve the possibility of *ex post* verification of product quality, coupled with either the possibility of redress (as in the case of a guarantee for faulty goods) or a product or agreement where there is the possibility of repetition (as in the purchase of toothpaste or the weekly record of a sales person). This means though that with non-standard goods, such as healthcare or political leaders, the possibilities for reducing the problems created by AI are much less apparent.

## 6.5  Agency and government

In the introduction, we remarked on the fundamental differences between the causes of market failure discussed in earlier chapters and AI. In this section, we examine some of the consequences of this difference. Chapter 9 takes the issue further.

### Asymmetric information and the benevolent government

A useful starting point is the welfare-maximising government. We saw in Chapter 4 that in order to implement the efficient level of a public good, a government must know the valuation placed upon that good by its citizens. That information is private, so there is an agency problem, which in some cases, such as quasi-linear preferences, can be overcome (by the Clarke tax, for instance). More generally, though, AI represents a complication that adds to the costs of government intervention, whether the market failures are public goods, externalities or increasing returns, where firms' costs are often private knowledge.

The problem of AI is also at the heart of the equality–efficiency trade-off. If a government could observe all actions and abilities directly, such as how rich an individual is and how hard they work, then, in principle, it could remove the incentive effects of benefits and taxation. In practice, costless monitoring is not feasible. To see what happens when AI intervenes, let us return to the principal–agent example given in the previous section and examine the effects of social insurance. Now, however, we shall view the agent as working for themselves, so that the figures in the table (repeated below) represent gross income. Under these circumstances, the expected utility (shown in the final column) from working hard ($e = 1$) is greater than that from idleness ($e = 0$), so the agent will set $e = 1$. Income is risky, so if a social insurance system is instituted, with the government as a benevolent principal, then in theory the agent will gain. Suppose that there are a large number of agents who are *ex ante*, identical and who face independent risks. The social insurance scheme consists of a tax on income of 50 if income is 400 and a benefit paid out when income is 100 and set so that the scheme breaks even. If the benefit is set on the basis that $e = 1$ then it amounts to 150, giving a net income of 250.

Table 6.2 shows that the typical individual has a higher expected utility under this scheme, but note that the incentives have now changed; the individual will prefer low effort, as the social insurance scheme has induced a moral hazard.

However, now, if effort is low, then gross income will be 100 with a frequency of 3/4 rather than 1/4. So, instead of breaking even, the social insurance scheme will

**Table 6.2**  Moral hazard in social insurance

|  | Low | Medium | High | Expected utility |
|---|---|---|---|---|
| Probability | 1/4 | 1/2 | 1/4 | |
| No insurance | | | | |
| Effort = 0 | 100 | 100 | 400 | 12.5 |
| Effort = 1 | 100 | 400 | 400 | 13.5 |
| Social insurance | | | | |
| Effort = 0 | 250 | 250 | 350 | 16.5 |
| Effort = 1 | 250 | 350 | 350 | 14.0 |

have an expected deficit of 100. Reducing inequality in the presence of AI therefore reduces effort. This trade-off is encountered throughout public sector economics in general and is explored further in Chapter 16 in particular.

### Asymmetric information within government

Unfortunately, the problems created for the public sector by AI do not stop there. When an economy enters a recession, it may be due to the failings of politicians or it may be the result of an unfortunate external shock. When a regulated water company proposes higher prices, it may be because weak management has no control over costs, or it may be the unavoidable results of changing weather patterns. So there are agency relationships within the state, and the government itself can be seen as the agent of the electorate (see Chapter 9, Table 9.1 for a list of such relationships).

Whether these agency relationships are the source of inefficiency depends, as with other such relationships, on whether agent and principal share the same goals. If the politician's only desire is to maximise welfare and if the civil servant's aim is only to serve, then there is no problem. In Chapter 1 we stated our view that individuals are not always self-serving, but to the extent that they are, then AI is a source not only of market failure, but also of government failure.

## 6.6  Conclusion

As we have shown in this chapter, an understanding of AI is a necessary element of the core of public sector economics. The issues raised here are taken further in the rest of the book. In Chapters 8 and 9 we look at models of government behaviour where individuals are assumed to be primarily self-interested and agency problems are to the fore. In Chapter 16 on social insurance on the other hand, it is private citizens who are the agents and the redistributing government is the principal. Because AI problems do not vanish when an activity is taken over by the state, we might ask, how then are the boundaries of the state to be set? In Chapters 21 and 22 on privatisation and regulation we look at this issue in detail. Finally, one area where the benefits of intervention perhaps outweigh the costs is in healthcare, where AI provides the major economic justification for some state control.

## Summary

- Asymmetric information occurs when one individual knows something that others do not. When actions are hidden then we have a situation of moral hazard; when knowledge is hidden we have adverse selection.

- Moral hazard implies that if full insurance is offered to risk-averse agents, then they will lower the effort they devote to reducing the chances of 'bad' states of the world such as sickness, unemployment or low profits.

- Adverse selection may imply that no competitive equilibrium exists. In the context of the public sector economics, however, a more likely implication is a distributional one, involving the cream-skimming of low risks by the private sector.

- The formal and informal incentives offered in the marketplace can reduce or even eliminate the costs of AI for some commodities.

- AI is not always diminished by state intervention; government has its own agency problems.

- Moreover, one of the most significant of agency problems may be between the electorate and its representatives.

## Questions

1. What is the difference between moral hazard and adverse selection? Give an example of each.

2. In the state space diagram, what happens to the budget line when the price of insurance rises? What happens to the demand for insurance?

3. Is there no efficiency–equity trade-off when there is no AI problem?

4. 'Formal reward schemes undermine the goodwill and teamwork necessary for the delivery of quality public services.' In what contexts is this most likely to be true?

5. List some examples of how AI in general and agency issues in particular will affect policies designed to reduce externality problems.

6. For the example shown in Table 6.2, how high can the tax be before the agent switches to low effort?

7. Why should a government economist need to understand the problem of asymmetric information?

## Further reading

Most intermediate microeconomic textbooks now have a chapter on AI. Other useful sources are the survey articles by Rees (1987, 1989) listed below. Almost any issue of the *Journal of Public Economics* or the *Journal of Health Economics,* for instance, confirms the importance of the topic, which is nowhere used as intensively as in the theory of regulation (see the references for that chapter).

# References

Akerlof, G. (1970) 'The market for "Lemons" ', *Quarterly Journal of Economics* 84, 488–500.

Atkinson, A.B. (1995) *Incomes and the Welfare State*, Cambridge: Cambridge University Press.

Fama, E. (1980) 'Agency problems and the theory of the firm', *Journal of Political Economy* 88, 288–307.

Glennerster, H. (1995) *Paying for Welfare*, Hemel Hempstead: Harvester Wheatsheaf.

Katz, M.L. and Rosen, H.S. (1988) *Microeconomics*, 3rd edn, London: McGraw-Hill.

Klein, B. and Leffler, K. (1981) 'The role of market forces in assuring contractual performance', *Journal of Political Economy* 89, 615–41.

Nelson, P. (1970) 'Information and consumer behaviour', *Journal of Political Economy* 78, 311–29.

Newbery, D. (1988) 'Missing markets', in F. Hahn (ed.) *The Economics of Missing Markets, Information and Games*, Ch. 10, Oxford: Oxford University Press.

Rees, R. (1987) 'The theory of principal and agent, Parts I and II', in J. Hey and P. Lambert (eds) *Surveys in the Economics of Uncertainty*, Oxford: Blackwell.

Rees, R. (1989) 'Uncertainty, information and insurance', in J. Hey (ed.) *Current Issues in Microeconomics*, Ch. 3, Oxford: Macmillan.

# CHAPTER 7

# Cost–Benefit Analysis

## Key concepts

| | | |
|---|---|---|
| potential Pareto improvement | Kaldor–Scitovsky paradox | opportunity costs |
| shadow prices | transfers | time preference |
| non-marketed goods | travel cost method | hedonic pricing |
| contingent valuation | CEA | |

## 7.1  Introduction

Cost–benefit analysis (CBA) is probably the tool used most widely by applied economists. As is obvious by the title, the costs of a project are deducted from the benefits and if the result is positive, then the project should proceed. In general, the distribution of costs and benefits amongst individuals will be uneven, so that some individuals may lose, even if the sum of the benefits outweighs the costs. To say that a project should proceed because the benefits exceed the costs therefore means adopting what is known as the potential Pareto improvement (PPI) as the welfare criterion.

Users of CBA include the European Investment Bank, when deciding whether or not to offer loans and grants for regional development, the Department of Transport in the UK (roads), Overseas Development Agency (overseas aid), the Environmental Protection Agency in the USA and the World Bank (aid for development). The concept of CBA is easy to grasp, but the practice is a far more subtle affair. In this chapter, we consider some of the main issues involved in CBA, both in the theory underlying it and in the practicalities of estimating benefits and costs.

## 7.2  Potential Pareto improvements

If a social welfare function is available to judge changes in society, then a project should go ahead if and only if social welfare rises or

$$\Sigma \Delta W_i \geq 0 \qquad (7.1)$$

(where the $\Delta W_i$ are the changes in welfare for individuals, $i$). However, the rule generally used in CBA is that projects should proceed provided that

$$\Sigma \Delta y_i \geq 0 \qquad \qquad \textbf{(7.2)}$$

Here the $\Delta y_i$ are income-based measures of changes in individual welfare, as measured by compensating variation or surplus. Now, in principle, as long as this sum is positive, the winners from the project could employ lump-sum transfers to compensate the losers and everyone would still gain. Hence the criterion is called a **potential Pareto improvement** (PPI) or sometimes, the Kaldor criterion, after its originator. There are two problems with the PPI. The first and fundamental problem is that the projects approved using the rule summarised in equation (7.2) may not accord with the projects yielding positive values for equation (7.1). In particular, with a concave social welfare function, the PPI rule will be biased against projects which benefit those on lower incomes, meaning that it will tend to reject projects which pass the test in equation (7.1), whilst accepting some projects which fail equation (7.1). To see this, recall that the change in welfare for individual $i$ is equal to the change in income multiplied by the social marginal utility of income (SMUI) for that person, so that equation (7.1) becomes

$$\Sigma SMUI_i \Delta y_i \geq 0 \qquad \qquad \textbf{(7.3)}$$

Consider the project summarised in Table 7.1, for a society consisting of two individuals, where the SMUI for someone on a low income is twice that for someone who is richer. The PPI rule used in CBA produces a figure for the net gain of 50, suggesting that the project should proceed, whereas, with the project, social welfare falls by 50. In theory it is possible to use welfare weights to adjust the CBA, an idea discussed in the next section. However, in practice, adjustment is rarely executed.

The second problem with PPI is illustrated in Figure 7.1, which shows two utility possibility frontiers, one for a world in which a new bridge is built and one without. Position A is the position of the two individuals in the absence of the bridge, C represents the outcome with the bridge. We can see that C is not a Pareto improvement over A, but if the bridge was built we could transfer income from individual 1 to person 2, reaching position B, for example, which is Pareto-preferred to A. Thus, building the bridge is a PPI. However, by transferring income from individual 1 to person 2 in the world with no bridge, we can reach D, for example, which is Pareto-

---

**Potential Pareto improvement**

Occurs when, in principle, the winners from a project could compensate the losers, so that all gain

---

**Table 7.1** Cost–benefit analysis and social welfare

|  | $\Delta y$ | SMUI | $\Delta W$ |
|---|---|---|---|
| Low income | −100 | 2 | −200 |
| High Income | +150 | 1 | +150 |
| Total | +50 |  | −50 |
| Decision | Proceed |  | Stop |

preferred to C. Thus, not building the bridge is a PPI over the world with the bridge. This result is known as the **Kaldor–Scitovsky paradox**. It means that the PPI can produce contradictory results.

Of course, if the utility possibility frontiers did not cross we would not have the paradox, but unfortunately it is relatively easy to give examples which produce crossing utility possibility frontiers. Suppose that only individual 1 would make direct use of the bridge, to buy fresh flowers from agent 2. However, fresh flowers are a luxury good and at low levels of income (and therefore utility), individual 1 will not buy. Both are better off with the bridge, when agent 1 is relatively rich, because individual 2 sells their flowers and 1 buys them. If the bridge is not built, no flowers are bought, but the cost of the bridge does not have to be borne, so both agents are better off for low levels of $U^1$. In Figure 7.1, the move from A to C would therefore be a PPI, but then so would C to A. In fact, only if Engel curves (income expansion paths for demand) are linear and parallel[1] for all agents can the Kaldor–Scitovsky paradox be ruled out. However, for small projects the impact on prices is likely to be modest, in which case the chances of a paradox are limited.

In summary, the main weakness of the PPI criterion is its unfairness; compensation is not actually paid and so the distribution of benefits from projects does not accord with the social welfare function. However, not paying compensation does have its advantages, the main being simplicity. Because of transaction costs and preference revelation problems, trying to ensure that the distribution of benefits maximised social welfare would undoubtedly lead to a significant rise in the cost of many proposals.

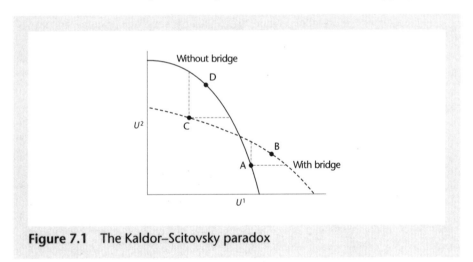

**Figure 7.1** The Kaldor–Scitovsky paradox

## 7.3 Opportunity costs and CBA fundamentals

### The market and CBA

The first crucial lesson of CBA is that, in the absence of market failure, the market does its own cost–benefit analysis. How? Consider the proposal to increase marginally the production of a commodity. CBA says that the project should proceed if the benefits of the increase exceed the costs, i.e. if the social marginal benefits are

[1] So that transfers of income between individuals lead to no changes in aggregate demand and hence no changes in relative prices.

greater than social marginal costs. In the absence of externalities, social marginal cost (SMC) equals private marginal cost. Meanwhile the social marginal benefit (SMB) is just the price, which equals the private marginal benefit if there is no monopsony. In short, if there is no market failure:

$$SMB - SMC > 0 \Leftrightarrow P > MC$$

This means that a project should proceed if and only if it is profitable, but this is exactly the same circumstance when a project would proceed if it was left to the profit-maximising firms of the private sector. For small projects, a separate CBA-based decision rule only makes sense in the context of market failure.

## Taxes and transfers

CBA is about assessing the real benefits of a project and the real resources required. Transfers of money between people arising as a result of the project count as equal and opposites and so cancel out. Figure 7.2 illustrates the point for a competitive market, where a new bridge will allow access by producers from across the river, lowering the supply curve from S to S' and hence the equilibrium from E to F. Consumer surplus rises from AEB to ACF and total producer surplus changes from EDB to CFD (see Box 5.1 for a reminder of this concept), so that the net rise in surplus is EFD and if it is larger than the cost of the bridge, the project should proceed. However, the change in total surplus hides the fact that the existing suppliers lose from the lower prices. Previously their surplus was EDB, but with the bridge in place it becomes CGD, a loss of BEGC. Their loss is the consumers' gain, a transfer which cancels out in the CBA.

One of the most common source of transfers arises from taxation. Any money flowing into government coffers represents a loss for some taxpayers. But it also represents a gain to other citizens, either through higher benefits, reduced debt or some other means. The losses and the gains cancel out, leaving only the effects of the taxes on real variables to be considered in the CBA.

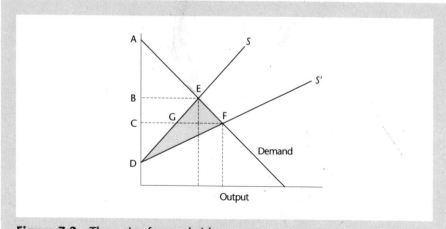

**Figure 7.2** The gains from a bridge

## Shadow prices and unemployment

Market failure means that market prices do not reflect marginal values. For instance, if the price of a unit of electricity is 5 pence, but the production of the electricity produces a rise in acid rain that we value at 1p, then the marginal benefit of electricity is not its market price, but 4 pence ($= 5 - 1$), which we call its **shadow price**. Suppose that Jane will be offered a job at £200 per week under a proposed project. Presently she is unemployed, and does work around the house that is valued at £40 per week. If she becomes employed, then the value of the output lost (i.e. the true costs) of taking her on is £40. This figure is the shadow price of employment, not the wage she will be paid. That £200 is just a transfer from the employer to Jane and so disappears from the analysis. Only if there is no involuntary unemployment will the shadow wage equal the market wage.

As well as in the examples of externalities and unemployment, shadow prices are also widely employed in the assessment of projects in developing nations, where often the foreign exchange regime means that imported and exported goods do not trade at their world prices. Shadow prices are fundamental to CBA, but estimating them is often difficult.

**Shadow price**

The true or opportunity cost of a resource

## Income distribution

As we have already noted, the PPI criterion does not take into account the distributional effects of the project. Ideally, projects should be evaluated on the basis of the change in social welfare, in other words, using equation (7.1) rather than equation (7.2). When distributional weights are introduced, transfers can no longer be ignored. Instead, if £1 is viewed as worth more to someone poor than it is to someone rich, then this should be reflected in the weights attached to costs and benefits and transfers. Not weighting is equivalent to the assumption that the current distribution of income is optimal and the project has only a negligible impact on incomes.

## Discounting

The benefits of a new road will be felt over many years. Somehow we have to sum the future benefits (and costs if there are any). Usually this is done through discounting. For instance, if the costs are incurred only in year 0 of a project and the benefits flow subsequently we have:

Net present value = NPV = $-C0 + B0 + B1/(1 + r) + B2/(1 + r)^2 + \ldots$

where $C0$ is the cost in year 0 and $Bi, i = 1, \ldots$, is the benefit in year $i$, with $r$ as the discount rate. A higher value of $r$ will favour projects where the payoffs are immediate (or the costs are loaded towards the end), while lower values will mean projects where the benefits are distant are more likely to be approved. Currently the UK government uses a real rate of return of 8% as the discount factor for most projects. The value of $r$ used will therefore influence which projects are adopted.

There are two main arguments for discounting and therefore two main schools of thought on the appropriate discount rate. First, whether because of impatience or

**Rate of time preference**

How much extra income a consumer requires in one year's time in order to give up £1 today

**Rate of capital productivity**

The value of the extra goods which can be produced in one year's time if £1 is invested in their production today

uncertainty, most people prefer to have £1 now rather than in the future. This is the **time preference** argument. Second, because capital is productive, £1 now can produce more than £1 in a year's time. For instance, a farmer who sows a bag of seed may reap a whole field of wheat in the following harvest. This is the **capital productivity** argument. In a Robinson Crusoe economy without market failure, the two figures will be the same in equilibrium, an argument illustrated by Table 7.2. Suppose $r > \rho$, where $r$ is the time preference discount rate and $\rho$ is the rate of increase of capital productivity, and Crusoe cuts future consumption by £1. Since future consumption is cut, current saving can be reduced by $1/(1 + \rho)$, since investing $1/(1 + \rho)$ now would produce £1 in one year's time. Crusoe therefore gets a rise in current consumption of $1/(1 + \rho)$ and a reduction of 1 in the future, valued at $1/(1 + r)$, giving a net rise in well-being.

Similarly, if $\rho > r$, Crusoe can reap the rewards of delaying consumption and investing in the future. While this leads to $\rho = r$ in equilibrium, with market failure or taxes the two rates will usually diverge. The correct rate to use then depends on the project and its financing. For instance, suppose a project diverts resources away from an investment that could have produced a rate of return of $\rho$ in one year. Then $\rho$ is the discount rate to be used. Alternatively, suppose the project reduces current consumption, then $r$ should be the discount rate used.

Some critics argue that no discount rate should be used, since using any positive rate raises the attractions of using a natural resource (or any other resource) now rather than in the future. Positive discount rates are therefore seen as inimical to environmental conservation. This criticism applies to the time preference argument, but not to the capital productivity motive for discounting. Further, the time preference rate used is only too high if present generations undervalue the consumption of future generations. If altruism links generations, then it is possible (though not certain) that the welfare of future generations is reflected in choices made by individuals in the present.[2]

To summarise, underlying both the shadow price and the discounting arguments is a concept fundamental to economics: opportunity cost. In CBA it is opportunity costs (and benefits) which should be employed in the appraisal, not market values if these are different.

**Table 7.2** Discounting in the Robinson Crusoe economy

| | Change in current consumption | Change in future consumption | Value of net change | |
|---|---|---|---|---|
| $r > \rho$ | $1/(1 + \rho)$ | $-1$ | $\dfrac{1}{1 + \rho} - \dfrac{1}{1 + r} = \dfrac{(r - \rho)}{(1 + r)(1 + \rho)}$ | $> 0$ |
| $\rho > r$ | $-1$ | $(1 + \rho)$ | $-1 + \dfrac{1 + \rho}{1 + r} = \dfrac{(\rho - r)}{(1 + r)}$ | $> 0$ |

## An example: *The Wensum Dam*

These principles are illustrated in the example of a new dam which will displace agricultural land but provide valuable electricity:

---

[2] This issue is taken up in more detail in Chapter 23 on the environment.

## The Wensum Dam

Benefits:     Increased hydroelectric production, valued at £1.5m/year in perpetuity

Costs:

| | |
|---|---|
| The land costs | £3m |
| Lost production on the land | £0.05m per year in perpetuity. |
| Materials | £10m |
| Labour, 100,000 days @£50 per day | £5m |

Income tax is at 20p in the £ and the project will be financed using bonds, which will crowd out investment yielding 10% return.

A financial appraisal by a private firm undertaking the project would be:

$$15m - 10m - 3m - 5m = \qquad\qquad £3.0m \text{ loss}$$

where the 15m = 1.5/0.1 – the stream of £1.5m per year discounted at 10%. A cost–benefit analysis would be:

$$15m - 10m - 0.5m - 5m + 1m = \qquad\qquad £0.5m \text{ surplus}$$

The differences between CBA and financial appraisal arise because:

(a) the cost of land is a transfer – what matters is the value of lost production;
(b) income tax which transfers £1m of the cost of labour back to the government.

As a result, the PPI decision rule would be to proceed with the dam, whereas a private firm would decide against the project.

## 7.4 Risk

Most projects involve an element of risk. Roads are built on the basis of forecasts of traffic which may under- or overestimate true growth. Power stations must be constructed before the price of electricity is known with certainty. A crucial question is therefore, How should the CBA be adjusted to deal with risk? There are two main positions. First, that the rate of return used in public and private sector appraisal should be the same, on the grounds that a lower rate for the public sector would lead to a switch away from private sector projects with a higher average rate of return. The second is that the government should use a lower discount rate on the grounds that it is so much larger than any private corporation and so can cope with uncertainty much more easily; it can 'self-insure' across a large number of independent projects.

**Arrow–Lind Theorem**

Implies that the risk-free discount rate should be used for projects where the risks are spread widely across society

The fundamental insight here is called the **Arrow–Lind Theorem**, after its proponents. The idea is illustrated in Figure 7.3, which draws on Figure 6.1 and shows a utility function for an individual at different levels of wealth. Suppose they currently have income $Y$ and they are offered a risky project, which will give them an extra £100 if it succeeds, but which will entail a loss of £100 if it fails. The chance of success is greater than 50%, so if they take on the project their expected income, $EY_1$, is higher than current income. However, in the figure, the individual is sufficiently risk averse that the expected utility from the project, $EU_1$, is less than $U(Y)$, so they prefer not to take on the project. Now suppose this individual were to share the project with another (identical) citizen. Their gains if the project succeeds would be halved, but so would their losses if the project failed. Expected income $EY_2$ is now smaller, compared to $EY_1$, but, because of the lower risk, we can see from Figure 7.3 that now the project is preferred to the status quo, that is $EU_2 > U(Y)$.

In summary, the Arrow–Lind Theorem states if the returns from a project are (a) uncorrelated with national income and (b) they are spread across a large number of people, then the aggregate risk premium tends towards zero, so that the correct discount rate to use is the no-risk rate. Now projects in the private sector will typically fail on at least one of these counts, so the public sector discount rate should be smaller than its private sector counterpart. It sounds like public sector projects will crowd out private sector projects with a higher rate of return. This is true, but the public projects will be preferred in the same way that many people will prefer a sure thing which guarantees them £100, to a lottery where they win £120 with probability ½, but only £85 the rest of the time. The lottery has a higher return, but its associated risk makes the sure thing preferable.

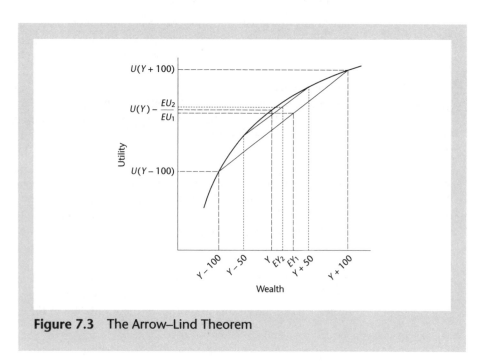

**Figure 7.3**  The Arrow–Lind Theorem

## 7.5  Estimating benefits

Often, the hardest part of CBA is the estimation of the benefits from the project. If there are no market failures, the marginal benefit of a good is just its price. So, as we have already noted, we could use the signals provided by the market to carry out a cost–benefit analysis. Unfortunately, since most of the goods involved in CBA are usually (though not always) non-marketed, there is no readily available method of identifying the value potential consumers place on the commodity. A number of techniques are used, none of which are perfect. The methods fall into two main categories: revealed preference and stated preference. The former uses information about actual behaviour to infer values for the good under question; the latter is based upon asking consumers to rank or value goods in hypothetical markets. Obviously, if the exchange is hypothetical, then the answers produced may be highly unreliable, but researchers are often forced to use stated preference methods by the limitations of the revealed preference approach.

## Revealed preference methods

### Market behaviour

Ideally there is some related good which is marketed. For instance, private healthcare demand may reveal something about values for publicly provided healthcare. Unfortunately, market behaviour reveals little of the value placed on many public goods and for these more indirect methods are required.

### Travel cost

Individuals can reveal the value they place upon a good by the amount of time they are willing to devote to its consumption. For instance, Ahmed catches a train to see a free exhibition at the National Gallery. If the fare is £20, then he would be willing to pay at least £20 to see the exhibition in the absence of travel costs. This is the basis of the **travel cost** method.

Suppose there were four equal-sized towns along the route to the gallery. The total cost for someone visiting from town $i$ would be the monetary costs of the visit ($m_i$) plus the time costs (expressed in £) or,

$$m_i + t_i w$$

where $t_i$ is the travel time from the $i$th town and $w$ is the opportunity cost of time. Suppose that, for the four towns, the proportion of the population and total costs visiting the gallery are (0.1, 10), (0.06, 15), (0.04, 20) and (0.02, 30). For instance, 6% of the population visit from the second town and their travel cost is £15. Note that as the costs rise, the numbers visiting dwindle. Essentially, these are observations on a demand curve and we can plot them (see Figure 7.4, where the crosses represent observations), then use regression to discover a line of best fit. If town sizes differ, then adjustments must be made and we would also want to gather data on the age, sex, income, etc., of the visitors to control for these variables in the estimation procedure.

> **Travel cost**
>
> A method for valuing amenities based on the distance people travel to enjoy them

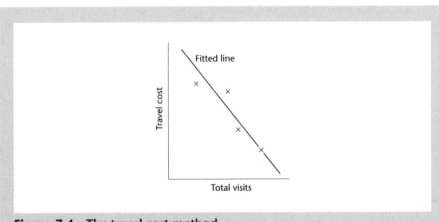

**Figure 7.4  The travel cost method**

The method yields an estimate of the consumer surplus, but it omits the benefits to non-users of the facility. For instance, I might have no intention of visiting a nature reserve where birds can be observed, but nevertheless might place some value on the existence of the reserve as a sanctuary for migrating fowl. The other major drawback is that we need to have an estimate of the opportunity cost of time. For someone who can choose their own hours freely at a fixed rate of reward, then the opportunity cost is just the hourly wage. But many people are not in this position. Moreover, some might actually enjoy the travel, rather than seeing it as time lost. Estimation of the $w$ is therefore fraught with difficulties, and authorities who use it in their CBA (e.g. the Department of Transport) are usually forced to make an uneasy compromise on the figure employed.

## Hedonic pricing

> **Hedonic pricing**
>
> A method for valuing amenities based on the implicit prices revealed by the marketplace

Houses with a sea view cost more than those without; detached cost more than semi-detached; three-bedroom semis fetch a higher price than two bedrooms. In each case, the value placed on the amenity (a sea view, no shared walls, an extra bedroom) is revealed by supply and demand and is known as **hedonic pricing**. The method can sometimes be extended to deal with environmental amenities such as noise and air pollution. Houses neighbouring an airport generally sell at a discount to identical buildings away from the flight path. The value that people place on quiet can be revealed by the choices they make.

For example, using ordinary least squares on 634 single family households in Los Angeles Metropolitan area in 1977–8, David Brookshire *et al* (1982) estimate that the elasticity of house price with respect to suspended particulate (i.e. smog) levels is about –0.22. In other words, a 1% rise in particulate levels would lead to a 0.22% drop in the price of a house in the affected zone. The problem with the hedonic pricing method is that other factors affect house prices too. Disentangling them is most difficult when the sample size is small compared to the number of factors and, in particular, when two factors are correlated across the sample. For instance, rural areas usually suffer less crime compared to urban districts and houses situated in the country usually have better views than their city counterparts. Hedonic pricing may be used in this instance to place a value on living in the country, but not on the separate components of the amenity, reduced crime and a better view.

## Stated preference methods

> **Contingent valuation**
>
> A method for valuing amenities based on individual's stated willingness to pay (or willingness to accept compensation)

Unfortunately, with many amenities it is not possible to use one of these ingenious revealed preference methods. Instead, we have to rely on individuals answering hypothetical questions designed to reveal the value they would place on the good if it was marketed. In environmental economics, in particular, this technique is widely employed (though controversial) and is called **contingent valuation** (CV). Similar methods are employed to evaluate safety improvements and in healthcare.

We saw in Chapter 4, on public goods, that individuals have incentives to misrepresent their preferences for collective goods. Someone asked 'what are you willing to pay for cleaner beaches?', but told that they would not actually have to pay anything, would have an incentive to overstate their valuation. Similarly, if asked the same question, but told that they would have to pay, then there is an incentive to free-ride on other people.

The preferred method of eliciting values is therefore an alternative technique known as *dichotomous choice*. Respondents are simply asked 'are you willing to pay x?', with x varied over the sample, and a bid curve[3] is estimated. The procedure is similar to that employed in the travel cost method, though the demand curve estimated is compensated, rather than Marshallian.

While the dichotomous choice technique overcomes the problems of strategic bias in CV responses, a number of other problems remain, not least the tendency for individuals to give similar willingness to pay (WTP) figures for a large project (e.g. 'save endangered species') and its component parts (e.g. 'save the whale'). Known as part–whole bias or the embedding problem, this is one of a variety of difficulties with the CV technique which mean its results must be treated with caution. Nevertheless, its use is spreading and is mandated, for instance, in several pieces of US environmental legislation.

One final alternative to stated and revealed preference methods should be mentioned. It is based on estimating the value of production gained or lost as a result of a scheme. For instance, instead of measuring the value of a life implicitly from risk-averting behaviour or explicitly through a WTP questionnaire, an estimate of the typical value of production lost through a death may be employed. Usually, production-based measures will underestimate figures obtained by methods which focus on the consumer.

## 7.6  Cost–benefit analysis in practice

In this section and the next, we illustrate the application of the CBA techniques using three examples. We begin with a well-known example showing the difference between private profitability and social desirability.

### Example 1. The Channel Tunnel

A fixed link between France and Britain was proposed as long ago as the Napoleonic era, but it is only in the 1990s that it became reality. Eurotunnel constructed a 50 km twin-bore rail tunnel (with a third, service tunnel running between) linking Folkestone and Calais. The potential benefits of the Tunnel arise from two sources and are shown in Figure 7.5. First, the Tunnel lowers the marginal cost of travelling between the two countries. Second, it adds a new competitor, placing downward pressures on prices. As a result of these two effects, the price falls from $P^0$ to $P^1$ while crossings rise, yielding the gain depicted by the shaded area. Against this must be placed the costs of construction.

Kay et al. (1989) provide estimates of the benefits of the new link, using data from Eurotunnel's prospectus and the ferry operators. They assumed that the Tunnel would open seven months after Eurotunnel's planned date of May 1993 and that the Tunnel would take most of the traffic from the existing ferry operators, as well as some from nearby ports and air routes across the Channel. Their estimates are given in Table 7.3, which uses a 5.5% discount rate and shows the high social benefits from the Tunnel. The private benefits to Eurotunnel were more precarious, and highly sensitive to minor changes in the assumptions, such as a delay in the completion date.

---

[3] A bid curve shows the proportion of the population who state they are willing to pay x for different levels of x. The area under the bid curve is then the mean willingness to pay. See Hanley and Spash (1993) for example.

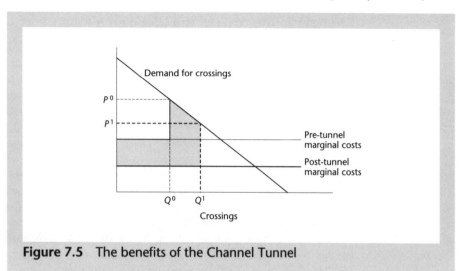

**Figure 7.5** The benefits of the Channel Tunnel

**Table 7.3** The anticipated costs and benefits of the Channel Tunnel

| £m 1994 | Social benefits | Private benefits |
|---|---|---|
| Consumers | 31,039 | |
| Ferry operators | –1,577 | |
| Tunnel operator | 18,336 | 15,942 |
| Air/rail Companies | –4,143 | |
| Cost | –11,839 | –11,839 |
| Total | 31,816 | 4,103 |

Source: Kay *et al.* Table 3, 1989

Although the Tunnel did make a delayed start in 1994, only 82,000 passengers used it in that year (Department of the Environment, 1997), and numbers did not begin to rise significantly until the EuroShuttle service began in June 1995. This and cost overruns have made heavily negative the private net benefits to Eurotunnel's investors. Just as passenger numbers have fallen below the estimates used in Kay *et al.* (1989), so prices have failed to fall in the manner anticipated. They predicted average prices for cars crossing the Channel to fall from £115.42 (1994 prices) to £50.72 for users of the ferry and to £41.44 for those switching to the Tunnel. In fact by 1998, the standard mid-summer price for crossing was £220 for both ferry and Tunnel users and there was no price, at any time of day or year, close to the figures anticipated.

Good practice in CBA includes carrying out sensitivity analysis. Kay *et al.* (1989) consider a variety of pricing outcomes and conclude that although the price affects the distribution of the benefits (higher prices create producer surplus rather than consumer surplus), overall, the enormous cost savings from the Tunnel mean that the net social benefits are not sensitive to changes in the price structure. With hindsight therefore, from a private perspective, the Tunnel should not have been constructed, but its social benefits far outweigh the costs.

### Example 2. The costs of the US Clean Air Act of 1981

The act required firms to reduce emissions of six major pollutants. The thirteen industries directly affected included motor vehicles, chemicals and metal manufacturing. Compliance costs over the period 1981–90 were estimated at $648bn (at current prices) by the Environmental Protection Agency (EPA), with the figures calculated by examining the six industries directly affected and multiplying the rise in cost by the original output level. These numbers overestimate the costs of the regulation, since they do not allow for reductions in use by the consumers. However, there are two elements omitted from the cost estimates. The regulations have a differential impact on the sectors of the economy, thus there are substitution effects between sectors. Second, if the regulations raise the costs of, say, cars, then this raises factor prices for industries apparently unaffected by the regulations. Thus, there are the general equilibrium consequences and some of these were substantial. For instance, in the directly affected sectors, Motors and Electrical Utilities, prices rose by 36.63 and 44.41%, respectively. Meanwhile, prices also rose in the indirectly affected parts of the economy, such as Food and Financial and Real Estate, where prices rose by 8.38 and 5.12%, respectively (Hazilla and Kopp, 1990). Because of the size and variety of effects following the regulations, partial equilibrium analysis therefore gives an inaccurate picture. Using a general equilibrium model, the authors estimate the total costs to be around $977 per capita. By 1990, the rise in prices was equivalent to a drop in GNP of approximately 6%.

The example does not give an estimate of the benefits of the Clean Air Act. Perhaps they were greater than 6% of GNP. In fact, estimates of the benefits of tighter air quality controls suggest that the benefits are often lower than the costs. For instance, in *Science* (1991) Alan Krupnick and Paul R. Portney estimated the value of tighter air quality controls in the Los Angeles region to be around $3bn versus the $10–13bn costs. This does not mean that all environmental projects fail the cost–benefit test.

## 7.7 Cost-effectiveness analysis (CEA)

**Cost-effectiveness analysis**

An appraisal method which finds the least cost means of achieving a specified object

Unlike CBA, in **cost-effectiveness analysis** (CEA) no attempt is made to estimate the benefits side of the equation. Instead, the technique is used to find the lowest cost method of reaching a particular goal, for instance a reduction in vehicle emissions. CEA is widely used in arenas such as healthcare, safety and the environment, usually on the grounds that valuing lives or unspoilt wilderness is inherently difficult. Moreover, many individuals would not agree with the act of placing a monetary value on a life or an endangered species, arguing that lives and other commodities are incommensurate and that therefore a full CBA is inappropriate. This ignores the point that many routine choices, such as driving a car, involve trade-offs between safety and consumption. In other words, the benefits of life-saving are implicitly weighted against the costs, even if individuals are not prepared to make explicit comparisons. Despite this argument, CEA does not carry the same political risk as CBA and is therefore more widely accepted as a decision-making aid.

For instance, since President Reagan's Executive Order 12291 of 1981, regulatory agencies in the US were required to choose alternatives on the basis of their net benefits to (US) society, except when directed by legislation. In practice, the US Congress has often chosen to force through statutes which give no opportunity for evaluation of the costs and benefits. The EPA still has to carry out CBA for a significant number of proposals, but in some instances it has fallen short of a full CBA and used CEA instead, as the next example illustrates.

### Example 3. Banning asbestos

Asbestos comes in a variety of forms, some of which are more dangerous than others. The EPA estimated the costs of banning asbestos in particular uses and compared this with the lives which would be saved in order to obtain a 'cost per statistical cancer avoided ($m 1987)'. Decision-making purely on cost-effectiveness grounds would lead to a ban for all sources of asbestos which had a cost of banning below a planned level. As can be seen from Table 7.4, there is a link between exemption and cost, but it is not uniform. In some cases, such as special industrial gaskets, the cost per statistical cancer of a ban is lower than that for some of the uses (e.g. asbestos-coated shingles) which were subject to a ban.

From the example, we can see that although cost–benefit ideas do influence the policy process, other factors matter as well. In this case, lobbying by the relevant industry groups also had an impact on the final shape of the ban.

**Table 7.4**   Costing an asbestos ban

| Item | Cost per statistical cancer ($m 1987) |
|------|---------------------------------------|
| Categories subject to phase-down/ban | |
| Drum brake linings | 1.1 |
| Drum after market | 0.1 |
| Roof coatings | 40.0 |
| A/C shingles | 120.0 |
| A/C pipe | 61.0 |
| Brake blocks | 0.3 |
| Categories exempt | |
| Asbestos diaphragms | >6,000 |
| Missile liners | 6,000 |
| Special industrial gaskets | 15.0 |
| Reinforced plastic | 90.0 |

Source: Luken and Fraas, Table 4, p. 104, 1995

## 7.8  Conclusion

Fundamental to the notion of CBA is the idea of shadow pricing: that resources should be valued at their opportunity cost and not at the market price, unless the two are equal. In principle, all economic decision-making could be taken using CBA. The allocation of resources to healthcare rather than education, the weight given to defence expenditure rather than transport, could all be the subject of CBA. In practice, CBA is largely confined to decision-making at a fairly routine level, such as road building in the UK, or the World Bank's loans for development projects. It is worthwhile listing some of the main reasons why this is so:

- the difficulty (if not the impossibility) of calculating benefits and costs in many instances;
- the commensurability of different kinds of benefits (saving lives or the natural world, for instance) is not universally accepted;
- the unwillingness or inability of CBA practitioners (i.e. economists) to explain and justify their practices;
- the difference between 'ought' and 'is', whether a government proceeds with a policy depends not only on whether the benefits exceed the costs, but also on the distribution of those benefits and costs across society.

The next two chapters are particularly concerned with the last argument. As we shall see, losers with loud voices may out-shout quiet winners and see off a project which passes the CBA test. Conversely, projects may be approved by government which would never overcome a CBA hurdle.

## Summary

- In the absence of market failure, profitability provides the correct CBA.
- For a scheme to pass a potential Pareto improvement test, the sum of compensating variations must be positive.
- A project which raises social welfare may fail the PPI criterion; a scheme which passes the PPI test may lead to a reduction in social welfare.
- The PPI test may be inconsistent – a proposal and its reversal may both meet the criterion.
- The shadow price of a commodity is its opportunity cost. In CBA, all goods, whether consumed now or in the future, should be valued at their shadow prices.
- The difficulty of measuring benefits limits the use of CBA.
- Cost-effective analysis is designed to find the minimum cost of meeting a given target and may be more acceptable when benefits are hard to measure or seen as incommensurate with costs.

## Questions

1. When will projects tend to pass a PPI test, but fail a social welfare test?
2. Explain the Kaldor–Scitovsky paradox.
3. If a tax is placed on a good, why is the revenue generated not counted as a loss of surplus?
4. Re-evaluate the Wensum Dam scheme if the government cuts the rate of income tax to 10%. What assumptions are you making about the labour market?
5. Will a project that wins a CEA test also always win a CBA test against the same set of alternatives?

**6.** The CBA rule states that all projects for which benefits exceed costs should proceed. How do you think the rule should be amended if a government has a fixed budget out of which projects must be financed?

## Further reading

There are many good texts on CBA, including those by Sugden and Williams (1978) and the collection of surveys edited by Layard and Glaister (1994). The argument that producer surplus should not be accorded the same status as its consumer counterpart, advanced by Mishan (1968), is also discussed in those references. Much recent work on CBA has involved its application to environmental issues, an area usefully surveyed by Hanley and Spash (1994) who also provide an overview of the various methods of benefit estimation discussed in this chapter. Meanwhile healthcare applications can be found in Sloan (1996). The appraisal of the financially disastrous Channel Tunnel project is provided by Kay et al. (1989), while the UK Treasury (1984) is the UK government's official manual of project appraisal. For understandable reasons, we have not covered project appraisal in developing countries; Little and Mirrlees (1970) is a good reference on the subject, with their assessment of the impact of the book, which was written for the World Bank, summarised in Little and Mirrlees (1996).

## References

Arrow, K. and Lind, R. (1970) 'Uncertainty and the valuation of public investment decisions', *American Economic Review* 60, 364–78.

Boadway, R. and Bruce, N. (1984) *Welfare Economics*, Oxford: Blackwell.

Brookshire, D.S., Thayer, M., Schulze, R. and d'Arge, R. (1982) 'Valuation of public goods', *American Economic Review* 72, 165–77.

Department of the Environment (1997) *Transport Statistics for Great Britain*, London: Government Statistical Services.

Hanley, N. and Spash, C. (1993 *Cost Benefit Analysis and the Environment*, London: Edward Elgar.

Hazilla, M. and Kopp, R.J. (1990) 'Social cost of environmental quality regulation: A general equilibrium analysis', *Journal of Political Economy* 98(4), 853–73.

Kay, J., Manning, A. and Szymunski, S. (1989) 'The economic benefits of the Channel Tunnel', *Economic Policy* 8, 211–34.

Krupnik, A. and Portney, P.R. (1991) 'Controlling urban air pollution – a benefit–cost assessment', *Science*, 252, 522–8.

Layard, R. and Glaister, S. (1994) *Cost Benefit Analysis*, 2nd edn, Cambridge: Cambridge University Press.

Little, I. and Mirrlees, J.A. (1974) *Project Appraisal and Planning*, London: Heinemann.

Little, I. and Mirrlees, J.A. (1994) 'Project appraisal and planning twenty years on', in R. Layard and S. Glaister, *Cost Benefit Analysis, Ch. 6*.

Luken, R.A. and Fraas, A.G. (1995) 'The US regulatory analysis framework: A review', *Oxford Review of Economic Policy* 9(4), 96–111.

Mishan, E.J. (1968) 'What is producer's surplus?', *American Economic Review* 58, 1269–82.

Sloan, F.A. (ed.) (1996) *Valuing Health Care*, Cambridge: Cambridge University Press.

Sugden, R. and Williams, A. (1978) *Cost Benefit Analysis*, Oxford: Oxford University Press.

UK Treasury (1984) *Investment Appraisal: A Guide for Government Departments*, London: HMSO.

# Public Choice

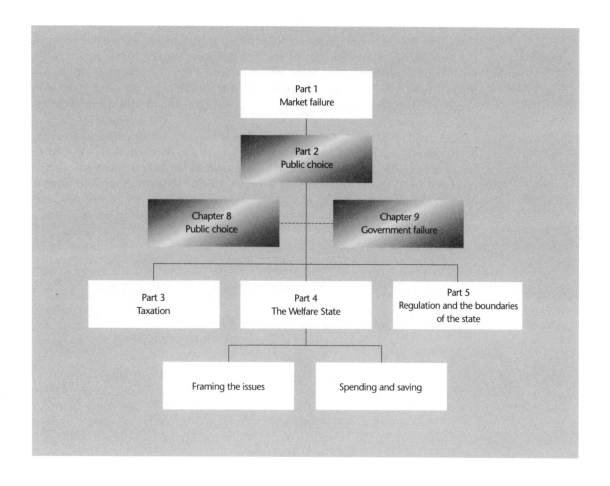

The market failure model of the first part of this book provides a template of what governments *should* do, but does not always provide a reliable guide to what governments *actually* do, or to the reasons why. The theory of public choice, sometimes called the 'economics of politics', is an alternative tool for understanding government actions, based on the assumption that individuals pursue their own selfish ends in or out of government. As you will see, sometimes it yields predictions similar to those of the market failure model, but in many cases it does not.

We split the analysis of public choice into two parts. Chapter 8 introduces some of the fundamental theories, such as the rational voter model, before outlining the predictions of public choice theory for behaviour in direct democracies. In practice though, most government is through elected representatives. Chapter 9 therefore builds on its predecessor and examines the problems created by the agency relationship within the public sector.

By the end of this part of the book you should have a good idea about the concept of *government failure*, an important counterweight to the view that it is only markets which are imperfect. So together with ideas drawn from the first part, you will have most of the conceptual tools required to work your way through the applied material of the remainder of the book.

# Public Choice

## Key concepts

| | | |
|---|---|---|
| the rational voter model | ethical voter | median voter |
| representative democracy | majority voting | direct democracy |
| civic duty | minimax | income and voting |

## 8.1 Introduction

Public choice theory provides an economic model of these political decision-making processes. We could think of public choice theory in the following way:

Input: → Democratic Process → Output:
Voters                                              Public Policy

The obvious question facing individuals is, Why vote? accepting that many people do vote and knowing that in many modern democracies the political process is based upon majority voting. We have the following question to ask about this process: Is majority voting a satisfactory method? By that we mean, do the decisions reached reflect the preferences of voters? And, since most democracies use a system of majority voting, is majority voting an efficient method of collective decision-making?

## 8.2 Democratic process

### Why vote? Rational voter

**Paradox of voting**

People vote, even though the expected utility of voting is apparently negative

Public choice theory utilises a microeconomic theory of voting behaviour, referred to as the rational voter model. The decision to vote is assumed to reflect the expected utility from doing so. Downs (1957) sets out the classic account of the rationality of voting and gave his name to the famous paradox – **the paradox of voting** – that it could not be considered rational to vote, yet many people do.

Imagine that there is a policy that a voter would like to see implemented or a party that the voter would like to win the election, X. Each voter therefore calculates the value of that policy being implemented, which yields utility $U(X)$. The model argues that the voter will also calculate the likelihood $P$ that their vote is decisive and will make a difference to the outcome of the election $0 \leq P \leq 1$. The value of $P$ will reflect the size of the electorate and how close the election is. From Mueller (1991), assuming that all voters are identical, the formula for the probability, $P$, of being decisive is approximately:

$$P = \frac{3e^{-2[(N-1)(q-1/2)]^2}}{2\sqrt{2\pi(N-1)}}$$

where $q$ is the voters' expectation of the proportion of votes each party is likely to get and $N$ is the size of the electorate. We can see that $P$ will be highest when the election is close, $q = 0.5$ and if the electorate is small; this is illustrated in Box 8.1. Finally, we must also consider the cost of voting, $C$; this includes the time spent considering the various alternatives and their likely impact on the voter as well as the opportunity cost of the time spent voting. So the expected utility from voting is $E(U) = P[U(X)] - C$.

---

**BOX 8.1**

## The futility of voting

We can illustrate the futility of voting with several examples. Suppose that the value from having your preferred candidate in power is £1,000 over 5 years and that the costs arise simply from the time allocated to voting. If the value of your time is £10 per hour and voting takes half an hour, then the cost is £5. Finally, the probability any given voter votes one way is ½.

*Case One* – A relatively small electorate of 50,000, this may represent a local election.
Using Mueller's formula, the probability that you are decisive is 0.0027. Putting all the elements together:

$$E(U) = 0.0027 \times 1,000 - 5 = -£2.30$$

*Case Two* – The situation gets worse when a much larger electorate is involved. In a national election with 100,000,000 voters, the probability of being decisive falls to about 0.00006:

$$E(U) = 0.00006 \times 1000 - 5 = -£4.90$$

*Case Three* – Finally, let us consider a student election where the benefits and costs associated with voting are much smaller, for instance a benefit of £100 but cost of voting of £1. We also expect a much smaller electorate, let us say 1,000 voters, so the probability of being decisive is much greater $P = 0.02$:

$$E(U) = 0.02 \times 100 - 1 = 1.00$$

Of the three cases considered, this is the only one in which it is worth voting!

---

Since any individual is unlikely to affect the outcome, $P$ is very small and, taking into account the cost associated with voting, the expected utility is negative, $E(U) < 0$, and it is irrational to vote. However, many people choose to vote. This is the 'Paradox of Voting', that people do it when they should not, i.e. they are not 'rational'.

Much of what has been said applies particularly to countries with a majority voting or first-past-the-post system. It can be rational to cast a vote for a minority party under some systems of proportional representation, since there is a greater chance that your party will have a representative elected than under majority voting, although, of course, the difficulties of coalition making mean that the policies which you feel distinguish your preferred party from the others may not actually be implemented.

Evidence supports the 'Paradox of Voting': people do vote and we provide some explanations for this below. One response to this would be to completely abandon the public choice approach. Alternatively, one might argue that it is still interesting to examine and test the other predictions of the model. This will give us some indication of whether a microeconomic approach to voting behaviour has any validity. For example we can ask the following questions, Is the turnout higher when the costs of voting are lower? or when the outcome is uncertain? or higher amongst those who have most to gain? McLean (1987) provides a broad-brush account of the empirical evidence, stating that 'Turnout is lower when it is wet than dry, when voting is expensive (as in the USA) than when it is cheap (as in the UK), when the result is not expected to be close, and amongst the poor compared to the rich.' However, Dunleavy (1991, p. 83) provides examples in which the probability of being decisive has little effect on voting behaviour.

> If probabilities of influencing election outcomes are very influential in shaping voters' decision to participate, the proportion of people voting should be inversely related to the size of the electorate . . . turnout should be less at national than local or regional elections . . .. In practice, this pattern rarely occurs in liberal democracies. In some countries, such as West Germany and France . . . turnout levels are high across all elections. . . . In other countries, like the United States and Britain, there are major differences in turnout but the pattern of variation is the opposite of what a public choice approach suggests – turnout levels at local elections are often up to half those at national elections.

Although in these cases the value of the outcomes, $U(X)$, differs. For example, local authorities have greater power in France than in the UK.

## Minimax strategy

An alternative model of voting behaviour considers the act of voting in an uncertain world. The decision to vote is made under conditions of uncertainty, therefore agents may not act to maximise expected utility, but are instead motivated by the desire to minimise regret. Imagine two states, $S_1$ where the vote has no impact and $S_2$ where the vote has an impact. We now examine the value of regret associated with each choice, vote or abstain, under the two states. In $S_1$ the outcome is independent of the voter's strategy, therefore a vote results in regret $C$, the cost of voting, and there is no regret if the voter abstains. If instead we are in the second state, $S_2$, the vote is decisive, then there is no regret associated with voting, but if the voter abstains there would be a value of regret equal to the utility we would have attained less the cost of voting, $U - C$.

|        | $S_1$ | $S_2$   |
|--------|-------|---------|
| Vote   | $C$   | 0       |
| Abstain| 0     | $U - C$ |

Since agents act to avoid maximum regret (to avoid abstaining in state $S_2$), the dominant strategy is always to vote, since the voter does not know whether $S_1$ or $S_2$ prevails. This is an extreme risk-avoiding strategy and the voter places the same value on each of these states occurring, although as we know from our earlier discussions, $S_2$ is unlikely to arise. Also, as Mueller (1991, p. 353) points out, such a strategy would lead to some unlikely forms of behaviour:

> Suppose, for example, that a voter is indifferent between the Republican and the Democratic candidates. His minimax strategy is then to abstain. Suppose now that the Nazi party enters a candidate. Now the minimax criterion forces the voter to the polls to avoid the possible, although highly unlikely, event that the Nazi candidate will win, *and will do so by only one vote.*

## Ethical voter

Earlier models have treated voters as being self-interested. An alternative explanation of voting behaviour is that voting is a consequence of altruism. In this case, the voter is not only interested in the impact of the vote on his or her own utility, s/he is also affected by the utility of others. So the voter's objective function is $O_i$

$$O_i = U_i + \theta \Sigma U_j$$

When $\theta = 0$, the voter is selfish but if $\theta = 1$, the voter is altruistic. Once $\theta > 0$, the expected utility from voting rises and the individual is more likely to vote.

This model can also explain other apparent irrational behaviour, such as a wealthy person voting for a party which will implement a progressive tax scheme. This voter may well find that their own income is lower if the party wins the election, but that once the tax revenue is redistributed, the incomes of many others will rise and this greater equality increases the utility of our altruistic voter.

## Individuals derive utility from voting and other explanations

Many political scientists and sociologists have difficulty in accepting the simplistic choice model presented above, as an adequate explanation of voting behaviour, not only because of the paradox of voting, but because the model takes no account of factors such as citizenship, political activism, strategic behaviour by voters, family traditions, the values within society, the structure of society, or political partisanship.

These arguments suggest that we should include the utility that voters may get from taking part in the democratic process in our expression for the expected utility of voting. There are several ways in which individuals may derive utility from the act of voting. First, voting is seen as a right and a civic duty. It provides an occasion for individuals to participate in and shape their society and so they should do their duty in voting. This is certainly something that had a very powerful effect on black voters in the first election in South Africa after apartheid was dismantled. In addition, voters may believe that it is important to vote in order to preserve democracy, particularly bearing in mind the historical struggles for suffrage. One may also gain utility simply from the act of expressing one's political preferences. Another less powerful argument might be that voting is a social activity; one may meet friends on the way to the election or share a car to the polling station. The likelihood of seeing friends and neighbours on one's way to the polling station may provide a further motivation, that of being seen to do one's duty. Finally, once you have voted, you will not be bothered by canvassers encouraging you to go out to vote!

Another important argument might be that ideology dominates rational decision-making. Those who are committed to a set of policies or principles might cast a vote in favour of a political party, regardless of the chances of the policy being implemented. Even if you know that a party has no chance of forming a government, so $PU(X)$ is very small indeed, you still vote for that party on the basis of conviction, or because you want to show that nationally there is support for that party. This explains voting for a small or single-issue party such as an environmental party or a third party in what is nationally a two-party race.

Given these arguments, it seems that voting yields a positive utility $D$ and there is an additional benefit from voting:

$$E(U) = P[U(X)] - C + D$$

This certainly increases the likelihood of $E(U) > 0$, making voting a more rational activity. On the whole, it will be difficult to measure $D$, particularly since it is a proxy for so many factors and this may diminish the value of the approach. However, studies have been conducted to examine the effect of civic duty and evidence suggests that this has a positive impact on the likelihood of voting.

# 8.3 Public choice mechanisms

**Direct democracy**

Where issues are decided directly by the electorate

**Representative democracy**

The electorate votes for a representative to reflect their views and make decisions on a range of issues

Our starting point will be that of a **direct democracy**, where individuals are asked to cast their vote on levels of public expenditure. This system is much more likely to be used in determining local rather than national levels of expenditure. Elections or referendums of this sort are used in Switzerland and California. Of course, most decisions are taken under a system of **representative democracy** where the votes are cast for parties with a set of policies. The elected representatives are then delegated to make decisions concerning levels of public expenditure. The problems associated with delegation are discussed in Chapter 9. Here we consider what public choice mechanisms are available and assess whether they will lead to an outcome which accurately reflects the views of the electorate.

## Arrow's Impossibility Theorem

**Condorcet paradox**

Majority voting can fail to satisfy the Arrow criteria, producing non-transitive (i.e. contradictory) social choice

In Chapter 3, we identified a set of desirable criteria that a method of social choice should satisfy and, according to Arrow's Impossibility Theorem, no social choice mechanism exists which satisfies these criteria. No constitutional or public choice rule will satisfy these criteria either. To illustrate this, we return to the **Condorcet paradox** of majority voting. Imagine three voters A, B and C, who each rank three alternative policies x, y and z in the following manner.

| A | B | C |
|---|---|---|
| x | y | z |
| y | z | x |
| z | x | y |

Majority voting will produce the following results:

x $P$ y by a majority (A and C);

and  y $P$ z by a majority (A and B).

If we impose collective rationality, transitivity implies that x $P$ z. But, x $P$ z is only true for A. So, when we impose transitivity, then A is a dictator. If, instead, we continue to use majority voting, z P x by a majority (B and C), now our results fail the condition of transitivity. With this simple example, we have shown that majority voting fails to satisfy the Arrow criteria.

There are alternative voting systems, discussed in Cullis and Jones (1992) or Musgrave and Musgrave (1989). The Arrow result is general and other voting systems also fail to satisfy the Arrow criteria. Despite this, there may be reasons to prefer these alternatives to majority voting. One reason is that votes within a majority voting system only involve pairwise comparisons, as above. This is not true of the alternatives, such as plurality voting where each option is given a score according to the ranking of preferences (1 if first best, 2 if second best and so on, the option with the lowest number of points wins), or point voting where voters rank alternatives by allocating a fixed number of points amongst the available options (here the option with the highest score wins). In fact these voting systems yield the same results as majority voting when only two outcomes are considered. A further advantage of point voting is that it allows voters an opportunity to voice the intensity of their preferences. For example, if voter A above were to allocate six points to the available options, given her preferences she might cast the following vote x = 3, y = 2 and z = 1. But if she had very strong preferences for x, then she might vote in a different manner, x = 5, y = 1 and z = 0, and so on. Given this, it may be tempting to argue that point voting provides a better representation of the voters' preferences. However, we have assumed that voters are honestly revealing their preferences and not behaving strategically in order to influence the outcome. This raises the possibility of forming coalitions or logrolling, which are discussed in Chapter 9. The opportunities for strategic voting are greater under a voting system which is sensitive to intensity of preferences. Given this, a system such as majority voting where the results are less likely to be influenced by strategic voting may be preferred.

## Majority voting and single-peaked preferences

However, majority voting does not always result in the Condorcet paradox. Let us compare the following sets of preferences $P_1$ and $P_2$.

|   | $P_1$ |   |   |   | $P_2$ |   |
|---|---|---|---|---|---|---|
| A | B | C |   | A | B | C |
| x | y | z |   | x | y | z |
| y | z | x |   | y | z | y |
| z | x | y |   | z | x | x |

x P y   by a majority (A and C)        y P z   by a majority (A and B)
y P z   by a majority (A and B)        z P x   by a majority (B and C)
z P x   by a majority (B and C)        y P x   by a majority (B and C)
Non-transitive                          Transitivity holds

When preferences are given by $P_1$ then we have the problem of non-transitivity, but when preferences are given instead by $P_2$, majority voting is transitive and satisfies the Arrow criteria. The difference between $P_1$ and $P_2$ can be seen as one of multi- and single-peaked preferences. This is illustrated in Figure 8.1, where the rankings by each voter of the three outcomes are represented. The first set of preferences $P_1$ are shown on the left-hand side of Figure 8.1 and the second set of preferences $P_2$ are shown on the right-hand side.

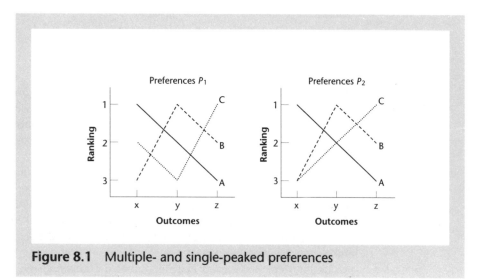

**Figure 8.1**  Multiple- and single-peaked preferences

We can see that under the first set of preferences $P_1$, whilst voters A and B have **single-peaked preferences**, those of voter C are multiple-peaked (forming a trough shape), whereas under the second set of preferences $P_2$, all of the voters have single-peaked preferences. If we could eliminate the possibility of **multiple-peaked preferences**, then we would also find that majority voting would no longer suffer from the Condorcet paradox. To see what this might mean, consider the following illustration:

x – large government budget
y – medium government budget
z – small government budget

For those voters whose most preferred outcome is x (a large budget), it seems natural to assume that the second most desirable outcome would be y (a medium budget), and the least desirable outcome would be z (a small budget). Similarly, if z (a small budget) is the most desirable outcome, y (a medium budget) would seem to be the obvious choice as the second most desirable outcome and x (a large budget) the least-preferred outcome. If we return to the case of majority voting not being transitive, we see that consumer C has the following rankings: z – small budget; x – large budget; y – medium budget. These could be classified as all-or-nothing preferences and it seems unlikely that a voter would have such a ranking. Within this example, it seems acceptable to rule out the possibility of multi-peaked preferences. This is because the choices in this case involved comparisons of different levels of expenditures on the same thing.

However, let us consider instead the example given by McLean (1987). In McLean's example Liverpool City Council was trying to make a decision concerning the best use of reclaimed land on the banks of the Mersey.[1] The three options were x - developing the land into an open park space, y – building council housing and z – selling for private housing development. The parties had the following preferences:

---

[1] This site was eventually redeveloped as the site for the very successful International Garden Festival.

| Liberals | Labour | Conservatives |
|----------|--------|---------------|
| x | y | z |
| y | z | x |
| z | x | y |

Here the Conservatives displayed multi-peaked preferences, but unlike our first example these are not a set of preferences that could be dismissed as unlikely. This is because the options involve ranking different types, not levels, of expenditure and the voter with multi-peaked preferences can no longer be dismissed as having all-or-nothing preferences.

Using this example, we can illustrate a further aspect of the Condorcet problem. When there are more than two possible outcomes and there are multi-peaked preferences, if the Council attempts to make a decision between these three policies, the outcome will depend on the order in which the votes were taken. So, if the first vote occurs between open spaces and council housing and the second between council and private housing projects, the outcome will be that open spaces are preferred to private housing. However, if instead we voted on open spaces and private housing the outcome would be reversed. Majority voting in this example is cyclical. Therefore unless preferences are single peaked, the outcome of majority voting will depend upon the order in which the votes are taken on the pairs of options under consideration; this is an example of agenda setting, which is discussed below.

## Majority voting and the median voter

In this framework attracting the median voter is the key to electoral success. If we return to the example where levels of government expenditure were ranked, we find a clear illustration of the power of the median voter. Assuming single-peaked preferences, we can see that B is the median voter. B's most preferred outcome is y, a medium-sized government budget. y is also the second most desirable outcome for the other voters. So, the most preferred outcome of the majority vote will be y. This is shown in Figure 8.2, where there are $n$ voters with single-peaked preferences. The

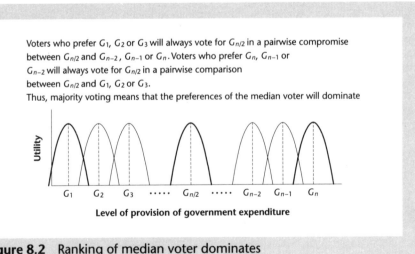

Voters who prefer $G_1$, $G_2$ or $G_3$ will always vote for $G_{n/2}$ in a pairwise compromise between $G_{n/2}$ and $G_{n-2}$, $G_{n-1}$ or $G_n$. Voters who prefer $G_n$, $G_{n-1}$ or $G_{n-2}$ will always vote for $G_{n/2}$ in a pairwise comparison between $G_{n/2}$ and $G_1$, $G_2$ or $G_3$.

Thus, majority voting means that the preferences of the median voter will dominate

Level of provision of government expenditure

**Figure 8.2** Ranking of median voter dominates

median voter ($n/2$) will vote for a level $G_{n/2}$ of the public good/expenditure. When $G_{n/2}$ is compared with a much lower level of provision such as $G_1$, the median voter and all of those who prefer a higher level of provision will vote for $G_{n/2}$. Equally, when $G_{n/2}$ is compared with a much higher level of provision such as $G_n$, the median voter and all those who prefer a low level of provision will vote for $G_{n/2}$. Therefore, under majority voting, the level of provision preferred by the median voter will win any pairwise comparison. The **Median Voter Theorem** is that: under majority voting the outcome with the most votes will be that preferred by the median voter.

This is a very powerful result and the implications are discussed below. However, the Median Voter Theorem does not only apply to a direct democracy. In a representative democracy, political parties will develop a portfolio of policies to maximise their chances of being elected, by choosing policies that will appeal not only to those at the extreme ends of the divide, but also to those in the middle. This is discussed in Chapter 9.

**Median Voter Theorem**

Under majority voting, the outcome chosen will be that preferred by the median voter

## 8.4 Inefficiency with majority rule

We now raise the question of whether the majority voting mechanism itself leads to an efficient outcome. There are also the issues of whether public production leads to an efficient allocation of resources and whether the decisions made by elected representatives result in an efficient outcome, which are discussed in Chapter 9.

### Public choice theory of public expenditure

Assume the voter casts a ballot on grounds of self-interest. Then they will vote for a level of public expenditure or provision of public goods where utility is maximised (see Figure 8.3).

Voters' preferred outcomes will reflect the fact that some individuals may like or use publicly provided goods more than others and that incomes differ; for example, amongst those with a low income the marginal utility of government expenditure may be high, but ability or willingness to pay low; alternatively for those with a high income the marginal utility of government expenditure may be low, but willingness

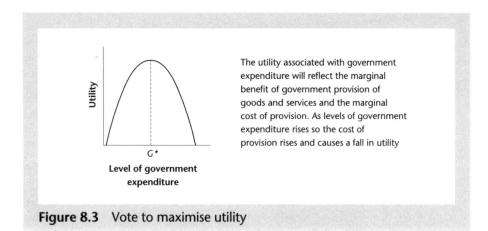

The utility associated with government expenditure will reflect the marginal benefit of government provision of goods and services and the marginal cost of provision. As levels of government expenditure rises so the cost of provision rises and causes a fall in utility

**Figure 8.3** Vote to maximise utility

to pay high The voting behaviour across income groups may vary according to the method used to pay for the public provision.

## Cost under a uniform tax

All consumers pay the same amount, therefore the cost to each voter is $C/N$, where $C$ is the total cost and there are $N$ voters. The cost to the median voter is $c_{med} = C/N$.

## Cost under a proportional tax

The cost to each voter is $c_i = tY_i$, where $t$ is the rate of taxation on income $Y_i$. Richer households pay more than poorer households. Assuming that a tax is only collected to finance public expenditure, therefore $C = \Sigma c_i = \Sigma t Y_i = t \Sigma Y_i$. Therefore, the tax rate is set so that $t = C/\Sigma Y_i$. The cost to the median voter is $c_{med} = tY_{med} = [C/\Sigma Y_i] \times Y_{med}$.

When income is normally distributed $Y_{med} = Y_{mean} = (1/N) \times \Sigma y_i$, the cost to the median voter will be the same under a lump-sum or proportional tax system (see Figure 8.4). But if the income distribution is skewed, as is typically the case, $Y_{med} < Y_{mean}$, the cost to the median voter will be lower under a proportional tax system. Therefore, the median voter will vote for a higher level of public provision under a proportional tax.

## Inefficiency under direct democracy

### Excessive supply

Under majority voting with a proportional tax system, the outcome is likely to be oversupply. This is shown in Figure 8.4 and occurs if the median voter has lower than average income. This situation is at its worst under a progressive tax system, where the marginal cost to the individual of public expenditure rises with income.

### Pareto efficiency

In Chapter 4, we saw that, because public goods are non-rival, it is necessary to consider the sum of the marginal valuations, therefore the Pareto efficiency condition for the supply of a public good is $\Sigma MRS = MRT$. Majority voting will reveal the value that the median voter places on the public good, $MV_{n/2}$, and the level of provision of the public good will therefore be $n \times MV_{n/2}$. Pareto efficiency would require that $n \times MV_{n/2} = \Sigma MV$. Rearranging this condition gives $MV_{n/2} = (1/n) \times \Sigma MV = MV_{mean}$, which is the requirement that the median preferences equal average preferences, therefore the outcome is only efficient when preferences are distributed symmetrically.

### Agenda setting

Systems where individuals vote over all possible pairs of options simultaneously are rare. Often the set of possible votes is defined by the Chair. If cycles are produced by majority voting, then any element in the cycle can be made the winner by a suitable choice of agenda. For instance if we get xPyPzPx . . . then if the Chair wishes to have x chosen, the agenda should read: 1. x versus y, 2. y versus z and then end there.

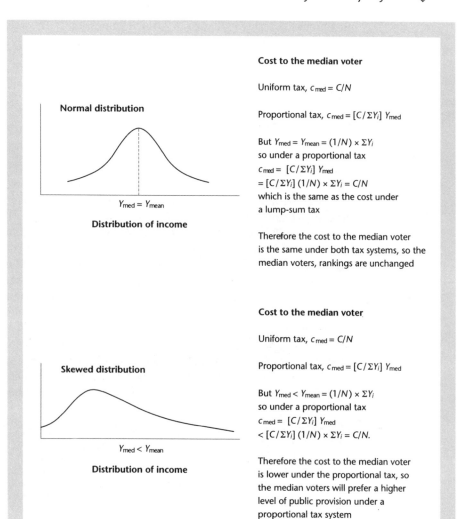

**Cost to the median voter**

Uniform tax, $c_{med} = C/N$

Proportional tax, $c_{med} = [C/\Sigma Y_i]\, Y_{med}$

But $Y_{med} = Y_{mean} = (1/N) \times \Sigma Y_i$
so under a proportional tax
$c_{med} = [C/\Sigma Y_i]\, Y_{med}$
$= [C/\Sigma Y_i]\,(1/N) \times \Sigma Y_i = C/N$
which is the same as the cost under
a lump-sum tax

Therefore the cost to the median voter
is the same under both tax systems, so the
median voters, rankings are unchanged

**Cost to the median voter**

Uniform tax, $c_{med} = C/N$

Proportional tax, $c_{med} = [C/\Sigma Y_i]\, Y_{med}$

But $Y_{med} < Y_{mean} = (1/N) \times \Sigma Y_i$
so under a proportional tax
$c_{med} = [C/\Sigma Y_i]\, Y_{med}$
$< [C/\Sigma Y_i]\,(1/N) \times \Sigma Y_i = C/N.$

Therefore the cost to the median voter
is lower under the proportional tax, so
the median voters will prefer a higher
level of public provision under a
proportional tax system

**Normal distribution**

$Y_{med} = Y_{mean}$

**Distribution of income**

**Skewed distribution**

$Y_{med} < Y_{mean}$

**Distribution of income**

**Figure 8.4**  Distribution of income and cost to median voter

## *Misrepresentation*

A further problem arises because individuals may have incentives to influence the outcome by lying about their preferences. Suppose two individuals vote over three options. Social choice is by majority rule, but in the case of a tie, then all top-ranking options face an equal chance of being chosen. If they vote honestly, then there is a 50% chance that x is chosen and a 50% chance of y. Suppose that B is almost indifferent between y and z, but really hates the x option, then by voting for z over y, B ensures that x is chosen with only 1/3 probability. The option z is now chosen with probability 1/3 as well, but z is Pareto inferior to both x and y; misrepresentation can therefore also be a source of inefficiency.

|   | x | y | z |
|---|---|---|---|
| A | 1 | 2 | 3 |
| B | 3 | 1 | 2 |

In a proposition closely related to Arrow's Impossibility Theorem (see Chapter 3), it can be shown that, provided there are more than three options and two people involved, any social choice rule must be dictatorial if it is to satisfy the Pareto principle and the universal domain assumption, but remain immune to manipulation via misrepresentation (see Campbell (1992) for a proof).[2]

## The costs of making decisions

We have seen that majority voting can lead to Pareto inefficiency. Why not use a unanimity rule then, since this ensures that only Pareto improvements are approved? Many negotiations over the future of the European Union take place in the Council of Ministers, with one representative drawn from each of the Member States. For some areas of decision-making, such as defence and foreign policy or the accession of new members, each country has a veto, so that unanimity is required. Unanimity may produce only Pareto improvements, but it is a costly way to make decisions; obtaining consensus can be a long-winded affair, involving logrolling, the bundling of proposals and side payments to Member countries who might lose from an unalloyed proposal. However, unanimity rules with side payments encourage misrepresentation and it is only under restrictive conditions (such as those governing the Clarke–Groves tax discussed in Chapter 4) that efficiency and honesty can be guaranteed. Increasingly, the Council uses a form of qualified majority voting. In doing so the Member states are trading off one source of efficiency (creating a Pareto improvement) against another (choosing an option sooner rather than later). This trade-off is depicted in Figure 8.5, which is based on Buchanan and Tullock's (1962) original

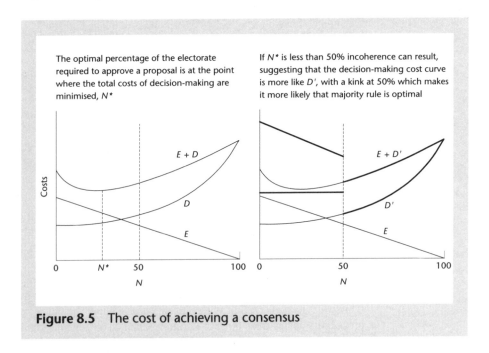

**Figure 8.5** The cost of achieving a consensus

---

[2] You might wonder how this squares with the Clarke–Groves tax explored in Chapter 4, where truth-telling was a dominant strategy for all. One of the assumptions of that model is that preferences are single peaked (everyone has one ideal level of provision of the public good and deviations from that level reduce well-being), which means that the universal domain assumption does not hold.

arguments. Along the bottom is the proportion of the electorate, $N$, required to give their approval if a motion is to pass. The curve $D$ shows the decision-making costs associated with requiring a larger proportion of the electorate to agree to a proposal. $E$, meanwhile, represents the external costs of making decisions which lead to losses of welfare for some individuals. Total costs are minimised at $N^*$, which defines the optimal number of votes required for a policy to be approved. Nothing about this diagram suggests that $N^*$ corresponds to the majority rule which is the norm in most democracies. For this to be the general case, there would have to be a kink at the 50% point and one reason to expect a kink of this kind is provided by the observation that if the optimal decision rule allowed policies to pass with less than 50% of the vote, then both a proposal and its rejection could be approved. For instance if only 30% of the vote was required, both building a new bridge and not building the same bridge could be passed. This suggests that the $D$ curve is more like $D'$ in Figure 8.5 – dropping at 50% as the possibility of incoherent social choice is removed and this feature would tend to push the optimum rule towards majority voting, as it does in the right-hand panel of Figure 8.5 where $E + D'$ is minimised at $N = 50\%$.

There is a similar trade-off involved between direct democracy, where everyone gets to vote, but negotiations can be costly and delay implementation, and representative democracy where decisions can be made more quickly, but there is a further argument in favour of representative democracy. It is probably not because it produces inefficient outcomes that direct democracy is so rare, but rather because of the costs of organising decisions and the need for supervision of the executors of any laws passed. If a decision is made to set up a new pension system or tax petrol, someone must organise the implementation. In a world not populated by saints, that individual requires monitoring, but supervision is a public good if a project will benefit many people and so will tend to be undersupplied. Electing representatives, part of whose job it is to monitor government agencies, can reduce the problem, provided that the elected agents and the bureau do not collude to further their own aims at the expense of the public. The possibility that they might suggests that, having examined the demand side of the public policy equation, it is now time to examine the suppliers of policies: politicians, their parties and the civil servants.

## 8.5 Conclusion

In this chapter we examined an economic model of the political process. The incentive to vote is modelled in terms of expected utility. However, we saw that the expected utility associated with an individual vote influencing the outcome of an election was very small indeed, leading to the 'Paradox of Voting': that people vote even when it is not rational to do so. The model can be extended to take account of the other aspects of voting which may yield utility, belief in democracy or viewing voting as one's civic duty, for example, and we also encountered other microeconomic models in which voting could be seen as a rational strategy. Having identified that individuals will vote, we then turned to the question of whether the political process will deliver what the voters want. According to Arrow's Impossibility Theory, no choice rule will satisfy the Arrow criteria. This was illustrated by the Condorcet paradox of majority voting. This paradox was shown to be associated only with multi-peaked preferences, which in some cases could be ruled out. Once we had shown that in certain cases, majority voting could be a satisfactory method, we identified other aspects of the political system such as logrolling or coalition forming, which do suggest that the political system is unlikely to lead to outcomes which the voters desire.

This chapter has also shown us that, even with direct democracy, inefficient levels of provision of a public good will be standard under most tax systems. Under proportional taxation, for instance, provision will tend to be excessive, provided the median voter has an income lower than the mean. There are other potential sources of inefficiency under majority rule such as agenda setting and misrepresentation. An additional inefficiency arises in that the cost of securing a majority does not minimise the costs of democratic decision-making. The whole rationale for government involvement is that the market may fail to provide an efficient level of certain goods, yet in this chapter, we have considered the inefficiency of the democratic process itself. The matter of the efficiency of public production is considered in Chapter 9.

## Summary

- Public choice theory is a microeconomic model of the political decision-making process.
- It is irrational to vote if the only reason for doing so is in the belief that a single vote will influence the outcome of the election.
- The 'Paradox of Voting' is that people do vote even though it is irrational.
- There may be additional utility associated with the act of voting which makes voting a rational strategy (belief in democracy or viewing voting as one's civic duty).
- Other microeconomic models, including regret theory, support the argument that voting is rational.
- The Condorcet paradox showing that majority voting fails to satisfy the Arrow criteria, is only true if preferences are multi-peaked.
- Majority voting can lead to an inefficient outcome under direct democracy.

## Questions

1. Is it ever rational to vote?
2. Are multi-peaked preferences in some sense irrational?
3. Why is the outcome of majority voting dominated by the preferences of the median voter?
4. How might the tax system and the distribution of income influence voting behaviour?
5. Can majority voting deliver an efficient outcome?
6. Will the political marketplace produce what the public wants?

# Further reading

Mueller (1991) or Sugden (1981) provide comprehensive coverage of the area of public choice and the problems which arise under a direct or representative democracy. A much shorter account of the role of public choice in understanding the economics of the public sector is the survey piece by Borooah (1993). Accessible accounts of the role of public choice in the field of political science can be found in Dunleavy (1991) or McLean (1987).

# References

Borooah, V.K. (1993) 'Public choice: an introductory survey', in P.M. Jackson (ed.) *Current Issues in Public Sector Economics*, pp. 132–55, London: Macmillan.

Buchanan, J.M. and Tullock, G. (1962) *The Calculus of Consent*, Ann Arbour: University of Michigan Press.

Campbell, D.E. (1992) *Equity, Efficiency and Social Choice*, Oxford: Clarendon Press.

Cullis, J. and Jones, P. (1992) *Public Finance and Public Choice*, 1st edn, London: McGraw Hill.

Downs, A. (1957) *An Economic Theory of Democracy*, New York: Harper and Row.

Dunleavy, P. (1991) *Democracy, Bureaucracy and Public Choice*, London: Harvester Wheatsheaf.

McLean, I. (1987) *Public Choice: an Introduction*, Oxford: Blackwell.

Mueller, D.C. (1991) *Public Choice II*, Cambridge: Cambridge University Press.

Musgrave, R.A. and Musgrave, P.B. (1989) *Public Finance in Theory and Practice*, 5th edn, London: McGraw Hill.

Sugden, R. (1981) *The Political Economy of Public Choice*, Oxford: Blackwell.

# CHAPTER 9

# Government Failure

## Key concepts

| | | |
|---|---|---|
| distribution of preferences | costs of voting | agency |
| bureaucracy | rent seeking | spatial competition |
| institutional failure | | |

Some useful definitions: *Pure democracy:* You have two cows. Your neighbours decide who gets the milk. *Representative democracy*: You have two cows. Your neighbours pick someone to tell you who gets the milk. *Bureaucracy:* You have two cows. At first the government regulates what you can feed them and when you can milk them. Then it pays you not to milk them. Then it takes both, shoots one, milks the other and pours the milk down the drain. Then requires you to fill out forms accounting for the missing cows. *Bureaucratic socialism*: You have two cows. The government takes them and puts them in a barn with everyone else's cows. They are cared for by ex-chicken farmers. You have to take care of the chickens the government took from the chicken farmers. The government gives you as much milk and eggs the regulations say you should need. *Surrealism*: You have two giraffes. The government requires you to take harmonica lessons. (Jackdaw, *The Guardian*, 1 May 1996)

## 9.1 Introduction

**Government failure**

When government actions fail to promote efficiency

Market failure occurs when the competitive system is unable to deliver Pareto-efficient outcomes. **Government failure** is defined analogously, when the activities of the state lead to Pareto inefficiency. Some economists include distributional inequity in the list of failures achieved by markets. Similarly Wolf (1988), amongst many others, argues that 'distributional inequity' should also be included as a category of government failure, when the activities of governments tend to reward special interest or confer power and privilege on individuals without merit. Politicians who use public office to offer interest-free loans to cronies many not create a Pareto inefficiency, but there is still a failure, in the sense that such redistribution of wealth may not accord with any principles of social justice.

Government failure springs from two main sources. First, the procedures of a democratic system and rules of voting can lead to Pareto-inefficient outcomes, even in direct democracy. We examined this problem in Chapter 8. A second and perhaps more serious source of failure is the fact that the actions of the state are usually executed by an intermediary, the bureaucracy, and that in most OECD countries, democracy is not direct but involves representatives who enact laws on behalf of the voters. Bureaucrats and politicians act as agents of the electorate and, as we shall see, this produces inefficiencies (see Box 9.1 for a discussion of inefficiency). Now, if governments fail as well as markets, then normative policy analysis has to be comparative, weighing up the deficiencies of each, but it is important to remember that other alternatives to the market exist, such as families and the voluntary sector. In the final section of this chapter, we therefore take a brief look at these options and their weaknesses.

---

**BOX 9.1**

## What do we mean by inefficiency?

As we have seen in our discussion of the Coase Theorem in Chapter 5, there is a powerful argument that if an outcome is not Pareto efficient, then everyone can gain from reforming it. Taken to its logical conclusion, we end at the Panglossian proposition that 'everything which is, is efficient'. Often linked to the Chicago school of public choice, associated with the Nobel laureates Ronald Coase, Gary Becker and George Stigler, under this view, efficiency becomes an axiom, meaning that any apparent inefficiency must be due to the failure of the observer to include outputs or transaction costs or from mis-specifying the information available to the agents involved. For instance, cheating in the Prisoner's Dilemma does not lead to an *inefficient* result, because the cooperative outcome is viewed as not feasible, given the cost of drawing up a contract for its enforcement.

The Virginia school of public choice (which can line up Nobel Prize winners Douglas North and James Buchanan on its side) agrees that within a given institutional framework, Pareto efficiency must be an implication of rational behaviour, but argues that outcomes can be judged as inefficient if there are feasible changes in institutions which would yield Pareto improvements. For instance, Crew and Rowley (1988) state:

> Institutional constraints, however, may well impede the attainment of efficiency gains potentially available within a different set of rules or constitutional conditions. In such circumstances, what is is not efficient *if meta-level changes are feasible*. (p. 54)

This is the notion of efficiency adopted in this book, although it is not completely satisfactory since it leaves unanswered the question of why efficient institutional reforms are not pursued.

---

One point worth stressing is that the form of government inefficiency will depend in part on the constitutional structure of a country. The UK, for instance, has no written constitution, within a parliamentary system with two main and cohesive political parties elected on a first-past-the-post system. The actions of the European Union are constrained by enabling Treaties between the Member States and, for major decisions, largely by the rule of unanimity within the Council of Ministers, although this is changing. In the USA, power is split between the President, the judiciary (backed by the constitution) and the legislature, where party loyalties are weak. The result is that the US system has far more 'veto points' in the decision-making process than the European Union, which in turn has more such points than the UK. As a consequence, we might predict that lobbying would be directed mainly at the government in the UK, but be spread more evenly across the organs of state in the USA. Similarly, we might predict that it is both easier to initiate policy in the UK, compared with the European Union or the USA, and also to reform it, once the need for adaptation is apparent to the governing party. This dependence of behaviour on the incentives created by the constitutional framework of a country does not invalidate public choice theory, but it does mean that comparing evidence and theories across countries has to be done with a great deal of caution.

With a half-century of big government behind us, there is now an extensive literature on the theory and practice of non-market failure. This chapter cannot provide a full survey of the subject. Instead it should give you an introduction to this field, to its main models and insights, which are then applied in subsequent chapters, notably those on regulation and privatisation. However, the idea of government failure, just like that of market failure, is fundamental to an understanding of the economics of the public sector, so ideas introduced in this chapter permeate the whole of the book.

## 9.2 Agency problems

As we saw in Chapter 6, an agency relationship, a situation where one individual or group has to act on behalf of another individual or group, leads to inefficiency if: (1) there is asymmetric information between agent and principal, (2) the goals of the agent and principal differ, and (3) if costless observation by the principal of the activities of the agent is not possible. In representative democracy, there are several agency problems acting simultaneously, as Table 9.1 suggests. In fact, the picture is not as simple as presented in the table; there are agency problems within organisations, between the senior executives and their workers, as well as between organisations, and very often it is not clear exactly who the principals are. Ministers in government will owe allegiance both to their party and to the country at large, while the bureaucracy will be overlooked by both politicians and voters.

**Table 9.1**  Agency problems in government

| Principal(s) | Agent |
| --- | --- |
| Electorate | Government |
| Politicians | Bureaucracy |
| Bureaucracy | Regulated sectors |
| Senior ministers | Junior ministers and government MPs |
| Party supporters | Party politicians |

## Politicians and their parties

**Representative democracy**

Government through elected representatives rather than by direct voting

**Representative democracy** does not necessarily mean party political systems, but in most OECD countries political representation is organised through parties. The simplest model of political parties shows that the agency problem need not always lead to voters' wishes being distorted, in the sense of producing an outcome which matches the preferences of the median voter. In the basic Hotelling model there are five key assumptions: (1) everyone votes, with a single electoral roll; (2) there are two parties, each of which can adopt any political platform; (3) each party cares only about being elected; (4) upon election it carries out its promised platform; and (5) the fixed preferences of the electorate can be lined up along a single dimension and are single peaked. Under these circumstances, whatever the shape of the density function of preferred positions, each party adopts the preferred position of the median voter. Political competition thereby restores the pivotal role of the median voter revealed in Chapter 8.

The argument is illustrated by Figure 9.1, which shows the distribution of voters' preferred outcomes, along some scale. Assumption 5 means we can depict preferences in this way and, combined with assumptions 1 and 4, means that each voter will offer his or her support to the party whose platform is nearest. If the two platforms are L and R, for instance, the Left-wing party will get all voters to its left and those up to halfway between L and R, while the Right-wing party will get the remainder. Either party can increase its support by moving towards the other, which by assumptions 2 and 3 they will tend to do. In equilibrium, they both have platforms at M, the position of the median voter, and so both earn 50% of the votes, though of course it does not matter which is elected.

The evidence from Pommerehne (1978) on voting in Switzerland suggests that the median voter has only limited explanatory power in representative democracies. Relaxing the assumptions of the basic Hotelling model therefore seems desirable and, as might be expected, leads to more complex and more realistic predictions.

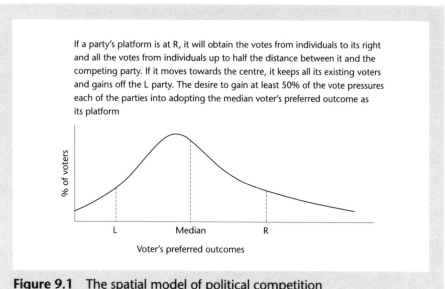

If a party's platform is at R, it will obtain the votes from individuals to its right and all the votes from individuals up to half the distance between it and the competing party. If it moves towards the centre, it keeps all its existing voters and gains off the L party. The desire to gain at least 50% of the vote pressures each of the parties into adopting the median voter's preferred outcome as its platform

**Figure 9.1** The spatial model of political competition

### Alienation (relaxing assumption 1)

Suppose your preferred platform is communist, should you vote for a social demo-cratic party? You may feel that it is not worth it, because it is only marginally better than the alternatives on offer. Thus, as parties move to the centre, they may lose voters at the edges. If the density function has a single hump and is symmetric and the party loses votes if it is more than a fixed distance from the platform, then the Median Voter Theorem will still hold. If however the distribution is asymmetric, the equilibrium will shift towards the mode and if there are a number of humps, the parties may end up away from the median and closer to one of the humps.

### Rationality of voting hypothesis (relaxing assumption 1)

If policies are close together, this reduces the incentive to vote and leads to some of the issues discussed in section 8.2. However, the Median Voter Theorem will still tend to hold, albeit there might only be one person voting in equilibrium.

### Credibility (relaxing assumption 4)

The agency relationship between a government and its electorate means that it is not possible for the latter to force an elected party to stick to its manifesto commitments. If a party can move its position at any time, we might not trust it to carry out its promises once elected. Thus in a system where no-one is exactly sure where the median voter is, so that initial party platforms were guesses which were then amended in the light of election results, convergence on the median voter position might be slow. Paradoxically therefore, if parties are seen to just care about the number of the votes cast for them and therefore bend their policies to the views of the electorate, they might receive weaker support than if they appeared committed to a particular policy. The idea of commitment is important in many areas of economics, but note one important point: if it is not possible to precommit a candidate or party to a particular policy, then the important component in elections may not be the plat-forms, but whether the candidates are trustworthy.

### Party workers and candidates (relaxing assumption 3)

Parties are more likely to be successful if they can energise resources. Resources are most likely to be attracted to a fixed platform. If individuals with extreme views (in the sense of further away from the opposing party) are more likely to supply resources (i.e. time and money) a party may be forced to trade off political popu-larity with voters against popularity with its own core supporters. This may pull both parties away from the median voter position. Similarly, if the candidate/ manifesto must be selected before being presented to the election and the vote over candidates is taken internally, the candidate chosen may hold the views of the median party member rather than those of the median voter. Against this, of course the party should anticipate that its candidate may not get elected in these circumstances and this will encourage it to amend its rules to favour the median voter position. The point here is that party members (a) want their party to be elected and (b) want it to hold to their preferred policies. In practice, there is a trade-off between the two which may lead to an outcome where parties do not compete for the median voter.

## Information and preference manipulation (relaxing assumption 5)

Elected parties have access to the immense resources of government; they can influence the supply of policy-related information to the electorate control; they can use the organs of the state to reward their supporters and build defences against potential challengers. They can also try to influence the preferences of pivotal voters, for example through party-political advertising disguised as government information. Dunleavy (1991) provides a taxonomy of means by which elected parties can attempt to influence future voting (see Table 9.2).

**Table 9.2** Influencing future voting

| Technique | Example |
| --- | --- |
| Partisan social engineering | Privatising social housing |
| Adjusting social relativities | Tax cuts for supporters, which increase future party funding |
| Context management | News management during wars |
| Institutional manipulation | Changing electoral boundaries; 'reforming' institutions which provide support for opponents |

What limits the government are constitutional safeguards, the scepticism of the electorate and the competing efforts of other parties, but the key point here is the relative power of government compared to the opposition, or as Downs (1957) put it:

> Every government is the locus of ultimate power in society, i.e. it can coerce all other groups into obeying its decisions, whereas they cannot coerce it . . . .. Thus the government is a particular and unique agent. (p. 23)

In other words, the power of government means that it can act more like a principal than an agent.

## Proportional representation (PR) (relaxing assumption 2)

Political competition under first-past-the-post electoral systems encourages existing parties to gravitate towards the middle of the political spectrum, but the method of converting votes into representatives also erects barriers to entry for new parties. This is primarily because at low levels of support a voter is extremely unlikely to see his or her vote turned into representation. In the UK for instance, the Liberal Democrats (and their predecessors) have regularly scored 15–20% of the vote in General Elections, but gained less than 5% of seats available in the House of Commons. PR removes or diminishes entry barriers, thereby encouraging competition between many parties with fixed positions, rather than between a few parties with variable positions. Despite this difference, William Riker (1962) argued that both types of electoral system would tend to yield two parties or coalitions of parties of approximately equal size. In his view, the value to being in government is a fixed prize, $P$, which must be shared amongst the $N$ members of the winning coalition. Once the coalition has a majority and captures $P$, any increase in its size dilutes the payoff of $P/N$ per member. This idea of 'minimum winning coalitions' has been extended by Axelrod (1970) who argues that coalitions will tend to be connected along the left–right axis. A coalition of communists and fascists would be unstable for instance. In practice, the two central parties (e.g. Socialists and Christian Democrats in many European countries) tend to be the largest, with a combined vote which far exceeds 50%, implying that the minimum-connected-winning coalition hypothesis adds little to the simpler theory proposed by Riker.

### Logrolling (relaxing assumption 5)

**Logrolling**

Vote trading amongst elected representatives and political parties

When a coalition forms with a 'you scratch my back, I'll scratch yours' philosophy, it is called **logrolling**. As an example, suppose that each agent's payoff from a school or hospital can be measured in pounds.

|   | School | Hospital | Neither |
|---|--------|----------|---------|
| A | 500 | –400 | 0 |
| B | –400 | 500 | 0 |
| C | –400 | –400 | 0 |

In pairwise comparisons, Neither wins over School by 2 votes to 1, Neither wins over Hospital by 2 votes to 1 and Hospital and School tie, but the important point is that the Neither option wins. However, if A and B make an agreement (or join a 'public expenditure party') to vote for each other's favoured option, then both hospital and school are built even though the total payoff is negative. Buchanan and Tullock (1962) therefore argued that this tendency for logrolling coalitions to form means that public expenditure will tend to be inefficiently high.

There are two important conclusions for this section. First, the agency nature of parties and government means that both have some power to pursue their own ends. Second, the relative power of government gives it some ability to change the rules of the game in its favour. But within the state there is another agency problem of potentially equal importance, which we now consider.

## Bureaucracy

The term 'bureaucracy' refers to the parts of the state responsible for implementing policy and for serving the government in its formulation of policy. Bureaucrats therefore include doctors in the NHS, teachers and the police as well as civil servants working in ministries such as the Treasury. As with any other individuals, members of the bureaucracy will have preferences which may not accord with the goals of the government of the day. These include personal advancement, salary, influence, sphere of control and any other factor which motivates human beings. Their motives need not be selfish. For instance, someone working for the Department of Transport may feel that road safety is undervalued by society and push for higher expenditure on this area. The members of the agency typically have knowledge about their area which is superior to that held by members of the public or by politicians. The net result is another form of government failure, because this asymmetric information gives them the ability to push the agency in directions which do not maximise social welfare and their motivation gives them the direction to go.

## 9.3 The monopoly bureaucracy

The simplest and most influential model of bureaucracy is due to William Niskanen (1968), who argued that members of the bureaucracy typically gain from increases in their budget, which they will therefore seek to expand. With monopoly power, they will be able to extend the size of their fiefdom until the government is indifferent between having the bureau and abolishing its functions altogether – this is known as **monopoly bureaucracy**. Suppose that the marginal benefit (MB) for the good supplied by the bureau is given by $MB = a - bQ$ and its average and marginal cost is $c$ (with $a > c$). The net benefit of output $Q$, illustrated in the top half of Figure 9.2, is therefore,

$$-\frac{bQ^2}{2} + (a - c)Q \tag{9.1}$$

and the optimal level of output of the bureau is at the point where net benefits are maximised or $MC = MB$. This leads to an output of $(a - c)/b$, shown as $Q^*$ on the figure. However, the bureau will set its output at the point where net benefits are driven down to zero, or $Q^M = 2(a - c)/b$. At this point, which is twice the optimal level of output in the case illustrated, the gains to society from producing up to $Q^*$ (the shaded triangle above the marginal cost line) are matched by the losses from producing from $Q^*$ up to $Q^M$ (the triangle below the cost line), so that society will be indifferent between having the service provided by the bureau or doing without altogether. In other words, the bureau has full monopoly control over its output.

Tests of this basic model are rare, but McGuire (1981) notes that one of its implications is that, provided $2c > a$, a 1% reduction in marginal cost should lead to a rise in output of greater than 1%. In Figure 9.2, this is suggested by the shift of the marginal cost curve $c$ to $c_1$ which pushes up output to $Q^{M1}$. Data on US government agencies suggests only small increases in output following cost reductions. Against this, Romer and Rosenthal's work (1979, 1982) on school budget-setting in Oregon, USA, provides some evidence that the budget-maximising model performs better than the

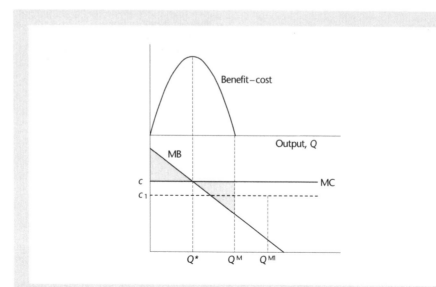

**Figure 9.2** Niskanen's monopoly bureau model

simple median-voter story[1] in explanations of public expenditure in at least one context. Within Oregon, maximum school budgets are set by law. Denote this by *F*. However, school boards can then propose a higher level, which is voted on in a referendum, with *F* as the alternative fallback level. Suppose that the median voter's optimum expenditure level is *M*, possibly larger than *F*, as in Figure 9.3 which shows the net benefit curve of school expenditure for the median voter. If $M > F$, a budget maximising school board will propose an expenditure of *B*, such that the median voter is indifferent between *B* and *F*, but with *B* higher than *M*. The theory therefore predicts:

1. if *F* is bigger than *M*, then no referendum will be proposed and the school board will set expenditure at *F*;

2. if *M* exceeds *F* a budget will be proposed (and passed in the referendum) at a level higher than *M*;

3. if *M* exceeds *F*, the proposed budget *B* will be *decreasing* in *F*.

The last, paradoxical point can be understood from further study of Figure 9.3, where a rise in the fallback level to *F'* means that highest expenditure acceptable to the median voter falls to *B'*. Meanwhile, the median-voter model predicts:

1. expenditure will be at *M*;

2. if $F > M$, there will be a referendum.

Note that this means that the median-voter model does not predict any link between either *F* and the act of having a referendum or between *F* and the proposed level, given that a referendum occurs. During the seven-year period studied, 57 observations involved no referendum, with the local school boards involved setting an average level of expenditure at 99.1% of the maximum legally allowed. This is evidence against the median-voter model, but when the authors used 111 observations to construct a regression model of the relationship between *F* and *B* across the school

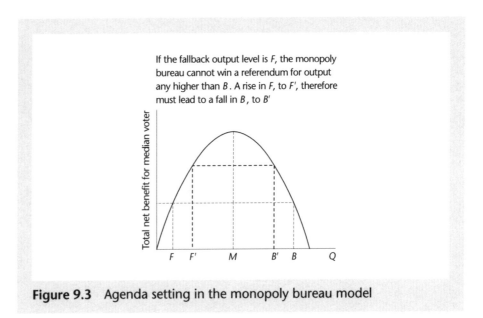

**Figure 9.3**  Agenda setting in the monopoly bureau model

---

[1] This work also provides evidence of the inefficiency created by the ability to control agenda setting.

districts where referenda were successful in 1971–2, they found a positive relationship, not the negative coefficient predicted by the budget-maximising model.

Thus neither the budget-maximising story nor the simple median-voter model perform particularly well. The authors argue that the results are compatible with the maximising model, provided there is uncertainty over voter turnout, but clearly the crudest Niskanen model is rejected.[2] Some further evidence is provided by referenda over changes to the tax base (i.e. $F$) itself. If $F < M$, the budget maximiser will actually want a lower $F$, so as to increase $B$ in any subsequent election. Voters would be expected to reject such a change, so that we would expect referenda on tax-base changes to be rare, even with uncertainty about voter turnout. Over three years, out of 300 school districts, only 31 tax-base referenda were executed, but none involved proposals to lower the tax base.

Wider support for the budget-maximisation model is rare. There are a number of reasons why the basic model performs poorly. First, it is wrong to see bureaucracies as monolithic, with policy made and implemented by one agent. Instead, the bureau is the usual mix of overlapping fiefdoms found in large private sector corporations. This means that simple budget maximising is wrong for a number of reasons. First, budget size is a public good for the organisation and, as such, individual managers will limit their supply of activities to this goal. Second, to some extent costs will be under the control of the bureau, so that the agency may prefer to see rises in costs (e.g. through overhiring, perks and salaries above market values) rather than increases in output, a form of inefficiency often called x-inefficiency. The bureau might therefore be technically and cost inefficient as well as distorting allocation. Third, most of the theory and evidence relating to bureaucratic behaviour relates to an American context, where arguably the greater separation of powers between legislature and executive and the weakness of political parties gives bureaux greater power, compared to Europe where governments typically have a much stronger control over the legislature.[3] Finally, not all managers and employees will actually share the goal of budget maximisation.

On this last issue, Patrick Dunleavy (1991) makes it clear that different types of agency will provide different types of incentives for inefficient behaviour. Some bureaux are *delivery* agencies, where the output of the agency is also the final consumption good of the programme. Hospitals provide an example of this type. Second there are *regulatory* agencies whose work consists of monitoring parts of the private sector. Third there are *transfer* agencies where most of the expenditure is simply passing through, only a relatively small proportion is kept back to cover staff costs and this is often only weakly linked to the size of the overall programme budget. For example, the budget of the Social Security Ministry is the entire expenditure on social security, but most of this just passes through the hands of the civil servants involved; they do not really spend it. They may gain satisfaction from *shaping* the total expenditure of the agency in particular ways rather than maximising it. Then there are *contracts* agencies (for instance part of the Ministry of Defence) which subcontract the actual production of the good and supervise its production. Thus warships are built on Clydeside, but their production is supervised by the Navy and the Ministry of Defence. Finally there are *control* agencies, such as the Treasury and the National Audit Office (NAO), whose functions are to watch over the activities of other bureaucracies. With these, as with regulatory agencies, a relatively high proportion of

---

[2] Essentially budget setters trade off the possibility of defeat at higher levels of $B$, against their gains from the larger budget.
[3] Of course this may reduce the power of bureaux, but increase the ability of governments to reward their own supporters.

the nominal budget will actually be spent in-house. Some support for this more complex picture of government agencies is provided in Dunleavy (1991). In particular, he argues that in the budget-maximising model, the core of a ministry should grow over time as civil servants attempt to extend their empire of spending. However, in the bureau-shaping model, it is control that is sought by the servants of the state, so that any expansion should take place away from the centre at the implementation level. Certainly, between 1961 and 1981, the proportion of the total UK labour force employed in the Civil Service fell from 2.7 to 2.6%, while the percentage employed in local government (including the National Health Service) rose from 10.1 to 15.6% (see Table 8.4 in Dunleavy, 1991). However, this is inconclusive, because it may just mean that the power to expand budgets was exerted by front-line delivery agencies, rather than the centre.

While evidence on the goals of public agencies does not support one single model of behaviour, a clearer picture of inefficiency is delivered by the literature studying the relative costs of public and private firms supplying similar goods. In an influential survey of over fifty studies into comparative costs, covering activities from banks to refuse collection, from hospitals to electricity generation, Borcherding, Pommerehne and Schneider (1982) found only two instances where public production is less costly than private alternatives and over forty in which the private sector supplies equivalent goods at significantly lower cost. Their conclusion, that the difference is driven by the degree of competition, so that the cost difference between public and private corporations is negligible when both operate in competitive markets, is denied in a later survey by Aidan Vining and Tony Boardman (1992), who use data from the 500 largest non-financial corporations in Canada to argue that both state-owned corporations and firms with a mixture of private and public shareholders had significantly lower efficiency as compared to private firms, even after allowing for the degree of competition.[4] They conclude that 'where competition is normatively appropriate, private ownership is preferable from an efficiency perspective' (Vining and Boardman, 1992, p. 226).

In summary, different kinds of agencies may lead to different kinds of distortions rather than excessive output. Greater x-inefficiency, damaging cross-agency competition and other activities may lower output below the figure predicted by Niskanen's model, but the main conclusion of public choice models of the monopoly bureau stands: it is difficult to align the incentives within the organisation with those of society as a whole.

## Limiting the agency problem

Agency is central to the issues of regulation and privatisation, so we shall explore it further in Chapters 21 and 22. For now, we note that limiting the problems created by agency means either reducing the degree of asymmetric information or bringing the goals of the principal and agent into line. The latter can occur through direct means (i.e. the preferences of the agent change to match more closely those of the principal), or indirectly via incentives.

### Measures to alter preferences

These measures include altering the preferences of civil servants through recruitment procedures which select for a desire to serve and through the establishment of a prevailing public-service ethos. In theory, altering preferences can solve the agency

---

[4] To the extent that public firms supply public and non-marketed goods, then the measures of efficiency used by Vining and Boardman (log of sales/employees and log of sales/assets) would be inappropriate.

problem. In practice obstacles remain; doctors socialised so that they put their patients first may seek ever higher levels of healthcare expenditure, while loyal civil servants may be manipulated by less scrupulous politicians. Mechanisms for altering the preferences of politicians are less obvious. Offering honours for public service and limiting the ability of retiring politicians to work for firms they previously regulated can filter out individuals aiming to use public office purely as a means to riches.

### Measures to reveal information

These measures include Freedom of Information Acts, but there are limitations; typically the monitoring of government activity is a public good and therefore likely to be under-supplied by individuals. Another approach is therefore the creation of agencies whose prime function is to monitor and evaluate the work of other parts of the bureaucracy. In the UK, for example, the NAO, established in 1983, is responsible for certifying the government accounts and for investigating the economy, effectiveness and efficiency of government departments and other public sector bodies. Meanwhile the Audit Commission (also established in the wake of the 1983 National Audit Act) is responsible for overseeing the work of local authorities and, since 1990, for reporting on the activities of the National Health Service. A third means of reducing asymmetries in information is to create competition in services. Provided returns to scale are not large, this can raise efficiency, since it makes comparative information available to the principal. Suppose the output, $y$, of an agent depends in part on effort $e$ and part on a random effect, $u$, which has an expected value of 0 (see Chapter 6). With two agents instead of one, if the random effect is common to both agents, then the difference in output will reveal which agent has supplied the highest effort. As the correlation between random elements falls, then it becomes less and less certain that the agent with the highest output has supplied the greatest effort. If there is no correlation between random elements, then incentive schemes based upon comparative performance become worthless.

### Measures to tighten incentives

These measures include performance pay schemes and privatisation, which expose the public firm to the stronger sanctions of the marketplace. To work, however, it has to be the case that profit maximisation and the public interest are at one, and this need not be the case if there is market, as well as government, failure. For politicians, raising the sanctions for malpractice and corruption and increasing the resources devoted to their exposure may limit some agency problems.

## 9.4　Rent seeking

**Rent seeking**

Investing resources to gain special privileges and hence monopoly rents

Rent is income from a service over and above its opportunity cost. A monopolist safe from the threat of entry obtains rent by virtue of its power over the market, as does a film star who works for $10m per film, but could only earn a pittance outside the movie industry. The term **rent seeking** (first used by Nancy Krueger, 1974), is a unifying concept in public choice theory, summarising the idea that individuals will seek to influence public policy so as to serve their own goals. The politician who enjoys high office and wishes to be re-elected is rent seeking, as is a coalition of garment manufacturers seeking to have textile imports curtailed. Rent seeking arises partially out of the agency problem, since the monopoly power of bureaucracies and governing parties enables them to exchange rents for political or financial support, but it can also be present in a direct democracy; witness the huge expenditures made by coalitions in the referenda of California and other US states.

In addition to the deadweight loss associated with any monopoly or other restriction granted by the government, the costs of rent seeking include the investments made in securing the rent. For instance, suppose GlobalTV and Euroscreen are two identical firms competing to obtain a monopoly TV network licence worth $M$. Both can put either $L$ (which is less than $M$), into lobbying or nothing. If one invests more in rent seeking than the other, it will gain the prize, but if both put in the same investment there is an equal chance of gaining the licence. Payoffs are then

|  |  | GlobalTV | |
| --- | --- | --- | --- |
|  |  | Invest nothing | Invest $L$ |
| Euroscreen | Invest nothing | $M/2, M/2$ | $0, M - L$ |
|  | Invest $L$ | $M - L, 0$ | $M/2 - L, M/2 - L$ |

This is a Prisoner's Dilemma with 'Invest $L$' as the dominant strategy for both players. The total cost of the rent seeking is therefore the deadweight loss from the monopoly plus $2L$. Notice that there is nothing in the argument stopping $2L$ being more than $M$, so that the gains to the winner need not offset the losses to the loser. In addition, to these direct costs we should add any costs attached to actions undertaken by government in response to rent seeking and distortions to the activities of third parties.

What rents are allocated? First, note that all rents imply losers as well as winners. It may be the case that although the losers forfeit rents, they gain from other aspects of the policy. For instance, the licensing of doctors raises doctors' incomes but leads (hopefully) to higher quality and greater faith in physicians. Second, the laws and regulations granting rents are often in the form of public goods; they are *inclusive*. For instance, the licensing of doctors or quotas on imports yield benefits for all doctors and all producers of goods in competition with imports. It follows that on both sides of the policy battlefield there will be free riding. Rent seeking by individuals tends therefore to be rare. Instead, the primary seekers of rents are interest groups, organisations such as Greenpeace, the British Medical Association, unions, farmers' associations and other coalitions which may have other reasons for their existence, but which also aim to steer public policy in a particular way.

## Interest groups and success in rent seeking

In most democracies, interest groups are a powerful force, but their activities need not be inimical to welfare. Gains from their existence include the information they discover and provide about the costs and benefits of policy options, as well as the monitoring of agencies and politicians. Furthermore, the policies supplied as a result of lobbying may well raise welfare if, for example, they lead to the reduction of negative externalities or the supply of public goods. In fact, an interest group is more likely to be successful in its aims when these yield a Pareto improvement.

The economic theory of rent seeking by interest groups has been developed by Olson (1967, 1982) (see Box 9.2) and Becker (1983), amongst many others. For an interest group to achieve its aims, it has to be stable enough to survive the long process of organising, raising funds and persuasion, but in order to be successful, it has to convince the electorate or politicians to put its policies in place and these two elements may conflict. Thus, a coalition is more likely to be stable if:

- Its membership is small.
- It supplies private goods to its members (thus reducing free-rider problems).
- It is homogeneous so that policy conflicts are minimised.
- Organisational costs are low, which is likely to be true with smaller and more homogeneous groups, but also when the coalition is urban rather than rural.
- The potential payoff per member from success is large and certain.

On the other hand, a policy is more likely to be passed:

- The closer it is to a Pareto improvement.
- If the coalition opposing it is weak.

Big coalitions therefore tend to be successful, but can be unstable, while smaller groups suffer less from free riding, but may not draw on wider support or indifference. The theory is therefore unable to predict whether it is consumer (typically large, small gains per person, heterogeneous) or producer groups (small, homogeneous, large gains per agent) which will triumph, but the empirical literature on the subject is dominated by examples drawn from producer groups rather than consumers, suggesting that free riding is the crucial factor determining the success or otherwise of a coalition. Alternatively, it may be that, for most policy changes, the vast majority of voters are intramarginal, in the sense that they are unlikely to switch support from one party to another over a single issue, whereas support from producer groups is more mobile and it is this which gives them their power.

---

**BOX 9.2**

## Rent-seeking example: The rise and decline of nations

In order to gain wealth an individual may invest his or her time into extending the production possibility frontier or into diverting resources from other individuals. The first form of rent seeking is productive for society, whereas the second is not, but Mancur Olson (1982) argues that, in a stable society, over time the relative cost of diversionary rent seeking drops and so resources are switched away from growth-producing activities. Unproductive rent seeking rises as coalitions merge and learn effective ways of obtaining rents, while other groups become entrenched opponents of the reforms which could lead the economy along more productive paths. Olson (1982) uses the relatively strong post-war performance of the German, Italian and Japanese economies to support his thesis, arguing that the destruction of political institutions in the defeated nations also destroyed the power of interest groups, whereas poor growth in the USA, Australia, New Zealand and the UK was in part due to the continuity of social structures in these countries.

Testing Olson's theories at the macroeconomic level is difficult, not least because indices of institutional stability and sclerosis have to be constructed. Choi (1983) constructs an index of sclerosis (IS) for eighteen OECD countries, which, for a given country, is increasing in the number of years since major disruptions, the size and the length of the disruption. Using per capita income growth from 1950 to 1973 as the dependent variable, $Y$, he obtains the following typical equation ($t$ statistics in brackets),

$$Y = 7.75 - 0.074IS \quad R^2 = 0.59$$
$$\quad (8.81) \quad (4.78)$$

While these results are clearly consistent with the Olson hypotheses, they are not *tests* of his ideas, since there are many other competing theories whose explanatory power is not examined. A more microeconomic approach is taken by Murrell (1983) who compares rates of industry growth in the UK and Germany, arguing that the gap between relative rates of growth in young and old industries should be higher in the UK (where interest groups have had a longer time to establish themselves in old industries) compared to Germany. In fact, for 1969–73 (the years studied), this was true in well over 50% of the cases studied.

One problem with the Olson thesis has been the dramatic downturn in the fortunes of countries such as Japan, Germany and France and the relative improvement in growth rates in the USA and the UK. In Olson (1996) he extends his arguments to deal with the eurosclerosis phenomenon, arguing that interest groups have reached maturity in the economies of continental Europe, but that, at least to some extent, the power of interest groups is cyclical; a long period of economic stagnation leads to their entrenched power being challenged by a reforming leader, such as Margaret Thatcher in the UK. This interpretation of events has not gone unchallenged, partially because it makes the theory almost immune to testing, but also for its broad-brush nature (see Paque, 1996, for instance for a detailed critique of the relevance of the theory for the post-war German experience).

## 9.5 Comparing institutions

In the last few chapters we have seen that both markets and government are subject to failure, in the sense that neither can supply the Pareto-efficient outcomes of competitive general equilibrium theory. This makes essentially comparative the normative issue of whether an activity should be undertaken or regulated by the government. Yet the options are often wider than 'government versus market' would suggest. Voluntary organisations such as charities and mutuals supply a significant proportion of services in most societies, particularly in the fields of healthcare and social services and of course much in the way of economic activity takes place inside the household and between members of families. These two other types of institution provide alternatives to government and profit-maximising firms.

That we need to consider these alternatives should be obvious, not least because of the increasing attention paid in political debate to the family and to activities produced largely outside the marketplace. For instance, the teaching of 'morality' to children occurs within schools (government production), within families (home production) and within many religious organisations. Similarly, the care of the elderly, the young or the infirm is partially carried out by the market, partially by the state, but mainly within the family. Policies to cope with the increasing number of elderly frail citizens in most OECD states therefore face a choice in the mix of organisations involved.

Application of economic reasoning to the family is contentious. Moreover, standard economic models of the household (e.g. Cigno, 1992) provide a poor guide to the kinds of economic activities which will be provided within families. Ben-Porath (1980) provides a useful alternative to the standard view, when he argues that families will exchange the sort of goods internally where the *identity* of the supplier is important. Why is this? We have already noted that an agency problem exists if there is asymmetric information and if the goals of the agent and principal differ. Altruism is one means by which the goals of principal and agent can be married and is therefore a particularly efficient means of solving agency problems where the scope for opportunism (sometimes called moral hazard with guile) is so extreme as to limit the value of any formal incentive system. But to trust an agent, the principal has to be confident of the agent's altruism. Ben-Porath argues that we can usually be more confident about altruism from family members than outsiders.

The second area of advantage for families again arises out of altruism. In Chapter 2 we examined the problem of merit goods, commodities where preferences do not accord with welfare. This distinction between preferences and welfare is not sufficient for the principle of consumer sovereignty to be abrogated; we have first to be sure that some other individual (the agent) has a clearer idea of the person's best interests and, second, that there is no agency problem, that the agent, given power over the individual's consumption, will not use that power to personal advantage. Family members are the people most likely to be able to solve this potential difficulty, to know what is best for a small child or a senile relative.

Examples of goods where identity is important therefore include some aspects of child-rearing, care of the elderly and the long-term sick. This does not mean that such goods must be provided within the family, nuclear or extended, but it does imply that any policies designed to alter the role of the state or the market in this area will also have implications for the provision of services within the family. A state which, for instance, lowers the resources going to carers, may increase the demand for its own nursing care services.

Not-for-profit organisations are a hybrid form, with their members and employees sharing some of the altruistic motives of family members, but within an institution closer to a traditional firm in its organisation. Since they are not subject to the full rigours of the marketplace, they are likely to suffer from the same kinds of internal agency problems as the state. Their advantage is therefore limited to those arenas where rightly or wrongly individuals would not trust profit-maximising firms: typically goods such as healthcare, where quality is difficult or even impossible to monitor by the consumer.

Families also face limitations: even the most extended families would struggle to run Siemens or Shell for instance, and if a wider proportion of economic activities were organised within families, then it is likely that they would be plagued by all the traditional forms of market failure. In summary we have four types of organisations (and many variants on each), each with their own limitations and proficiencies, reviewed in Table 9.3. Markets, for instance, have powerful incentives for efficiency, in that competition limits the scope for rent seeking within firms; governments can overcome the free-rider problems associated with public goods and non-depletable externalities, but suffer from agency problems.

**Table 9.3** Four forms of institutional failure

| Institution | Efficiency advantages | Source of main failures |
| --- | --- | --- |
| Markets | Limiting agency problems | Public goods<br>Externalities<br>Increasing returns<br>Asymmetric Information<br>Merit goods |
| Governments | Overcoming free-rider problem<br>Economies of scale | Preference aggregation<br>Bureaucracy agency problems<br>Agency problems with politicians<br>Rent seeking |
| Families | Altruism when identity is important | Increasing returns |
| Not-for-profits | Altruism | Agency within organisation |

## 9.6   Conclusion: the political marketplace

Analogies can be drawn between the operations of a government and a market. In both individuals exchange; in the market it is usually goods for money; in politics, policies are traded for votes or for support. Exchange in the marketplace is a source of efficiency, except when market failures intrude. Similarly, exchange within politics can yield efficiency, but it need not do so.

Government failure occurs for two main reasons: preference aggregation methods which do not (and cannot) guarantee that social choices maximise welfare and the agency relationship which exists between the citizenry and the organs of the state. This chapter has explored some of the forms and consequences of government failure, but you will meet many more in subsequent sections of the book. For instance, some further examples of rent seeking will be encountered in the chapters covering the environment and regulation; the choice of taxes will be influenced by politicians' desire to mislead the public about the tax burden. One fundamental implication of government failure which runs throughout the book is that market failure is a necessary reason for government intervention to be Pareto improving, but not a sufficient reason.

## Summary

- Government failure means the inability of the state to achieve a Pareto-efficient outcome and to redistribute income in a fair manner.
- Failure may arise even with direct democracy, but is more likely to occur with representative systems where asymmetric information between the citizens and their agents (politicians and bureaucrats) combines with the public-good nature of monitoring.

- Privatisation, agencies established to monitor other government departments, re-election for politicians and constitutional limitations may all act to limit the degree of government failure.
- The ability of a coalition to win acceptance of its proposal depends on the size of its support, and the losses faced by losers from its policy.
- The ability of a coalition to survive depends inversely on its size and heterogeneity, but positively with the size of the payoffs from success.
- These features suggest why coalitions of producers tend to be more successful than coalitions of consumers, so that regulation is biased towards protecting the interests of firms, and why policies, once enacted, tend to be difficult to reverse.
- Non-market failure is not confined to government. Institutions such as families and charities are also unable to achieve Pareto efficiency alone. Reforming or altering the incentives faced by one type of institution will have implications for all other types of institutions and these effects may well be unforeseen and long term.

## Questions

1. What are the key differences between representative and direct democracies?
2. Is it more productive to view government as the principal or as the agent?
3. In the Romer and Rosenthal model of school boards in Oregon, what would be the consequences of a rise in the marginal cost of education?
4. Why are most successful interest groups coalitions of producers?
5. When does the Median Voter Theorem hold true?

## Further reading

The best and most comprehensive survey of public choice theory is the book by Dennis Mueller (1988). Alternatives include Iain McLean's (1981) book, which is directed more towards politics students, and the slim volume by van den Doel and van Velthoven (1993), while for up-to-date applications see the journal, *Public Choice*. For a different kind of perspective on government, from a Marxist position, see Foley (1978). For the theory of bureaucracy, Patrick Dunleavy (1991) provides a useful overview, while Wolf's (1988) book looks at the boundaries between market and state. The paper by Mancur Olson in Crafts and Toniolo (1996) gives an up-to-date summary of his views on economic sclerosis in a European context. Eggertson (1993) surveys the emerging economics of institutions and Nancy Folbre (1992) provides an economic analysis of the family, together with a survey of the emergence of Welfare States in the OECD, from a feminist perspective.

# References

Axelrod, R. (1970) *Conflict of Interest*, Chicago: Markham. ˈ

Becker, G. (1983) 'A theory of competition among pressure groups for political influence', *Quarterly Journal of Economics* 98, 371–400.

Ben-Porath, Y. (1980) 'The F-connection: families, friends and firms and the organization of exchange', *Population Development Review* 6(1), 1–30.

Borcherding, T. (1985) 'The causes of government expenditure growth: a survey of the U.S. evidence', *Journal of Public Economics*, 891–901.

Borcherding, T., Pommerehne, W.W. and Schneider, F. (1982) 'Comparing the efficiency of private and public production: the evidence from five countries', *Zeitschrift für Nationalekonomie* 89, 127–56.

Buchanan, J. and Tullock, G. (1962) *The Calculus of Consent*, Ann Arbor: University of Michigan Press.

Choi, K. (1983) 'A statistical test of Olson's model', in D.C. Mueller, *The Political Economy of Growth*, pp. 57–78, New Haven: Yale University Press.

Cigno, A. (1992) *The Economics of the Family*, Oxford: Clarendon Press.

Craftz, N. and Toniolo, G. (eds) (1996) *Economic Growth in Europe Since 1945*, Cambridge: Cambridge University Press.

Crew, M.A. and Rowley, C.K. (1988) 'Towards a public choice theory of monopoly regulation', *Public Choice* 57, 49–67.

Downs, A. (1957) *An Economic Theory of Democracy*, New York: Harper and Row.

Dunleavy, P. (1991) *Democracy, Bureaucracy and Public Choice*, Hemel Hempstead: Harvester Wheatsheaf.

Eggertson, T. (1993) *Economic Behaviour and Institutions*, Cambridge: Cambridge University Press.

Folbre, N. (1992) *Who Pays for the Kids?*, London: Routledge.

Foley, D. (1978) 'State expenditure from a Marxist perspective', *Journal of Public Economics* 9, 221–38.

Krueger, N. (1974) 'The political economy of the rent-seeking society', *American Economic Review* 64, 291–303.

McGuire, T. (1981) 'Budget-maximizing government agencies: an empirical test', *Public Choice* 36(3), 313–22.

McLean, I. (1981) *Public Choice: An Introduction*, Oxford: Blackwell.

Mueller, D.C. (1983) *The Political Economy of Growth*, New Haven: Yale University Press.

Mueller, D.C. (1988) *Public Choice II*, Cambridge: Cambridge University Press.

Murrell, P. (1983) 'The comparative structure of the growth of the West German and British manufacturing industries', in Mueller (1983) pp. 109–131.

Niskanen, W. (1968) 'The peculiar economics of bureaucracy', *American Economic Review*, Papers and proceedings, 58, 293–305.

Olson, M. (1967) *The Logic of Collective Action*, New Haven: Yale University Press.

Olson, M. (1982) *The Rise and Decline of Nations*, New Haven: Yale University Press.

Olson, M. (1996) 'The varieties of eurosclerosis: the rise and decline of nations since 1982', Ch. 3 in N. Crafts and G. Toniolo (eds) *Economic Growth in Europe Since 1945*, Cambridge: Cambridge University Press.

Paque, K.-H. (1996) 'Why the 1950s and not the 1920s? Olsonian and non-Olsonian inter-pretations of two decades of German history', Ch. 4 in N. Crafts and G. Toniolo (eds) *Economic Growth in Europe Since 1945*, Cambridge: Cambridge University Press.

Peacock, A. (1980) 'On the anatomy of collective failure', *Public Finance*, 33–43.

Pommerehne, W.W. (1978) 'Institutional approaches to public expenditure', *Journal of Public Economics* 9, 163–201.

Riker, W.H. (1962) *The Theory of Political Coalitions*, New Haven: Yale University Press.

Romer, T. and Rosenthal, H. (1979) 'Bureaucrats versus voters: on the political economy of resource allocation by direct democracy', *Quarterly Journal of Economics* 93, 563–87.

Romer, T. and Rosenthal, H. (1982) 'Median voters or budget maximizers: evidence from school expenditure referenda', *Economic Inquiry* 20, 556–78.

van den Doel, H. and van Velthoven, B. (1993) *Democracy and Welfare Economics*, 2nd edn, Cambridge: Cambridge University Press.

Vining, A.R. and Boardman, T. (1992) 'Ownership versus competition, efficiency in public enterprise', *Public Choice* 73(2), 205–39.

Wolf, C. (1979) 'A theory of non-market failure', *Journal of Law and Economics*, 107–40.

Wolf, C. (1988) *Markets or Governments: Choosing Between Imperfect Alternatives*, Cambridge, MA: MIT Press.

# Taxation

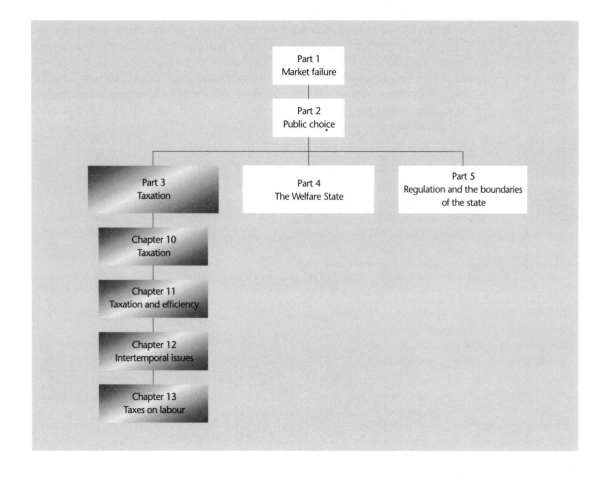

Part 1
Market failure

Part 2
Public choice

Part 3
Taxation

Part 4
The Welfare State

Part 5
Regulation and the boundaries
of the state

Chapter 10
Taxation

Chapter 11
Taxation and efficiency

Chapter 12
Intertemporal issues

Chapter 13
Taxes on labour

In 1997, the UK government took over £270bn from taxes and social security contributions. Expenditure must be financed and by far the largest part of it is financed through taxation, but there are many different forms of taxation and the use of each of them has different implications for incentives, efficiency and equity.

Chapter 10 provides an overview of the topic, defining the different types of taxes, setting out some of the main principles behind tax policy and describing the central features of the UK tax system.

Chapters 11 to 13 then look deeper into the impact of taxes on a market economy. The first of these three chapters is concerned with the issue of *incidence* – who really bears the burden of a tax, and the question of *efficiency* – how we measure the costs of taxes and how taxes can be designed to minimise those costs. Chapters 12 and 13 then apply these ideas to the savings decision and labour supply, respectively. As such, they provide the backdrop to the social policy and pensions and ageing chapters of the next part.

# Taxation

---

## Key concepts

| | | |
|---|---|---|
| direct taxation | incentives | evasion |
| costs of taxation | avoidance | hypothecation |
| indirect taxation | tax reform | globalisation |

---

## 10.1 Introduction

Taxation is an important political and economic issue. Few would regard paying tax as something that they like or choose to do, but most regard it as a requirement of citizenship. Tax contributions, at the very least, finance public services such as security and in many cases also pay for health, education and welfare programmes. In this sense, taxation is political. Political considerations determine the level of state expenditure and who should pay. The tax system is not only a means of raising finance to provide public goods, it is also a redistributive tool. It follows that the tax system can reflect ideological positions such as 'to each according to their needs, from each according to their means'. However, in the last twenty years, particularly in the UK and the USA, the dominant political philosophy has been that of the New Right. Central to this have been the notions of individual choice and freedom. The implications for the public sector have been a reduction in the involvement of the state in the economy and a commitment to reducing taxation. A further factor leading to change in the tax system has been the growth of the global economy. Multinational firms can choose where to locate and, in an attempt to make domestic industry internationally competitive, governments have responded by reducing the rates of Corporation Tax.

Given that taxes alter the choices made, governments may use tax policy to achieve objectives other than raising finance or redistribution. For example, in Sweden, tax policy is used to facilitate labour-market participation amongst mothers, whereas in Germany, tax policy is used to support a more traditional model of the family, by encouraging mothers to remain at home. Thus, tax policy may reflect elements of national culture and the values of society other than equity or individualism.

In the following sections, the desirable characteristics of a tax system and issues which have influenced recent trends in taxation are identified. This is followed by a discussion of the main forms of taxation and recent trends in taxation. We go on to examine the budgetary process.

## 10.2 Tax systems

The theoretical issues and the empirical evidence relating to taxation will be discussed in subsequent chapters in this part. In the discussion throughout this part, it will also be clear that taxes may influence the choices that consumers make and that some taxes may be set with this in mind, for example environmental taxes which place high taxes on fuel use in order to reduce consumption. Here, we shall concentrate on the design of the tax system.

### Desirable features of tax systems

In his seminal work on public finance, Musgrave (1959), drawing on the eighteenth century philosopher/economist Adam Smith (1910), identified a set of requirements for a 'good' tax system. Although not universally accepted, they represent a set of principles by which a tax system might be judged. The following represent some general features of tax systems which are usually considered desirable, given that a government needs to raise revenue.

#### Efficiency

**Efficiency**

An efficient tax does not result in a loss of Pareto efficiency; however, most taxes will result in a loss of efficiency and an optimal tax is one which is designed to minimise such losses

Taxation raises **efficiency** considerations. We know from Chapter 3 that Pareto efficiency requires that prices should reflect marginal costs, but most forms of taxation (Income Tax, expenditure tax) will actually drive a wedge between prices and marginal costs. So, unless governments tax endowments, commonly referred to as lump-sum taxes, taxation will result in a loss of efficiency. Our concern for efficiency reflects the principle that, given a revenue target, a tax should be designed to cause least harm. This issue will be explored in more detail in the chapters that follow.

#### Equity

Both horizontal and vertical equity represent value judgements. Horizontal equity requires that there should be equal treatment of those who are in relevant respects the same. Thus tax treatment should disregard gender, ethnicity or religious conviction. In general, tax systems do satisfy horizontal equity in these respects. However, individuals with otherwise identical characteristics face differential tax treatment according to marital status or age. A Married Couple's Tax Allowance, for example, creates differential tax treatment for single and married people. This is becoming less common across the OECD, although in some countries it remains an important part of government policy aimed at encouraging and supporting marriage and the family. Larger tax allowances may also be given to older workers, usually as part of a policy to protect against pensioner poverty.

#### Simplicity and low administrative cost

A desirable feature of a tax system is that it is simple and easy to administer; however, this is not always easy to achieve. The costs associated with collecting taxes will rise where there are more people or types of goods facing special tax treatments, if there are more differential rates and more tax-raising bodies (e.g. local, federal, central). It is this sort of concern that has resulted in support for simple taxes such as the 'flat tax' – a tax with a single marginal rate (see Hall and Rabushka, 1983).

---

**BOX 10.1**

## What is a progressive tax?

Many tax systems directly address the issue of vertical equity by using the tax system to redistribute income. This is often considered to be a political decision. A redistributive tax system generally uses progressive taxes, where the marginal rate of tax is greater than the average rate and where the average rate of taxation is rising. Three examples or progressive tax schedules are illustrated below.

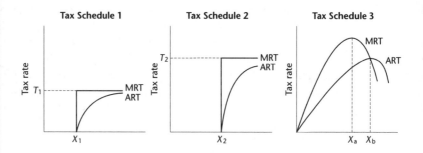

Both tax schedules 1 and 2 represent single tax rates, where the marginal rate is greater than the average rate. Under schedule 1, income levels below $X_1$ are tax free and income above and including this level is taxed at a rate $T_1$. The marginal rate of taxation, MRT, the rate at which the last unit of income is taxed, is constant for incomes above $X_1$. The average rate of taxation, ART = $T_1(X - X_1)/X$, when $X \geq X_1$, and zero otherwise, is always rising. Tax schedule 2 is characterised by a rise in the level of tax-free income ($X_2 > X_1$) and a rise in the marginal tax rate ($T_2 > T_1$). The ART is also rising, but at a steeper rate, so we can argue that this schedule is more progressive than the first. Finally, tax schedule 3 is non-linear. The marginal rate of tax rises and is at its highest rate when income reaches $X_a$. The ART is also rising when the MRT is rising, but continues to rise beyond $X_a$. The ART reaches a maximum level at $X_b$. Beyond this, MRT < ART, so this tax schedule is only progressive for $0 \leq X \leq X_b$. In contrast, a regressive tax is one in which the average rate of taxation falls with income, while a proportional tax is one where the average rate of tax is constant as income rises.

It is unlikely that a tax system will reflect all of these properties. A trade-off will occur between efficiency and vertical equity and also horizontal equity and simplicity.

## Tax base and tax unit

**Tax base**

Extent or area of economic activity on which tax is payable

The tax paid depends upon what is defined as taxable, the **tax base**. One approach to measure the means of a household is by its resources. The resources available to a household are the income that it earns, the interest or returns on any assets and the capital value of the assets themselves. These form the tax base under an Income-Tax scheme. Alternatively, an individual's means could be measured by his or her level of expenditure and consumption, thus, those with higher levels of consumption will pay more tax. Levels of consumption form the tax base for an expenditure tax. Whatever definition is used, the size of the tax base will also be affected by the size and extent of tax allowances (income-based) or number of goods covered (expenditure-based), this is discussed below.[1]

**Taxable unit**

The unit upon which the tax authorities assess and levy taxation

A second factor which determines tax liability is the definition of the **taxable unit**: household, couple or individual. Historically, women were treated in tax law as dependants and the higher tax allowance given to married men reflected the 'burden' of a wife. Whilst the Married Couples' Tax Allowance remains in most tax systems, its value has diminished and most households are given the option of choosing whether to be taxed individually or as a couple. By introducing marriage as a relevant issue in determining tax liabilities, the government can provide financial **incentives** to encourage particular family structures. In Table 10.1, we illustrate the effect of different tax units on overall liability. If total household income is £30,000 and the tax unit is the married couple, then tax liability would be £6,000. If the tax unit were the individual, then the tax liability would depend on levels of individual earnings. If both partners earn the same income, £15,000, they would each be liable for £3,000 and the total tax liability would be £6,000. Here, they are indifferent between being married and remaining unmarried. If instead, the woman was not earning but her partner earned £30,000, his tax liability would be £6,750, which is higher than if they were taxed as a couple. They now have an incentive to get married!

**Incentives**

The effects of taxes and other prices on behaviour

**Table 10.1** Tax effect of marriage

| Tax unit | Household | Earnings (£) | Tax on individual (£) | Total tax (£) |
|----------|-----------|--------------|-----------------------|---------------|
| Single | Anand | 15,000 | 3,000 | |
| | Beth | 15,000 | 3,000 | 6,000 |
| Single | Anna | 0 | 0 | |
| | Ben | 30,000 | 6,750 | 6,750 |
| Married | A and B | 30,000 | | 6,000 |

Figures based on a tax allowance of £3,000 per person, which is transferable when married, and a 25% tax rate

---

[1] A comparison of expenditure and income approaches is given in Chapter 12.

## Types of taxes

**Direct tax**

Paid to the tax-collection authorities by the taxpayer on whom the tax is levied

Taxes are usually classified according to point at which they are actually paid. In the UK, **direct taxes** are paid to the Inland Revenue by the individual taxpayer upon whom the tax is levied; for example in the UK under Pay As You Earn (PAYE), Income Tax is paid directly from a person's income. **Indirect taxes** are paid by consumers upon the goods that they purchase; the tax is thus collected by firms and retailers, who then pass on the tax revenue to the Customs and Excise; the main indirect tax in the UK is Value-Added Tax (VAT). National Insurance Contributions (NICs) are also taxes on income; the National Insurance scheme is discussed in detail in Chapter 16. NICs are paid as a percentage of earnings. They are made by both employees and employers as insurance against loss of income of the employees due to unemployment, ill-health and retirement. NICs are not collected by the Inland Revenue, but by the Contributions Agency. However, in the March 1998 budget, it was announced that in order to reduce the administrative costs for firms, the Inland Revenue will collect NICs in future.

**Indirect tax**

Paid to the tax-collection authorities by a third party who collects the tax from the taxpayer

### Taxation of income and wealth

These are direct taxes on households. There are often measurement problems, which reduce the effectiveness of these taxes. Although it should be easy to measure earned income – most people work and are on company payrolls – it is hard to calculate income for groups such as the self-employed, especially in small enterprises where salaries are not paid and it is difficult to distinguish between revenue, operating profits and income. It is also difficult to assess accurately levels of income in the less formal sectors of the economy, often referred to as the 'black' or 'parallel' economy, where employees are not on a formal payroll, hours might be low or highly variable and wage payments are made in cash.

Taxing wealth may prove to be even more difficult. In general, it is not so much the value of wealth that is taxed, but rather changes in the value which are actually realised. For example, if one owns stocks in a company, there are two ways in which the stocks yield value: the first is from any dividend paid out by the company, which is typically taxed as a source of income; the second is through growth in the stock market quotation. As a stock appreciates in value, although the wealth of the holder has risen, they only have that wealth at their disposal if they sell the asset. These are taxed as capital gains. Of course, there are other assets which do not have stock market quotation, such as property and art, where the value cannot be as easily measured. Such assets may be unique and there is no share price to indicate value. A further source of changes in wealth are inheritances and gifts. In the UK, Inheritance Tax can be avoided by transferring assets more than seven years before death.

### Taxation of goods and services

These are indirect taxes levied on expenditure by households; the revenue is collected by firms and then paid to the government. It is often easier to administer expenditure taxes than taxes on income and wealth because there are fewer problems associated with measurement. However, the issues raised by the black economy still remain, since not all transactions appear in company accounts. A general expenditure tax will result in a higher tax burden for those with greater levels of expenditure, but it is regressive; the average rate of tax is higher for those on low incomes because they allocate a higher proportion of their income to expenditure on goods.

---

**BOX 10.2**

## The following are issues that arise when collecting taxes on *income and wealth*

● *Which sources of income are taxed as income?*

Wages and salaries form only part of the returns to employment. Many employment packages include fringe benefits such as health insurance or pensions provisions and company cars. All OECD countries include income from employment, net business income, rent income and public pensions as taxable income, but exclude employer's contributions to health insurance and pension schemes. There is a more mixed treatment of other fringe benefits. In the UK, company cars have recently become subject to tax in response to arguments from the environmental lobby, and other benefits, such as workplace nurseries, are taxed too.

● *How should the tax liabilities of households be calculated?*

This is really a matter of identifying the appropriate tax unit: individuals, married couples or entire families. In each case, the incomes are aggregated according to the appropriate tax unit. In some cases, where couples have a joint income, but are taxed as individuals, the income is equally split and then taxed. When the tax system is progressive, this reduces their total tax liability. In general, OECD countries have moved towards a system of individual taxation.

● *What form should tax relief take?*

Generally, households can earn a certain level of tax-free income, known as tax relief. There are two types of tax relief: standard tax relief is available to all taxpayers and is independent of expenditure or family status, whereas nonstandard relief is given according to the level of certain expenditures, such as charitable donations, made by the taxpayer. Standard tax relief is given in several ways. Most countries employ a system of tax allowances, whereby a level of income is set, up to which no tax is paid. An alternative is a system of tax credits. Here each individual or household is allocated a tax credit which is deducted from the final tax liability. Under this system, it is possible that the value of the tax credit exceeds that of the tax liability; in such circumstances, the taxpayer would receive the difference. Finally, tax relief can occur in the form of a 0% starting rate of tax.

● *How many tax rates?*

Most OECD countries have simplified their income tax systems by reducing the number of tax bands. The top and bottom marginal rates have fallen in most countries.

---

### Taxes on organisations

These are mainly taxes on firms. Organisations such as charities are not usually liable for tax. Firms are taxed according to their income, that is the level of profit, by Corporation Tax. They are also taxed on their use of factors of production, notably labour and energy. It is possible to argue that governments never actually tax firms, because firms simply pass on any taxes to consumers. We shall examine this further in Chapter 11.

**BOX 10.3**

## The following issues arise when collecting taxes on *expenditure*

- *Should all goods be taxed?*

Under a general expenditure tax, all goods face the same rate of taxation, though in practice some goods may be exempt or zero rated. By imposing a zero rate on goods which constitute a high share of low-income budgets, the system becomes more progressive. For this reason food and children's clothing are zero rated in the UK.

- *Same rate for all goods?*

Governments may set lower rates in order to encourage certain forms of expenditure, for example books and newspapers are zero rated supposedly for educational reasons. Alternatively, higher rates may be set to discourage certain forms of behaviour. This is one reason why higher rates are levied on tobacco and alcohol.

- *How can rates be set to maximise revenue?*

The revenue raised by a tax may not rise as the tax rate increases. The reason for this is simple: in some cases people stop buying the good, so this effect will reflect the elasticity of demand. Since governments use taxes to raise revenue, it is tempting to set the highest taxes on goods with the least elastic demand. This is another explanation for the higher rates of taxation on tobacco and alcohol, although this may result in loss of efficiency.

A further issue relates to whether firms should be taxed at all, i.e. are firms really a separate entity? After all, most firms are owned by domestic residents who themselves are liable for the taxes on households described above. However, firms benefit enormously from public expenditure. For example, a high-quality infrastructure reduces the costs faced by the firm, thereby facilitating production and trade, and firms benefit from the availability of a healthy and well-educated workforce. This introduces one justification of taxation of firms. Also, while many firms are domestically owned, some firms are foreign owned and their owners are not liable for household taxes; levying taxes on firms ensures that all who benefit from public expenditure also contribute towards financing that expenditure. Finally, in many cases governments want to influence the decisions that are made by firms, particularly those relating to location, and so Corporation Tax is a valuable policy instrument.

A full OECD classification of types of taxation is presented in Box 10.5. This is the basis for international comparisons of tax systems, although domestic classifications may differ.

### Typical taxpayer

A typical taxpayer is entitled to some tax-free earnings, which is given by their tax allowance. In the recent past, tax allowances in the UK have made no allowances for children, but this will change with the new Working Family Tax Credit (WFTC – discussed further in Chapter 17). The WFTC replaces tax allowances and Family

BOX 10.4

## The following issues arise when considering taxes on *organisations*

- *Globalisation*
The global economy has made it easier for companies to avoid paying taxes in high-tax economies. As a consequence, the tax base is reduced and the tax burden is transferred on to the immobile rather than the mobile. This is discussed further in Chapter 24.

- *Impact of taxation on investment*
Investment can be encouraged if capital expenditure is given preferential tax treatment. In the UK, this is achieved by using tax credits or allowances for capital expenditure or capital depreciation.

- *Choice of factors of production*
Since a tax on a factor of production alters the relative price of the factors, it follows that the employment decisions of firms can be affected by the tax system.

- *Location of firms*
A key aspect of regional policy is to offer tax incentives, such as lower rates of Corporation Tax in a set-up year or larger allowances for capital investment, to encourage firms to set up in particular regions.

Credit and is intended to increase the incomes of households in employment with children and will be administered as a tax credit. Tax relief is given for certain work-related expenses (e.g. tools, subscriptions to professional bodies), some savings (pensions, PEPs/TESSAs/ISAs – see Box 12.1) and on mortgages (MIRAS, although this is being reduced). Married couples do enjoy distinct tax treatment; the Married Couples Allowance (MCA) is £1,830, but this is restricted relief and limited to 15%, i.e. £274.50; in the March 1998 budget it was announced that in future this will be limited to 10%.

The rates for Income Tax in the tax year 1998/99 are given below:

Tax year 1998/99
| | |
|---|---|
| Basic Personal Tax Allowance | £4,045 |
| 20% Income Tax | £4,045–£8,145 |
| 23% Income Tax | £8,145–£30,145 |
| 40% | £30,145 and above |

The National Insurance rates for both employees and employers are given in Table 10.2. These are the standard rates for employees who are not contracted out of the State Earnings-Related Pension Scheme (SERPS – see Chapter 18).

Combining both forms of taxation on income, we can estimate the weekly tax on income. Some examples are given in Table 10.3. As monthly income rises, so does the household tax liability. A married couple have a slightly lower tax liability than a single person.

**BOX 10.5**

## OECD classification of taxation

**1000 Taxes on income, profits and capital gains**
 1100 Individual taxes on income, profits and capital gains
   1110 On income and profits
   1120 On capital gains
 1200 Corporate taxes on profits and capital gains
 1300 Unallocatable as between 1100 and 1200

**2000 Social security contributions**
 2100 Employees
 2200 Employers
 2300 Self-employed or non-employed

**3000 Employers' payroll or manpower taxes**

**4000 Taxes on property**
 4100 Recurrent taxes on immovable property
   4100 Households
   4120 Other
 4200 Recurrent taxes on net wealth
   4210 Individual
   4220 Corporate
 4300 Estate, inheritance and gift taxes
   4310 Estates and inheritances
   4320 Gifts
 4400 Taxes on financial and capital transactions
 4500 Non-recurrent taxes
   4510 On net wealth
   4520 Other non-recurrent
 4600 Other

**5000 Taxes on goods and services**
 5100 Taxes on production
   5110 General taxes
     5111 Value-added taxes
     5112 Sales taxes
     5113 Other
   5120 Taxes on specific goods and services
 5200 Taxes on use of specified goods
   5210 Recurrent taxes
   5220 Non-recurrent taxes

**6000 Other taxes**
 6100 Paid solely by business
 6200 Other

**Table 10.2**  National Insurance Contributions

| Not contracted-out standard contribution rates | Employee | | Employer |
|---|---|---|---|
| | First £64 weekly | Over £64 weekly | On all earnings |
| Weekly £64–£109.99<br>Monthly £278–£476.99<br>Annually £3,328.00–£5,719.99 | 2.0% | 10.0% | 3.0% |
| Weekly £110.00–£154.99<br>Monthly £477.00–£671.99<br>Annually £5,720.00–£8,059.99 | 2.0% | 10.0% | 5.0% |
| Weekly £155.00–£209.99<br>Monthly £672.00–£909.99<br>Annually £8,060.00–10,919.99 | 2.0% | 10.0% | 7.0% |
| Weekly £210.00–£485.00<br>Monthly £485.00–£910.00<br>Annually £10,920–£25,220 | 2.0% | 10.0% | 10.0% |
| Weekly over £485<br>Monthly over £2,102<br>Annually over £25,220 | 2.0% | 10.0% | 10.0% |

Source: Contributions Agency Website

**Table 10.3**  Estimates of tax liability on income

| Monthly household income | £500 | | £1000 | | £2000 | |
|---|---|---|---|---|---|---|
| Weekly tax on income | Single | Married | Single | Married | Single | Married |
| Income Tax | £6.95 | £3.29 | £32.08 | £28.39 | £85.13 | £81.48 |
| National Insurance | £5.14 | £5.14 | £16.68 | £16.68 | £39.76 | £39.76 |
| Total | £12.09 | £8.43 | £48.73 | £45.07 | £124.89 | £121.24 |
| Marginal tax rate | 30% | 30% | 33% | 33% | 33% | 33% |

Source:
These calculations were made using the IFS model, How Did the Budget Affect You? IFS, Budget Homepage, July 1998. They do not include estimates of the tax relief associated with mortgages or pensions, nor estimates of indirect taxes

## 10.3  Taxes in the UK and other countries

### The contribution of taxes to the budget in the UK

Using the OECD tax classification, we can see from Table 10.4 that Income Tax remains the largest single tax in the UK, although by the early 1990s it accounted for less of total receipts than in the 1960s. Value-Added Tax (VAT – tax code 5110) and National Insurance Contributions (NICs – tax code 2000) each raise about one-sixth of revenue. The capital taxes, Capital Gains and Inheritance Tax, make a very small contribution. Taxes on companies, Corporation Tax and employer social security contributions, raise around 15% of total receipts. Revenue from Corporation Tax peaked in 1985, but by 1992 had fallen to the low levels of the 1960s and 1970s. Total social security contributions have remained fairly steady. Taxes on property and wealth have yielded less and less of revenue at each point since 1965. Finally, taxes on expenditure are gradually generating a greater proportion of government revenue.

**Table 10.4**  Proportion of total revenue raised by each tax type – UK

| Code | Tax | 1965 | 1975 | 1980 | 1985 | 1990 | 1995 |
|------|-----|------|------|------|------|------|------|
| 1100 | Individual income | 29.8 | 37.9 | 29.8 | 27.1 | 28.6 | 26.6 |
| 1200 | Corporate profits | 7.1 | 6.7 | 8.3 | 12.5 | 10.9 | 9.2 |
| **Total 1000** | | **37.0** | **44.5** | **38.2** | **39.6** | **39.5** | **35.8** |
| 2100 | Employee's social security | 7.2 | 6.6 | 6.7 | 8.1 | 6.5 | na |
| 2200 | Employer's social security | 7.6 | 10.3 | 9.5 | 9.0 | 9.9 | na |
| **Total 2000** | | **15.4** | **17.4** | **16.6** | **17.9** | **17.1** | **17.2** |
| **Total 3000** | | **0.0** | **0.0** | **4.2** | **0.0** | **0.0** | **0.0** |
| **Total 4000** | | **14.5** | **12.7** | **12.0** | **11.7** | **8.6** | **6.4** |
| 5110 | General commodity | 5.9 | 8.8 | 14.4 | 15.2 | 16.5 | 18.3 |
| 5120 | Specific commodity | 24.9 | 14.8 | 13.1 | 13.7 | 12.6 | 14.2 |
| **Total 5000** | | **33.0** | **25.4** | **29.2** | **30.7** | **30.5** | **32.5** |

Source: Revenue Statistics of OECD Member Countries (1963–93), Table 60 and IMF, Washington, Government Finance Statistics Yearbook, Table S2, p. 4, 1997
na = not available

## Comparison with other OECD countries

Compared with its European partners, Britain is a lower tax country. However, the tax burden in the UK still exceeds that of the USA and Japan. From Table 10.5, we see that in most OECD countries, including Japan and the USA, taxes have increased more rapidly since the late 1970s.

A comparison of the relative importance of direct and indirect taxes, social security contributions, Corporation Tax and taxes on wealth within the OECD is shown in Figure 10.1. Taxes on income and profits are the major source of government revenue in Canada, Japan, Sweden, the UK and the USA, whereas in Ireland, expenditure taxes provide the greatest source of revenue, while in France and Germany, social security contributions form the most important tax in terms of revenue raised. Taxes on property and wealth by comparison raise rather little revenue. There is no general movement within the OECD in the direction of taxing income rather than expenditure, though this is certainly the trend in the UK. Indeed, in Ireland, the reverse is true.

Multinational firms can organise their activities in such a way as to minimise their tax bills. One response of governments to the growing importance of multinationals whose activities are geographically mobile has been to reduce the rate of Corporation

**Table 10.5** Tax revenue as % GDP in OECD countries

|             | 1970 | 1975 | 1980 | 1985 | 1990 | 1994 |
|-------------|------|------|------|------|------|------|
| Australia   | 24.2 | 27.5 | 28.4 | 30.1 | 30.7 | 29.3 |
| Austria     | 35.7 | 38.6 | 41.2 | 43.1 | 41.3 | 43.2 |
| Belgium     | 35.7 | 41.8 | 44.4 | 48.1 | 45.1 | 46.5 |
| Canada      | 31.3 | 32.4 | 31.6 | 33.1 | 36.5 | 32.1 |
| Denmark     | 40.4 | 41.4 | 45.5 | 49.0 | 48.7 | 51.3 |
| Finland     | 32.5 | 37.7 | 36.9 | 40.8 | 45.4 | 47.2 |
| France      | 35.1 | 36.9 | 41.7 | 44.5 | 43.7 | 44.2 |
| Germany     | 32.9 | 36.0 | 38.2 | 38.1 | 36.7 | 39.2 |
| Greece      | 25.3 | 25.5 | 29.4 | 35.1 | 37.5 | na   |
| Ireland     | 29.7 | 30.0 | 32.4 | 36.1 | 35.3 | 37.1 |
| Italy       | 26.1 | 26.2 | 30.2 | 34.5 | 39.1 | 42.3 |
| Japan       | 19.7 | 20.9 | 25.4 | 27.6 | 31.3 | na   |
| Netherlands | 37.0 | 42.9 | 45.0 | 44.1 | 44.6 | 47.0 |
| New Zealand | 27.4 | 31.1 | 32.9 | 33.3 | 37.4 | 36.9 |
| Norway      | 39.3 | 44.9 | 47.1 | 47.6 | 46.3 | 47.0 |
| Portugal    | 23.1 | 24.7 | 28.7 | 31.6 | 31.0 | 32.6 |
| Spain       | 16.9 | 19.5 | 24.1 | 28.8 | 34.4 | 35.0 |
| Sweden      | 39.8 | 43.4 | 48.8 | 50.0 | 55.6 | 50.3 |
| UK          | 36.9 | 35.5 | 35.3 | 37.9 | 36.4 | 34.1 |
| USA         | 29.2 | 29.0 | 29.3 | 28.7 | 29.4 | na   |

Source: Revenue Statistics of OECD Member Countries (1963–94), Table 1
na = not available

Tax in order to entice them to locate in their country (see Table 10.6). The fall in the rate of Corporation Tax in Ireland is particularly noticeable and this is discussed further in Chapter 24.

## 10.4 Current issues

### Improving incentives

#### *Improving work incentives*

The belief that high rates of income taxation, particularly for those on higher incomes, act as a disincentive to work has become increasingly widespread in recent years, although, as we shall see in Chapter 13, there is little empirical evidence to support the view that Income Tax has a strong disincentive effect for those in full-time employment on income above benefit levels. However, governments in most countries have reduced their upper rates of Income Tax. In addition, there are concerns that taxation, in combination with the withdrawal of state support for those

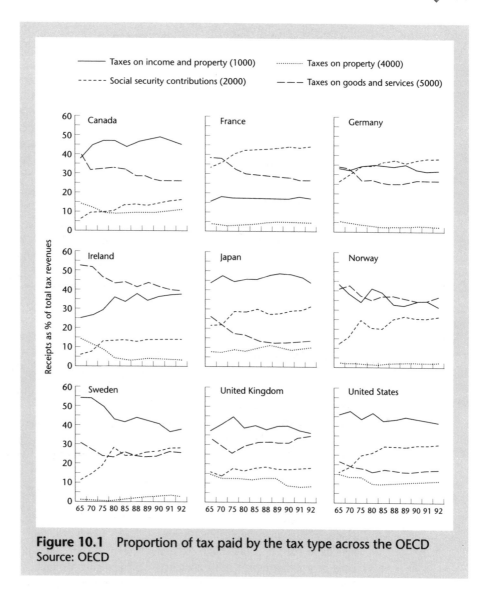

**Figure 10.1** Proportion of tax paid by the tax type across the OECD
Source: OECD

moving into work, results in very high marginal rates of taxation, often in excess of 70%, which creates a poverty or unemployment trap (see Chapter 13). One method of reducing this problem is to unify the tax and social security systems, as has been done in The Netherlands and Scandinavia, or to integrate partially the systems using refundable tax credits, which is the case in Canada and the USA and the WFTC scheme in the UK. A further option, which has been suggested in New Zealand and been the subject of an experiment in New Jersey, in the USA, is negative Income Tax schemes. These options are discussed in Chapter 17.

## Improving incentives to invest and save

Some forms of investment have been given a more favourable treatment under the tax system. For example, many countries provide tax relief on mortgages so as to encourage home ownership; tax relief is often also given on pension contributions.

**Table 10.6** Statutory corporate tax rates 1980–96

|           | 1980 | 1990 | 1996  |
|-----------|------|------|-------|
| Australia | 50   | 39   | 36    |
| Canada    | 46   | 38   | 38    |
| France    | 50   | 37   | 33    |
| Germany   | 56   | 50   | 45    |
| Ireland   | 45   | 10   | 10    |
| Italy     | 25   | 36   | 37    |
| Japan     | 40   | 40   | 37.50 |
| Spain     | 33   | 35   | 35    |
| Sweden    | 57   | 30   | 28    |
| UK        | 52   | 34   | 33    |
| USA       | 46   | 34   | 35    |

Source: IFS *Green Budget Summer 1997*, Table 5.1, 1997b

## Reconnecting taxes

In most OECD countries, governments have committed themselves to reducing the burden of taxation. However, the tax shares of GDP have remained relatively constant over the last twenty years. Part of the appeal to the electorate of the New Right agenda of reducing taxes was that more and more people resented paying taxes. One explanation of this is that the link between the collection of taxes and how the revenue is spent has been lost. Whereas historically taxes were raised to finance particular objectives, primarily war efforts, in recent times the public sector has grown steadily and taxes are collected for a myriad of purposes.

This can be illustrated in the UK. In the post-war period when the Welfare State was established, there was a consensus that the nation as a whole should take responsibility for rebuilding. However, in the late 1970s and early 1980s that consensus seemed to break down. To many it seemed that taxes disappeared into a black hole of government. The processes by which governments arrive at the levels of expenditure or priorities within government are not very transparent; all that the public see of the process is the result of Cabinet discussions at budget time.[2] Voters may also be unaware of the widespread benefits that they receive via the tax system. For example, in addition to the benefits associated with the Welfare State, tax subsidies are available for home and car ownership and university education.

The following are some of the solutions which have been put forward to address this problem.

### Hypothecation

**Hypothecated taxes** are levied on particular activities and the revenue raised is ring-fenced so that it can only be used to finance expenditure on that good. Thus,

**Hypothecated taxes**

Hypothecated taxes are levied on particular activities and the revenue is ring-fenced so that it can only be used to finance expenditure on that good

---

[2] Although this may change: a recent reform to the budgetary process is the replacement of the annual spending round agreeing financial settlements for each government department with three-yearly budget settlements. The aim is to avoid uncertainty and to allow departments to engage in longer term planning.

hypothecation may establish a closer connection between those who finance and those who use a public service. One example is the TV licence system in the UK, under which only users pay for the service and the revenue raised from the tax is used to finance the BBC. Another example is the tax on cinema tickets levied in the 1940s which was used to finance the British film industry.

The principle could be extended to other publicly provided goods such as the public highway system. The main users of roads are car owners and all car owners pay car tax. Proponents of hypothecation would argue that the revenue raised from the road tax should be earmarked for transport policy and perhaps used to finance future developments in the highway system. Furthermore, a truly hypothecated tax would reflect the extent and wear and tear of use and the result would be a much higher rate of tax for lorries and road haulage vehicles. One argument that is often put forward in the UK by the medical profession is that smokers and drinkers should pay higher rates of tax because they require greater medical care as a consequence of chest and liver complaints resulting from their consumption of tobacco and alcohol. By taxing the consumers, it would be possible to use the revenue to pay for the additional medical care that they may require.

However, opponents of a hypothecated tax argue that pure public goods cannot be financed in this manner. From our earlier discussion of public goods in Chapter 4 we know it is not always feasible or desirable to charge for a public good at the point of use. As a consequence, many public goods are financed through general taxation because only the government can enforce payment and overcome the free-rider problem.

### More direct democracy

Some of the above problems may be overcome if citizens feel that they can contribute more directly to the decision-making processes over levels of public provision. In California and in many other US states, citizens can propose and vote on tax legislation. Within Switzerland referenda are often held at canton level on revenue raising and expenditure decisions. The London Borough of Tower Hamlets also held votes on the level of its local tax rates. Decentralisation of government, returning the decisions over local levels of expenditure to local communities, may reconnect revenue raising to service provision.

## Taxation in the global economy

Changes in technology, greater capital mobility and communications have strengthened the trend towards the 'global economy'. In this environment, it is easier for companies to avoid paying taxes in high-tax economies. This is partly because the rate of corporate taxation influences location decisions, but also because globalisation has created a growing number of multinationals. These vast organisations with processes located in a number of countries can use transfer pricing, or report profits in offshore tax havens to reduce their tax liabilities. It is argued that such companies will be attracted to countries with tax regimes that levy a lower statutory rate and have a broader tax base (as compared with a narrower base with a much higher rate). This is partly because they tend to pay a lower share of their revenue in tax under these regimes, but also these types of tax regimes facilitate transfer pricing, whereby the multinationals shift income into low-tax regimes and shift high costs or expenditures which are deductible against tax into high-tax regimes. The impact of this is to transfer the tax burden on to the immobile rather than the mobile. This means that the burden of taxes falls on labour, consumers and national companies. This is discussed further in Chapter 24 although, as we saw in Figure 10.1, the proportion of tax revenue collected from corporations is low.

Other than reducing Corporation Tax and engaging in tax competition, governments can deploy the following means to deal with the problems of taxation in a global economy.

### Double tax treaties

These are bilateral arrangements between two countries, A and B, which set out tax liabilities for a company operating in both countries. Such arrangements do not eliminate the attraction to a company of organising its tax affairs to take advantage of low rates in particular countries, but a double tax treaty between high and low Corporation Tax countries may limit this activity, by requiring that in order for a firm to take advantage of the low-tax regime a certain proportion of its business activities must take place in the low-tax country.

### The 'California option'

In California, Corporation Tax is levied on the share of business that takes place in the State rather than the level of profits recorded. This means that the level of revenue is not affected by transfer pricing or offshore profits. This tax legislation is being contested by several large companies.

### Linking corporate tax to economic benefits

In this instance, the problem associated with globalisation is that decisions concerning the location of companies may be sensitive to the rates of Corporation Tax. One way around this may be to establish a clear link between the levels of tax and the benefits of government expenditure, such as the provision of public goods, transport system, infrastructure, a trained workforce or a low-crime area.

## Tax evasion and avoidance

**Tax avoidance**

The legal arrangement of one's financial affairs so as to minimise one's tax libaiblity

**Tax evasion**

The illegal arrangement of one's financial affairs so as to minimise tax liable

**Tax avoidance** is the legal arrangement of one's affairs so as to minimise one's tax liability. This contrasts with **tax evasion** which is the illegal rearrangement of one's affairs so as to minimise liability. It is commonly argued that whilst the rich taxpayer can employ an accountant to take advantage of legitimate methods of reducing tax liability (tax avoidance), the only means available to the poor taxpayer is the black economy (tax evasion). Although resources can be deployed to reduce the loss of revenue associated with evasion or avoidance, there is clearly a trade-off between the costs of detecting evasion or closing tax loopholes and the value of lost revenue. In fact, Peacock and Shaw (1982) argue that tax evasion does not necessarily result in lost revenue. This perverse result occurs, however, only if all of the income that is not paid in tax is spent in the domestic economy

In our discussion of the taxation of companies, we saw that the rise of multinational firms and increasing globalisation have meant that firms can arrange their affairs in such a way to be taxed in the country with the most favourable tax regimes. It is estimated that transfer pricing costs the US Treasury up to $35 billion a year. Studies in the UK found that in the early 1980s only two of the top twenty firms paid

Corporation Tax and that 40% of firms paid no Corporation Tax in 1980. The latter figure fell to 22% in 1985, but rose again substantially in the early 1990s. In fact, experience shows that Corporation Tax revenues are greatest under a regime with a wide tax base and low tax rates. The 1987 OECD report on international tax avoidance and evasion quotes the rather dated Gordon Report (late 1970s) on the rapidly increasing use of tax havens such as the Bahamas, Bermuda, the Cayman Islands and Panama.

In the UK, Tutt (1989) asserts that the corporate sector is the main source of lost revenue associated with tax avoidance. He argues that, whereas in the area of personal tax, avoidance is the preserve of the wealthy, this is not the case for the corporate sector. According to Tutt, the scale of avoidance rose throughout the 1980s. In the July 1997 budget, the Chancellor announced a number of measures designed to tackle Corporate Tax avoidance, focusing on loopholes which allowed tax allowances to be aggregated and transferred. It was also announced that the Inland Revenue will carry out a review and any tax loopholes identified by this review would be closed in future budgets.

Since tax evasion is illegal, it is difficult to estimate its extent. Several figures in the literature act as bench marks: 'The Chairman of the Board of the Inland Revenue suggested in 1979 that the black economy might be 7.5% of national income' and 'Smith (1986) . . . concluded that "an act of faith" was required to support any belief that the black economy could account for more than 5% of national income' (both taken from Kay and King, 1990).

The variation in the figures reflects the variation in the methods that are used to estimate the size of tax evasion. At a macroeconomic level, there is the comparison between actual transactions and the volume of notes and coins in circulation or discrepancies between the employment, expenditure or output measures of GDP. Micro-economic studies consider the reported income and expenditure levels for households, although it would be surprising if anyone engaging extensively in black economy activities would truthfully reveal their income and expenditure levels in a survey.

There is certainly a perception of a large black economy. This is in part because in recent years there has been a rise in the number of people in employment without an equivalent rise in the level of tax collected. Hakim (1989) argues that this has arisen because people mistakenly assume that everyone with a job is liable for Income Tax or NICs. Many of the newly created jobs, particularly in the service sector, are either badly paid or offer low hours and as a consequence the earnings are not above the tax thresholds.

## 10.5  Budgetary process

### Taxation in Britain 1979–97

The Conservative governments between 1979 and 1997 introduced a significant number of reforms to the tax system. These changes were in part driven by an ideological commitment to lower taxation, so as to give the individual greater control over his or her income and reduce the role of the state, and by the belief that taxes on income reduced work incentives. Over this period there were also substantial compositional changes in the form of taxation, a large reduction in the share of Income Tax, offset by a growth in VAT. After eighteen years in government, it is by no means clear that the Conservatives had actually reduced levels of taxation (see IFS, 1997a).

Total tax receipts in the UK in 1997/98 reached £300 billion or approximately £7,500 for every adult in the UK. Between 1978/79 and 1997/98, the tax burden as a share of GDP has risen slightly, from 34.25 to 36.25% (see Table 10.7). However, it could be misleading to take the period as a whole. Since tax receipts and the size of the social security bill are cyclical, we should recognise the pressure imposed on the public finances by the recession of the 1990s. In fact the tax level fell substantially between 1979 and 1993/94, but since then rates rose in order to improve public finances.

**Table 10.7** Government revenue in 1997/98 and 1978/79

|  | £bn 1997/98 | % of revenue 1997/98 | £bn 1978/79 | % of revenue 1978/79 |
|---|---|---|---|---|
| Income Tax | 71.8 | 24.0 | 20.2 | 29.0 |
| National Insurance Contributions (NICs) | 49.1 | 16.4 | 11.1 | 15.6 |
| Value-Added Tax (VAT) | 50.7 | 16.9 | 6.6 | 7.8 |
| Fuel duties | 19.6 | 6.5 | 2.8 | 3.8 |
| Tobacco duties | 8.4 | 2.8 | 2.4 | 3.7 |
| Alcohol duties | 6.1 | 2.0 | 10.4 | 3.5 |
| Vehicle excise duties | 4.5 | 1.5 | 0.5 | 1.7 |
| Council Tax | 10.6 | 3.5 | na | 9.2 |
| Other customs and excise | 6.4 | 2.1 | na | 2.6 |
| Capital Gains tax | 1.1 | 0.4 | 0.6 | 0.6 |
| Inheritance Tax | 1.6 | 0.5 | 0.4 | 0.5 |
| Stamp duty | 2.7 | 0.9 | na | 0.6 |
| Corporation Tax | 27.2 | 9.1 | 4.9 | 6.0 |
| Business rates | 14.6 | 4.9 | na | na |
| Petroleum Revenue Tax | 1.6 | 0.5 | na | 0.3 |
| Oil royalties | 0.3 | 0.2 | na | na |
| Other taxes and royalties | 5.5 | 1.8 | na | 3.5 |
| Total taxes and NICs | 282.1 |  | 59.9 |  |
| Other receipts | 17.2 | 5.7 | 4.5 | 11.7 |
| General government receipts | 299.4 |  | 64.4 |  |

Source: IFS, Table 1.1, April 1997 and Revenue Statistics of OECD Member Countries, 1965–80, Table 59
na = not available

## The 1979–97 tax changes in more detail

Having described the general trends in taxation associated with Conservative governments between 1979 and 1997, we can now look in more detail at the changes which have produced the greatest effect on revenue, namely those affecting households. These relate to personal Income Tax and the shift towards indirect tax.

## Fewer and lower marginal rates of personal Income Tax

In 1978, there were twelve tax bands with marginal rates rising from 25 to 83%. By 1997, there were only three: a lower rate of 20%, a basic rate of 23% and a higher rate of 40%. In the very first Conservative budget in 1979, the higher rates of Income Tax were reduced and the basic rate fell from 33 to 30%. The 1986 budget cut the basic rate from 30 to 29%. This was reduced again in the following budget to 27% and fell again to 25% in the 1988 budget. It was in the same budget that the Chancellor, Nigel Lawson, abolished all higher rates above 40%. Since 1988, there have been fewer changes in Income Tax. In 1992, a new 20% lower rate of Income Tax was introduced. In following budgets, the income band for the lower rate was increased and in 1995 the basic rate fell from 25 to 23%.

## A shift towards indirect taxation

In 1978, some goods were exempt from VAT, and VAT was levied at three rates: zero on necessities, 8% on most goods and 12.5% on luxuries. In the 1979 budget, the principle of a higher rate on luxuries was abandoned and all goods liable for VAT were taxed at a new higher rate of 15%. This trend was reinforced by the further increase in the standard rate of VAT in 1991 to 17.5 per cent. It was announced in 1993 that VAT would be extended to a previously untaxed good, heating fuel. This measure, planned for 1995, was roundly condemned as being highly regressive, hitting the poor and particularly pensioners. Rather than risk the unpopularity of charging VAT on heating at the full 17.5%, the Conservative Chancellor, Kenneth Clark, imposed a lower rate of 8%. Although the measure is regressive, it is seen by some as desirable on environmental grounds. The regressive effects could be countered by increasing transfer payments.

## Smoothing the profile of NICs

In 1978, NICs were collected at a single rate on all incomes between £43 and £325 (in 1989 prices). Over this period, two main packages of reform of the system of NICs were implemented. The underlying aim was to avoid sudden or large jumps in the marginal rates of contributions. In the early Conservative budgets, the rates of NICs rose. This exacerbated a problem of very high marginal rates of taxation faced by the low paid. In the 1985 budget, the Chancellor, Nigel Lawson, replaced the single rate of 9% on weekly pay of £43 and above with graduated rates of 5% on weekly pay £43–£75, 7% on weekly pay £75–£115 and 9% on weekly pay above £115. Although these reforms addressed the problem of very high marginal rates for those earning around £45 per week, they did create problems for those whose weekly pay was around the new tax thresholds. This was addressed in 1989 by a simplified system whereby all employees pay a rate of 2%; a rate of 9% is paid on weekly earnings between £43 and £150. Although the value of the thresholds has risen, the principle of this system remains, including the upper earnings limit on NICs. The effect of these measures on budget constraints is illustrated below in Figure 10.2 and is slightly adapted from Dilnot and Webb (1989).

## Local taxation

In 1990, local authority domestic rates, the traditional means by which local authorities raised finance, were replaced by the Community Charge or 'poll tax'. The government argued that it should be regarded as a tax which would increase the accountability of local government to their electorates. The Community Charge provoked

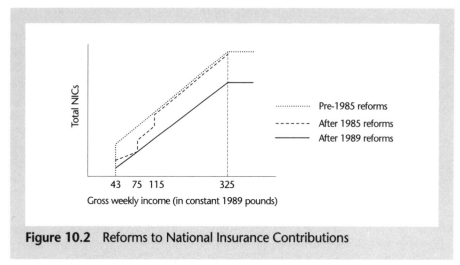

**Figure 10.2** Reforms to National Insurance Contributions

considerable opposition, leading to its withdrawal and replacement with a tax related to property values, the Council Tax, but with a discount for single-adult households.[3]

## Other measures

The real value of the ceiling for mortgage interest relief (MIRAS) was allowed to decline, and relief restricted to the base rate in 1991 (since 1991, the value of MIRAS has been further eroded). In common with other OECD countries, there was a change in tax treatment of married couples. Independent taxation of husband and wife was introduced in 1990 and since then the value of the MCA has fallen. New tax-favoured assets (see Box 12.1 in Chapter 12) were introduced in order to encourage savings: Personal Equity Plans (PEPs, 1986), exempting both dividends and capital gains from managed equity investments in quoted companies; Tax Exempt Special Savings Accounts (TESSAs, 1990), effectively exempting interest on time deposits. All are subject to restrictions on both the assets that can be held and the length of the holding period.

## A Labour budget

For most of its years in opposition, Labour supported a more progressive Income Tax system. However, it was widely believed that this commitment was the main reason that Labour were once again rejected by the electorate in 1992. After a fourth successive election defeat, Labour were forced to reflect on their policy in areas such as public finance and public ownership and the outcome was a change of emphasis in policy. Labour retained a commitment to 'social justice', but the means would be through opportunity and training, rather than a heavily redistributive tax system. Instead of 'common ownership' of the means of production, Labour argued that the state should work alongside and regulate industry. In addition, in order to defend themselves against the accusation that they were always a tax-and-spend party, Labour committed themselves to the existing levels of government expenditure and promised that there could be no rise in the basic rate of Income Tax during the first two years of a Labour government.

---

[3] Most of the opposition to the 'Poll Tax' took the form of non-compliance and demonstrations. One demonstration in Central London ended in violence and the government was faced with the fact that their reform of local authority finance had led to riots in the streets.

Given these changes, it was not clear how different a Labour budget would be from a Conservative budget. There was some uncertainty as to whether the newly elected government would actually depart from any existing policy. The main tax measures introduced are shown in Box 10.6.

**BOX 10.6**

## Main tax measures of the Labour budget 1 July 1997

- *Heating and lighting*
Cut in VAT on fuel and power from 8% to 5% from September 1997; gas levy reduced to zero from April 1998.

- *Industry*
Corporation Tax cut by 2%; the tax fell to 31% for large firms and to 21% for small business and tax allowances on new investment to double for one year.

- *Windfall Tax on privatised utilities*
The electricity companies to pay £2.1 billion, the water companies to pay £1.65 billion and other privatised companies (including BT, BA and BAA) to pay £1.45 billion.

- *Advanced Corporation Tax*
Abolition of 20% tax credit on dividend income for pension funds and other non-charitable companies.

- *Housing*
Mortgage Tax Relief fell from 15% to 10% from April 1998, costing mortgage holders £10 a month. Stamp duty up to 1.5% on house sales above £250,000 and to 2% for sales over £500,000. £200 million extra council borrowing for housing in 1997 and £700 million in 1998.

- *Motoring*
Prices up by 4p a litre on all fuels from 6pm on Budget Day. Car tax rose to £150 from 17 November 1997.

- *Duties*
Rise of 19p on a packet of 20 cigarettes from 1 December 1997 and an increase of 19p on a bottle of spirits, 1p on pint of beer, 4p on bottle of wine and 1p on alcopops, from 1 January 1998.

- *Tax relief*
Abolition of tax relief on health insurance for over 60s.

- *Tax avoidance*
A new programme was announced projecting a catch of £1.7 billion over four years.

- *Welfare to work*
Organised programme for unemployed people aged 18–25. Includes a £75 subsidy to firms to employ older long-term jobless and threat of withdrawal of benefits if opportunities are not taken up.

- *Lone parents*
£200 million allocated to help find work for 1 million parents whose 2 million children are at school. Also more generous allowances for those on benefit. Also a programme to train 50,000 people as child-care assistants.

### Likely effects of the 1997 Labour budget

- *Households*: Only a small proportion of the additional revenue raised in this budget comes from households. The main direct effects on households are the changes in duties on tobacco, alcohol and petrol, the rise in car tax and the reduction in MIRAS. When assessing the actual costs to households, it is not so much income levels but consumption patterns and household type that determine the cost. For example, pensioners will experience the lowest costs because they do not have outstanding mortgages, tend not to drive cars, are non-smokers and drink less. The biggest losers will tend to be two-earner couples with children, since such households have a mortgage and possibly two cars. Other budget measures, such as the Welfare-to-Work programme and the assistance provided to lone mothers, will have greatest impact on those in the lowest income groups. Finally, it is not clear what impact the new tax measures affecting the corporate sector will have on households. For example, will the Windfall Tax lead to a rise in prices charged by the utility industries?

- *Firms*: It was claimed that the aim of this budget was to improve investment and to achieve stability. According to the Inland Revenue, the cuts in Corporation Tax will benefit around 500,000 companies. The new tax levels will make the UK a more attractive place for multinationals, since it now has one of the lowest tax rates in the OECD. Small and medium-sized businesses will benefit the most, particularly from the doubling of the rate of capital allowances. It is hoped that these measures will lead to a boost in investment.

  The change in Advanced Corporation Tax (ACT) ends the system whereby tax advantages encourage firms to pay out profits in dividends rather than reinvest. Assuming that the response of firms to this measure is to reinvest profits, this is consistent with the notion of a budget which encourages investment. However, this change does mean a loss in income for the companies involved, estimated to be between 5 and 10% of pension schemes' income. Pension companies argue this will affect many holders of personal pensions who may find a shortfall in their final pension income. Those most likely to be affected are younger people who have yet to accrue substantial assets. People in company pension schemes are less likely to be affected because many of these schemes have substantial surpluses which have enabled companies to take holidays from contributions. Some have argued that some pension providers may be forced to top up pension contributions, which is at odds with the stated desire to improve investment. Overall, the fall in Corporation Tax and the change in capital allowances aim to improve the climate for investment and so the final effect is only likely to be moderated rather than eliminated by the change in ACT.

- *Environment*: The budget contains measures which are likely to have contradictory effects on the production of carbon dioxide ($CO_2$) emissions. The reduction in VAT on fuel is likely to lead to a rise in use, resulting in an additional 1.64 million tonnes of $CO_2$. On the other hand, within 'Welfare-to-Work' it is proposed that employment will be generated by a scheme to insulate the houses of pensioners, which may result in lower fuel consumption. However, the increase in both the price of petrol and levels of car tax will make car use more expensive. One additional measure intended to encourage the use of low emission was a reduced licence fee for vehicles which comply with this.

- *Welfare*: Several measures were introduced aimed at reducing the nation's welfare bill. The most significant of these is the 'Welfare-to-Work' programme, the primary intention of which is to reduce youth unemployment. The scheme will provide education or training for those without qualifications and employment experience for those with qualifications. There will be an element of choice in terms of work experience in the private sector, voluntary sector or as part of the environmental task force, but anyone refusing all of these options will face cuts in their benefits. A further measure aimed at reducing the number of long-term unemployed is an employment subsidy to any employers who take on someone who has been unemployed for more than two years.

Another set of policies intending to reduce welfare dependency are those relating to lone mothers. The proposals announced in the Budget are that lone mothers will receive help and support in training and finding employment, and, probably most importantly, that they should receive financial support for child-care expenses. The financial support will be an extension of the existing policy of disregarding a proportion of child-care expenses when benefit payments are calculated. The disregard will rise from £60 to £100 a week, the effect of which is to increase the level of earnings before benefits are withdrawn. It will not be compulsory for lone mothers to enter the labour market, although at the stage when the youngest child reaches school age, the mother will be required to attend a job search interview. At the job search interview, it will be stressed that the family will be better off if the mother is in employment. The Policy Studies Institute has estimated that the benefit is a rise in income of £50 a week. One possible difficulty associated with getting more lone mothers into the labour market is the well-documented shortage of affordable child care. The Chancellor addressed this with a first move towards a national child-care policy, by announcing that as part of the 'Welfare-to-Work' programme, 50,000 young people will be trained as child-care assistants.

### Choices for the future

Suppose that Labour want to reduce the tax liabilities for those on low incomes in order to further reduce the disincentives associated with moving from unemployment into employment. Several options are examined in Box 10.7; each involves a cost to the Treasury of £1 billion. Under the current system, the personal allowance is £4,045 and this is kept constant under all of the proposals. There are several other measures that could be used to achieve the same aims, for example an increase in tax allowances.

Naturally, further tax cuts would involve greater costs to the Treasury. We can see in Table 10.8 the costs of extending each of these proposals. The distributional effects of each of these proposals is assessed in the IFS *Green Budget Summer 1997*. It concludes that whilst Labour's favoured policy of introducing a 10% rate would result in a more progressive tax system, extending tax allowances would achieve similar results and be administratively less costly.

## 10.6 Conclusion

In this chapter we have seen that, over the last twenty years, governments are collecting the same or even a greater proportion of GDP in tax. The main change in

BOX 10.7

## Proposals to reduce Income Tax liabilities for the low paid

Proposal 1 – Cutting the lower rate to 19%.

Proposal 2 – Introducing a new lower rate of 10% which would be levied on the first £375 of taxable income and then imposing the existing 20% rate on income between £4,420 and £8,145.

Proposal 3 – Replacing the lower rate of 20% with a 10% rate and extending the income band on which the basic rate is applied. Now the 23% rate would be applied on income between £5,195 and £30,145.

These proposals are all illustrated below and compared against the current system.

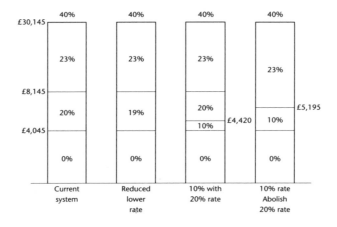

Source: IFS *Green Budget Summer 1997*, Figure 4.9, 1997b

### Table 10.8

| Revenue cost | Proposal 1 | Proposal 2 | Proposal 3 |
|---|---|---|---|
| | Reduced lower rate (%) | Income level at which starting rate 10% can be applied, with 20% rate (£) | Income level at which starting rate 10% can be applied, abolishing 20% rate (£) |
| £1.0bn | 19 | 375 | 1,150 |
| £2.0bn | 18 | 750 | 1,450 |
| £4.0bn | 16 | 1,600 | 2,100 |
| £8.0bn | 12 | 3,400 | 3,600 |
| £9.5bn | 10 | 26,100 | 26,100 |

Source: IFS *Green Budget Summer 1997*, Table 4.1, 1997b

tax in the UK has been the transfer of the tax burden from direct to indirect tax. Looking across the OECD, we find that the common trends are a simplification of the Income Tax system (reduction in the number of rates and cuts in the upper rates) and reduction in the rates of Corporation Tax in response to globalistion.

When discussing the desirable features of a tax system, it was argued that a tax system should be designed to minimise efficiency losses. This is an issue that will receive attention in subsequent chapters. We will consider not only how the dead-weight loss or excess burden of a tax can be measured, but also the circumstances in which these losses will be greatest. It was also mentioned that a tension may occur between some of the desirable features, for example between equity and efficiency. This trade-off equity and efficiency was first introduced in Chapter 3 and will now be discussed in more detail.

## Summary

- Desirable features of a tax system include minimal loss of efficiency, low administrative costs and that the system should take account of issues of both horizontal and vertical equity.
- Across the OECD most tax revenue is raised through taxes on households, Income Tax and expenditure tax.
- In response to the global economy, governments around the world have reduced rates of tax on business, so the level of tax revenue raised by Corporation Tax is falling.
- In the UK, the tax reforms of the Conservative government have led to a shift from direct towards indirect taxes; however, over the nineteen years of Conservative government (1979–1997) tax rates rose on average.

## Questions

1. Why might it be difficult for the tax authorities to design a tax which satisfies all of the desirable features of a tax system?
2. What link, if any, exists between the size of the tax base and the existence of tax allowances?
3. Critically assess the case for a hypothecated tax system.
4. Does globalisation reduce the revenue raising ability of governments?
5. Is Britain a low-tax economy?
6. What tax measures should the government implement if it wishes to reduce the tax paid by those on low income?

## Further reading

The best source for statistics on the level of taxation in the UK is the Inland Revenue and, for international comparisons, the OECD (1987, 1993 and 1994). The Institute for Fiscal Studies publishes excellent summaries and assessment of recent tax policy; see Giles and Johnson

(1994) and *Election Special*, March (1997a); the IFS also produces a budget publication, the IFS Green Budget (1997b), and has an excellent website. For a comprehensive review of the theoretical issues relating to taxation, see Devereux (1996) or Kay and King (1990), and for a useful discussion of the options for tax reform, see Keen (1991).

# References

Devereux, M.P. (ed.) (1996) *The Economics of Tax Policy*, Oxford: Oxford University Press.

Dilnot, A. and Morris, C.N. (1983) 'The tax system and distribution 1978–1983', *Fiscal Studies*, May, 4(2), 55–64.

Dilnot, A. and Webb, S. (1989) 'Reforming national insurance contributions: a progress report', *Fiscal Studies*, May, 9(2), 38–47.

Giles, C. and Johnson, P. (1994) *Taxes Down, Taxes Up: the Effects of a Decade of Tax Changes*, Institute of Fiscal Studies, Commentary, 41, February.

Hakim, C. (1989) 'Workforce restructuring, social insurance coverage and the black economy', *Journal of Social Policy* 18(4), 471–503.

Hall, R.E. and Rabushka, A. (1983) *Low Tax, Simple Tax, Flat Tax*, New York: McGraw-Hill.

IMF Government Finance Statistics Yearbook (1997) IMF, Washington.

Institute of Fiscal Studies (1997a) *Election Special*, March, London: Institute of Fiscal Studies.

Institute of Fiscal Studies (1997b) *Green Budget Summer 1997*, July, London: Institute of Fiscal Studies.

Kay, J.A. and King, M.A. (1990) *The British Tax System*, 5th edn, Oxford: Oxford University Press.

Keen, M. (1991) 'Tax reform', *Oxford Review of Economic Policy*, Autumn, 7(3), 50–67.

Mulgan, G. and Murray, R. (1993) *Reconnecting Taxation*, London: DEMOS.

Musgrave, R.A. (1959) *The Theory of Public Finance*, New York: McGraw-Hill.

OECD (1987) *International Tax Avoidance and Evasion: Four Related Studies*, Paris: OECD.

OECD (1993) *Taxation in OECD Countries*, Paris: OECD.

OECD (1994) *Revenue Statistics of OECD Member Countries*, Paris: OECD.

OECD (1997) *Revenue Statistics of OECD Member Countries 1965–80*, Table 59, Paris: OECD.

Peacock, A.T. and Shaw, G.K. (1982) 'Tax evasion and tax revenue loss', *Public Finance* 37(2), 269–78.

Smith, A. (1910) *Wealth of Nations*, Book V, Chapter II, Part II 'On taxes', London: Everyman's Library.

Smith, S.R. (1986) *Britain's Shadow Economy*, Oxford: Oxford University Press.

Tutt, N. (1989) *The History of Tax Avoidance*, London: Wisedene Limited.

# Tax Incidence and Efficiency

## Key concepts

| | | |
|---|---|---|
| elasticity | incidence | equivalent variation |
| compensating variation | producer surplus | consumer surplus |
| deadweight loss of taxation | | |

## 11.1 Introduction

We have seen that governments raise revenue by levying taxes on many areas of economic activity. In this chapter, we examine the effect of taxation levied in goods markets. Such taxes can be levied in several ways: either as taxes on particular goods, general expenditure taxes, taxes on factors of production, or as taxes on profits or revenue of firms. Even when a tax is directed at a particular area of economic activity, whilst the tax may be collected from the main agents involved, the cost of the tax may actually fall on others. It is for this reason that economists are concerned with who actually pays a tax, the tax incidence. For example, if there is a tax on labour, this naturally adds to the cost of production and is collected from the employer, so it may be paid through a squeeze on profits. Alternatively, the employer may employ less labour, thus passing the cost of the tax onto the employees, or respond by raising prices, passing the cost of the tax onto the consumer. Usually, the incidence of taxation is shared, so we examine which factors influence the distribution of this. A second key issue is that non-lump-sum taxation creates a gap between prices and marginal costs, and so results in a loss of Pareto efficiency. We also want to examine what losses in economic efficiency are caused by taxation. This discussion will inform our choice of optimal tax rules: how to raise a given level of revenue, creating the least distortion in the economy.

## 11.2 Incidence, partial equilibrium[1]

**Tax incidence**

The degree to which the imposition of a tax is reflected in the price paid by consumers and the price received by producers

We have just argued that economists are interested in the question of **tax incidence**, that is, 'on whom does the tax burden fall?' Let us take the example of a tax on a good. The marginal cost of production rises from MC to $MC_T$ and so the supply curve shifts up, as shown in Figure 11.1. The firm may pay the whole value of the tax itself. In this case, the price faced by the consumer would be unchanged; it may instead attempt to pass some (or all) of the tax onto the consumer. The extent to which as a result price rises reflects the elasticity of demand for the product.

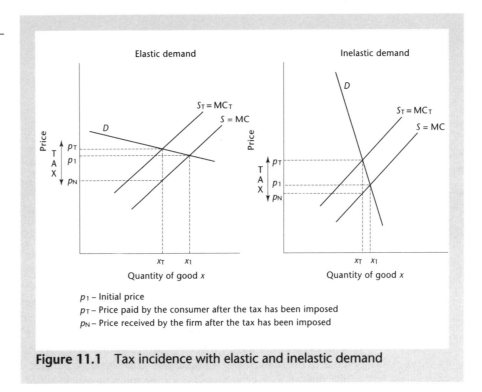

$p_1$ – Initial price
$p_T$ – Price paid by the consumer after the tax has been imposed
$p_N$ – Price received by the firm after the tax has been imposed

**Figure 11.1**   Tax incidence with elastic and inelastic demand

### Elasticities

When demand is inelastic, we know that if the price rises, demand does not fall by much, but if demand is elastic, even a small rise in price will result in a large fall in demand. It follows that the rise in price for the consumer price, once a tax is imposed, is greater when demand is inelastic than when demand is elastic. This is shown in Figure 11.1, where the rise in price for the consumer is the gap between the post- and pre-tax price, $p_T - p_1$, and the effect for the producer is the gap between the pre-tax price and the marginal cost of the post-tax output, $p_1 - p_N$. It is clear that the rise in price to the consumer is greater when demand is inelastic and that the effect on the producer is greater when demand is elastic.

From Figure 11.1, we see that when a tax is levied, the market price will rise and that the quantity traded in the market will fall from $x_1$ to $x_T$. This represents a loss in

---

[1] Students may find it useful to refer back to a microeconomics text (for example Katz and Rosen, 1998, Chapter 4 or Varian, 1996, Chapter 10).

both consumer and producer surplus. It follows that the loss of consumer surplus will be greatest when demand is elastic and the loss of producer surplus will be greatest when demand is inelastic.

Our discussion of taxes on goods has assumed that the tax is levied on producers and the effect has been captured in our simple models by a shift in the supply curve. But we have seen that the burden of these taxes may fall on both the producer and the consumer. Since the burden of the tax is shared, we can equally consider a tax on goods which is levied directly on the consumer. In our simple model, this would result in a shift in the demand schedule.

## Taxing inelastic goods

Although, in most cases, the incidence of taxation is shared, there are some cases where the cost falls entirely upon the consumer or upon the producer. When the supply schedule is perfectly elastic, the cost of the tax falls entirely upon the consumer (see Figure 11.2). The producer still receives the pre-tax price, $p_N = p_1$, and the consumer pays the higher price $p_T$; the increase in price $p_T - p_1$ is the value of the tax. In this case, there is no loss in producer surplus, only a loss in consumer surplus.

There is another case where the cost of the tax also falls entirely upon the consumer, which is when the demand schedule is perfectly inelastic.

There are also two extreme cases when the price paid by the consumer does not rise at all and the full cost of the tax falls on the producer. In Figure 11.3, we illustrate the example of a perfectly inelastic supply schedule, where the amount supplied is independent of price.

Finally, the entire cost of the tax falls on the producer when consumer demand is perfectly elastic. In this case, there is no loss of consumer surplus, only producer surplus. The consumer still pays the pre-tax price, $p_T = p_1$, and the producer receives the lower price $p_N$; the fall in the price received by the producer is the value of the tax, $p_1 - p_N$.

In Chapter 10, we commented that governments may choose to target inelastic goods for higher rates of taxation. When demand or supply is inelastic, the quantity traded is independent of the rate of tax. However, the cost of taxation falls entirely on the consumer if demand is inelastic and on the producer if supply is inelastic.

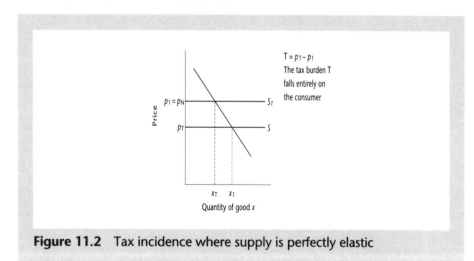

**Figure 11.2**  Tax incidence where supply is perfectly elastic

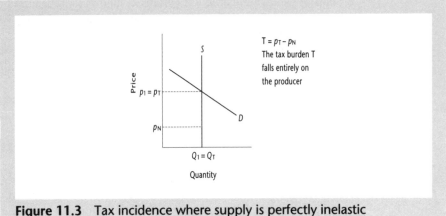

**Figure 11.3**  Tax incidence where supply is perfectly inelastic

### Short- and long-run effects

The impact of taxation on demand in the longer run will depend on the extent to which there are substitutes for the taxed good. In the case of a tax on a good, as the tax creates a price differential between the taxed good and substitutes, we would expect to see a displacement in demand away from the taxed good towards the untaxed, and hence relatively cheaper, substitute. The timescale over which substitution occurs reflects the stocks of the taxed good which the consumer currently holds and the frequency of purchase. Assuming that the consumer has no stocks and buys the taxed good frequently, we would expect a rapid response. Conversely, the response will be much slower if the consumer holds stocks of the taxed good or if the good is purchased less frequently. As demand changes, so we would expect to see the number of firms in the industry to adjust.

When we consider the longer run impact of a tax on a factor of production, we can see that similar considerations apply. The ease with which a firm can replace the taxed factor with relatively cheaper untaxed factors will reflect the degree of substitutability of the factors involved and the elasticity of supply of factors, that is, the extent to which the factors can be considered fixed or flexible factors of production. It is usual to think of capital and labour as substitutes and also to consider the stock of capital as fixed in the short run. A tax on either factor would leave demand for capital unchanged in the short run and the longer run effect would depend on the $MRS_{LK}$ (see Figure 11.4). In this example, we are assuming that the firm intends to produce the same level of output, therefore the demand for factors must be interpreted as *conditional*.[2] Further responses to the tax, which are not examined here, would be for the firm to reduce output, a scale effect, or to increase price.

### Specific and *ad-valorem* taxes

We have seen that the incidence of taxation will depend upon the elasticity of demand and that the impact in the longer term depends upon supply conditions and the relationship between the taxed good and other non-taxed goods. The next question to ask is whether the form of taxation makes a difference. We examine the impact of two types of taxation, specific and *ad valorem*.

---

[2] Demand for the factor is therefore conditional upon the given level of output.

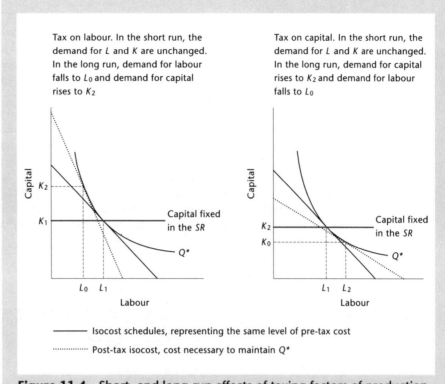

Tax on labour. In the short run, the demand for $L$ and $K$ are unchanged. In the long run, demand for labour falls to $L_0$ and demand for capital rises to $K_2$

Tax on capital. In the short run, the demand for $L$ and $K$ are unchanged. In the long run, demand for capital rises to $K_2$ and demand for labour falls to $L_0$

——— Isocost schedules, representing the same level of pre-tax cost

··········· Post-tax isocost, cost necessary to maintain $Q^*$

**Figure 11.4**  Short- and long-run effects of taxing factors of production

### Specific tax

The **specific tax**, $t$, levies the same level of revenue per unit regardless of the number of units traded, $p_T = p + t$. Under a specific tax, the demand schedule shifts in Figure 11.5 ($D$ to $D_{ST}$).

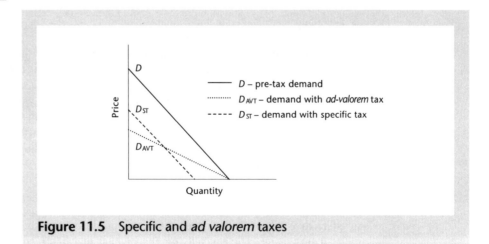

**Figure 11.5**  Specific and *ad valorem* taxes

### Ad-valorem tax

**Ad-valorem tax**

An *ad-valorem* tax is levied as a % of the value of units

Under an ***ad-valorem*** tax, $t$, the revenue per unit depends on the value of units sold, $p_T = p(1 + t)$. The value of the tax is highest when the price of the good is highest (conversely, the value of the tax is lowest when the price of the good is lowest), so the demand schedule swivels downwards from the axis where price is zero, $D$ to $D_{AVT}$ in Figure 11.5.

An *ad-valorem* tax is levied as a percentage of the value of the good being taxed. We want to compare this with taxes that we have already considered which are levied at a single rate, specific or unit taxes. In the competitive environment, in order to raise the same revenue, a unit or specific tax must be set at a higher level than an *ad-valorem* tax. In Figure 11.6, $D_{ST}$ and $D_{AVT}$ are set to raise the same level of revenue at $E_T$, the quantity traded has fallen from $x_1$ to $x_T$ and the price has risen from $p_1$ to $p_T$. Both taxes raise revenue of $p_T - p_N$. However, when we compare the rates at which each of the taxes are set as a proportion of the pre-tax price $p_1$, we find that the unit tax is $E_1E_{ST}$ and the *ad-valorem* tax is $E_1E_{AVT}$. So, the specific tax is set at a higher level than the *ad-valorem* tax.

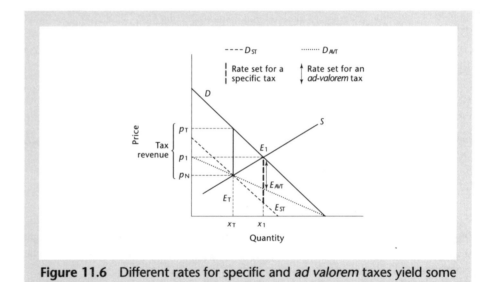

**Figure 11.6** Different rates for specific and *ad valorem* taxes yield some revenue

## Monopoly

The analysis so far has assumed a perfectly competitive environment; we now examine the effect of alternative market structures. The impact of the tax on price depends on the shape of the monopolist's demand and marginal cost schedules. If the demand schedule is linear and marginal cost is constant, the tax would cause a shift up in the marginal cost schedule, as in Figure 11.7. The new profit-maximising point is $E_T$, where $MC_T = MR$. The price rises from $p_1$ to $p_T$, and with a linear demand schedule $\Delta p = 0.5t$. The price rise under a monopoly may actually be smaller than that which occurs in a competitive market.

## Taxes on profits

An alternative to taxing the goods that firms produce is for the government to tax profits instead. Here the tax falls on the owners of capital, the shareholders. The

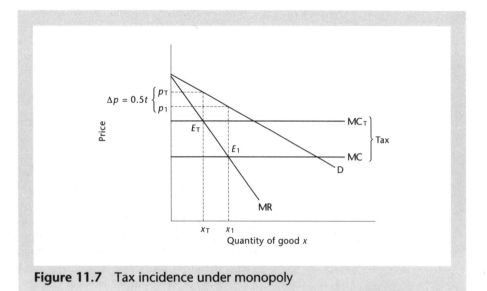

**Figure 11.7** Tax incidence under monopoly

impact of a profits tax on the behaviour of firms will depend on the objectives of the firm; for example whether they are profit maximisers or revenue maximisers.

### Profit maximisers

When a firm is a profit maximiser, any tax on profits, lump sum or proportional, will leave the profit-maximising level of output unchanged. This is shown in Figure 11.8. Pre-tax profits are given by $\pi_1$ and the profit-maximising level of output is $x_1$. A lump-sum tax would cause the post-tax profit schedule to shift down to $\pi_L$; the profit-maximising level of output is unchanged at $x_1$. Finally, a proportional tax would create the post-tax profit schedule $\pi_P$; again the profit-maximising level of output is unchanged at $x_1$.

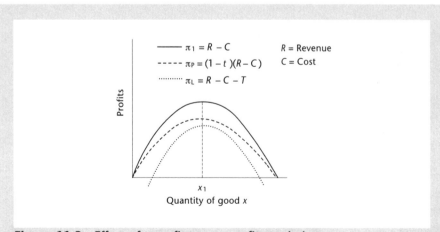

**Figure 11.8** Effect of a profit tax on profit maximiser

When a firm is a profit maximiser, a profit tax will leave the profit-maximising level of output unchanged. This implies that the price will be unchanged and so the cost of this tax falls entirely on the firm. The fact that this tax does not cause output or price to change implies that in this particular case, a tax on profits creates no excess burden. This is presumably the justification for the claim that Labour's Windfall Tax on the excess profits of the utility industries will not have an effect on consumers.

### Revenue maximisers

A firm which seeks to maximise revenue usually does so facing the constraint of achieving a minimum level of profits. This is usually interpreted in the following manner: a manager of a firm may see revenue as the best indicator of the market power and prestige of the firm; however, she or he is still accountable to the shareholders of the firm, whose primary concern is the level of profits that the firm makes. Hence, a manager can only pursue higher revenue if profits are sufficiently high to satisfy the shareholders. The profit constraint may or may not be binding. In Figure 11.9, the revenue-maximising level of output is $x_1$; at this level of output the firm makes a level of profit $\pi_1$. We also illustrate two minimum profit levels; the profit constraint $\pi_L$ is not binding, since the level of profit made at the revenue-maximising level of output is $\pi_1 > \pi_L$. So this profit constraint does not alter the revenue-maximising level of output $x_1$. However, the second profit constraint $\pi_2$ is binding; since the profit made at the revenue-maximising level of output is not sufficient, $\pi_1 < \pi_H$, the firm now reduces output to $x_0$.

We can now see that taxing profits may cause a revenue-maximising firm to change its optimising level of output. The optimising level of output would fall if the profit tax created a binding profit constraint. This is shown in Figure 11.10. Let us assume that the pre-tax profit of a revenue-maximising firm, $\pi_1$, were equal to the level of profits required by the shareholders, $\pi_C$, so the profit constraint is not binding. Under a lump-sum tax, the profits will fall to $\pi_1 - T < \pi_C$, and so the profit constraint is now binding and output will fall to $x_0$. Equally, under a proportional

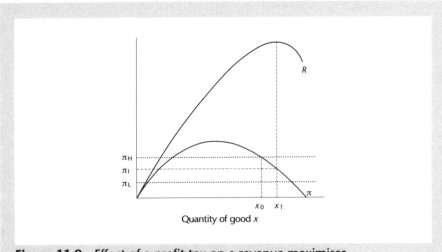

**Figure 11.9** Effect of a profit tax on a revenue maximiser

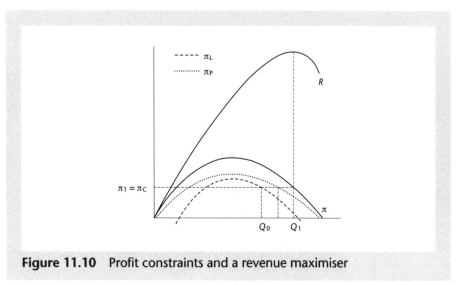

**Figure 11.10** Profit constraints and a revenue maximiser

tax, the profits will fall to $\pi_1(1 - t) < \pi_C$; again the profit constraint is now binding and output will fall.

## 11.3 General equilibrium incidence

Our analysis so far has been partial equilibrium, but usually when a tax is imposed there are effects in related markets. A tax on petrol, for instance, will have implications for prices and output in the transport sector as well as in the energy market. To understand the incidence and welfare implications in full, we therefore require a general equilibrium approach.

Figure 11.11 provides an example of the value of looking at the whole economy in the case of a tax on a good, X. Suppose that this is one of two goods produced in the economy (Y is the other) and that they are both produced using labour and capital, under conditions of constant returns to scale. Capital and labour are in fixed supply, so as in Chapter 2, the possible combinations of the inputs can be depicted in an Edgeworth box. In Figure 11.11, the curve connecting $O_X$ to $O_Y$ is the contract curve, the locus of technically efficient combinations of inputs. At $O_X$, all inputs are used in the production of Y and at $O_Y$, all resources are used in the production of Y. In the case shown, production of X is more labour intensive than Y, meaning that at any point along the locus, the labour to capital ratio ($L/K$) is higher for X than it is for Y. We know that in the standard model, a tax on X raises its consumer price relative to the price of Y, thereby lowering demand and the price received by producers; but what implications does this have for the factor markets? Suppose initially output was at A. Since the tax lowers demand for X, we must move down the contract curve towards $O_X$, say to B. At this point, the tangent between the two isoquants must be flatter than it was at A.[3] Now, in a competitive market, the absolute value of MRTS (the slope of the isoquants) will be equal to $w/r$, the ratio of the wage to the cost of

---

[3] With constant returns to scale, along any ray from the origin, such as $O_X$A, the slope of all the X isoquants must be the same. In particular the slope of the X isoquant at C must be the same as the slope at A. But then this means that the slope of the same isoquant at B must be shallower.

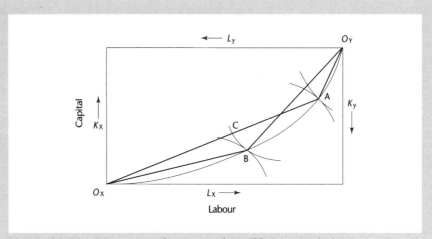

**Figure 11.11** Tax on good x, general equilibrium analysis

capital. Thus if the slopes of the isoquants are shallower at the new equilibrium, then wages must fall relative to the returns on capital. In short therefore, the burden of a tax on the labour-intensive good falls partly on its consumers (something we knew from partial equilibrium modelling) and partially on the suppliers of labour (something we can only deduce from general equilibrium reasoning). Meanwhile, owners of capital gain. These events are not surprising; the rise in the price of X reduces demand for it, thereby reducing demand for the factors used in its manufacture. Since it is relatively labour intensive, it is wages which fall relative to $r$.

**Stolper–Samuelson Theorem**

A tax on a good X which is factor intensive in factor A results in a transfer in income from the owners of factor A to the owners of factor B, because of the fall in the return to factor A

This result, known as the **Stolper–Samuelson Theorem** after its originators, provides a *qualitative* prediction of the effects of a tax on one commodity in a *simple* model. Other results are available for the qualitative effects of taxes on factors[4] and taxes on factors specific to one industry. However, often we wish to have *quantitative* predictions about the consequences of a tax in a far more *complex* world, where formal results are elusive. Economists have therefore developed more sophisticated models, most of which are now computer-based.

A prototype of this approach is the Harberger model (1962, 1974). As above, there are two goods X and Y, produced using two factors $K$ and $L$. Good Y is capital intensive and produced by the corporate sector; good X is labour intensive and produced in the non-corporate sector. Harberger uses the model to explore a number of issues of incidence, amongst the effect of the introduction of a corporation tax in the corporate sector, which he treats as a tax on the use of capital in that sector.

Recall from Chapter 2 that in a competitive equilibrium:

$$\frac{w}{r} = \text{MRTS}_{LK}{}^X = \text{MRTS}_{LK}{}^X$$

where $\text{MRTS}_{KL}{}^i$ is the marginal rate of technical substitution between capital and labour in industry, i. This produces the familiar locus of profit-maximising input combinations, $O_X A O_Y$ along which the MRTSs are equal for the two goods. A tax on capital employed in the production of Y raises the price of capital for that industry and leads to new profit-maximising conditions:

---

[4] Of course with fixed factor supplies, a tax on a factor falls entirely on that factor even in a general equilibrium model.

$$\frac{w}{r} = \mathrm{MRTS}_{LK}{}^{X}; \qquad \frac{w}{(1 + t)r} = \mathrm{MRTS}_{LK}{}^{Y}$$

where $t$ is the rate of Corporation Tax. With capital and labour perfectly mobile, each must earn the same net reward in each sector, so that $w$ and $r$ must be the same in both industries. As a result, in any new profit-maximising combinations of inputs, the MRTS is higher in industry X: $\mathrm{MRTS}_{LK}{}^{X} = (1 + t)\mathrm{MRTS}_{LK}{}^{Y}$. Point B in Figure 11.12 is one such combination and more generally the revised locus is $O_X B O_Y$ in Figure 11.12. As can be seen, apart from the endpoints, allocations on the locus are technically inefficient: less can be produced in total, compared to the no-tax outcome. Whether, overall, demand for capital rises or falls depends on two forces. First, the tax leads to a *factor substitution* effect away from capital and toward labour. Second, the tax raises the price of good Y relative to X. This leads to an *output* effect, resulting from the decline in demand for Y and rise in demand for X. Since Y is capital intensive, in this case demand for capital falls, but if X was the capital-intensive product, then the outcome would be ambiguous. In other words, the general equilibrium approach tells us that a tax on capital in one sector may in theory lead to a rise in the after-tax price of capital.

By assuming a constant elasticity of substitution production function and using the stylised facts of the American economy, Harberger (1962) was able to produce estimates of the actual incidence of capital taxation, but though useful for exploring the issues and as a pedagogical device, this basic model is obviously highly limited. Attention is restricted to a two-sector model, factors of production are considered to be homogenous, there are no unemployment or dynamic effects and all competition is perfect. No allowances are made for different skill levels of labour, nor for various types of capital. In practice, sectors of the economy where production is capital intensive tend to employ very sophisticated capital and a highly trained workforce, where labour and capital are complements. In sectors which are less capital intensive, the firm does not require a highly skilled workforce to operate the capital equipment, and in these sectors of the economy, labour and capital tend to be substitutes.

In section 7.6, we have already encountered an example of later developments in modelling incidence in a general equilibrium framework. There a *computable general*

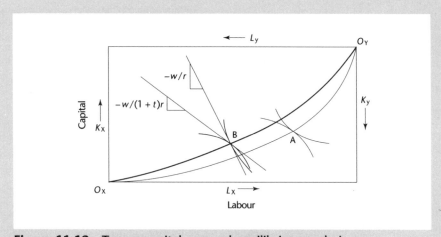

**Figure 11.12** Tax on capital, general equilibrium analysis

*equilibrium* (CGE) model was used to analyse the impact of the Clean Air Act on over twenty different sectors of the US economy. CGE models, which use computers to find numerical values for the general equilibrium, have been used in a wide variety of contexts, including analysing international trade treaties (see for instance Hertel, 1997), the consequences of global warming (see Chapter 23), as well as taxation.

To summarise: the general equilibrium approach enables us to trace the effects of government policy through the entire economy. As the cases chosen illustrate, doing this reveals the limitations of the partial equilibrium approach.

## 11.4 The costs of taxation

**Deadweight loss**

A measure of the loss of economic efficiency associated with the imposition of a tax

Recall, from Chapter 3 that the efficiency cost of distortionary taxation is measured using the concept of **deadweight loss** (DWL). Figure 11.13 reproduces the second way of representing this loss. In this figure, DWL is measured by AB, the difference between the revenue raised by the lump-sum tax, $T$ and the distortionary tax on $x$ of $t$ per unit. Up until now in this chapter and elsewhere in the book, we have measured the burden of taxation using the concept of consumer surplus, based on areas under market demand curves. In this section, we wish to reconcile these two approaches, in order to clarify the forces which determine the DWL.

Note first that in Figure 11.13 the value of the lump-sum tax has another interpretation. Suppose that the individual was asked to hand over some of their original income, $M_0$, in order to prevent the distortionary tax being imposed upon them. The maximum amount they would be willing to pay would leave them indifferent between facing this deduction and having the distortionary tax, $t$, imposed upon them. This amount is termed the **equivalent variation** (EV) of the price rise associated with the imposition of the tax. As can be seen from Figure 11.13, EV is equal to the

**Equivalent variation**

The change in income required to leave the consumer on the new indifferent curve, but without experiencing the tax change

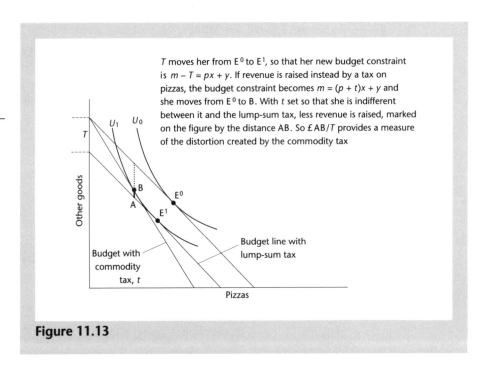

$T$ moves her from $E^0$ to $E^1$, so that her new budget constraint is $m - T = px + y$. If revenue is raised instead by a tax on pizzas, the budget constraint becomes $m = (p + t)x + y$ and she moves from $E^0$ to B. With $t$ set so that she is indifferent between it and the lump-sum tax, less revenue is raised, marked on the figure by the distance AB. So £AB/$T$ provides a measure of the distortion created by the commodity tax

**Figure 11.13**

lump-sum tax, because deducting $T$ places the individual on the indifference curve, $U_1$. Since EV = $T$ it follows that DWL is also the difference between EV and $tx_1$.

Figure 11.14 shows another way of representing EV. The top half of the figure is almost identical to Figure 11.13, except that to keep it simple, much of the labelling has been omitted. In the bottom portion of the figure, the market demand, *DD*, is derived in the standard way. So that, at a price $p + t$, for instance, demand is $x_1$. The curve through A and C, meanwhile, is a **compensated demand** curve, defined as the demand for X where the consumer is compensated for price changes so as to keep them on the same indifference curve, in this case, $U_1$. Tax revenue is $tx_1$ or the area HAFG, so that as usual the loss of consumer surplus from the distortionary tax is the area ABF. What about the DWL?

In fact, the DWL for the tax rise is just the area ACF. To see this, consider a marginal rise in the price from $p$ of 1 unit. Compensation of $x_0^c$, the extra cost of buying the original bundle, enables the individual to stay on the same indifference curve. Similarly, for another price rise of 1 unit, the compensation required is given by the compensated demand at that price. Increasing the price until we reach $p + t$ reveals the total amount of compensation required to be the area GCAH. However, the tax raises available revenue of only HAGF, so that even if this tax revenue is given to the consumer she or he is worse off by ACF, the deadweight loss.

There are a number of general lessons to be learnt from Figure 11.14. First, DWL and the loss of consumer surplus are not exactly equal. Second, for a rise in taxation with a normal good, ABF always exceeds ACF, so that the loss of consumer surplus is

**Compensated demand**

The substitution effect-only demand schedule, measuring the change in demand caused by the change in relative price, but at constant utility

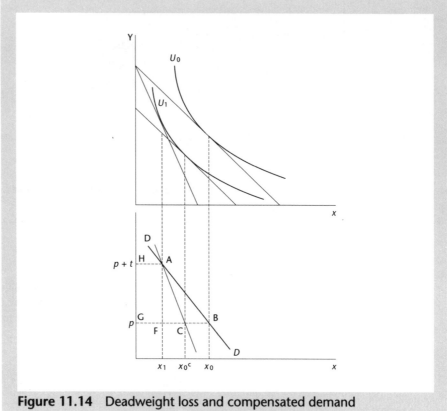

**Figure 11.14** Deadweight loss and compensated demand

an overestimate of the cost of distortionary taxation. Third, the difference between the two areas is due to the difference between the points B and C, which, in turn, is due to the difference between $x_0^c$, the demand for $x$ on the compensated demand curve at price $p$, and $x_0$ the market demand at the same price. Since the cause of the difference between the two curves is the fact that income is higher with the market demand curve, the difference between B and C is therefore due to the income effect. If the income elasticity of demand for $x$ is small, therefore, or $x$ occupies only a small place in the budget, then B and C will be sufficiently close together for the loss of consumer surplus to be an accurate approximation to the DWL.[5] Fourth, the area DWL is equal to the price change multiplied by the change in compensated demand caused by the price change. So DWL is obviously bigger when the tax is greater, but it is also increasing in the size of the substitution effect. If a good has few close substitutes (e.g. housing or food), then the substitution effect will be small and so will be the deadweight cost of distortionary taxes. Conversely, if the good has many substitutes (e.g. one brand of confectionary bar), the substitution effect will be larger, the effect on demand of changing price will therefore also be larger and consequently so will be the DWL. Box 11.1 shows how approximate values of DWL can be calculated.

**BOX 11.1**

## Estimating the size of the deadweight loss

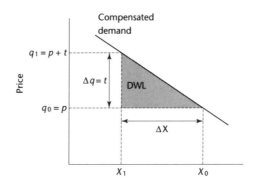

Recall that Δ denotes change, so $\Delta q$ is the change in price and $\Delta x$ is the change in quantity.

### Approximations

We have seen that the DWL of a tax is given by an area under the compensated demand curve, as in Box 11.1, but it would be more useful if we could calculate it for specific instances. In Box 11.1, DWL for a tax which raises the price from $p_0$ to $(p_0 + t)$ is given by the shaded triangle under the compensated demand curve:

$$\text{DWL} = \tfrac{1}{2}(q_1 - q_0)(x_0 - x_1) = -\tfrac{1}{2}\Delta q \Delta x$$

where as usual the Δ mean 'change in'. To make sense of this formula, we need to

[5] See Willig (1976).

replace the change in price, $\Delta q$, and the change in quantity, $\Delta X$. Now, $\Delta q$ is just the tax, $t$. Meanwhile, by definition, the own-price elasticity of the compensated demand curve is $\varepsilon^c = \left| \dfrac{\partial x}{\partial q} \dfrac{q}{x} \right|$, but $\dfrac{\Delta x}{\Delta q} \approx \dfrac{\partial x}{\partial q}$ so for small changes in the price, $q.\Delta x/x.\Delta q = -\varepsilon^c$ or $\Delta x = -\Delta \varepsilon^c X \Delta q/q$. Putting this together:

$$\text{DWL} = \tfrac{1}{2} \left( \frac{t}{q} \right) xt\varepsilon^c = \tfrac{1}{2} \left( \frac{t}{P+t} \right) \varepsilon^c = \tfrac{1}{2}*tax\ rate*compensated\ elasticity*revenue$$

since $R$ is just $tX$. It is easy to see from this formula that the DWL is higher when revenue is greater, when the tax rate is bigger and when the compensated elasticity is large. Since revenue is increasing in the tax rate (at least for small taxes), then the DWL is approximately a function of the *square* of the tax rate, meaning that the efficiency loss from a tax rate of 20% is roughly four times the loss from a rate of 10%.

We can produce a similar approximation for the MCPF, the marginal cost of public funds. Recall that this is the extra DWL created when £1 of extra revenue is raised (see Box 11.2).

---

**BOX 11.2**

# The marginal cost of social funds

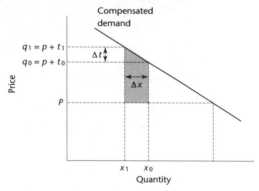

The shaded area in the figure shows the change in DWL from a small increase in the tax rate of $\Delta t$. This is approximately $-\Delta xt$ which is equal to $-t\, \Delta t \dfrac{\partial x}{\partial q}$ or $\dfrac{t}{q} \times \Delta t \varepsilon^c$

What about the change in revenue, $R$? Just as a monopoly which raises its price gains extra revenue from the sales it keeps, but loses money from the loss of some custom, so a government which raises taxes by $\Delta t$ gains revenue of $\Delta tx$ on the demand which remains, but loses revenue $t\, \Delta x$ *from the decline in demand. The net change is therefore $\Delta tx(1 - t\varepsilon^c/q)$.*

Putting this together we get:

$$\text{MCPF} \approx \frac{\Delta tx\, \dfrac{t}{q}\, \varepsilon^c}{\Delta tx \left( 1 - \dfrac{t}{q}\, \varepsilon^c \right)} = \frac{\dfrac{t}{q}\, \varepsilon^c}{1 - \dfrac{t}{q}\, \varepsilon^c}$$

As with the DWL, therefore, a rise in the tax rate or an increase in the compensated elasticity raises the marginal cost of public funds.

## 11.5 Optimal taxation

We have just seen that the efficiency cost of taxation is measured by the value of the DWL and that in general the DWL will vary between goods. A key question which arises from this observation is whether there is a pattern of tax rates which will minimise the DWL associated with raising a given amount of government revenue. This is known as the problem of optimal taxation and was first examined by Frank Ramsey (1927) at the behest of Pigou.

Suppose that we were to change the tax system, deciding to raise an extra £1 of revenue from taxation of good x, simultaneously lowering the amount of revenue gained from taxing good y by £1. Overall there would be no change in government revenue, but what would be the change in DWL? By definition, the increase in DWL from raising taxes on x would just be the MCPF for x. Similarly the drop in DWL from reducing taxes on Y would just be the MCPF for y. As a consequence, then, DWL would rise if the MCPF was higher for x than for y, and fall if the converse was true. So to minimise DWL, we require that the cost of raising an extra £1 of revenue should be the same for all taxes: MCPF should be constant.

Rearranging the formula for MCPF from Box 11.2, we obtain:

$$\frac{t}{q} = \frac{k}{\varepsilon^c}$$

where $k$ is a constant which reflects the amount of revenue the government seeks to raise. This particular formula is known as the inverse elasticity rule; it requires that goods which have few substitutes should be taxed more highly than goods where the substitution effect is large. It is such a simple rule because we have simplified the analysis a great deal. In particular, the formula given assumes constant producer prices (or a 100% Corporation Tax) and assumes that there are no cross-price effects between goods. More general models produce much more complex formulae which reflect these complexities (see Myles, 1996, for instance).

Perhaps more importantly, the rule is concerned only with efficiency and not with equity. When taxes are chosen to maximise an inequality-averse social welfare function, taxes should be set in such a way that a less than proportionate move occurs along the compensated demand schedules of goods which are disproportionately consumed by those on low incomes (Diamond and Mirrlees, 1971). In other words, the rule of taxing goods with inelastic demand more highly is modified by a principle of taxing goods with lower income elasticities more lightly. These rules may conflict; food has a low income elasticity, but it also has few substitutes!

Finally, our discussion in Chapter 10 showed that the kind of differential taxation typically implied by optimal tax rules is administratively complex and costly to collect. It is also often seen as undesirable because it may clash with principles of horizontal equity.

## 11.6 Conclusion

We began with a partial equilibrium treatment of taxation of goods. Within this framework, we saw that even if the tax is levied on the producer, the cost is likely to be shared between the producer and the consumer. One option available to government is to tax profits rather than the goods themselves. This might ensure that the cost falls only on the producer. In fact, the cost falls only on the owners of the firm when the firm is a profit maximiser or if the firm is a revenue maximiser unconstrained by post-tax profits. However, a tax does not have an isolated impact; there are spillover effects from one market to another. Using a general equilibrium framework, the Stolper–Samuelson Theorem shows not only the incidence of a tax but also its effect of the distribution of income.

The second important question addressed in this chapter was that of measuring the size of the welfare loss associated with taxation, the deadweight loss. The deadweight loss is measured by comparing a lump-sum tax which does not affect the Pareto efficiency conditions and a proportional tax which does. The size of the deadweight loss depends upon the rate of tax and the compensated demand elasticity, the substitution effect. Given a measure of the deadweight loss, it is possible to consider the design of the tax system. In Chapter 10, we stated a general principle that a tax system should be designed to cause least distortion. However, the implication of this would be for differential taxation; not only would this be admistratively costly but would also be inequitable.

Many of the issues raised in this chapter, particularly those relating to measuring the size of the deadweight loss, will form part of the discussion in the following chapters, where we consider the effect of taxation on savings and on labour supply.

## Summary

- Taxes affect the prices paid by consumers and the prices received by producers; the tax incidence will reflect elasticities of demand and supply.

- An *ad-valorem* tax can raise the same revenue as a specific tax whilst being set at a lower rate.

- A tax on profits will not affect the optimal output and will not cause prices to rise.

- Taxes in one section of the economy have a spillover effect, so a general equilibrium analysis is important.

- Welfare losses created by the rise in price can be measured by the loss in consumer surplus or by the compensating and equivalence variations.

- Non-lump-sum taxes cause a deadweight loss; size of the deadweight loss is given by the rate of tax and the compensated demand elasticity, the substitution effect.

- Optimal taxation would impose differential rates of taxation which are inversely related to the elasticity of compensated demand.

## Questions

1. Under what circumstances is the full value of tax borne by (a) the consumer and (b) the producer?

2. What is the difference between the effect of a specific tax and an *ad-valorem* tax?

3. Is a profit tax non-distortionary?

4. Why is a general equilibrium approach to the effect of taxation valuable?

5. Outline the Stolper–Samuelson Theorem.

**6.** In this chapter we have discussed two methods of measuring the size of the deadweight loss. How are they related?

**7.** Explain the trade-off between efficiency and administrative simplicity in the case of taxation on goods.

## Further reading

Students wishing to supplement their reading on the partial equilibrium analysis of tax incidence should consult a microeconomic text such as Katz and Rosen (1998) or Varian (1996) or public sector texts such as Brown and Jackson (1990) or Cullis and Jones (1992). Atkinson and Stiglitz (1980) has a more advanced treatment of tax incidence under general equilibrium. For a survey of results obtained using early CGE models, see Shoven and Whalley (1984).

http://www.agecon.purdue.edu/centers/gtap/ is the website for the Global Trade Analysis project (Hertel, 1997), which aims to provide researchers worldwide with a common CGE framework. A summary of the lessons learnt for policy from the optimal tax literature can be found in Heady (1993).

## References

Atkinson, A.B. and Stiglitz, J.E. (1980) *Lectures in Public Economics*, Maidenhead: McGraw-Hill.

Brown, C.V. and Jackson, P.M. (1990) *Public Sector Economics*, 4th edn, Oxford: Blackwell.

Corlett, W.J. and Hague, D.C. (1953) 'Complementarity and the excess burden of taxation', *Review of Economic Studies* 21, 21–30.

Cullis, J. and Jones, P. (1992) *Public Finance and Public Choice: An Analytical Perspective*, 1st edn, London: McGraw-Hill.

Diamond, P.A. and Mirrlees, J.A. (1971) 'Optimal taxation and public production', I and II, *American Economic Review* 61, 8–27, 261–78.

Harberger, A.C. (1962) 'The incidence of the corporation income tax', *Journal of Political Economy* 70, 215–40.

Harberger, A.C. (1974) *Taxation and Welfare* Boston, Little, Brown.

Heady, C. (1993) 'Optimal taxation as a guide to tax policy', *Fiscal Studies* 14, 15–43.

Hertel, T.W. (1997) *Global Trade Analysis: Modeling and Applications,* Cambridge: Cambridge University Press.

Katz, M.L. and Rosen, H.S. (1998) *Microeconomics*, 3rd edn, London: McGraw-Hill.

Myles, G. (1996) *Public Economics*, Cambridge: Cambridge University Press.

Ramsey, F.P. (1927) 'A contribution to the theory of taxation', *Economic Journal*, March, 37, 47–61.

Shoven, J.B. and Whalley J. (1984) 'Applied GE models of taxation and international trade', *Journal of Economic Literature* 22, 1007–51.

Varian, H.R. (1996) *Intermediate Microeconomics*, 4th edn, London: Norton.

Willig (1976) 'Consumer surplus without apology', *American Economic Review*, 66(4), 589–97.

# CHAPTER 12

# Intertemporal Issues

## Key concepts

Ricardian Equivalence
endogenous growth
Registered Asset
   Expenditure Tax

expenditure tax
government budget
   constraint

intertemporal
   substitution
fiscal illusion

## 12.1  Introduction

People save for three main reasons: because the pattern of their desired consumption does not match the flow of their income; to pass on bequests, and for precautionary reasons, since it is not possible to insure against all eventualities. Goods consumed at different points in time can be viewed as different commodities in the same way that, say, beer and wine are different and so, just as taxes affect the decision of how much beer or wine to consume, they also influence the pattern of consumption over time. Governments might wish to alter this pattern for a number of reasons: if individuals are myopic, then perhaps they need fiscal incentives to save; and if there are borrowing restrictions or other capital market imperfections, then the tax system can sometimes offer an alternative means of matching income to desired expenditure. Taxing savings might also be part of a system of redistribution in some circumstances and, as we shall see in Chapters 16, on social insurance, and 18, on pensions, taxes and benefits, may also offer an alternative to private precautionary saving. Governments may also wish to influence the intertemporal allocation of consumption for more public choice reasons; a society composed largely of old people may tax the young, or borrow money internationally and leave the debt to future generations. Conversely, a society where the young have the upper hand may penalise those with pensions.

Humans are not squirrels; goods unconsumed are not normally stored for future consumption, like nuts for winter. Instead they form the basis of capital accumulation, which determines the future productive capacity of the economy. Governments therefore have a second class of reasons for affecting the intertemporal allocation of consumption, provided doing so changes investment and the capital stock. It is often argued that more saving, more investment and more growth[1] are good things in themselves and therefore the case for subsidising saving is unarguable but, as with all other interventions in a market economy, the case for altering the rate of return to saving must rest on market imperfections. Nevertheless, increasing concern over low savings rates, low investment and low growth is common to many Western countries. In the UK, for instance, it has long been recognised that the ratio of investment to GDP is much lower than in other similar countries, as Table 12.1 shows. Countries are ranked by their investment to GDP ratios in 1990. Except for 1960, when it would be second to bottom, whatever year was used as the baseline, Britain would occupy the bottom position.

Similarly, concern has been expressed about low and declining savings rates in a number of countries, including the UK and the USA. Table 12.2 illustrates some of the issues, showing that there is no universal down-trend and that, even in some of the countries which saw a collapse of savings in the 1980s, rates have subsequently recovered. Where they do show a decline, these figures provide evidence of a reduction in personal saving rates. There are a number of possible explanations for such a drop. First, in property or stock market booms, like those of the late 1980s, the return to existing assets might outperform expectations, leading to windfall gains and consequent reduction in saving. Second, many countries deregulated credit markets during the same period, reducing borrowing restrictions which led to a one-off readjustment of consumption plans. Third, a rise in government saving, or government commitment to pensions, for example, may lead to a reduction in private saving. Finally, as a population ages, it will tend to dissave as retired people cash in their carefully acquired assets.

In the case of the Scandinavian countries (Denmark, Norway, Sweden and Finland), for instance, Lehmussaari (1990) argues that the sharp drop in personal

**Table 12.1** Investment/GDP percentages (1985 prices)

| Year | 1950 | 1960 | 1970 | 1980 | 1990 |
|------|------|------|------|------|------|
| Japan | 17 | 26 | 40 | 34 | 39 |
| Korea | na | 7 | 22 | 28 | 37 |
| France | 22 | 25 | 31 | 27 | 27 |
| Germany | 28 | 32 | 32 | 27 | 26 |
| Italy | 24 | 34 | 31 | 27 | 25 |
| Australia | 30 | 31 | 31 | 28 | 24 |
| Ireland | 18 | 17 | 27 | 27 | 23 |
| Netherlands | 26 | 27 | 30 | 23 | 22 |
| Norway | 32 | 30 | 34 | 30 | 21 |
| USA | 25 | 21 | 20 | 20 | 20 |
| Denmark | 18 | 26 | 30 | 18 | 20 |
| UK | 11 | 17 | 20 | 16 | 19 |

Source: Penn World Tables at http://bizd.ac.uk/dataserv/penn.htm

---

[1] We shall see later in this chapter there is no necessary causal link from saving to investment to growth.

**Table 12.2** The decline of savings ratios

| Year | 1985 | 1990 | 1994 |
|------|------|------|------|
| Denmark | –10.4 | –3.6 | –4.4 |
| Finland | 8.0 | 3.8 | 4.4 |
| France | 9.7 | 7.6 | 9.2 |
| Germany | 11.4 | 13.8 | 11.5 |
| Italy | 18.9 | 18.0 | 14.5 |
| Japan | 15.6 | 14.1 | 14.7* |
| Netherlands | 11.1 | 15.5 | 11.2 |
| Sweden | 2.4 | –0.3 | 8.6 |
| USA | 8.6 | 6.3 | 6.1* |
| UK | 6.3 | 3.2 | 5.6 |

\* = 1993 figures
The figures are net household savings as a percentage of disposable household income for three recent years
Source: OECD, Table 6.16, 1996

savings was due to the progressive elimination of credit restrictions in the late 1970s and early 1980s. In Denmark, the private saving rate collapsed from 13.3% in 1984 to 4.1% in 1986, while Norway saw a swing from 9.5% in 1984 to –1.8% by 1986, largely as a result of the reduction of the down-payment required for house purchases. Like many other countries, France also experienced an easing of consumer credit constraints and an associated drop in personal savings rates in the 1980s. Ostroy and Levy (1995) have modelled savings over the period and conclude that the reversal of the trend in the 1990s represents an increase in precautionary saving in the face of raised labour market uncertainties, an explanation which may also account for the recent rise in UK savings rates.

In this chapter we look at two main topics: the effect of different taxes on savings and consumption, and the link between public policy, particularly tax policy, and long-term growth. We do so for the reasons outlined in previous paragraphs, but also as a building block for the analysis of savings and pensions policies which follows in Chapter 18.

## 12.2 Intertemporal choice and taxes

We begin by setting out the standard model of consumer choice, as applied to intertemporal decision-making. The model has two standard roles: first, in depicting the young consumer who borrows against future earnings, perhaps to finance their education or buy a house, and second, in depicting a working individual planning their retirement.

### The theoretical effects of taxes on savings

Figure 12.1 provides the starting point for most theoretical models of savings behaviour. It shows the choice facing a consumer who receives income $m^1$ in period 1, when he or she is young, and $m^2$ when old, in period 2, and must allocate this income to consumption, $c^i$, $i = 1, 2$. In the basic model, capital markets are free from imperfection, which means first, that the return, $r$, on income saved when young also represents the cost of borrowing and second, that there are no restrictions on borrowing, no liquidity constraints. Letting saving be $s$ (which if negative will actually be borrowing), then in the first period, consumption plus savings must equal total income, while in the second period consumption will be equal to income plus any returns from savings or minus any repayments of loans which have to be made. Or

$$c^1 + s = m^1$$
$$c^2 = m^2 + (1 + r)s$$

Because of the perfect capital markets, we can eliminate $s$ to produce:

$$c^2 = m^2 + (1 + r)(m^1 - c^1)$$

The slope of the budget line is therefore $-(1 + r)$. An individual who neither borrows nor saves has consumption exactly equal to their income in each period. This pattern of consumption leaves them at their *endowment point*, shown in Figure 12.1. Individuals who borrow in the first period will have consumption in the first period which exceeds their income. They lie to the right of the endowment point in the figure, while savers will lie to the left. In Figure 12.1, the individual consumes less than they earn in period 1, leaving them on indifference curve $U^1$ with savings of $S_A$. If the rate of return on assets decreases, the budget constraint pivots around the endowment point and produces a substitution effect away from saving (A to B) and an income effect which reduces consumption in both states of the world and therefore increases saving (B to C), yielding a new savings level of $S_C$, on indifference curve $U^2$. The net effect on saving is therefore indeterminate, although it is typical to assume that the supply of savings curve is upward sloping; empirical work supports that notion.

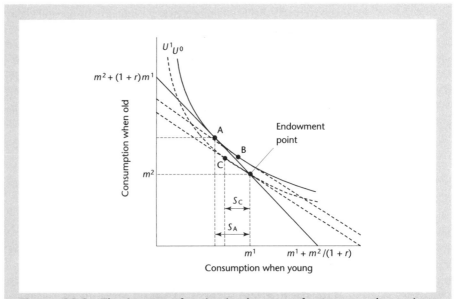

**Figure 12.1** The impact of a rise in the rate of return on the savings decision

Figure 12.2 shows the effects of taxes on savings. If a tax of $t$ is levied on incomes $m^1$ and $m^2$, then the budget constraint moves inward from $DD$ to $FF$. Its equation becomes:

$$c^2 = (1-t)m^2 + (1+r)[(1-t)m^1 - c^1]$$

The endowment point therefore moves inwards, from A to B in Figure 12.2, and the consumer moves to $E^1$, but the slope of the budget line remains unchanged and there is no distortion, no excess burden.[2] More often, Income Tax is charged on all income regardless of source, so that the individual pays tax on $m^1$ and $m^2$, but must also pay tax again on the savings they make out of their first period income, when they are cashed in. This means that £1 which is saved will be taxed twice: once as income in first period and once when the savings are cashed in the second period. The budget constraint becomes:

$$c^1 = (1-t')m^1 - s$$

$$c^2 = (1-t')[m^2 + (1+r)s]$$

where $t'$ is the tax rate which raises the same revenue as $t$. Eliminating $s$ produces:

$$c^2 = (1-t')\{m^2 + (1+r)[(1-t')m^1 - c^1]\}$$

from which we can see how income saved is taxed twice. The slope of the budget constraint therefore becomes $-(1-t')(1+r)$, reducing the incentive to save. Figure 12.2 shows the excess burden associated with this type of distortionary tax; at $E^2$ the tax revenue has the same net present value (NPV) as the lump-sum tax which produced $E^1$ as the consumer optimum.[3] The individual is therefore worse off with

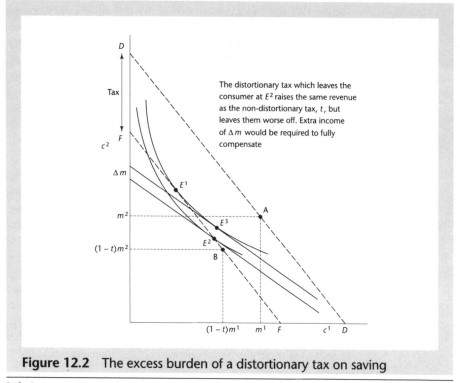

**Figure 12.2** The excess burden of a distortionary tax on saving

[2] If $m^i$ represents income from labour supplied instead, then there may be an excess burden arising from a distortion of the income–leisure choice.
[3] When taxes accrue at different dates, then, just as with other forms of economic flow, they have to be discounted in order to be comparable.

the distortionary tax and would have to receive the sum $\Delta m$ to place them back on the original indifference curve at $E^3$. $\Delta m$ is therefore the excess burden. As with the taxes examined in Chapter 11, the greater the substitution effect, the larger is the excess burden of the tax. Thus, just as income taxes reduce labour supply compared to revenue-equivalent lump-sum taxes, distortionary taxes of this kind reduce savings compared to non-distortionary taxation, but it is the compensated elasticities which determine the size of the resulting welfare loss.

## Expenditure and income taxes

**Expenditure tax**

A tax on expenditure rather than income. Thus, a tax which avoids taxing savings twice

**Registerd Asset Expenditure Tax (RET)**

An expenditure tax where saving in registered schemes attracts tax relief, but withdrawals are taxed

**Pre-paid Expenditure Tax (PET)**

An expenditure tax where only income from labour and transfers are taxed

The reduced incentive to save is created because it is *income* which is taxed. If, instead, it is **expenditure** which is taxed, then the distortion can be avoided. In fact, taxes which do not distort the savings decision can be designed in two ways. First, only consumption or expenditure can be taxed. This means that savings are untaxed until they are cashed in. Alternatively, all income (other than that from previous saving) can be taxed, but savings are not taxed again when consumed. The first form of expenditure tax is called a **Registered Asset Expenditure Tax (RET)**. It is implemented by having the various forms of saving registered and giving tax relief when individuals place their income into these assets. Withdrawal from the savings scheme triggers the tax payment. The second form of tax is called a **Pre-paid Expenditure tax (PET)**, because tax is paid only once, on income from labour, gifts and bequests. In both cases, income is only taxed once in its life. Under the conditions of certainty outlined above, these types of expenditure taxes are equivalent and also equivalent to a simple VAT on consumption. When the rate of return on savings is uncertain, they need not be equivalent *ex post*, because in the RET the government shares some of the risk, whereas in the PET it is the individual who bears the risk and so reaps the reward.

Ever since Kaldor (1955) there has been a long academic debate over the merits of an expenditure tax rather than a tax on income. What is notable about this discussion is how little influence it has had on government tax policy. As we shall see, neither tax has clear-cut efficiency advantages, so that arguments in favour of the expenditure tax have increasingly turned on issues of equity and administrative simplicity.

### Efficiency

All taxes (other than lump-sum) affect choices and behaviour, so in making a choice between two alternatives, we need to consider which creates least distortion. At first sight it might appear that an expenditure tax creates least distortion because it does not tax savings, so it will not affect incentives to save. However, both taxes affect labour-supply decisions. Thus, it is necessary to consider the Second Best solution, which as we saw from Chapter 2, does not necessarily imply that imposing the remaining Pareto efficiency conditions is optimal. It follows that since both expenditure and income taxes distort other choices such as labour supply, the Second Best solution is not necessarily the expenditure tax. More generally, optimal taxation requires heavier tax rates on goods with higher income elasticities and lower compensated elasticities, and this message has no straightforward implications about whether double taxation of savings is preferable to no distortion of the intertemporal allocation of consumption.

### Equity

Supporters of expenditure taxes argue that the best means of comparing individual well-being is via consumption levels. If one person spends much more than another, then it can be concluded that they are better off. This argument suggests that the expenditure tax is more equitable than its alternative because it comes closer to taxing according to economic well-being.

There is also an horizontal equity argument in favour of the expenditure tax: if there are two individuals with the same lifetime income, but one individual saves more early on in life, so as to consume more at a later date, an income tax penalises the saver, compared to a consumption tax, which has the same yield (in NPV terms) whenever consumption is undertaken. Against this, the vertical equity argument is that Income Tax is superior since it allows progressive taxation. However, progressive taxation is perfectly possible with expenditure taxes by, for instance, giving individuals a tax allowance (the basis of the flat rate tax system as advocated by Hall and Rabushka, 1983) and taxing income from work, but using either the PET or RET method to avoid taxing savings twice.[4] Alternatively, as we saw in Chapter 10, some progressivity can be achieved by using zero rating for necessities or possibly introducing higher rates for luxury goods. So, in short, there are equity arguments on either side of the debate.

## Administration

The administrative argument centres on the treatment of income from assets under Income Tax and in the difficulty of finding an accurate account of total income, particularly amongst the self-employed or those with several sources of income. In any period, income $m = w + rW + g$, where $w$ = wages, $r$ = return on wealth, $W$, and $g$ = gifts and bequests. Taxing $w$ and $g$ is relatively straightforward, but taxing income from assets requires the tax authorities to know the change in the value of the assets. If the assets are not liquid, this may be difficult and, furthermore, cashing in some portion of the assets in order to pay Income Tax may impose significant cost on the taxpayer. For instance, if an individual owns a house which rises in value by £20,000 in one year, but has no other liquid assets, then that person may have to sell the house in order to pay the tax on its increase in value. Fundamentally, therefore, the problems arise because of capital market imperfections; if all assets were traded in thick markets, then valuation would not be problematic and if there were no borrowing constraints, the householder could take out a loan against the house in order to pay off the tax accruing from its rise in value.

Both PET and RET avoid the problems created by imperfect capital markets. With the PET, the capital gains on the house or other asset are untaxed, so changes in the value of assets do not concern the tax authorities. With the RET, income from assets only faces taxation when they are cashed in,[5] in which case the individual has the necessary tax in liquid form and the tax inspectors know the value of the tax base from the size of the cash pile.

In practice most tax systems are hybrids, Income Tax bases with elements of RET and PET that limit the double taxation of some savings and thereby come close to expenditure taxation (see Box 12.1) . Where they differ from either option is in the differential treatment of assets. Some, such as housing or the lump-sum element of pensions in the UK, escape taxation altogether, with partial or full tax deductibility

---

[4] Part of wage income represents the return on human capital. Investment in education could be treated as a registered asset.

[5] Bequests and gifts of assets might be problematic. Under PET there is no difficulty, but with a RET simplicity could only be preserved if the recipient was liable for all future taxation.

upon purchase, but no taxation when sold. Other assets, such as ordinary savings accounts, face double taxation. By taxing different activities under a variety of tax schedules, there is a loss in efficiency, because the post-tax marginal returns will no longer be equal. Table 12.3 shows an enormous range in the taxation of different forms of savings assets in the OECD. For an average worker within the UK, for instance, rates range from a subsidy of −10.2% for some forms of pensions savings to a tax of 38.2% on bank deposit accounts. In Germany, and many other countries, the range is still larger. Arguably, it is this distortion of the returns to different forms of saving that represents the greatest argument in favour of either an expenditure tax or an income tax.

## 12.3  Debt and the government budget constraint

In the previous section we examined the intertemporal decision-making of a single consumer, but governments too can use capital markets to reschedule their income

---

**BOX 12.1**

### PEPs, PETs, ISAs, RETs and TESSAs

In the hybrid tax system of the UK, Personal Equity Plans (PEPs) and Tax Exempt Special Savings Accounts (TESSAs) provide examples of how governments attempt to raise savings rates and also how an expenditure tax might be implemented. With PEPs, introduced in 1987, savers may place up to £9,000 each year into the purchase of shares and bonds. Any income or capital gains from the investment is then untaxed. There are restrictions on the investment: savers may only invest up to £1,500 each year in assets outside the European Union and if they wish to use up the full PEP allowance, £3,000 must be placed in the shares of a single company. Because savers are only allowed to invest through one investment management company each year (except for the £3,000 single company part of the savings plan), tax administration costs are kept down. TESSAs, which started in 1991, have a similar tax status to PEPs, but are registered, interest-bearing accounts, where the saver must commit his or her funds for a minimum of five years in order to avoid paying tax on the returns.

Other countries have similar savings vehicles: in France for example, *plan d'épargne en actions* (PEAs) closely resemble PEPs, except that, like TESSAs, there is a minimum holding period, while *plan d'épargne populaire* are tax-exempt savings accounts.

Unless there is a specific desire to promote one form of saving over another, PEPs and TESSAs seem to impose an unnecessarily large number of restrictions on the ability of individuals to manage the portfolio of their savings. An alternative is the Individual Savings Account (ISA), to be introduced by the Labour government in 1999, in which a tax-free 'umbrella' is placed over a number of different types of asset, including savings accounts and investments in shares.

All these savings vehicles therefore share the idea of a registered asset with the RET form of the expenditure tax, but, in common with PET, it is the returns from investing which are untaxed and not the initial income diverted into saving.

**Table 12.3** Variable taxation of assets in the OECD

| Asset | Bank deposits | Direct share purchases | Pensions (deductible premiums, standard tax payout) | Owner-occupied housing, with local property taxes |
|---|---|---|---|---|
| Australia | 42.8 | 37.3 | –7.9 | 26.9 |
| Denmark | 67.6 | 18.6 | 15.6 | 38.0 |
| Finland | 28.2 | 29.0 | 31.6 | na |
| France | 38.8 | 10.0 | 0 | 22.7 |
| Germany | 53.6 | 9.7 | 0 | –14.4 |
| Italy | 56.9 | 11.8 | na | 27.0 |
| Japan | 25.1 | 10.7 | na | 38.2 |
| Netherlands | 57.1 | 12.8 | 0 | 32.3 |
| Sweden | 56.9 | 40.8 | 17.9 | 46.5 |
| USA | 36.9 | 29.0 | 0 | 18.4 |
| UK | 33.4 | 10.0 | –10.2 | na |

na = not applicable
The figures are marginal tax rates for average production workers in 1993, see source for further details
Source: Robson, Table 1, 1995

and expenditure. Typically, governments can raise revenue in three main ways: through charges for goods and services, through taxes and by issuing debt.[6] In order for consumers to take up this debt, interest must be offered, possibly alongside an offer to redeem (buy back) the bonds at a later date. In the two-period model, for instance, the government might issue debt of $b$ in one period, and then in period 2, pay the owners of the bonds $(1 + r)b$ to redeem it. What effect on consumer behaviour does the method of financing government expenditure have? Suppose the government is planning expenditure. It can finance this with a lump-sum tax in the first period of $T$. The first period budget constraint becomes $c^1 = m^1 - s - T$, and if there are no imperfections in the capital market, the overall budget constraint is:

$$c^2 = m^2 + (1 + r)(m^1 - T - c^1) \tag{12.1}$$

Alternatively, it can borrow money, $b$, and pay off the debt in the second period (plus the interest which accrues), with a tax of $T'$. With deficit financing of this kind, the consumer has only $m^1 - b$ left after purchasing the bond in the first period, but gains $(1 + r)b$ in the second period, at which point $T'$ must be paid. The overall budget constraint for the individual is:

$$c^2 = m^2 - T' + (1 + r)b + \underline{(1 + r)(m^1 - b - c^1)} \tag{12.2}$$

---

[6] Printing money adds a further option which will not be considered in this book, although for many governments this has been historically a significant source of income.

Here the underlined portion of the equation represents the consumer's return from first period saving. Just as the consumer's budget constraint is binding, so the **government budget constraints** must hold. It follows that $b = T$, since the loan from consumers must cover the cost of the public expenditure if a tax is not levied. In the second period, it must also be true that $T' = (1 + r)b$, because the tax revenue must cover the cost of paying off the debt. The two budget constraints represented by equations (12.1) and (12.2) are therefore the same, and government financing options are therefore *equivalent*, in the sense that whether the government covers the cost of its expenditure in the first period or delays it to the second, the consumer's optimal consumption plan is unchanged. In one sense this result, known as the **Ricardian Equivalence Theorem**, is completely general; altering the timing of taxation for a given level of expenditure has no impact on the consumer's consumption, however many time periods are involved. If taxes are levied in period 1, then the consumer reduces savings to pay them; if taxes are delayed by forty years, the consumer saves by buying bonds sufficient to pay off the taxes when they are levied. However, this result does depend on five key assumptions: non-distortionary taxation, perfect capital markets, the absence of risk, no fiscal illusion and an infinite life span for the consumer. We now explore each of these in turn.

1. **Non-distortionary taxation.** As we have seen in the previous section, if taxes are not lump-sum, then incentives are potentially altered, making consumer behaviour dependent on the form of finance used.

2. **Perfect capital markets.** The result depends on the ability of consumers to borrow or save so as to offset the effects of the government's actions. If there are borrowing constraints, a tax of $T$ in period 1 need not be equivalent to a tax of $(1 + r)^n T$ in period $n$, because, to pay the former, the consumer may be unable to borrow further in period 1 and must therefore reduce consumption instead. The non-neutrality of debt policy in the case of borrowing constraints can be seen in Figure 12.3, where A is the endowment point in the absence of taxation. Perhaps because she engaged in studying in period 1, the consumer receives most of her income in the second period of her life, but in the situation illustrated she is unable to borrow at all and her budget constraint is therefore the heavy line through A. Her chosen consumption pattern, given these restrictions, is A. Now suppose the government can either levy a tax $T$ in period 1, or borrow and levy $(1 + r)T$ in period 2. For simplicity, we assume that the government borrows abroad.[7] Since both taxes have the same NPV, both have the same consequences for the budget constraint, *in the absence of borrowing constraints*. However, with the borrowing constraint, a period 1 tax lowers her first period income to $m^1 - T$ and leaves the endowment point at B. Her new budget constraint is therefore the heavy line through B and her new optimal consumption is also at that point. Alternatively, levying the tax in the second period would move the endowment point to C, on a higher indifference curve compared to B, although still constrained. Effectively, the government borrows on her behalf, relaxing the constraint she faces. As a result, she prefers the second period tax to the first period, and more to the point, the timing of the tax clearly does have an impact on her consumption behaviour. It is no longer neutral.

---

[7] Obviously it cannot borrow from the consumer, since she would have either to go into debt to purchase the bond or reduce her period 1 consumption still further below its optimal level.

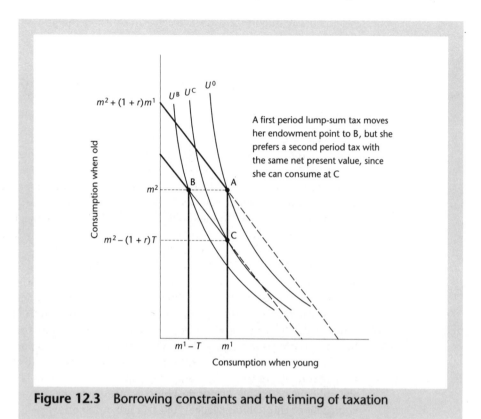

**Figure 12.3** Borrowing constraints and the timing of taxation

3. **Full insurance.** If it is not possible to insure against future uncertainties such as the real rate of return on bonds then, in a risky world, the behaviour of a risk-averse person will be affected by the timing of taxation.

4. **No fiscal illusion.** Fiscal illusion occurs when, either because of the complexities of the tax system or through ignorance, voters do not fully understand the implications of tax and expenditure changes for the government budget constraint. As a result, consumers may not make the offsetting changes in their savings behaviour required for the theorem to hold, because, for instance, they do not anticipate that a rise in government spending means an increase in taxes at a later date.

5. **Infinite lives.** Individuals have only a finite life span. Delaying the implementation of the tax beyond the end of their life gives a boost to lifetime wealth, compared to the case where the tax falls within their life. Simultaneously, the person who does face the tax will suffer a drop in lifetime wealth. In general therefore, with finite lifetimes, borrowing by governments will not be completely offset by individuals. However, if the first person is altruistic towards the second, and plans to leave them money, then they may simply respond to the introduction of the delay by reducing their bequest by an amount equal to the discounted value of the tax. If such altruism between generations is missing, then again the Equivalence Theorem will not hold.

These five assumptions are unlikely to hold in practice, meaning that the Equivalence Theorem provides a set of bench marks rather than a prediction about how an economy operates. It points to one important conclusion: that to some extent the savings decisions of the individual consumer can offset those of the government. This is particularly important when we come to consider the provision of state pensions, which we shall do in Chapter 18.

## 12.4 The long-run consequences of tax policy

### Savings and investment

It is often argued that savings should be subsidised so that investment rises as a result, thereby raising the growth rate. The argument has grown stronger in the wake of dramatic reductions in the savings ratio in a number of OECD countries, mentioned in the introduction, and has provided much of the impetus behind tax-based methods to raise savings, such as PEPs and TESSAs (see Box 12.1). The force of the argument rests on three foundations: higher growth is desirable; higher savings leads to higher investment, and higher investment raises the growth rate. All three assumptions are problematic, as we shall now see.

First, it is not automatically true that higher growth is a good thing. Raising capital accumulation means reducing consumption, but it is only consumption that provides well-being. If Crusoe sets aside more of his crop to provide seed for the following year, he can raise the rate of growth of his miniature economy, but if he sets aside too much, then he will starve to death before the new crops can be harvested. An increase in investment above the level set by the market can only be desirable if the social rate of return to investment is larger than the private rate of return, i.e. if there is market failure of some kind. Such a gap may arise for a number of reasons, such as the public good nature of certain kinds of investment in research, infrastructure or education or through tax wedges, but it is not automatic.

Second, does higher saving lead to greater investment? In an economy marked by complete capital mobility, which is the case for most OECD countries, there should be no link between the level of domestic saving and investment, as Figure 12.4 shows. The real rate of return, $r^*$, is dictated by competition for funds in world capital markets; $I(r)$ is the investment function, $S(r)$ is the supply of domestic savings, $I^E$ is the resulting equilibrium investment level. A subsidy to the domestic savings function, $S$, pushes it out to $S'$, raising the amount of investment funded at home from $S^E$ to $S^{E'}$, but having no impact on the equilibrium level of $I_E$.

While this must be the base case in a world of mobile capital, Feldstein and Horioka (1980) present evidence from sixteen OECD countries in support of a positive link between domestic savings and investment. Regressing I/GDP on S/GDP, they obtain a 'savings retention coefficient' of 0.887, results confirmed by later studies, which have typically found coefficients in the range 0.7–0.9. The term 'Feldstein–Horioka paradox' has been attached to this result, indicating the puzzle that it represents to economists. There are a number of possible explanations for a positive relationship between savings and investment for a single country, but none can currently be seen as compelling.[8]

Whatever the reason for the apparent positive relationship, even if we take the paradoxical result as fact, then the choice between subsidising investment and savings does not automatically favour the latter. To the extent that total supply of funds for investment is more elastic than the domestic savings function, raising the return

[8] One candidate explanation is that perfect capital mobility is true for short-term investment in liquid assets such as currencies, and not for long-term investment in physical assets, but this ignores the links between the two provided by stock exchanges. See Devereux (1996) for discussion of this and alternatives.

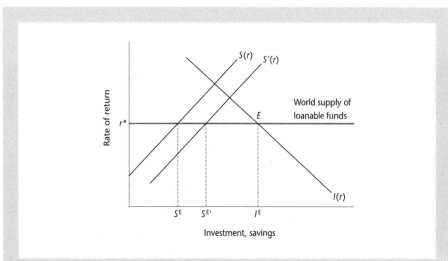

**Figure 12.4** Why subsidising domestic saving may have no impact on the investment

on domestic saving will still only have a limited impact on investment.[9] However, against this, since a proportion of investment is financed abroad, a portion of any direct subsidy to investment will provide transfers to foreign taxpayers, whereas a savings subsidy will transfer government revenue only to domestic consumers.

## Taxes to raise growth

The third link in the chain is that between investment and growth, but, just as higher saving does not necessarily imply higher investment, higher investment may not mean higher growth. This surprising result comes from the neoclassical growth model first proposed by Robert Solow and illustrated in Figure 12.5. In this constant returns to scale and closed economy world, invested savings are employed to raise the capital to labour ratio ($k$), to replace existing capital which depreciates at a rate $\delta$ and to extend capital provision for a population which grows at a rate $n$. Output per head is $f(k)$, out of which the population saves a proportion $s$, giving total investment of $sf(k)$. If this total is bigger than $(n + \delta)k$, the amount required to cover depreciation and the additions to the population, then the capital to labour ratio rises, but as it does so, diminishing returns to capital mean that marginal units of capital are not as productive as the average. Eventually, savings just match the capital required to serve population growth and cover depreciation and the economy is in equilibrium at $k^*$. If the capital to labour ratio starts out higher than $k^*$, then the capital to labour ratio declines over time until $k^*$ is reached. In equilibrium, therefore, capital per person is constant, which means that GDP per head is also constant. National income grows at a rate $n$, as population grows, but there is no increase in income per head.

What happens if the propensity to save increases from $s$ to $s'$? Investment also increases, as in Figure 12.5, and for a time growth rises, but in the long run it settles down to $n$ once more, albeit at a higher value of $k^*$ and therefore at a higher per

---

[9] Both savings and investment are relatively interest-rate inelastic, which suggests that large subsidies are required if any significant change in investment is to be achieved.

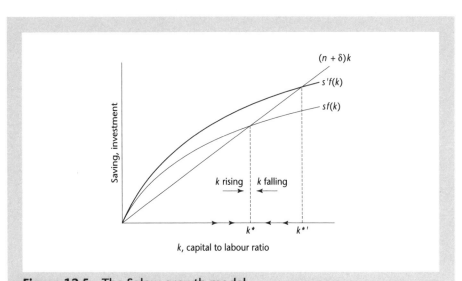

**Figure 12.5** The Solow growth model

capita income level. The lesson is that government policy cannot change the equilibrium growth rate by raising capital accumulation, except in the short run, though of course this short run may actually last many years.

Nevertheless, it might be argued that higher income per head in equilibrium, plus the chance of higher growth along the route to equilibrium, is reason enough for subsidising saving. This argument is wrong. Savings in this model are rather mechanical; society simply sets aside a fraction $s$ of income in each time period, but if that savings rate represents the optimising decision of a single agent, distributing consumption over his or her (infinite) lifetime, then there is no market failure reason for government to intervene. Arguments for intervention must rest on (a) the view that agents discount the future at the wrong rate or (b) that there are distortions in the economy which reduce the rate of saving compared to its optimal level or (c) that there are external benefits from investment omitted from the calculations of private agents. The last of these ideas has always been controversial in economics, though in recent years it has received more and more attention, particularly by macro-theorists interested in understanding technical progress.

## Endogenous growth

Justifiably seen as the engine of modern growth, technical progress is absent from the basic model outlined above. In early modifications of the basic Solow story, technical progress was added as an exogenous element, meaning that government policy could not alter an equilibrium growth rate of per-capita income fixed at the rate of technical progress, $g$. More modern approaches have attempted to incorporate innovation into the model itself (hence **'endogenous growth theory'**), in two main ways. Recall that in the basic model the economy converges to $k*$ because of diminishing returns. Instead, if there were constant returns to $k$, then there would be no equilibrium in the Solow sense; per-capita income would continue to grow. In the *broad capital* approach (see for instance Rebelo, 1991), it is argued that many investment goods have external benefits so that, while for the individual firm investing in training or research and development there are diminishing returns to that invest-

**Endogenous growth**

Growth theories in which the level of innovation is explained within the model

ment, the same is not true for the economy as a whole. In addition to the goods mentioned, broad capital includes other forms of education and basic scientific research as well as investment in infrastructure.

Now, constant returns for a factor are a strong claim and one largely unsupported by the evidence on growth accumulated to date. However, as long as broad capital reduces the severity of diminishing returns, the spurt of out-of-equilibrium growth produced by an increase in the rate of accumulation may be very long lasting.

The alternative route to endogenous growth, particularly associated with the work of Grossman and Helpman (1991), is sometimes called *endogenous innovation*. In their model, firms innovate if they anticipate profits from doing so. Undertaking research and development produces output in two forms: first, a form specific to the individual firm which enables it to improve its product or lower its cost and second, an external benefit in the form of general knowledge available to all organisations. Because this second form of output is non-excludable, firms will tend to underinvest compared to the social optimum, or will tend to skew their efforts towards knowledge, the benefits of which are appropriable.

Research and development often represents a fixed cost. Consider a firm which is planning an innovation of cost $F$, which will lower marginal costs by $\Delta c$. If its market share is $m$ and total market output is $Q$, then (roughly) the change in profits will be $\Delta cmQ - F$, which is increasing in its market share, and in the size of the market. Investment will therefore tend to increase as market power rises and through international trade, provided the total number of firms remains constant (so that $Q$ rises, but $m$ remains unchanged). Policy-makers therefore face a classic Second Best dilemma: increased concentration reduces static efficiency, but may produce long-term gains.

The costs of making the investment will be lower with a highly educated workforce, particularly those working in R&D. Meanwhile, returns will be more appropriable with a well-functioning intellectual property rights system and when there is fast dissemination of new products. As with the broad capital models, there must be constant returns to a factor (R&D effort) in the system if growth is to be truly endogenous but, as we have already noted, even if returns are diminishing, the period of raised out-of-equilibrium growth following a rise in accumulation may be extended compared to the basic Solow model.

In short, therefore, endogenous growth theory provides a link between public policy and growth rates and also a rationale for intervention in the shape of the external benefits of R&D, investment and education; but is the theory true? The lessons provided by the evidence on growth are somewhat unclear, not least because much of the available data is drawn from the post-war 'Golden Age' of growth or the catch-up growth of East Asian economies, neither of which represents experiences likely to be repeated by the rich nations. Typical results are those reported by Levine and Renelt (1992), who use data from 1960 to 1985 to obtain results of the form

GDP growth per head = −0.83 − 0.35GDP1960 − 0.35POP + 3.17SEC + 17.5INV

where GDP1960 is real GDP per capita in 1960, POP is the rate of population growth, SEC is the proportion of the population completing secondary education and INV is the investment ratio, I/GDP. Taken at face value, this suggests that higher investment in human capital and non-human capital should lead to higher growth, though it does not say whether the social rate of return exceeds the private rate. DeLong and Summers (1991) separate out investment into equipment and non-equipment and find social rates of return much higher on the former (at around 30% gross) and much higher than the private rate of return. Later work on this issue by Oulton and Young (1996), using substantially the same data, produces apparently opposite conclusions.[10] They find that the gross social rate of return on equipment investment is around 26%, but when the rate of depreciation of 15% is subtracted, the resulting net social return of 11% is not statistically significant from a private cost of capital of between 1.5 and 4%.[11]

Public policy conclusions may therefore be far more complicated than a simple injunction to subsidise investment. Certain forms of investment may have much greater external effects than others, calling for a policy of differential subsidisation, while there are other crucial aspects of the growth process. For instance, it should be remembered that part at least of the difference in country growth rates arises from differences in the efficiency with which new capital is employed. As Crafts (1991) points out, during 1958–72, German investment rates exceeded the UK's by only 25%, yet the rise in net output per unit of investment was 90% higher in Germany.

## 12.5 Conclusion

The economics of saving reveals a number of commonly held views to be untrue: it is a fallacy that as the real rate of return rises, savings must increase; it is a fallacy that if savings rise, then so must investment; it is a fallacy that a rise in investment must lead to an increase in equilibrium growth rates. We have also seen in this chapter that the actions of individuals can at least partially undo the effects of changes in government borrowing and saving, so that aggregate saving and borrowing remains unaltered. This has important implications for the understanding of social insurance and pensions, because it means that, when modelling changes in government behaviour, we cannot assume that the actions of private individuals will remain unchanged. These issues will be explored further in Chapters 16 and 18.

---

[10] They also find that education attainment has no significant impact on growth rates.

[11] Lack of statistical significance here means that we are not 95% sure that the gap between private and social returns has not arisen through chance. There is a question whether an estimated gap of 7–9.5% between private and social rates of return is *economically* significant, in the sense that it is sufficiently large to justify a policy gamble on subsidies to investment of some kind.

## Summary

- Individuals save as a precaution against future uncertainties, to pass on bequests after their death and to smooth consumption over the lifecycle.

- The last twenty years have seen declines in the savings ratio in many of the richer countries, partly because of the removal of borrowing restrictions.

- Within standard consumer theory consumption at different dates simply represents different commodities and savings are the vehicle for achieving a desired pattern of consumption.

- A rise in tax on savings creates a substitution effect away from saving and, for net savers, an income effect which raises saving. The overall consequences for saving are therefore ambiguous. In practice, aggregate savings rise with the real rate of return, albeit with a low elasticity.

- Expenditure taxes remove the double taxation of saving created by income taxation and offer administrative advantages over income taxes in their treatment of capital gains.

- The Ricardian Equivalence Theorem proposes that changes in debt-financed government expenditure will be offset by private savings. It provides a benchmark model for the interaction of government and individual behaviour.

- In an open economy with perfect international capital mobility, there should be no link between the level of domestic savings and investment. However, in practice the link is present and apparently robust.

- If technical change is exogenous, increases in investment have no permanent effect on the growth rate. If technical progress is endogenous, higher investment can alter the equilibrium growth rate.

- Endogenous growth theories suggest that some forms of capital, such as human capital, R&D and infrastructure, have external effects stronger than other types of asset. This suggests that the size of subsidies to investment should differ between types of capital.

## Questions

1. What has happened to I/GDP ratios since 1945? What has happened to S/GDP?

2. Why do individuals make bequests? What would you expect to be the consequences of an inheritance tax on savings behaviour?

3. In the UK, individuals can save up to £9,000 per year in a personal equity plan (PEP). Any income from the PEP is untaxed. Does this policy fit the PET model or the RET model of an expenditure tax?

4. How can individuals offset the savings and borrowing behaviour of governments?

5. What reasons are there for assuming that the equilibrium rate of return on investment is fixed by world markets?

6. Suppose that worldwide, governments imposed a subsidy to saving. Trace the impact of this on investment and growth in the world economy. Would you expect a similar effect if the subsidy was confined to the European Union?

7. Can governments use the tax system to raise the long-run growth rate?

# Further reading

Taxes and saving are surveyed well by Boadway and Wildasin (1994), with the open economy aspect covered in Devereux (1996). The most recent suggestions for reforming UK taxation along PET lines can be found in the Institute for Fiscal Studies (1994). Barro (1974) is the starting point for modern discussion of Ricardian equivalence, with Buchanan (1976) providing a counterblast in favour of the fiscal illusion view. The formal analysis of savings in a dynamic economy becomes sophisticated very quickly; Myles (1995) is a clear introduction. The endogenous growth literature increases at an annual rate far exceeding that of the economies it seeks to dissect. The *Oxford Review of Economic Policy* 1992 Winter issue is devoted to the subject, Crafts (1996) discusses the evidence from an economic historian's perspective, Mankiw (1995) and Barro and Sala-I-Martin (1995) are topical alternatives and Grossman and Helpman (1991) bring together most of their important ideas on the relationship between innovation and growth. Copies of the Penn World Tables can be found at http://bized.ac.uk/dataserv/penn.htm.

# References

Barro, R.J. (1974) 'Are bonds net wealth?', *Journal of Political Economy* 82, 1095–117.

Barro, R.J. and Sala-I-Martin, X. (1995) *Economic Growth*, New York: McGraw-Hill.

Boadway, R. and Wildasin, D. (1994) 'Taxation and saving', *Fiscal Studies* 15, 19–63.

Buchanan, J. (1976) 'Barro on the Ricardian Equivalence Theorem', *Journal of Political Economy* 84, 337–342.

Crafts, N. (1991) 'Reversing relative economic decline: the 1980s in historical perspective', *Oxford Review of Economic Policy* 7(3), 81–98.

Crafts, N. (1996) 'Post-neoclassical endogenous growth theory: what are its policy implications?', *Oxford Review of Economic Policy* 12(2), Summer, 30–47.

DeLong, J.B. and Summers, L.H. (1991) 'Equipment investment and economic growth', *Quarterly Journal of Economics* 106(2), 445–502.

Devereux, M. (1996) 'Investment, savings and taxation in an open economy', *Oxford Review of Economic Policy* 12(2), Summer, 90–109.

Feldstein, M. and Horioka, C. (1980) 'Domestic savings and international capital flows', *Economic Journal* 94, 613–29.

Griffith, R., Sandler, D. and van Reenen, J. (1995) 'Tax incentives for R and D', *Fiscal Studies* 16(2), 21–44.

Grossman, G.M. and Helpman, E. (1991) *Innovation and Growth in the World Economy*, Cambridge, MA: MIT Press.

Hall, R. and Rabushka, A. (1983) *Low tax, simple tax, flat rate*. New York: McGraw-Hill.

http://bized.ac.uk/dataserv/penn.htm

Institute for Fiscal Studies (1994) *Setting Savings Free*, London: IFS.

Kaldor, N. (1955) *An Expenditure Tax*, London: Allen Unwin.

Lehmussaari, O.P. (1990) 'Deregulation and consumption: saving dynamics in Nordic countries', *IMF Staff Papers* 37(1), 71–93.

Levine, R. and Renelt, D. (1992) 'A sensitivity analysis of cross-country growth regressions', *American Economic Review* 82(4), 942–63.

Mankiw, G. (1995) 'The growth of nations', *Brookings Papers on Economic Activity* 275–310.

Myles, G. (1995) *Public Economics*, Cambridge: Cambridge University Press.

OECD (1996) *Historical Statistics*, Paris: OECD.

Ostroy, J.D. and Levy, J. (1995), 'Household saving in France: stochastic income and financial deregulation', *IMF Staff Papers* 42(2), 375–97.

Oulton, N. and Young, G. (1996) 'How high is the social rate of return?', *Oxford Review of Economic Policy* 12(2), 48–69.

Rebelo, S. (1991) 'Long run policy analysis and long-run growth', *Journal of Political Economy* 99(3), 500–21.

Robson, M.H. (1995) 'Taxation and household saving: reflections on the OECD report', *Fiscal Studies* 16(1), 38–57.

# Taxes on Labour

## 13.1 Introduction

For most governments, income tax is the largest single source of revenue (see Figure 10.1). It is also an essential policy tool, whether the policy objective is the redistribution of income or supply-side macroeconomic policy. One fear of policy-makers is that high levels of income taxation will result in a reduction in hours worked. This is the disincentive effect of taxation and is of obvious interest to governments because of the implications for revenue. To see if these fears are grounded, we need to model the impact on individual decision-makers and, in particular, we need to consider a model of labour supply.

The efficiency loss associated with taxation is another important issue examined in this chapter. The debate over the size of the loss is not the same as that concerning the extent of incentive effects. A tax with no incentive effects, which does not cause individuals to alter their labour supply, may still cause a substantial loss in efficiency.

Finally, we consider the likely effects of transfers from governments to individuals, asking whether welfare payments create or sustain dependency on the state, thus providing a framework to analyse the effectiveness of social policy, discussed in the next part.

## 13.2 Modelling labour supply[1]

We typically assume that supply curves are upward sloping, which suggests that there will be an increase in the supply of labour if the wage rate, the reward for hours worked, increases. However, real world evidence is mixed. Some studies suggest that labour supply is inelastic with respect to the wage (vertical) or even that labour

---

[1] This model of labour supply will be familiar from consumer theory (see Katz and Rosen, 1988, or Varian, 1996).

supply displays negative wage elasticity (is backward sloping). Labour supply behaviour differs across groups. For example, the labour supply behaviour of married women is very different to the labour supply behaviour of married men, and the labour supply of single parents is different to that which is observed in two-parent families.

To understand these divergent observations, we utilise the standard model of consumer choice, in which an individual is assumed to maximise utility, subject to a budget constraint. The choice concerning labour supply results from a trade-off between leisure and income or consumption. Throughout, it will be assumed that leisure and income are normal goods. The trade-off exists because our time is divided between two activities, paid work and leisure. Paid work involves giving up leisure time, but yields an income which enables consumption. We shall see that as a result the final decision reflects individual preferences, the wage rate and unearned income.

## Trading off leisure for income

We shall use the following notation:

$T$ – a time endowment which reflects the total number of hours available to the individual (usually thought of as 24 hours);

$I_U$– an income endowment which represents the level of unearned income (possibly inherited income or income from social security payments);

$L$ – the number of hours of leisure enjoyed by the individual;

$w$ – the hourly wage rate earned by the individual;

$H$– the number of hours worked by the individual, his or her labour supply;

$I_E$– the earned income $wH$;

$I$ – total income $I_U + I_E = I_U + wH$.

The individual makes a choice between leisure, $L$, and income, $I$. This choice will imply the supply of hours, since for a given time endowment $T$, $H = T - L$. Clearly, any number of hours worked implies giving up hours of leisure and the individual is compensated for this by a wage rate, $w$, which then adds to income. It is in this sense that the wage rate is the price of leisure.

### Preferences

We assume that the individual prefers more of both leisure and income, $U(L,I)$ (see Figure 13.1). The slope of an indifference curve is the marginal rate of substitution between income, $I$, and leisure, $L$, defined as $\text{MRS}_{IL}$. A low $\text{MRS}_{IL}$ gives a shallow slope for indifference curves, reflecting a low value for leisure. This means for each hour of leisure lost, the individual only needs to be compensated with a small rise in income to keep utility constant. A high $\text{MRS}_{IL}$ gives a steep slope for indifference curves, reflecting a high value for leisure. In this case, for each hour of leisure given up, the individual must be compensated with a large rise in income to keep utility constant.

### Budget constraint

The consumer has a total income $I = I_U + wH$ but, since $H = T - L$, we can rearrange

$$I = I_U + w(T - L) = I_U + wT - wL \tag{13.1}$$

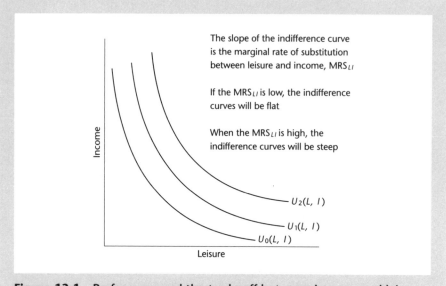

**Figure 13.1** Preferences and the trade-off between income and leisure

This budget constraint simply says that our income combines any unearned component with the full value of the time endowment (that is, what could be earned if, for example, the individual worked for the full twenty-four hours) less the amount that is 'spent' on leisure. Equation (13.1) is often reinterpreted further in terms of choices and endowments, $I + wL = I_U + wT$, where the left-hand side represents 'purchases', as the consumer buys income and leisure, and the right-hand side represents the value of the consumer's endowments. However, returning to equation (13.1), we have a simple linear equation, where $I_U + wT$ is the intercept and $-w$ is the slope. We

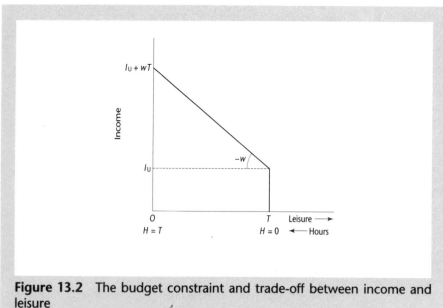

**Figure 13.2** The budget constraint and trade-off between income and leisure

can see in Figure 13.2 that when $L = 0$, we are at the intercept which represents the level of income attained when the individual enjoys no leisure time and works for the whole of their time endowment, i.e. $H = T$. When $L = T$, we find ourselves at the other extreme, where the whole of the individual's time endowment is taken up by leisure and he or she supplies no labour at all, i.e. $H = 0$.

Using this framework, we can examine the following issues: whether an individual participates in the labour market; the number of hours supplied (see Box 13.1); and the response to changes in the wage rate and rate of taxation.

---

**BOX 13.1**

## Hours supplied

The choice problem facing our consumer is:

Maximise utility $U(L, I)$, subject to a budget constraint $I = I_U + wT - wL$

There is plenty of scope for differing preferences, which allows for quite different choices of hours by different individuals at a given wage.

In the examples below, the point of tangency is at point E, the optimal choice for leisure is $L*$ and income $I*$. Since the number of hours worked is given by $H = T - L$, we can find the optimal labour supply $H*$. Were the consumer to have shallow indifference curves (a low taste for leisure), the optimal choice of leisure would be lower and hours supplied higher (see left-hand panel below), and if instead the indifference curves are steep (a high taste for leisure), the optimal choice of leisure would be much higher and hours supplied lower (see right-hand panel, below).

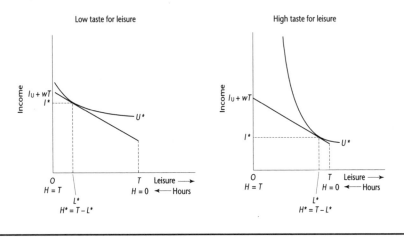

---

## Income and substitution effects

### *Responses to wage changes*

A change in the wage rate will cause the budget constraint to swivel around the endowment income point, since $I_U$ is unchanged. If the initial wage is $w_0$ and the new wage is $w_1$, $w_1 < w_0$:

the initial budget constraint is $I_0 = I_U + w_0 T - w_0 L$

and

the new budget constraint is $I_1 = I_U + w_1 T - w_1 L$

We can see in Figure 13.3 that in both cases the time endowment point (where $L = T$ and $H = 0$) is unchanged because the endowment income $I_U$ has remained the same, but that the intercept (where $L = 0$ and $H = T$) and the slope have altered, since the change in the wage rate has decreased the income gained from working for each hour of the time endowment.

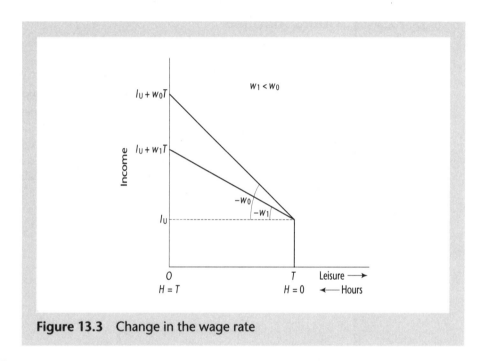

**Figure 13.3   Change in the wage rate**

**Substitution effect**

Measures the change in demand due to new relative prices assuming constant utility

**Real income effect**

The change in demand caused by a change in spending power, holding money income constant

We measure the response to a wage change using the substitution and income effects which are formalised in the Slutsky equation and shown in Figure 13.4. The **substitution effect** measures the change in demand for leisure due to the change in relative prices (the slope of the budget constraint), holding utility constant, which is represented by $\partial L/\partial w |_U$. This is always negative because the change in leisure has the opposite sign to the change in the wage rate. An *increase* in the wage rate means a rise in the price of leisure makes leisure relatively more expensive and so *reduces* demand for leisure. A *cut* in the wage rate means a fall in the price of leisure makes leisure relatively less expensive and so *increases* demand for leisure. This is the movement from point $E_0$ to $E_1$, in Figure 13.4.

The **real income effect**, or the conventional income effect, is the change in demand for leisure, assuming that the full value of money income is unchanged, $-\partial L/\partial I \times L$. Since leisure is a normal good, this is also always negative, because the change in demand for leisure has the opposite sign to the change in the wage rate. An *increase* in the wage rate makes real income fall and so *reduces* demand for leisure. A *cut* in the wage rate makes real income rise and so *increases* demand for leisure.

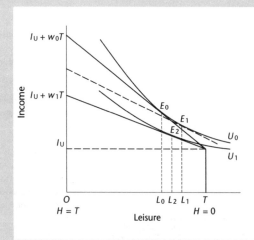

The substitution effect is the change in demand for leisure when the wage rate falls, with constant utility, $L_0$ to $L_1$

The income effect is the change in demand for leisure when the fall in the wage rate causes a cut in income and utility changes, $L_1$ to $L_2$

In this example, the substitution effect dominates the income effect and the overall effect of a fall in the wage rate is an increase in the demand for leisure $L_0$ to $L_2$, that is a fall in the number of hours of labour supplied

**Figure 13.4** An example of the substitution and income effect where the substitution effect dominates

**Money income effect**

The change in demand caused by the increase in the value of the time endowment

The **money income effect**, or the endowment effect, is the change in demand for leisure, given the change in money income or the change in the full value of the time endowment, $\partial L/\partial I \times T$. This is always positive, as the change in demand for leisure has the same sign to the change in the wage rate. Therefore, an *increase* in the wage rate causes money income to rise and so *increases* the demand for leisure. Equally, a *cut* in the wage rate leads to a fall in money income and so *decreases* the demand for leisure.

The combined income effect is

$$-\frac{\partial L}{\partial I} L + \frac{\partial L}{\partial I} T = (T - L) \frac{\partial L}{\partial I} = H \frac{\partial L}{\partial I}$$

which is positive. We know that $\partial L/\partial I$ is positive because leisure is a normal good. The combined income effect will be greater when the number of hours already worked, $H$, is large or when the $\partial L/\partial I$ is big.

This is shown by the movement from $E_1$ to $E_2$ in Figure 13.4. The income effect counters the substitution effect, so the final effect on the demand for leisure (and on labour supply) will depend on whether the income effect dominates the substitution effect.

In this example, the fall in the wage rate from $w_0$ to $w_1$ causes an increase in demand in leisure $(\dot{L}_0 - L_1)$ because of the substitution effect (leisure has become cheaper and so the individual consumes more). The combined income effect is the reduction in demand for leisure $(L_1 - L_2)$, which occurs because income has fallen and the individual consumes less of all goods. But the substitution effect dominates the income effect, so the overall effect is that the response to a fall in the wage rate is an increase in the demand for leisure, which is a fall in hours supplied, consistent with an upward-sloping labour supply schedule.

In our second example, in Figure 13.5, the combined income effect dominates the substitution effect. The net effect of the fall in the wage rate is that the demand for leisure falls from $L_0$ to $L_2$, so there is a rise in hours supplied. So, in this example, the labour supply schedule is downward sloping.

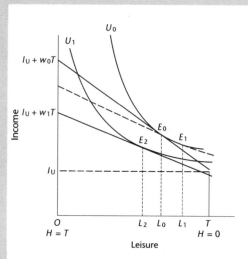

The substitution effect is the change in demand for leisure when the wage rate falls, with constant utility, $L_0$ to $L_1$

The income effect is the change in demand for leisure when the fall in the wage rate causes a cut in income and utility changes, $L_1$ to $L_2$

In this example, the substitution effect is dominated by the income effect and the overall effect of a fall in the wage rate is a fall in the demand for leisure $L_0$ to $L_2$, that is a rise in the number of hours of labour supplied

**Figure 13.5** An example of the substitution and income effects where the income effect dominates

The Slutsky equation formalises the response to a change in the wage rate ($\partial L/\partial w |_{Iu}$ is the final change in demand for leisure in response to a change in the wage rate, holding unearned income constant)

$$\frac{\partial L}{\partial w} \bigg|_{Iu} = \frac{\partial L}{\partial w} \bigg|_{U} + H \frac{\partial L}{\partial I}$$

$$\qquad\qquad \text{SE} \qquad\quad \text{IE}$$
$$\qquad\qquad \text{-ve} \qquad\quad \text{+ve}$$

where SE is the substitution effect and IE is the income effect.

To summarise, a rise in the wage rate will only lead to an increase in labour supply if the substitution effect dominates the income effect. This is only the case for the first of the three labour supply schedules shown in Figure 13.6. Should the income

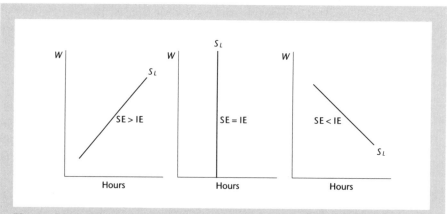

**Figure 13.6** The impact of the income and substitution effects on labour supply schedule

effect exactly counter the substitution effect, then the labour supply schedule will be inelastic and a change in the wage rate will have no effect on the number of hours supplied. Finally, when the income effect dominates, we observe a backward-bending labour supply schedule. Here, the rise in the wage rate results in a fall in the number of hours supplied. From the Slutsky equation, we can see that the income effect is likely to dominate when the hours of labour already supplied are large, so we would expect the income effect to be larger for those in full-time employment. It follows that those groups most likely to be attracted by a higher wage into the labour market, or to work longer hours, are those who are currently working few hours or on lower incomes.

### Taxation and labour supply

Having examined the basics of labour supply, the model can now be applied to examine the likely effects of taxation upon labour supply decisions. The UK tax schedule for 1997/98 is illustrated in Box 13.2.

**BOX 13.2**

## UK tax system

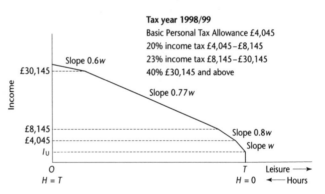

Tax year 1998/99
Basic Personal Tax Allowance £4,045
20% income tax £4,045–£8,145
23% income tax £8,145–£30,145
40% £30,145 and above

**Tax reforms**

*Increasing the tax allowance*: This will increase the section on the budget constraint where no tax is paid (see Figure (a) below).

*Reducing the starting rate*: This will increase the return for hours worked at the lower sections of the budget constraint (see Figure (b) below).

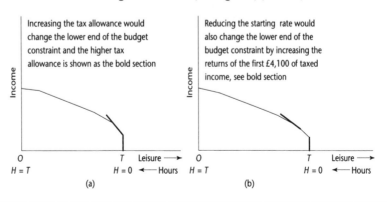

(a)                              (b)

## Lump-sum tax

Recall that **lump-sum tax** is paid regardless of income level or hours of labour supplied. Given a lump-sum tax $S$, the budget constraint becomes

$$I = I_U + wT - S - wL$$

There is no change in the slope, because the return to each extra hour worked, the wage rate, is the same (see Figure 13.7). The response to the introduction of a lump-sum tax is given by the income effect alone; since there is no change in the price of leisure, the substitution effect is zero. So the impact on labour supply is unambiguous; the fall in income causes a fall in demand for leisure and a rise in labour supply.

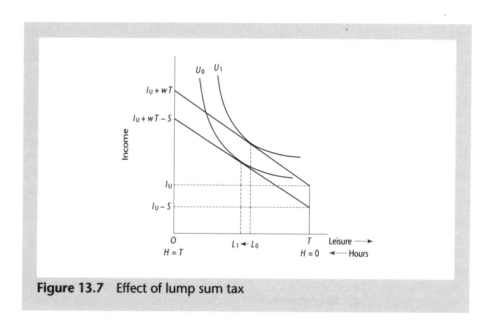

**Figure 13.7**  Effect of lump sum tax

## Proportional tax

Introducing a **proportional tax** on earned income has much the same effect on the budget constraint as reducing the wage rate. In this simple model, for a tax rate $t$, the individual would pay tax at a level $tw$, leaving a net wage of $w - tw = w(1 - t)$. This would result in a budget constraint,

$$I = I_U + w(1 - t)T - w(1 - t)L$$

As we have seen before, this leaves the endowment point unchanged, but the fall in the effective wage rate reduces the income obtained for each hour worked (see Figure 13.8).

The response to a proportional tax is the same as the response to a change in the wage rate; labour supply will fall if the SE > IE, be unchanged if SE = IE and rise if SE < IE. A perennial debate concerns the disincentive effects associated with Income Taxes. The claim that higher taxes reduces labour supply provides one justification

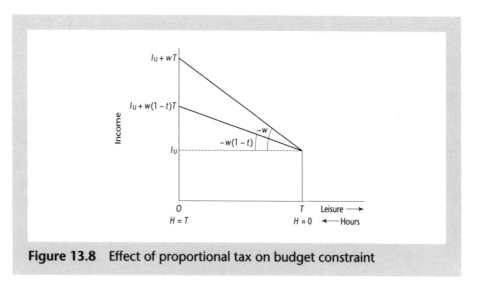

**Figure 13.8** Effect of proportional tax on budget constraint

for the reduction in Income Tax rates discussed in Chapter 10. Turning the argument around, for there to be incentive effects associated with lower taxes or higher wages, it is necessary that the labour supply schedule is upward sloping, that is, the substitution effect dominates the income effect. However, there is no theoretical reason for this to always be the case.

## 13.3 Income Tax and inefficiency

### Deadweight loss

Returning to the arguments introduced in Chapters 3 and 11, a proportional tax will create distortion because it alters marginal values. The distortionary effects which give rise to efficiency losses are associated with the change in the return to each extra hour worked the wage rate. In order to measure this efficiency loss, we need to compare the outcomes under the two tax regimes (see Figure 13.9).

Let us first consider the effect of the proportional tax. The initial choice point was at $E_1$ on $U_1$; in response to the tax our individual moves to point $E_0$ on indifference curve $U_0$. We now want to compare this outcome with that of a lump-sum tax, which is imposed at such a level that consumers are indifferent between the two taxes, so the new choice point should also lie on $U_0$. Such a tax is shown and the new choice point is $E_2$. When we compare the demand for leisure and hence the labour supply under these tax systems, we find that, when the proportional tax is imposed, the demand for leisure rises, from $L_0$ to $L_1$, so labour supplied falls, but, when the lump-sum tax is imposed, the demand for leisure falls from $L_0$ to $L_2$, so the supply of labour rises.

Now let us compare the revenue raised under each tax system. We know that, under the proportional tax system, the revenue raised or the tax paid depends on the number of hours worked, but under a lump-sum tax system the revenue is constant and independent of the number of hours worked. As we have already identified, the optimising response to a proportional tax is to reduce hours worked, thus reducing

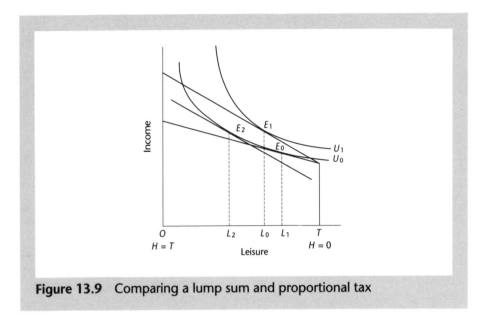

**Figure 13.9** Comparing a lump sum and proportional tax

the tax paid and the revenue available to government. We can measure this, by finding $tw \times H$, which is the vertical distance from $E_0$ to the original budget constraint, $E_0A$, in Figure 13.10. The revenue from a lump-sum tax is constant, FA, in Figure 13.10. So, more revenue is raised by the lump-sum tax. This is because under the proportional tax system the substitution effect leads the individual to demand more leisure, because the opportunity cost associated with leisure has fallen and the consequence is a fall in the supply of labour. The gap in revenue $E_0F$, in Figure 13.10, is a measure of the deadweight loss (DWL).

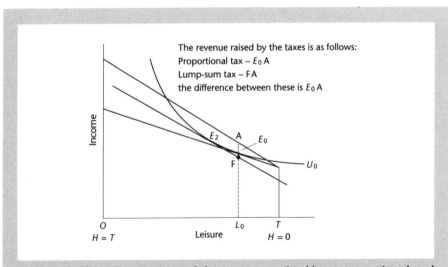

**Figure 13.10** A comparison of the revenues raised by a proportional and a lump sum tax between which consumer is indifferent

As we saw in Chapter 11, the DWL is greater when there is a large substitution effect and here it is measured as the area under the **compensated labour supply** schedule.

**Compensated labour supply**

The substitution effect-only supply schedule, measuring the change in supply caused by the change in relative prices but at constant utility

## Inefficiency and incentives

We have seen that the efficiency loss occurs because of the change in marginal values associated with a proportional tax. However, we must be careful not to confuse this with the overall labour supply response to the same change in the return to each extra hour worked. For example, although we may observe labour supply, which is completely inelastic, so the introduction of a tax does not cause labour supply to change; this does not mean that the tax is not distortionary. In the event of inelastic labour supply schedules, the distortion still occurs because of the substitution effect, even though this effect may be exactly countered or dominated by the income effect. The same is true if we consider a backward-bending labour supply schedule. In this case the introduction of the tax causes overall labour supply to rise, but the inefficiencies remain.

We can see this in Figure 13.11, when we compare the response to a tax on the labour supply schedule, $S_L$, with that on the substitution effect-only supply schedule, the compensated supply curve, $CS_L$. We start with a wage rate $w$ and labour supply is $H_1$ and consider the impact of the Income Tax $t$.

In each case the substitution effect-only response is the same: labour supplied falls from $H_1$ to $H'$ and the DWL is the shaded area under the compensated supply curve, $CS_L$. We also see that the income effect is always positive and counters the substitution effect: in the first example, where the supply curve is upward sloping, the final labour supply is at $H_0$; in the second case labour supplied is unchanged and in the third case labour supply has risen. The key point is that the welfare loss is the same, whilst the labour supply response reflects the extent of the income effect, so taxes may create inefficiencies at the same time as providing incentives to work harder.

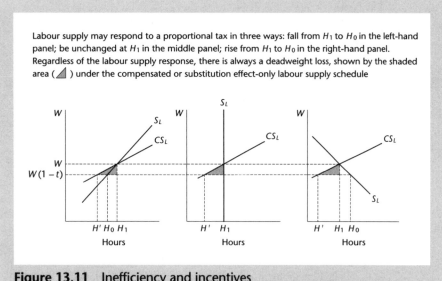

Labour supply may respond to a proportional tax in three ways: fall from $H_1$ to $H_0$ in the left-hand panel; be unchanged at $H_1$ in the middle panel; rise from $H_1$ to $H_0$ in the right-hand panel. Regardless of the labour supply response, there is always a deadweight loss, shown by the shaded area ( ◢ ) under the compensated or substitution effect-only labour supply schedule

**Figure 13.11** Inefficiency and incentives

## Size of efficiency loss

We have argued that the efficiency loss rises with the tax rate and the size of the substitution effect. The DWL is the triangle under the compensated labour supply schedule, between $H_1 - H'$ and $w - w(1 - t)$, in Figure 13.11. This triangle will be larger if the compensated supply schedule is more elastic or if the tax rate is greater. In fact, the magnitude of the DWL is given by the following (see Box 13.3 for proof)

$$DWL = 0.5 \times t \times \eta^{CS} \times R$$

where $t$ is the tax rate, $\eta^{CS}$ is the elasticity of the compensated labour supply schedule (which is the size of the substitution effect) and $R$ is the revenue raised.

Using this measure, it is clear that the efficiency loss rises with a higher marginal rate of taxation $t$. This provides further evidence of a trade-off between equity and efficiency (see discussion in Chapter 3). A progressive tax system (which typically uses higher marginal tax rates) is a tool for greater equity, but will result in a higher efficiency loss.

---

**BOX 13.3**

# Estimating the size of the deadweight loss

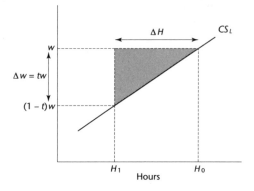

DWL = ½ΔwΔH, but ΔH = ηΔwH/w and Δw = tw, so DWL = ½twηΔwH/w = ½ tηtwH = ½tηR, where R = twH and Δ denotes change.

If $t = 0.25$ and $\eta^{CS} = 0.1$, then the DWL would be 1.25% of revenue raised.

If instead $\eta^{CS} = 0.5$, the DWL would be 6.25% of revenue raised. Finally, if $\eta^{CS} = 0.9$, the DWL would be 11.25% of revenue raised.

---

## Estimates of labour supply

Empirical evidence on labour supply elasticities shown in Table 13.1 is mixed. What is clear is that, within certain groups, supply elasticities are similar, but that there are big differences between the groups. Generally, there are significant differences in labour supply behaviour across gender and household composition. The labour supply of married men tends to be inelastic, with low elasticities of the compensated labour supply schedules. Married women, on the other hand, tend to have very elastic labour supply schedules, with high elasticities of the compensated labour supply schedules. The labour supply elasticities of lone mothers are even larger.

This empirical evidence suggests that female labour supply is much more responsive to changes in the budget constraint. So if the employer or the government wanted to encourage or discourage female labour supply, it could do so by altering incentives; that is, changing the net reward of an hour in the labour market. What we can also see is that these estimates suggest a much greater loss of efficiency associated with a proportional tax on female labour supply; a 25% tax rate would result in an approximate efficiency loss of 1.25% of revenue for men and one of 11.25% of revenue, for women.

**Table 13.1**

| Author | Country | Total elasticity | Subs. effect | Income effect |
| --- | --- | --- | --- | --- |
| *Husbands' labour supply elasticities* | | | | |
| Hausman (1981) | USA | 0.03 | 0.95 | −0.92 |
| Ashworth and Ulph (1981) | UK | −0.33 | 0.29 | −0.62 |
| Atkinson and Stern (1980) | UK | −0.16 | −0.09 | −0.07 |
| Blundell and Walker (1982) | UK | −0.23 | 0.13 | −0.36 |
| *Wives' labour supply elasticities* | | | | |
| Cogan | USA | 0.65 | 0.68 | −0.03 |
| Hausman (1981) | USA | 0.45 | 0.90 | −0.45 |
| Arafat and Zabalza (1986) | UK | 0.68 | 0.62 | −0.06 |
| Blundell and Walker (1982) | UK | 0.43 | 0.65 | −0.22 |
| Blundell *et al.* | UK | 0.33 | 0.52 | −0.19 |
| *Lone mothers' labour supply elasticities* | | | | |
| Hausman (1980) | USA | 0.53 | 0.65 | −0.18 |
| Bingley *et al.* | UK | 0.76 | 1.28 | −0.52 |
| Jenkins (1992) | UK | 1.44 | 1.68 | −0.24 |

Source: Blundell, Tables 4.6, 4.7 and 4.8, 1993

## 13.4 Transfer payments and labour supply

By making an allowance for unearned income, we have already given a potential role for transfer payments or social security payments. There are two main concerns associated with transfer payments. The first is, when an individual receives an unearned income from the government, the likelihood of that individual entering the labour market is reduced. The second is that, even if the individual enters the labour market, the rate of benefit withdrawal creates disincentives to labour supply. Both of these problems could lead to problems of benefit dependency.

**Participation decision**

The decision made by an individual about their entry into the labour market

### Participation

The **participation decision** reflects a comparison between monetary values of time spent in and outside the labour market. Each individual has a reservation wage, $w^*$, which is also referred to as the shadow price of leisure. They will choose to supply labour if the market wage they receive exceeds the value of their reservation wage. Hence, an individual will participate, that is supply their labour, if $w > w^*$.

The wage rate clearly identifies the monetary value of time spent in the labour market. The reservation wage is the monetary value of time spent outside of the labour market and calculating this is slightly more complicated. The reservation wage will obviously include the value of unearned income. It will also reflect both time constraints, perhaps associated with caring for children or elderly relatives and financial constraints, such as mortgages. The reservation wage will rise if unearned income rises or if more time needs to be spent in the home, but will fall if there are greater financial outlays. In Figure 13.12, we see two examples of non-participation in the labour market. The reservation wage is sketched as the dashed line, which is tangent to the indifference curve at the point where the individual does not participate, $H = 0$. Any wage above the reservation wage will encourage participation, $H > 0$. Thus, there are then two main reasons why an individual chooses to not work: either their reservation wage is high or their expected market wage is low.

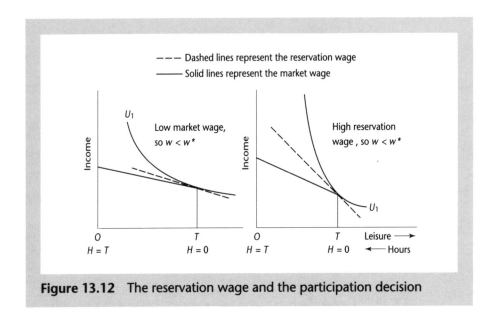

**Figure 13.12** The reservation wage and the participation decision

## Benefit traps

A further problem occurs when benefits are means tested. The budget constraint is non-linear in this case, because recipients of the benefits face very high rates of marginal tax as the benefits are withdrawn. In exceptional cases a **poverty trap** may occur (see Figure 13.13). This is characterised by earned income initially adding to unearned income with hours worked and then income falling due to the withdrawal of benefits. Total income eventually rises above the pre-withdrawal level, as earned income will continue to rise as hours are increased. There is no incentive to work between these two points of equal income. As a consequence we expect that individuals will either choose not to work or to only supply a small number of hours so that income does not reach the level at which benefits are withdrawn. These cases are illustrated in Figure 13.13. An **unemployment trap** arises if income falls as soon as the individual enters the labour market.

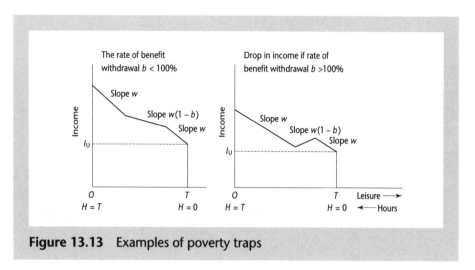

**Figure 13.13** Examples of poverty traps

The problem of a poverty or unemployment trap arises if the rate of withdrawal of benefits has the impact of a marginal rate of taxation in excess of 100%. The 1988 Social Security reforms (often referred to as the Fowler Reforms, see Box 13.4) attempted to eliminate marginal rates of taxation in excess of 100%; this was successful, but the cost was to increase the numbers experiencing marginal tax rates of 75–80% (see Table 13.2). Such high rates of tax create strong disincentive effects amongst the group of people who we saw from the Slutsky equation (those with low hours supplied and low incomes) are most responsive to incentives. This is another dilemma facing government. A means-tested benefit should be the most effective way to direct welfare support to those most in need, but the consequence of high rates of tax as the benefits are withdrawn may create a benefit trap.

Empirical evidence (see discussion in Layard *et al.*, 1991) suggests that there is a small positive correlation between levels of benefit payments and economic inactivity, but that there is no strong evidence that the level of benefit payment has an impact on the duration on persistence of economic inactivity.

**Table 13.2** Marginal net income deduction rates, in thousands

|        | 1985 | 1993/94 | 1994/95 | 1995/96 |
|--------|------|---------|---------|---------|
| 100% + | 70   | 0       | 0       | 10      |
| 90% +  | 130  | 75      | 90      | 100     |
| 80% +  | 290  | 170     | 355     | 420     |
| 70% +  | 290  | 525     | 600     | 615     |
| 60% +  | 450  | 540     | 620     | 630     |
| 50% +  | 680  | 540     | 625     | 630     |

Source: The Government's Expenditure Plans 1996/97, Social Security Departmental Report, Figure 19

## Example of the poverty trap

Prior to 1988:

|  | Gross income | £50 | £80 | £100 | £120 |
|---|---|---|---|---|---|
| plus | Child benefit | 11.70 | 11.70 | 11.70 | 11.70 |
|  | rent rebate | 13.84 | 10.09 | 7.32 | 3.91 |
|  | rate rebate | 4.55 | 3.35 | 2.41 | 1.21 |
|  | Family income supplement | 20.75 | 5.75 |  |  |
|  | Free school meals | 5.00 | 5.00 |  |  |
| less | Income tax | 0.89 | 9.89 | 15.89 | 21.89 |
|  | National Insurance | 4.38 | 7.00 | 8.75 | 10.50 |
| Net | Income | 100.57 | 99.00 | 96.79 | 104.43 |

[1] The 1998 Fowler/Moore Reforms: eliminated >100% tax rates, [2] Family Income Supplement was replaced by Family Credit, see Chapter 17.

## Fixed costs of employment

**Fixed cost of employment**

Once a person enters the labour market, they may incur one-off expenditures unrelated to the number of hours they work

It should be recognised that entering employment may be a costly exercise; work clothes must be bought, travel expenses incurred and more importantly for those who have been acting as carers, usually for children, alternative (and often expensive) arrangements must be made. These **fixed costs of employment** are often thought of as fixed payments, which do not vary with the wage rate. If we call the fixed cost $F$, the effect can be seen in Figure 13.14 and the budget constraint is now $I = I_U - F + wT - wL$.

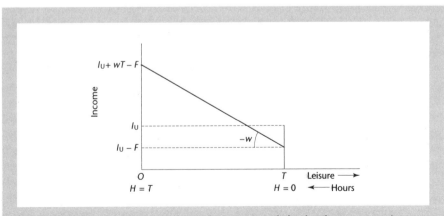

**Figure 13.14** Fixed costs of employment and the budget constraint

This is likely to result in another disincentive effect, which is likely to be exacerbated by low anticipated wage rates and the high fixed costs of employment (particularly full-time employment) associated with child-care. These disincentive effects are more likely to affect women, particularly lone mothers and women whose husbands are unemployed. We see in Table 13.3 below that in 1984 40% of lone mothers faced marginal rates of taxation at 50% or above.

**Table 13.3**

| Marginal tax rate in 1984 | % of single parents in Britain |
| --- | --- |
| 0 | 6 |
| 9 | 6 |
| 10–38 | 5 |
| 39 | 32 |
| 40–49 | 4 |
| 50 | 20 |
| 51–69 | 7 |
| 70–79 | 9 |
| 80–99 | 3 |
| 100+ | 9 |

Source: Atkinson, Table 5.2, 1993

## 13.5 Conclusion

In this chapter we have considered the impact of Income Tax upon the behaviour of individuals. The response to an Income Tax will reflect the relative strengths of the income and substitution effects, so that a conventional labour supply schedule will only occur if the substitution effect dominates the income effect. Estimates of labour supply elasticities show that, amongst men, supply elasticities are small, suggesting a limited response to an Income Tax. The estimates of supply elasticities for women are much larger and positive; as a consequence female supply is more responsive to incentive efforts. Given this, the effect of the tax reforms during the 1980s on work incentives is uncertain. The biggest reductions in Income Tax were amongst those at the upper end of the income distribution. The revenue collected from this group has risen, but Dilnot and Kell (1988) argue that this can be attributed to factors other than incentives. They suggest that hours of work have remained fairly constant, but that remuneration packages of top earners have probably changed, resulting in greater income rewards rather than fringe benefits, which attracted preferential tax treatment. Finally, we considered the impact of welfare payments on labour supply. We found that it is not the payments themselves that might create supply disincentives, but the fact that welfare payments are means-tested. Means-testing transfer payments results in a withdrawal of payments once income reaches a certain level; this withdrawal acts as a tax and we found that many claimants face a tax rate of 70–80%. The likely impact of welfare payments upon labour supply provides a useful insight for the design of social policy, discussed in Chapter 17.

## Summary

- The labour supply response to a change in the wage rate or the introduction of a proportional Income Tax will be determined by the relative strengths of the income and substitution effects.
- A conventional labour supply schedule arises when the substitution effect dominates; supply is inelastic if the substitution and income effects counter each other and the labour supply schedule is backward bending if the income effect dominates.
- Estimates of labour supply elasticities suggest that male labour supply is inelastic and that female labour supply exhibits a large positive elasticity.
- The efficiency loss associated with a proportion tax reflects the size of the tax and the elasticity of the compensated labour supply schedule.
- There is a smaller gender gap in the compensated labour supply elasticities; estimates fall between $0.1 < \eta^{CL} < 0.9$.
- The efficiency loss associated with a progressive tax system is greater than that with a single rate.
- The withdrawal of means-tested benefits acts as a tax, often in excess of 70%, on those in receipt of welfare payments, creating a welfare trap and efficiency losses.

## Questions

1. Are there disincentives associated with income taxation?
2. The Laffer curve suggests that as tax rates rise, the tax revenue initially rises and then falls. Sketch this and outline the assumptions which it makes about labour supply behaviour.
3. Why is there a welfare loss associated with a proportional tax?
4. What factors influence the size of the deadweight loss associated with a proportional tax?
5. What is a poverty trap? How does this differ from an unemployment trap?
6. Which groups in society face the greatest disincentives associated with taxation?

## Further reading

For those who are unfamiliar or a little rusty with the model of labour supply, it is worth returning to an intermediate microeconomic text such as Katz and Rosen (1998) or Varian (1996). Blundell (1992 or 1993) provides an excellent survey of empirical work on labour supply. For more details on poverty traps and work incentives, see Parker (1995) or Walker (1993).

# References

Atkinson, A.B. (1993) 'Have social-security benefits seriously damaged work incentives in Britain?', in A.B. Atkinson and G.V. Mogenson (eds) *Welfare and Work Incentives: A North European Perspective*, pp. 161–91, Oxford: Clarendon Press.

Atkinson, A.B. and Mogenson, G.V. (eds) (1993) *Welfare and Work Incentives: A North European Perspective*, pp. 161–91, Oxford: Clarendon Press.

Blundell, R. (1992) 'Labour supply and taxation: a survey', *Fiscal Studies*, August, 13(3), 15–40.

Blundell, R. (1993) 'Taxation and labour-supply incentives in the UK', in A.B. Atkinson and G.V. Mogenson (eds) *Welfare and Work Incentives: A North European Perspective*, pp. 135–60, Oxford: Clarendon Press.

Dilnot, A. and Kell, M. (1988) 'Top-rate tax cuts and incentives: some empirical evidence', *Fiscal Studies*, November, 8(4), 70–107.

Heady, C. (1993) 'Optimal taxation as a guide to tax policy: a survey', *Fiscal Studies*, February, 14(1), 15–41.

Katz, M.L. and Rosen, H.S. (1998) *Microeconomics*, 3rd edn, London: McGraw-Hill.

Layard, R., Nickell, S. and Jackman, R. (1991) *Unemployment: Macroeconomic Performance and the Labour Market*, ch. 5, Oxford: Oxford University Press.

Parker, H. (1995) *Taxes, benefits and family life: The Seven Deadly Traps*, Research Monograph 50, London: Institute for Economic Affairs.

'The Government's Expenditure Plans 1996/97', Social Security Department Report. Norwich: The Stationery Office.

Varian, H.R. (1996) *Intermediate Microeconomics*, New York: Norton.

Walker, I. (1993) 'Income taxation, income support policies and work incentives in the UK', in Jackson, P.M. (ed.) *Current Issues in Public Sector Economics*, pp. 31–57, London: Macmillan.

PART 4

# The Welfare State

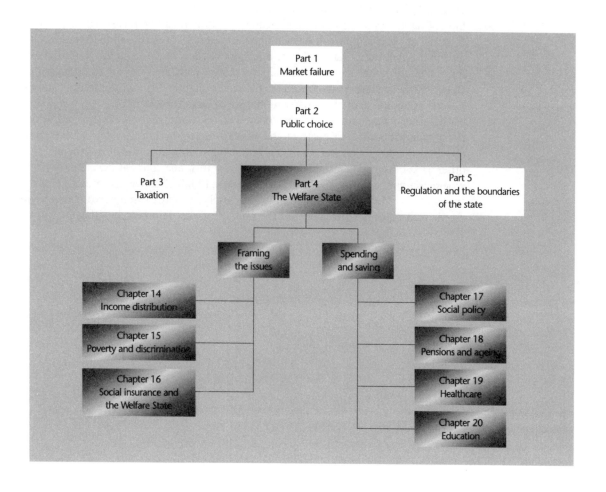

Part 1
Market failure

Part 2
Public choice

Part 3
Taxation

Part 4
The Welfare State

Part 5
Regulation and the boundaries
of the state

Framing
the issues

Spending
and saving

Chapter 14
Income distribution

Chapter 15
Poverty and discrimination

Chapter 16
Social insurance and
the Welfare State

Chapter 17
Social policy

Chapter 18
Pensions and ageing

Chapter 19
Healthcare

Chapter 20
Education

If importance is measured by expenditure, then the Welfare State is by far the most significant part of government activity. In the UK, £2 out of every £3 spent by the government is on the Welfare State. It is also the area of public expenditure most subject to scrutiny, where the ceaseless march of reforming ministers has had the least effect on the growth of aggregate expenditure.

The seven chapters of this part are divided into two. The first three chapters are general, offering a background to the debate on the size and shape of the Welfare State. Chapter 14 looks at income inequality – how it can be measured, what are its component parts and how it has changed. Chapter 15 does the same for poverty and discrimination, then Chapter 16 provides an overview of the different potential roles for a Welfare State. Each of these chapters also considers the forces changing the shape of the Welfare State, from globalisation (Chapter 14) and the feminisation of poverty (Chapter 15) to the changing nature of risks (Chapter 16).

The other four chapters (Social Policy, Pensions and Ageing, Health and Education) examine specific aspects of the Welfare State, taking up some of the issues raised in the previous three chapters, but also building on some of the themes from other parts of the book. Much of Chapter 17, for instance, looks at the benefit system, where an understanding of the efficiency costs of high effective tax rates is central to the analysis. Meanwhile, Chpapter 18 is closely related to Chapter 6, since asymmetric information is the source of the bulk of market failure in healthcare.

# Income Inequality

## Key concepts

| | | | |
|---|---|---|---|
| Lorenz curve | Gini coefficient | inequality aversion | lifecycles |
| globalisation | equivalised income | wage gap | Eurosclerosis |

## 14.1 Introduction

The majority of this chapter is devoted to two topics: first, to the depiction of the income distribution and the measurement of inequality, and second, to exploring the factors behind the sharp rise in UK income inequality over the last twenty years.

As Figure 14.1 shows, in any society, incomes are determined by a multitude of factors, meaning that in turn the distribution of incomes is the outcome of a very complex process. Government policy is only therefore one of a number of influences on the income distribution. In a perfectly competitive market, individuals will expect to receive the marginal product of the factors they supply, so the immediate

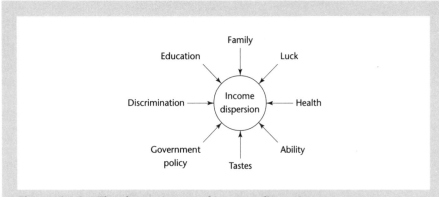

**Figure 14.1**  The determinants of income dispersion

determinant of the income distribution is the distribution of marginal products across individuals. However, these in turn will be affected by the past decisions of individuals about savings, investment in education, or in job search, by the educational and other decisions made on their behalf by their parents, by their innate ability and by elements of chance. Income will also be determined by tastes, in that the patient saver is likely to have a higher income in the future than the spendthrift, and that someone with a high taste for consumption will tend to work more hours than someone with a preference for leisure. Meanwhile, living standards (as opposed to pure income) will also be influenced by our choices (and constraints) over who we live and share incomes with. In short, like everything else in the competitive general equilibrium, income inequality is determined by the interplay between tastes, technology and endowments.

Imperfect competition breaks the link between marginal products and earnings. Meanwhile bequests and transfers from relatives, alongside government actions (especially, but not exclusively, the tax and transfer system), weaken the link between incomes from factor supplies and total income. As a result, the competitive model may provide only a weak guide to what eventually determines the distribution of income.

## Lifecycle issues

The individual's income is also normally dependent on what stage they have reached in the lifecycle. Figure 14.2 shows a heavily stylised summary of one person's life, divided into three sections: childhood, working life and retirement. In childhood, lacking income and without access to capital markets, they can spend only the pocket money granted to them by their parents. Income and expenditure change sharply once they gain employment. For a time, perhaps, expenditure outstrips income, as they borrow to buy a car or other consumer durables. Later on, they are net savers, preparing for retirement, which is marked by a drop in income (and a switch in its sources, from labour to capital market). Expenditure also falls (and may still lie below income, if the individual continues to save for precautionary reasons, as many pensioners do). Consumption meanwhile is much smoother than either expenditure or income; when young, it is parents who provide; later on, consumption for our individual is based on their own expenditure and on the flow of in-kind services from assets purchased previously, such as a car, furniture or a house. For this reason, it initially trails behind expenditure, but then overtakes it later in life. Now, of course individuals differ and there are many possible events left out of this fiscal biography, from unemployment and divorce to bequests from dead relatives, but it does have important implications for income inequality. Even in a country where lifetime incomes are completely equal, there is likely to be considerable inequality in current income, purely because of variations in the age of individuals. Demographic changes can therefore lead to changes in measured income inequality, but not necessarily in the lifetime well-being of any individual.

The data shown in this chapter takes incomes at a single time, but for some purposes a picture of lifetime inequality is more suitable. For instance, students are poor when viewed at a single point in their lives, but will usually have above-average incomes for their lifetime. If capital markets are perfect, then consumption and therefore living standards will be more closely related to lifetime income than to income for one particular week or year, implying that the acceptability of the 'snapshot' approach as a measure of living standards depends on the degree of imperfection in the capital market.

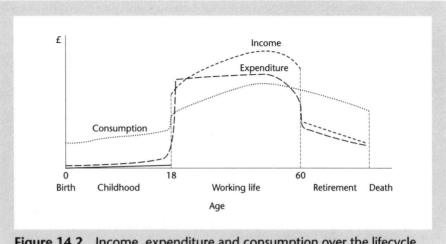

**Figure 14.2** Income, expenditure and consumption over the lifecycle

## 14.2  Measuring inequality

We have already seen that incomes can be unequal and yet there may be no loss of social welfare (compared to the optimum) as a result, even when viewed by the most ardent Rawlsian. This arises partly because of the lifecycle, but also because tastes for income and leisure differ. It follows that when we measure inequality of income, we have first to decide why we are measuring it. A purely statistical summary of the distribution of income leads to one approach, while measures which purport to show the loss of social welfare from inequality need something more sophisticated.

### Lorenz curves

**Lorenz curve**

This shows the cumulative percentages of total income owned by cumulative percentages of the population

The simplest way to depict inequality uses the **Lorenz curve** (see Figure 14.3), which plots cumulative population on the x axis against cumulative share of total income on the y axis. If incomes in a society are completely equal, then the poorest individual has the same income as the richest, meaning that the Lorenz curve is a line at 45°. If, though, one person has all the income and all others have none, then the curve follows the x axis until 100 is reached, at which point it jumps up the y scale to 100%.

More generally, if £1 is transferred from someone with a higher income to someone with a lower income, then the new Lorenz curve lies above the old. Conversely, if one Lorenz curve lies above another, then it can be obtained from the first by a sequence of income transfers from rich to poor. We can see this in Figure 14.4. In the lower diagram, the distribution of income is shown before and after £1 is transferred from someone at $Y_H$, above the mean income line, to someone at $Y_L$, an equal distance below (so that mean income is unchanged). This transfer reduces the frequency of people with incomes $Y_H$ and $Y_L$ by 1 and raises the number of individuals with incomes $Y_H - 1$ and $Y_L + 1$ by 1, creating the 'steps' in the income distribution. The effects of this on the Lorenz curve are traced in the top portion of the figure, where $C_L$ represents the cumulative percentage of the population with incomes below $Y_L$ (the area to the left of $Y_L$ in the lower diagram) and $C_H$ shows the percentage of the population with incomes below $Y_H$ (the area to the left of $Y_H$ in the

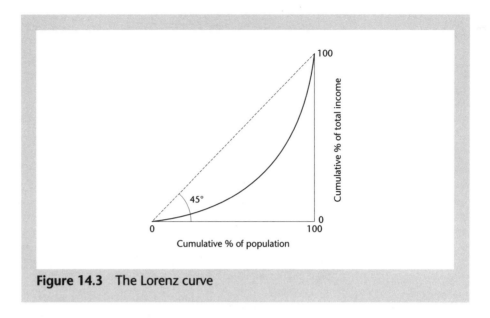

**Figure 14.3**   The Lorenz curve

bottom diagram). The heavy line thus shows how the cumulative percentage of total income is altered. Below $C_L$ and above $C_H$ there is no change but, between the two, cumulative income rises by £1, lowering the area between the Lorenz curve and the 45° line.

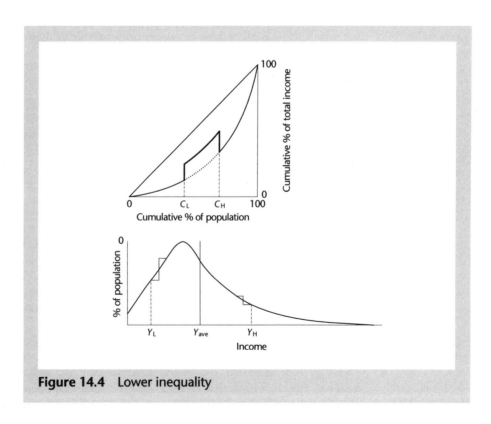

**Figure 14.4**   Lower inequality

## The link to social welfare

We saw in Chapter 3 that most measures of social welfare rise when well-being is spread more evenly across society. It follows that, if (1) income is a good measure of individual well-being and (2) social welfare is only a function of individual well-being, then £1 transferred from someone rich to someone poor raises social welfare. So if Lorenz curve A lies closer to the 45° line compared to curve B, then social welfare is higher (see Figure 14.5) for all concave social welfare functions. Of course, Lorenz curves may cross; B and C do. Curve B shows more equality than C at lower levels of income, but more inequality at higher levels, so it is not possible to tell which represents higher social welfare without knowing the underlying welfare function. A Rawlsian, or someone else who is extremely inequality averse, will see distribution C as representing lower social welfare.

In many instances we wish to compare inequality or welfare across time or countries. If it is only inequality that is under the spotlight, then Lorenz curves provide a convenient method. However, once we begin to make welfare comparisons, extra assumptions creep in; income must be a good measure of well-being and to be comparable across time or between different societies, any adjustments for inflation or differences in purchasing parity must be made. More fundamentally, mean income will typically differ, and we would want a social welfare measure which reflected that, but not differences in population. The **generalised Lorenz curve** continues to plot cumulative percentage of the population along the bottom, but now cumulative total income as a proportion of average income forms the y axis. If one country's generalised Lorenz curve lies above another's, then it is as if we are saying that every person in the first country has a higher income than the corresponding person in the second country.

**Generalised Lorenz curve**

A Lorenz curve with right-hand scale values multiplied by average income

## Measures of inequality

Since the area above the Lorenz curve shrinks as inequality falls, one obvious candidate for a summary measure is this area as a proportion of the total area under the

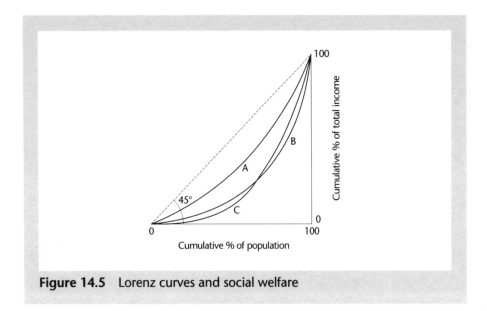

**Figure 14.5** Lorenz curves and social welfare

**Gini coefficient**

The area between the Lorenz curve and the 45° line expressed as a fraction of the total area under the 45° line

45° line, a statistic called the **Gini coefficient**. More formally, if there are $n$ individuals with incomes $y_i$ ($i = 1, \ldots, n$ and $y_i < y_j$ for $i < j$) and mean income is $\bar{y}$, the Gini coefficient is:

$$G = 1 + \frac{1}{n} - \frac{1}{n^2\bar{y}} (y_1 + 2y_2 + \ldots + ny_n) \tag{14.1}$$

If $G = 1$, then one individual has all the income; if $G = 0$ then all individuals have the same income. The Gini coefficient is the most commonly employed measure of inequality, but it is hard to interpret as a welfare measure, because the weight placed on an individual's well-being depends on how far up the ranking they are and not on their income as such (you can see this in equation (14.1)). Some measures have been developed which are explicitly based upon social-welfare indices, the most famous of which is Atkinson's measure:

$$A = 1 - \left( \Sigma_i \frac{y_i^{1-e}}{\bar{y}} \right)^{\frac{1}{1-e}} \tag{14.2}$$

We have already encountered $1 - A$ as a measure of social welfare in Chapter 3. The higher the value of $e$, the greater the sensitivity of the measure to transfers between rich and poor (greater inequality aversion). If $e = 0$, for instance, then changes in the distribution of income do not alter the value of the index. If $e = \infty$, then we have a Rawlsian measure, where only transfers to the individual with the lowest income alter A.

These measures embody two different approaches to the issue of inequality measurement (statistical and welfare, respectively), but to some degree they are both *ad hoc*. A third approach asks what the desirable features of an inequality measure are and then finds the class of indices which fit. Write $I(Y)$ as the inequality index associated with a vector of incomes, $Y = (y_1, y_2, \ldots y_N)$, then the following list of axioms are often proposed for $I(Y)$:

(A) *Anonymity Axiom.* The inequality measure is not altered by a change in the labelling of households.

The next axiom states the conditions under which the measure of inequality should be expected to go down.

**Transfer Axiom**

Obeyed by inequality measures which fall when income is transferred from rich to poor

(T) *Transfer Axiom.* Suppose that we have two vectors of household incomes, $Y^A$ and $Y^B$, with the same mean income, and that $Y^A$ can be derived from $Y^B$ via a series of transfers from rich to poor. Then $I(Y^A) < I(Y^B)$.

An index having this property is called Schur convex, since its value is lowered by any process of averaging. A third axiom underlies the idea that we should be able to compare inequality in two countries by normalising the vector of incomes in any country, using average income.

(R) *Relativity Axiom.* If all incomes are multiplied by $a > 0$, then the index should be unchanged. That is, $I(aY) = I(Y)$.

Both the Gini coefficient and the Atkinson index satisfy A, T and R, but it is sometimes argued that an index should be *decomposable,* meaning that the index for a society can be represented as the sum of the indices for sub-groups within that society, weighted by the total income of individuals in each group, plus an index for the inequality between sub-groups. This is convenient if, for example, we wish to know what proportion of inequality across Europe arises because of inequality within its Member States and what proportion is due to inequality between Member States. Let the vector of incomes in a sub-group $i$ composed of $H^i$ members be $Y^i$ and let the proportion of total income attributable to this group be $w^i$, with its mean income as $m^i$ then we have:

(D) *Theil Decomposability Axiom.* An index $I(Y^1, \ldots, Y^N)$ satisfies D if it can be written as:

$$I(m^i e^1, \ldots, m^N e^N) + \sum_{i=1}^{i=N} w^i I(Y^i) \tag{14.3}$$

The vector $e^i$ is $(1,1, \ldots, 1)$ (with $i$ elements in total), so that $m^i e^i$ is a vector representing the sub-group, but with all individuals within that sub-group having the same income. The first term in equation (14.3) represents inequality between groups, while the second is the sum of inequality within groups, with each group weighted by its relative contribution to total income. Only one index satisfies A, I, R and D and that is Theil's Entropy Index,[1] which is:

$$T = \frac{1}{N \log N} \sum_{i=1}^{i=N} \frac{y_i}{\bar{y}} \log \frac{y_i}{\bar{y}} \tag{14.4}$$

where $N$ is the number of households in total.

In this section, we have seen that there are a number of inequality measures on offer. All satisfy A, I and R, so that if the Lorenz curve for country A lies inside that for country B, or the curve for a given country at time $T$ lies inside that for time $S$, then they will record inequality as lower in A compared to B and lower at time $T$ compared to $S$. However, when Lorenz curves cross (which they often do), the different indices may disagree about which case represents higher inequality.

## 14.3  Practical issues

The representation of inequality in a Lorenz curve or through a summary measure such as the Gini coefficient involves a host of practical choices about whether to use the household or the individual as the unit of analysis, whether to use post- or pre-tax income, and so on. In general, the best depiction of inequality will depend on the purposes of the investigation. Some of the main issues are discussed below.

### Household composition and equivalence scales

It is possible to construct inequality measures based upon individual income or to look at the distribution across households. Households normally pool some of the income of their constituent parts, and also achieve returns to scale through the provision of joint goods (e.g. heating). Thus measures based upon household income normally show a more equal spread of incomes than measures based on the

---

[1] Despite its unique ability to satisfy all four axioms, the Theil measure is only usually employed when decomposability is an important requirement. This partly reflects the fact that the index does not have a simple economic interpretation.

individual, and measures based on income per person underestimate the standard of living of individuals who do not live alone.

In applied analysis, it is usual to suppose that all members of a household share the same standard of living, then to try to find ways of comparing the living standards of different types of households, for instance single people versus couples. The *equivalent income* of an individual is then the income required to give him or her the same standard of living as a couple.[2] In a similar way, the equivalent income for families with children can be compared to that of couples without children. The theory of **equivalence scales** is based on the idea that a household of two adults, for instance, probably needs very little extra in the way of housing space or heating, compared to a single person, but obviously is likely to want about twice as much food in order to achieve the same standard of living. One way to compare the living standards of households of different sizes is therefore to adjust the utility function used. If $U(x,y)$ is used for an individual, $U(x/a, y/b)$ is used for two people, where $a$ and $b$ are coefficients which show how much extra of that particular good two people require compared to one person. In the example, $x$ might be heating, in which case $a = 1$, and if $y$ is food, $b = 2$ would be a good approximation.

There is an alternative and perhaps more useful way of stating the same thing. Suppose $p$ is the price of $x$ and $q$ is the price of $y$, then the two-person household's optimisation problem is to maximise $U(x,y)$ subject to $apx + bqy \leq$ income. In other words, prices are altered rather than needs. Figure 14.6 illustrates the answer for different households to the question, How much income is required to reach a given standard of living? We first take a standard of living, defined by the indifference curve, $U$. We then find the lowest income, such that a particular household can just reach $U$ given their adjusted prices. For household 0 facing prices $p$ and $q$, equivalent income $E^0$ is required, but for household 1 facing prices $ap$ and $bq$, $E^1$ is needed to get them on the same indifference curve. If we take household 0 as the reference point for the construction of an equivalence scale, we can say that for every £1 required by it to reach $U$, household 1 requires $e = E^1/E^0$. In practice, $e$ will vary as prices and $U$ alter, but in applied estimates of equivalence scales it is more usual to assume that $a = b$, so that one household's living expenses are a simple multiple of the reference household. This is very much an approximation, since for many goods, needs in multiple-person households are not a simpe multiple of needs in a one-person house-hold. For instance, adding a baby to a two-adult household has an enormous effect on nappy consumption, but not on whisky.

There are other more traditional means of approaching the idea of equivalence scales, based on the approach of Engels who argued that households which spent the same proportion of their budget on food (a clear necessity) would have the same standard of living. Instead of food, a wider basket of necessities could be selected as the reference bundle, as in Figure 14.7. Here, $S_0$ shows the share of income $Y_0$ spent on necessities by the reference household of two adults. At the same income, the two adult and one child household spend $S_1$ on food, but if they had income $Y_1$ they would spend the same share as the two adults. In the Engels approach, therefore, $Y_1 - Y_0$ provides a measure of the extra income required by the household with the child to match the welfare of the two adults.[3]

**Equivalence scale**

A means by which standards of living across household types may be compared

---

[2] In the charts displayed in this chapter, it is assumed that a single person requires 0.61 of the income of a couple in order to achieve the same living standard; thus two cannot quite live as cheaply as one.

[3] A slightly different and perhaps more intuitive approach was taken by Rothbarth (1941), who argued that the two households would have the same living standard if the adults in the household with the child could purchase the same *level* of adults-only goods, such as alcohol and tobacco.

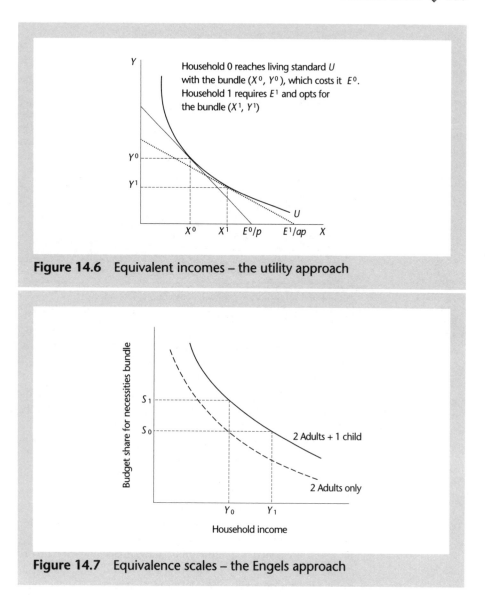

**Figure 14.6** Equivalent incomes – the utility approach

**Figure 14.7** Equivalence scales – the Engels approach

Equivalence scales have been estimated for many types of households in most developed countries with most modern researchers using the utility-based method to estimate equivalence scales. Table 14.1, drawn from Banks and Johnson (1994), summarises some estimates for the UK (one utility-based, the other using Engels' method) and compares them to the equivalence scales implicit in the social security benefit, Income Support, which effectively assumes that there is a fixed cost of children and that the marginal child adds less than this to the cost of living of a household. Comparisons with the researchers' estimates are therefore made with both the average cost of an extra child in the Income Support figures and with the marginal cost. We can see that, though all the estimates agree that children are costly and that this cost rises with their age, there is a wide range of estimates over their actual cost, ranging from 18% of an adult (Blundell and Lewbel, 1984, cost of a child 0–2 years old) to over 100% (official estimates with fixed costs for children aged 16 plus).

**Table 14.1** Equivalence scale estimates for the UK

| Household | Scales Implicit in Income Support | | Blundell and Lewbel (1984) | Banks and Johnson (1994) |
|---|---|---|---|---|
| | No fixed costs of parenthood | With fixed costs of parenthood | Utility approach | Engels' method |
| Single person | 0.64 | 0.64 | – | – |
| Two adults | 1.00 | 1.00 | 1.00 | 1.00 |
| Plus one child | | | | |
| Under 11 | 1.22 | 1.36 | 1.09 (0–2 yrs) | 1.12 (0–2 yrs) |
| 11–15 | 1.32 | 1.46 | 1.14 (3–5 yrs) | 1.22 (3–5 yrs) |
| 16–17 | 1.38 | 1.52 | 1.16 (6–10 yrs) | 1.37 (6–10 yrs) |
| 18 | 1.50 | 1.64 | 1.36 (11+ yrs) | 1.41 (11–16 yrs) |

Source: Banks and Johnson, from Tables 2, 3 and 4, 1994

How does the choice of equivalence scale affect inequality measures? Typically, larger households have bigger incomes than smaller ones, so that small equivalence scales reduce inequality indices, but larger adjustments bring the equivalised incomes of larger households below those for smaller households, which pushes up the inequality measure. There is therefore a U-shaped relationship between the size of the equivalence scale and the inequality index.

One problem with the equivalence-scale approach is the underlying assumption that all members of a household share the same standard of living. In practice, resources within the household may be shared unequally and this means that inequality may be underestimated as a result. Evidence on intrahousehold inequality is hard to gather, but some inferences may be drawn from expenditure patterns. If a household pools all its income, then expenditure on private goods should be unaffected by who earns the wage, but as Martin Browning *et al.* (1994), among others, have demonstrated, expenditure patterns are related to who brings in the money. For instance, in their study of clothing expenditure within two-adult Canadian households, Browning *et al.* (1994) found that a 1% rise in the ratio of the woman's earnings to the man's led to a 0.13% rise in the ratio of expenditure on women's clothing to men's. Overall, therefore there is good reason to believe that income is not shared equally within the household, but little data is available on the exact division.

## Taxes and benefits

It is possible to use incomes either before or after adjustment for taxes and transfers. A Lorenz curve for before-tax incomes shows the level of inequality produced by the market. However, we have to remember that this is an *equilibrium* outcome; removing taxes and benefits has implications for wages, private savings and so on. Within some groups, such as pensioners, many individuals have zero gross income because they rely on government provision. Removing government pensions would lead to massive changes in private savings behaviour and therefore dramatically alter the shape of the distribution of gross income.

Households also derive benefits from government expenditure on goods such as healthcare and education, as well as from direct cash transfers. In addition, the benefits of public goods such as defence should also be included in any measure of well-being. Adjusting net incomes for in-kind benefits is difficult, not least because we know little about the distribution of benefits for many public goods, but also because in the absence of markets for the goods and services provided by the government, it is hard to place a value on the benefits of private goods.[4] In most standard analysis of the income distribution, benefits-in-kind are omitted, but doing this will generally lead to an overestimate of the degree of inequality in society, since the pattern of consumption of public services is fairly egalitarian (see LeGrand, 1982). Conversely, a reduction in public expenditure may lead to an unnoticed rise in inequality.

## 14.4 International comparisons and recent trends

The OECD consists of over twenty Member States, ranging the USA to Turkey, from Sweden to Japan. Making accurate comparisons of inequality between these countries is almost impossible.[5] Data sampling methods differ widely between countries, as does the accuracy of reported incomes. The unit of analysis also differs; in some countries, it is the individual, in others the household. Countries such as Sweden, with a high proportion of in-kind benefits, are difficult to place alongside societies such as Japan or the USA where market income more accurately reflects total income. Household size also varies between countries, as do demographic factors such as the proportion of elderly in the population, so that two similar Gini coefficients may hide a substantial difference in the living standards or lifetime inequality of the nations. Under these circumstances, what conclusions can we take from international comparisons? First, if measured inequality is consistently higher in country A compared to country B and the gap cannot be explained by differences in sampling method, demographics, etc., then we are entitled to conclude that A is more unequal than B. Second, and perhaps more importantly, we can compare trends and try to understand why trends differ, when developed countries face many of the same economic forces.

### Recent trends

Figure 14.8 shows the recent experience of a number of OECD countries, as measured by post-tax Gini coefficients. As might be expected, the USA stands out as the nation with the highest inequality of the group and Sweden consistently scores lowest, with Norway just behind. We have just noted the difficulty of comparing inequality between nations, so that while it is probably safe to conclude from this figure that the USA is more unequal than Sweden or Norway, conclusions about the relative ranking of countries within the middle of the pack are much less certain. The lower figures for Sweden are partly due to impact of taxes and benefits, but even before taxes its Gini coefficient is well below that for other countries. Smeeding *et al.* (1990, Table 2.2), for instance, indicate that the lowest quintile of families in Sweden had 9.4% of total equivalised income, in 1979, compared to 5.1% for the equivalent US quintile and

---

[4] Tim Smeeding (1985) estimates that up to 28% of income for the elderly in the USA represents transfers-in-kind.

[5] Smeeding *et al.* (1990) report on the Luxembourg Income Study, which standardises income data from many countries, rendering it more comparable, but still subject to a fair degree of uncertainty.

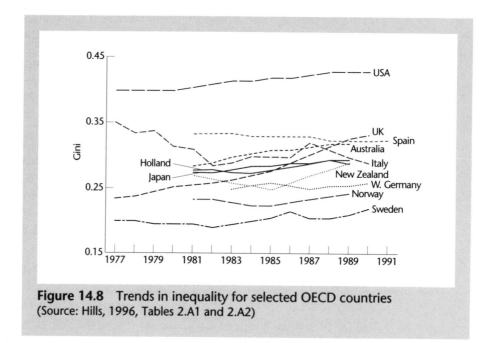

**Figure 14.8** Trends in inequality for selected OECD countries
(Source: Hills, 1996, Tables 2.A1 and 2.A2)

7.9% in West Germany. The respective Gini coefficients were 0.249, 0.371 and 0.363. The Swedish tax and transfer system also had the biggest impact on the lowest quintile, pushing up its income share to 10.6% compared to 7.5% and 6.1% for Germany and the USA, respectively. Low post-tax inequality may therefore be correlated with low pre-tax inequality.

Over the time period, inequality is roughly constant for most countries, although both Spain and Italy show downward trends, the latter with a great deal of fluctuation. Although countries such as the USA, Australia and New Zealand have experienced mild rises in inequality, the sharpest change faced by any nation is signalled by the upward trend in the Gini coefficient for the UK, which achieves the rise from second lowest to second highest in the space of under fifteen years.

More detail on the recent experience of the UK is provided by Figure 14.9, which shows Lorenz curves for the UK, using equivalised incomes for households in three years. The curve for 1991 lies outside the curves for 1979 which, in turn, lies outside the curve for 1961. Thus we can say unequivocally that inequality has risen and not just the Gini coefficient. This process reversed a much longer trend of declining inequality, as Figure 14.10 suggests. In this figure, the Gini coefficient for the UK shows a declining trend until the mid-1970s and, subsequently, a steep climb. The share of income going to the bottom 10% of households begins at 4.22% of total income, rises slightly to a peak of 4.82% (in 1973), but is roughly constant until 1980, when it begins to fall towards its 1991 value of 3%. The picture at the top of the income range is more erratic, but is roughly constant until the early 1980s, after which it climbs to a 1991 value of 25%.

## Women and men

Comparing the relative fortunes of men and women is difficult, if not impossible. Many men and women share a household and as we have already mentioned,

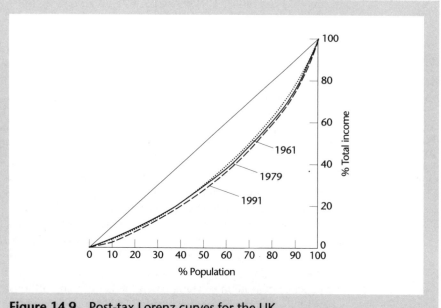

**Figure 14.9** Post-tax Lorenz curves for the UK
(Source: Goodman and Webb, 1994, Statistical Appendix, Figure 2.3)

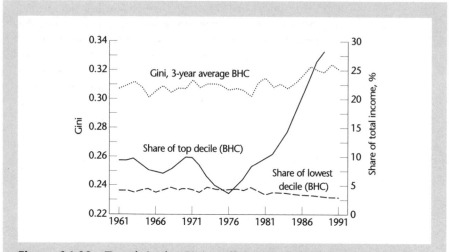

**Figure 14.10** Trends in the Gini coefficient and decile income shares
(Source: Goodman and Webb, 1994, Statistical Appendix, Figures 2.1 and 2.2;
BHC = Before Housing Costs)

intrahousehold transfers raise the living standards of the poorer member of the
household and reduce it for the richer member, although of course, many couples
would not see it in such individualistic terms. Household income will almost certainly omit the value of home-based production (e.g. in the rearing of children), thus
giving a potentially false picture of the balance of transfers within the household.
Data for intrahousehold transfers is rarely available and so we are left to fall back on
information provided in the market.

Figure 14.11 shows that average wages for women in full-time employment have risen slowly relative to their male equivalents. Data presented in this way does not allow for differences in education, training, experience and occupational choice, and so on. Adjusting for these effects still shows a significant **wage gap** between men's and women's incomes. However, we should not view this adjusted gap as a 'true' measure of discrimination, since it may be that some of the forces which bar women's progress in the labour market also hinder them in their experience of education and other factors affecting incomes (see Chapter 17).

Since women on average have lower wages than men, the increase in income inequality seen in the UK over the last twenty years will have tended to push earnings apart. But female labour participation has moved steadily upwards and the women have closed the difference in educational attainment. So has the earnings gap closed or not? Data from the Family Expenditure Survey (FES), the General Household Survey (GHS) and the British Household Panel Survey (BHPS) provides some evidence.

According to the FES, in 1973, the average hourly earnings of a woman working full-time were 59% of average male earnings, a figure which climbed to 70% in the late 1970s (perhaps because of the introduction of the Sex Discrimination and Equal Pay Acts in 1975) and which, after a plateau in the 1980s, has now reached 77%. The experience of women working part-time is different, although it was not until the late 1970s that the figures for part- and full-time working women began to diverge. They dropped from a peak of 68% (of male full-time earnings per hour) to the low 60s where they have since more or less remained; the 1993 figure was 63%.

These changes are reflected in women's ranking relative to men in the male earnings distribution. In 1973, more than 50% of full-time women earned less than the 10th percentile of the male earnings distribution. Meanwhile, 90% earned less than the median man and only 2.3% had incomes which would have placed them in the top decile of the earnings league table for men. However, 1993 shows a different story at the lower end of the distribution, with only 25% of women earning less than the 10th percentile of the men, but still 75% of full-time women earned less than the

### Wage gap

The difference between men's and women's average incomes, usually expressed as a percentage of average male earnings

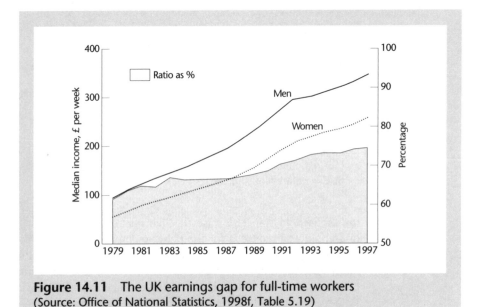

**Figure 14.11** The UK earnings gap for full-time workers
(Source: Office of National Statistics, 1998f, Table 5.19)

median male and the proportion of women receiving more than the bottom 90% of men had inched up to 2.5%. The rise in inequality during this period affected both men and women; whereas the 10th percentile of full-time women (men) saw earnings growth of 62% (18%) between 1973 and 1993, the rise was 93% (49%) at the 90th percentile. Again, part-time women fared more poorly, with rises of 38% and 50% at the two markers.

These figures illustrate the two opposing forces of catch-up and rising inequality, but they do not reveal whether the catch-up is due to reduced discrimination or other changing features of the labour market. Consequently, we return to this issue in section 17.6.

### Ethnic minorities in the UK

Most of the available data on income and wealth comes from the Inland Revenue or surveys where questions of ethnicity are not raised, with the result that we know very little about the interracial distribution of income in the UK. What little information we have mostly comes from the GHS which does ask questions about both income and ethnicity. The accuracy of this information is limited by the small size of the sample and the fact that ethnic minorities represent only 6% of the UK population and hence only around 6% of the sample. Figure 14.12 summarises the little we know and suggests a heterogeneous rather than homogeneous picture. For the population as a whole, 20% should lie in each quintile, implying that people of Pakistani/Bangladeshi origin are significantly overrepresented in the poorest fifth of society and all ethnic minorities are underrepresented in the richest fifth.

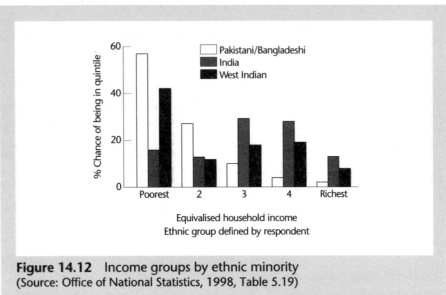

**Figure 14.12** Income groups by ethnic minority
(Source: Office of National Statistics, 1998, Table 5.19)

## 14.5 Explaining the trends

We have seen that several countries, notably the UK, but also Australia, the USA and New Zealand, have seen steady rises in inequality over the last fifteen to twenty years. Identifying the immediate sources of these changes is relatively straightforward.

## The immediate causes

We said in the first section of this chapter that incomes are mainly determined in factor markets, so it is there that we must go to search for the proximate causes of the changes, which divide into four categories as shown in Table 14.2.

In analysing trends in men's wages, for instance, Gosling *et al.* (1994) note that prior to 1975, young men could expect to earn more than their predecessors upon entry to the labour market. Since then men without an education or a skill have fared no better than their forbearers, whereas educated men have continued to show gains on earlier generations. However, the returns to education cannot explain all of the dispersion; the variance of incomes of men with the same education has also shown a steady rise. Participation by married women in the labour market has increased, but in the poorest families women are still less likely to work. Rises in unemployment,

**Table 14.2** The proximate causes of rising income inequality in the UK

| Category | Proximate Causes |
|---|---|
| Widening gap between high- and low-wage earners | Rising relative return to education, coupled with a collapse in wages for the unskilled and semi-skilled |
| | Tax and benefit changes favouring the affluent (e.g. drops in highest rate of Income Tax, the switch to indirect tax which is less progressive in its impact – see Tables 14.3 and 14.4) |
| | End of 1970s income policies (which tended to squeeze incomes) |
| | Declining importance of trade unions, leading to greater dispersion in semi-skilled workers, particularly in non-unionised sectors |
| Widening gap between those in and out of work | Tightening of benefit eligibility, tying of benefit level to RPI rather than average earnings (e.g. UB for a single person was 41% of average disposable income in 1970 and just 30% in 1992) |
| | Rising participation of labour market participation by women, leading to increasing numbers of two-earner and no-earner households |
| | Tying of state pensions to prices rather than earnings. From 1983 to 1993, the value of a basic state pension for a single person fell from 45% of per capital disposable income to 38% |
| Rising numbers without income from work | Increase in unemployed, compared to 1970s and earlier |
| | Increases in numbers of pensioners (most of whom have below-average incomes) |
| | Rise in single-parent families, with head not in paid employment |
| | Increase in number of long-term sick/disabled |
| Rising dispersion in investment income | 1980s property boom led to rising property income for owner–occupiers |
| | Rising proportion of retired with occupational pension (up from 44% in 1979/80 to 55% in 1988/89), with a wide dispersion in terms of pensions |

Note: Some of the changes could be classified under multiple headings

**Table 14.3** Changing tax rates in the UK

|  |  | 1975 | 1985 | 1995 |
|---|---|---|---|---|
| Income Tax | Basic rate (%) | 33 | 30 | 25 |
|  | Highest rate (%) | 83 | 60 | 40 |
|  | Personal Allowance | £2,834 | £3,445 | £3,445 |
|  | Married Allowance* | £1,175 | £1,950 | £1,720 |
|  | MIRAS ceiling | £125,960 | £46,800 | £30,000 |
|  | MIRAS rate | Marginal rate | Marginal rate | 15% |
| National Insurance | (%) | 9 | 9 | 10 |
| Indirect taxes | VAT rate (%) | 8 | 15 | 17.50 |
|  | VAT domestic fuel (%) | 0 | 0 | 8 |
|  | Excise, 20 cigarettes | £0.12** | £0.81 | £1.13 |
|  | Excise, spirits, bottle | £10.00 | £7.38 | £5.55 |

All figures at 1995 prices
* Separate taxation introduced in 1990/91 – earlier figures are for Additional Personal Allowance
** Figures for 1977 (prior to this, cigarettes were taxed on a weight basis)
See also Chapter 10

when combined with this skewed increase in female participation, mean a decline in the percentage of one-earner couples from 45% in 1975 to 29% in 1993 (Hills, 1996, p. 49).

## Government policy

It is clear from the previous section that some of the changes in inequality are the result of government policy. Tax policy has also influenced the pattern of incomes, as Tables 14.3 and 14.4 show. Since the government chooses the legislation it enacts, we might argue that these factors are exogenous, but it can also be argued that the trade-off between equality and efficiency has moved against the pursuit of equality. For instance, the returns to education and skill have grown in the last twenty years, opening up the gap in wages between skilled and unskilled. And, as populations have aged, the cost of eliminating pensioner poverty has risen.[6]

In the next section, therefore, we examine some of the arguments over whether the equality–efficiency trade-off is changing. Because of its importance, it is an issue we return to in Chapters 15–20, where some of the more specific aspects of the debate are covered.

## 14.6  Fundamental causes

Identifying fundamental causes of these changes is difficult; it requires us to construct counterfactual worlds by identifying some of the underlying causes as

---

[6] This issue is taken up in Chapter 18.

**Table 14.4** Winners and losers from tax changes, 1985–95

| Decile | % Gaining | Average gain/loss wk (£) | Average gain/loss (% net income) |
|:---:|:---:|:---:|:---:|
| 1 | 7 | –3.0 | –2.9 |
| 2 | 13 | –1.4 | –1.4 |
| 3 | 23 | –1.8 | –1.5 |
| 4 | 40 | –1.1 | –0.8 |
| 5 | 50 | 0.7 | 0.4 |
| 6 | 57 | 1.6 | 0.7 |
| 7 | 64 | 3.1 | 1.2 |
| 8 | 69 | 4.4 | 1.5 |
| 9 | 72 | 6.3 | 1.8 |
| 10 | 76 | 31.3 | 5.8 |
| All | 47 | 4.1 | 1.7 |

All figures at 1995 prices
Source: Giles and Johnson, Table 3, p. 11, 1995

endogenous and others as exogenous. Nevertheless it is important, for precisely the same reason; if we wish to know what policy responses are possible and which are desirable, then we require some idea of what it is a government can influence within an economy. We can classify the fundamental causes into four classes: individual preferences, demographic changes (such as an ageing population or changes in household structure), technology and external factors, such as globalisation. Government policy itself is not exogenous; it depends on the preferences of the electorate, and the other factors influence each other over the long run. Figure 14.13 summarises the possibilities. The original equality–efficiency frontier is shown as $OO$ and the degree of equality is $Q^0$. If equality has declined (to $Q^1$), it can be due to one of two reasons (or both, they are not mutually exclusive). The cost of pursuing equality at the expense of efficiency may have risen, as shown in the left-hand diagram, where, with the same political preferences at work, the new level of equality is $Q^1$. The right-hand panel outcome shows the alternative, where the trade-off has not changed, but preferences have; perhaps individuals have become more ideologically opposed to the Welfare State, or have revised their estimates of its cost.

The debate over whether the Welfare State remains affordable is common to all Western nations, with many Anglo-Saxon politicians arguing that continental Europe will have to follow the examples of Britain, America and New Zealand in pursuing vigorous welfare pruning. The difficulty of agreement on the causes of the changes is exemplified by the debate over the Welfare State in Sweden (see Box 14.1), a country which has long provided a model of a prosperous nation with a high degree of equality. Most authors agree that Sweden has underperformed relative to its natural comparators, but are split on whether the Welfare State has been a cause of that decline.

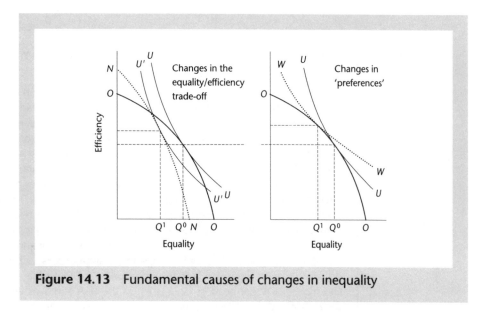

**Figure 14.13** Fundamental causes of changes in inequality

## Globalisation

**Globalisation**

The process by which the world economy becomes more integrated

One popular argument is that the trade-off has turned against the pursuit of equality because of global competition from newly industrialising nations. It is usual to base the globalisation argument upon the factor price equalisation hypothesis of international trade theory, combined with modern growth theories. These theories rest on the idea that consumers in developed nations are unwilling to substitute lower quality for lower price. Thus to gain access to a market, a new supplier must meet some quality threshold. However, producing reliable quality is complex, requiring an educated workforce, infrastructure (roads, power, etc.), learning by doing, and so on, all of which mean that high-quality/knowledge-intensive goods are less threatened by global competition compared to commodities produced largely by unskilled labour.

Once a country faces competition from developing nations (so the argument goes), two things may happen: a reduction in wages or unemployment. Unemployment is more likely to result when a country has inflexible labour markets because of minimum wage legislation, worker protection, union power and an effective welfare safety net. Thus continental European countries (so the story goes) have faced higher unemployment, whereas the USA and New Zealand have seen wages fall. The UK seems to have had both.

### Background evidence

Nickell and Bell (1995), for example, divide their sample of countries in two: the USA, Japan, Norway and Sweden, which have seen a small rise in overall unemployment, but a higher rise in unemployment amongst the unskilled, and the UK, Spain, Germany, Canada and The Netherlands, which have endured a higher increase in unemployment, with both skilled and unskilled suffering. Overall, they estimate that around 20% of the rise in UK male unemployment over the last twenty years is due to a decline in demand for unskilled workers. Nevertheless, it is hard to blame

| BOX 14.1 | **Has the trade-off turned against equality? – Sweden** |

The consensus on Swedish economic performance is that it has lagged behind that of other rich nations and that, as a result, Sweden's ranking in the per-capita GDP league tables has slipped from 6th to 7th place in the early 1970s to 17th position by 1994 (Henreksen, 1996). This fact is disputed by some; Walter Korpi (1996), for instance, argues that Swedish performance has not been materially worse than that of the other European nations, pointing out that between 1973 and 1989 Swedish growth of GDP per capita was 1.7% per annum, compared to 1.6% for Germany, the UK, Denmark, The Netherlands, France and Switzerland. These two years are significant, representing trough and peak, respectively, and over other time periods Swedish per-capita growth looks less respectable, falling consistently below the OECD average (e.g. 1970–91 OECD average was 2.11, European OECD average was 2.04 and Sweden was 1.5% per annum, Henreksen, 1996). One problem with simply comparing growth rates is that richer countries do tend to grow more slowly than poorer ones,[7] so that other countries which had higher GDP per head in 1970, such as the USA and Switzerland, have also shown lower than average growth rates. More relevant therefore is the fact that Sweden has slipped down the rankings; convergence should lead to bunching rather than overtaking.[8] Swedish growth does seem to have lagged, but even this does not imply that the Welfare State has caused the decline. Cross-sectional studies are equivocal on the impact of the size of the public sector on growth (see Atkinson, 1995, or Levine and Renelt, 1992, for instance), which is understandable because there may be positive consequences for growth of higher government spending on education or infrastructure, say. In a survey of the extensive literature on the subject, Agell *et al.* (1996) state that, once variations in initial GDP have been controlled for, there is no relationship at all between tax share and growth rates and, moreover, once demographic factors enter the regression, there is a small *positive* relationship between tax share and growth in OECD countries over the period 1970–90. Agell (1996) argues that the case for Swedish sclerosis is therefore not a dynamic one (the Welfare State causing lower growth rates), but a static one (the Welfare State lowering efficiency). On this issue, the evidence must be provided by microeconomic investigation. For the individual with average earnings in 1991, the marginal tax rate from all sources of taxation is approximately 62%. Even with a low compensated labour supply elasticity of 0.05 (see Chapter 13), the marginal cost of public funds (MCPF) is 9.6. With the higher elasticity of 0.11, the MCPF rises to 21.1, meaning that for every extra Swedish Krona raised by the government, the extra excess burden is 20.1 Krona (Agell, 1996). The lack of incentives to combat moral hazard may also impose costs on sickness funds and saving.

In summary, the case that Sweden has faced lower growth rates as a result of its Welfare State is not overwhelming, but the country has slipped down the league table of GDP per capita. There is clearer evidence of a static efficiency loss and some suggestion that this loss has become worse as the century has progressed.

---

[7] This may still be consistent with sclerosis if the cause of subdued growth is the size of a Welfare State swollen by prosperity.

[8] Korpi (1996) argues that most of this slide down the table is recent and due not to sclerosis, but to the fiscal policies which Swedish governments have pursued in the mistaken belief in the existence of Eurosclerosis.

trade with developing nations, since it makes up only a small proportion of total expenditure, as Table 14.5 illustrates.

The UK has one of the largest rises in import penetration of the European Union countries, but total imports from developing nations are still below 3% of GNP. Note though that the greater the convergence of wages between developed and developing nations, the smaller will be the rise in import penetration; in the extreme, UK wages might fall to Chinese levels, at which point the Chinese would have no cost advantages and import penetration could be zero. Thus import penetration may be a poor guide to the consequences of trade for the unskilled.

**Table 14.5** Imports from developing nations

| Imports from developing nations/GNP % | 1970 | 1990 |
|:---:|:---:|:---:|
| USA | 0.4 | 2.5 |
| EU | 0.5 | 2.1 |

## Factor content analysis

**Factor content analysis**

Using input–output relationships to predict changes in demand for inputs

Changes in trade patterns do not tell us much about the resultant changes in the demand for different types of labour, but crude estimates of the impact of globalisation can be obtained using a technique called **factor content analysis**. In the basic version of the technique, the effective increase in the supply of unskilled workers is estimated by summing the changes in net imports for each sector multiplied by a coefficient, $a$, indicating the amount of unskilled labour per unit of output in the *developed* nation. Wood (1995) criticises this approach, and uses the value of $a$ in *developing* nations, modified in two ways: first, to allow for the fact that, with higher wages, developed nations would tend to use more skilled labour than developing nations in the production of the imported goods, and second, to adjust for the drop in demand from the higher prices which would result if developed nations produced the goods themselves. As can be seen from Table 14.6, these different approaches yield significantly different estimates, but they share the conclusion that unskilled labour bears the brunt of changes in the global economy. In addition to the direct effects of trade changes, Wood lists two further factors which might have added to the impact: first, defensive innovation in threatened sectors, leading to a substitution away from

**Table 14.6** The impact of globalisation on labour demand

| % change in labour demand manufactured goods, 1990 | Sachs and Shatz (USA) | Wood (all developed nations) |
|:---|:---:|:---:|
| All | –5.7 | –10.8 |
| Skilled | –4.8 | 0.3 |
| Unskilled | –6.2 | –21.8 |

Source: Wood, Table 1, 1995

unskilled labour, and second, service industries, many of which are also tradeable (e.g. tourism, key punching), but for which data is much harder to gather.

Some critics dismiss the factor content method; after all, taste and technology changes could also have caused the changes in imports and exports, not competition from developing nations. Alternatively, it can be argued that the factor content method is irrelevant. Trade theory predicts that relative factor rewards will only change in response to differential productivity changes or following changes in the relative prices of goods (i.e. in this case, rises in the relative prices of knowledge-intensive goods). Thus it is goods' prices which should be examined and not factor content changes. Unfortunately, data for goods' prices is less reliable, but even so, some attempts have been made to use it. Putting computer prices to one side, Sachs and Shatz (1994) find that import prices have risen more slowly for labour-intensive goods and, on the domestic (i.e. USA) front, prices in skill-intensive industries have risen more quickly.

If unskilled labour is displaced, then it should find its way into other sectors, as firms substitute towards the now cheaper factor. However, the proportion of skilled workers has risen steadily in most sectors, an important point which suggests that technical progress favours the skilled and perhaps obviates the need for a trade-based explanation of labour market changes.

The arguments over global competition are complex and the assembly and analysis of the evidence is at a preliminary stage. It seems that trade factors can explain some of the increase in wage inequality, and certainly more than was once thought. Meanwhile, the differential impact of technical progress is also a significant component of the rising gap between unskilled and skilled.

## 14.7 Conclusion

It seems that inequality in the UK has risen for a number of reasons. Some of these reasons have raised the cost of maintaining traditional levels of inequality. Anticipating and reacting to these forces, the Conservative government chose greater inequality rather than measures which would have raised the fraction of GNP devoted to the Welfare State. Inequality has also risen in other countries. Whether the countries of continental Europe will be forced to allow the same rise in inequality is less clear; the impact of globalisation is as yet small and its proponents may have overemphasised the dangers it poses for the Welfare State.

The next chapter is complementary to this one in that it is concerned with poverty, a concept distinct from inequality, but nevertheless related. In Chapters 16–20 we then examine specific aspects of the Welfare State. In reading those chapters, keep in mind that many of the forces which affect the equity–efficiency trade-off at the general level examined in this chapter are also prominent at more detailed levels of government expenditure.

## Summary

- Income inequality arises from a variety of factors including differences in innate ability, the return to education, luck, home environment and stages of the lifecycle, as well as from government policy.

- The Lorenz curve provides a simple way of depicting inequality. It plots the cumulative share of total income against the cumulative fraction of the population, with members of the population ranked by income. Complete equality produces a 45° line for the Lorenz curve.

- Various summary measures of inequality are available. The most widely employed is the Gini coefficient which is the ratio of the area between the Lorenz curve and the 45° line, measured as a fraction of the total area beneath the 45° line.

- For most OECD countries there has been no clear-cut trend in income inequality over the last twenty years. In Britain over the same period there has been a sharp and persistent rise in inequality.

- In the UK, the gap between women's wages and men's has slowly declined, but by 1996 the mean full-time female worker still earned only 77% of her male counterpart.

- Evidence on the relative incomes of ethnic minorities in the UK is limited, but it consistently points to a significant gap between white and non-white earnings.

- The immediate causes of the rise in UK income inequality include the rise in the relative returns to education, government tax and benefit policy and demographic trends, such as the increase in lone parenthood and the rise in the numbers of pensioners.

- Debate over the fundamental causes of the changes continues. Some commentators blame a rise in global competition for the increase in inequality, but there is little evidence that this accounts for a substantial proportion of the developments observed over the last two decades.

## Questions

1. How can we compare inequality (a) between countries and (b) over time?

2. What advantages does the Gini coefficient have over other measures of inequality? What disadvantages does it have?

3. An index of inequality is constructed based on unequivalised individual incomes at a particular moment. Would the index be higher or lower if (a) lifetime income was used, (b) if equivalised income was employed and (c) if household income was used instead?

4. Why is the degree of import penetration by developing nations not a measure of the impact of globalisation on developed economies?

5. Why has inequality risen in the UK so dramatically? Why has it not risen in other European countries?

# Further reading

Atkinson (1983) is a good general source on the economics of inequality. Banks and Johnson (1994) have an up-to-date discussion of equivalence scales. Goodman and Webb (1994) provide an overview of trends in UK inequality and Harkness (1996) is a topical summary of pay gap issues. More on UK inequality can be found in Hills (1996) and for international comparisons, see Hills (1996) and Atkinson (1996), while Smeeding *et al.* (1990) give background detail on the whole issue of international comparisons. More generally, the Institute of Fiscal Studies provides regular commentaries on the changing shape of the UK income and wealth distribution (a topic not explored here) and the *Review of Income and Wealth* provides up-to-date material on a wide range of countries. Hills (1996) provides a summary of the reasons for the change in the UK distribution. A good place to enter the debate on the effects of globalisation is the collection of articles by Freeman (1995), Richardson (1995) and Adrian Wood (1995), in the *Journal of Economic Perspectives*. Also relevant is the 1995, 11(1) issue of the *Oxford Review of Economic Policy*, particularly the articles by Nickell and Bell (1995) and, on one potential type of solution, by Lars Calmfors and Per Skedinger (1995). The issue of whether the trade-off between equality and efficiency has turned against the former is covered in Atkinson (1995), and for the case of Sweden in the interchange between Korpi (1996), Agell (1996) and Henreksen (1996); see also Lundberg (1985) and Lindbeck *et al.* (1993).

# References

Agell, J. (1996) 'Why Sweden's Welfare State needed reform', *Economic Journal* 106, 1761–72.

Agell, J., Lindh, T. and Ohlsson, H. (1996) 'Growth and the public sector: a critical review essay', *European Journal of Political Economy*, 8, 44–61.

Atkinson, A.B. (1983) *The Economics of Inequality*, Oxford: Oxford University Press.

Atkinson, A.B. (1989) *Poverty and Social Security*, Oxford: Clarendon Press.

Atkinson, A.B. (1995) 'The Welfare State and economic performance', *National Tax Journal* 48, 171–98.

Atkinson, A.B. (1996) 'Seeking to explain the distribution of income', Ch. 2 in J. Hills (ed.) *New Inequalities: The Changing Distribution of Income and Wealth in the United Kingdom*, Cambridge: Cambridge University Press.

Banks, J. and Johnson, P. (1994) 'Equivalence scales and public policy', *Fiscal Studies* 15, 1–24.

Barro, R.J. (1990) 'Government spending in a simple model of endogenous growth', *Journal of Political Economy* 98(5), 103–25.

Blau, F. and Kahn, L. (1992) 'The gender earnings gap: some international evidence', *American Economic Review* 82, 533–8.

Blundell, R. and Lewbel, A. (1984) 'The information content of equivalence scales', *Journal of Econometrics* 50, 49–68.

Browning, M., Bourguignon, F., Chiappori, P.-A. and Lechene, V. (1994) 'Income and outcomes: a structural model of intrahousehold allocation', *Journal of Political Economy* 102, 1067–96.

Calmfors, L. and Skedinger, P. (1995) 'Does active labour-market policy increase employment? Theoretical considerations and some empirical evidence from Sweden', *Oxford Review of Economic Policy* 11(1), 609–19.

Freeman, R. (1995) 'Are your wages set in Peking?', *Journal of Economic Perspectives* 9(3), Summer, 15–32.

Giles, C. and Johnson, P. (1995) *Taxes up, taxes down: The effects of a decade of tax changes*, Institute for Fiscal Studies, Commentary No. 41.

Goodman, A. and Webb, S. (1994) *For richer, for poorer: the changing distribution of income in the UK, 1961–91*, Institute for Fiscal Studies, Commentary No. 42.

Gosling, A., Machin, S. and Meghir, C. (1994) *What Has Happened to Wages?*, Institute for Fiscal Studies, Commentary No. 43.

Harkness, S. (1996) 'The gender earnings gap: evidence from the UK', *Fiscal Studies* 17, 1–37.

Henreksen, M. (1996), 'Sweden's relative economic performance: lagging behind or staying on top?' *Economic Journal* 106, 1747–60.

Hills, J. (ed.) (1996) *New Inequalities: The Changing Distribution of Income and Wealth in the United Kingdom*, Cambridge: Cambridge University Press.

Johnson, P. and Webb, S. (1991) *UK Poverty Statistics: A Comparative Study*, Institute for Fiscal Studies, Commentary No. 27, May.

Korpi, W. (1996) 'Eurosclerosis and the sclerosis of objectivity: on the role of values among policy experts', *Economic Journal* 106, 1727–47.

LeGrand, J. (1982) *The Strategy of Equality*, London: George Allen Unwin.

Levine, R. and Renelt, D. (1992) 'A sensitivity analysis of cross-country growth regression', *American Economic Review* 82, 942–63.

Lindbeck, A., Molander, P., Persson, T., Peterson, O., Sandmo, A., Swedenborg, B. and Thygesen, N. (1993) 'Options for economic and political reform in Sweden', *Economic Policy* 17, 219–64.

Lundberg, E. (1985) 'The rise and fall of the Swedish model', *Journal of Economic Literature* 23, 1–36.

Nickell, S. and Bell, B. (1995) 'The collapse in the demand for the unskilled and unemployment across the OECD', *Oxford Review of Economic Policy* 11, 40–62.

Office of National Statistics (1998) *Social Trends 1997*, London: Stationery Office.

Richardson, J.D. (1995) 'Income inequality and trade: how to think, what to conclude', *Journal of Economic Perspectives* 9(3), Summer, 33–55.

Rothbarth, E. (1941) The measurement of change in real income under conditions of rationing, *Review of Economic Studies* 8, 34–55.

Sachs, J. and Shatz, H. (1994) 'Trade and jobs in United States manufacturing', *Brookings papers on economic activity*, 1, 1–84.

Smeeding, T. (1985) *Alternative Methods for Valuing Selective In-Kind Transfers and Measuring Their Impact on Poverty*, US Bureau of Census, Technical Report No. 50.

Smeeding, T., O'Higgins, M. and Rainwater, L. (1990) *Poverty, Inequality and Income Distribution in a Comparative Perspective*, London: Harvester Wheatsheaf.

Snower, D. (1993) 'The future of the welfare state', *Economic Journal* 418, 700–17.

Wood, A. (1995) 'How trade hurt unskilled workers', *Journal of Economic Perspectives* 9(3), Summer, 57–80.

# Poverty

## 15.1 Introduction

In his seminal work on poverty in York in 1899,[1] Seebohm Rowntree (1901) identified a lifecycle pattern of poverty. People are at greatest risk of poverty when their
needs exceed their resources, that is during childhood, early parenthood and in
retirement. Nearly a century later, these remain the periods of the lifecycle associated
with the greatest risk of poverty. Though many of the factors identified by Rowntree,
namely unemployment, ill-health and low savings for retirement, remain significant,
their relative importance has changed, with some diminishing. For example, in the
first Rowntree study, large family size was a key contributory factor towards poverty
in childhood and early parenthood, but poverty in these periods of the lifecycle is now
more likely to be associated with family breakdown.

Any discussion of poverty must begin with the question of how poverty is defined
and how it can be measured. Only then is it possible to consider recent trends in
poverty and to identify the groups most at risk and how poverty has changed over time.

## 15.2 Defining poverty

There are different views on the appropriate definition of poverty. Some regard
poverty as an absolute concept which reflects subsistence and which remains

---

[1] This was the first of three studies. The surveys (1899, 1935 and 1950) were very extensive; the first
surveyed approximately 11,000 households, the second surveyed approximately 16,000 households and the
third approximately 16,000 households.

constant over time, whereas others argue that poverty is a relative concept and its meaning varies both across societies and over time. Measures of poverty, rather like social welfare, should be seen as reflections of differing views on social justice.

## Poverty lines

**Poverty line**

Measures the level of income below which an individual or household is considered to be experiencing poverty

Whatever definition of poverty is used, a **poverty line** identifies a level of income which is considered to be necessary to prevent poverty. As we shall see, many argue that whether or not a person experiences poverty is largely a matter of her or his ability to afford food, clothes and accommodation. However, other factors also affect well-being. A person's income level may be sufficient to prevent hunger, but not high enough to ensure adequate nutrition. An unbalanced diet may result in chronic health problems or shorter life expectancy. Equally, although a family may have a home, factors such as the location, the local infrastructure and the quality of the housing also have an impact on their quality of life. In the case of rural living, access to local services such as health and education may be problematic, while in the case of inner-city developments, the quality of health and educational services may be poor and the absence of banking facilities and low-cost food outlets may cause further difficulties.[2]

## Absolute poverty

**Absolute poverty**

Where income is not sufficient to ensure physical well-being – food, clothing and shelter

This approach regards poverty as a fixed standard. An **absolute poverty** line is measured as the level of income necessary for the bare necessities of life: food, clothes and shelter. The Rowntree studies referred to above have been highly influential. Rowntree (1901) considered that primary poverty exists when a family does not have a sufficient income to maintain physical efficiency. He used the work of nutritionalists to identify the nutritional levels necessary to maintain body weight and used this to estimate the minimum dietary needs of a family. Taking the cost of housing as given, Rowntree defined a poverty line as the income net of rent necessary to purchase food, clothes and heating. His poverty line for a family with three children was 17s. 8d: 12s. 9d for food, 2s. 3d for clothing, 1s. 10d for fuel and 10d for household sundries. He considered that a family whose income net of rent fell short of this was experiencing primary poverty.

The notion of a poverty line linked to primary or absolute poverty proved extremely popular, since it vindicated the minimal assistance such as that provided by the Poor Law in the UK. It also heavily influenced later reforms to the Welfare State. During the Second World War and based on evidence from Rowntree's second study, Lord Beveridge proposed a subsistence budget of 53s. 3d per week for a family with three children, with an allowance for food of 31s.[3] The same principle which informed the levels of assistance set out in the Beveridge report remained in place until the mid-1980s.[4] According to Townsend (1993) this concept of poverty was also a

---

[2] Many high-street banks have withdrawn branches and cashpoint machines from inner-city areas. Large supermarkets are usually located on the outskirts of towns and easy access to these requires having a car or a regular public transport system. Thus it may not be possible for those on low income to buy their weekly shopping in supermarkets. They are usually reliant on local corner stores, where prices are high and availability of fresh produce is much more limited.

[3] Townsend (1979) claims that in 1938 evidence shows that most working-class households spend a much lower proportion (41%) of their income on food than the minimum set out in these subsistence poverty lines.

[4] 'In the mid-1980s the British Government formally abandoned the subsistence standard which had prevailed in principle since the acceptance of the Beveridge Report' (Townsend, 1993 with D. Gordon). This decision is outlined in the 1985 Green Paper on Social Security.

successful export. The notion of subsistence was used to set the 'poverty line' in South Africa, India, Malaysia, Canada and the USA.

However, there are problems in measuring absolute poverty. First, Townsend (1979) argues climate is a key consideration in setting a subsistence level of calorific intake. In Northern Europe it is estimated that the minimum daily needs are 2000 calories, but in warmer climes 1000 calories are considered sufficient, therefore the poverty line should vary with climate. Second, estimates of subsistence reflect a minimum calorie intake based upon average needs and are not sensitive to the activities or occupations of the individuals involved. For example, an adult involved in heavy manual work would require a diet with a higher calorific intake than another adult engaged in non-manual employment. Finally and most importantly, the requirements for subsistence will also change over time. For example, the clothing allowance for a woman identified by Rowntree (one pair of boots, two aprons, one second-hand dress, one skirt made from an old dress, one-third of the cost of a new hat, shawl and jacket, two pairs of stockings, a few unspecified underclothes and a pair of old boots used as slippers) is clearly a bench mark which has changed over time and culture. Similar arguments can be made over diet, particularly since the foodstuffs which formed the bulk of the diet even ten or twenty years in the past may no longer be widely available in food outlets. In conclusion, even an absolute measure of the income necessary to prevent poverty will differ across countries, its value will rise with inflation and it should also reflect developments in what constitutes subsistence.

## Relative poverty

The discussion so far has shown that defining absolute poverty can be problematic. Thus an alternative measure of poverty considers the position of the individual *relative* to the society within which they live. **Relative poverty** measures the level of income necessary not only for subsistence but which also enables participation in that society:

> Individual, families and groups in the population can be said to be in poverty when they lack the resources to obtain the types of diet, participate in the activities and have the living conditions and amenities which are customary, or at least widely encouraged or approved, in the society to which they belong. (Townsend, 1979, p. 31)

**Relative poverty**

Where income is not sufficient not only to ensure physical well-being but also to allow participation in society

A useful example is tea, which has no nutritional value (and so would be excluded from a diet concerned only with subsistence), but is regarded as essential in many societies because of its role in social customs.[5] The subjective nature of this measure means that it is not an easy matter to reach agreement on what is an appropriate relative poverty line.

Estimating a poverty line based on a relative definition of poverty requires a method of measuring not only the income necessary for a physical life, but for participation in society as well. For example, when Rowntree conducted his second survey in 1935, he included factors which reflect the ability to participate in society: radio, newspapers, presents for the children and the cost of taking a holiday. Townsend's approach is to identify an index of deprivation and then trace the relationship

---

[5] Rowntree (1901) certainly regarded his estimated primary poverty line as an absolute minimum which would not allow for social participation. He wrote 'It would suffice only for the bare necessities of merely physical efficiency in terms of health' p. 142. 'A family living on the scale allowed for in this estimate must never spend a penny on railway fare or omnibus. They must never go into the country unless they walk. They must never purchase a halfpenny newspaper or spend a penny to buy a ticket for a popular concert' p. 167.

between the value of the index and income. He finds that the value of the index rises as income falls and that at a given level of income, 150% of the level of supplementary benefit,[6] the index rises sharply as income falls (see Figure 15.1).

The index of relative poverty used by Townsend (1979) in this study includes measures of diet (for example, not having a cooked breakfast or a Sunday joint), material well-being (for example, the household does not have a refrigerator or does not have sole indoor use of four amenities (flush WC, sink and water, bath or shower, cooker)) and social well-being (for example, has not had an afternoon or evening out for entertainment in the last two weeks, has not had a relative/friend to their home or been to the home of a relative/friend for a meal/snack in last four weeks or has not had a week's holiday away from home in last twelve months). Piachaud (1981) argues that the measures reflect household or individual choice and are not necessarily indicators of deprivation. As an observer in the late 1990s, we would probably regard not having a cooked breakfast or a Sunday joint as a matter of personal choice or the result of a busy, but not necessarily impoverished, lifestyle. Piachaud also questions the emphasis placed by Townsend upon style of living. He argues that deprivation is also a matter of conditions in the workplace, the living environment and public services.

Just as measures of absolute poverty need to adjust over time, so must measures of relative poverty. In a later study of household poverty in the Greater London region in 1985–86, Townsend (1993) reports an index of multiple deprivation, using thirteen sources of deprivation to measure material and social deprivation.[7] The thirteen categories and sample questions are given in Table 15.1. This index takes account of deprivation in the work environment and poor access to public services (thus addressing some of Piachaud's concerns outlined above). Using this index, it was concluded that households needed an income equivalent to 166% of the level of supplementary benefit (on average) in order to avoid poverty. Background studies for

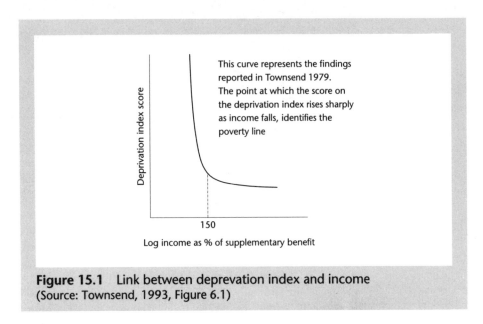

This curve represents the findings reported in Townsend 1979. The point at which the score on the deprivation index rises sharply as income falls, identifies the poverty line

Deprivation index score

150

Log income as % of supplementary benefit

**Figure 15.1**  Link between deprevation index and income
(Source: Townsend, 1993, Figure 6.1)

---

[6] Supplementary benefit (SB) became Income Support (IS) after the 1988 Social Security Reforms. It is the basic level of welfare payment provided by the state.
[7] The full index is presented in Appendix 3.3 of Chapter 3 in Townsend (1993).

**Table 15.1** Index of deprivation used for the Greater London Survey of Poverty 1985–6

| Index | % of population |
|---|---|
| *Material deprivation* | |
| Dietary – No fresh meat or fish most days of weeks (also offer vegetarian alternative) | 13.2 |
| Clothing – Inadequate protection against severe cold | 5.6 |
| Housing – Overcrowded (fewer rooms, excluding kitchen and bathroom, than persons) | 9.2 |
| Home facilities – No washing machine | 24.4 |
| – No central heating | 32.1 |
| Environment – Nowhere for children under 5 (5–10) to play safely | 39.1 (37.2) |
| Location – Doctor's surgery or hospital outpatients dept not within 10 minutes' journey | 8.5 |
| – No shops for ordinary household goods within 10 minutes' journey | 4.1 |
| Work – Polluted air, dust, noise, vibration, extreme temperatures | 24.9 |
| *Social deprivation* | |
| Employment rights – Subject to one week's termination of employment or less | 26.7 |
| – Faces discrimination (sex, race, age or disability) | 8.3 |
| Family activity – If family has children, children not had outing in last year | 26.1 |
| Integration into community – Alone and isolated from people | 9.4 |
| Lack of formal participation – Did not vote at last election | 31.1 |
| Recreational – No holiday away from home in last 12 months | 29.8 |
| Educational – No formal qualification | 31.9 |

Source: Townsend, Appendix 3.3, 1993

the London Weekend Television programmes 'Breadline Britain' conducted in 1983 and 1990 produced similar results.[8]

## Outcome measures of poverty

**Poverty and capabilities**

The poverty line is measured in terms of commodities needed to reach a minimal level of well-being

A further contribution to the debate on defining poverty relates to whether poverty should be defined in terms of goods and income at all. Sen (1983) argues that the definition of poverty should always represent an absolute concept, but not as a matter of physical subsistence, rather in terms of their **capabilities**, 'at the risk of oversimplification, I would like to say that poverty is an absolute notion in the space of capabilities but very often it will take a relative form in the space of commodities or characteristics'. pp. 71–4. He goes on to argue that,

[8] Mack and Lansley (1985, 1992). They find a poverty line at 135% of SB in 1985.

in a poor community the commodities or resources needed to participate in community activities might be very little indeed. . . . For richer communities, however, the nutritional and other physical requirements (like clothing) were typically already met, and the needs of communal participation – while absolutely no different in the space of capabilities – would have a much higher demand in the space of commodities and that of resources. (pp. 71–4)

Sen rejects a purely relative approach to poverty, because this would leave us with the notion that the problem of starvation is purely a relative one. He also thinks that much poverty in Western societies can be given an absolute basis. The foundation of his argument is the notion of *capabilities*. These are somewhat like the characteristic approach to consumer behaviour. A bike gives a person the capability to move around, but if the same person is paraplegic, then the bike is useless in this regard. Likewise in order to be educated (in the widest sense of the word), a Western child may need access to a television in a way that a child in India does not. Thus the capabilities (education, transport) are absolute, but the commodities required to achieve them are not. At the same time, Sen makes a distinction between *absolute satisfaction* and the relative position that may be required to achieve this level. If a society's average standards of dress determine whether or not someone at a job interview will be employed, then falling below the relative minimum sartorial standard will lead to a loss of absolute consumption.

While Sen and Townsend argue vigorously over their relative positions, in some senses they are quite close. Both end up with a relative notion of poverty, but notice that Sen is saying that the core capabilities which determine whether someone is deprived or not are absolute; it is their representation in commodity space that is relative to a society and a time period. Townsend though is arguing that even the core capabilities are in some sense relative to a particular society. At a practical level, Sen's poverty line is likely to suffer from some absolutist drag. If 50% of the British population were poor at the turn of the century, then that proportion has diminished. With Townsend, however, there is no reason why an increase in the riches of a country may have no effect on the proportion in poverty.

## 15.3  Measuring poverty

The poverty lines derived by Rowntree (1901, 1941) and Townsend (1979, 1993) are based on a 'scientific' study of what level of income is necessary to sustain physical life (Rowntree) and physical and social life (Townsend). These studies have been used by governments to identify the minimum income standard (MIS) and the level of social assistance, although the actual level of income considered to be the MIS or awarded as welfare payments is the result of political decision-making. It is for this reason that Sen (1985) argues that the level of poverty should not be measured by the level of income paid out in welfare payments. Such a measure is very sensitive to changes in the political environment. Suppose a government were to reduce the value of welfare payments. By this measure, the incidence of poverty would fall. If instead welfare payments became more generous, the incidence of poverty would rise.

It should be clear that a poverty line drawn on the basis of a relative definition of poverty, although closely related to inequality, is a distinct concept. Where income inequality is greatest, we are also likely to find larger numbers of households experiencing relative poverty. Given this and the difficulty of classifying a satisfactory index of deprivation, governments use the 'poverty line' of the level of income which is half the national average. This is of course not a poverty line, but it is used as an approximation. Similarly, whilst the European Union and the United Nations identify poverty according to a relative definition, that is, in terms of 'living in a manner compatible with human dignity' and 'to take part in the life of the community' and describing the poor as 'persons whose resources are so limited as to exclude them from the minimum acceptable way of life in the Member State in which they live', they also take half the national average income as a measure of poverty. As we argued in Chapter 14, it is important that we treat such international comparisons with some caution.

## Desirable features for poverty measures

A measure of poverty should give an indication of both the numbers of households experiencing poverty and the extent of the poverty which they experience. Morris and Preston (1986) provide an extensive survey of measures of poverty and inequality. Suppose that there are $n$ individuals, $I = 1, \ldots, n$. Each has income $y_i$, which, when listed all together in a vector, can be denoted by $y$. A poverty line is defined, $\pi$, and given the income distribution plus this line, any poverty measure should be able to produce a number – the poverty index. Thus we can think of a poverty index as a function $P(y,\pi)$. Sen (1976) identifies the following axioms for a desirable measure of poverty:

*Focus Axiom.* If x and y are two income distributions with x obtained from y by changing incomes of the non-poor only, then $P(x,\pi) = P(y,\pi)$. Any measure of poverty should, other things being equal, be unchanged if the income of a non-poor household changes.

*Monotonicity Axiom.* If x is obtained from y by a loss of income among the poor, then $P(x,\pi) > P(y,\pi)$. Any measure of poverty should, other things being equal, rise if the income of a poor household falls.

*Weak Transfer Axiom.* If x is obtained from y by transferring incomes among the poor in such a way that (a) only two people are affected and (b) the gap between their incomes is higher under x than it is under y, then $P(x,\pi) > P(y,\pi)$. Any measure of poverty should, other things being equal, be sensitive to transfers of income between the poor. Suppose the following were to occur: a transfer from the very poorest household to a less poor household; this is certainly a worsening of the extent of poverty, and the poverty measure should reflect this.

Of the three, it is the last axiom that is the most contentious, since it seems to be an argument about inequality rather than poverty. Sen argues it measures relative deprivation and it is also due to 'diminishing marginal utility of income' effects. In addition to the three axioms, there is a fourth, purely technical one that we all assume anyway. It will not be referred to again.

*Anonymity or Symmetry.* If x is obtained from y by a permutation of incomes, then $P(x,\pi) = P(y,\pi)$.

## Headcount and other measures

**Headcount ratio**

Proportion of households whose income falls below the poverty line; measures the incidence of poverty

The **headcount ratio**, $H = q/n$, simply measures the proportion of households experiencing poverty, where $q$ is the number of households whose income level falls below the poverty line, $\pi$, and $n$ is the total number of households. This measure is easily calculated and satisfies the Focus Axiom, but it fails both the Monotonicity Axioms and the Weak Transfer Axiom. Under the headcount, if, all other things being equal, the income of an already poor household were to fall, then there would be no change in the number of households below the poverty line and hence no change in the headcount, thus failing the Axiom of Monotonicity. The headcount is also not sensitive to transfers of income between the poor. If a transfer from the very poorest household to a less poor household were to occur, the number of households experiencing poverty is unaltered. Hence the headcount fails the Weak Transfer Axiom.

**Poverty gap**

Spread of incomes falling below the poverty line measures the depth of poverty

The **poverty gap** $Q = 1/q\Sigma\ (\pi - y_i)$ is a measure of spread, where $\pi$ is the value of the poverty line and $y_i$ is the income levels of those below the poverty line. This measure does satisfy the Focus and Monotonicity Axioms: $Q$ is unaltered by changes in incomes above $\pi$ and $Q$ would fall if any $y_i$ falls. But any transfers of income between the poor would cancel each other out and $Q$ would remain constant, so failing the Weak Transfer Axiom.

**Sen poverty index**

Ranks the level of poverty amongst the poor

Sen suggests an alternative measure which satisfies the above axioms. **Sen's indices** rest on the notion of ranking the poverty of the poor. Each individual is lined up, with those on the lowest income given the highest rank. So if $q$ people are poor, the person with an income closest to $\pi$ is given a rank of 1, and so on. Then each individual's poverty gap is given a weighting equal to their rank. Again, the idea of this approach is to capture the relative deprivations involved in poverty: those with the lowest incomes are given the highest weighting. The result is:

$$S(y,\pi) = H\left[I + (1-I)G_{\mathrm{p}}\left(\frac{q}{q+1}\right)\right]$$

$$P_{\mathrm{SEN}} = H\left[Q + (1-Q)\,I_{\mathrm{GIN}}\right]$$

where $H$ is the headcount ratio, $I$ is the poverty gap ratio (the second one mentioned above) and $G_{\mathrm{p}}$ is the Gini coefficient for the poor (see Chapter 14).

It is important to realise that an element of arbitrariness exists with all measures of poverty. First, Sen argues that we need to rank individuals' poverty in some way and that ranking according to rank in the poverty order is the simplest way forward and gives weight to notions of relative deprivation. Second, when all the poor have the same income, he argues that the correct measure is one based on the product of the headcount ratio and the income gap ratio, which gives the aggregate income gap for the poor as a proportion of total income. Again, this has something to commend it, but there is no law that forces us to accept Sen's measure (or any other).

## Equivalence scales

In constructing a poverty line for households, the measure must reflect the size and composition of that household. It is necessary, therefore, to use equivalence scales which weight the needs of each adult and child. Buhman et al. (1988) show the sensitivity of measures of poverty to the choice of equivalence scales (see Table 15.2). The differences between equivalence scales can be summarised by the following: equivalent income = total income/$n^s$, where $n$ is the family size and $s$ represents the elasticity of family needs relative to family size. When $s = 0$, no adjustment for family size is made, and when $s = 1$, a complete adjustment is made so the equivalent income is per-capita income. Buhman et al. (1988) take four categories of equivalence scales: subjective scales, based on what is needed to live; observed equivalence scales,

**Table 15.2** Proportion of households with income below 50% of median, by equivalence scale

|  | Subjective $s = 0.25$ | Observed $s = 0.36$ | Official $s = 0.55$ | Statistical $s = 0.72$ |
|---|---|---|---|---|
| USA | 17.9% | 17.8% | 17.2% | 17.2% |
| Australia | 16.0% | 14.8% | 12.3% | 11.7% |
| UK | 15.2% | 14.0% | 11.4% | 8.1% |
| Canada | 15.0% | 14.4% | 13.2% | 12.3% |
| Switzerland | 10.5% | 9.8% | 8.5% | 8.3% |
| Norway | 10.3% | 8.9% | 5.1% | 5.1% |
| Sweden | 7.9% | 6.5% | 5.4% | 5.3% |
| West Germany | 7.6% | 6.6% | 5.2% | 5.4% |
| Netherlands | 7.3% | 7.2% | 8.0% | 8.8% |

Source: Atkinson, Table 2, 1990, based on Buhman *et al.* (1988)

based on empirical studies of consumption patterns; official equivalence scales, used in domestic policy-making; and statistical equivalence scales, used in international studies of poverty by the OECD.

The measured incidence of poverty in the UK and Norway halves when the statistical equivalence scale is used instead of a subjective equivalence scale. The incidence of measured poverty also falls in Australia, Canada, Switzerland, Sweden and West Germany. Only for the USA and The Netherlands does the measured incidence of poverty seem to be independent of the choice of equivalence scales. Despite this evidence, Townsend (1993) notes that in Britain the Department of Social Security maintains the view that the choice of equivalence scales is immaterial.

Johnson and Webb (1991) illustrate the importance of the choice of equivalence scales when they attempt to make sense of three apparently contradictory studies of poverty in the UK. All of the studies used the same UK data; two reached the conclusion that the poor are getting poorer, the third showed rising real incomes for the bottom decile. Some of the differences arise due to the differences in the definitions of income used and also according to whether levels of expenditure provide a better indication of the position of the poor than income. But a significant part of the differences arises as a consequence of the choice of equivalence scales.

## 15.4 Recent trends in poverty

In 1935, thirty-six years after his first study of poverty, Rowntree argued that the position of the working class had remained unchanged, that poverty was endemic, with approximately 30% of families living on incomes below his minimal poverty line. The Labour government elected in 1945 expanded the Welfare State in the UK, which it was hoped would eliminate want. In his third study in 1950 Rowntree concluded that the combination of growing affluence and the Welfare State meant that no family would live a life of need. However, this post-war optimism has been short-lived. In the 1960s, evidence began to emerge of malnutrition in young children. In their report *Poverty and the Poorest,* Abel-Smith and Townsend (1965) drew attention to the plight of low-income working families and shortly after this, the influential Child Poverty Action Group was established. Recent studies show not only that poverty remains, but that it has worsened over the last twenty years. The studies conducted in 1983 and 1990 for the London Weekend Television programmes 'Breadline Britain' (Mack and Lansley, 1985, 1992) concluded that poverty in the UK rose from 7.5 million (14% of households) in 1983 to 11 million (20% of households) in 1990. Recent evidence also shows that the Welfare State in the UK is not as effective at preventing child poverty as those in Europe. The UNICEF report (1993) *Child Neglect in Rich Nations,* showed that the USA and UK had much higher rates of child poverty than other OECD countries, contrasting the European model of child welfare with the 'neglect filled' Anglo-American model.

## Poverty in the UK

Table 15.3 shows the steady worsening of the incidence of poverty throughout the 1980s. There is evidence of an improvement in the position in 1993/4 where the percentage of households experiencing poverty fell to 19% (before housing costs) and 24% (after housing costs). Evidence from *Households Below Average Income* (*The Guardian,* 17 October 1997, 'Figures back Major's more equal claim') show that this trend has continued. By 1994/5, the percentage of households experiencing poverty was 16% (before housing costs) and 22% (after housing costs). However, this is still double the incidence of poverty reported for 1979 (7% before and 9% after housing costs).

During the 1980s and into the 1990s, earnings in the UK grew at a faster rate than that at any comparable period since 1945; average earnings have risen by 39% since 1979. It might be expected that by the early 1990s fewer households would fall below the minimal standards for poverty set in 1979. However, Table 15.4 shows in fact that by 1992/3 a higher number of both children and adults fall below the 1979 poverty

**Table 15.3** Individuals living below 50% of average earnings (including the self-employed)

|        | Before housing costs | | After housing costs | |
|--------|----------------------|------------|---------------------|------------|
|        | Numbers (millions) | Percentage | Numbers (millions) | Percentage |
| 1979   | 4.4  | 8  | 5.0  | 9  |
| 1981   | 4.7  | 9  | 6.2  | 11 |
| 1987   | 8.7  | 16 | 10.5 | 19 |
| 1988/9 | 10.4 | 19 | 12.0 | 22 |
| 1991/2 | 11.7 | 21 | 13.9 | 25 |
| 1992/3 | 11.4 | 20 | 14.1 | 25 |
| 1993/4 | 10.7 | 19 | 13.7 | 24 |

Source: DSS, *Households Below Average Income.* Walker and Walker (1997), Table 2.1

**Table 15.4** Children and adults in households below 1979 fixed-income thresholds (after housing costs)

|  | 1979 | 1992/3 |
|---|---|---|
| *Children* | | |
| Below 1979 poorest decile median | 860,000 | 1,180,000 |
| Below 50% of 1979 average income | 1,430,000 | 1,940,000 |
| *Adults* | | |
| Below 1979 poorest decile median | 2,000,000 | 2,970,000 |
| Below 50% of 1979 average income | 3,850,000 | 4,100,000 |

Source: DSS, *Households Below Average Income*, Tables 11–2 and 11–5

lines. This is the result of the growing inequality of the distribution of income and of the falling levels of income (after housing costs) amongst those in the poorest decile (see the discussion of growing inequality over this period in Chapter 14).

In the UK childhood poverty is rising; the number of children living in households which are dependent upon benefits has risen for all age groups (see Table 15.5).

**Table 15.5** Number of children dependent upon benefits

|  | Aged under 10 | Aged 10–13 | Aged 14–16 |
|---|---|---|---|
| *Income Support* | | | |
| 1979 | 574,000 | 236,000 | 135,000 |
| 1989 | 1,463,000 | 384,000 | 250,000 |
| 1994 | 2,080,000 | 629,000 | 369,000 |
| *Housing Benefit without Income Support* | | | |
| 1989 | 187,000 | 69,000 | 51,000 |
| 1994 | 284,000 | 104,000 | 61,000 |

Source: Hansard 19–7–95, cols 1477–80

## Poverty in Europe

Britain has a greater proportion of children living in poverty than any other European Union nation (see Figure 15.2). As we argued in Chapter 14, it is important that we treat international comparisons of poverty with some caution, as most are relative measures and relate to average income within a country. This is illustrated in Figure 15.3.

Table 15.6 shows the composition of poor households across Europe (figures for the USA and Canada are also included). In most countries, the elderly make up just over one-third of the poor households; Italy and The Netherlands are exceptions to this (less than 15%). Britain has a smaller proportion of households without children in poverty than other European Union countries (around 20%). Nearly two-thirds of the households experiencing poverty in the North European countries (Denmark,

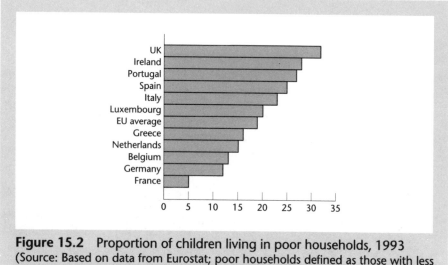

**Figure 15.2**  Proportion of children living in poor households, 1993
(Source: Based on data from Eurostat; poor households defined as those with less than 50% of net average income across the EU)

Norway and Sweden) are single childless households. In Denmark, Finland and Sweden, very few households with children are poor (less than 10%), reflecting the priorities of the Welfare State and the high protection given to children. Couples with children make up the largest single groups experiencing poverty in Italy and Spain (around 40%). In most European countries there are few lone parents; however, in Austria, Canada, the UK and the USA, over 10% of households experiencing poverty are headed by single parents.

Table 15.7 shows that the UK has one of the highest incidence of poverty before benefits and direct tax. Only Sweden and Belgium have a higher proportion of households with incomes below the national average. The incidence of poverty after benefit and direct tax is lower (see Table 15.7). This supports the argument that the Welfare States across Europe do alleviate poverty. The Welfare State in the UK seems to be least effective, since the proportion of households remaining in poverty after benefits and direct tax is at 23%, the highest in Europe.

In making international comparisons of poverty, it is important to be aware of how sensitive the comparisons are to the measure of poverty being used. Figure 15.3 illustrates the different results that are achieved when different measures of poverty are applied across Europe (data from the Luxembourg Income Study, 1985). According to national figures, poverty appears to be concentrated in France, Spain, Italy, UK and Germany. The position is somewhat different when we apply a European Union poverty line. Although the relative position of Italy and the UK remains similar, a greater concentration of poverty is found in the traditionally poor countries, Spain, Greece and Portugal, and a reduced concentration of poverty is found in France and Germany. Neither measure indicates a high incidence of poverty in The Netherlands, Denmark, Republic or Ireland or Belgium. Notice that there are slight differences in the ranking between the UK and Spain in Figure 15.3b and Table 15.7; in Table 15.7 the figures are much more recent.

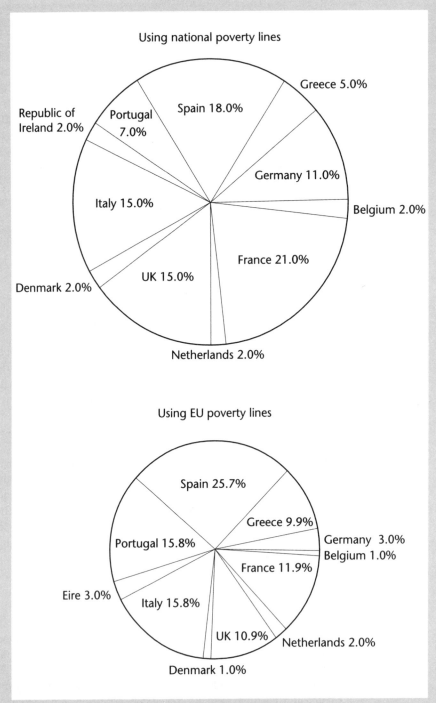

**Figure 15.3** Distribution of poverty in Europe
(Source: Atkinson, 1990, Figure 1)

**Table 15.6** Composition of poor households after direct tax and social security benefits. Equivalent income less than 50% of the average

| Circa 1990 | Aged | | No children | | Parents | | Other | Total |
|---|---|---|---|---|---|---|---|---|
| | Single | Couple | Single | Couple | Single | Couple | | |
| Austria | 21.7 | 10.0 | 26.0 | 8.0 | 14.1 | 17.0 | 3.2 | 100 |
| Belgium | 18.0 | 16.6 | 14.0 | 20.2 | 4.3 | 20.5 | 4.5 | 100 |
| Denmark | 16.2 | 3.0 | 61.7 | 6.9 | 3.5 | 7.4 | 1.2 | 100 |
| Finland | 29.6 | 2.1 | 46.9 | 8.2 | 2.5 | 7.6 | 3.1 | 100 |
| Germany | 21.0 | 8.1 | 25.7 | 22.4 | 4.3 | 14.5 | 3.9 | 100 |
| Italy | 9.0 | 5.8 | 5.0 | 26.5 | 0.4 | 42.1 | 11.2 | 100 |
| Netherlands | 4.9 | 7.7 | 37.2 | 16.2 | 9.1 | 23.3 | 1.6 | 100 |
| Norway | 30.2 | 2.0 | 50.7 | 1.1 | 9.6 | 5.8 | 0.6 | 100 |
| Spain | 6.5 | 19.7 | 5.3 | 15.9 | 1.7 | 40.1 | 10.7 | 100 |
| Sweden | 16.1 | 0.8 | 72.6 | 3.4 | 1.4 | 5.8 | 0.0 | 100 |
| UK | 26.7 | 14.7 | 14.1 | 9.8 | 10.4 | 18.9 | 5.4 | 100 |
| USA | 16.6 | 6.8 | 23.0 | 7.7 | 12.5 | 20.9 | 12.4 | 100 |
| Canada | 5.0 | 2.4 | 41.5 | 10.8 | 14.1 | 20.1 | 6.1 | 100 |

Source: Bradshaw and Chen, Table 5, 1997

**Table 15.7** Households with incomes below 50% of average national equivalent income

| | Before benefits and direct taxes | After benefits and direct taxes |
|---|---|---|
| UK (1991) | 38.1 | 23.0 |
| Germany (1989) | 32.7 | 17.5 |
| Spain (1990) | 33.1 | 16.0 |
| Italy (1991) | 27.2 | 9.6 |
| Finland (1991) | 24.6 | 9.6 |
| Netherlands (1991) | 33.0 | 9.3 |
| Sweden (1992) | 41.4 | 9.1 |
| Denmark (1992) | 36.9 | 8.2 |
| Belgium (1992) | 38.3 | 7.1 |

Source: Bradshaw and Chen, Tables 2 and 3, 1997

## 15.5 The changing nature of poverty

In the past, both at the time of the Rowntree studies (1899, 1935 and 1950) and of the Beveridge Report (1942), there was a large working class and possibility of poverty was a real threat for many of its members. The working class is now much smaller, with a shift in occupational distribution away from manual employment and a growth of employment in the non-manual service sector. Figure 15.4 illustrates the composition of poverty from Rowntree's first two surveys (1899 and 1935) and data from 1979 and 1987.

## Labour market

The main pressure causing families to enter into poverty occurs through loss of earnings, either through unemployment or inability to work due to ill-health. Poverty can also occur though low pay in households where the main earners are in

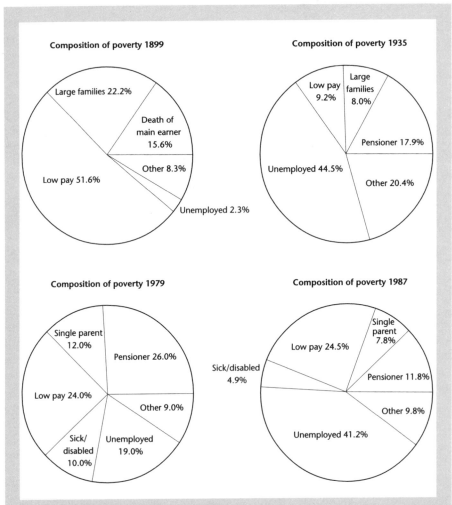

**Figure 15.4** Changing composition of poverty
(Source: Hills, 1993, Figure 26 and Oppenheim, 1990. Single parents – taken from those not in full-time employment. Other – men aged 60–64, widows, students, people temporarily away from home, people who are unemployed but not available for work)

employment. In the 1899 Rowntree survey, low pay accounted for over 50% of the households experiencing poverty. By 1935, unemployment was a much greater problem, accounting for 44% of the household experiencing poverty. Unemployment remains a problem but it is cyclical; we can see this through the rising impact of unemployment between 1979 and 1987. One cause for concern in many OECD countries has been the rising number of the long-term unemployed. Over this period, low pay accounted for a quarter of households experiencing poverty. Ill-health of the main earner does place pressure on household finances, but it is now less of an issue partly because the welfare system provides protection for the long-term sick. Also the shift in employment away from traditional industries, such as coal and steel, has led to a decline in the number of industrial accidents which result in incapacity to work. The labour market creates particular difficulties for female employment. The high cost of child-care and low pay within employment combine to keep many women out of the labour market. There is evidence of occupational segregation. Women tend to be employed in jobs where the conditions are more flexible and thus more conducive to combining employment and motherhood. However, if demand for such jobs exceeds supply, the likely outcome is for wages in these jobs to fall.

Unemployment and low pay also contribute towards pensioner poverty. Saving during the working life is more difficult for those with disrupted careers or whose employment has been in low-paid jobs. These groups will mostly rely upon state provision for their retirement, which is no longer indexed to average earnings, only inflation. This consigns many to the lower end of the income distribution.

## Feminisation of poverty

In the UK, the households experiencing poverty are more likely to be headed by women than by men. This reflects the fact that most households experiencing poverty are either single-parent families or single pensioners (pensioner poverty is discussed in Chapter 18). Where women are the head of a single-parent family,[9] it is very difficult for them to enter the labour market, particularly when their children are at pre-school ages. Figure 15.5 illustrates these effects, using the theoretical framework used in Chapter 13. Assuming that the single parent must arrange for child care as soon as she enters the labour market, child-care cost $C$, the unearned income falls $(I_U - C)$ when hours worked is positive. The effect that this has on labour market participation will reflect the wage that the single parent is able to command in the labour market. In Figure 15.5, where the single parent enters the labour market with an hourly wage $w_1$, the impact on labour supply is small because the single parent is able to earn more in employment when $H > H_1$. If, however, the market wage is lower, $w_2 < w_1$, the effect is greater. Income in employment is only greater than income outside the marketplace when hours are very high, $H > H_2$. Naturally, the extent of the disincentives will depend on the size of the child-care costs.

Another aspect to the feminisation of poverty is illustrated by the position of women in households where the husband is unemployed. In such households, the woman herself is also likely to be unemployed. There are competing explanations for this. The first highlights the interaction of the household benefit entitlements and the incentives for the wife to enter the labour market. Assuming that benefits are means-tested, once the husband is unemployed, any household income associated

[9] Although there are single-parent families headed by men, these form a very small minority. Single mothers include never marrieds, divorced, separated and widows.

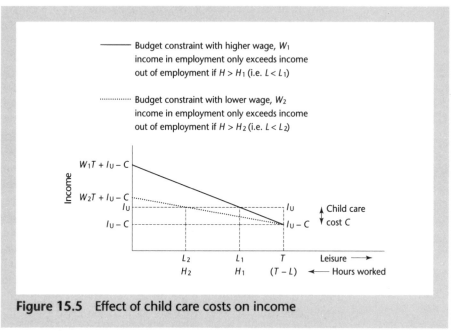

**Figure 15.5** Effect of child care costs on income

with the wife's employment may reduce the household benefit income. This reduces the incentives to enter the labour market. A second consideration is the likelihood that a wife, whose husband is unemployed, will be able to find employment herself. The fact that her husband is unemployed reflects the state of the local labour market and suggests that she may not be able to find employment (see Connolly, 1997).

An important aspect is the relatively poor position of women employed in the labour market, as we saw in Chapter 14; despite a narrowing of the gender pay gap which occurred after anti-discrimination legislation in 1976, a sizeable gender pay differential remains. It seems that low pay, particularly amongst women in part-time employment, does contribute to the feminisation of poverty. This raises the question of why the gender pay differential exists; one explanation is that women experience discrimination in the labour market and this is discussed further in Chapter 17.

## Demography

Demographic trends are an important factor, leading to changes in the nature of poverty. Recent demographic trends include an ageing population, smaller families and more single-parent households. Based on the evidence of Rowntree's 1935 survey (see Figure 15.4), one would expect that an ageing population would lead to an increasing incidence of poverty (see Chapter 18). At the time of Rowntree's surveys, it was common to have large families; these accounted for 22% of those experiencing poverty in 1899, but had fallen to 8% in 1935 (see Figure 15.4). Family size was often associated with poverty because of the pressures on family resources. In the post-war period, family size has fallen and is no longer a main factor in explaining poverty. O'Higgins and Jenkins (1990) argue that recent trends in family size have made it more difficult to use equivalence scales accurately.[10] Whilst family size has fallen,

---

[10] 'Given both the rate at which average household sizes are changing and the apparent increase in the average household size of those in poverty, there is clearly need for caution if basing poverty population estimates on household numbers.' (O'Higgins and Jenkins, 1990)

there has been a growth in the numbers of single-parent families; they account for 12% of poverty in 1979 and 8% in 1987 (discussed above).

## 15.6 Conclusion

In this chapter we have discussed in some detail the work conducted by Seebohm Rowntree. His work is particularly useful, because it illustrates the difficulties associated with measuring poverty and the changing nature of poverty. In Rowntree's work, the definition of poverty used was an absolute measure. However, the argument that being poor means more than an inability to afford a subsistence diet is persuasive that is, poverty should be a relative concept. More recent work views poverty as a relative concept. Rowntree's work had a strong influence on the Beveridge model of social insurance upon which the British Welfare State was based. In his third study in 1950, Rowntree concluded that the combination of growing affluence and the Welfare State meant that no family would live a life of need.

However, poverty, particularly childhood poverty, is still with us. In the UK, the incidence of poverty has more than doubled since 1979. There are several underlying trends. The first is the worsening position of the unskilled. Those without qualifications are now the group most likely to experience poverty, because they are more likely to become unemployed or be in low-paid employment. The second is the feminisation of poverty. Women who are single pensioners are less likely to have private pension provisions and those who head single-parent families face significant barriers to entry into the labour market. The position of women is exacerbated by the persistence of a gender pay differential; in particular a much larger pay gap exists between men in full-time employment and women in part-time employment.

In Chapter 17, we shall examine the policies that are in place to eliminate poverty and examine the success of the UK government in achieving this aim.

## Summary

- A poverty line is the minimum level of income necessary to avoid poverty.
- Absolute poverty is a measure of the ability to provide the bare essentials for life.
- Relative poverty measures not only physical but also social well-being.
- Most studies use 50% of the median income as an indicator of the poverty line.
- In the UK between 1979 and 1994, the number of households with incomes below the poverty line doubled.
- In 1993, the The UK had the highest incidence of child poverty in the European Union.
- Traditionally, those most likely to experience poverty are the unemployed, the low paid and pensioners dependent on a state pension.
- Households headed by women are now the household type most at risk of poverty.

## Questions

1. Is it possible to derive a single universal measure of absolute poverty?
2. To what extent is a relative measure of poverty simply a reflection of the degree of income inequality?
3. Why is simply counting the number of households which fall below the poverty line not acceptable as a measure of poverty?
4. How does the incidence of poverty in Britain compare with other OECD countries?
5. Account for the increasing incidence of poverty amongst female-headed households.

## Further reading

More detailed accounts of the causes of poverty can be found in Alcock (1993) or Atkinson (1990, 1995). The classic reference on whether poverty is an absolute or relative concept is Townsend (1979). Morris and Preston (1986) provide an excellent survey of the various measures of poverty and inequality. Evidence on recent trends in poverty can be found in Townsend (1993) and Walker and Walker (1997).

## References

Abel-Smith and Townsend, P. (1965) *Poverty and the Poorest,* London: G. Bell and Sons.

Alcock, P. (1993) *Understanding Poverty,* London: Macmillan Press.

Atkinson, A.B. (1990) *Comparing Poverty Rates Internationally: Lessons from Recent Studies in OECD Countries,* Welfare State Programme Working Paper 53, Suntory–Toyota International Centre for Economics and Related Disciplines, London: London School of Economics.

Atkinson, A.B. (1995) *Incomes and the Welfare State: Essays on Britain and Europe,* Cambridge: Cambridge University Press.

Beveridge, W. (1942) *Report on Social Insurance and Allied Services,* Cmd 6404, London: HMSO.

Bradshaw, J. and Chen, J. (1997), 'Poverty in the UK: a comparison with nineteen other countries', *Benefits* 18, 13–17.

Buhman, B., Rainwater, L., Schmaus, G. and Smeeding, T.M. (1988) 'Equivalence scales, well-being, inequality, and poverty', *Review of Income and Wealth* 34, 115–42.

Connolly, S. (1997) 'A model of female labour supply in which supply is dependent upon the chances of finding a job', *Applied Economics* 29, 1379–86.

Desai, M. and Shah, A. (1988) 'An econometric approach to the measurement of poverty', *Oxford Economic Papers* 40, 505–22.

DSS, *Households Below Average Income,* Tables 11–2 and 11–5, Norwich: The Stationery Office.

DSS, *Households Below Average Income,* Table 2.1, Norwich: The Stationery Office.

'Figures back Major's more equal claim' *The Guardian,* 17 October 1997.

Hansard, 19–7–95, cols 1477–80, London: HMSO.

Hewlett, S.A. (1993) *Child Neglect in Rich Nations,* UNICEF, New York.

Hills, J. (1993) *The Future of Welfare,* York: Joseph Rowntree Foundation.

Johnson, P. and Webb, S. (1991) *UK Poverty Statistics: A Comparative Study*, Institute for Fiscal Studies, Commentary No. 27.

Mack, J. and Lansley, S. (1985) *Poor Britain*, London: Allen and Unwin Press.

Mack, J. and Lansley, S. (1992) *Breadline Britain in the 1990s*, London: Harper Collins.

Morris, N. and Preston, I. (1986) 'Special Issue', *Bulletin of Economic Research* 38(4).

O'Higgins, M. and Jenkins, S. (1990) 'Poverty in the EC: estimates for 1975, 1980 and 1985', in R. Teeken and B. Van Praag (eds) *Analysing Poverty in the European Community*, pp. 187–211, Eurostat.

Oppenheim, C. (1990) *Poverty the Facts*, London: Child Poverty Action Group.

Piachaud, D. (1981) 'Peter Townsend and the holy grail', *New Society* 57, 419–21.

Rowntree, B.S. (1901) *Poverty: A Study of Town Life*, London: Macmillan Press.

Rowntree, B.S. (1941) *Poverty and Progress: A Second Social Survey of York*, London: Longman Press.

Rowntree, B.S. and Lavers, G. (1951) *Poverty and the Welfare State*, London: Longman Press.

Sen, A.K. (1976) 'Poverty: an ordinal approach to measurement', *Econometrica* 44(2), 219–31.

Sen, A.K. (1983) 'Poor relatively speaking', *Oxford Economic Papers* 35, 153–69.

Sen, A.K. (1985) 'A sociological approach to the measurement of poverty: a reply to Peter Townsend', *Oxford Economic Papers* 37, 669–76.

Townsend, P. (1979) *Poverty in the United Kingdom: A Survey of Household Resources and Living Standards*, London: Allen Lane and Penguin Books.

Townsend, P. (1993) *The International Analysis of Poverty*, Hemel Hempstead: Harvester Wheatsheaf.

Townsend, P. (1996/7) *A Poor Future: Can We Counter Growing Poverty in Britain and Across the World?*, Lemos Crane in association with The Friendship Group.

Veit-Wilson, J. (1994) *Dignity Not Poverty: A Minimum Income Standard for the UK*, Published for the Commission on Social Justice, London: Institute for Public Policy Research.

Walker, A. and Walker, C. (eds) (1997) *Britain Divided: The Growth of Social Exclusion in the 1980s and 1990s*, London: Child Poverty Action Group.

# CHAPTER 16

# Social Insurance and the Welfare State

## Key concepts

| | | | |
|---|---|---|---|
| social insurance | adverse selection | moral hazard | risk pooling |
| myopia | incentives | forced saving | Welfare State crisis |

## 16.1  Introduction

In Chapters 1 and 10, we have seen that most governments within the OECD take a large proportion of national GDP in taxation. By far the largest proportion of this revenue is then transferred directly to other citizens through the institution called the 'Welfare State'. Redistribution on this scale has a major impact on income inequality and poverty. This chapter and those which follow are concerned with the 20–25% of GDP churned in this way. What exactly counts as the Welfare State differs from country to country and also from writer to writer, because of the variety of functions which shelter under the umbrella of the term. In Table 16.1, compiled by the European Union, expenditure on pensions, healthcare, benefits for the invalid or disabled, unemployment insurance, housing expenditure and transfers to families and children are grouped together under the social protection heading. Some writers would also add spending on education and training to this list, while others would concentrate on cash benefits, to the exclusion of healthcare and housing.

We have spread discussion of the Welfare State over the four chapters which follow. In this one, we concentrate on three main issues: the different roles of the Welfare State; the efficiency arguments for social insurance, and the challenges and pressures on a system designed to cope with the risks of the early part of the twentieth century, not with the realities of the twenty-first century.

### The role of the Welfare State

As we have already noted, what counts as welfare differs from person to person and from country to country. This partly reflects different aspects of the role of the Welfare State, which we can divide into efficiency-enhancing, redistributive and regulatory.

**Table 16.1** Social expenditure in the European Union

|  | B | DK | D | GR | E | F | IRL | L | NL | P | S | UK |
|---|---|---|---|---|---|---|---|---|---|---|---|---|
| Social protection %GDP | 26.4 | 32.4 | 29.7 | 15.5 | 23.2 | 29.2 | 20.5 | 23.7 | 31.9 | 17.6 | 39.7 | 26.7 |
| **% by function** | | | | | | | | | | | | |
| Old age | 34.5 | 33.9 | 30.6 | 55.7 | 30.7 | 20.5 | 21.9 | 31.8 | 31.7 | 33.3 | 47.8 | 40.1 |
| Sickness | 22.9 | 18.8 | 26.8 | 14.8 | 25.3 | 26.4 | 29.7 | 24.8 | 22.2 | 30.7 | 24.8 | 19.2 |
| Invalidity/ disability | 8.9 | 8.4 | 8.8 | 9.8 | 7.8 | 5.7 | 6.9 | 11.2 | 22.4 | 11.7 | – | 11.7 |
| Survivors | 10.8 | 0.1 | 10.2 | 10.5 | 9.7 | 7.1 | 6.2 | 15.0 | 5.4 | 7.3 | – | 1.3 |
| Maternity | 0.90 | 1.7 | 0.7 | 0.5 | 0.9 | 1.4 | 2.1 | 1.5 | 0.6 | 0.9 | 3.4 | 1.3 |
| Unemployment | 10.0 | 12.6 | 6.7 | 3.4 | 20.6 | 6.8 | 14.5 | 0.9 | 9.2 | 4.9 | 8.5 | 6.1 |
| Housing | – | 2.6 | 0.8 | 0.57 | 0.4 | 3.1 | 3.0 | 0.2 | 1.1 | 0.0 | – | 7.0 |
| Occupational accidents/ diseases | 1.9 | 0.9 | 2.9 | 0.1 | 2.2 | 1.9 | 0.5 | 3.3 | – | 2.1 | 2.2 | 0.4 |
| Miscellaneous | 1.4 | 4.6 | 2.5 | 4.1 | 1.0 | 1.5 | 2.1 | 0.1 | 2.7 | 2.9 | 0.6 | 1.6 |
| Active job markets | 1.7 | 6.3 | 2.8 | – | 2.6 | 1.5 | 2.6 | 0.2 | – | 1.7 | – | 1.1 |
| Family | 7.0 | 10.1 | 7.3 | 0.6 | 10.6 | 8.1 | 10.6 | 11.2 | 4.9 | 4.6 | 12.7 | 10.2 |

Source: Eurostat (1996), pp. 16–17. B = Belgium, DK = Denmark, D = Germany, GR = Greece, E = Spain, F = France, IRL = Ireland, L = Luxembourg, NL = Netherlands, P = Portugal, S = Sweden, UK = United Kingdom

## Social insurance: The efficiency role of the Welfare State

**Social insurance**

An insurance system organised by the state in which premiums are related to ability to pay

Chapter 6 explained how market failure arises in the presence of asymmetric information. When private insurance markets fail, **social insurance** may be able to step into the breach. Section 3 of the chapter covers this role.

## Social protection: The redistributive role of the Welfare State

Although some part of the Welfare State can be viewed as efficiency-enhancing, nevertheless there is a substantial residue for which redistributive explanations are more natural. Philosophical views on what kind of redistribution is desirable have implications for the role of the Welfare State.

- *Safety net.* The most basic view is that the state's role is to provide a rudimentary standard of living below which its citizens should not fall, regardless of the causes of their poverty. As we mentioned in Chapter 3, there are several quite different underpinnings for this opinion. One recognises no inherent duty of one human being for the well-being of another, but notes that social order may require some safety net. Social security may be the price to be paid for safe streets. The second is for equality in principle, but views the efficiency costs of redistribution as too high to be worth paying above a basic minimum. Although the UK's welfare state has drawn closer to the safety net model in the last twenty years, its clearest expression can probably be found in the American system.

- *Redistributive*. At the opposite extreme are Welfare States founded on a belief in the desirability of equality. Associated with high marginal rates of taxation on higher earners, married to extensive transfers and a range of services in-kind such as healthcare, housing and community care, Scandinavian countries, particularly Sweden, are often seen as models of this design, but the UK prior to the late 1970s would also qualify.

- *Enabling*. A third view favours equality of opportunity rather than equality of outcome. Under this opinion, the state should make efforts to equalise opportunities open to its citizens, perhaps by investing in education and training or through the provision of subsidised child care for lone parents wishing to rejoin the labour market. Alternatively, proponents of the enabling Welfare State might simply view it as an effective means of achieving equality of outcomes, along the lines of the proverb, 'give a person a fish and they eat for a day; give them a fishing boat and they eat for life.' Due to increasing disillusionment with traditional redistributive policies, political parties of the Centre-Left, such as the UK's Labour Party, have begun to advocate a Welfare State whose role is primarily enabling.

### The Nanny state: The regulatory role of the Welfare State

The first two roles embody a respect for the principle of consumer sovereignty. However, consumers are often viewed as myopic, as poor planners of their futures. A significant proportion of government activity is therefore directed towards overriding or influencing individual choices, especially savings decisions – hence the term, the **Nanny state**. Compulsory pensions and compulsory health insurance are examples of policies associated with this approach. As a result, welfare expenditure can be limited (see the example of Singapore discussed below), even though the pattern of consumption which results might be similar to that produced by more traditional models of the Welfare State.

**Nanny state**

A Welfare State which compels its citizens to make provision for life risks such as ill-health, old age, etc.

## Citizenship and exclusion

Many Welfare States have declared goals which go beyond those listed above, such as reducing exclusion and enhancing citizenship, which can be understood as a combination of civil, political and social rights. According to Pierson (1991) (see Table 16.2), for instance, the most limited concept of citizenship, such as that which existed in the eighteenth century, only reflects individual freedoms such as free speech. By the late nineteenth century and early twentieth century, a more extensive concept of citizenship evolved, representing political freedom and the ability to vote. Finally, with the creation of the Welfare State, citizenship began to include social rights, for example through the establishment of a universal and free health and education system.

A welfare system where social rights are based on contributions made while in employment excludes those who, for whatever reason, are not in continuous full-time employment. This has obvious gender implications particularly in a society where women have important caring roles as mothers and carers of the elderly or sick within the family, and have typically been employed in the home rather than in the labour market. The disabled form another group that could be disenfranchised if citizenship is based on rights accrued in the labour market. In fact any group which

| Table 16.2 | The growth of citizenship in Britain | | |
|---|---|---|---|
| | Civil rights | Political rights | Social rights |
| Characteristic period | Eighteenth century | Nineteenth century | Twentieth century |
| Defining principle | Individual freedom | Political freedom | Social welfare |
| Typical measures | *Habeas corpus*; freedom of speech, thought and faith; freedom to enter into legal contracts | Right to vote; parliamentary reform | Free education; pensions; healthcare; the Welfare State; payment for MPs |

Source: Pierson, Table 1.2, p. 23, 1991

can be termed as 'outsiders' can also be excluded. For example, race can be considered the single most visible demonstration of national citizenship and used as a test for exclusion from welfare services.

## 16.2 Social insurance

It is quite easy to insure a car or against holiday illness, but to get adequate cover for major life risks such as unemployment or divorce can be impossible. Often this kind of insurance is simply not provided by the private sector or myopia may limit its take-up. Instead, governments take the lead role in many forms of insurance, either providing the cover themselves in the form of the Welfare State, or indirectly, by organising and regulating the voluntary sector. Since Bismarck created the beginnings of the German welfare system in the 1880s, with three acts covering healthcare (1883), accident (1884) and invalidity insurance (1889), the extent of government involvement in social insurance has grown enormously, as the introduction to this chapter showed.

In keeping with the multiple roles outlined in the previous section, social insurance has aims which go beyond those of private alternatives, including the desire to build social unity. In the words of the 1944 White Paper on Social Insurance, 'concrete expression is thus given to the solidarity and unity of the nation' (Atkinson, 1993, p. 23). Second, as we have already mentioned, social insurance usually offers protection against risks which the private sector is loath to cover. The motives for social insurance are therefore a combination of efficiency and equity. Most systems usually involve redistribution as well as insurance; in other words some contributors can expect to be net winners or losers over their lifetime. For the moment we will concentrate on the insurance aspect and on the efficiency arguments which support it.

### The value of social insurance

Bird's (1995) work on risk in the USA and West Germany provides a pioneering insight into the value of social insurance. He estimates a model of income risk for the USA and (West) Germany using panel data from 1983 to 1986. For a large sample of people in the two countries, the volatility of their income is compared, before and after taking into account social insurance. To measure the costs of this volatility, a constant relative risk aversion utility function (i.e. $U(y) = (y^{1-e})/(1-e)$, where $e$ is the degree of relative risk aversion) is used with $e = 1.5$ (estimates of $e$ usually range from 1.5 to 5; the higher figure would place a much higher valuation on insurance). As in Chapter 6 where the demand for insurance was outlined, the cost of risk is measured by the **risk premium**, the amount a risk-averse person is willing to pay to avoid all risk.

**Risk premium**

A measure of the cost of risk, the maximum amount of income a risk-averse person is willing to sacrifice to eliminate all risk

In Table 16.3, market income is income before taxes, benefits and any other transfers the individual pays or receives. Typically, this is far more volatile than incomes after transfers (disposable income), so the risk premium for market incomes is much higher. The table tells us that the median American benefits to the tune of about $300 per year from social insurance.

When aggregated over 238 million Americans and 61 million Germans, we get the figures depicted in the lower half of the table. There are a number of things to note. First, the expected transfers do not add up to zero. This is because some portion of the taxes received by the governments goes on items such as defence and education, but Bird misses out of the equation the benefits of state spending on these goods. Nevertheless, for the bottom 80% in both Germany and the USA, the overall welfare change is clearly positive. The gain arises in two parts: lower income groups receive benefits from the redistributive effects of social insurance (i.e. the first column of numbers); middle-income groups gain from increased security. This suggests why it is not only low-income groups who are in favour of the Welfare State; large sections of the middle classes benefit as well. The final point worth noting is the redistributive element; although social insurance offers protection, its benefits are strongly skewed away from those with high incomes.

**Table 16.3** The value of social insurance for two OECD countries

| Sample medians of | USA ($) | Germany (DM) |
|---|---|---|
| Cost of market income risk | 1,456 | 2,002 |
| Cost of disposable income risk | 1,150 | 1,135 |
| Absolute difference | 306 | 867 |
| Relative (%) | 21 | 43 |

| | Aggregate impact between pre- and post-distribution income (Billion(s) 1986 currency) | | |
|---|---|---|---|
| Country and quintile | Aggregate expected transfer | Aggregate value of increased security | Aggregate welfare change |
| **USA ($)** | | | |
| Lowest 20% | +31.2 | +4.6 | 35.8 |
| Middle 60% | −29.9 | +22.2 | −7.3 |
| Upper 20% | −159.5 | +7.4 | −152.1 |
| **Germany (DM)** | | | |
| Lowest 20% | +49.9 | +7.5 | +57.4 |
| Middle 60% | −40.6 | +41.5 | +0.9 |
| Highest 20% | −149.9 | +10.7 | −139.2 |

Source: Bird, Tables 1 and 2, 1995

### Lifecycle redistribution

This conclusion partly reflects the drawbacks of a snapshot approach. People usually have changing resources over their lifetime. For instance, students are typically poor at the time of their studies, but can expect to earn more and hence pay more taxes later in their lives. Thus, in a Welfare State, much of what the average citizen pays in taxes or social security benefits is returned to them in some form or other over the course of their lives. Aspects of this are emphasised in the work of Falkingham and Hills (1995) on the UK welfare system. In a large-scale simulation exercise, they model 4,000 hypothetical life histories, examining what each individual pays into the Welfare State and receives in return. Out of the average £133,000 received by an individual in benefits over a lifetime, £98,000 is self-financed, meaning that individuals are paying in to the tax and benefit system at one stage in their lives, in order to receive back monies at other stages. Only the poorest 10% are less than 50% self-financing. So the figures in Bird's tables probably overplay the degree of redistribution, when viewed from a lifetime perspective.

## 16.3 Market failure and social insurance

If, as the figures of the previous section suggest, social insurance is so valuable, then why can it not be provided by the private sector? In Chapter 6 we listed five reasons which needed to be fulfilled if full insurance was to be made available in competitive markets. These included the absence of asymmetric information, the availability of insurance provision and the absence of myopia on the part of the consumer. The first of these is fundamental and was examined in detail in that chapter, so here we concentrate on the remaining two conditions.

### The availability of insurance

**Risk pooling**

The sharing of gains and losses amongst more than one person

**Diversification**

The exchange of different risks, so as to reduce total individual risk

In the competitive model of insurance, consumers buy cover, off-loading the risks onto insurance companies. Yet, insurance companies are owned by consumers, so why should they be prepared to accept the transfer of risks? One answer is that owners and customers might be different kinds of people. The risk-averse might buy insurance, the risk-neutral or risk-loving might supply it. A better answer is that insurance companies provide vehicles for the **risk pooling** and for **diversification**. With broken legs, for instance, the probability of one individual having a break in one year is likely to be uncorrelated with the chance of another individual suffering the same accident in the same year. If, for instance, there is a 1% chance of an individual suffering a broken leg which will cost £1,000 to mend, then in a town of 100,000 people we can be almost certain that the total costs of broken legs per year will be close to £1 million. If the citizens each own one share in the Broken Leg Repair Company, which insures all individuals in the town, then each can be almost certain of facing a cost of £10 per annum. In return, they are covered against possible expenditure of £1,000. Pooling therefore reduces the uncertainty over the costs and provides a rationale for insurance companies being willing to take on risks.

The key assumption here is that the risks are uncorrelated. Unfortunately, some of the most important risks do not fall into this category. The swings of the business cycle mean that unemployment rises and falls across the whole economy; inflation destroys the value of all monetary assets simultaneously. The greater the positive correlation, therefore, the smaller the degree of protection against risk which can be provided by the market. This does not mean that the government can magically step in and provide full insurance. However, through its size (and its coercive powers), the state has a far greater ability to spread risk than private insurance companies of limited means. Therefore, while full insurance is not feasible, there is some scope for social insurance to improve upon that offered by the market.

There is another reason for social insurance in the case of macroeconomic risks such as unemployment. The paying out of unemployment insurance will typically lead to a rise in aggregate demand, since it represents a transfer from someone with a higher income (lower marginal propensity to consume) to someone with a lower income (and hence a higher marginal propensity to consume). In turn, under Keynesian views of the economy, this rise in aggregate demand leads to a reduction in the probability of someone else being unemployed. Thus there is an external benefit from unemployment insurance which will be ignored by individual private insurers because of their small size. The net effect of the externality is the underprovision of insurance, relative to the social optimum, which again provides some reason for government intervention.

## Perceptual bias

In order to decide whether or not to purchase insurance, the risk-averse consumer must have some idea of the benefits of doing so. These benefits depend on the probability of the loss occurring and the size of the loss, as well as the degree of risk aversion and the cost of insurance. While the individual might have an accurate picture of the last three items in this list, they are unlikely to know exactly what the chances are of ill-health or unemployment. Experience might teach them and, if they are particularly astute, they might be able to deduce the risk probabilities from the insurance premiums, provided the insurance industry is competitive and has no costs other than paying out for losses. Evidence tends to suggest that individuals are not particularly good at estimating risk probabilities, suffering from at least two major forms of bias, illustrated by Figure 16.1.

Figure 16.1 shows the tendency for individuals to overestimate the probabilities attached to rare events, in this case the causes of death. Closer reading also reveals a tendency to overestimate probabilities when the events have a high profile (murder or car accidents) and underestimate the more commonplace ways of dying. While this suggests the desirability of restricting the marketing of insurance policies designed to play on our fears of suffering a dramatic death, it does not point to the need for wholesale intervention.

Myopia or short-sightedness is another and more significant form of perceptual bias. Many of the most expensive risks, such as old age or illness, tend to occur towards the ends of our lives. Insuring against them takes place when we have income from employment, earlier on, but myopia means we discount the future too heavily when allocating resources between consumption and savings/insurance. The result is a shortfall when income is needed. This myopia may arise from the sheer difficulty of planning over long time horizons and imagining our future needs, or it may arise through *cognitive dissonance*, a form of wishful thinking where chances of bad events occurring are subjectively reduced. Either way, it leads to individuals being underinsured compared to what they would choose if they could see the future without blinkers.

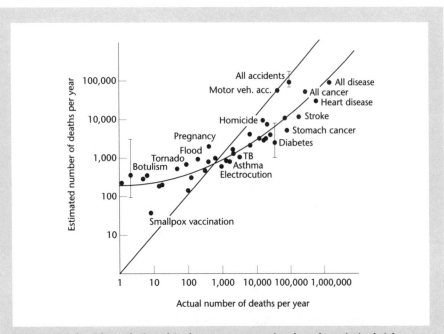

**Figure 16.1** The relationship between perceived and statistical risk probabilities
(Source: Slovic *et al.*, 1980)

## Market failure and major risks

This section has explained the main market failures associated with insurance, but how do life risks map onto this list? Table 16.4 lists some of the major unexpected alterations to the standard of living that we face in a typical lifetime. For each risk, the most important sources of market failure are identified. Any such table is, at least to some extent, subjective, but note that we are not claiming (for instance) that myopia is not important in disability insurance, only that adverse selection is likely to be the major source of problems.

The optimal solution to these market failures might not be social insurance. In the final line of the table, a tentative identification of the appropriate intervention has been made. Some comments on this are in order. When moral hazard is the only problem affecting private insurance markets, the case for government provision depends mainly on moral hazard being less prevalent when the state offers insurance, instead of the market. This might or might not be the case (hence the question mark in the table). Governments have stronger monitoring powers compared to private insurance companies, and so are theoretically able to detect moral hazard more easily. Moreover, there may be greater shame attached to cheating a social insurance scheme and also greater outrage against people who do so, both of which would serve to limit moral hazard. Against this, social insurance schemes are constrained by political factors, specifically the provision of a safety net for all citizens, which limits the ability to control disincentive effects.

Moral hazard therefore does not evaporate when the insurance is social rather than private. So a government which provides insurance against unemployment or disability must still find incentives to limit the problem. In Chapter 6, we saw that the costs of moral hazard are determined by the degree of risk aversion, the costs of effort

**Table 16.4** Market failures and the major life risks

| | Moral hazard | Adverse selection | Myopia | Positive correlation |
|---|---|---|---|---|
| Inflation | | | ● | ● |
| Divorce | ● | ● | ● | |
| Children | ● | ● | ● | |
| Ill-health | | ● | | |
| Disability | | ● | | |
| Unemployment | ● | ● | | ● |
| Old age | | | ● | |
| Appropriate intervention | Social insurance? | Adjusted capitation payments; compulsory pooling | Compulsory insurance | Social insurance |

(or any other factor which affects the chances of a loss) and the sensitivity of the probability, $p$, to changes in effort. If the marginal costs of effort are high and small changes in effort lead to large changes in $p$, then the gap between utility with and without the loss must be high, in order to limit the extent of moral hazard. Conversely, if the situation is reversed and $p$ is insensitive to $e$, but the marginal costs of effort are low, then the problem of moral hazard is smaller and more easily dealt with. Unfortunately, we do not know much about the shape of the $p$ and cost functions, but views on their shape often determine opinions on social insurance. Those who believe that effort levels are sensitive to incentives will argue that the gap between unemployment benefit and market wages should be large in order to deter shirking, or that couples who divorce should be much worse off than when married. Conversely, those who advocate benefit levels close to wages believe that the disincentive effects of unemployment insurance are minimal.

There are two main means of dealing with adverse selection. The traditional method is compulsory pooling, whereby private insurers are forbidden to discriminate on the basis of risk categories, or the government provides the insurance and chooses not to make premiums depend on easily identifiable risk factors, such as age or past claims. The second method is rarer and involves providing subsidies to insurers to insure certain higher risks so that there is no incentive to cream-skim. An interesting recent example of this approach is the reforms to the Dutch health system, discussed in Chapter 19.

With myopic behaviour, we have already noted that a compulsory savings system is one potential solution, so it is only with positively correlated risks such as unemployment that socially provided insurance is the obvious means of intervention. However, the Welfare State is not simply a provider of insurance, it also redistributes income. Inevitably, insurance and redistributive motives interact and this alters the case for state intervention. A society which, for instance, promises every citizen some basic standard of living creates problems of moral hazard for an insurance system. Recall that the degree of moral hazard reduces as the gap widens between income with and without a loss, because the incentive to skimp on effort is lowered. Now, the level of income out of work which might be required to force all the able-bodied to work could well be below that tolerable in a society which seeks to protect the vulnerable. The provision of a safety net might therefore make it unprofitable for private insurers to offer cover for risks with a significant moral hazard problem, leaving a gap which could be filled by social insurance.

In summary, social insurance is desirable when certain forms of market failure, such as positive correlation, are present, or the pursuit of redistributive goals reduces the availability of private insurance. But social insurance does not eliminate problems of moral hazard and so creates its own form of government failure.

## 16.4 The Welfare State and social insurance in practice

As we have emphasised, real-world social insurance does not resemble the competitive insurance model. The transfers of the Welfare State arise from a mixture of often ill-defined motives including social insurance, compulsory saving and pure redistribution. Typically, these motives are all present in the operations of any Welfare State. In addition, some social insurance benefits, such as medical care, are often paid out in kind. Separating out the components of the system is not always easy either; for instance the difference between saving and insurance is often narrower than at first appears. Saving is putting aside income for a contingency (e.g. old age) which we know *will* occur; insurance is putting aside income for contingencies which *may* occur. However, it is almost certain that an individual will require healthcare at some time in their life, thus health insurance is almost health saving. And people die before claiming pensions (pension funds rely on this fact when calculating the benefits to the survivors), making saving for retirement more like insuring against not dying.

### Distinguishing the components

In a pure saving scheme, the benefits available to a contributor are limited to the accrued value of their investments; in a pure insurance scheme, working on an actuarially fair basis, the expected payout from the scheme to an individual should be equal to his or her contribution. For both saving and insurance systems therefore, the expected payout to an individual should be closely linked to contributions, but in redistributive schemes payouts are *negatively correlated* with incomes (which typically have a positive link to contributions). Normally, though not exclusively, eligibility for the transfer is not dependent on contribution under pure redistribution, whereas contributing provides a passport to social insurance.

|  | **Pure insurance** | **Pure redistribution** |
|---|---|---|
| **Eligibility** | Dependent on contribution | Not dependent on contribution |
| **Expected payout** | Matches contribution; typically contribution related to income | Inversely related to income; typically inversely related to 'contributions' |

The following three case studies illustrate how social security systems can differ. At a risk of extreme simplification, they can be characterised as examples of social insurance (Germany), compulsory saving (Singapore) and redistribution/safety net (UK).

### United Kingdom

Approximately half (46.7% according to the Department of Social Security) of all benefits are *Contributory Benefits*, financed through National Insurance Contributions (NICs), where eligibility is dependent upon people's national insurance records (for example, the retirement pension and the State Earnings-Related Pensions Scheme (SERPS)). The remaining are non-contributory, paid from general taxation. Of the non-contributory benefits most are *Income Related* (33.7% of the total), where eligibility depends upon means. The remainder are *Contingent Benefits*, where eligibility depends upon circumstances alone (such as Child Benefit), accounting for 19.5% of expenditure.

Social insurance contributions are paid in two forms in the UK: via National Insurance (NI), payable by most of the employed and their employers into the National Insurance Fund (NIF), and through general taxation, paid into the Consolidated Fund. Likewise, benefits are paid out by the NIF and from general taxation. The main benefits include Income Support (a safety net benefit for those without any other form of entitlement); Family Credit, a supplement to earned income for those on low incomes; the Basic Pension; Child Benefit, payable to all families with children; Incapacity Benefit and Disability Living Allowance; Housing Benefit and Council Tax Benefit, payable to help low-income households with housing costs; and Job Seekers' Allowance (JSA), which replaced Unemployment Benefit in 1996. Table 16.5 shows the breakdown of expenditure by what the Department of Social Security calls 'client groups'. See Chapter 17 for more on the details of the benefit system.

This separation of social insurance from general taxation and redistributory policy is more apparent than real and has become increasingly so over the years. NI is really a tax, albeit with a few wrinkles. Its separate identity makes the headline figure for Income Tax lower. However, on the benefits side, there are distinctions to be drawn between the benefits paid out of the NIF and those paid from the Consolidated Fund. The latter are non-contributory, which means that the citizen need not have paid anything into the tax system in order to qualify for a benefit. For instance, qualification for receiving Child Benefit depends only on having a child. With contributory benefits paid out of the NIF, such as Unemployment Benefit, beneficiaries must have paid NI in order to receive payment and the level of payment was traditionally linked to the level of contribution. This link has been increasing eroded. JSA, for instance, is paid at a single rate, while the flat-rate component of the state pension is linked to the retail price index rather than average earnings.

The UK government has been a pioneer in limiting the growth of the Welfare State. Table 16.6 lists some of the measures aimed at cutting the NI budget.

### Germany

Whereas the link between premium paid and benefits received has almost vanished in the UK, in Germany the contributory principle forms the backbone of the system. Membership of the four types of insurance fund, covering pensions, sickness, unemployment and accident insurance, is compulsory for the economically active, producing coverage rates of around 95% for sickness and accidents and 85% for pensions. (Long-term care is a fifth branch of the system, currently being introduced (see Chapter 18).) The funds are financed equally by levies on employees and their employers, with the exception of accident insurance, funded solely by employers. The government regulates contribution and benefit rates, but the funds themselves (one

**Table 16.5**   Social expenditure in the UK in 1994–5

| Beneficiary | £million |
|---|---|
| Elderly people | 38,430 |
| Sick and disabled | |
|     Long term | 20,270 |
|     Short term | 670 |
| Family benefits | 16,510 |
| Unemployed people | 9,400 |
| Widows and others | 1,920 |
| Total | 87,200 |

Source: The Government's Expenditure Plans, Figure 8, 1996

**Table 16.6**   Cutting back on benefits in the UK

| Benefit | Main cut |
|---|---|
| Retirement pension: flat rate | Uprating linked to retail prices rather than average earnings |
| Earnings-related retirement pension (SERPS) | Based on lifetime earnings instead of best 20 years |
| Invalidity pension | Was untaxed and included earnings-related component Replaced by the flat rate and taxable Incapacity Benefit |
| Unemployment benefit | Abolition of earnings-related element, duration cut to 6 months; replacement by Job Seekers Allowance; lower rate for under-25s and tightening of eligibility rules |
| Widows benefits | Abolished for childless women under 40 |

Source: Webb, Table 2, 1995

for each of the four risks) are administered jointly by unions and employers under the supervision of the government. A multitude of funds exist, organised on occupational or regional lines for example, but unemployment insurance is organised by a single body, the Federal Labour Office.

A key aspect of the German system is the close link between contributions and benefits and the legal nature of this entitlement. For instance, with long-term disability, the pension is equal to roughly two-thirds of earnings in the year prior to the illness or accident. Meanwhile, gross benefits from unemployment insurance are around 40% of gross wages prior to redundancy. After 312 days of claims, when entitlement to insurance ends, unemployment relief offers support still closely tied to previous earnings, at around 90% of the level of unemployment insurance.

With its strong relationship between earnings from employment and benefits, the German system is heavily centred on the labour market. Those too young for the labour market, or with intermittent periods of contribution, must rely on eligibility via a spouse or parent. For those inadequately served by insurance, such as single parents, and those with low incomes, assistance comes in several forms: via tax allowances, child benefits and through the *Sozialhilfe* (social assistance), which offers a safety net organised and financed by local government, with benefits based upon individual need. Overall, roughly one-third of total social security expenditure is by the government, with employees and employers making up the remainder.

The German system, which has provided a model to other social security programmes around the world, is much closer to the insurance model than the UK system. Despite this, the overall level of inequality and poverty within Germany is well below that of the UK, where the gap between average wages and the safety net provided by the state has grown sharply in the last twenty years. The system is not without its problems, which include:

- The extra costs imposed by unification between East and West, particularly given the high level of unemployment in the former East Germany.
- Some groups do relatively less well out of a system based on paid employment. Retired women (since women have lower incomes), and those outside the labour market, for instance caring for children or infirm relatives, who again tend to be women, are among the parts of German society relatively poorly served.
- The large number of funds creates fragmentation and inertia within the system, while the separation of state spending between local and central government creates incentives for each to offload welfare costs onto the other.
- The fact that it is mainly directed towards social insurance rather than poverty alleviation means that there are some perverse incentives created by the interaction between different parts of the fragmented system. For instance, Evans (1996) gives the example of a hypothetical male German receiving their *Arbeitslosengeld* insurance payments as the result of losing one job. Taking a low-paid part-time job does not remove his entitlement to benefit, but once he exceeds 19 hours a week all payments are lost, creating a deep poverty trap.

In addition, the German Welfare State has been blamed for low growth and rising unemployment, in much the same way as the UK system, and also faces the problems of funding care for the elderly and the sick in the future.

## Singapore

South Korea, Hong Kong, Taiwan and Singapore have been described as *oikonomic* Welfare States (from the Greek, *oikos*, meaning household), marked by two principles: reliance on the family as the main source of income security, and the use of welfare primarily to service growth. With the strong growth record of south-east Asia, policy-makers in Europe and North America have seen Singapore as a possible model for the future. In outline, the system relies heavily on **compulsory saving**, providing a good example of the Nanny Welfare State and is as follows.

**Compulsory saving**

A policy tool used by the Nanny state

### Old age and invalidity

The central plank of the structure is the Central Provident Fund (CPF). The scope of the fund has gradually been extended, but currently both employee and employer contribute 20% of wages. Interest is paid on savings, or they may be used for housing, certain forms of investment, as well as transfers to parental Retirement Accounts and loans for higher education (repayable within ten years). After the age of 55, some of the deposits can be withdrawn, but enough must be left in to provide for retirement. Currently roughly one in five members of the labour force is outside the scheme, while many of those in the scheme have only limited savings within the scheme because of low lifetime earnings. Outside the CPF scheme, tax allowances are available to the disabled who work and also to their siblings if they share accommodation. Similarly, offspring can receive payments for buying homes close to elderly parents.

### Healthcare

The CPF also includes a component called Medisave, into which 6% of wages are put aside to cover the hospital costs of the insured and his or her immediate family. In addition for long-term illnesses, there is a voluntary scheme called Medishield which covers outpatient treatment and surgery for those under 65.

### Safety net

The Public Assistance Scheme provides a safety net, with payments of 69% of the Minimum Household Expenditure level (set by the government), available to those unable to work, including the elderly poor, the disabled, the chronically ill and the vagrant. Those judged able to work (and the criteria are tightly drawn) are offered interest-free loans to start their own business. A safety net of sorts is also in place for the provision of healthcare, with state-provided subsidised services for the poor and complete waivers for the most destitute. Such waivers are only available if stringent conditions are satisfied. Employment of any member of the family is reason enough for disqualification.

Overall, by the 1990s less than 2% of GDP was spent by the government of Singapore on health and social security.

At one level, the differences between these countries are illusory; all rely on compulsion, whether through taxation, contributions to an insurance fund or contributions to the CPF. Moreover, since the average citizen pays for her- or himself over a lifetime, contributions to the various funds must be high in order to finance the desired benefits. Comparison of contribution rates is not straightforward, but for instance in the UK, an employee on £20,000 per year who is not contracted out of the SERPS, pays 9% of their salary into the NIF, with another 10.4% added by their employer. Healthcare spending is funded out of general taxation, but is roughly equivalent to a 10% Income Tax, meaning that 29.4% of income is being paid towards health and contributory benefits. According to Clasen and Freeman (1994), in Germany 37.4% of income goes into sickness, unemployment and pension funds, split equally between employee and employer, while we have already noted that a Singaporean contributes around 40% of income. All these numbers are high and the differences between them do not mainly represent differences in efficiency, but in the generosity of the benefits. In addition, as we have seen, the three systems do differ in the degree to which they address aims of insurance and redistribution. Finally, given that Singapore has the highest contribution rates, but also the highest growth, while the UK has the lowest contribution rates, but is also the poorest of the three countries, it seems likely that any negative link between welfare spending and growth must be connected to the *form* rather than the level of spending.

## 16.5 The crisis in the Welfare State

One of the most reliable features of the twentieth-century economy has been the steady rise in social expenditures in the richer nations of the world (see Table 16.7). Across the OECD, spending on pensions, unemployment benefit and support for the sick, the disabled or the disadvantaged has grown to be the largest component of public spending. This immense growth in expenditures has been caused by a variety of trends, including an ageing population, rises in equilibrium unemployment and the decline of the traditional two-parent family. In the UK, where social security represents the greatest single element in the government budget, the large size of the Welfare State stands accused of simultaneously undermining growth, destroying competitiveness and corrupting the moral fabric of society.[1]

In section 6 of Chapter 14 we saw that movements in inequality arise either through an alteration in the trade-off between equity and efficiency or as a result of changing views on where society should be on that locus. It is not surprising therefore that many of the forces which have created the changes in inequality are also responsible for the increased pressure on the Welfare State. In the remainder of this section, we consider three of those forces: changes in the economy, demographic trends and ideological shifts.

**Table 16.7**  Social security spending as % of GDP for selected OECD countries

|              | 1960 | 1970 | 1980 | 1990 |
|--------------|------|------|------|------|
| Canada       | 8.0  | 8.1  | 9.9  | 12.9 |
| Denmark      | 7.4  | 11.6 | 16.6 | 18.4 |
| France       | 13.6 | 17.0 | 19.2 | 21.2 |
| Italy        | 9.8  | 12.4 | 14.1 | 18.2 |
| Japan        | 3.8  | 4.6  | 10.1 | 11.5 |
| Netherlands  | –    | 17.4 | 25.9 | 25.8 |
| Spain        | 2.3  | 8.5  | 16.0 | 15.9 |
| Sweden       | 8.0  | 11.1 | 17.6 | 19.5 |
| UK           | 6.9  | 8.7  | 11.7 | 11.4 |
| USA          | 5.3  | 7.9  | 10.9 | 11.2 |
| W. Germany   | 12.5 | 13.1 | 16.5 | 15.2 |
| EC           | 10.6 | 13.1 | 15.9 | 17.1 |
| OECD         | 6.9  | 9.1  | 12.7 | 13.7 |

'Social security' = benefits for sickness, old age, family allowances, social assistance grants and unfunded employee welfare benefits paid by general government
Source: OECD, Table 6.3, 1995 and earlier years

---

[1] For instance, Frank Field (who was to serve as a Labour minister for State 1997–8) writes that the welfare budget: 'appears out of control; undermines good government; is increasingly destructive of honesty, effort, savings and thereby of self-improvement' (Field, 1996, p.8).

## Economic and demographic pressures

The modern welfare systems of Europe came into maturity during the immediate post-war period. Those years have been dubbed the 'golden years' of growth by economic historians and are now widely seen as a deviation from trend growth, caused by a variety of factors unlikely to reoccur, including the high ratio of human capital to physical capital available at the start of the era, trade liberalisation and the opportunities for the technological catch-up of the USA. Alongside high growth, the period was also marked by low rates of unemployment and poverty, as well as a relatively youthful workforce. In short, the years after 1945 were not just golden years of growth, they were also golden years for the Welfare State and about as likely to reoccur. Thus one possible reason for the crisis is simply that the original designers of the Welfare State based their plans on unsustainable assumptions about growth and unemployment.

To be sustainable in an actuarial sense, the demand for payouts from an insurance system must be matched by the supply of incoming revenues. By the late 1970s, rates of economic growth began to slow and, as the second and third columns of Table 16.8 illustrate, unemployment rose. In addition to changing economic conditions, demographic trends meant the size of the retired population rose along with life expectancy, while changes in family circumstances led to a greater number of divorces and a concomitant rise in the number of single parents.

To be politically sustainable, a Welfare State has to be seen to be achieving its declared goals, but despite the increase in redistribution effort, as measured by social security spending, there has been no accompanying reduction in inequality (see Chapter 14). Figures for poverty (see Chapter 15) tell a similar story. Therefore, one further reason for dissatisfaction with traditional models of the Welfare State is the

**Table 16.8** Economic and demographic pressures on the Welfare State

| | Average rates unemployment | | % of population aged 65 or over | | % of population aged 75 or over | | % of lone parents | |
|---|---|---|---|---|---|---|---|---|
| | 1975–80 | 1980–93 | 1960 | 1990 | 1960 | 1990 | 1980 | 1990 |
| Denmark | 6.4 | 9.6 | n/a | 15.5 | n/a | 6.9 | 12 | 18 |
| France | 5.4 | 9.6 | 11.6 | 14.0 | 4.3 | 6.8 | 7 | 13 |
| Germany | 3.0 | 7.2 | 10.6 | 15.3 | 3.4 | 7.4 | 9 | 12 |
| Greece | 2.0 | 7.5 | 8.1 | 13.7 | 3.0 | 6.0 | n/a | 5 |
| Italy | 7.3 | 10.3 | 9.1 | 14.4 | 3.0 | 6.3 | 4 | 7 |
| Netherlands | 3.6 | 9.0 | 8.6 | 12.8 | 2.8 | 5.3 | 8 | 10 |
| Spain | 7.4 | 18.9 | n/a | 13.2 | n/a | 5.4 | 3 | 5 |
| Sweden | 1.6 | 3.1 | 11.8 | 17.8 | 4.1 | 6.8* | 18 | 19 |
| UK | 5.1 | 9.6 | 11.7 | 15.6 | 4.2 | 6.8 | 12 | 19 |
| USA | 6.8 | 7.1 | 9.2 | 12.8 | 3.1 | 5.0* | 22 | 25 |

\* Refers to 1986
n/a = not available
Source: George and Taylor-Gooby, Tables 1.3, 1.6 and 1.7, 1996

lack of a rise in equity in return for the loss of efficiency associated with high spending on social protection.

## Ideological shifts

One proposed explanation of this lack of return is traditionally associated with the New Right, members of which argue that the Welfare State has undermined traditional sources of income insurance, such as the family (see Box 16.1). Such views are obviously controversial and they mark a shift in the debate beyond that normally encountered in economic approaches, because they suppose that preferences are, in the long run, endogenous to the economic system.

**BOX 16.1**

# The rise of New Right ideology

New Right thinkers claim not only that the Welfare State undermines economic growth and political legitimacy, but that it weakens traditional ways of community and family life. They argue that the incentives created by safety nets have rewarded behaviour such as unemployment or single parenthood. Thus, over time, social norms have shifted in a way that places an increased burden on the Welfare State.[2] Many also argue that it is necessary to break up the state's monopoly of welfare provision in order to create enhanced roles for private and voluntary sector alternatives and to allow welfare 'consumers' to exercise greater choice among different welfare options. In the UK, the ideas of the New Right came to political prominence when Margaret Thatcher became leader of the Conservative Party. In her view, the post-war political consensus was the result of Conservatives mistakenly making too many compromises with parties of the Left. Under her leadership, the Conservative Party argued that the role of the state in the economy should be dramatically reduced. Such ideas were not new. In 1969, Henry Drucker wrote that: 'There is mounting evidence that government is big rather than strong; that it is fat and flabby rather than powerful; that it costs a great deal of money but does not achieve much'. Margaret Thatcher (1993) herself held a dismissive view of social policy: 'welfare benefits, distributed with little or no consideration of their effects on behaviour, encouraged illegitimacy, facilitated the breakdown of families, and replaced incentives favouring work and self-reliance with perverse encouragement for idleness and cheating.'

Criticism of the Welfare State has not only come from the Right. Marxists have criticised it for propping up capitalism, while from the Liberal Left, there have been concerns that the Welfare State was repressive, stigmatising and controlling. Others have stated that the Welfare State is insensitive to issues of gender and race and not sufficiently redistributive. Nevertheless, as we shall see in Chapter 17, it is the views of the New Right which have been most influential in shaping the pattern of reforms.

---

[2] The most forthright articulation of this view can be found in the work of writers such as David Green (1996), Charles Murray (1994) and Patricia Morgan (1996) (see also further reading for references).

## New challenges for the social insurance model

An insurance scheme can only be effective when (a) the insured circumstances cover the greatest risks, (b) when these circumstances are short-lived and (c) where the insured have the wherewithal to cover the premiums. However, in recent years, the importance of the traditional risks (such as short-term unemployment or industrial accidents) has declined, while new risks have arisen, such as lone parenthood, which can last for many years, and are often faced by individuals who do not have access to labour market income. As a result, social insurance systems founded in the first part of the twentieth century have faltered. Table 16.9 illustrates this, building on the lessons of Chapter 15 and showing how those in receipt of retirement pensions in the UK make up a declining proportion of the bottom decile of the income distribution, to be replaced by the long-term unemployed and lone parents. Four key trends can be identified which undermine the effectiveness of the social insurance model of the Welfare State.

- *Changing family structure.* While the system insured against loss of income due to sickness, unemployment or retirement, it did not insure against family break-down, currently one of the main causes of lone parenthood, and therefore of poverty because lone parents have an increased risk of experiencing poverty. More-over, lone parenthood is a long-term condition, likely to last years rather than months. Smaller household and family size also makes it harder for the family to provide a substitute form of insurance for its members.

- *Gender.* The poverty associated with lone parenthood is one consequence of a system based on a traditional view of the household, with a male wage earner and a female homemaker. The husband made the NI payments and his wife's welfare entitlements were usually dependent upon his contributions. Consequently, very few women had welfare entitlements in their own name, leaving many financially vulnerable not only to the direct effects of divorce already mentioned, but also to the impact of unemployment and retirement later in life.

- *Changing employment structure.* As we saw in Chapter 14, widening wage inequality, the switch to part-time working and an increase in long-term unemployment have all been part of labour market trends. However, when first constructed, the insurance system assumed something close to full employment with earnings levels sufficient to build up a reasonable pension. Consequently, many individuals on low wages or with only intermittent income from work cannot contribute at a level which frees them from the threat of poverty.

- *Disabled.* Finally, the Beveridge social insurance model only provides support for those who have been employed and then become unable to work due to illness or industrial injury.

The immediate consequences of these trends is that individuals and families find that the insurance system cannot protect them from the risk of poverty. Meanwhile, the insurance fund runs at a deficit and must either be topped up from general taxation (in which case it ceases to be social insurance and becomes a safety net) or limit the protection it affords or find new means of raising income. The switch to non-contributory benefits, depicted in Table 16.9, illustrates the first of these policies at work; the cuts in benefit eligibility shown in Table 16.6 provide examples of the second.

**Table 16.9** Composition of the bottom income decile, UK 1970–90

|  | 1970 | 1980 | 1990 |
|---|---|---|---|
| **Contributory benefit recipients** | **59%** | **57%** | **30%** |
| Retirement pensioners | 47% | 39% | 22% |
| Long-term sick | 3% | 4% | 3% |
| Short-term sick | 1% | 1% | 1% |
| Widows | 3% | 2% | 1% |
| Unemployed | 5% | 11% | 3% |
| **Non-contributory benefit recipients** | **41%** | **43%** | **70%** |
| Long-term sick | 0% | 1% | 1% |
| Unemployed | 3% | 13% | 17% |
| Lone parents | 11% | 16% | 23% |
| Full-time workers | 22% | 7% | 13% |
| Other | 5% | 5% | 15% |
| **Total** | **100%** | **100%** | **100%** |

Source: Webb, Table 1.9, p. 26, 1994

## 16.6 Conclusion

In summary therefore, there are three main aspects to the crisis of the Welfare State: cost, protection and legitimacy. Its size and cost continue to increase, while the degree of protection it affords its citizens seems to decline. Meanwhile, more and more people doubt whether it can do the job it was created for, or question whether that job is itself worthwhile. We have seen in this chapter that there are solid efficiency reasons for government intervention in insurance and that wide sections of society do obtain benefits from the income-smoothing features of social insurance. Nevertheless, the end of the golden years means that the cost of social insurance has risen, leaving richer nations with the choice between lower protection against risks or accepting the higher cost of the Welfare State. In the chapters which follow, we examine this painful dilemma in more detail.

## Summary

- Social insurance is a concept which mixes goals of insurance with those of redistribution.
- Private markets for insurance face efficiency problems of moral hazard and adverse selection, as well as failing to cope adequately with individuals' myopia or with positively correlated risks.

- Despite the failings of the market, publicly provided insurance is not always necessary, since other measures such as compulsory saving can sometimes rectify the limitations of the market.

- Publicly provided insurance may face many of the same problems as its private counterpart, notably in dealing with moral hazard. It is also limited in its ability to deal with some positively correlated risks.

- The risk-reduction benefits of social insurance are apparently shared across most of society, as are the benefits of redistribution over the lifecycle. Both these factors go some way to explaining why the Welfare State continues to gain support from the middle classes.

- Nevertheless, mounting concern over the size of the Welfare State has led to reform and pressures for further changes.

- The UK welfare system has moved away from its social insurance basis and towards a safety net model.

- Reforms which involve simply transferring the cost of welfare to the private sector do not solve the incentive problems of social insurance.

- The reduction of moral hazard and limiting redistribution are the key arguments for cuts in the Welfare State.

- Conversely, those who believe that moral hazard/incentive problems are not significant, and who believe in redistribution, are likely to be against cuts.

## Questions

1. What market failures limit the insurance cover offered by private schemes?
2. Is cream-skimming inefficient or inequitable or neither?
3. What are the arguments for compulsory saving schemes? What are the arguments against?
4. How can we measure the impact a government has on the insurance system?
5. Why might moral hazard increase over time?
6. Why has the Welfare State grown?

## Further reading

Microeconomic textbooks such as Gravelle and Rees (1992) provide the theory essential for an understanding of insurance markets. Barr (1994) yields more detail on the UK system and on the philosophy lying behind social insurance. Bird (1995) is an interesting attempt to estimate the value of social insurance. Field (1996) provides one example of the convergence of Right and Left over the future of welfare in the UK. Murray (1994) provides a gloomy prognosis for the UK from the American critic of the Welfare State.

# References

Atkinson, A.B. (1989) *Poverty and Social Security*, Oxford: Clarendon Press.

Atkinson, A.B. (1993) 'Private and social insurance and the contributory principle', Ch. 2, in N. Barr and D. Whynes (eds), *Current Issues in the Economics of Welfare*, Basingstoke: Macmillan.

Atkinson, A.B. (1995) 'The Welfare State and economic performance', *National Tax Journal* 48, 171–98.

Baldwin, S. and Falkingham, J. (eds) (1994) *Social Security and Social Change: New Challenges to the Beveridge Model*, Hemel Hempstead: Harvester Wheatsheaf.

Barr, N. (1994) *The Economics of the Welfare State*, 2nd edn, London: Weidenfeld and Nicolson.

Barr, N. and Whynes, D. (eds) (1993) *Current Issues in The Economics of Welfare*, Basingstoke: Macmillan.

Bird, E.J. (1995) 'An exploratory comparison of income risk in Germany and the United States', *Review of Income and Wealth* 41(4), 405–26.

Clasen, J. and Freeman, R. (1994) *Social Policy in Germany*, Hemel Hempstead: Harvester Wheatsheaf.

Drucker, P.F. (1969) 'The sickness of government', *Public Interest* No. 14, Winter, 3–23.

Eurostat (1996) *Facts through Figures*, OOPEC: Luxembourg.

Evans, M. (1996) *Means Testing the Unemployed in Britain, France and Germany*, London School of Economics: Welfare State Programme WSP/117.

Field, F. (1996) *Stakeholder Welfare*, Institute for Economic Affairs, Choice in Welfare Series, No. 32.

Falkingham, J. and Hills, J. (eds) (1995) *The Dynamics of Welfare: The Welfare State and the Life Cycle*, Hemel Hempstead: Prentice Hall/Harvester Wheatsheaf.

George, V. and Taylor-Gooby, P. (1996) *European Welfare Policy: Squaring the Welfare Circle*, Basingstoke: Macmillan.

Glennerster, H. (1995) *Paying for Welfare*, Hemel Hempstead: Harvester Wheatsheaf.

Gravelle, H. and Rees, R. (1992) *Microeconomics*, London: Longmans.

Green, D.G. (1996) *Community Without Politics*, Institute for Economic Affairs, Choice in Welfare Series, No. 27.

H.M. Treasury (1996) *Government Expenditure Plans*, London: Stationery Office.

Morgan, P. (1996) *Who Needs Parents?*, Institute for Economic Affairs, Choice in Welfare Series, No. 31.

Murray, C. (1994) *The Underclass: The Crisis Deepens*, Institute for Economic Affairs, Choice in Welfare Series, No. 20.

OECD (1995) *Historical Statistics*, Paris: OECD.

Pierson, C. (1991) *Beyond the Welfare State: The New Political Economy of Welfare*, London: Polity Press.

Slovic, P., Fischoff, B. and Lichtenstein, S. (1980) 'Facts versus fears: understanding perceived risk', in R. Schwing and W.A. Albers Jr (eds) *Societal Risk Assessment: How Safe is Safe Enough?*, pp. 9–34, New York: Plenum Press.

Thatcher, M. (1993) *The Downing Street Years*, London: Harper Collins.

Webb, S. (1994) 'Social insurance and poverty alleviation: an empirical analysis', in S. Baldwin and J. Falkingham (eds), *Social Security and Social Change: New Challenges to the Beverage Model*, pp. 11–28, Hemel Hempstead: Harvester Wheatsheaf.

Webb, S. (1995) 'Social security policy in a changing labour market', *Oxford Review of Economic Policy* 11(3), 11–26.

# Social Policy

## 17.1 Introduction

This chapter will discuss the current state of social policy and recent trends in demand for social provision. This is the largest area of government expenditure and we discuss the attempts taken by governments in the UK to reduce expenditure on social policy. Despite these reform measures, welfare expenditure has continued to rise, which is not surprising, given that most of the factors behind the rise continue to press. As we saw in Chapter 16, these include an ageing population, changing family composition and the rise in unemployment. However, as we saw in Chapters 14 and 15, the UK has experienced a growing gap between rich and poor and an accompanying rise in the persistence of poverty. This raises a final controversial issue: if we assume that the primary aim of the Welfare State is the prevention of poverty, why has the welfare system failed to cure many of the ills it aims to address?

## 17.2 Policies to combat poverty

Social policy includes a range of measures that can be used to reduce poverty and inequality. There are some elements of social policy which are universal, for example health and education, which are discussed in later chapters. The policies discussed in this section are concerned directly with the elimination of poverty and the reduction of inequality and are more or less targeted at those on low incomes and those without incomes.

## Contingent benefits

**Contingent benefits**

Welfare payments made to all who fall in a particular group

A **contingent benefit** is a welfare payment which is made to all individuals or households in a particular state; such payments can be justified when there is a strong link between the given state and the incidence of poverty.[1] In Chapter 15 we saw that whilst the composition of the poor has changed over time, households in certain circumstances are more likely to experience poverty (during retirement, parenthood or spells of ill-health, for example). Given this, an anti-poverty social policy might include contingent welfare payments for such groups, for instance state pensions, Child Benefit or disability benefits. An attraction of contingent benefits is that the payments are independent of income, so there is no impact on work incentives; the households will not lose entitlement if they find a job, change job or increase their hours of work. In addition, the administrative costs of contingent benefits are relatively low. Contingent benefits are simple to assess, individuals or households either do or do not exhibit the required characteristic,[2] and cheap to administer: the same payment is made to all. Finally, since contingent benefits are available to all in a given state, there is little stigma attached to making a claim, so the take-up rate is very high. As a consequence, governments can be sure that were a retired person or parent in poverty, their situation would be eased once the contingent benefit is paid. However, whilst those with certain characteristics are more likely to experience poverty, it is unlikely that the particular characteristic is exclusively exhibited by the poor, thus a contingent benefit may be paid to rich as well as poor households.

## Income-related benefits

**Income-related benefits**

Welfare payments made only to those whose income falls below a certain level

As the factors leading to poverty are in fact more complex than a single characteristic and may change over time, and the financial resources that are available to combat poverty are limited, governments may prefer to combat poverty using **income-related** or means-tested **benefits**. These are welfare payments which are made to individuals or households whose income (earned income and savings) falls below a certain level; these benefits are targeted at the poor. Should the claimants' circumstances improve (for example, experience a rise in income), they will lose their entitlement to income-related benefits. Because entitlement and amount paid have to be assessed on the basis of individual circumstances, it is more costly to administer a means-tested benefits system. Kay and King (1990) estimate that the average administrative cost of £1 paid in income-related benefits is ten times that of £1 spent on contingent benefits. However, this form of welfare payment has the attraction of being more targeted; they are only paid to those in need. Although means testing is often considered to be a more effective method of preventing poverty, one drawback of the system is that some households who are entitled to the benefits fail to apply; take-up rates are less than 100% (see Table 17.1).[3] For example the fact that take-up rates are low for Income Support and Family Credit may be a cause for concern. These benefits are discussed in more detail in section 17.5.

---

[1] Barr (1993) gives the following example: if only redheads are poor, all redheads are poor and it is impossible to change the colour of your hair, then a welfare payment contingent on having red hair would be an effective anti-poverty strategy.

[2] Once a person is in a state such as retirement or parenthood, they are entitled to the contingent benefit and they are unlikely to change states for possibly twenty years.

[3] Perhaps they find the administrative process off-putting, resent the scrutiny of officials or find the process of making the claim demeaning. Many households may be entitled to very small amounts and so the cost of form-filling outweighs the benefit of the additional income.

**Table 17.1** Take-up rates of means-tested benefits

|  | Estimated take-up (%) | Average weekly payment (£) |
| --- | --- | --- |
| Income Support | 88–92 | 49.40 |
| Family Credit | 82 | 46.30 |
| Housing Benefit | 93–97 | 35.70 |
| Council Tax | 71–79 | 6.30 |

Source: *Social Security Statistics 1996/97*, Tables H4.01, H4.02, H4.03 and H4.04

An anti-poverty strategy should be designed so that state intervention cures rather than causes poverty. In particular, for the young and able-bodied, social policy should not deter individual effort and lead to a situation where households are better off living on welfare. So it is important to consider the likely effect of the combined benefit and tax system upon work incentives. Whereas contingent benefits which are not linked to income are unlikely to affect work incentives, income-related benefits effectively impose high rates of taxation.[4] Atkinson (1995) argues that 'the means testing approach necessarily penalises personal effort. Even if the poverty trap no longer involves marginal rates of taxation in excess of 100%, the marginal rates are still higher than those levied on the rest of the population.' This problem was illustrated in Chapter 13.

## Workfare

**Workfare**

Welfare payments are made under the condition that the recipients work or undertake education/ training

One critique of many welfare systems is that they encourage a culture of dependency amongst welfare recipients. In particular, recipients who are unemployed receive welfare payments under the condition that they are available for work, which means that they cannot offer themselves for employment in the voluntary sector nor can they use their time to gain qualifications or skills. Essentially, they are paid to do nothing other than search for employment. **Workfare** requires that recipients offer something in exchange for their welfare support. This is usually employment, but it may also include training. The justification for workfare is twofold; one is ideological, that welfare support should not be a passive activity, that welfare recipients have the right to financial support, but also the responsibility to society to offer something in exchange for that support. The second justification is associated with the poor levels of skills amongst the unemployed and the damage that prolonged spells of economic inactivity does to future employment chances. The combination of employment and welfare means that individuals maintain contacts with the world of work. Alternatively, the combination of training and welfare allows individuals to address their lack of skills. It is expected that both of these will enhance future employment prospects. The pro-workfare view is challenged on several fronts. The first is that the requirement that welfare recipients should be employed is unrealistic; not all welfare recipients are in a position to work, the disabled or mothers of preschool children for example. Second, it can be demeaning, as the jobs offered by workfare are often low grade and may even harm future employment prospects. Finally, the requirement of workfare means that less time can be spent on effective job search.

---

[4] In the framework introduced in Chapter 13, contingent benefits only result in an income effect and not a substitution effect, but a means-tested benefit will result in both an income and substitution effect.

## Integrating the tax and benefit system

One problem facing many poor households is that once they find a job, not only do they lose entitlement to income-related benefits, they also start to pay taxes. Therefore, governments need to carefully consider the design of the tax system. Options put forward include a negative income tax or tax credit scheme.

### Negative income tax

**Negative income tax**

Combines the tax and welfare system; Income Tax is paid when income is above a minimum and welfare payments are received at the same rate, if income falls below the minimum

Under a **negative income tax** scheme each taxpayer or welfare recipient is assessed by a single body, thus combining the administration of tax and benefits. Given a rate of tax $t$, the amount of tax paid is given by the following $T_i = t(Y_i - Y_A)$, where $Y_i$ is income and $Y_A$ is the tax threshold. Taxes are only paid when $Y_i > Y_A$; when $Y_i < Y_A$ the individual or household has a negative tax liability and receives an income from the state. When the household has no earned income $Y_i = 0$, their negative tax liability is $tY_A = Y_{min}$ (the minimum income necessary). Under a negative tax system, post-tax income is $Y_{net}$, where

$$Y_{net} = Y_i - t(Y_i - Y_A)$$
$$= Y_i(1 - t) + tY_A$$
$$= Y_i(1 - t) + Y_{min}$$

This is shown in Figure 17.1. There are clear incentives to work; a higher gross income always leads to a higher net income.

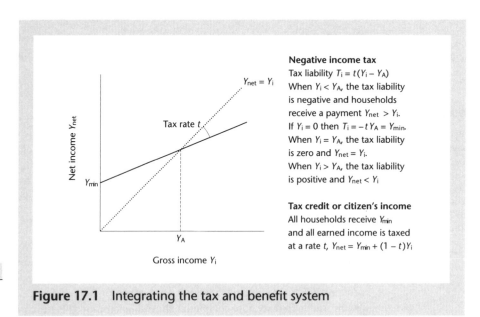

**Figure 17.1** Integrating the tax and benefit system

### Tax credit

**Tax credit**

Each tax unit is allocated a tax allowance which is credited against their tax bill when tax is due, but is paid out if income falls below the tax threshold

Most income tax systems allow for some tax-free income, typically an annual sum, usually referred to as a tax allowance. An alternative would be to offer a **tax credit** to all taxpayers on a weekly basis. In the case of those in employment, this would allow for tax-free earnings; taxes would only be paid once tax liabilities exceed the value of the tax credit. Payments would be made to those whose tax liabilities fall below the value of the tax credit. However, a tax credit system is unlikely to provide a high enough income to eliminate poverty. For example even a very high tax allowance of £4,000 would only provide a starting weekly income of £76.92. The effect of a tax credit system can also be seen in Figure 17.1. Here $Y_{min}$ is the weekly tax credit and tax is paid at a rate $t$ on all earned income. However, tax allowances are only available to those in employment (see Chapter 10). This scheme could be extended to non-taxpayers by offering a citizen's income, whereby all citizens receive a fixed weekly income from the state which replaces all income-related benefits. A citizen's income has a very similar effect: post-tax income is $Y_{net} = Y_{min} + Y_i(1 - t)$.

Schemes such as a negative income tax or tax credit would reduce the tax liabilities of those on low incomes but, in order to be self-funding, these schemes would require a much higher rate of tax on those in employment.

## Minimum wage legislation

In addition to fiscal measures which have greatest effect on preventing poverty amongst those outside of the labour market, the government can prevent low pay by intervening directly in the labour market. Most European countries and the USA have minimum wage legislation which requires that employers pay wage rates above a certain level. In discussing the likely effects of a minimum wage, attention has tended to focus upon the likely effects on employment. By setting a wage above the market clearing rate, employment is expected to fall, but the amount of unemployment created will depend upon the wage elasticity of demand for labour (which itself reflects the elasticity of demand for the final product, the elasticity of substitution of labour for other factors of production, the availability of substitutes and the labour costs as a proportion of overall costs) and the degree of power held by the employer in the factor market. Any rise in unemployment which is attributable to the minimum wage certainly raises questions about its effectiveness as an anti-poverty tool. However, assuming for a moment that out-of-work benefits offer sufficient protection against poverty, we can focus our attention on the degree to which a minimum wage prevents in-work poverty. The impact will be felt by different groups of workers according to the level at which the minimum wage is set. With a relatively low minimum wage, the groups most likely to be covered are women or young workers in very low paid jobs, usually in catering or cleaning.[5] Although such a low minimum wage increases the income of the workers covered, it may have a more limited effect in terms of reducing overall poverty. This is because these workers are often in households where there is another earner. However, in the case of groups such as lone mothers, a combination of minimum wage legislation and subsidised child care can be an effective anti-poverty tool. Only when a minimum wage is set at quite a high level, when it covers men in low-paid occupations such as farming, does it reduce household poverty. Of course, when the minimum wage is set at these high levels, the loss of employment is likely to be much higher. Our arguments suggest that a minimum wage may have limited impact as an anti-poverty tool, but it can be effective as a policy aimed at reducing income inequality, because it limits the degree of vertical inequality (the gap between the rich and poor) but also horizontal inequality (the gap between men and women).

---

[5] Young workers under 20 are often excluded from minimum wage legislation, partly to protect their opportunities for training.

## 17.3 Welfare State in the UK

The modern day social security system remains based on the Beveridge Report (Beveridge, 1942), which established a social insurance system protecting households from the insurable risks of poverty (see Chapter 16 for a detailed discussion of social insurance). The scheme was intended to provide support to those groups identified by Rowntree (1941, see Chapter 15), as those most in need of social welfare, namely, the elderly, sick, unemployed and families on low incomes. Insurance against loss of income in the circumstances of unemployment, ill-health and retirement was provided through NICs. Expenditure on social security has risen sevenfold since the inception of the Welfare State and as we saw in Table 16.7, expenditure on social security has accounted for a growing proportion of central government expenditure (CGE) and gross domestic product (GDP).

### Current expenditure

By 1996/7 the total welfare expenditure of the government had reached £142.5 billion: £93.4 billion was spent on social security, £34.9 billion was spent on health and £14.2 billion was spent on education and employment. The main areas of expenditure are shown in Figure 17.2.

This section will concentrate on the social security system (pensions and the pressures created by an ageing population are discussed in Chapter 18, health is discussed in Chapter 19 and education in Chapter 20). Rates of benefit payment are presented below in Table 17.2. In calculating the rates for households, the Department of Social Security uses equivalence scales to identify the adult equivalent size of household (see discussion in Chapter 14).

Predicted government expenditure and number of claimants for 1996/7 are presented in Table 17.3. What is noticeable is that, whilst in most cases the level of

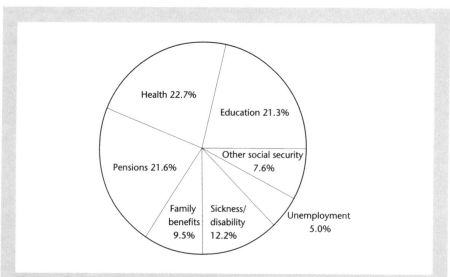

**Figure 17.2**  Government welfare spending 1996/7
(Source: Public Finance Trends 1996, Table 2.2 and Government Expenditure Plans 1996–9, Social Security Departmental Report, Figure 8)

**Table 17.2**   Main benefit rates, £ per week

| Benefit | Household type | November 1978 | April 1995 | April 1996 |
|---|---|---|---|---|
| Retirement pension | Single person | 19.50 | 58.85 | 61.15 |
| | Married couple | 31.20 | 94.10 | 97.75 |
| Unemployment Benefit | Single person | 15.75 | 46.46 | 48.25 |
| | Married couple | 25.50 | 75.10 | 78.00 |
| Invalidity/Incapacity Benefit | | 19.50 | 58.85 | 61.15 |
| Disability Living Allowance | Care component | – | 46.70 | 48.50 |
| (Highest rate) | Mobility component | – | 32.65 | 33.90 |
| Attendance Allowance | Highest rate | 15.60 | 46.70 | 48.50 |
| Child Benefit | First child | 4.00 | 10.40 | 10.80 |
| | Subsequent children | 4.00 | 8.45 | 8.80 |
| One-parent Benefit | | 2.00 | 6.30 | 6.30 |
| Income Support | Couple, two children* | – | 122.60 | 126.30 |
| | Pensioner couple** | – | 101.05 | 104.10 |
| Family Credit | | – | 56.50 | 58.20 |

\* One child under 11, one child 11–15
\*\* Aged 60–75, non-disabled
– Benefit introduced in 1988
Source: *The Government's Expenditure Plans 1996/97*, Figure 20.

expenditure is higher where there is a large number of claimants, the benefit with the largest number of claimants is the Social Fund, where the amounts being paid out are relatively small. The current UK benefit system is discussed in section 17.8, where benefits are categorised by function in Table 17.11 and the eligibility conditions are outlined.

## Beneficiaries

Approximately 96% of the social security budget is spent on benefit payments. In 1996/7, the largest single group in receipt of benefits were the elderly. Roughly one-quarter of benefit payments are made to the sick or disabled, while one-fifth of welfare payments are made to low-earning families (see Figure 17.3).

Comparing Figures 17.2 and 17.4, we can see that the share of welfare expenditure accounted for by health has remained fairly constant from 1951/2 to 1996/7. Housing now accounts for a much smaller share, reflecting the post-war housing boom. The share of social security expenditure has risen.

Looking at most recent trends, over the past twenty years it is clear that the elderly have always been the single largest group in receipt of benefits (see Table 17.4), while the sick and disabled are gradually accounting for a greater proportion of benefit payments. The cyclical nature of the social security budget is also clear. For example, during the recessions of the 1980s benefit payments to the unemployed accounted for a rising proportion of all benefit groups. The proportion of welfare payments made to families has remained fairly constant, though this disguises an important trend, namely, the rising number of lone-parent families dependent upon benefits.

**Table 17.3** Cash benefits, UK 1996/7

| | Numbers in 000s | Expenditure in £ millions |
|---|---|---|
| *Contributory benefits* (i.e. from the National Insurance Fund) | | |
| Retirement pensions (including lump-sum payments) | 10,537 | 31,851 |
| Widows Benefit etc. | 301 | 1052 |
| Job Seekers' Allowance (Unemployment Benefit) | 2072 | 999 |
| Incapacity Benefit | 2373 | 7767 |
| *Non-contributory benefits* (i.e. those from the Consolidated Fund) | | |
| *Contingent benefits* | | |
| Non-contributory retirement pension | 28 | 171 |
| War pensions | 327 | 1419 |
| Child Benefit and One-parent Benefit | 8051 | 7072 |
| Disability Living Allowance | 518 | 4361 |
| Severe Disablement Allowance | 349 | 893 |
| Industrial Injury Benefit | 245 | 661 |
| Attendance Allowance | 1108 | 2421 |
| Invalid Care Allowance | 357 | 768 |
| *Income-related benefits* | | |
| Income Support | 9587 | 1,4061 |
| Family Credit | 725 | 2047 |
| Housing Benefit | 4776 | 1,1523 |
| Social Fund | 7297 | 539 |
| Disability Working Allowance | 12 | 25 |
| Council Tax Benefit | 5614 | 2361 |

Source: Compiled using *The Government's Expenditure Plans 1996/97*

**Table 17.4** Trends in welfare recipients

| Beneficiaries | 1978/9 | 1983/4 | 1987/8 | 1992/3 | 1996/7 |
|---|---|---|---|---|---|
| Elderly | 55% | 50% | 49% | 47% | 44% |
| Sick/disabled | 16% | 14% | 17% | 22% | 25% |
| Family | 16% | 17% | 18% | 17% | 19% |
| Unemployed | 8% | 16% | 14% | 13% | 9% |
| Others | 5% | 3% | 2% | 1% | 3% |

Source: Calculated from *Growth in Social Security* (1979–1993), Table 3 and *Social Security Statistics 1996/97*, page 3, 'Benefit Expenditure'

The number of lone parents has continued to rise. By 1993, 14% of all households with dependent children were single-parent households and 66% of single-parent households were dependent upon Income Support (Glennerster, 1995). Lone parents are usually described as a homogeneous group; in fact it is a very diverse group. Lone parenthood arises due to marital breakdown, death of spouse or having children outside of marriage. The majority of single-parent households are created by divorce

(60%). One-third have never married, the remainder have been widowed. The rising number of lone parents can be explained by both the increase in divorce rates (the divorce rate has more than doubled since the 1960s, in 1992 173,000 marriages ended in divorce) and the increase in numbers of children born outside of marriage (the number of births outside of marriage has risen from 8% of all births in the 1960s to 36% of all births in the 1990s).

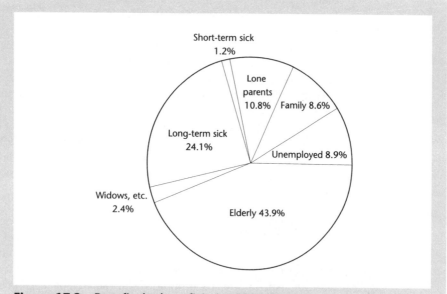

**Figure 17.3** Benefits by beneficiaries 1996/7
(Source: *Social Security Statistics 1996/97*, page 3, 'Benefits Expenditure')

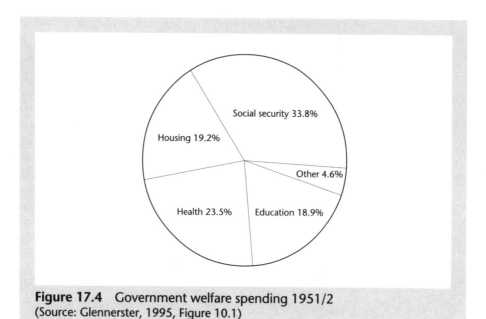

**Figure 17.4** Government welfare spending 1951/2
(Source: Glennerster, 1995, Figure 10.1)

## 17.4 Welfare reform

Welfare expenditure has accounted for a growing share of GDP. As we have argued in Chapter 16, by the late 1970s the Welfare State had come under significant economic and demographic pressure. The IMF rescue package in 1976 probably marks the starting point for reform of the welfare system in the UK. It was at this stage that many began to view the Welfare State as a barrier to economic growth. Although very few reform measures were actually implemented, the Labour government froze the real value of departmental budgets and welfare expenditure stabilised. During the 1980s, the welfare system came more under sustained ideological attacks from the New Right, which created an anti-welfare climate of opinion, but did not translate into radical policy until the late 1980s. In fact, Clarke and Langan (1993) argue that over the 1980s the Conservative government proceeded in a cautious fashion, focusing on areas where resistance was weakest (housing) and where anti-welfare prejudice was strongest (benefits for the unemployed). They refer to Le Grand (1990) who suggests that the services used most extensively by the middle class survived best over the 1980s. It was only after three election victories that the Thatcher administration tackled the areas of welfare where the middle-class support was strongest: education and health.

### Conservative reform

During their eighteen years in office, the Conservative government rejected the possibility of raising more revenue to finance the Welfare State focusing, instead, upon reducing expenditure. Their initiatives in the area of social policy had the following objectives:

- to reduce the disincentive and dependency creating effects of benefits;
- to create a more efficient benefits system by 'targeting' benefits at the most needy; and
- to encourage moves away from the State as the primary agency of social insurance.

*Reducing disincentives.* Disincentives to employment were thought to occur because it was both too easy to claim benefits and the level of benefits was too high. One attempt to reduce disincentives was the tightening of the conditions of eligibility for Unemployment Benefit, requiring that claimants need to prove that they were 'genuinely seeking work'. In addition some groups, such as the young and long-term unemployed, were compelled to attend training courses or face loss of benefits. Another measure taken to reduce disincentives was to reduce the replacement ratio.[6] The replacement ratio in the UK is much lower than in other European Union countries (see Table 17.5). In 1980, the Conservative government introduced legislation which meant that the value of most benefit payments increased with price inflation and not with wage inflation (see discussion in Chapters 14 and 16). The decision to index pensions to RPI rather than to earnings was particularly controversial, because it meant that those at the end of their working life who had made NICs could no longer share in the growth of income experienced by the working population.

---

[6] The replacement ratio is the ratio between average rates of benefit payments and wages.

**Table 17.5** Replacement ratios for household types before housing costs, May 1992

|  | Single people | | Couples | | |
|---|---|---|---|---|---|
|  | No children | One child | No children | One child | Two children |
| Belgium | 66 | 70 | 59 | 63 | 66 |
| Denmark | 65 | 70 | 67 | 68 | 69 |
| France | 73 | 74 | 72 | 70 | 72 |
| Germany | 63 | 71 | 63 | 71 | 75 |
| Greece | 35 | 38 | 34 | 38 | 42 |
| Ireland | 39 | 44 | 51 | 54 | 58 |
| Italy | 35 | 39 | 38 | 41 | 43 |
| Luxembourg | 84 | 86 | 82 | 86 | 86 |
| Netherlands | 74 | 76 | 75 | 76 | 77 |
| Portugal | 65 | 66 | 65 | 66 | 67 |
| Spain | 67 | 72 | 63 | 72 | 74 |
| UK | 21 | 32 | 31 | 42 | 48 |
| EU average | 57 | 62 | 58 | 62 | 65 |

Source: Fawcett and Papadopoulos, Table 2, 1991

*Targeting benefits.* According to Clarke and Langan (1993):

> this principle was most clearly articulated in the review of Social Security which reported in 1985 (DHSS, 1985). The resulting legislation reduced the value of SERPS-based pensions, restructured Supplementary Benefit (with particular impact on what were termed 'special needs payments'), replaced Family Income Supplement (paid to low earning households) with family credit and froze the value of Child Benefit, thus moving family support increasingly away from universal benefits to means tested ones.

In another move intended to target benefits more effectively, charges for a variety of social services were introduced, from which only those on low incomes were exempt. These included increased prescription charges, introducing charges for home support services for the elderly and abolishing free eye tests and dental treatment. The government also reduced expenditure by limiting the service provided, for example phasing out of maintenance grants to university students, ending the subsidy for school meals and making benefit income taxable.

*Encourage moves away from the state as the primary agency of social insurance.* When the Conservative government first proposed that private insurers should take over the responsibility of providing sickness and pension insurance, the private sector was reluctant to participate. The insurers main concern was the government's requirement that the insurance should be universal, and that it should include good and bad risks (see Chapter 6 for a discussion of market failure in the provision of insurance). Other initiatives included tax exemptions for the over 65s who took out private health insurance.

A further issue which concerned the Conservatives over this period was the administrative complexity of the system. Whilst some benefits are targeted at particular groups, for example the retirement pension and Child Benefit, others are available to all those with low incomes (Income Support, Housing Benefit and Council Tax Benefit). Thus households with low income are usually entitled to a number of benefits. This created a complex system, particularly because the conditions for eligibility are often benefit-specific. For example, both Income Support and Housing Benefit are means-tested. Households claiming Income Support would usually be entitled to Housing Benefit, but Housing Benefit is also available to some households whose income level lies above the Income Support threshold. Attempts have been made by the Department of Social Security (DSS) to create a less cumbersome system and a number of reforms were implemented in the 1988 Social Security Act. These concentrated on reducing the number of benefits available and the problems created by the unemployment or poverty trap.[7] (The 1988 reforms are discussed below.) A consequence of the 1988 reforms and general social security policy over the 1980s was a change in emphasis in benefit payments. Fewer resources were used to finance contingent benefits and more resources were channelled into income-related or means-tested benefits.

## 1988 social security reforms

The 1988 social security reforms were intended both to simplify the benefit system and to eliminate the problem of marginal tax rates of over 100% for those on benefits.[8] The main simplification took the form of unifying the benefit entitlements of those in and outside employment. Thus Income Support both tops up the incomes of low-paid workers and is paid out as an income for those outside of the labour market while Family Credit is paid to low-income families in employment. Eligibility conditions were unified and it was intended that the final, post-benefit income for both groups should be the same. The reforms also addressed the issue of the poverty or unemployment trap (for a further discussion of this see Chapter 13).

## Income-related versus contingent benefits

Attention has already been drawn to the change in emphasis in the form of welfare payments made. The Beveridge welfare system provided benefits which were state-contingent, such as Child Benefit and basic state pension. The advantage of these benefits was their administrative simplicity and high take-up rate. The disadvantage was that contingent benefits were paid regardless of individual need and consequently paid to less needy middle- and high-income households, which the Conservative government regarded as an inefficient use of resources. The Conservatives argued that since the Welfare State exists to prevent poverty and to provide a safety net, only low-income families should be entitled to welfare payments. Accordingly they introduced greater targeting and means testing of benefits. In practical terms,

---

[7] An illustration of an unemployment/poverty trap was given in Chapter 13. These are characterised by income falling as hours of work rise and occur in welfare systems where benefit payments are means-tested.
[8] Also already defined as the 'Fowler reforms' after the Secretary of State for Social Security at the time, Norman Fowler. A full account of the sources of poverty traps is given in Parker (1995).

this was achieved by freezing the value of the contingent benefits and increasing the value of means-tested benefits.

However, many would question the assertion that the only function of the Welfare State is to prevent poverty. As we saw in Chapter 16, the Welfare State performs a number of other roles including: smoothing income over the lifecycle; ensuring household income in the event of loss of income (but not necessarily poverty) due to sickness, unemployment or death; redistribution towards those with dependents; and establishing citizenship, regardless of gender, ethnicity or disability. Once these other functions are taken into account, it is by no means clear that the critique of the inefficiency of the existing system holds.

The other problems associated with greater reliance on means testing have also been discussed:

- That the problems associated with the unemployment/poverty trap become more acute. Atkinson (1995, p. 296) argues that

  the means testing approach necessarily penalises personal effort. Even if the poverty trap no longer involves marginal rates of taxation in excess of 100%, the marginal rates are still higher than those levied on the rest of the population . . . I find it strange that a government so concerned with incentives should not see that reliance on means testing has such a counter productive effect.

- The problem of low take-up of means-tested benefits (see Table 17.1).

In summary, by the late 1970s UK governments had abandoned full employment as a key policy objective. Over the 1980s, the welfare benefit system was reformed to tighten up eligibility, to reduce the disincentive effects of excessive benefit levels and to make the system more efficient by targeting the most needy. Expenditure on universal or contingent benefits fell, and was targeted instead on households with low incomes, families and the disabled. Along with welfare reform the Conservative government also attempted to deregulate the labour market (the abolition of the Wages Councils and anti-union legislation). As we saw in Chapter 16, these measures have contributed towards the growing level of inequality. In addition, the incidence of poverty and levels of welfare expenditure have continued to rise.

## 17.5 Current welfare system

The main benefits are presented in Table 17.6. We then outline some of the main benefits, focusing upon the eligibility criteria.

### Income-related benefits

#### Job Seekers' Allowance (JSA)

The JSA was introduced in October 1996 to replace Unemployment Benefit and Income Support for unemployed people. Entitlement to the JSA is dependent upon whether the claimant is unemployed, capable of work, available for work and actively seeking work. These conditions are formalised in a Jobseekers' Agreement which clarifies the conditions of availability for work and outlines the steps that the unemployed person will take to find work. There are two rates for the JSA: the income-based rate and a basic rate. The income-based rate is paid for a period up to six months to those who have made sufficient NICs; this is equivalent to Unemployment

**Table 17.6** Main benefits categorised by function

| Income-related benefits | Sickness and Incapacity benefits |
|---|---|
| Job Seekers' Allowance | Statutory Sick Pay |
| Income Support | Incapacity Benefit |
| Retirement pension | Severe Disablement Allowance |
| Housing Benefit | |
| Council Tax Benefit | *Disability benefits* |
| | Attendance Allowance |
| *Family benefits* | Mobility Allowance |
| Family Credit | Disability Living Allowance |
| Child Benefit | Disability Working Allowance |
| One-parent Benefit | Invalid Care Allowance |
| Widows Benefit | War Pensions |
| Guardian's Allowance | Industrial injuries |
| Statutory Maternity Pay | |
| Maternity Allowance | *Welfare-to-Work* |
| Working Family Tax Credit | |

Benefit, although the period over which the payments are made has been reduced from twelve to six months. The basic rate, which is non-contributory and means-tested, is paid to those who have not met the contributions criteria and to those who have been unemployed for a period longer than six months. This is essentially Income Support and claims are made through that route.

### Income Support

Income Support replaced Supplementary Benefit in 1988. It is means-tested and payable to anyone over the age of sixteen who is not working more than sixteen hours a week. It is paid to the following groups who are not required to be actively seeking work: pensioners, single parents and those unable to work and also to the unemployed under the conditions of the JSA described above. The payment is assessed on the basis of household resources and responsibilities and is intended to top up household income to the level that the state regards as the minimum upon which that household could live. Income Support does not cover rent or Council Tax. Support for these comes from Housing Benefit and Council Tax Benefit.

Whilst Income Support does provide maintenance for children, some limits are placed on the support for a claimant household where one parent is absent. In such cases, the claimant may be required to make an application for child maintenance from the absent parent through the Child Support Agency (CSA). The CSA is discussed in more detail under family policy.

### Retirement pension

See Box 18.1 for a full discussion of the state pension.

### Housing Benefit and Council Tax Benefit

These are both means-tested benefits. Recipients of Income Support are eligible for Housing Benefit. Some households which are not in receipt of Income Support are eligible for both of these benefits. Housing Benefit provides low-income households with financial assistance in paying for their accommodation, known as 'eligible rent'.[9] The 'eligible rent' reflects the local rents and the housing needs of the claimant. New rules have been introduced to limit the value of 'eligible rent' for young claimants. Since 1996 the maximum benefit paid to single young people (under 25) has been set at the cost of renting a single room with shared facilities. Council Tax Benefit is designed to help people on low income pay their Council Tax; from Table 17.1 we know that take-up of this benefit is particularly low.

### Social Fund

Claims can be made to the Social Fund for one-off non-repayable awards to help households in particular circumstances: pregnancy (up to £100 towards the cost of items for the new baby); or death (contribution towards a low-cost funeral). Cold weather payments (£8.50 in 1996) are paid automatically to any households in receipt of Income Support if the temperature falls below 0°C for seven consecutive days. In addition, loans are made to help families with purchases that are not easily covered within a weekly budget, for example, the purchase of a fridge or a washing machine. The Social Fund was established by the 1988 social security reforms and replaced 'special needs payments'.

## Family benefits

### Family Credit

Family Credit was introduced in 1988 replacing Family Income Supplement. This is a means-tested benefit intended to provide financial support for households with children. Eligibility requires that the claimant is employed for sixteen or more hours a week and that the household includes at least one child under the age of sixteen. Family Credit can be claimed by both one- and two-parent households. In 1999 this will be replaced by the Working Family Tax Credit (see below).

### Child Benefit

Child Benefit replaced Family Allowance in April 1977. Under Family Allowance, a payment was made to families with two or more children; Child Benefit is paid for all children under the age of sixteen. A higher rate is paid for the first child and the same rate is paid for all younger children (see Table 17.2). The benefit will be paid to families with older children 16–19 when the child is engaged in full-time education (up to A-level standard) and to families with children 16–17 waiting to take up a place on a youth training scheme. Until the Budget in March 1998, lone parents received an additional payment, One-Parent Benefit. This was abolished for all new claimants on the grounds that it unfairly discriminated against two-parent families.

### Working Family Tax Credit

This will be introduced in 1999 and will replace Family Credit (see Table 17.7 for a comparison of the two schemes). All families where the main earner works more

---

[9] The benefit covers any payment which is necessary to secure the accommodation (for example mooring charges for house boats and site fees for mobile homes), but not living costs such as heating.

**Table 17.7** The proposed reforms of the 1998 Budget: Working Family Tax Credit

| 2 Adults; 2 Children < 11 | | Family Credit | WFTC |
|---|---|---|---|
| Payment if | 30 > hours > 16 | £71.75 | £78.50 |
| Payment if | hours > 30 | £0 | £10.80 |
| Taper begins at | | £77.15 | £90 |
| Taper rate | | 70% | 55% |

\* + 20% rise in Child Benefit (universal)
\*\* 70% tax break for child-care costs < £150 per week, for families < £14,000 (per year)
Source: Treasury, 1998 Budget Website

than sixteen hours a week will receive a tax credit (the value will reflect the size of household). An additional tax credit is to be paid to lone mothers working more than sixteen hours a week and to couples where both partners work more than sixteen hours a week, to reduce the burden of the costs of child care. The rate of withdrawal of the tax credit will be lower than that for Family Credit (55% rather than 70%), leaving families better off and with improved work incentives (see Figure 17.5).

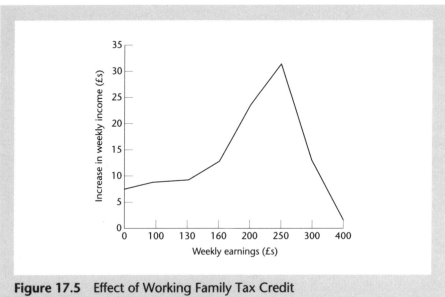

**Figure 17.5** Effect of Working Family Tax Credit
(Source: Treasury, 1998, Budget Website)

## Incapacity and disability benefits

Incapacity Benefit replaced Sickness Benefit and Invalidity Benefit in April 1995. It is a contributory benefit and is paid to those who are assessed as being incapable of work. In the first instance (the first six months) incapability is assessed on the basis of an 'own occupation' test. Beyond this incapability is assessed on the basis of an 'all work' test. During the first six months, claimants receive Statutory Sick Pay[10] and a lower rate of Incapacity Benefit; beyond this only a higher rate of Incapacity Benefit. People with severe disabilities or an illness requiring significant care may also be entitled to other benefits including Severe Disability Allowance, Disability Living Allowance, Attendance Allowance and Invalid Care Allowance. (See *Social Security Statistics* for details of entitlement and rates.)

## Welfare-to-Work

The 'Welfare-to-Work' programme introduced in the 1997 July Budget aims to reduce the nation's welfare bill, with the primary intention of reducing youth unemployment, and is an example of a workfare scheme, discussed in section 17.2. The scheme will provide education or training for those without qualifications and employment experience for those with qualifications. Choice can be exercised as to whether work experience is to be found in the private sector, voluntary sector or as part of the environmental task force, but refusal of all of these options will lead to cuts in benefit. A further measure aimed at reducing the number of long-term unemployed is an employment subsidy to any employers who take on someone who has been unemployed for more than two years.

Another set of policies intending to reduce welfare dependency relates to lone mothers. Lone mothers will receive help and support in training and finding employment, and, most importantly, financial support for child-care expenses. The latter will be an extension of the existing policy of disregarding a proportion of child-care expenses when benefit payments are calculated. The child-care relief will rise from £60 to £100 a week, resulting in an increase in the level of earnings before benefits are withdrawn. It will not be compulsory for lone mothers to enter the labour market, although at the stage when the youngest child reaches school age, they will be required to attend a job search interview. At the job search interview it will be stressed that the family will be better off if the mother is in employment. One possible difficulty associated with getting more lone mothers into the labour market is the shortage of affordable child care. The Chancellor addressed this with a first move towards a national child-care policy, by announcing that as part of the 'Welfare-to-Work' programme, 50,000 young people will be trained as child-care assistants.

## EU social policy

Most of the early work of the European Union in the field of social policy related to equal opportunities. A truly social dimension was only established under the presidency of Jacques Delors (President of the European Commission 1985–92).[11] Delors was the champion of the Social Chapter (see Box 17.1). The Social Chapter itself was not binding upon all Member States; however, all but Britain signed up. Shortly after its election the new Labour government announced its intention to sign.

---

[10] Paid by the employer for a period up to six months. Not all employees are entitled to Statutory Sick Pay. They may not have been with the current employer for long enough. In this instance they would usually receive the higher rate of Incapacity Benefit.

[11] By the late 1980s, within continental Europe, it was clear that the single European market could have a negative impact on levels of employment and workers' rights. The French and German governments were keen to establish a social dimension to the European Union, in order to balance these effects.

BOX 17.1

## Provisions of the Social Chapter of the Single European Act 1985

Freedom of movement of EC citizens within the Community.

Equitable wages sufficient to enable a decent standard of living.

Rights for part-time and temporary workers.

Improved living and working conditions involving the progressive harmonisation of holiday entitlements, etc.

Adequate social protection for those both in and out of work.

Freedom of association and collective bargaining.

The right to vocational training.

Equal treatment for men and women.

Adequate participation of employees in the affairs of the company that employs them.

Satisfactory health and safety at work.

Protection of children and adolescents at work.

Proper retirement pensions.

Integration of disabled persons into the world of work.

Source: Wise and Gibb, p. 160, 1993

Whilst the Commission clearly felt that social protection contributed to economic performance and growth, there were concerns that diversity of welfare provision between Member States could hamper the development of a single market. Initially, *social dumping*, which became an issue when Spain, Greece and Portugal joined the European Union, was the main concern. These countries are low-wage economies, with high levels of poverty and limited welfare provision. The fear in the other countries was that within a single market, firms would move from within Europe into these countries and thus dilute standards of social protection across Europe. *Social tourism* is an associated problem. The freedom of movement of workers across Europe could mean that workers in countries with high rates of unemployment would be tempted to move from their own country into others with more generous welfare provisions.

The Social Chapter was intended to set out minimal levels of social welfare rather than to achieve harmonisation of social policy. Welfare provision in many countries, for example Germany, exceeded those set out by the Social Chapter. The emphasis was on identifying certain employment rights and social welfare that satisfy the needs of social citizenship. On the basis of these general principles, the European Union issued several Directives on rights for part-time and temporary workers, the length of the maximum working week and maternity leave. There has been no Directive on a minimum wage, although legislation does exist in most Member States. The European Union has had a significant effect on poverty through its anti-poverty programmes and regional policy.

Social Europe was strengthened at the Amsterdam Summit in the summer of 1997. More emphasis was given to the employment measures within the Stability and Growth Pact, for example, the development of a 'skilled, trained and adaptable workforce' and an employment summit was planned to investigate a possible role for the European Investment Bank to finance job-creation projects. For the first time, the Treaty clearly states that the European Union can take action to outlaw all discrimination based on 'sex, racial or ethnic origin, religion and belief, disability, age or sexual orientation'.

## 17.6 Citizenship and the Welfare State

The Welfare State is not only concerned with poverty; it also addresses the issues of citizenship and social exclusion. We consider here the areas of social policy which are intended to reduce the incidence of childhood poverty and address gender and racial discrimination.

### Family

In Chapter 15, we referred to the Rowntree studies of poverty which were so influential in drawing attention to the problems of poverty and in the design of the Welfare State. The third Rowntree study found a much lower incidence of poverty, mainly amongst the elderly, and concluded that the Welfare State had eliminated poverty in young families. However, in the 1960s evidence of malnutrition in young children began to emerge. Initially campaigners sought to increase the value of the Family Allowance, which was established in 1946 and paid for the second and each subsequent child. The first change (under a Labour government in 1967) was an increase in the payments to larger families; allowances were increased for the fourth and subsequent children. The second was to implement means-tested benefits, the family income supplement (under a Conservative government in 1970), whereby a higher family allowance was paid to mothers and the increase taxed back from average taxpayers. The move towards means testing was opposed by the Labour Party and when they returned to power in 1974, they introduced legislation which replaced all previous child and family benefits with a single non-means-tested Child Benefit for each child.

In 1985, the Department of Health and Social Security report *Reform of Social Security* (Cmnd 9517/8/9) (DHSS, 1985) argued that the existing system did not effectively target the groups most in need. In particular, it was found that in relation to other groups, households with young children were at greater risk. One characteristic of the resulting reforms was the increase in resources targeted at families, such as Family Credit. Despite this, the number of children in households experiencing poverty has continued to rise over the last twenty years. One explanation for this is the rising rate of family breakdown and the resulting increasing incidence of female-headed households dependent upon benefits. As discussed in Chapter 16, a factor contributing towards welfare dependency is the poor availability of affordable child care. The Conservative government began to address the issue of the cost of child care with the introduction of a child-care allowance in 1994/5. More recently, the value of the child-care allowance has been increased as part of the 'Welfare-to-Work' programme. A further aspect of the 'Welfare-to-Work' programme is the attempt to address the low skills base amongst lone parents. This mirrors the highly successful scheme piloted in New Jersey in the United States.

Commitment to family values is a part of modern political philosophy. One aspect of this is the emphasis on the responsibility of the parent rather than the state for the cost of child maintenance. In response to rising divorce rates and the increasing reliance of lone parents on Income Support, the Child Support Agency (CSA) was established by the 1990 Child Support Act in order to compel absent parents, usually fathers, to provide financial support for their children. The effect of the CSA was greatest for those women receiving benefits, since only those whose husbands had defaulted on maintenance payment in the previous six months and those women who had been the victim of domestic violence would be automatically entitled to child maintenance from the state. For mothers who received Income Support, when the father paid child maintenance, the effect was a 100% tax on their Income Support. The activities of the CSA were extremely unpopular amongst absent parents, partly because the CSA usually only had details of the fathers who were already contributing child maintenance, while making little progress towards tracing fathers who failed to contribute. Moreover, the settlements arrived at by the CSA ignored any arrangements that the couple had already agreed upon.[12]

## Gender discrimination

| **Discrimination** |
| --- |
| Different treatment independent of productive characteristics, but due instead to non-productive characteristics such as gender, race or religious belief |

In Chapters 14 and 15, we saw that women earn less than men and that households headed by women are at greater risk of poverty. One of the explanations for the low levels of pay for women is that they experience **discrimination** in the labour market. The same is also true for many other groups who face discrimination on the grounds of race, age, disability, sexual orientation or religion. Discrimination occurs in the labour market when individuals receive differing rewards on the basis of a characteristic, or set of characteristics, which have no bearing on their ability to perform the task in question. Measuring the extent of discrimination is very difficult because it may be that some of the pay differential that exists between workers does reflect differences in their productive characteristics. To find pure discrimination, we need to identify the extent to which individuals with identical characteristics are rewarded differently, that is whether women or non-whites with the same qualifications and employment histories as men or whites earn less. One way of doing this is to identify an earnings equation for each of the groups, and then consider the difference in earnings between the groups; this is illustrated for the gender pay differential in Figure 17.6[13]

$$\log w_M = a_M + b_M C_M + e_M \qquad \text{Earnings equation for men}$$

$$\log w_W = a_W + b_W C_W + e_W \qquad \text{Earnings equation for women}$$

where $a_i$ and $b_i$ are parameters, $C_i$ are the levels of productive characteristics and $e_i$ represents the error terms, $i = M, W$.

In Figure 17.6, the average productive characteristics for women and men are given ($C_{AVW}$ and $C_{AVM}$, respectively), where $C_{AVW} < C_{AVM}$. This reflects that men do on average have longer employment histories and higher levels of qualifications and

---

12 Of particular concern was that the CSA ignored any 'clean-break' settlements, whereby a lump-sum settlement, usually a house, was made instead of regular child maintenance payments. In January 1995, new legislation was introduced to take account of such settlements. A Green Paper published in July 1998 proposed the following simplifications: a non-resident parent should pay 15% of net income for one child, 20% for two and 25% for three or more. Those on low incomes or with second families would make reduced payments.

13 An identical approach is used to examine the extent of other forms of discrimination.

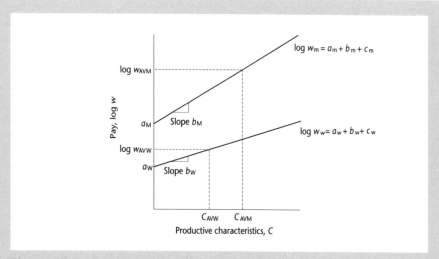

**Figure 17.6**  Disaggregating the gender pay gap

training. Given these average characteristics, we can see how a gender pay gap emerges, $\log w_{AVM} > \log w_{AVW}$. The question is, how much of this gap is due to discrimination?

The gender pay gap can be disaggregated as follows:

$$\log w_M - \log w_W = (a_M - a_W) + b_M C_M - b_W C_W + e_M - e_W$$
$$= (a_M - a_W) + b_M C_M - b_W C_M + b_W C_M - b_W C_W + (e_M - e_W)$$
$$= (a_M - a_W) + b_W (C_M - C_W) + (b_M - b_W) C_M + (e_M - e_W)$$

The above formulation allows us to separate the effects of differing characteristics $(C_M - C_W)$ and of differing rewards for the same characteristics $(b_M - b_W)$. The part of the pay gap which can be explained is given by $(C_M - C_W)$, the gap in productive characteristics, although this may also reflect some discrimination, for example in access to training. The rest, $(a_M - a_W)$ and $(b_M - b_W)$, can be attributed to pure discrimination.

Using the General Household Survey (GHS) and the British Household Panel Survey, Susan Harkness (1996) employs this method to calculate the following breakdown of the wage gap between men and women in full-time employment and between women in full- and part-time employment, see Table 17.7. Note that the pay gap ($\log w_i - \log w_j$) between men and women in full-time employment has narrowed between 1974 and 1992–3, whereas the pay gap between women in full- and part-time employment has widened. She concludes that the level of discrimination against women in full-time employment has dropped over the period and that the opening of the pay gap between women in full- and part-time employment is due to the difference in the characteristics of the two groups of women and not to the additional discrimination faced by women seeking part-time work.

Economic theory offers the following accounts of discrimination: where the tastes of employers, employees or customers mean that they do not wish to employ, work with or be served by a particular group; under conditions of asymmetric information, employers uncertain of worker quality make judgements on workers from particular groups (i.e. women are less reliable because they have to take time off to look after

**Table 17.8** Inequality and the gender earnings gap

| | Men (i) and women (j) full-time | | | Women full-time (i) and part-time (j) | | |
|---|---|---|---|---|---|---|
| | 74 | [Year] 83 | 92–3 | 74 | [Year] 83 | 92–3 |
| $\log w_i - \log w_j$ | 0.408 | 0.318 | 0.221 | 0.072 | 0.194 | 0.204 |
| $(b_i - b_j)C_i$ | 0.362 | 0.293 | 0.203 | −0.016 | 0.051 | −0.044 |
| $b_j(C_i - C_j)$ | 0.046 | 0.025 | 0.018 | 0.018 | 0.043 | 0.249 |

Source: Harkness, Table 6(a), 1996

children) which may be true on average, but not necessarily true of an individual; this is known as statistical discrimination. Finally, monopsonists can discriminate between groups of workers with differing labour supply elasticities. It seems that discrimination persists in circumstances where the firm or workers are protected from competition or where informational problems exist.

## Racial discrimination

In Britain, non-whites tend to earn less than white workers and have a higher likelihood of experiencing unemployment. Blackaby *et al.* (1995) provide the following evidence from the GHS, 'Not only did the white–black wage differential increase from 7.3% in the 1970s to 12.1% in the 1980s, but also the difference in the unemployment rate increased from 2.6% to 10.9%'. However, as we discussed in Chapter 14, data limitations mean that it is not possible to use the sort of analysis that has been conducted to examine the gender discrimination (discussed above) to measure racial discrimination in Britain. Therefore, in this section we provide some descriptive statistics which give an impression of the position of ethnic minorities in the labour market in Britain.

**Table 17.9** Unemployment rates (%) by ethnic origin, and age groups, spring 1995

| Ethnic origin | All | Men | Women |
|---|---|---|---|
| All | 10 | 11 | 7 |
| White | 9 | 11 | 7 |
| Non-white | 21 | 25 | 16 |
| Black | 26 | 33 | 17 |
| Indian | 14 | 16 | 12 |
| Pakistani/Bangladeshi | 28 | 29 | 24 |
| Mixed/other | 19 | 22 | 16 |

Source: HMSO, Table 10, 1997
All ethnic categories self-defined

In Chapter 14, we saw the importance of distinguishing between 'black' workers. For example, in Figure 14.12, only some ethnic minority groups are overrepresented in the bottom quintile, although all are underrepresented in the top quintile. Similar results can be found in the unemployment rates across ethnic groups (see Table 17.9). The rate of unemployment is much higher amongst the black and Pakistani/Bangladeshi communities.

Table 17.10 compares the unemployment rates across age groups. Looking at the whole working population, the unemployment rates for non-whites are higher than that for whites, but the gap is much greater amongst the younger age groups.

The unemployed tend to have lower levels of qualifications than those in employment. Table 17.11 shows that the proportion of unemployed without qualifications is much higher amongst non-white communities. However, it also shows that black workers who are unemployed are more highly qualified than white workers.

Turning now to rates of pay, Table 17.12 shows that the pay differential between white and non-white is sensitive to ethnic groups and gender. The overall white/non-white pay differential is greatest for those from the Pakistani/Bangladeshi community and narrowest for those from the Indian community. The same general trends are also true when looking at the white/non-white pay differential for men. An interesting development has occurred in the white/non-white pay differential for women, while white women earn more on average than women from the Indian or Pakistani/Bangladeshi communities; by 1994/5 they were earning slightly less than

**Table 17.10** Unemployment rates (%) by ethnic origin, and age groups, spring 1995

| Ethnic origin | All | 16–24 | 25–34 | 35–44 | 45–59/64 |
|---|---|---|---|---|---|
| Black | 24 | 39 | 27 | 17 | 15 |
| Indian | 12 | 23 | 11 | 8 | 11 |
| Pakistani/Bangladeshi | 27 | 39 | 21 | – | – |
| Mixed/other | 16 | 27 | 14 | 13 | – |
| White | 8 | 14 | 8 | 6 | 6 |

Source: HMSO, Table 4.15, 1996      – not available
All ethnic categories self-defined

**Table 17.11** Rates of unemployment (%) by qualifications by ethnic origin, spring 1995

| Ethnic origin | Higher (A-level or above) | Other | None |
|---|---|---|---|
| Black | 16 | 25 | 35 |
| Indian | – | 12 | 19 |
| Pakistani/Bangladeshi | – | 27 | 34 |
| Mixed/other | 12 | 17 | – |
| White | 4 | 8 | 14 |

Source: HMSO, Table 4.16, 1996      – not available
All ethnic categories self-defined

**Table 17.12** Average hourly pay by ethnic origin, and gender, winter 94–autumn 95

| Ethnic origin | All | Men | Women | Gender pay gap |
|---|---|---|---|---|
| White | £7.73 | £8.34 | £6.59 | 0.79 |
| Black | £6.88 | £7.01 | £6.71 | 0.96 |
| Indian | £7.12 | £8.01 | £5.75 | 0.72 |
| Pakistani/Bangladeshi | £6.43 | £6.87 | £4.78 | 0.70 |
| Mixed/other | £7.32 | £7.70 | £6.66 | 0.86 |
| Ethnic pay gap | | | | |
| White/Black | 0.89 | 0.84 | 1.02 | |
| White/Indian | 0.92 | 0.96 | 0.87 | |
| White/Pakistani/Bangladeshi | 0.83 | 0.82 | 0.73 | |
| White/other | 0.95 | 0.92 | 1.01 | |

Source: HMSO, Table 4.17, 1996
All ethnic categories self-defined

the other groups of non-white women. A gender pay gap also exists across ethnic groups; this is narrowest in the black community. More recent evidence from the Employment Policy Institute,[14] shows that black women have now overtaken both white women and black men in terms of average pay. They quote the following figures of hourly pay in 1997: £6.10 – black women, £5.85 – black men and £5.19 – white women.

In conclusion, in general non-whites are paid less and are more likely to experience unemployment. The pattern does vary across ethnic group and gender. One reason for this may be that different groups face differing attitudes and have different experiences of discrimination, both in the labour market and in schools. Other explanations include variations in employment opportunities (for example, the rate of self-employment is higher in the Indian community than in the other non-white groups) and in the quality of education received. The last factor has proved to be very important in explaining the white/non-white wage differential in the USA. Non-white pupils tend to be educated in schools with lower levels of expenditure per head and higher pupil : teacher ratios.

## Anti-discrimination legislation

Low pay and employment in low-status jobs are both consequences of discrimination in the labour market. Whilst other factors, such as social norms and differences in qualifications, may also contribute to low pay and status, there is evidence that much of the pay gap which exists between men and women and between white and black workers can be attributed to discrimination in the labour market. Legislation was introduced in the UK in the 1970s (the Sex Discrimination and Equal Pay Acts in 1975) to protect female and non-white workers, but its effect has been limited. Harkness (1996) shows that most of the narrowing of the gender pay gap which has occurred since 1970 was achieved in the years immediately following the legislation.

---

[14] *The Guardian*, 15 July 1998, p. 23, 'Black women take pole position on pay'.

According to the FES, in 1973 the average hourly earnings of a woman working full-time were 59% of average male earnings, a figure which climbed to 70% in the late 1970s (perhaps because of the introduction of legislation) and which, after a plateau in the 1980s, has now reached 77%. The experience of part-time women is different, although it was not until the late 1970s that the figures for part- and full-time women workers began to diverge. They dropped from a peak of 68% (of male full-time earnings per hour) to the low 60s where they have since more or less remained (the 1993 figure was 63%).

Since the early 1980s, very little progress has been made. An explanation for this can be found in the wording of the original legislation: differences in pay between workers doing the *same job* were outlawed. However, in the labour market female and non-white workers are both horizontally and vertically segregated from white male workers in terms of the actual jobs that they do. Female employment tends to be concentrated in industries such as catering, cleaning and clerical work where few men are employed, but when they do work in industries with a higher concentration of male employment such as finance and banking, women tend to be employed as tellers and men in a managerial capacity. A similar situation exists for non-white workers. The implication of this is that pay gaps did not remain in the few cases where women or non-whites were employed in the same job as white men, but could persist in general because most women and non-whites were employed in different jobs. The situation has altered recently as some groups have taken discrimination cases to the European courts where the emphasis is not on employers paying different rates for the *same job*, but for jobs of *equal value*. This notion of equal value has widespread implications in the area of pay. When the European Economic Community was established, France had a particularly strong protection of the rights of women in the workplace. They were concerned that this would place France at a disadvantage once a common market was established. As a consequence, the articles within the Treaty of Rome which relate to social policy include strong anti-discrimination measures. The European Court of Justice has extended the scope of these measures. For example, as new initiatives are established, the Court considers the possible impact of the measure on equal opportunities. European anti-discrimination policy was further strengthened by the Amsterdam Treaty in the summer of 1997.

Discrimination does not only imply that these groups are lower paid, it also has implications for employment rights, eligibility for employer-provided sickness and maternity benefits and access to company pension schemes. These sorts of protection are often only provided to full-time employees who have been employed with the company for a given period of time.[15] Such conditions frequently mean that these rights are not extended to women and non-whites, because they are more likely to be employed on a part-time basis or have shorter tenure. Some of these benefits have recently been extended where it was possible to prove that the conditions had the effect of discriminating against women.[16]

Outside of the labour market, women and non-whites can find themselves vulnerable. For example, women are much less likely than men to have private or company

---

[15] These rights may also be restricted to those whose earnings lie above a certain threshold. Some part-time employees may share the right of full-time employees, but only when they have completed a longer tenure with the current employer.

[16] This argument was particularly effective where the rights were only available to full-time employees; given the concentration of women in part-time employment, it was argued that the result was discriminatory.

pensions (37% of women compared with 61% of men) and non-whites are more likely to experience unemployment; the rate of unemployment is particularly high within the West Indian and Bangladeshi communities. Discrimination against non-whites can occur within the welfare system, particularly where access to a service or benefit is dependent upon nationality. Despite the fact that a large proportion of the black community in this country was born and brought up in Britain, racist attitudes mean that a person with a non-white skin is not regarded as British. In this respect, colour of skin can be used by racist officials as an opportunity to question legal right of residence. This climate of suspicion may lead to non-whites choosing not to use services to which they are legally entitled, relying instead upon community-based voluntary organisations or on family provision.[17] Some of the eligibility criteria have also resulted in poor welfare provision for the non-white communities. For example, just as the contributions criterion for a pension results in many women receiving a lower final pension, the same is true for families who came to Britain in the 1950s. Immigrant households can also find themselves at a disadvantage in the allocation of social housing. In areas where supply is limited, there are waiting lists for houses and priority given to those who have lived locally.

## 17.7 Conclusion

Over the last twenty years, the UK government has been committed to reducing the size of the welfare bill. However, demographic trends and the economic climate have meant that a greater number of pensioners, single-parent families and unemployed people have become dependent upon state benefits, and the welfare bill has risen rather than fallen. The fact that welfare reforms have failed to prevent further growth in social security expenditure does not mean that nothing has changed. The welfare system is now selective rather than universal and the state is no longer a monopolist in welfare provision. Whilst the state remains the main welfare provider, the support it provides is now targeted at those in greatest need. Tax incentives which have been offered to encourage private health insurance and pension provision have contributed to the rising private provision of welfare. Finally, a third form of welfare provision has re-emerged: support through the voluntary sector. Associated with these changes are the problems of higher marginal tax rates on the poor than on the rich and the concerns of a multi-tier welfare system.

In 1994, a European Union report, *Social Protection in Europe*, p. 86, compared levels of social expenditure across Member States and concluded that, 'contrary to the view put forward by the New Right, a high level of social protection is not an obstacle to economic development.' In the same year, an OECD report, *New Orientations for Social Policy*, p. 10, asserted that:

> Because the elderly need not fear serious deprivation, their adult children are freed to work, raise their children, and to take advantage of opportunities and to make a contribution to society that might otherwise be denied them; the unemployed are provided with income not only for survival, but also to permit time to search for a job appropriate to their skills, or to acquire new skills; public intervention in education and support for children is an investment in tomorrow's resources, and in everyone's futures; provisions for health care are an investment in the productive capacity of

---

[17] In many non-white communities there is a much greater reliance upon the informal sector.

human resources. Together, these and other benefits of social policies contribute to a more efficient and a more just society.

## Summary

- The Welfare State protects households against poverty, provides insurance against loss of income due to unemployment, ill-health and old age and establishes citizenship.
- The social security budget accounts for roughly one-third of central government expenditure and 10% of GDP.
- The system is based upon a model of social insurance amongst the employed male population; however many of the claimants are female and are likely to have disrupted labour market careers.
- The value of certain benefits has fallen and eligibility conditions were tightened in order to reduce the disincentive and dependency creating effects of benefits.
- The system was reformed by 'targeting' benefits at the most needy, instead of making universal payments.
- Incentives were introduced in order to encourage moves away from the state as the primary agent of social policy.

## Questions

1. Outline the argument behind the paradox that whilst means-tested benefits are targeted to those most in need, universal benefits may be more effective at alleviating poverty.
2. Can workfare be the future of welfare?
3. To what extent does a minimum wage hurt those it aims to help?
4. Define discrimination. Has legislation eliminated the problem of gender discrimination?

## Further reading

Barr (1993) is an excellent reference point for the theory of social policy and evaluation of policy measures. Glennerster (1995) provides a comprehensive history and analysis of British social policy. Baldwin and Falkingham (1994) and Hills (1993) discuss the pressures facing the modern Welfare State. The First Report of the Low Pay Commission (1998) provides a comprehensive account of empirical evidence of the impact of minimum wage legislation and a discussion of the appropriate rate and coverage of a minimum wage in the UK.

## References

Abel-Smith, B. and Townsend, P. (1965) *Poverty and the Poorest: A New Analysis of the Ministry of Labour's Family Expenditure Surveys 1953–54 and 1960*, London: Bell.
Alcock, P. (1996) *Social Policy in Britain: Themes and Issues*, London: Macmillan Press.

Atkinson, A.B. (1995) *Incomes and the Welfare State: Essays on Britain and Europe*, Cambridge: Cambridge University Press.

Baldwin, J. and Falkingham, S. (eds) (1994) *Social Security and Social Change: New Challenges to the Beveridge Model*, Hemel Hempstead: Harvester Wheatsheaf.

Barr, N. (1993) *The Economics of Welfare*, Oxford: Oxford University Press.

Beveridge, W. (1942) *Report on Social Insurance and Allied Services*, Cmd 6404, HMSO.

Blackaby, D.H., Clark, K., Leslie, D.G. and Murphy, P.D. (1995) 'The changing distribution of black and white earnings and the ethnic wage gap: evidence for Britain', *Conference Paper*, October 1995, Employment and Education Economics Group.

Clarke, J. and Langan, M. (1993) 'Restructuring welfare: the British regime in the 1980s', in A. Cochrane and J. Clarke (eds) *Comparing Welfare States: Britain in International Context*, London: Sage in association with The Open University.

Department of Health and Social Security Report (1985) *Reform of Social Security*, Cmnd 9517/8/9.

Department of Social Security (1993) *The Growth of Social Security 1978/79–1992/93*, HMSO.

Department of Social Security (1995) *Social Security Statistics 1996/97*, Stationery Office.

EU (1994) *Social Protection in Europe*, Brussels: Commission of the European Community.

Fawcett, H. and Papadopoulos, T.N. (1991) *West European Politics*, July, 20(3), 1–30.

The First Report of the Low Pay Commission (1998) 'The National Minimum Wage', London Stationery Office.

George, V. and Taylor-Gooby, P. (eds) (1996) *European Welfare Policy: Squaring the Welfare Circle*, London: Macmillan.

Glennerster, H. (1995) *British Social Policy Since 1945*, Oxford: Blackwell.

Harkness, S. (1996) 'The gender earnings gap: evidence from the UK', *Fiscal Studies*.

Hills, J. (1993) *The Future of Welfare: A Guide to the Debate*, York: Joseph Rowntree Foundation.

HMSO (1996) *Social Focus on Ethnic Minorities*, London: HMSO.

HMSO (1997) *Ethnic Minorities*, London: HMSO.

HM Treasury, 1998 Budget Website.

HM Treasury (1979) *The Government's Expenditure Plans 1980–81*, 1.

HM Treasury (1995) *The Government's Expenditure Plans 1996/97*, Figure 20.

HM Treasury (1996) *The Government's Expenditure Plans 1997/98*.

International Labour Office Report (1984) *Into the Twenty-First Century*.

Kay, J.A. and King, M.A. (1990) *The British Tax System*, 5th edn, Oxford: Oxford University Press.

Le Grand, J. (1990) in J. Hills (ed.) *The State of Welfare: The Welfare State in Britain Since 1974*, Oxford: Oxford University Press.

Leibfried, S. (1993) 'Towards a European Welfare State', in C. Jones (ed.) *New Perspectives on the Welfare State in Europe*, London: Routledge.

Oaxaca, R. (1973) 'Male-female wage differentials in urban labour markets', *International Economic Review*, 693–703.

OECD, *New Orientations for Social Policy*, 2, Paris: OECD.

Parker, H. (1995) *Taxes, Benefits and Family Life: The Seven Deadly Traps*, Institute of Economic Affairs, Research Monograph 50.

Pierson, C. (1991) *Beyond the Welfare State: The New Political Economy of Welfare*, Cambridge: Polity Press.

Rowntree, B.S. (1901) *Poverty: A Study of Town Life*, London: Macmillan Press.

Rowntree, B.S. (1941) *Poverty and Progress: A Second Social Survey of York*, London: Longman.

Rowntree, B.S. and Lavers, G. (1951) *Poverty and the Welfare State*, London: Longman Press.

*The Guardian*, 15 July 1998, p. 23, 'Black women take pole position on pay'.

Webb, S. (1994) 'Social insurance and poverty alleviation: an empirical analysis', in J. Baldwin and S. Falkingham (eds) *Social Security and Social Change: New Challenges to the Beveridge Model*, Hemel Hempstead: Harvester Wheatsheaf.

Wise, M. and Gibb, R. (1993) *Single Market to Social Europe*, Harlow: Longman.

# CHAPTER 18

# Pensions and Ageing

## Key concepts

| | | |
|---|---|---|
| annuities | pay-as-you-go | moral hazard |
| demographic time bomb | funded pensions | aged dependency ratio |

## 18.1 Introduction

Pensions are the prime means by which *individuals* stretch income over the lifecycle, but in most OECD countries pension systems are heavily regulated and/or funded by the *government*. In the UK, for instance, state pensions represent nearly 10% of government expenditure, while a quarter of all government spending in Italy is on pensions. Most countries depend on pay-as-you-go (PAYG) pension systems, in which payments to pensioners are financed by taxing current workers. If the government budget is to balance then we must have $twL = pD$, where $L$ is the number of workers who earn $w$ each, $t$ is the payroll tax rate they face and their payments are used to endow $D$ pensioners with an income of $p$. Rearranging we get:

$$t = \frac{p\,D}{w\,L} \tag{18.1}$$

**Aged dependency ratio**

The ratio of those retired to those adults under retirement age

So the burden of the pension system rises as the old **aged dependency ratio** ($D/L$) increases or with a growth in the relative generosity of benefits, $p/w$. Both these factors have been at work in OECD countries, but, except in the very long run, governments have only the power to control the second.

In this chapter, we consider some of the problems faced by pension systems, concentrating on the dilemmas posed by ageing populations, but also considering the impact of the changing nature of a society where work patterns are becoming less coherent and where women are becoming more financially independent. One of our themes is that the dilemmas are not just the obvious ones of efficiency versus vertical equity, but also that of equity between the sexes, in the provision of pension benefits, and also in the question of who will care for the increasing numbers of the very old, many of whom require some physical support.

## 18.2  Pensions, market failure and equity

### What are pensions?

**Annuity**

A yearly income guaranteed until death

The typical pension is an **annuity**, a promise to pay a fixed annual amount for as long as the individual lives. Sometimes there are survivor's benefits, for widows, for instance, built into the pension; sometimes the payment is at least partially index-linked and there may be a lump-sum paid out at the time when the pension is claimed, but the common element in all pension schemes is that they provide for the elderly at a time in their lives when they have little or no labour market income.

**Pay-as-you-go (PAYG)**

A pension system in which current pensions are paid from tax receipts

**Funded pensions**

Pensions paid out as the return on investments

While the basic idea of the pension is simple, actual models are extremely diverse (see Box 18.1 for some details on the UK system). In the **pay-as-you-go (PAYG)** model, usually government organised, payments to current pensioners are funded out of the contributions of working members. In **funded pension** schemes, usually privately organised, the pension funds are invested in assets and it is the return from these which provides for retirement. With the introduction of a funded scheme, today's young save and receive benefits tomorrow, but today's retirees receive nothing, because there is no fund to pay them interest. With a PAYG system, the older generation obtains an immediate benefit from the taxes paid by the young. Therefore the introduction of a PAYG system can produce a Pareto improvement as long as the sum of the rates of growth of the population and real wages is greater than the rate of interest. It is this 'social security paradox' (Aaron, 1966) which provides the impetus to PAYG schemes worldwide.

Schemes can be occupational, usually organised around a workplace or union, or personal, arranged directly between the individual and an insurance company or other financial institution. A defined benefit (DB) scheme pays out according to a formula, usually related to the number of years that individual has worked and salary in the final years of employment; in a defined contribution (DC) scheme, the individual receives whatever return has been achieved on the funds invested on his or her behalf. Typically occupational pensions tend to be DB, while personal pensions are almost always DC. Both types of scheme involve risks: DB schemes are usually less portable, so that individuals suffer if they switch jobs or final salary is low; with DC schemes the level of the pension depends on the position of the stock market come retirement.

### Market failure

The market failures associated with pensions are limited, but nonetheless important. Authors such as Barr (1994) emphasise the fact that the value of the pension is affected by the rate of inflation, so that only governments are able to offer complete insurance against changes in prices. If it was only this kind of market failure that affected the pensions system, then the selling of index-linked gilts by governments could remedy the problem and limit the extent of government intervention.

Myopia is perhaps a more fundamental justification for government action. The pension-planning individual is asked to choose between consumption now or consumption delayed thirty or forty years into the future. It would not be surprising if he or she was to behave more like the proverbial grasshopper than the ant, opting for immediate pleasure over a secure future. This makes pension planning something of a merit good, but as with the previous argument, this form of market failure does not justify wholesale provision of pensions by the state. It suggests that compulsory

## BOX 18.1

# The UK pensions system

Pensions provision in the UK is based on two tiers, with the first level provided by the basic pension (plus benefits which are means-tested) and a second tier, called SERPS – the State Earnings-Related Pension Scheme – out of which individuals may opt if they have an occupational or a private pension which can guarantee them the same minimum level of benefits in retirement.

### The bottom tier

To get the full basic pension, a person must have paid National Insurance Contributions (NICs) on income in excess of the Lower Earnings Limit (LEL) for 9/10 of their working life. Contributions are made on an individual's behalf during education, unemployment and periods of disability, while for those who have taken time out from the labour market to bring up children or care for dependants, Home Responsibilities Protection (HRP) can reduce the years required to obtain the full pension. Smaller periods of contribution lead to the pension being reduced pro rata, down to one-quarter of the full amount. The LEL and therefore the basic pension is indexed to the retail price index.

Pensioners on low incomes, which certainly includes anyone with just the basic pension or less, are also eligible for Income Support, Housing Benefit (provided they are in receipt of at least some retirement pension) and Council Tax Benefit. Income Support provides the safety net and typically provides an income 10–20% higher than the full basic pension.

### The second tier

NICs also go towards the second tier of provision, membership of which is also compulsory. However, individuals can choose between staying in SERPS or opting out into an approved alternative, which may be either a DC or a DB scheme.

Pensions entitlement from SERPS is complicated and has been changed several times since the inception of the scheme in 1978. Currently, for each working year the LEL contributions are deducted from the total NICs made and earnings above the Upper Earnings Limit (UEL) are ignored. The sum remaining is then revalued at retirement using an index of average wages. The final pension paid is an average of these average annual contributions, with each year currently weighted by 1/80 (set to decline to 1/244 by 2028). Added on to this regime is a multitude of transitional arrangements covering the various reforms enacted since 1978 and which make the value of the SERPS pension sensitive to date of birth.

### Alternatively

For someone opting out of SERPS, a DB scheme must guarantee a minimum pension (GMP) roughly equal to the SERPS entitlement foregone. In return, the employee receives a reduction of NICs of 1.8% of salary (up to the UEL) and employer's NICs are reduced by 3% between the LEL and the UEL. With DC schemes, there is no immediate discount and no GMP, but minimum contributions must be equal to the rebate given to those contracting out and, at the end of each year, this rebate is added to the employee's pension scheme by the exchequer.

planning may be in order, perhaps accompanied by the regulation necessary to avoid the mis-selling of personal pensions seen in the UK in the late 1980s.

### Equity

Some of the vertical equity arguments for government intervention are an extension of those employed to justify redistribution over the life course in general. A government which seeks equality of outcomes will wish to see individuals having equal access to resources at all stages of their lives. However, in a society which favours equality of opportunity, state-provided pensions may not be mandated. Instead, opportunities would be offered to individuals earlier in their lives and if some fail or do not take advantage of those opportunities, then there is no reason why other individuals should support them in their old age.

One form of equity which might be thought desirable is equity between generations. With a funded system, pensioners' incomes are related to national income earlier in their lives, when they were working. With a PAYG scheme, today's pensioner's living standards are not tied to yesterday's output, providing one argument in favour of PAYG and against funded systems.

Horizontal equity, between men and women, is a growing issue with pensions. There are conflicting notions of fairness at work. First, we have seen in previous chapters that women earn less than men. Second, women typically also have fewer years of full-time work. Both of these effects serve to lower women's retirement income compared to men's. Traditionally, some of this inequality between the sexes would be mitigated by income sharing within households, but with the rise in the rate of divorce,[1] increasing numbers of women will miss out on this shelter. As a result of this, retirement poverty in the UK is heavily skewed towards women; out of 1.5 million pensioners receiving Income Support in 1993, 1.1 million were single women (Johnson *et al.*, 1996). Against this, women live longer than men, and until recently retired earlier. Thus in an actuarially fair pension system, for a given annuity, women would pay premiums up to two-thirds higher than men (Barr, 1994), but in fact with most PAYG and occupational pensions they effectively pay the same price for the annuity.

## 18.3 The OECD's demographic time bomb

The ageing of the OECD countries has already been discussed in this book. Over the next fifty years, aged dependency ratios, $D/L$ from equation (18.1), will rise for the richer countries. While all countries face this **demographic time bomb**, there are notable differences in the extent of the threat. Some countries, notably the UK, Sweden and Germany, already have a high dependency ratio, but will nevertheless see some growth in the proportion of over 65s in the next fifty years (though in the short term, the aged dependency ratio will fall in the UK). Others, such as Italy, France and especially Japan, will see comparatively youthful populations age rapidly, while a third group of countries, including the USA, Australia and Canada, will age more slowly, perhaps because of the steady inward flow of migrants. Table 18.1 illustrates the situation, while Box 18.2 explores the implications of ageing for two pension systems.

**Demographic time bomb**

The growing proportion of retired people in OECD countries

---

[1] Division of pension rights is not typically a part of divorce settlements in the UK, although the law is in the process of change.

**Table 18.1** Percentage change in over 65s and dependency ratio

| Country | Over 65s | | Aged dependency ratio | |
|---|---|---|---|---|
| | 1990–2010 | 2010–2030 | 1990–2010 | 2010–2030 |
| UK | –1 | 35 | –3 | 39 |
| France | 22 | 33 | 17 | 46 |
| Germany (West) | 21 | 10 | 37 | 42 |
| Italy | 22 | 17 | 28 | 37 |
| USA | 18 | 65 | 2 | 69 |
| Japan | 71 | 2 | 82 | 8 |
| OECD | 28 | 36 | 19 | 45 |

Source: Fry *et al.*, Table 3.3, 1990

---

**BOX 18.2**

# Ageing and pension systems

**Italy.** The Italian pensions system is organised around providential schemes, which though originally funded in nature had become PAYG by the end of the 1960s. According to Jappelli and Pagano (1994), by 1990 13.9% of Italian GDP was devoted to state retirement benefits. In the largest scheme, the Istituto Nazionale della Providenzia Sociale (INPS), covering the majority of employees, subscribers contributed 25% of earnings to a scheme where benefits exceeded contributions by 33,000 billion Italian lire (about £1.8 billion). To cover projected rises in benefits fully would mean contribution rates rising to nearly 60% of earnings by 2025. Amongst the causes of this crisis were terms which meant that someone with a full 40 year history could achieve a pension of up to 80% of pre-retirement earnings, indexed against earnings, with a survivor's pension of 60% of the spouse's plus 20% for orphans (Disney, 1996).

In 1992, reforms designed to limit expenditures included:

- Raising the retirement age to 65 for men and 60 for women.
- Pensions normally index-linked to prices rather than earnings.
- Pension determined by average career earnings indexed by inflation plus 1%, rather than the last five years of earnings.
- Raising the minimum period of service from fifteen to twenty years.

These and other measures are estimated to cut the payroll burden by 17.5% points of income (Disney, 1996), still not large enough to eliminate the gap between contributions and payout, but later efforts to reduce benefits further have run into the sand with teachers, amongst others, in rebellion (*The Guardian*, 19 May 1997).

**Japan.** As with Italy, the Japanese pension system was created at a time when it was one of the fastest growing economies in the developed world, with one of the youngest workforces. It is rapidly becoming one of the oldest nations, with a high proportion of the very elderly (Ogawa and Retherford, 1997), combined with stagnant growth. Originally, the Japanese pension system was funded, but the ratio of reserves to annual expenditure is low and falling, down to 5.8 in 1990 and projected to diminish still further to 1.3 in 2020 (OECD, 1990).

The Japanese system is similar to the UK's, in that contributions are earnings-related, and benefits come in two forms: a basic element and an earnings-related component, from which about 30% of private sector employees contract out. As the figures below (from Takayama, 1992) suggest Japanese society faces a difficult choice between much higher social security rates or less generous retirement benefits, which at one time could exceed 80% of average lifetime gross earnings, but which since 1985 are currently capped at 68%.

|  | 1990 | 2010 | 2030 |
|---|---|---|---|
| **Basic/flat-rate tier** | | | |
| No. of pensioners (million) | 12.7 | 26.1 | 29.9 |
| Support ratio (contributors/claimants) | 5.2 | 2.5 | 2.1 |
| Flat-rate contribution index (1990 = 100) | 100 | 233 | 253 |
| **Earnings-related** | | | |
| No. of pensioners (million) | 4.6 | 11.9 | 13.3 |
| Support ratio | 6.4 | 3.9 | 2.2 |
| Expenditure (trillion yen, 1989 prices) | 12.6 | 31.4 | 31.7 |
| Contribution rate from earnings | 12.4% | 27.5% | 31.5% |

Since it is the workforce who produce the economic 'cake' of GDP which is then shared between the entire population, there are essentially three responses to the ageing trend. First, the slice of the cake taken by each individual pensioner could fall. Second, the slice taken by each worker could diminish. Obviously a combination of both these options is also possible and has been the most common response by governments to date (Box 18.2 and Table 18.3 provide examples). The final response is to raise the size of GDP relative to what it would otherwise be.

## The issue of funded versus PAYG schemes

One reform often countenanced is a switch away from PAYG towards the funded model. Governments such as the UK's have pursued this option with some vigour, but it is not clear how it fits with the three responses just listed. In fact, such a switch probably solves the *government's* problem, but may have little or no impact on *society's* position, since as already intimated, the essential dilemma created by an ageing population is how to share out a shrinking cake, not how to finance the pensions system. We can see this more clearly by way of an example.

Suppose society consists of equal numbers of workers and pensioners. Workers produce £30,000 per year and we make the preliminary assumption that the type of pension system has no impact on that figure. We shall suppose, for the sake of the example, that all individuals prefer completely smoothed consumption. In a funded system, the pensioners own tokens or money which they use to buy the output off workers. The workers sell because this money represents their generation's future pensions, so in equilibrium each worker consumes £15,000, and sells £15,000 worth of output to a pensioner. In a PAYG system, the same pattern of consumption is reached, but this time the government taxes workers at 50% and gives the result to pensioners.

Under both systems, workers and pensioners have the same consumption, £15,000, but what happens now if there are two pensioners for each worker, because each person now lives for three equal periods, during only one of which they work? The fundamental problem is that the same output must now be shared between three people (the 'shrinking cake' problem). Under the PAYG system for instance, a tax rate of two-thirds would lead to an equal split between all three people. Under the funded system, the worker now sells two-thirds of output to obtain rights to £20,000 in return, which is then cashed in over the remaining two periods of life. Thus both funded and PAYG can produce the same outcome.

It is clear therefore that in the steady state, any difference between PAYG schemes and funded pensions must arise out of the incentives each offers to individuals to work and invest. Let us take the incentive to work first. The PAYG system relies on taxes to pay for pensions. If pensions are contributory, then a 'tax' of two-thirds and a savings rate of two-thirds are equivalent as long as the individual understands how the contributions they pay now will yield a pension in the future. It might be thought, though, that a payment through the state is more at risk than a payment from a pension fund. After all, the pension received in retirement from a PAYG scheme must depend on the willingness of future taxpayers to vote for a reduction in their own living standards. However it is also true that future taxpayers could vote for the taxes on capital income which would also eliminate net returns from pension funds. And, of course, funded schemes have their own risks from the variable performance of world stock markets. Both methods of funding pensions therefore bring with them risks for savers.

What about the incentive to save? We saw in Chapter 12 that if a government raises lump-sum taxes $T$ on workers who then receive a pension of $(1 + r)T$ when they retire, where $r$ is the market interest rate, then this will produce a one-for-one reduction in savings. Thus PAYG appears to result in substantially less saving than a funded system. There are some caveats worth mentioning. If the taxes raised are greater than savings, or if there are distortionary taxes, then the reduction in saving will not be pound-for-pound. The same is true if behaviour is myopic (which is the justification for government intervention in the first place), so that individuals do not connect the tax now with their future pensions and continue to save. Conversely, if generations are altruistically linked, then, as we saw with the Ricardian Equivalence Theorem in Chapter 12, adjustments to bequests and gifts can undo any attempted intergenerational redistribution, leaving savings unaffected by a switch to PAYG.

Nevertheless, Feldstein (1974) reported evidence for the US economy which suggested that the American pension programme, Old Age and Survivors Insurance (OASI), lowered private savings substantially. Later work uncovered serious errors in his estimation and more recent figures put the OASI-induced depression of total wealth at around 5% (Beach *et al.*, 1984); still significant, but not overwhelming.

Even if aggregate savings are reduced, that does not mean that investment falls. In Chapter 12 we also encountered the idea that, for a small country, with perfect capital mobility, the level of saving and the rate of investment need not be connected. Moreover, it is possible that a tax-financed pension system may mimic a funded system if pension benefits are introduced slowly and the government invests the initial gap between commitments and income, or uses it to finance capital products and then issues debt and uses the receipts to build the capital stock. However, although initially some tax-based schemes were designed to act like funded systems, over time the funded aspect of most government pension systems has been eroded through over-optimistic indexing and commitments made to income maintenance (the Italian system discussed in Box 18.1 provides a good example). It is also true that there is a fallacy of composition with the small-country argument; most of the economically developed world is ageing and most state pension schemes are unfunded, thus if *world* saving drops, then *world* investment must also be constrained.

There is another important factor to consider. In a world populated by individuals with finite lifetimes, savings perform two functions: for individuals they allocate consumption across time; for society, they provide the means to build the capital stock. These functions need not mesh. Thus, in equilibrium, the capital stock may be too low, compared to the level which maximises per capita consumption (the '**Golden Rule**' level), or it may be too high, with consumption below its maximum because too much of each year's production is devoted to maintaining the existing capital : labour ratio. Perversely, therefore, lower investment may be a good thing.[2] Feldstein (1977) has argued the opposite, pointing to the gap between the rate of return on capital and growth rates as evidence that higher investment could raise consumption. While some scepticism has been expressed about his position (see Boadway and Wildasin, 1994, for instance), few economists would argue that in fact the capital stock is too high. Nevertheless, it is precisely in an ageing population that it would be optimal for capital accumulation to decrease.

So, in short, the argument in favour of funding is that it makes the cake bigger, but the argument, though persuasive, is not watertight. Ultimately it rests on the PAYG scheme producing a lower capital stock and as we have seen, the evidence on this is sparse. There is also another problem: the transitional burden of moving from one form of scheme to another may be immense. Recall, that if the rate of growth of the economy is independent of the form of the pension system, a Pareto improvement is possible from the move from a funded to a PAYG system. It follows that even if funding raises long-run per-capita consumption, reversing the move may lead to some generations losing, particularly those whose taxes go to pay older people with PAYG pensions, but who must fund their own pensions out of their own savings.

To see this, let us return to the two-period example and consider a switch to a funded system from PAYG as in Table 18.2. In the first period, the working generation must pay a tax of £15,000 to cover payments to existing pensioners, but it knows that it will receive nothing from taxes during its old age. So even if the working generation puts aside half of its remaining £15,000 for retirement, its lifetime consumption will have been halved. In period 2, the generation which was young in period 1 is now old and receives back the fruits of its funded pension, £7,500. Meanwhile, later generations then break even, funding their own pensions, but paying no tax.

What happens if funding raises GDP? For there to be no lifetime loss of consumption for no generation, the return on investment must be at least 100%. That way the working generation in period 1 can invest all its after-tax income, live off air and consume £30,000 during retirement. Obviously, less dramatic transitions from PAYG to funding can cushion the blow for the generations caught between the two schemes, but improved growth rates have to be substantial if no one is to lose out.

**Golden Rule capital stock**

The capital stock at which consumption per person is maximised

---

[2] This kind of argument rests on there being diminishing returns to capital. See Chapter 12 for the counterview, put forward by endogenous growth advocates, that positive external effects put investment below its optimal level.

**Table 18.2**  Switching to a funded system

|  |  | Period 1 (£) | Period 2 (£) | Period 3 (£) |
|---|---|---|---|---|
| Young | Wage income | 30,000 | 30,000 | 30,000 |
|  | Tax | 15,000 | 0 | 0 |
|  | Savings | 7,500 | 15,000 | 15,000 |
|  | Consumption | 7,500 | 15,000 | 15,000 |
| Old | PAYG pension | 15,000 | 0 | 0 |
|  | Funded pension | 0 | 7,500 | 15,000 |

## Other options

We have seen that switching from PAYG to funded systems for pension financing cannot defuse the demographic time bomb, as long as the rate of growth of the economy is independent of the type of pension system. And, even if the growth rate is higher with a funded scheme, major costs would have to be imposed on any generation which financed the birth of a new funded scheme for itself, while simultaneously paying for current pensioners through taxation. This makes major pension reform politically unpopular and so most OECD countries have concentrated on lowering the exchequer cost of PAYG schemes, by raising contribution rates, increasing retirement ages and lowering the generosity of benefits. Simultaneously, elements of funding have been introduced by encouraging individuals to opt out of the state-run schemes. Table 18.3 summarises some recent reductions in pension benefits across the European Union.

The fact that populations are ageing is a consequence of something which we would normally see as a boon: an increase in life expectancy. However, in this section we have seen that if lives lengthen, but years of work do not and productivity does not rise, then the goods and services we produce must be stretched over more years; average consumption must fall. PAYG systems based on over-optimistic assumptions about population growth and economic growth have had difficulty coping with these demographic realities and, as we have seen in this section, there are no magic solutions to the problem.

## 18.4  Pensioner poverty in the UK

Over time, pensioner incomes in the UK have risen faster than average incomes, with much of this improvement occurring in the 1980s, when large numbers began claiming from their occupational pensions (Johnson *et al.*, 1996), but Britain is still less generous towards its pensioners than most other rich countries and thus has a much higher proportion of pensioners living in poverty.[3] Figures produced by the OECD (using data from the Luxembourg Income Study) make this clear (see Table 18.4).

---

[3] Since it has one of the highest proportions of over 65s in the OECD, it therefore offers something of a model of how to keep down the exchequer cost of an ageing population.

**Table 18.3** Reducing pension benefits in the European Union

| Country (dates of recent major reforms) | Dependency ratio | | Benefit indexation changed | Retirement age raised | Replacement rates reduced | Public employees' benefits curtailed |
|---|---|---|---|---|---|---|
| | 1990 | 2030 | | | | |
| Austria (1985, 1988, 1993) | 0.33 | 0.59 | Scaled down by 0.1% for each 1% unemployment | Stricter controls on early retirement | From average of last 5 working years to best 15 | Raised contributions |
| Finland (1996) | 0.21 | 0.43 | From 0.5 price inflation + 0.5 wage inflation to 0.8 and 0.2, respectively | Cuts in pension paid to early retirees | From last 4 years to last 10 years | Reduced benefits, retirement age raised to private-sector level |
| France (1993) | 0.31 | 0.50 | Tied to prices rather than wages | | From best 10 years to best 25 years | Under consideration |
| Germany (1989, 1996) | 0.36 | 0.79 | From gross wages to wages net of taxes or contributions | From 60 (women) and 63 (men) to 65 (both) | | |
| Greece (1990, 1992) | 0.21 | 0.43 | Tied to public sector rather than private sector wages | To 65 for men and women | To average of last 5 years, from last 2 years | Minimum service and minimum retirement ages raised |
| Italy (1992, 1995) | 0.35 | 0.77 | Linked to prices rather than wages and life expectancy at retirement | From 55 to 60 (women); from 60 to 65 (men) (private employment) | Linked to lifetime contributions capitalised at GDP growth rate | |
| Portugal (1993) | 0.2 (1987) | 0.25 (2020) | | From 62 to 65 (women) | From best 5 out of last 10 years to best 10 out of last 15, indexed on prices | Special benefits and contribution rates eliminated |
| UK (1986, 1995) | 0.48 | 0.64 | Linked to prices rather than wages | From 60 to 65 (women) | From best 20 years revalued to lifetime earnings revalued | |

Note: these changes are not comprehensive and nearly all are being implemented gradually
Benefit indication = rate at which pension benefits increased each year
Replacement rate = pensions as a proportion of preretirement income
Source: European Commission, 1996

**Table 18.4** Risk of poverty (probability of less than one half of median income, 1978–80)

| Country | Poverty measure | Elderly | Total |
|---------|-----------------|---------|-------|
| Canada | Pre-transfer | 55.0 | 20.1 |
| | Post-transfer | 11.5 | 12.1 |
| Germany (West) | Pre-transfer | 74.5 | 21.1 |
| | Post-transfer | 9.2 | 5.5 |
| UK | Pre-transfer | 69.7 | 21.9 |
| | Post-transfer | 18.0 | 8.8 |
| USA | Pre-transfer | 57.7 | 22.6 |
| | Post-transfer | 20.0 | 16.9 |
| Australia | Pre-transfer | 66.1 | 21.4 |
| | Post-transfer | 5.3 | 10.9 |
| Sweden | Pre-transfer | 85.5 | 28.0 |
| | Post-transfer | 0.1 | 5.5 |

Source: OECD, Table 4.2, 1988

While the pre-transfer figures indicate that Britain has an average proportion of the elderly living in poverty, the post-transfer figure is worse than any other country apart from the USA. At the bottom of the pile, pensioners reliant on the basic state pension or Income Support have witnessed the opening of a gap between them and the rising numbers receiving investment income or income from occupational pension schemes, because of the indexing of pensions on prices rather than average earnings. As a result, after housing cost, incomes for those in the top quintile of pensioners have risen by 65% between 1979 and 1993, compared to only 10% for those in the bottom quintile (Dilnot *et al.*, 1994, Table 2.7). Meanwhile, over the same period, the basic pension fell from 20% of average male earnings to 15%.

A number of options have been put forward for reducing pensioner poverty. All of them are expensive to the Treasury, though the impact on work and retirement incentives is less clear.

## Uprating the basic pension

There are two main ways the pension could be upgraded. First, its current level could be increased, but inflation still used as the index for uprating. Second, annual increases could be tied to average earnings rather than prices. Obviously various combinations of these two approaches are also possible, as are more generous programmes.

Doubling the basic pension, as advocated by the Trades Union Congress (TUC), amongst others, would not double its cost to the government, since around one-third of the money would return in the form of taxes and reductions in social security benefits such as Income Support and Housing Benefit. Johnson *et al.* (1996) estimate that, even allowing for this partial cost reduction, doubling the basic pension would be the equivalent of adding around 9% to the National Insurance rate. Moreover, lower income pensioners would lose existing means-tested benefits, thereby gaining little, while higher income groups would keep nearly all of the increase. As a result, at 1995 prices, the richest 600,000 pensioners would receive, on average, nearly £3,000 per head per year, while the poorest 2.7 million would, on average, net only £1,600 each year (Johnson *et al.*, 1996).

Indexing on average earnings would be cheaper in the short run, but more expensive in the long run. The basic state pension currently accounts for about 10% of government expenditure, or £26.9 billion in 1994–5, which would rise to £97.4 billion in 2050–1, if real earnings rise at 1.5% per annum, compared to £42.3 billion if the basic pension remained tied to prices (Johnson *et al.*, 1996, Table 4.1). This is a considerable hike. According to equation (18.1), if $p/w$ is constant, then the burden of pensions will not rise, provided the labour force, $L$, increases faster than the number of dependents, but as we know $L/D$ is expected to fall. Financing the uprating according to earnings would therefore lead to a 7 point rise in NICs compared to a 4% fall if prices remained the guide.

As with increasing the basic pension, returning to an earnings-based index would benefit those with additional incomes disproportionately. Those who did not qualify for a full basic pension or who were reliant on other forms of state support would not get the full benefit of any increases.

This kind of problem is familiar from Chapter 17. Reforms aimed at helping people who are poor, but which are universal in character, such as rises in the basic pension, often have their largest impact on the incomes of the not-so-poor. They are therefore expensive for every £1 of poverty alleviation achieved.

### Replacing the basic pension

A second category of reform aims to replace the basic pension altogether. As we saw in Box 18.1, the basic pension rate lies below the Income Support floor.[4] One means of reducing poverty slightly for those eligible for Income Support but non-claimants would be to scrap the basic pension altogether. The argument against this route is precisely the fact that many pensioners, though eligible, do not currently claim the extra help to which they are entitled. Income Support carries with it a stigma which deters many claimants. In addition transferring all payments to Income Support would reduce, if not eliminate, social solidarity aspects of the state pension scheme.

**Citizen's Pension**

A pension designed to give a minimum income to all

A second alternative is the **Citizen's Pension**, given to all, regardless of work history, gender, etc. Currently, most men qualify for the basic pension, but out of 6.1 million female pensioners in 1993, only 1.7 million received the full basic pension as a result of their own NI payments. The gaps in qualification arise because in the past married women were able to opt for a lower rate of NIC which in return gave them no eligibility to a basic pension in their own right. Other women had incomes which fell below the LEL line or were out of the labour market, but with the tying of the basic pensions to prices, with increased labour market participation rates from women and with HRP, forecasts from the Government Actuary's Department suggest that all women will have some eligibility for a basic pension by 2010, with an average rate of benefit of over 90% by 2020. Since coverage would then be almost universal, one option is to eliminate all the complex contribution rules and introduce a Citizen's Pension. For those currently claiming pensions, this would not have much of an impact on pensioner poverty, even if it

---

[4] Note that because they face different incentives, the Income Support levels set for pensioners and non-pensioners can be different, as they are in practice.

were enacted immediately. Much of the net £2 billion it would cost to finance (Johnson *et al.*, 1996) would accrue to those already well-off, principally women with no basic pension in their own right married to men with pensions.

One familiar method of making benefits for the poorest more generous, while limiting the cost to the state, is to means-test those benefits. This is the Minimum Pension Guarantee (MPG) reform advocated by Atkinson (1994) and analysed in Dilnot *et al.* (1994). If the pension is reduced by £x (the 'taper rate'), for every extra £1 available to the individual, then this creates a disincentive to save, especially for the poorest households, so as with other forms of redistribution there is a trade-off between equity and efficiency. Atkinson (1994) suggests one means of reducing this problem, by only counting pension income in the means-test. Savings and earned income would not count, while the compulsory nature of the pensions system would stop people switching their assets out of their 'pension account' and into their 'savings account'.[5] Johnson *et al.* (1996) simulate the effects of an MPG set at 20% of average male earnings with investment income and earnings disregards of £20 and £100 per week, respectively. With a taper rate of 1, such a move would cost around £2.9 billion per annum, compared to £3.4 billion with the rate set at 0.75 and £4.4 billion for a rate of 0.5. In all three cases, it is the bottom three deciles of pensioners who would gain the most.

In summary, with basic pensions tied to prices rather than earnings and with rising inequalities between rich and poor for those in work, the extent of pensioner poverty is likely to increase in the UK. As we have seen in this section, there are a number of ways the current basic pension could be reformed so as to reduce this poverty. All of them are potentially expensive, though the cost is reduced significantly if retirement pensions are means-tested.

## 18.5 The changing face of society

At the beginning of this chapter we stated that many pension systems were built around a particular view of society, one in which women were largely dependent on men for their incomes and where lengthy job tenure made occupational schemes with defined benefits the best choice for many. Both these features are changing. Reduced security and shorter job tenure are stereotypical trends in the modern labour market. Both seem to be occurring, though the trend is much weaker than the media might suggest.[6]

Typically, the traditional DB occupational pension has only limited portability. There is usually a 'vesting' period at the beginning of the job, where if the employee leaves, she or he loses all pension contributions. Meanwhile pension levels are usually tied to final years of salary. This makes portable schemes (which tend to be DC) more attractive for younger people and also for individuals who are likely to change jobs or, as is the case with many women, have extended periods out of the job market or in part-time work.

One aspect of the case for back-loading, associated with most DB schemes and created by tying pension benefits to final years of salary, is that firms are more likely

---

[5] Currently, many individuals take part of their supplementary pension in the form of a tax-free lump-sum. Stopping this would raise about £1 billion per annum and close one loophole in the MPG system.

[6] In a recent examination of UK evidence, for instance, Burgess and Rees (1996) find no trend in average job tenure for women and a small drop in average job tenure for men, from 10.5 to 9.4 years over the 1975–92 period. The one group with more significant reductions in job tenure were low-income males.

352 ◆ Pensions and Ageing

to invest in training if they know workers are less likely to leave (see Lazear, 1985). Workers are more likely to stay if higher pay is associated with longer tenure and this is exactly what most occupational DB schemes do. However, Dorsey (1995), in a survey of the evidence, suggests little empirical support for this proposition.

The argument, in a less certain world, therefore seems to be in favour of a switch away from pensions tied to the individual firm, which means either towards government-organised schemes such as SERPS or towards more personal pensions.[7] We have already seen that in practice most state-organised schemes are PAYG and there is a pronounced desire to move away from PAYG. Personal schemes, though funded, have some noticeable drawbacks which are worth listing. First, they are typically expensive, with much higher administrative charges compared to state-organised systems.[8] Second, the prime market failure with pensions is myopia and cognitive failure; many individuals have great difficulty in understanding the future consequences of their financial plans. In a survey of US employees asked about their pension rights in the event of job termination, estimates of benefits exceeded their true value by a factor of four (Dilnot *et al.*, 1994). Meanwhile, insurance companies in the UK are facing a government-enforced payout of £2 billion to individuals who, in the late 1980s, were persuaded to switch out of occupational pensions into private pensions in the mistaken belief that they were enhancing their retirement income. This suggests that one of the benefits of company or government-run schemes is that they help restrict the damage done to our future prospects by our cognitive limitations.

Given that they are more likely to switch jobs and are likely to spend significant time away from the labour market, women's demand for flexibility in retirement planning is greater than most men's. This is reflected in Table 18.5, where three things are evident. First, the pension coverage of younger women is much greater than older cohorts, but still does not match male levels. Second, the proportion of women taking out personal pensions and SERPS is higher than that for men. This is partly due to access to occupational pension rights, partly a matter of preference for

**Table 18.5** Pension choices in the UK, 1992–3 (thousands)

|       |            | SERPS | Personal pension | Occupational pension | All  |
|-------|------------|-------|------------------|----------------------|------|
| Women | Aged 21–30 | 350   | 800              | 900                  | 2100 |
|       | Aged 51–60 | 450   | 50               | 600                  | 1150 |
|       | All 21–60  | 2200  | 1550             | 3550                 | 7400 |
| Men   | Aged 21–30 | 500   | 1000             | 1150                 | 2650 |
|       | Aged 51–60 | 350   | 200              | 1050                 | 1600 |
|       | All 21–60  | 1250  | 2600             | 5700                 | 9550 |

Source: Johnson *et al.*, Tables 5.3 and 5.4, 1996. Note that the original figures were drawn from a number of sources and are therefore subject to some imprecision

---

[7] Note that DC schemes can be organised through the company. Although comparatively rare in the UK, they are increasingly common in the USA.
[8] Disney (1996) calculates administrative charges for the US OASI at 1% of income per annum, compared to 10–13% for private sector funds.

flexibility, given likely patterns of job tenure. Third, there is a shift towards personal pensions amongst younger cohorts for both women and men.

When personal pensions mature, the individual must buy an annuity. In the UK, for instance, there are strict limits on the ability of the new retiree to spend the lump sum in other ways.[9] One of the issues faced by governments concerns whether the price paid for the annuity should reflect survival risks; whether, in other words, the price should be higher for women. Because they are covered by equal pay legislation, in occupational schemes all pensioners who have made the same contributions receive the same benefits. Thus men subsidise women, although historically fewer women have been members of occupational schemes, so the extent of this subsidy is limited. A trend towards personal pensions, with a free market in annuities, would therefore see women losing and men gaining. Restricting annuity pricing according to gender would limit this transfer, but might lead to adverse selection and ultimately separating behaviour, with men avoiding annuities.

In this section we have seen that the changing nature of society alters the relative demand for different types of pensions. In turn this raises questions about equity, particularly between the sexes, a subject that has implications for our next topic.

## 18.6 Care and the elderly

Table 18.6 shows that in OECD societies it is not simply the aged dependency ratio that is rising; the numbers of the over 75s and over 80s are also increasing. Many though by no means all of the very old have some demand for care. Care covers a spectrum of possibilities. At one end we have the arthritic older citizen who requires some help with cleaning or gardening; at the other end is something else close to full-time nursing. Typically, therefore, government responsibility for organising and funding care lies somewhere between social security and health ministries. This gives incentives for the separate organisations to attempt to off-load responsibility by attempting to redraw the lines dividing 'care' from 'healthcare'. Similarly, if healthcare is free at the margin, whereas care expenses are out-of-pocket, then there is an incentive for

**Table 18.6** The pattern of ageing in five OECD countries

| | % population over 65, over 75 and over 80 | | | | | | | | | | | |
|---|---|---|---|---|---|---|---|---|---|---|---|---|
| | 1960 | | | 1970 | | | 1980 | | | 1991 | | |
| | 65 | 75 | 80 | 65 | 75 | 80 | 65 | 75 | 80 | 65 | 75 | 80 |
| W. Germany | 10.2 | 3.3 | 1.4 | 13.2 | 4.3 | 1.9 | 13.9 | 5.8 | 2.6 | 15.4 | 7.2 | 3.8 |
| Italy | 9.2 | 3.1 | 1.3 | 10.9 | 3.8 | 1.8 | 13.6 | 4.9 | 2.3 | 15.4 | 6.3 | 3.1 |
| Japan | 5.7 | 1.7 | 0.7 | 7.1 | 2.1 | 0.9 | 9.1 | 3.1 | 1.4 | 12.6 | 5.0 | 2.5 |
| Sweden | 11.8 | 4.1 | 1.9 | 13.8 | 4.9 | 2.3 | 16.4 | 6.4 | 3.1 | 17.7 | 8.1 | 4.4 |
| UK | 11.7 | 4.1 | 1.9 | 13.0 | 4.7 | 2.3 | 14.9 | 5.7 | 2.7 | 15.8 | 7.0 | 3.7 |

Source: OECD, Table a1.1.7, 1.6, 1.5, 1993

---

[9] Following the 1995 Pensions Act up to 25% of the value of a pension fund can be taken in lump-sum form.

individuals to portray demand for care as demand for healthcare. Thus there is a major moral hazard problem with any system which attempts to distinguish for policy purposes between healthcare and care.

Second, not all individuals require care and many individuals will need only limited help, even at the very end of their lives. Thus, the demand for care is essentially demand for care insurance. Again if full insurance is provided, then a problem of moral hazard is created.

The third issue is that, to a large extent, care is provided by family members, who thereby share in the benefits when or if the state takes over the burden. This also gives rise to a moral hazard problem, since there is an incentive for families to off-load care of their elderly relatives onto the state. The theory underlying this is provided by Figure 18.1, which depicts a family choosing between devoting resources to the care of an elderly member of the family or consuming resources themselves. In the absence of state help, family provision of care is $C^0$, from a budget constraint AA. If the government makes available support in the form of care $C^g$, the family's budget constraint moves out to ABB. There is a net rise in total care going to the dependent member to $C^1$, but the family's contribution falls to $C^{1f}$. If, though, the removal of the dependent into voluntary or private care means that family-supplied care is not feasible, then the heavy line represents the budget constraint faced by the family. Here, B (on the indifference curve $U^2$) is the outcome, with no family-supplied care and total care given to the dependent falling from $C^0$ to $C^{gm}$ meaning that the other family members are better off, but the dependent relative is worse off compared to the no-subsidy case.

It is misleading to represent the family as always having a single set of well-defined preferences. In practice, the goals of one member of the family may clash with another and within the family it is largely, though not exclusively, women who

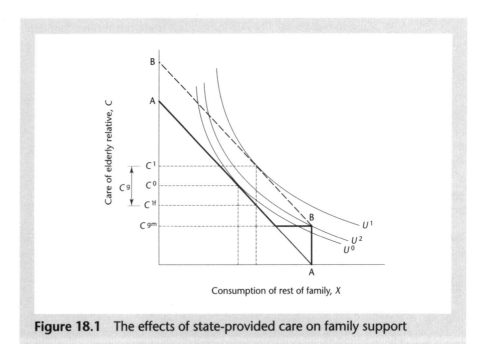

**Figure 18.1** The effects of state-provided care on family support

provide physical care. So, in the absence of social or private insurance, an increasingly frail population means an increasing burden on women rather than men.[10]

For the UK, Laing (1993) estimates the cost of state and private care at £9 billion, compared to a £32 billion figure for the cost of unpaid and informal family support, suggesting large scope for the substitution of the market or the state for families in the provision of care. He also links the rise in the numbers of elderly going into care in the 1980s to the availability of financial support in the shape of Supplementary Benefit/Income Support. Figure 18.2 provides supporting evidence. From April 1983, retired individuals qualifying for Supplementary Benefit (which later became Income Support) with assets worth less than £3,000 could claim the cost of fees for private or voluntary residential care. As the chart shows, expenditure exploded, despite the later implementation of much tighter rules governing eligibility.

As with the general problem of increasing dependency rates, there is no magic fix. Three types of solution are possible: a funded and possibly privatised system where premiums reflect risks, a PAYG system and a funded system with risk pooling.

The extent of private provision of care insurance is currently limited. This reflects partly the cost. Actuarially fair lifetime insurance to cover care and residential home costs in the UK would mean investing a lump-sum premium of £19,000 at age 65 for men and £37,200 for women, according to Tania Burchardt (1996). As those figures suggest, full-scale privatisation of this kind would also involve a substantial re-distribution from women to men, but such privatisation would not be sustainable, as long as the NHS offers something of an alternative and a safety net is provided to those without the assets to finance care.

In the UK, the previous government favoured a privately funded system, whereby individuals were given incentives for taking out private insurance in the form of a rise in the assets disregarded when considering eligibility for government-supported, but means-tested residential care. For every £1 of cover taken out, £1.50 of capital could

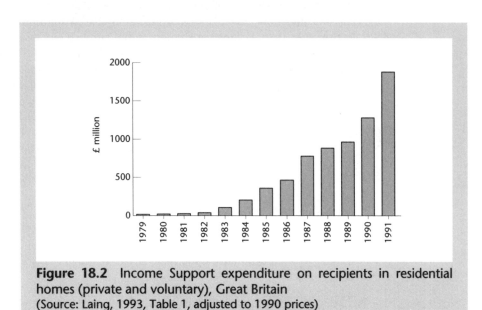

**Figure 18.2** Income Support expenditure on recipients in residential homes (private and voluntary), Great Britain
(Source: Laing, 1993, Table 1, adjusted to 1990 prices)

---

[10] Of course even with private or social insurance picking up the tab, most care workers remain women.

be disregarded. Experience with similar schemes in the USA (Glennerster, 1996) suggests low take-up rates, even given the offer of high subsidies, and this is likely to be the case wherever the state offers close substitutes for free.

A PAYG system which is demand-led offers potential for the enormous substitution of state support for family provision, but it also provides the opportunity to deliver an integrated service which does not waste expensive healthcare when all that is needed is a little help. Glennerster (1996) suggests a slightly different model for the UK, in which GP fundholders would receive a **capitation allowance** and be allowed to purchase services, medical and non-medical, for their patients. As with healthcare, GPs would therefore act as gatekeepers, rationing provision and thus limiting the problem of moral hazard. Individuals could still buy top-up services or private insurance, but the basic provision of care would become an adjunct of the health system. One danger of this approach lies in the priorities of the GP, who might prefer medical support to other forms of care and limit access to resources for individuals with surviving or at least local relatives.

**Capitation allowance**

Payment proportional to the number of patients registered

The third approach, more suited to funded social insurance systems, is to create an adjunct to social security. This was the option presciently chosen by the Dutch in 1968, who added a 0.5% charge to social insurance, shared between employer and employee. Later on though, to keep the fund in balance, the contribution rate has had to be increased to 4.5% and a form of rationing instituted, with local commissions assessing need on an individual basis (Glennerster, 1996). Meanwhile, in 1995 Long-Term Care Insurance was added as the fifth leg of the German social insurance system. Together, employers and employees pay 1.7% of earnings (up to a ceiling). The Federal government pays the cover for the unemployed and those with incomes below a threshold have their contributions paid by the state. Living expenses must still be paid out of pensions, but cover extends to home as well as institutional care.

Japan has made steps in the same direction, but perhaps scared by the Dutch experience, with its spiralling costs, Japan has also made tentative moves in the opposite direction, towards supporting family-based solutions. The 'Golden Plan', instituted in 1980, is aimed at supporting the family by increasing the availability of heavily subsidised home-help, short-term stay facilities and daycare centres for the elderly.[11] On the face of it, if there is one country where families might be expected to take on the physical and financial burden of care of the elderly, it is Japan, since a higher proportion of pensioners co-reside with their offspring than in any other rich nation. However, this figure is on the decline, as is the possible supply of female relatives for care. Between 1967 and 1995, the percentage of women between 40 and 49 in paid employment rose from 24 to 53% in Japan and in the long run, Ogawa and Retherford (1997) estimate that the ratio of non-working women aged 40–49 to those bedridden or suffering from senile dementia will fall from 14.3:1 in 1990 to 2.2:1 in 2025. Meanwhile, the proportion of respondents answering 'good custom' or 'natural duty' to the question 'What is your opinion about children caring for their elderly parents?' fell from 80 to 47% over the period 1963–96. Based on this evidence and looking at Table 18.7, it seems therefore that family-based care for the very old is unlikely to be a sustainable option for the future, unless heavily subsidised.

---

[11] This appears to have been partly motivated by the moral hazard problem of families using the healthcare system as an alternative to purchasing care. Ogawa and Retherford (1997) point out that copayments for hospital stays are around Yen 39,000 per month (around £200 at 1996 exchange rates), compared to Yen 60,000 for intermediate care nursing homes, giving incentives for families to place sickly relatives in hospital.

**Table 18.7**  Generations together? Pensioners living with their children in six OECD countries

| | % pensioners living in three-generation households, 1990 | % pensioners co-residing with children, 1988 |
|---|---|---|
| Japan | 32 | 65 |
| Germany | 3 | – |
| France | – | 18 |
| USA | 1 | 15 |
| UK | 1 | 10 |
| Sweden | – | 5 |

Source: Ogawa and Rutherford (1997)

## 18.7  Conclusion

Pensions form the largest element in the government budget. Population ageing thus has major implications for public finance, especially since demographic trends are one of the features of the economy least controllable by the state. As we have seen, the tax burden created by PAYG pension schemes is only one aspect of the implications of an ageing population; equity between the sexes and the care of the frail elderly are also important dimensions of the problem. In Chapter 19 we will also see that an ageing population has major consequences for the health services as well.

## Summary

- Pensions are the means by which individuals smooth consumption across the working and retired parts of their lives.

- Pensions form the largest component of public sector spending in the UK and many other OECD countries. Most state-run schemes are pay-as-you-go (PAYG), meaning that they are paid out of current tax or social security income.

- The major justification for state involvement in pension planning is myopia on the part of its citizens. While this justifies regulation and possibly compulsory saving, it does necessarily imply that the government itself should supply the pension.

- It is possible to achieve a Pareto improvement with a PAYG pension scheme, compared to a funded system. However, with PAYG schemes, governments have often made promises about the generosity of benefits, which have been expensive to fulfil.

- Despite the spread of occupational pensions, many pensioners live in poverty. A means-tested pension system would have the greatest impact on pensioner poverty, but would strike at the universal character of the basic pension.

- Although changes in job tenure have been quite small, trends in the labour market point to a greater role for personal pensions and a diminishing place for the traditional occupational pension scheme.

- The increasing numbers of the frail elderly have raised the demand for care in most OECD countries. The large costs involved in care have tended to fall on social security, healthcare budgets or family members.

## Questions

1. What, if any, are the significant market failures affecting the pension market?
2. For what areas of risk are defined benefit safer than defined contribution schemes? For what areas are they more risky?
3. Why can PAYG schemes produce a Pareto improvement over funded schemes?
4. 'Women earn less than men. So it is only fair that in most pension schemes men subsidise the pensions of women.' Do you agree?
5. Suppose a population is ageing. What does the Median Voter Theorem predict will happen to the state pension if the median voter is (a) retired or close to retirement or (b) in their twenties?

## Further reading

Disney (1996) is a good source for the theoretical ideas underpinning this chapter, with Myles (1996) as a more advanced alternative. The classic articles on which both books draw, on the interaction between social security, saving and growth, are Samuelson (1958) and Diamond (1965). The debate on the impact of PAYG pensions on aggregate saving was kicked off in Feldstein (1974). Disney (1996) is also a good source for the policy options open to the richer nations, while Dilnot et al. (1994) and Johnson et al. (1996) draw on the expertise of the Institute of Fiscal Studies to examine the UK's position in detail. Johnson et al. (1996) also devote some space to considering gender issues in pensions. For the debate on financing care, see Glennerster (1996).

## References

Aaron, H. J. (1966) 'The social insurance paradox', *Canadian Journal of Economics* 32, 371–4.

Atkinson, A.B. (1994) *State Pensions for Today and Tomorrow*, London: Suntory–Toyota International Centre of Economics and Related Disciplines, Welfare State Programme, Discussion Paper WSP/104/LSE.

Barr, N. (1994) *The Economics of the Welfare State*, 2nd edn, London: Weidenfeld and Nicholson.

Beach, C.M., Boadway, R.W. and Gibbons, J.O. (1984) 'Social-security and aggregate capital accumulation revisited – dynamic simultaneous estimates in a wealth-generation model', *Economic Inquiry* 22(1), 68–79.

Boadway, R. and Wildasin, D. (1994) 'Taxation and savings', *Fiscal Studies* 15, 19–63.

Burchardt, T. (1996) 'What price security: assessing private insurance for long-term care, income replacement during incapacity and unemployment for mortgagors', Welfare State Programme, WSP/129, STICERD, LSE.

Burgess, S. and Rees, H. (1996) 'Job tenure in Britain 1975–92', *Economic Journal* 106, 334–44.

Creedy, J. and Disney, R. (1989) 'Can we afford to grow older?', *European Economic Review* 33, 367–76.

Diamond, P.A. (1965) 'National debt in neo-classical growth model', *American Economic Review* 55, 1126–50.

Dilnot, A., Disney, R., Johnson, P. and Whitehouse, E. (1994) *Pensions Policy in the UK: An Economic Analysis*, London: Institute for Fiscal Studies.

Disney, R. (1996) *Can We Afford To Grow Older?*, Cambridge, MA: MIT Press.

Dorsey, S. 'Pension portability and labor market efficiency: a survey of the literature *Industrial and Labor Relations Review* 42(2), 276–92.

European Commission (1996) 'Ageing and pension expenditure prospects in the Western world', *European Economy*, Reports and Studies No. 3.

Feldstein, M. (1974) 'Social security, induced retirement and aggregate capital accumulation', *Journal of Political Economy* 84, 331–6.

Feldstein, M. (1977) 'Does the USA save too little?', *American Economic Review, Papers and Proceedings*, February, 67(1), 116–21.

Fry, V., Smith, S. and White, S. (1990) *Pensioners and the Public Purse: Public Spending Policies and Population Ageing*, Institute of Fiscal Studies, Report 36.

Glennerster, H. (1996) *Caring for the Very Old: Public and Private Solutions*, Welfare State Programme, WSP/126, STICERD, LSE.

*The Guardian*, 19 May 1997.

Jappelli, T. and Pagano, M. (1994) 'Government incentives and household saving in Italy', in J. Poterba (ed.) *International Comparison of Government Incentives and Household Saving*, Chicago: University of Chicago Press, 34–56.

Johnson, P., Disney, R. and Stears, G. (1996) *Pensions: 2000 and Beyond; Volume 2: Analysis of Trends and Options*, London: Retirement Income Inquiry.

Laing, W. (1993) *Financing Long-term Care: The Crucial Debate*, London: Age Concern England Books.

Lazear, E.P. (1985) 'Incentive effects of pensions', in D. Wise (ed.) *Pensions, Labour and Individual Choice*, Chicago: University of Chicago Press, 135–61.

Myles, G. (1996) *Public Economics*, Cambridge: Cambridge University Press.

OECD (1988) *Reforming Public Pensions*, Paris: OECD.

OECD (1990) *OECD Surveys: Japan 1989/90*, Paris: OECD.

OECD (1993) *OECD Health Systems*, Vol. 2, Paris: OECD.

Ogawa, N. and Retherford, R.D. (1997) 'Shifting costs of caring for the elderly back to families in Japan: will it work?', *Population and Development Review* 23(1), 59–95.

Samuelson, P.A. (1958) 'An exact consumption-loan model of interest, with or without the social contrivance of money', *Journal of Political Economy* 66, 467–82.

Scanlon, W.J. (1992) 'Possible reforms for financing long-term care', *Journal of Economic Perspectives* 6(3), 43–58.

Takayama, N. (1992) *The Greying of Japan: An Economic Perspective on Public Pensions*, Oxford: Oxford University Press.

# Healthcare

## 19.1 Introduction

In this chapter we examine the market failures in healthcare. As Table 19.1 suggests,[1] healthcare expenditures take up a substantial proportion of national income in most OECD countries and government involvement is significant. Rapid rises in healthcare prices and the consequences of an ageing population have pushed up spending, especially by governments, leading to mounting pressure for healthcare reform. Some countries, notably New Zealand, the UK and The Netherlands, have recently undertaken major reorganisations of their healthcare systems, while most others have introduced significant changes of one form or another, largely intended to limit the percentage of GDP and government expenditures devoted to healthcare and to raise the incentives for its efficient utilisation. However, we shall see how elusive are the twin goals of equity and efficiency in the healthcare domain.

## 19.2 The economics of healthcare

Healthcare is a special good in many ways, not least because of the degree of state intervention in its provision. Yet it is also unique in that it is not healthcare itself that matters for the patient, but health, an entirely different good. Healthcare is an input into health along with many other factors, such as nutrition, the physical environment and the human environment. In turn, health is an important element in our well-being or utility. We can depict the relationship as $U = U(X, f(Y, H))$, where $U$ is utility, $H$ is healthcare, $X$ is a bundle of consumption goods and $Y$ is a vector of

---

[1] Abbreviations in parentheses in Table 19.1 are used to identify countries in the figures elsewhere in the chapter.

**Table 19.1** Health expenditure in the OECD

| Country | 1960 % GDP | 1960 % G | 1970 % GDP | 1970 % G | 1980 % GDP | 1980 % G | 1990 % GDP | 1990 % G |
|---|---|---|---|---|---|---|---|---|
| Australia (AUS) | 4.8 | 47.6 | 5.6 | 56.7 | 7.1 | 62.9 | 8.3 | 68.0 |
| Austria (OS) | 4.4 | 69.4 | 5.5 | 66.7 | 7.7 | 68.8 | 8.4 | 67.1 |
| Belgium (B) | 3.4 | 61.6 | 4.2 | 87.0 | 6.5 | 83.4 | 7.9 | 88.9 |
| Canada (CA) | 5.3 | 42.7 | 7.2 | 70.2 | 7.5 | 74.7 | 9.5 | 72.2 |
| Denmark (DK) | 3.6 | 88.7 | 5.9 | 86.3 | 6.7 | 85.2 | 6.7 | 82.8 |
| Finland (FI) | 3.8 | 54.1 | 5.7 | 73.8 | 6.4 | 79.0 | 7.8 | 80.9 |
| France (FR) | 4.3 | 57.8 | 5.9 | 74.7 | 7.5 | 78.8 | 8.8 | 74.4 |
| Germany (WG) | 4.9 | 66.1 | 6.0 | 69.6 | 8.4 | 75.0 | 8.8 | 71.6 |
| Greece (GR) | 2.6 | 64.2 | 3.7 | 53.4 | 4.0 | 82.2 | 4.9 | 77.0 |
| Ireland (IR) | 3.8 | 76.0 | 5.1 | 81.7 | 8.1 | 82.2 | 7.6 | 74.8 |
| Italy (IT) | 3.6 | 83.1 | 6.6 | 86.4 | 6.6 | 81.1 | 8.1 | 77.6 |
| Japan (J) | 3.0 | 60.4 | 6.5 | 69.8 | 6.5 | 70.8 | 6.7 | 71.9 |
| Luxembourg (L) | – | – | 4.7 | – | 6.8 | 92.8 | 7.0 | 91.4 |
| Netherlands (N) | 4.0 | 33.3 | 5.9 | 84.3 | 8.0 | 74.7 | 8.4 | 71.3 |
| New Zealand (NZ) | 4.2 | 80.6 | 5.1 | 80.3 | 7.2 | 83.6 | 7.3 | 81.7 |
| Norway (N) | 3.2 | 77.8 | 4.9 | 91.6 | 7.1 | 98.4 | 8.0 | 95.3 |
| Portugal (P) | – | – | 3.0 | 59.0 | 5.1 | 72.4 | 6.1 | 61.7 |
| Spain (SP) | 1.6 | 58.7 | 3.6 | 65.4 | 5.4 | 79.9 | 6.4 | 80.5 |
| Sweden (SW) | 4.7 | 72.6 | 7.1 | 86.0 | 9.2 | 92.5 | 8.6 | 79.8 |
| Switzerland (SWI) | 3.3 | 61.3 | 5.1 | 63.9 | 7.0 | 67.5 | 7.9 | 68.3 |
| United Kingdom (UK) | 3.9 | 85.2 | 4.6 | 87.0 | 6.0 | 89.6 | 6.0 | 83.5 |
| USA (US) | 5.3 | 24.5 | 7.4 | 37.2 | 9.2 | 42.0 | 12.2 | 42.2 |

% GDP = Percentage of GDP devoted to healthcare
% G = Percentage of healthcare expenditure spent by government
Source: OECD, Table 1 and Table 7.1.1, 1993

consumption goods which affect health. Obviously there may be overlap between $X$ and $Y$; food provides vital nutrition as well as the pleasures of eating. There may also be conflict; a cream bun may add to happiness but simultaneously raise the risk of heart disease.

Uncertainty enters the relationship between health and healthcare in two profound ways:

- Medical science has only a limited understanding of the function $f$, which is characterised by a heavy degree of uncertainty and complex interactions between healthcare and other non-medical factors.

- Episodes of ill-health are intermittent and the causes varied. Demand for healthcare is therefore founded on a demand for health insurance, though what is supplied is more usually healthcare expenditure insurance.

The first observation means we should not take the relationship between healthcare and health for granted; most of the evidence suggests that the link between major therapies (e.g. heart surgery) and health is weak and often small, compared to the impact of non-healthcare factors such as nutrition. Figure 19.1 illustrates the weakness of the relationship between healthcare spending and infant mortality, suggesting the importance of non-medical factors for health. Meanwhile, for instance, in a survey of 30 hospital market areas in Maine, USA, McPherson (1990) notes a greater than 8.5-fold variation between the highest and lowest rates of surgical interventions for procedures such as tonsillectomies and knee operations, pointing to clinical uncertainty as the primary cause of the variation.

The second point implies that the insurance market failures created by asymmetric information, that we identified in Chapter 6, are likely to be present in the healthcare system as well.

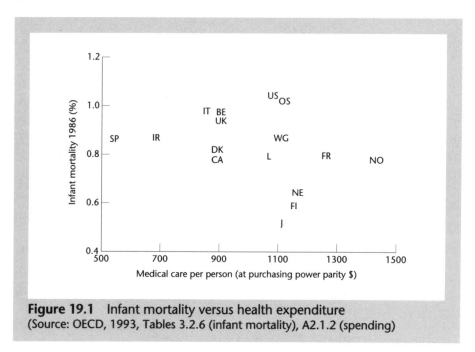

**Figure 19.1** Infant mortality versus health expenditure
(Source: OECD, 1993, Tables 3.2.6 (infant mortality), A2.1.2 (spending))

## The goals of healthcare

At least in principle, healthcare is a commodity like any other, so we would expect the goals to be equity and efficiency. With healthcare, however, some analysts go beyond the normal criterion of equity in welfare to equity in healthcare, an example of what Tobin (1970) denotes **specific egalitarianism**, meaning concern for equality in the distribution of resources for a particular good, rather than well-being in general. For instance, the UK's National Health Service (NHS), along with many other health services, was founded on the proposition of equal access to treatment.

It is worth recalling the lessons of Chapter 2, that efficiency divides into a hierarchy. A process is *technically efficient* if a given level of output could not be produced with less of any of the inputs; a process is *economically efficient* (cost efficient) if a given level of output is produced at minimum cost, given the price of factors (a cost-efficient process must therefore be technically efficient); and a distribution of resources between different processes is *allocatively efficient* if there is no other

**Specific egalitarianism**

A belief that some goods, but not necessarily all resources, should be spread equally across society

redistribution of resources that could make one person better off without making someone else worse off. It follows that if the distribution is allocatively efficient then it is economically efficient too.

In the context of healthcare, it is helpful to distinguish between two levels of allocative efficiency: at a lower level there is the decision to allocate funds between (say) heart operations and hip transplants, while at the top level there is the decision on the level of resources to be put in which promote health relative to other uses of government expenditure and private consumption.

### Rationing

In a free market, consumer behaviour determines what the allocatively efficient pattern of resources should be. Once markets are not used to allocate resources, then some other method must be used. In systems with global budgets, such as in Britain, rationing by waiting is the main method of allocation, which gives rise to some peculiar economics. Now we might expect that an increase in resources which raises the supply of operations will lead to a fall in waiting lists, but in fact this need not be the case. An increase in supply that causes average waiting times to fall will simultaneously increase the numbers joining the back of the queue. If this second effect outweighs the first, then a rise in the resources available to the NHS will lead to an increase in the numbers waiting for treatment. This is most likely to occur if the major delays are for minor illnesses and complaints, such as varicose veins. Even if waiting lists do not rise in total, the point is that, in a system organised by rationing, increases in resources may have only limited impact on waiting lists, because the increase has a positive impact not only on how fast people are processed, but also on how fast they join the end of the queue (see Lindsay and Feiganbaum, 1984).

When governments assume responsibility for controlling aggregate healthcare expenditure, the allocation of resources becomes a political issue. Most governments which intervene in healthcare have effectively dodged the macro-level allocation problem, instead setting the health budget on the basis of past allocations, the state of the economy, current demographic trends and public pressure, which is often related to the length of waiting lists. Hence debate rarely centres directly on allocative efficiency at the top level; rather, concern is over the percentage of GDP devoted to healthcare, the problem referred to in the introduction to this chapter.

## 19.3 Market failure and healthcare

The key analysis of why the market fails when it deals with healthcare is that of Arrow (1963). He argued that there are four characteristics that differentiated healthcare from standard commodities: interdependencies; returns to scale; supply-side restrictions and asymmetric information.

The first of these is an externality. Arrow argued that individuals care about the health of others. Since this is a general feeling of concern about the well-being of all members of society, the health of one agent becomes a public good and hence likely to be undersupplied by the private market. Thus, so the argument goes, healthcare should be subsidised, just like any other good that provides a positive externality.

There are returns to scale and scope in hospital services, meaning that in smaller cities and towns the local general hospital would have a monopoly if the provision of healthcare was left to the private market. There is an additional economy of scale which is potentially more serious; there is typically a significant learning curve associated with complex medical procedures. Surgeons who carry out a large number of similar operations have much smaller failure rates than those with a lower volume. Smaller hospitals may therefore have another penalty, which is all the more serious for being largely hidden from the consumer. Enthoven (1990) gives an example of death rates for open-heart surgery which fall well beyond the 150 operations per year point. In 1986, 36% of Californian hospitals performing open-heart surgery performed less than 150 per year, which, he argues, goes someway to explaining the high rates of death (17.6%) from coronary artery bypass graft surgery in California.

The third problem arises out of the effective monopoly that doctors hold over the supply of healthcare. In most countries (and certainly all in the OECD), only trained doctors can carry out a wide range of medical practices and in most countries only licensed individuals may call themselves doctors. The distinction is not obvious, but it is important. Someone might give themselves the title of doctor without attempting to engage in, say, surgery. Instead they might offer a range of therapeutic services not covered by law.

The consequences of these restrictions are compounded by the self-governing nature of the medical profession. In Britain, the General Medical Council is run by doctors to enforce medical codes of behaviour, but as in many other countries, this extends to restrictions on competition between doctors over and above those prescribed by law. Competition and advertising are deemed unethical and hence controlled by internal disciplinary proceedings. Arrow saw this as a cartel (a legal act of collusion) likely to raise the price of medical services for consumers. For this reason, there is a case for government intervention to restrict the powers of doctors. Yet note that it is the government that grants the monopoly in the first place.

Asymmetric information (see Chapter 6) is the usual justification given for this monopoly, and comes in many forms. First, if healthcare is provided by the market with private firms supplying insurance, there are three partners to the exchange: patients, doctors and the health insurers.[2] If the patients are fully insured, and doctors have no incentives to control costs, moral hazard problems emerge, leading to excessive treatment (compared to the case where patients pay the marginal cost of treatment) and poor cost control. For instance, Joseph Newhouse (1996) reports on one USA-based randomised experiment in which individuals were randomly allocated to two groups, one with full insurance and one to a policy with a large deductible. Health costs for the fully insured were 40% more than those with the deductible, with little or no measurable difference in health. Second, patients and doctors also know more about the nature of the illness than health insurers and hence this leads to adverse selection and potentially to exclusion and cream-skimming by insurers. Finally, the fact that doctors know more about medicine than patients may lead to **supplier-induced demand**, a situation where patients are encouraged to purchase more medical care than is strictly necessary. In the absence of restrictions on who can call themselves doctors, this asymmetry of information between patient and doctor might also lead to a lemons' problem in the supply of doctors, with patients unable to distinguish true physicians from charlatans.

For a standard commodity, all these afflictions would probably lead to regulation being the suggested mode of government intervention, but in the case of healthcare many governments go well beyond regulation, into production and finance. In part,

---

**Supplier-induced demand**

The ability of providers with monopoly information to promote excessive use of their service

---

[2] The consequences of this double agency problem are dealt with in Blomqvist (1991).

this is the consequence of the adverse selection problem already mentioned. Healthcare demand is closely linked to previous episodes of treatment and age. These variables (and others) are easily monitored, so that a private insurance company could easily screen out the high-cost cases and offer insurance only to those with a low chance of claiming. For instance, Manos Matsaganis and Howard Glennerster (1994) estimate that fundholding GPs in the UK could save £3,297 per annum on average by removing diabetics from their list of patients and £5,820 by removing clients with a history of heart trouble or a stroke. As we remarked in Chapter 6, this process of cream-skimming leads to inequitable treatment within a private system. There are two main solutions: regulations such that insurers are unable to discriminate between risks, or subsidies to high-risk cases (note, these subsidies may be implicit, as in the NHS).

Meanwhile, moral hazard is the enemy of efficiency within healthcare. A fully insured patient will have no incentive to limit their demands on the system; a doctor paid on a fee-per-episode basis will also have no incentive to control treatment. One way to limit moral hazard is through *co-insurance*, where the patient pays part of the cost of the treatment, but co-insurance on the scale required to overcome moral hazard by patients may lead to considerable inequity, as those unable to pay the fees because of low income limit their use of healthcare. In other words, equity may call for low rates of co-insurance, while efficiency demands a high rate. One consequence of this is that, at the macro-level, private healthcare with full insurance may be less efficient than a public system such as the NHS, which has the ability to curtail expenditures. Nevertheless, as we shall see, there is no magic cure for the market failures afflicting healthcare.

## 19.4 Healthcare systems and their weaknesses

The simplest way of categorising healthcare systems is to note that the *finance* for medical spending can be provided either privately or via the public purse and that the same is true for the actual *provision* of healthcare, yielding four polar cases. While a useful starting point, this classification system hides some important variations within its categories and also masks similarities. For instance, a system financed privately, but with compulsory contributions, as in Germany, has more in common with a healthcare service financed out of taxation than it has with a purely voluntary system, like that of the USA. A more useful classification scheme is provided by Table 19.2, which is based on work by Evans (1981) and the OECD (1992). Most countries are a mix of systems. In some cases (e.g. France), the mix is significant enough for the country to rate an entry in more than one category.

In a reimbursement system, patients choose their supplier or *provider* (doctor, hospital), incur medical bills, and then send these bills to insurance companies, the *purchasers*, for payment. Crucially, there is no direct connection between insurer and provider. Under direct contract models, the insurer (or the state) enters into contracts for the provision of services, monitors their provision and pays the bills, at rates agreed at the time the contract is signed. Providers may be other arms of the health service (as in the UK system) or run by municipalities, doctors' groups, other non-profit organisations or private suppliers. Under the integrated model, this arms-length rate relationship is abandoned, provider and purchaser become one, so that work-related payments ('fee for service') are usually absent.

Table 19.2 Classifying healthcare systems

|  | Reimbursement | Direct contracts | Integrated |
|---|---|---|---|
| Voluntary finance | Switzerland | Switzerland, USA | USA |
| Compulsory contributions or taxes | France, Belgium | France, Belgium, post-reform UK and NZ, Netherlands, Germany, Ireland, Canada, Japan | Pre-reform UK and NZ, Sweden, Spain, Ireland |

## Voluntary versus compulsory finance

The key difference between voluntary finance and compulsory systems is one of equity. In voluntary schemes, benefits are in proportion to the levels of premium, which, in turn, reflect the degree of apparent risk posed by the consumer. Compulsory contributions are usually related to income, but typically do not reflect risk and the benefits are unrelated to contributions. As such, the compulsory schemes which dominate OECD provision outside the USA score more highly on equity grounds compared to the systems of the USA where, for instance, 14% of the population has no health insurance and 60% of those below the Federal Poverty Line are not eligible for Medicaid, the main government-funded healthcare programme for the poor (OECD, 1994, p. 320).

## Compulsory finance with reimbursement

**Reimbursement system**

A healthcare system where patients are charged for services, but then reclaim their expenditure from insurers

A **reimbursement system** is one in which patients recover all their costs. Since the price of medical treatments is therefore effectively zero, there is an incentive for patients and their doctors to demand more healthcare than is optimal, for instance by asking for high-cost screening for low-risk ailments. Since the government or the insurance funds pick up the bill for all treatment, but have no direct contact with providers, there is little incentive for providers to control costs. This structure therefore tends to suffer from runaway costs and in its purest form has been largely abandoned, usually with the introduction of some form of cost-sharing between patient and insurer or by a move to greater contact between funding agency and service providers.

## Compulsory finance with contracting

The great advantage of the reimbursement system is that, by placing power in the hands of the consumer, medical services become patient-orientated. Contrast Belgium for instance, where patients have direct access to specialists as well as general practitioners (GPs), where GPs visit more patients at their homes than they see in the office and where patients rarely wait more than an hour between initial phone call to their GP and consultation; with the UK where GPs rarely make home visits, the waiting time for an appointment can be several days, and GPs act as

| Contract system |
| --- |
| A healthcare system in which providers (e.g. hospitals) enter into direct contracts with purchasers (e.g. insurers) over the services they will supply |

gatekeepers controlling access to specialists. **Contract systems** work by establishing close ties between suppliers and funding authorities, but almost inevitably this means a reduction in consumer choice and consumer power (although choice of GP is not normally a problem). In a contracting system, the insurer negotiates terms with hospitals and other service providers, setting rates for services and possibly also agreeing volume limits (as in the UK system). Insurers may also negotiate with doctors' associations to agree terms for GP treatment, perhaps involving capitation payments (a fixed sum per patient per year), rather than a fee-for-service agreement. Capitation and competition between service providers lower costs compared to the reimbursement system and if there are multiple insurance funds, then competition between them gives the consumer some power over the range and quality of treatment on offer.

### Compulsory finance with integration

Compared to a reimbursement system, contracting leads to lower administration costs, but higher negotiation costs, as organisations clash over the 'correct' price for a service. Providers (hospitals, for instance) will wish to charge as high a price as possible for their services and will therefore tend to overstate their costs to the purchasers (insurance companies or sickness funds), who will wish to drive down prices. Integration between the purchaser and provider does away with some, though not all, of negotiation costs and lowers administrative costs still further compared to the reimbursement model. In the integrated system, usually funded out of taxation, money does not follow the patient, therefore consumer choice is typically curtailed, with no choice of hospital or specialist, and expenditure priorities set by the providers. The effects on efficiency are mixed. There is little incentive for the provider to minimise costs or to allocate funds in ways which match consumer priorities. Thus cost inefficiency and low-level allocative inefficiency tend to proliferate. Against this, an integrated system allows economies of scale to be reaped and provides excellent opportunities for controlling the global budget. Note that we do not say that this leads to top-level allocative efficiency, since it may well lead to underspending on healthcare and long waiting lists as a result, one of the main criticisms directed at the UK's NHS.

## 19.5 Health expenditure escalation

To some extent, the problems of different healthcare systems reflect the weaknesses of their institutional form, but across the OECD there is general concern over expenditure escalation, the rising share of healthcare in government budgets and GDP. Table 19.3 illustrates three general points: first, healthcare expenditure has almost universally grown faster than other components of GDP; second, medical inflation has usually outstripped general inflation and third, the real resources devoted to healthcare have increased, even allowing for population growth. From 1975 to 1987, for instance, per-capita benefits rose by an average of 1.9% in the UK, 4.0% in Japan and 4.9% in France (OECD, 1990, p. 14), so in fact the figures in Table 19.3 represent something of a slow-down in growth rates. Now, the upward trend in per-capita expenditure is misleading as a measure of benefits, because of the effects of an ageing population, but what cannot be denied is the rising share of GDP taken up by

**Table 19.3**  Health expenditure growth in the OECD (% per annum, 1980–90)

| Country | Nominal expenditure growth | Domestic price growth | Medical-specific price rises | Healthcare volume growth | Population growth | Per-capita, benefits growth |
|---|---|---|---|---|---|---|
| Australia (AUS) | 11.8 | 7.3 | 0.3 | 3.9 | 1.5 | 2.3 |
| Belgium (B) | 7.9 | 4.2 | 0.6 | 2.9 | 0.2 | 1.2 |
| Canada (CA) | 10.7 | 5.1 | 1.8 | 3.5 | 1.0 | 1.5 |
| Denmark (DK) | 7.2 | 5.9 | 0.2 | 1.0 | 0.0 | 1.0 |
| Finland (FI) | 12.7 | 7.1 | 1.7 | 3.5 | 0.4 | 3.1 |
| France (FR) | 10.4 | 6.2 | –0.9 | 5.0 | 0.5 | 4.5 |
| Germany (WG) | 5.0 | 2.6 | 0.7 | 1.5 | 0.3 | 1.2 |
| Greece (GR) | 22.6 | 18.3 | –1.2 | 4.9 | 0.5 | 4.4 |
| Ireland (IR) | 7.7 | 6.8 | 2.2 | –1.3 | 0.3 | –1.6 |
| Italy (IT) | 14.8 | 10.0 | 0.6 | 3.8 | 0.2 | 3.5 |
| Japan (J) | 6.0 | 1.5 | 0.9 | 3.6 | 0.2 | 3.4 |
| Netherlands (N) | 4.4 | 2.0 | 0.5 | 1.8 | 0.5 | 1.3 |
| New Zealand (NZ) | 12.5 | 9.8 | 1.6 | 0.9 | 0.7 | 0.2 |
| Norway (N) | 10.0 | 7.6 | –0.6 | 1.7 | 0.3 | 1.4 |
| Portugal (P) | 22.6 | 17.1 | 0.4 | 4.3 | 0.0 | 4.3 |
| Spain (SP) | 14.4 | 8.9 | 0.4 | 4.6 | 0.4 | 4.2 |
| Sweden (SW) | 8.9 | 7.6 | –0.6 | 1.7 | 0.3 | 1.4 |
| United Kingdom (UK) | 9.8 | 6.1 | 1.3 | 2.1 | 0.2 | 1.9 |
| USA (US) | 10.4 | 4.1 | 2.7 | 3.3 | 1.0 | 2.3 |

Source: OECD, Table 2, 1993. Medical-specific price rises = excess of healthcare price increases over other goods

healthcare systems world-wide. The forces behind this rise can be divided into supply and demand components. As we shall see below, many of these forces mirror those encountered in the explanations of G/GDP growth discussed in Chapter 1.

## Demand side

### Ageing population

As we saw in Chapter 18, in most OECD countries the population is ageing. Older people have a higher demand for healthcare and this rises sharply with age, but especially beyond 75. Some rough calculations are made in Table 19.4, where aged dependency ratios (the ratio of the proportion of the population over 65 to the proportion under), for the years 1980 and 2030 (estimated), are displayed, alongside the relative per-capita healthcare expenditure on under and over 65s. The final two columns use these figures to calculate the resulting per-capita increase in health expenditure and, since it is largely those under 65 who finance healthcare, the extra per-capita cost to this group of the aged population. The per-capita increase in expenditure is an increasing function of the change in the aged dependency ratio ($A$) and the ratio of the cost of serving under and over 65s ($C$). In some countries, such as Japan, Finland and Canada, the high values of both $C$ and $A$ combine to give a sharp rise in per-capita healthcare expenditure. Other countries, such as Belgium and Italy, with low values of $C$ or countries with an already mature population, such as Sweden or the UK, escape any precipitate rise in healthcare costs.[3] Overall, though, these rises in expenditure only amount to about 0.4% per annum, which, looking back at the final column of Table 19.4, still leaves significant rises in per-capita benefits unexplained by population ageing.

**Table 19.4**  Ageing populations and rising healthcare expenditure

| | Aged dependency ratio (%) | | Ratio of per-capita healthcare costs over 65/ under 65 | Per-capita cost increase, 1980–2030 (%) | % rise in per-capita cost per person <65 |
|---|---|---|---|---|---|
| | 1980 | 2030 | | | |
| Australia | 14.77 | 35.22 | 4.9 | 24 | 46.09 |
| Belgium | 21.9 | 33.29 | 1.7 | 4 | 13.72 |
| Canada | 14.09 | 37.28 | 4.5 | 34 | 61.24 |
| Denmark | 22.25 | 36.44 | 4.1 | 17 | 30.58 |
| Finland | 17.69 | 39.74 | 5.5 | 35 | 60.29 |
| France | 21.89 | 35.78 | 2.4 | 9 | 21.42 |
| Germany | 23.39 | 43.56 | 2.6 | 13 | 31.47 |
| Ireland | 18.22 | 22.71 | 4.5 | 10 | 14.18 |
| Italy | 20.83 | 35.3 | 2.2 | 9 | 22.05 |
| Japan | 13.5 | 31.85 | 4.8 | 31 | 52.18 |
| Netherlands | 17.4 | 37.83 | 4.5 | 29 | 51.45 |
| New Zealand | 15.38 | 30.65 | 4.2 | 24 | 40.41 |
| Sweden | 25.4 | 35.41 | 5.5 | 14 | 23.10 |
| UK | 23.23 | 31.14 | 4.3 | 10 | 17.06 |
| USA | 17.06 | 31.65 | 3.9 | 18 | 32.71 |

Source: OECD, Tables 42 and 43 and own calculations, 1995

## Increasing wealth

Healthcare is a luxury good, in the sense that demand for it rises faster than income. As GDP rises, most incomes rise too, leading to an increase in the proportion of GDP devoted to healthcare. Of course, in many countries, there is no 'market' as such for healthcare; its level and price is determined in the political marketplace, but a rise in

[3] It is not clear why the value of $C$ varies so much between countries. It is probably partially due to what costs are included in healthcare (inclusion of nursing home costs raises $C$) and the nature of the different systems under study here. Countries such as the UK or Sweden, which rely on rationing to allocate resources, might be more inclined to prioritise the provision of acute services, meaning that the more minor ailments suffered by the under 65s and treated in demand-led systems such as Belgium or Italy, remain at the bottom of the queue.

incomes will still lead to pressure for a greater proportion of income to be spent on healthcare. Gerdtham *et al.* (1992), for instance, provide evidence on the factors determining healthcare spending and show the importance of national income as a factor. In a comparison of nineteen OECD countries for 1987, they construct the following regression equation which explains 92% of the variation in expenditure between countries:

$$HCE = 25.097 + 1.327GDP + 0.224IN - 0.524Public + 1.11Fee - 0.17Urban$$

All variables are in natural logs. HCE = healthcare expenditures per capita, IN = share of healthcare expenditure spent on in-patient care, Public = share of healthcare expenditure which is public spending, Fee = 1 when there is a fee for service for out-patient care and zero otherwise, and Urban = share of the population living in towns with populations in excess of 500,000. We can see that a 1% rise in GDP implies a 1.327% rise in healthcare spending. Figure 19.2 illustrates the relationship between GDP and healthcare spending.

Both this figure and the estimates of ·Gerdtham *et al.* (1992) are cross-sections across nations rather than over time and they do not explain why medical spending per head rises faster than income. They are also in reduced form, in the sense that the rise could also be due to supply-side effects, but combined with the data in Table 19.3, they do suggest that healthcare is unfairly singled out, because part of the explanation of the rising share of healthcare in GDP is similar to the reasons why the share of expenditure on travel and restaurant meals has increased.

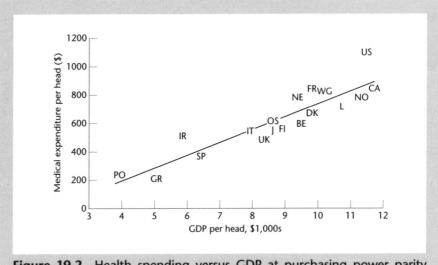

**Figure 19.2** Health spending versus GDP at purchasing power parity (PPP)
(Source: OECD, 1993, Tables A2.1.2 (spending), A1.2.11 (GDP per head) and A1.4.2 (PPP))

## Lifestyle changes

People in Britain, for instance, consume far less in calories than they did twenty-five years ago. Nevertheless the proportion of the population which is overweight continues to rise, principally because of changes in lifestyles; few jobs now involve heavy and repeated manual work and a variety of technological changes, from the wider availability of cars to the introduction of the remote controlled TV, means that more and more of the population are at risk from illnesses related to leading a sedentary lifestyle. This is partly a rational response to the increased protection afforded by medical care. In the introduction, we saw that $U = U(X,f(Y, H))$ summarises the relationship between healthcare and well-being. A rise in $H$, therefore, or a rise in the marginal effect of $H$ on $f$ (i.e. medical advances), can lead to a substitution away from $Y$ (other inputs to healthcare, such as exercise and a health diet) and towards alternative goods, in the same way that the introduction of the compulsory use of safety-belts leads to faster driving.

## Supply side

### Baumol effect

Providing healthcare is a labour-intensive activity, with the vast majority of costs arising from the employment of nurses and doctors. Labour-saving technical progress is limited compared to manufacturing industries such as cars or computers, so the relative price of healthcare tends to rise. If GDP $= pH + qY$ where $H$ is healthcare, $p$ its price, $Y$ is the output of other goods and $q$ a price index for these goods, then we can see that, even if $Y$ and $H$ do not change if the relative price of $H$ rises ($p/q$ rises), then the proportion of GDP devoted to healthcare spending must also rise. This is the Baumol effect (see Baumol, 1967) which, as we saw in Chapter 1, applies not only to healthcare, but to many service sectors in the economy.

### Technological feasibility

Normally technological improvements lead to a fall in cost and a consequential drop in market prices. If the good is inelastically demanded, as is healthcare, then the net result is the fall in total expenditure, illustrated in Figure 19.3, where the shift down

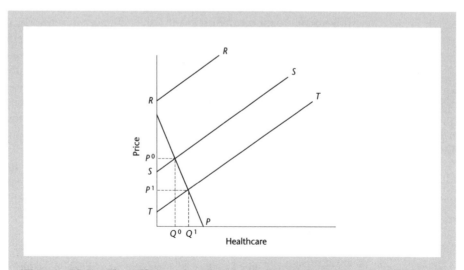

**Figure 19.3**  The effects of technological improvements on healthcare costs

of the supply curve is from $SS$ to $TT$ and leads to a fall in expenditure from $P^0Q^0$ to $P^1Q^1$. Many of the technological breakthroughs in healthcare, such as in transplant techniques and *in-vitro* fertilisation, mean that treatments can be offered for the first time. In this case, the supply curve moves down from $RR$ (or higher) to $SS$, where treatment becomes economic and expenditure rises from its former level of zero.

### Changing monopoly power

We have already seen that the Baumol effect leads to a rising relative price of healthcare over time, but if doctors or other healthcare workers gain more power, then this leads to still further rises in the price of healthcare. It is not clear why this factor should lead to continuing increases in the relative price of healthcare, rather than just a high but static level, but the OECD (1995) puts forward the argument that part of the startling rise in healthcare expenditure during the 1950s, 1960s and 1970s was due to the immaturity of the systems put in place by reforming governments in the wake of the Second World War. If this is the case, future rises in the relative price of healthcare could be expected to be small.

## 19.6 Quasi-markets and the reform of two healthcare systems

As we saw above, the three main problems of healthcare systems are expenditure escalation, poor incentives for cost efficiency and, in the case of integrated systems, low responsiveness to consumer needs (poor incentives for allocative efficiency). In this section, we examine reforms to two healthcare systems which have attempted to sharpen these incentives.

### Quasi-markets

It is an argument commonly made and encountered in the debate over privatisation for instance, that the market offers better incentives for cost efficiency compared to the public sector. Providers are also likely to be more sensitive to consumer preferences in a competitive environment, raising lower level allocative efficiency as well. However, as we have seen in section 19.3, with healthcare, markets are the source of the inefficiencies and not necessarily the cure. **Quasi-market** is a term used to describe a wide range of organisational forms which occupy the spectrum between traditional government bureaucracy and the competitive market. While quasi-markets are quite common in many countries, their use in the UK was pioneered by the Conservative government, which introduced them into many services where economic arguments or political necessity meant that full-scale privatisation was not an option. The introduction of quasi-markets has been a key aspect of reforms of the healthcare system in the UK, but other services, such as education (see Chapter 20) and personal social services, have also been transformed in a similar manner. Table 19.5 summarises some of the key features of competitive markets and their antithesis.

With quasi-markets, some element of the competitive process is introduced. In education for instance, parents are much more free to choose their child's school than used to be the case, whilst financial control over budgets has been devolved

**Quasi-markets**

The introduction of elements of the market into publicly provided or organised services

**Table 19.5** Quasi-markets

|  | Competitive markets | Traditional bureaucracies |
|---|---|---|
| Consumers | Choose supplier | Assigned to supplier |
| Allocation of goods | By prices | By rationing |
| Free entry and exit | Yes | No |
| Price-setting | By firms | By government |
| Bankruptcy and takeover of suppliers | Yes | No |

down to individual schools. However, governments typically retain control over the number of suppliers (e.g. schools or hospitals).

## Dutch reforms

The Dutch healthcare system provides an example of a set of pre-existing quasi-markets, where reforms have centred around the search for greater efficiency (see Table 19.6). Around one-third of the population (higher income groups, the self-employed and state government workers) have private insurance for medical expenses. Except for municipal employees (who have their own scheme) most of the rest are compulsorily insured by sickness funds. The insured are fully covered for all medical treatment and pay a contribution on an income-related basis. For employees, one-half of the premium is paid by employers. There is a general fund which receives the premiums plus a subsidy from the government (about 12% of its income) and then pays out to sickness funds for the costs of treatment. In addition to medical insurance, the AWBZ is a compulsory national insurance scheme which provides cover for nursing home care, psychiatric services and long-term institutional care. About 40% of all 'health' expenditure is financed through the AWBZ.

**Table 19.6** Sources of funds in the Dutch healthcare system

| Source of payment (corrected for transfers) | 1988 | 1992 |
|---|---|---|
| Government | 9.6 | 10.1 |
| Exceptional Medical Expenses (AWBZ) | 23.5 | 38.4 |
| Sickness Fund Insurance | 36.6 | 26.1 |
| Private Insurance | 20.4 | 16.7 |
| Residual Payments (by users) | 9.9 | 8.7 |
| Total | 100 | 100 |

Source: Schut, Table 1, p. 620, 1995

GPs receive an income based on capitation and specialists earn on a fee-per-service basis. Traditionally, insurers reimbursed the costs of hospitals, etc., without a contract with providers, putting The Netherlands in the compulsory/reimbursement category.

Within such a system, the goal of equity is met by the availability of insurance for all and the lack of any link between payments into the system and benefits from the system. Cost efficiency is poorly served however, since there are no incentives for consumers to moderate their demands, nor are there incentives for doctors or hospitals to limit treatment, since all costs are simply passed up the chain to the sickness funds and the general fund.

The Dutch government has tried again and again to reform the system, failing for a variety of reasons. The latest reforms, following the 1988 Dekker report, are slowly being implemented and are as follows:

- Open enrolment for health insurance every two years; all individuals would have to purchase insurance which would consist of a small flat-rate element (paid to the insurance company) and an income-related component (paid via taxes).

- Capitation payments to insurers from the government would be risk-adjusted to avoid cream-skimming. Profits made by insurers depend on the flat-rate premium charged and their payments to hospitals, doctors, etc.

- Insurers are freed to enter into contracts with providers, while price and capacity regulations have been relaxed to allow greater competition to develop. Insurers are also freed to run their own health operations (like Health Maintenance Organisations in the USA).

What incentives are created in this new model? Consider someone who has an expected cost of treatment per year of $T$ and is classified (on the basis of age and sex) into a risk class which means that they attract a capitation payment of $R$ (fixed by the government). The insurance company also receives a premium of $P$ from any customers it attracts. Expected profit for the insurance company is therefore $P + R - T$. Assuming that it has little monopoly power, the insurer can influence its profits in two main ways. It can put pressure on its suppliers of medical services to lower their costs, hence reducing $T$. In a competitive insurance market, this leads to falls in $P$, so that the consumer gains from the increased cost efficiency. Alternatively, if $P + R$ is lower than $T$ for some groups of individuals *and the insurer can spot such groups*, it can attempt to make demand for its services less attractive to them, for instance, by raising the level of co-payment. Avoiding cream-skimming therefore means getting the value of $R$ right for different risk classes and increasing the number of classes until there is no publicly available information that the insurers can use to skim the cream. Work by Van den Ven *et al.* (1994) suggests that the existing risk classifiers (age and sex) do not extract the maximum information available. In a survey based on the records of a panel of 14,000 privately insured individuals, they found that those who preferred an insurance policy without a deductible element to one with would typically cost the insurer 57% more in expenditure in the following year. Table 19.7 summarises how the insurer's profit from serving low risk (deductible) rather than high risk (no deductible) can be reduced if all available information is employed. So that, for instance, paying insurers according to average costs controlled for age and sex reduces the extra cost of the non-deductible policy to 32% of the cost of the deductible policy. Controlling for all the indicators listed reduces the gap to 8%. The key question, so far unresolved, is whether this gap is small enough to eliminate cream-skimming.

**Table 19.7** Eliminating adverse selection

| Risk adjustment | % over-compensation of insurers for high option compared to low option |
|---|---|
| None | 57 |
| Age/sex | 32 |
| Plus region and supplementary insurance | 28 |
| Plus health indicators (GP consultations, prescribed drugs, disability, days of illness and health change) | 14 |
| Plus last year's costs | 8 |

Source: Van den Ven *et al.*, 1994

## UK reforms

On 1 April 1991, the reforms defined in the previous year's National Health Service and Community Care Act came into being after a long period of concern and debate over the future of the NHS.[4] Years of rising expenditure had seemed to result only in lengthening queues (by the late 1980s waiting lists had risen enormously, with over 1 million people waiting for elective treatments) and increasing worries over the quality of treatment when it finally occurred. A second associated problem was the lack of control at the micro-level and particularly ignorance among practitioners and managers about effectiveness and costs. Finally, as an integrated service, the NHS was widely perceived as unresponsive to patient needs and inflexible.

A commonly held view, supported by the figures in Table 19.1, is that Britain *underspends* on healthcare compared to other countries, but there was no stated aim to increase the proportion of GDP devoted to the NHS. Instead, the stated aims of the reforms were:

- raising cost efficiency,
- increasing patient choice and
- production of necessary information for choice and cost efficiency.

The key reforms were at the hospital level where the purchaser and provider functions of health authorities were separated.[5] The changes to a quasi-market were gradual and cumulative, but currently District Health Authorities (HAs) purchase services according to the perceived pattern of demand within their own area. For instance, an authority decides how many hip transplants it wants to execute in a year and entertains bids for the contract. Providers are principally self-managing Hospital Trusts, which are formally independent of the HAs. Trusts have the powers to

---

[4] The system is being reformed again (see the next section).
[5] The NHS is organised on a two-tier basis: 190 District Health Authorities report to Regional Health Authorities, which are in the process of being abolished. Traditionally, the regions received the money, which was then allocated to districts according to their own formulae (e.g. where the hospitals happened to be). Under the new system resources are given to each region on a per-capita basis adjusted for age and health and with 3% extra given to the Thames (London) regions. Within the regions, resources will also be distributed on a weighted per-capita basis.

manage themselves and to bid for funds from the HAs. They also have the ability to enter into local labour and wage contracts, so that the NHS pay systems may gradually become regionalised. In 1991, 37 Trusts were created, with another 208 groups of hospitals breaking away from their HAs over the next three years (National Audit Office, 1995) and by 1995, only 17 acute hospitals in England and Wales were not Trusts.[6]

In drawing up the budgeting decision, a key separation is between emergency and non-emergency services. The former are (at least theoretically) demand-led, while the latter are subject to more formal agreements over volume. Initially, the annual contracts between purchaser and provider were based largely on volume (e.g. 2,000 hip replacements per year at a price of £x million), which places all the risk on the provider, but under guidance from the NHS Management Executive, such simple agreements have been eliminated and replaced with more sophisticated contracts which share risk.

The separation of purchaser and provider functions in districts created 'top-down' competition, but the reforms also included elements designed to create 'bottom-up' competition. Larger GP practices (greater than 7,000 patients) are now able to manage their own funds and buy services directly from hospitals and districts on a case-by-case basis. With few exceptions, these **fundholders** cannot buy all their services: only out-patient services, some in-patient and day-case treatments, directly requested diagnostic tests and community health services, such as counselling. In addition, the practices have more control over their internal budgets. According to a report on fundholding, around 2,000 out of 9,100 GP practices were fundholders by 1994, controlling around 9% of NHS resources, and serving around 30% of patients in England (National Audit Office, 1994).

**Fundholders**

Groups of GPs who receive a budget which they may use to purchase some medical services on behalf of their patients

## The impact of the reforms

There are four main areas of interest where we could anticipate some impact from the reforms: cost efficiency, quality, equity and patient choice. Yet, although these reforms represent the greatest changes to the NHS ever undertaken, they were not piloted and no institutions or programmes were created to evaluate their success. This is not surprising; reputations are damaged by failure, so we should expect self-interested politicians to seek to control the production and flow of information. Independent assessment work is therefore patchy and as yet incomplete, but consists of two elements: evaluation of the incentives created by the new system and more detailed work, gathering survey data to see whether outcomes match the predictions.

### Incentives for cost efficiency

In theory, creating hospital trusts should lead to a rise in competition for funds and therefore to greater cost efficiency. But outside the main metropolitan areas, there is typically only one main provider, limiting the scope for competition. In addition, hospitals are providing complex services to their purchasers, making standardisation difficult. In private markets where this occurs, long-term cooperation between provider of the commodity and the purchaser can lead to substantial cost savings. However, long-term cooperation reduces competition, meaning that effective competition can only occur when there are a large number of integrated purchaser–provider units competing for the consumer's money.

---

[6] Training costs for doctors and nurses, super-regional specialist centres and regional specialist centres have their own funding arrangements, linked more directly to the centre.

There is another important barrier to achieving cost efficiency in the NHS. One government report concluded, 'there is no accepted consistent way of grouping diagnoses for treatment into useful categories for contracting' and so, 'there is no consistent costing methodology in use on which to base prices' (National Audit Office, p. 6). In other words, the Trusts and the Districts do not have the information required to cost systematically the treatments they contract for. A method for grouping diagnoses, called Healthcare Resource Groups (HRGs), is under construction, but progress in its implementation has been slower than anticipated.

GP fundholders may be a more effective way of achieving greater efficiency, but the range of procedures over which they have purchasing control is limited. Moreover, there are some concerns over the size of the fundholders which mean that they have higher administrative costs compared to HAs and weaker bargaining power. In part, this has led to the reforms proposed by the Labour government (see below).

## Incentives for quality

If we wanted to model the health service of the past, we might view it as doctors maximising their own utility given the budget available. Although the contracts between HAs and hospitals do specify quality, the difficulties involved in measuring this suggest that the incentives now run the other way and that the new system encourages the maximising of the number of interventions, subject to a quality constraint and a budget. If quality stays where it was, then the number of operations can only rise through improvements in cost efficiency. If, though, the quality constraint is set lower, then the number of operations can rise still further. This potential for trade-off is seen most clearly in the demand for treatment by London teaching hospitals. These represent higher quality, but at higher cost, so there is therefore considerable conflict between clinical views (so refer the patient to London) and budgetary pressure (so treat locally).

## Incentives for equity

Traditionally, most concern about equity has been focused on equal access to treatment across social classes. Most post-reform worries have centred on patients of GP fundholders jumping the queue for hospital treatment, an issue of horizontal equity. Since fundholding practices tend to be larger than average and therefore more likely to be suburban, rather than inner-city, the link between household income and access to treatment may have been strengthened by the reforms. It was also anticipated that fundholding might lead to cream-skimming, since the limited budget available to GPs encourages them to save money by off-loading high-cost patients (e.g. those with a history of heart disease).

## Incentives for patient choice

As we saw above, in a true market, consumers make the choices, but unlike quasi-market reforms to education which created greater opportunities for parental choice, these changes fell short of giving power to patients. Instead, they entrusted GP fundholders with greater powers to make choices on patients' behalf. However, to the extent that GPs do aim to serve their patients, the increased choice available to GPs under fundholding provides patients with indirect power.

## Assessing the actual outcomes

Empirical evidence is still scarce, but there are clear signs of some major changes in the NHS; the mean length of waiting lists fell from 7.6 months in April 1991 to 4.8 months in December 1993 and in-patient numbers have risen by an average of 5.1% per year over the 1990–3 period. Figure 19.4 shows it is not hard to find one of the major causes. The early years following the reforms were accompanied by large injections of resources into the NHS, which eased the transition and attacked some of the underlying causes of consumer complaint.

Evidence on whether choice has increased is still limited. One study (see Robinson and Le Grand, 1993) found that: 10% of patients of fundholders were offered a choice of hospital and only 5% were offered a choice of consultant, but 90% of patients were happy with the decision made. This is not surprising, since it is GPs rather than patients who have the information required to make an informed choice. Cost and quality evidence is equally patchy, but Carole Propper (1996) did find some evidence of a downward movement in the prices charged for elective surgery. Meanwhile, one survey of 1,985 elderly patients conducted by Dee Jones *et al.* (1993) found no significant changes in the quality of non-clinical care over the period 1990–2. Information provided prior to hospitalisation was viewed as poorer in 1992, but on average, ward staff were seen as more informative in the post-reform year.

Studying whether Trust status or fundholding has brought benefits is much harder, since the organisations which elected to change their status in the immediate aftermath of the reforms were often the most dynamic parts of the NHS anyway. This creates a selection bias; Trust hospitals may be better run, but that might be because

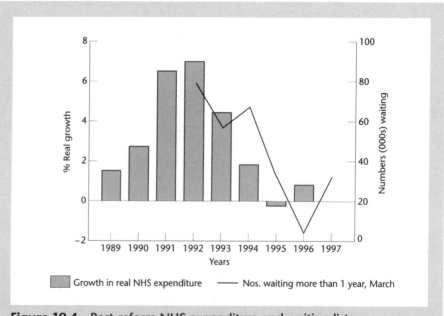

**Figure 19.4** Post-reform NHS expenditure and waiting lists
(Source: Office of National Statistics, 1997, Table 2.21 and Department of Health, 1998, Table 18)

they were the more efficient hospitals prior to the reforms and not because the changes made them more efficient. However, one major fear raised about fundholding has not occurred so far: Howard Glennerster and his colleagues found little evidence of cream-skimming in the post-reform period (Glennerster *et al.*, 1993).

In summary, it is too early to say that the reforms have achieved the goals set for them. The gains which are most apparent are due to the increased resources allocated to the post-reform NHS. As Figure 19.4 suggests, waiting lists have started to lengthen now that the growth of expenditure has settled back to a lower level.

## Reforming the reforms: the Labour government's plans

In the wake of their election in 1997, the Labour government has sought to modify the work of their predecessors (see Box 19.1), while maintaining the purchaser–

---

**BOX 19.1**

## Labour's plans: 'New Roles and Responsibilities'

Health Authorities (HAs)
- Will eventually lose commissioning responsibility.
- Together with local authorities, NHS Trusts and Primary Care Groups, HAs will be responsible for three-year Health Improvement Programmes – the framework for *local* NHS bodies. They will have to divide funds between Primary Care Groups equitably and act as their supervisor.

Primary Care Groups
- Based on around 100,000 patients per group.
- Groups of GPs take over commissioning from the HAs and GP fundholders.
- A single, unified budget for all services.
- Must work within the 'Health Improvement Programme', but no caps on sections of the budget.

NHS Trusts
- Parties to Health Improvement Programmes.
- Negotiate agreements on services with Primary Care Groups.
- 'More accountable', new statutory duties of 'quality and partnership'.

National Performance Framework
- Development of indicators in six areas: health improvement, fair access, effective delivery of appropriate healthcare, efficiency, patient/carer experience and health outcomes of NHS care.
- Powers of intervention for the Secretary of State into 'failing' parts of the NHS.
- New National Institute of Clinical Excellence and a Commission for Health Improvement.

Health Action Zones (HAZs)
- Ten areas from April 1998.
- 'Accent will be on partnership and innovation'.

provider split. They argue that the previous reforms created an unnecessarily bureaucratic health service, one that was divisive, with the patients of GP fundholders enjoying a favoured status and one that was out of touch with consumers. The reforms transfer commissioning responsibilities to large groups of GPs. This reinforces GPs' dual role as providers of medical care and as the managers of resources. Uncomfortable with the latter role, which might force them to take responsibility for rationing, GPs have signalled their resistance to the proposed changes.

The other central aspect of the proposals builds on the managerialist philosophy of the previous government, in raising the importance of monitoring and measuring achievement of objectives. As with the concept of Medical Audit introduced with the 1991 reforms, and the emphasis on costing care, the National Performance Framework proposals appear aimed at reducing uncertainty about the health function $f(H,Y)$ and raising cost and technical efficiency. And, as with the previous reforms, the patient largely remains a bystander in the process of the allocation of healthcare resources.

## 19.7 Conclusion

Along with other aspects of the Welfare State, healthcare has been scrutinised by cost-conscious governments keen to limit expenditure growth. In this chapter, we have seen that many of the forces propelling healthcare spending upwards are effectively unavoidable; the combination of an ageing population, income elastic demand and labour-intensive services is almost irresistible. Governments seeking to introduce incentives for greater cost efficiency are hampered by constraints familiar from our examination of other asymmetric information problems; full insurance implies moral hazard, but limiting insurance cover leads to inequity.

Encouraging efficiency while pursuing equity is as difficult in healthcare as it is in other sectors of the economy. Competition between insurers increases the pressures for cost efficiency, but it also tends to lead to cream-skimming of patients. The recent reforms to the Dutch system represent a bold attempt to reduce this trade-off. Meanwhile, the reforms in Britain mark a strong break with the traditional integrated model of the NHS. Both types of reform suggest convergence towards the compulsory/contract system, a process noted in a survey of healthcare trends across the developed world (OECD, 1994).

## Summary

- Healthcare is an input into health, along with many other factors. The relationship between health interventions and health is complex and poorly understood, even by doctors.

- The major cause of market failure in healthcare is asymmetric information between patients and doctors and between patients and insurers. In an insurance-based system, moral hazard tends to lead to excessive treatment and poor cost control. Adverse selection is less of an efficiency problem, however, and more of an equity issue, since insurers may often have information sufficient for cream-skimming to occur.

- The specific problems of healthcare systems tend to be institution-specific. Integrated systems such as the old NHS suffer from poor patient choice and low incentives for efficiency, but have good macro-budget controls. Meanwhile, reimbursement-based systems are good for patient choice, but create few incentives for cost control.

- A feature common to most OECD countries is the rising cost of healthcare, due to the rising volume of services provided and to healthcare inflation outstripping average price rises.

- Measures to tackle the problems of rising cost include the reforms which have moved the UK and New Zealand integrated services closer to the contractual model and the pioneering introduction of risk-adjusted capitation in The Netherlands.

- Demographic changes make it unlikely that OECD countries will be able to completely halt the growth in healthcare expenditures unless there is a dramatic extension in the use of formal rationing.

## Questions

1. Does adverse selection in healthcare insurance create an efficiency or an equity problem?
2. Why do healthcare costs tend to be higher under insurance-based systems?
3. Explain why doctors gain from regulation of their own profession.
4. 'Healthcare is a luxury good, so governments should not attempt to stop healthcare expenditure rising as a proportion of GDP.' Discuss.
5. Is it possible to make healthcare systems more sensitive to patients and yet still control costs?

## Further reading

For more on the basics of healthcare economics, the text by McGuire *et al.* (1988) provides a good introduction or go back to Arrow (1963). Useful overviews of the healthcare problems faced by developed countries can be found in the OECD (1990, 1992, 1993, 1994, 1995) references, while Gerdtham *et al.* (1992) provide a cross-sectional analysis of variations in healthcare expenditure. Bartlett *et al.* (1994) provide an introduction to the quasi-markets concept. The collection of papers edited by Robinson and Le Grand (1993) is the first systematic attempt to review the effectiveness of the UK healthcare reforms, while Van den Ven *et al.* (1994) and Schut (1995) provide information on changes in The Netherlands and OECD (1992, 1994) is a systematic survey of recent healthcare reforms across the OECD, though not an evaluation of their success. The last section of Besley and Gouveia (1992) summarises how public choice ideas can be applied to the healthcare arena.

# References

Arrow, K. (1963) 'Uncertainty and the welfare economics of medical care', *American Economic Review* 53, 941–73.

Bartlett, W., Propper, C., Wilson, D. and Le Grand, J. (1994) *Quasi-Markets in the Welfare State*, Bristol: SAUS Publications.

Baumol, W. (1967) 'The macroeconomics of unbalanced growth', *American Economic Review* 57, 415–26.

Besley, T. and Gouveia, M. (1992) 'Alternative systems of health care Policy', *Economic Policy* 19, 200–59.

Blomqvist, T. (1991) 'The doctor as double agent: information asymmetry, health insurance and medical care', *Journal of Health Economics* 10, 411–32.

Department of Health (1998) *Health and Personal Social Services Statistics for England*, London: The Stationery Office.

Enthoven, A.C. (1990) 'What Can the Europeans Learn from the USA?', in OECD (1990) 135–59.

Evans, R.G. (1981) 'Incomplete vertical integration: the distinctive structure of the healthcare industry', in J. van der Gaag and M. Perlman (eds) *Health, Economics and Health Economics*, Amsterdam: North-Holland, 44–60.

Gerdtham, U.-G., Sogaard, J., Andersson, F. and Jonsson, B. (1992) 'An econometric analysis of health-care expenditure: a cross-section study of the OECD countries', *Journal of Health Economics* 11, 63–84.

Glennerster, H., Manos, M., Owens, P. and Hancock, S. (1993) 'GP fund-holding: wild card or winning hand?', Ch. 4, in R. Robinson and J. Le Grand (eds), *Evaluating the NHS Reforms*, London: King's Fund Institute.

Jones, D., Lester, C. and Whitehouse, C. (1993) 'Monitoring changes in health services for older people', Ch. 6, in P. Robinson and J. Le Grand (eds), *Evaluating the NHS Reforms*, London: King's Fund Institute.

Lindsay, C.M. and Feiganbaum, B. (1984) 'Rationing by waiting lists', *American Economic Review* 74(3), 404–17.

Matsagannis, M. and Glennerster, H. (1994) 'Cream-skimming and fund-holding', Ch. 11, in W. Bartlett, C. Propper, D. Wilson and J. Le Grand (eds), *Quasi-Markets in the Welfare State*, Bristol: SAUS Publications.

McGuire, A., Henderson, J. and Mooney, G. (1988) *The Economics of Health Care*, London: Routledge.

McPherson, K. (1990) 'International differences in medical care practices', in OECD (1990) 17–28.

National Audit Office (1994) *General Practitioner Fund-holding in England*, London: HMSO.

National Audit Office (1995) *Contracting for Acute Health Care in England*, London: HMSO.

Newhouse, J.P. (1992) 'Medical care costs: how much welfare loss?', *Journal of Economic Perspectives* 6(3), 3–21.

Newhouse, J.P. (1996) 'Health reform in the United States', *Economic Journal* 106, 1713–24.

OECD (1990) *Health Care Systems in Transition*, Paris: OECD.

OECD (1992) *The Reform of Health Care Systems: A Comparative Analysis of Seven OECD Countries*, Health Policy Studies no. 2, Paris: OECD.

OECD (1993) *OECD Health Systems, Volumes I and II*, Health Policy Studies no. 3, Paris: OECD.

OECD (1994) *The Reform of Health Care Systems: A Review of Seventeen OECD Countries*, Paris: OECD.

OECD (1995) *OECD Outlook for the UK*, Paris: OECD.

Office of Health Economics (1997) *Compendium of Health Statistics*, London: The Stationery Office.

Propper, C. (1996) 'Market structure and prices – The response of hospitals in the UK National Health Service to competition', *Journal of Public Economics* 61(3), 307–35.

Robinson, R. and Le Grand, J. (eds) (1993) *Evaluating the NHS Reforms*, London: King's Fund Institute.

Schut, F.T. (1995) 'Health care reform in the Netherlands: balancing corporatism, etatism and market mechanisms', *Journal of Health Policy and Law* 20(3), 615–52.

Tobin, J. (1970) 'On limiting the domian of inequality, *Journal of Law and Economics* 13, 263–75.

Van den Ven, W.P.M.M., Van Vliet, R.C.J.A., Van Barneveld, E.M. and Lamers, E.M. (1994) 'Risk adjusted capitation – Recent experiences in the Netherlands', *Health Affairs* 13(5), 120–36.

Van Vliet, R.C.J.A. (1992) 'Predictability of individual health-care expenditures', *Journal of Risk and Insurance* 59(3), 443–60.

# CHAPTER 20

# Education and Training

## Key concepts

| | | | |
|---|---|---|---|
| merit good | vouchers | grants | student loans |
| myopia | vertical equity | horizontal equity | imperfect capital markets |
| specific training | human capital theory | general or transferable training | graduate tax |

## 20.1 Introduction

There are several potential sources of market failure in education: education and training are merit goods which may be undervalued by consumers, resulting in sub-optimal consumption; education and training confer external benefits; imperfections in the capital market make it difficult to borrow to finance investment in education; and finally, an asymmetry of information may exist between the providers and the consumers over the quality or standard of the good. It can also be argued that government intervention is justified on the grounds of vertical or horizontal equity. For example, government provision of education or regulation, such as a minimum school-leaving age, may be one means of redistributing income from rich to poor. It may also serve to improve equality of opportunity across the population.

In this chapter, we investigate whether underinvestment is a consequence of insufficient incentives to invest and examine some of the policy measures that may be implemented to encourage investment. We also assess recent reforms to the education system which introduced elements of a market system and aimed to improve educational quality and introduce greater choice. Given the large number of qualifications and awarding bodies in Britain, a glossary is given in Box 20.1.

## 20.2 Optimal investment

Private individuals or firms determine their optimal action by comparing the private costs and benefits of that action. However, there are other non-financial costs and benefits. The non-financial costs are often referred to as 'psychic costs', which may

**BOX 20.1**

# Glossary of educational terms for the UK

*England and Wales*

**GCSE** **General Certificate of Secondary Education**
The qualification obtained by most students at the legal school-leaving age (16). Students take GCSEs in up to ten subjects. These replaced Ordinary level and CSE qualifications in 1988.

**A-Level** **Advanced level General Certificate of Education**
Qualification obtained after two years of post-compulsory education (16–18). Students typically take three or four A-levels. A-level grades are the usual prerequisite for university entry.

**AS-Level** **Advanced Supplementary General Certificate of Education**
AS is same standard as A-level but represents half the study time. They were introduced in 1987 in order to encourage breadth in the post-16 curriculum.

*Scotland*

**Standards** **Standard Level of Education**
The qualification obtained by most students at the legal school-leaving age (16). Students take Standards in up to ten subjects.

**Highers** **Higher Level of Education**
Qualification obtained after one year of post-compulsory education (16–17). Students typically take five Highers. Highers are the usual prerequisites for university entry. In Scotland, the degree courses are a year longer (usually four rather than three years). A Scottish student wishing to attend an English University would stay at school for an additional year.

*Vocational*

**GNVQs** **General National Vocational Qualifications**
GNVQs are vocational qualifications which are offered as an alternative to the more academic A-levels or Highers.

**NVQs** **National Vocational Qualifications (SVQs in Scotland)**
Qualifications which are awarded on the grounds of work-based competences.

**BTEC** **Edexcel Foundation (BTEC) Qualifications**
England and Wales. Vocational qualifications combining knowledge and understanding with the application of skills. Emphasis is placed on teamwork and communication and work-related projects.

**CPVE** **Certificate of Pre-vocational Education**
Offered by schools as a vocational alternative to A-levels.

> *Education and training bodies*
>
> **LEA**      **Local Education Authority**
> Arm of local government which until the 1988 Education Reform Act ran and financed all state education (schools and polytechnics). LEAs retained a role after the 1988 Act as a central provider of certain education services such as peripatetic teachers and coordinator of supply teachers.
>
> **GMS**      **Grant Maintained Schools**
> Schools who after the 1988 Act chose to 'opt out' of LEA control. GMS status means that schools are managed by their own Board of Governors and financed directly from central government.
>
> **LMS**      **Local Management of Schools**
> Schools are largely independent of the LEA; they control most of their budget, but rely on a few services which are provided centrally by the LEA.
>
> **TECs**      **Training and Enterprise Councils**
> Local employer-led institutions in England and Wales with the responsibility for providing training for government training schemes for the unemployed. They have an additional role of identifying local training needs.
>
> **LECS**      **Local Enterprise Councils**
> The Scottish equivalent of TECs.

include the cost of hours spent studying and of not participating in social activities. There are also non-financial benefits: for example, higher qualifications also affect job quality; the working environment may be quieter or cleaner and the job may be considered to be more prestigious. There are also benefits such as the pleasure of engaging in education and the enhanced ability to communicate or to enjoy a wider range of interests. Therefore, whilst a private individual will only take account of the financial costs and benefits, optimal investment would take account of the psychic costs and benefits as well. Thus it is important to examine the costs and benefits associated with education and training, since the size of these determines the incentive to invest.

## Human capital theory

**Human capital theory**

Human capital is the set of characteristics which determine a worker's productivity, which can be enhanced through education or training

**Human capital theory** (HCT) models the education decision of individuals. HCT suggests that individuals have a stock of human capital which determines their productivity as a worker and hence their wage rate. They can enhance their stock of human capital through investment in education or training. Since there are both costs and benefits associated with investment in human capital, an individual's decision will involve a cost–benefit trade-off similar to that made in all investment decisions. Human capital theory treats the demand for education as an investment and not a consumption decision and ignores the non-pecuniary aspects.

The financial costs fall into two categories: direct costs and lost earnings over the education or training period. Direct costs are the costs of enrolment or tuition fees. These are the actual costs of receiving the education and training; the size of these costs reflects the nature of the skills being acquired. The costs of the loss of earnings over the education or training period will normally be largest for those in full-time education, who usually have limited employment opportunities. These costs may be much smaller for those undertaking training, depending on the extent to which worker productivity is affected. One of the main benefits of education or training is that the average level of pay increases with levels of education or training (see Table 20.1).

In Figure 20.1, we compare the earnings profile of an educated worker $Y_E$ with that of a non-educated worker. During the time in education $E^*$, the educated worker

**Table 20.1**  Effect of higher education on hourly wages at age 33

|  | Hourly wage £s Men | Hourly wage £s Women |
| --- | --- | --- |
| No university education | 10.18 | 6.61 |
| Non-degree higher education | 11.16 | 8.51 |
| Graduate degree | 11.62 | 9.71 |
| Post-graduate degree | 11.19 | 9.80 |
| Degree subject and effect on weekly pay by gender | % rise in weekly pay Men | % rise in weekly pay Women |
| Arts | –10 | 0.5 |
| Engineering | 0.6 | 2.1 |
| Education | 0.36 | 0.9 |
| Economics/accountancy/law | 10.4 | 2.4 |
| Other social sciences | 0.65 | 10.6 |
| Maths/physics | 0.9 | 1.6 |
| Chemistry/biology | –1.7 | –1.16 |

Compiled from Blundell *et al* (1997)

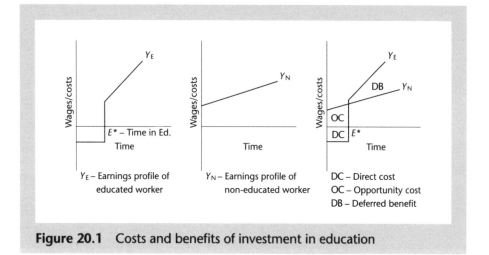

$Y_E$ – Earnings profile of educated worker

$Y_N$ – Earnings profile of non-educated worker

DC – Direct cost
OC – Opportunity cost
DB – Deferred benefit

**Figure 20.1**  Costs and benefits of investment in education

incurs direct costs (DC) and opportunity cost (OC) of lost earnings, but once he or she has completed the education, earnings will exceed those of the non-educated worker. An individual will find it worthwhile to invest in education if the deferred benefit (DB) exceeds the value of the costs.

A more general approach is to conduct a cost–benefit analysis (see Chapter 7 for more details), which compares the initial cost or outlay associated with the investment, $c$, with the net benefit or increment in terms of earnings (these may be positive or negative), $i_t$. The increments in earnings will be negative when there are forgone earnings (usually in the early years) and positive once the individual benefits from higher earnings. As in the basic model, investment will be made if the present value of the stream of increments exceeds the direct cost. That is, investment will occur if

$$\Sigma\, i_t/(1 + r)^t > c \qquad t = 0, \ldots, n$$

but no investment will occur if

$$c > \Sigma\, i_t/\, (1 + r)^t \qquad t = 0, \ldots, n$$

This tells us that for a large cost, $c$, a large increment, $i$, and a low rate of return, $r$, are required. It is also clear that investment is more profitable if there are a number of years, $n$, over which to yield the increments, $i$. If $n$ is small, or even zero, an individual would normally only consider costless investments.

Within this simple model we can see that investment will be low when the anticipated returns are low (due to discrimination, entry into low-pay occupations such as nursing, low motivation or ability, or lack of useful contacts) or an individual anticipates a disrupted labour market career (due to unemployment, ill-health or family formation). In addition, if there is uncertainty, the individual may be unwilling to undertake the costs. However, it is possible that an individual will see investment in education as the best method of protecting their position in the future, in the knowledge that traditionally those with higher levels of education and training are less likely to experience unemployment.

## Investment in training

We can use a cost–benefit model similar to that discussed above to analyse the decision by firms to invest in training. It is assumed that the firm aims to raise profits and that training increases marginal productivity in the post-training period. However, marginal productivity is lower in the training period, for two reasons. First, individuals are learning on the job and they often attend day- or block-release training courses. Second, overall productivity may be lower, since trainees need closer supervision than other workers. Therefore, if the marginal productivity of an apprentice/trainee is denoted $MP_A$, the marginal productivity of a non-trained worker is denoted $MP_N$ and the marginal productivity of a trainee is $MP_T$ we can say that $MP_A < MP_N < MP_T$. Investment occurs if the present value of the expected gains in productivity in the post-training period outweighs the present value of the loss in productivity during the training period. In Figure 20.2, investment should occur when the present value of the area DEFG exceeds the present value of the area ABCD.

In this model, we have only considered whether the benefits of higher productivity in the post-training period exceed the costs of lower productivity during the training period. But we have not addressed the issue of who actually incurs the cost of training. In a perfectly competitive market, the profit-maximising firm will pay a real

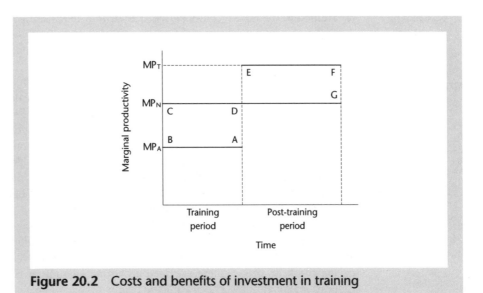

**Figure 20.2**   Costs and benefits of investment in training

wage equal to the marginal product of labour. So, the real wage for a trainee or apprentice is $W_A = MP_A$, the real wage for a trained worker is $W_T = MP_T$ and the real wage for a non-trained worker is $W_N = MP_N$. In this example, the worker bears the whole of the cost of the training (ABCD), but receives the whole benefit (DEFG) as shown in Figure 20.2.

It is possible that the cost of the training could be shared between the employer and employees. For example, the firm could pay the following real wages for an apprentice and a trained worker, $MP_A < W_A < MP_N$ and $MP_N < W_T < MP_T$; this is shown in Figure 20.3. Here the cost to the employee is the opportunity cost of a real wage below that of an untrained worker, $W_A < MP_N$, and the cost to the employer is the real wage paid above the marginal productivity of a trainee, $MP_A < W_A$. Benefits

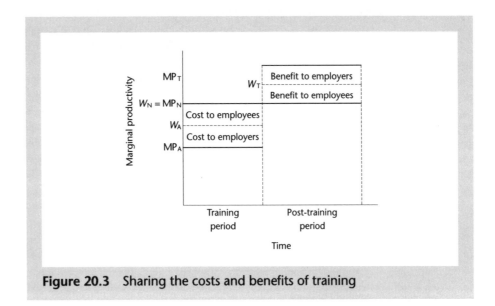

**Figure 20.3**   Sharing the costs and benefits of training

are accrued in the post-training period. The benefit to the employee is the real wage above the marginal productivity of an untrained worker, $MP_N < W_T$, and the benefit to the employer is the real wage paid below the marginal productivity of a trained worker, $W_T < MP_T$.

These arguments have focused upon the effects of training on a worker's own level of productivity. There are further benefits to the firm; in particular a more educated workforce tends to be more flexible and more adaptable. Its workers learn more easily and are more able to cope with changing working practices. Employers also find that employees who do learn quickly can then act as trainers themselves by helping their co-workers develop skills. Some skills have spillover effects, for example communication and IT skills. They not only enhance productivity within a particular job, but also increase productivity of others. Firms should take account of these effects when making their investment decisions.

Firms facing an uncertain future will have lower levels of investment. One of the key sources of uncertainty facing the firm will be due to labour market turnover. Once a firm has trained a worker, the firm is unable to prevent the worker from leaving the firm, unless there are special contracts bonding workers to firms. The implications for training are clear: if the firm is unable to ensure the future benefits of higher productivity, then it will be unwilling to bear the costs of the investment.

## 20.3  Market failure

If externalities exist, private costs and benefits may differ from the social costs and benefits, so that an action which is privately optimal will not be socially optimal. Externalities are not the only sources of market failure in the field of education. There are also problems of asymmetric information, failure in capital market and issues of equity.

### Social benefits

Where there are positive externalities associated with education and training, and, as a consequence, the market leads to underinvestment, government action may be necessary to internalise the externalities, or in other words, to improve the incentives to invest in education or training. The private benefits of education are, as we saw earlier, the gain in earnings associated with increased productivity. The social benefits include private benefits, in addition to the advantages to others (individuals or firms) of an educated workforce and population. Given the effect that education has on earnings, there is the immediate social benefit of additional tax revenue. Estimates of the private and social return of further and higher education are given in Table 20.2.

Empirical studies suggest that the greatest social benefits are associated with basic numeracy and literacy attained in primary education.[1] It is certainly true that these skills have enormous private benefits. They ensure that we can read bus timetables or instructions on setting the video, write shopping lists and check household bills; but these skills also help us in our dealings with the rest of society (our neighbours, the shops we go to, our places of employment). Thus they confer social benefits, and these increase as skills become widespread. For example, if one writes a letter of

---

[1] See Psacharopolous (1985), whose estimates also show that the returns to education are greatest in less developed economies.

**Table 20.2**  Returns to education 1981–5

|  |  | Private return | Social return |
| --- | --- | --- | --- |
| A-level |  | 6.0 (males) | na |
|  |  | 9.8 (females) | na |
| Degree-level | Social science | 32.5 | 12.0 |
|  | Engineering | 34.0 | 7.5 |
|  | Natural Science | 23.5 | 6.0 |
|  | Arts | 10.0 | 0.5 |
|  | All | 27.5 | 8.0 |

Source: OECD, *Economic Outlook, Table 17, 1995*
na, not available

complaint it is only effective if the recipient can read it! A voter needs to be able to read the ballot paper. These examples illustrate how basic literacy and numeracy skills facilitate communication, employment and democracy.

Our educational experience influences our conversations and our social circles; our school days form part of our common experience in our interactions with others. Therefore, education yields cultural benefits. Compulsory schooling also fulfils a role of childminder, thus allowing parents the opportunity to enter the labour market. Education also has intergenerational effects, since children's intellectual development is influenced by their parents' education. A child's educational attainment also reflects their parents' expectations which are in part determined by the parents' own level of educational attainment.

## Equity

Government action motivated by vertical equity should result in policy designed to redistribute income from rich to poor. Policy motivated by horizontal equity should include measures that ensure that all those with identical characteristics are treated in the same way.

### Vertical equity

Education in the UK, like health, can be described as a benefit in-kind, because it is provided by the government. Taxes are used to finance education and since the rich pay more in tax, it can be argued that the state provision of education does result in some redistribution. The redistributive effect is increased if the children of wealthier families attend private or independent schools. However, the greatest consumers of state education (and health) are members of the middle classes, since it is their children who take GCSEs, A-levels and degrees (see Table 20.3). This has prompted some economists to argue that state provision of education is a subsidy to the middle classes and that if state education is to be justified on the grounds of vertical equity, either the system must be reorganised so that education is only free for those in real financial need, or expenditure should be directed towards free provision of education not currently consumed by low-income households, such as nursery education (see Le Grand, 1987).

**Table 20.3** Consumption of education and health by social class

| Education | Per capita spend, % of mean | | | |
|---|---|---|---|---|
| | Primary | Secondary | University | Total |
| Professional | 90 | 88 | 272 | 128 |
| Intermediate | 102 | 99 | 172 | 121 |
| Skilled manual | 103 | 105 | 37 | 89 |
| Semi/unskilled | 103 | 103 | 50 | 84 |
| Health | Per capita spend, % of mean | Per person reporting illness, % of mean |
| Professional | 94 | 120 |
| Intermediate | 104 | 114 |
| Skilled manual | 92 | 97 |
| Semi/unskilled | 114 | 85 |

Source: Le Grand, Tables 3.1 and 4.1, 1982

Another argument is based on the distribution of income. Improving the skills base of the workforce through either education or training may reduce some inequalities in pay.[2]

### Horizontal equity

When we discuss horizontal equity, equal opportunities for those with identical characteristics, it is important to identify what we mean by identical characteristics. In the case of education, we usually mean ability and preferences. This means that there should be equality of opportunity and access in the area of education for all those of the same level of ability, so opportunities should not be influenced by irrelevant factors such as class, gender or ethnicity.

We have seen that there are both direct and opportunity costs associated with education and so, in a system rationed by price, financial considerations may mean that some cannot afford to enrol. It is also the case that expectations concerning the value of education may be influenced by class, gender or race. Free state provision of education and the legal requirement that all children should attend full-time education until age sixteen, ensure a degree of equality of opportunity. But the costs and uncertain benefits may deter some from enrolling in further or higher education.

## Asymmetric information

In Chapter 2, we introduced the concept of a merit good, one which consumers themselves may not fully appreciate. In the case of education, it is easy to see why the

[2] Blaug, Dougherty and Psacharopolous (1982) estimated that raising the school-leaving age in 1972 reduced income inequality amongst young workers by as much as 15%.

consumers, who are school children, might undervalue the good. It is also possible that their parents, who actually make the decisions, fail to appreciate the full benefits. One reason for this is that the benefits accrue over a long time. Education can improve employment opportunities and quality of life over a lifetime. It is also possible that families are unaware or uncertain of the benefits, and it is this lack of information that causes them to undervalue education. Finally, as with pensions and other investments with delayed returns, individuals may suffer from myopia. Fundamentally, myopia lowers the present value of any given stream of income, and in this context reduces the likelihood of investing in education or training. For a variety of reasons, then, there may be underinvestment in education. In the case of education, society requires that all children should attain a minimum standard. This is usually ensured by a statutory minimum school-leaving age.

A sub-optimal level of consumption may also occur when the consumer is uncertain of the quality of the education or training they receive or they obtain certificates that are not universally recognised; then underinvestment may occur. Conversely, if the consumer is uncertain of their own level of competence and they are paying fees to the provider, they may be persuaded by the provider to remain in education longer than necessary and so overinvestment occurs.

## Imperfect capital market

Anyone who invests in human capital must find some means of covering the costs of the investment. Just as firms reinvest profits or borrow from banks to finance their investment in physical capital, people will use savings or family income and borrow to finance human capital. However, they may find that banks are unwilling to lend without some guarantees concerning repayment. Banks may be happy to consider physical capital as collateral, because they can repossess and sell it, but this is not true of human capital. It is in this respect that the capital market may be imperfect. If the individual faces wealth constraints, then investment will be lower. There is also an equity issue; the problem of low investment may be exacerbated if family income is low. In such circumstances, borrowing may be even more difficult and families may prefer that children enter the labour market and add to household income (see Micklewright, 1989).

## General and specific training

**General training**

This increases the productivity of workers in all firms

The willingness of workers or firms to pay for training will depend on the value of the training in other firms. For example, workers may be persuaded to finance their training if the same skills can be used in many different firms. Firms, on the other hand, may only be prepared to pay for training which is of benefit exclusively to themselves. This raises the issue of whether training is general or specific. Let us take a productivity vector for a worker, $m$, across all firms, $j$:

$$P_m = (P_{m1}, P_{m2}, \ldots, P_{mj} \ldots)$$

**Specific training**

This increases the productivity of workers in the training firm only

A training scheme will enhance the worker's stock of human capital and increase their productivity both within the training firm and possibly also in other firms. Becker (1964) identified two forms of human capital: **general training** ($g$) which is equally valuable to all firms, and **specific training** ($s$) which is only of value in the training firm. If we assume for simplicity that the value of productivity before training is zero and the training firm is firm 1, then the impact of any training that the worker receives in the training firm will be:

$$P_m = (s + g, g, g, \ldots, g)$$

General training costs will not be borne by the firm, because it cannot recoup these costs by paying a wage below the value of the marginal product in the post-training period. It is unable to do this because general training can be used elsewhere and firms who have not paid for the training (and so do not need to recoup training costs) will poach the trained workers paying a wage equal to their marginal product in the post-training. This problem can only be overcome if the individual pays for the training period (see Figure 20.2), which may be problematic if access to capital is rationed, or if a way is found to ensure that all firms share the cost of all general training. Specific training costs will usually be shared between firm and employee, so the worker receives a wage, $W_A$, above their marginal product during the training period and a wage, $W_T$, below their marginal product in the post-training period (see Figure 20.3).

Stevens (1994) extended Becker's model by arguing that most training falls somewhere between these two extremes and is **transferable**, that is, of some value to some other firms but becomes less valuable as the activities of the firm diverge from those of the training firm. According to the Stevens model, firms are prepared to pay more towards less transferable training. Sub-optimal investment in general or transferable training and overinvestment in specific training and relative to general training will be the consequence of a failure to resolve the externality problem.

**Transferable training**

This increases the productivity of workers in the training firm and in those engaged in similar activities, but becomes less valuable as the activities of firms diverge from those of the training firm

## 20.4 Reform to the UK education system

In our discussion of underinvestment in education and training, we have seen that the cost of the investment may act as a disincentive and that this problem is particularly acute when investors are myopic or capital markets are imperfect. The following policy measures attempt to improve the incentives to invest in human capital by addressing the problem of cost and allowing individuals to overcome capital market failure. First, let us consider the evidence of underinvestment in education and training in the UK.

### Education in the UK

Over the last few decades there has been considerable debate concerning education and training in the UK, much of which has stemmed from concern that the existing system is failing to produce a well-trained and productive workforce. A great deal has been made of Britain's poor performance in this area relative to European competitors, such as Germany and France, and other OECD countries. In Table 20.4, a group of OECD countries are ranked according to their level of expenditure on education as a percentage of GDP. Public expenditure in the UK is lower than many of its competitors, but higher than in Germany and Japan. However, participation rates for 16–18 year olds in full-time education are much lower in the UK than in the other countries.

In Figure 20.4, comparing the proportions of the working population qualified at given levels of skills in the UK, France, Germany, Singapore and the USA in 1994, we

**Table 20.4** Expenditure on education across the OECD

| | Public expenditure on education | | | Participation 16–18 % of cohort | |
|---|---|---|---|---|---|
| | | Per capita £s | | | |
| | % GDP | Below HE | In HE | Full-time | All |
| | 1991 | 1990 | 1990 | 1991 | 1991 |
| Canada | 6.7 | 470 | 220 | 78 | 78 |
| Sweden | 6.5 | 420 | 90 | 76 | 76 |
| Denmark | 6.1 | 440 | 100 | 79 | 79 |
| Netherlands | 5.6 | 320 | 170 | 78 | 80 |
| USA | 5.5 | 450 | 140 | 75 | 76 |
| Belgium | 5.4 | 350 | 90 | 85 | 85 |
| France | 5.4 | 380 | 80 | 87 | 87 |
| UK | 5.3 | 340 | 90 | 43 | 76 |
| Australia | 4.7 | 280 | 140 | 61 | 76 |
| Spain | 4.5 | 200 | 40 | 63 | 63 |
| Germany | 4 | 270 | 90 | 89 | 89 |
| Japan | 3.7 | 250 | 30 | 61 | 63 |

HE = Higher Education
Source: OECD, *Economic Outlook*, Tables 13 and 14, 1995

find evidence of a skills gap between the UK and the rest. In the UK over 50% of the working population have at most the basic literacy and numeracy skills. This is higher than in any of the other countries. In Germany, for example, the proportion is only 30%. Also a smaller proportion of the workforce, about 27% in total, in the UK have standard or intermediate skills, compared with 56% in Germany. However, a larger proportion of the workforce in the UK have advanced skills, than in France, Germany or Singapore. The same cross-country comparisons made in the 1980s would reveal an even greater disparity (see recent studies by National Institute of Economic Research or House of Lords Report 1988). Figure 20.5 shows that the skills gap between the UK and others is much smaller for young people in the labour market, that is, 25–28 year olds, levels 1–4, as shown in Figure 20.4.

Recent evidence taken from *Training Statistics 1995* shows some improvements in qualifications amongst entrants to the labour market:

● Over half of GCSE results in 1995 were grades C or above;

● Over one-third of those aged 18–19 have gained a vocational qualification since leaving school;

● Over two-thirds of pupils leaving compulsory education in 1994 remained in education;

● The number of young people being qualified to NVQ level 3 has risen, representing progress towards the National Targets for Education and Training.

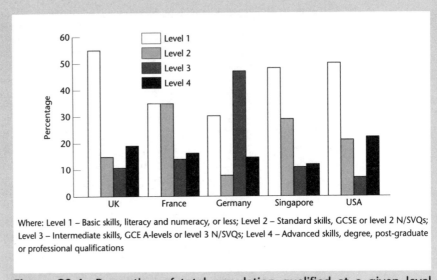

Where: Level 1 – Basic skills, literacy and numeracy, or less; Level 2 – Standard skills, GCSE or level 2 N/SVQs; Level 3 – Intermediate skills, GCE A-levels or level 3 N/SVQs; Level 4 – Advanced skills, degree, post-graduate or professional qualifications

**Figure 20.4** Proportion of total population qualified at a given level (1994)
(Source: CD-ROM, Twenty-five years of Social Trends)

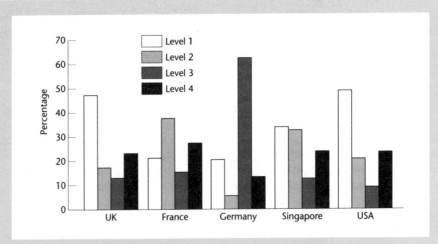

**Figure 20.5** Proportion of 25–28 year olds qualified to a given level (1994)
(Source: CD-ROM, Twenty-five years of Social Trends)

Rather less progress has been made in the area of training and of improving skill levels amongst the workforce as a whole, that is, in attaining the objective of lifetime learning. Again according to *Training Statistics 1995*, the proportion of the employed workforce qualified to NVQ level 3 has not changed. Moreover, workers most likely to receive training are young, those with qualifications and those in professional and associate professional occupations. In addition, little has been done to address what most commentators regard as the problem of insufficient private provision of training.

Partly as a result of the evidence of a skills gap, the British government of the 1980s introduced major changes in the control and financing of the provision of education. We shall focus on those that have been specifically designed to encourage enrolments in formal education and develop workplace skills. The 1988 Education Reform Act represents the first major change to the English state education system since the 1944 Act. Many of the measures in the 1988 Act had been implemented several years earlier in Scotland.

## The 1988 Education Reform Act

- The Secretary of State for Education was to establish a National Curriculum for all state schools and set attainment targets of knowledge which children were expected to reach at ages 7, 11, 14 and 16.
- The effectiveness of schools in reaching the attainment targets was to be assessed, pupils at ages 7, 11, 14 and 16 were to be tested on their knowledge and the results of these tests were to be published.
- The number of pupils per school was fixed at that of the 1979 pupil rolls.
- The Secretary of State for Education would approve budgets for each school, according to an agreed formula.
- If the majority of parents wanted, schools could choose to opt out of local authority control.
- Local authorities lost their control of polytechnics, which in later years would become universities.
- The grant-awarding bodies to universities were empowered to make awards on the grounds of conditions which they saw fit. Tenure for university teachers was abolished.

### Financing schools

Prior to the 1988 Education Reform Act, most state schools were funded and managed through the local education authority (LEA). The LEAs allocated money to schools to pay for their teaching staff and to cover the provision of books and equipment. Other services, such as school maintenance, careers advice and educational psychologists, were also provided by the LEA.

There were some exceptions: the Inner London Education Authority (ILEA) and Cambridgeshire Education Authority gave their schools more financial autonomy. It was this model that government hoped to encourage in the 1988 Act by offering schools the opportunity to opt out of LEA control.

The governors of all schools are required by law to consider each year whether they wish to take up the option of opting out. In order to do so, they must take a poll of all parents and a majority of parents must support the move for it to be agreed. A school which opts out receives 'grant-maintained status' and is then run by its board of governors. The school directly receives the money that would have been spent by the local authority on that school plus an amount which covers the value of other support services provided by the LEA. The school is then free to choose how it spends these resources and from whom it purchases additional services. By 1995, just over 1,000 schools from a pool of 25,000 primary and secondary schools had chosen to opt out.

One reason for the poor take-up was that in 1990 schools were given a third option which offered greater autonomy but maintained contacts with LEAs. The third way is the local management of schools, which gives schools control over their budget. The budget received by schools now includes at least 85% of the resources which were previously controlled by the LEA, thus allowing locally managed schools the sort of flexibility over the types and providers of services that a GMS school has, yet still relying on the LEA to centrally provide services such as educational psychology, supply teaching and peripatetic teachers for music, etc.

The standard funding formula means that schools receive an income to cover teaching costs based on the salary of an average teacher. Since older teachers cost more than the average and younger teachers less, there is an incentive for schools to save money by employing the young and the inexperienced.

## Parental choice

Schools must take any pupil who applies to them provided that would not mean that the school exceeds its 'relevant standard number' (rsn), a quota based on the number of pupils at the school in 1979 (when rolls were much higher). The rsn may be reduced upon application of the LEA to the Secretary of State. Previously when demand exceeded supply, schools could rank and select applicants on non-academic grounds, such as distance from the school. Since the 1988 Act, schools have been allowed to select candidates on academic grounds. In Scotland, there is evidence of parents taking advantage of the opportunity to select schools. See Adler and Raab (1988).

## Nursery education

The nursery voucher scheme provided parents with a voucher for pre-school education, which could be used in either a state or a private nursery. The intention was to encourage parents to enrol their children in pre-school education, since this has a variety of educational advantages, for example, an early start with reading. However, one drawback was that the vouchers only partly covered the cost of pre-school education and families had to finance the rest of the cost themselves and another was that the scheme did not address the issue of supply. In the areas where the scheme was piloted, there were simply not enough nursery schools and so places were rationed. The scheme has been abandoned by the new Labour government, although they retain the policy of guaranteeing a nursery place to all 3–5 year olds.

## Educational quality

One of the central ideas of the 1988 Act was to monitor and regulate the output of schools, but to leave each school to devise its own internal organisation. Thus financial decentralisation was accompanied by centralisation through the introduction of the National Curriculum, testing of children and the Office for Standards in Education (OFSTED) replaced Her Majesty's Inspectorate for Schools. In order to promote informed choice and hence lubricate the workings of the quasi-market, LEAs were required to compile and publish comparative tables of performance indicators for schools, including, for instance, the proportion of students achieving grades A–C at GCSE.

The league tables created the following incentives: since performance is ranked by outcomes and not by value added, a school's position in the league tables does not reflect improvement in educational attainment. If schools are judged on the basis of the league tables, then schools have the incentive to concentrate resources to competing for high-ability inputs (children) and to exclude low-quality inputs, rather than to maximise the value added. If a school is faced with closure, perhaps due to poor results or shrinking roles, it may decide to opt out. This would protect the school's resources and prevent them from being transferred to other more successful schools.

The combined effect is likely to be one where some schools have managed to capture the brightest children and are full, while others are underutilised and with weaker children. If this happens, competition between schools becomes rather limited, since parents will find that they effectively have no choice. An OFSTED report in June 1998 (OFSTED, 1998), which analysed the performance of 3,500 secondary schools in England, showed that the performance of most schools had improved, but that the performance of the better schools had improved at a faster rate than that of the worst schools, leading to an increasing gap in performance between the best and worst schools. The chief inspector for OFSTED argues in the report that it was assumed that the quasi-market would provide parental choice and drive up educational standards, and that market pressures would lead to the expansion of good schools and the closure of poor schools. In fact whilst competition does exist and schools often engage in fierce competition to attract the 'best' pupils, parents often find that they have no choice because of the limited number of places at the best schools. OFSTED concluded that 'The principle of parental choice has been frustrated because there have not been enough good schools and such schools have not been able for the most part to expand very greatly'.

The National Foundation for Educational Research (1997) conducted a comparative analysis of the performance of schools under the government league tables and two alternative measures of performance (see Table 20.5). The government league tables rank schools according to the percentage of pupils entered for GCSEs passing five or more at grades A–C. This does not reflect the performance of all of the students on the educational roll in a year, since some may not be entered by their schools. The average GCSE score is sensitive to this and gives a better account of how well the school is serving all of its pupils. Finally, a value-added index is calculated, which takes account of the type of pupils that attend the school and assesses, given the various educational difficulties that they may face, what would be their expected GCSE performance and how much better they can do. Some schools perform well according to all three measures. But the make-up of the top ten is quite different when we compare the first and third indices. Several of the best performing schools according to the 'value-added' index are inner-city comprehensives. The new Labour government has announced a pilot scheme to conduct a value-added analysis, which if successful will be extended.

**National Curriculum**

School curriculum followed by all children in compulsory education in England, Wales and Northern Ireland

## National Curriculum

There was some consensus on the need to establish a broad **National Curriculum**, but other measures, such as testing in schools of pupils as young as seven, were opposed within the education profession. All pupils in state schools must follow the National Curriculum. Schools must offer education in the following areas: English, mathematics, science, design and technology, information technology, history, geography, music, art, physical education and a modern foreign language. The overall content is specified by the National Curriculum, but teachers devise their own lesson

**Table 20.5** Top ten schools under different performance indicators

| Government league tables (% of pupils passing 5 GCSEs at grades A–C) | | Average GCSE point score (total point score A–G divided by no. of pupils on roll A* = 8, A = 7, B = 6, C = 5, etc.) | | 'Value-added' league table (points above expected average GCSE point score, taking account of poverty, special needs and English as second language) | |
|---|---|---|---|---|---|
| Old Swinford Hospital, Stourbridge | 98 | Cooper Co. and Coborn School, Upminster | 63.00 | Cooper Co. and Coborn School, Upminster | 19.66 |
| Watford Grammar School for Girls | 93 | Cardinal Vaughan, Kensington and Chelsea | 59.40 | Clapton School, Hackney | 17.19 |
| Cooper Co. and Coborn School, Upminster | 92 | Sacred Heart of Mary, Havering | 57.70 | Charles Edward Brooke Girls', Lambeth | 17.06 |
| Herts and Essex High School, Bishop's Stortford | 90 | Old Swinford Hospital, Stourbridge | 55.58 | Haggerston School, Hackney | 15.95 |
| Coloma Convent Girls' School, Croydon | 89 | Anglo-European School, Ingatestone | 55.27 | Sion Manning, Kensington and Chelsea | 15.77 |
| Emmanuel City Technology College, Gateshead | 89 | Presdales, Hertfordshire | 54.70 | Cardinal Wiseman RC School, Birmingham | 15.50 |
| Watford Grammar School for Boys | 89 | Watford Grammar School for Boys | 54.60 | Sacred Heart of Mary, Havering | 15.50 |
| Sexey's School, Bruton | 88 | Watford Grammar School for Girls | 54.60 | Hasmonean High School, Barnet | 15.24 |
| St. Albans Girls' School | 88 | St. Albans Girls' School | 54.20 | King David High, Liverpool | 14.98 |
| Queen Elizabeth Grammar School, Penrith | 88 | Dame Alice Owen's School, Hertfordshire | 53.80 | St. Thomas the Apostle, Southwark | 13.84 |

Source: Compiled using *The Observer*, 'Where to find real value for your children', 23 November 1997, p. l

plans. The attainment tests described above are intended to reflect the progress that each child is making at the various stages of the National Curriculum. National tests are set at the end of each key stage (key stage level 1 ages 5–7, level 2 ages 7–11, level 3 ages 11–14 and level 4 14–16) and the results are reported, thus allowing a comparison between schools.

In the 1997 Education White Paper *Excellence in Schools* (DOE, 1997), it is argued that despite the changes implemented in the 1988 Education Act, too many children are failing within the education system. Between 1991/92 and 1995/96 there was certainly an improvement in GCSE attainment. The number of pupils achieving 5 or more GCSE passes (grade G or better) rose from 82 to 86% and of these the proportion achieving a grade C or better rose from 38 to 45%.[3] However, the proportion who fail to attain GCSEs has remained constant at 8%. If we look at the performance of 7, 11 and 14 year olds in the National Curriculum tests, we find that roughly 80% of children at age 7 reach the expected standards; this falls to only 50–60% of 11 and 14 year olds achieving the expected standards. The White Paper also draws attention to a report in 1995 which identified the poor performance of pupils in mathematics in the UK relative to other countries; the relative performance in science and English is much better. An analysis of teaching methods suggests that schools in other countries spend a greater proportion of time on mathematics.

The new Labour government wants greater emphasis on the core skills of literacy and numeracy within the National Curriculum for primary schools. The Secretary of State for Education and Employment announced in January 1998 that a less demanding curriculum would be set for design and technology, history, geography, music, art and physical education, allowing more time to follow the curriculum in English, mathematics and science. Other policy initiatives intended to improve literacy and numeracy skills amongst primary school aged children include summer schools and homework clubs. The White Paper (DOE, 1997) also includes plans for reduction in classroom size, an intention to improve standards and a 'zero tolerance' of underperformance.

Employment-related education has been introduced into school teaching through development of Technical Vocational Education Initiatives (TVEIs) and the National Curriculum. TVEI develops skills for the working environment, emphasising science, technology and modern languages, and extends upon the requirement within the National Curriculum that emphasis should be placed on economic and industrial awareness, the intention being that students come to perceive school education as relevant to their future. Beyond this, it is now a requirement that children should have at least two weeks' work experience before leaving school.

## Vocational qualifications

There are a range of vocational qualifications (NVQs, BTEC and CPVE, see Box 20.1) which are now taught to 16–18 year olds in schools as less academic alternatives to A and AS levels. By developing these alternatives within schools, the government has attempted to ensure that vocational qualifications are seen as an equally valid route into further and higher education and to make post-compulsory education more attractive. There is some evidence that this has been successful, as in recent years there have been increasing numbers of young people remaining in education after age sixteen.

For those in employment, General National Vocational Qualifications (GNVQs) are awarded for competence in performing work-related tasks (see Table 20.8). They provide formal recognition for skills that are developed in the workplace. Skills are assessed according to frequency of use and difficulty, so there are a number of levels of proficiency. Some concerns have been raised over the reliability of assessment of these skills, particularly GNVQ levels 1 and 2. Assessment is conducted by supervisors in the workplace and they may not value the task or give the task their full attention. A further concern is that when the same schema is applied to skills across all

---

[3] Only one-third of pupils attained a grade C or better in both English and mathematics in 1996.

**Table 20.6** Link between educational and vocational qualifications

| Educational qualification | GNVQ – Level | Vocational skill |
| --- | --- | --- |
| National Curriculum | 1 | Routine tasks |
| GCSE | 2 | Operative/Craft |
| A-level | 3 | Technician/Advanced craft/Supervisor |
| Degree | 4 | Higher technician/Junior management |
| Post-graduate | 5 | Professional/Management |

Source: OECD *Economic Outlook*, Box 2, 1995

occupations. It is essential to identify the most general aspects of the skills, but this may render the qualification without substance for each particular industry.[4]

## Training

The main government initiative in the area of training in the 1980s was the creation of Training and Enterprise Councils (TECs) in England and Wales and Local Enterprise Councils (LECs) in Scotland, which it was hoped would act as a catalyst for employer-funded training. The TECs and LECs are employer-led bodies whose primary remit is to provide government training schemes; other main functions include promoting effective training by employers and individuals and providing practical help to local businesses. Given that TECs and LECs have no means to force companies to increase expenditure on training or to contribute to training programmes, they are not likely to succeed in achieving their wider goals.

During the 1980s, the government developed two main training schemes for the unemployed. First, the Youth Training Programme provided training and employment opportunities for unemployed young people. For each person on this scheme, firms received a subsidy for providing the training and the wage costs, which were at a level just above Income Support, from the government. The scheme not only raised the formal skills of entrants into the labour market, it also ensured a level of work experience which, it was hoped, would improve employment opportunities. Second, Employment Training was a scheme designed for the long-term unemployed. Those who have been unemployed for over a year were offered a Restart interview, which identified training needs and attempted to find work placements. The training element was reduced, but Restart offered work placements; workers on such placements received a bonus payment in excess of their Income Support and were given financial help to cover travelling expenses, etc. Job clubs were also set up with the intention of aiding job search. These schemes have been replaced by 'Welfare-to-Work'.

## 20.5 Student finance

As we saw earlier, when a student considers making an investment in post-compulsory education they face immediate costs and deferred benefits. Imperfections

---

[4] This is the criticism made by some major employers. The High Street chain BHS withdrew from the GNVQ system because it felt that the qualifications did not address the particular training needs of High Street retailers.

in the capital market mean that some students, particularly those from low-income families or those without collateral, may not be able to borrow to cover these costs. Governments face the following policy options when correcting this form of market failure: student grants, student loans or a graduate tax.

## Grants for post-compulsory education and training

Grants are a straightforward measure of reducing cost and sidelining the issue of imperfect capital markets. By contributing towards the costs of investment, the present value of the income stream associated with education is increased, thus improving the incentives to invest in education. Grants are often awarded to cover the direct costs of investment; for example, they cover university fees. Maintenance grants are also awarded to provide an income during a period of education. In Figure 20.6, we see that the direct cost of education is covered by a fees grant (FG) and the student is awarded a maintenance grant (MG), which reduces the opportunity cost (OC) of the investment. The grants reduce the cost of the investment and students are not reliant on family income or on borrowing to finance their education.

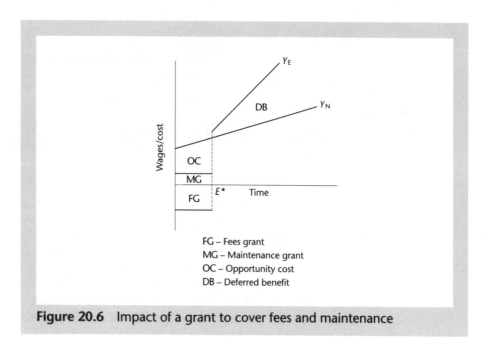

**Figure 20.6** Impact of a grant to cover fees and maintenance

## Loans for post-compulsory education and training

Alternatives to student grants still operate on the principle of reducing the cost to the individual associated with the investment, but where the student repays to the state the value of their financial support once they have graduated. These are intended to address the problem of imperfect capital markets in the area of investment in human capital. The government underwrites the scheme, so all those who apply for loans to finance education or training are entitled to them and there is no requirement for collateral to support the loan. The loan covers the direct cost of education and contributes to a student's living costs while they are in education. The effect on the costs faced by the student are identical to the grant system, that is, the loan reduces the opportunity cost (OC). However, the student has to repay the loan and this reduces their deferred benefit by loan repayment (LR). Having completed their education, the student pays a proportion of their income in loan repayments. The repayments are, in this case, linked to income and are only made when the loan is outstanding. This is illustrated in Figure 20.7.

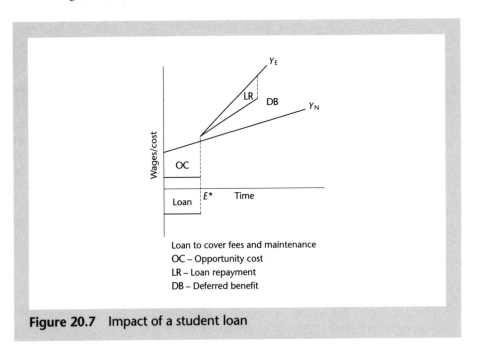

**Figure 20.7**   **Impact of a student loan**

## Graduate tax

Under a graduate tax, students receive financial support from the state which they repay via higher taxes. The advantage of this scheme is that it is not necessary to introduce an additional layer of administration which is needed to run a loan system. Under a graduate tax, all graduates are issued with a separate tax code and they repay the financial support by paying higher taxes. It is not expected that the graduate will only pay taxes equal in value to the financial support that they were given as students. This is illustrated in Figure 20.8. The financial support reduces the cost of the investment and the deferred benefit is reduced by a proportional tax, $t_g$, which is paid for the post-education working life.

## Student finance in the UK

Enrolments in post-compulsory education have been rising steadily. Until the late 1980s, students were financed through a system of grants which covered both fees and maintenance. This policy was costly for the government, particularly as the numbers of students enrolled in post-compulsory education rose. A further disadvantage was that financial support was provided to all and not only those with greatest financial need, which, as we saw in Table 20.3, resulted in a transfer to the middle class. In the mid 1980s, the student loan system was introduced and the real value of the maintenance grant fell. Students were encouraged to take out loans to maintain

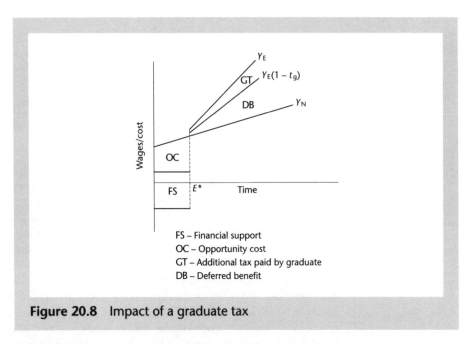

**Figure 20.8** Impact of a graduate tax

their real income. Loans were repaid over a five-year period once the course has been completed and repayments commence when income has risen above a certain level. The direct costs of fees were paid by the state and all students received a means-tested maintenance grant, the value of which was adjusted according to parental income. It was expected that parents would top up the income of students who did not receive the full value of the maintenance grant. The Dearing inquiry into university funding reported in 1997 and the new funding arrangements are discussed in Box 20.2.

Given the pressures on the government budget, it is likely that the current system will change. The key concerns are the likely effects on the total numbers of students enrolling in higher education and in particular on the numbers of students from low-income families. Other European countries provide less financial support. Most students work to support themselves during their time at university; this may adversely affect the numbers who successfully complete degrees (see Figures 20.4 and 20.5). In the USA, the fees at top universities are very high and all students finance their education through employment and borrowing, yet in our cross-country comparison of levels of qualifications, the USA has the highest proportion of the entire working population with degrees. Finally, we consider the system in Australia, which in 1989 changed from a grant to a loan system[5] and according to Australian government reports, this has allowed 30% more students from disadvantaged backgrounds to attend university.

## Financing training

Vouchers are an alternative method of reducing the cost of investment in education or training and have the added attraction of facilitating choice. This is a natural extension of the educational policies discussed above. The Training Credits Scheme

[5] The loans are repaid in the form of higher National Insurance Contributions.

BOX 20.2

# The Dearing Report into Higher Education

**Background to Dearing**

Over the 1980s, there was an enormous expansion in Higher Education (HE). Between 1976 and 1996 the number of full-time students in HE more than doubled, but the level of public funding per student almost halved. This left universities facing a crisis over funding levels.

**Dearing recommendations**

The Dearing committee was convinced of the case that students receive significant private benefits from investment in HE (see Table 20.1) and so should bear a greater proportion of the costs. Dearing recommended that all students should contribute towards their university fees. By transferring the burden of the cost to the individual this would also equalise the treatment of all students investing in post-compulsory education. This is an equity argument: students in further education, typically from lower income households, have always paid their own fees and it is only students in HE, predominantly from the middle classes, who benefit from state subsidy for the costs of education. In order to ensure that students from poorer backgrounds are not effectively disenfranchised, Dearing recommended that the means-tested maintenance grant should be retained. Further financial support should be provided through an expansion of the student loans system, with repayments at a lower rate of income than currently applied. Dearing also recommended that the government address the accounting anomaly that expenditure on student loans is treated as expenditure rather than allowing for the fact that loans are repaid over the longer term. When government expenditure and borrowing is being capped, this accounting practice places an unnecessary limit upon expenditure on HE.

The Dearing recommendations affect university funding in the following way: the student contribution towards fees could be used to boost investment in the university sector and the change in accounting procedure relaxes government spending targets.

**Government response**

The government does not plan to fully implement the Dearing recommendations: fees will not be universally applied (most students, 70%, will contribute £1,000 towards fees); maintenance grants will be discontinued; loans will be repaid at a lower percentage of income above £10,000 and government expenditure on student loans will be treated as such. Students whose parental income is below £23,000 will make no contribution, if parental income is between £23,000 and £35,000, students will make a partial contribution, and the full amount will be paid by students whose parental income is above £35,000. Repayments under the new system are shown below. Concerns that students from low-income families will be deterred from HE if they contribute towards fees led the government to link payment to parental income.

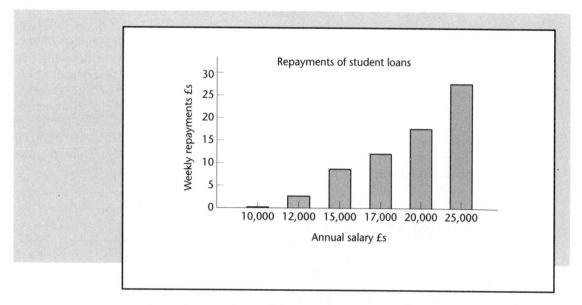

aimed to provide all 16–18 year olds with vouchers for training, so extending training opportunities and giving individuals control over their training. It was intended to correct the imbalance between state investment in formal education for the 16–18 age group and state investment in vocational training. This scheme has been replaced by 'Welfare-to-Work', discussed in Chapter 17.

Vouchers do not address the externality problem faced by firms over the provision of training. In the UK, the need to solve this problem was given prominence in a 1992 White Paper, *People, Jobs and Opportunity: Unlocking the Potential*, but the issue has not yet been resolved. Solutions may have to be found through the tax system. For example, in Britain in the 1960s and 1970s there was an Industrial Training Levy and in France and Australia, there are payroll taxes. In France, the net tax is the extent to which tax liability exceeds training expenditure, and firms whose training expenditure exceeds their tax liability may claim compensation from a training fund. Evidence suggests that the French training tax has resulted in much higher levels of investment in general training.

The results of such measures are as follows: the failure of any firm to provide training now imposes a cost on that firm rather than on the firms who do provide training; a concentration of training activity amongst those firms with a relative advantage (suggesting some idea of increasing returns in the provision of training). However, there is also the concern that governments should not only provide incentives for firms to raise their expenditure on training. They should also ensure the quality of training through appropriate certification of training programmes.

## 20.7 Conclusion

Education is a merit good, but this is only one reason for market failure. Other important factors include myopia, imperfect capital markets and uncertainty. Much of education policy is concerned with education quality and curriculum content. These issues were addressed in the 1988 Education Reform Act. Over the past twenty years enrolment in post-compulsory education has risen and one might be tempted to argue that this was a consequence of these reforms. However, other factors are at work: the virtual disappearance of the youth labour market and the growth in returns to education. The increasing number of university students has brought about a crisis in student finance. The difficulties that individuals face in financing their education caused by imperfect capital markets has resulted in government involvment. In the UK, universal grants were replaced by a hybrid system of grants and student loans; however since the Dearing Report it is planned that students will contribute £1,000 towards their fees and cover their maintenance income through student loans. Finally, state provision of education can be justified on the ground of both vertical and horizontal equity, although it may be argued that many education systems do benefit the rich and middle-income groups rather than the poor.

## Summary

- Education is a merit good. Individuals may undervalue education and, as a consequence, investment will be sub-optimal.

- Education and training yield positive externalities to fellow consumers and employees, to employers and to society as a whole. Since these social benefits are not included in a private cost–benefit analysis, the result will be sub-optimal investment.

- Investment in education is costly. Individuals may face difficulties in borrowing to cover the costs. If there are capital market imperfections, then investment will be sub-optimal.

- The benefits from education or training are long-term. When individuals are myopic or are uncertain about the future, they will underinvest in education.

- Firms will be unwilling to finance training if other firms can poach the trained worker without having to compensate for the training costs. This is a particular problem if the skills are general or transferable.

- Policies such as grants, loans and graduate taxes are designed to correct for failure in the capital markets. All of these schemes ensure that students are able to finance their investment and differ according to whether students repay the financial assistance and if so, how.

- Measures such as the National Curriculum and the broadening of post-sixteen qualifications have contributed towards increasing enrolments in post-compulsory education and higher levels of skills/qualifications amongst young workers in Britain.

## Questions

1. How will the following affect the individual's decision to invest in education? (a) An increase in enrolment fees, (b) a disrupted career, (c) making the decision in their teens, thirties or fifties.

2. Will firms invest in transferable training?

3. Outline the most serious forms of market failure in the area of education.

4. Why is the use of school league tables controversial?

5. How can a government choose between the various methods of student finance?

# Further reading

The National Insititute for Economic Research regularly publishes studies on skills, training and productivity. For more details on current educational policy, see the websites of the Department of Education, OFSTED or the National Foundation for Educational Research. The OECD is also a good source for comparative studies of educational policy and educational attainment.

# References

Adler, M. and Raab, G. (1988) 'Exit, choice and loyalty: the impact of parental choice on admissions to secondary schools in Edinburgh and Dundee' Journal of Education Policy, 3(2), 155–179.

Atkinson, A.B. (1983) *The Economics of Education*, London: Hodder and Stoughton.

Becker, G. (1964) *Human Capital*, New York: Columbia University Press.

Blaug, M. (1972) *An Introduction to the Economics of Education*, London: Penguin.

Blaug, M., Dougherty, C. and Psacharopolous, G. (1982) 'The distribution of schooling and the distribution of earnings: raising the school learning age in 1972', *Manchester School* 50, 24–40.

Blundell, R., Dearden, L., Goodman, A. and Reed, H. (1997) *Higher Education, Employment and Earnings in Britain*, London: IFS.

Cohn, E. (1979) *The Economics of Education*, Cambridge, MA: Ballinger.

Creedy, J. (1994) 'Financing higher education: public choice and social welfare', *Fiscal Studies*, August, 87–108.

The Dearing Inquiry (1997) 'Higher Education in the Learning Society', National Committee of Inquiry into Higher Education. London: Stationery Office, 1997.

Department of Education (1995) *Training Statistics 1995* London: Stationery Office.

Department of Education (1997) Education White Paper, *Excellence in Schools*, London: Stationery Office.

Department of Education, Webpage, *The School Curriculum: A Brief Guide*.

Department of Trade and Industry (1992) '*People, Jobs and Opportunity: Unlocking the Potential*' February, GM1810 London: Stationery Office.

*The Financial Times*, 21 May 1997, 'University degrees bring substantial returns', p.14.

Glennerster, H. (1995) *British Social Policy Since 1945*, Hemel Hempstead: Prentice Hall.

Glennerster, H. (1996) *Paying for Welfare: Towards 2000*, 3rd edn, Hemel Hempstead: Prentice Hall.

Le Grand, J. (1982) *The Strategy of Equality*, 91–107, London: Allen and Unwin.

Le Grand. J. (1987) 'The middle class use of British social services', in R. Goodin and J. Le Grand, *Not Only the Poor: The Middle Classes and the Welfare State*, London: Allen and Unwin.

Micklewright, J. (1989) 'Choice at sixteen', *Economica* 56, 25–39.

*The Observer*, 'Where to find real value for your Children', 23 November 1997, p. 1.

OECD (1995) 'Education and training in the United Kingdom', *Economic Outlook*, Paris: OECD.

OFSTED Report (1998) *Secondary Education: A Review of Secondary Schools in England 1993–97*, June.

Psacharopolous, G. (1985) 'Returning to education: a further international update and implications', *Journal of Human Resources* XX(4), 583–97.

Stevens, M. (1994) 'A theoretical model of on the job training with imperfect competition', *Oxford Economic Papers* 46(4), 537–62.

PART ....5...

# Regulation and the Boundaries of the State

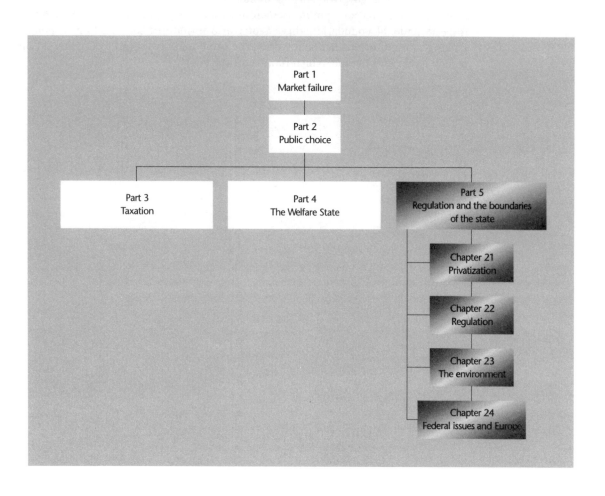

Part 1
Market failure

Part 2
Public choice

Part 3
Taxation

Part 4
The Welfare State

Part 5
Regulation and the boundaries
of the state

Chapter 21
Privatization

Chapter 22
Regulation

Chapter 23
The environment

Chapter 24
Federal issues and Europe

The final part of the book examines four areas of government activity where the state is in flux. Twenty years ago, nationalised industries dominated the industrial landscape. Today, only a rump of firms are socially owned in the UK. Over the same period, environmental policy has come to the fore, while as the European Union develops and national movements advance, the debate over the future role of the nation state grows.

As we explained in Chapter 1, governments do not just operate by taxing and spending; a large part of their influence on the economy is through regulation, so a second theme of this part is the use of regulation by the state as an alternative to other forms of control.

Chapters 21 and 22 consider privatisation and regulation, respectively. Changes to the latter in recent years have been driven by the consequences of the former, with the creation of large private-sector monopolies such as the water and electricity companies. Chapter 23 examines environmental policy and, since pollution rarely respects national boundaries, this chapter also introduces the question of policy-making in a multi-jurisdictional world. The same issue is central to Chapter 24 on federal issues and Europe, which rounds off the book.

# CHAPTER 21

# Privatisation and Social Ownership

## Key concepts

| | | | |
|---|---|---|---|
| ownership | delegation | X-inefficiency | natural monopoly |
| agency | efficiency | franchising | ideology |
| incentives | profit share | equity | regulation |

## 21.1 Introduction

Across Europe, government remains very important in the economy, both as a tax raising authority and in terms of the value of government expenditure, but its role as a producer is diminishing. In the UK in 1979, 11.5% of GDP was accounted for by state-owned industry. This figure had fallen to 7.5% in 1987 and to just 1% in 1990. Over this period, the state changed from being an *owner* of industry or a *producer* of goods, and became a *regulator* of the private providers of the same goods. The issues associated with regulation are discussed in Chapter 22. This trend is world-wide. It has been estimated that between 1985 and 1993, governments in 100 countries raised some $328 billion by selling state-owned firms to private investors.[1] In September 1997, the Chinese government announced a wide-ranging privatisation programme, intending to transfer the ownership of thousands of state-owned companies to the private sector. The UK has played a pioneering role in this trend. By 1993, privatisation had raised £40 billion, and the figure is closer to £60 billion in 1996/7. In fact, the perceived success of the UK privatisation programme has been used to justify such programmes in other countries. To a certain extent, the UK model has become a paradigm for other privatisations.

We have emphasised that privatisation is a world-wide phenomenon and governments have reacted to a combination of the pressures illustrated in Figure 21.1. However, significant cross-national differences remain; in particular, privatisation has been implemented by governments of different political complexions. For

---

[1] See Adam *et al.* (1992) and the OECD reports (1993 and 1997) for a discussion of privatisation in developing and transition economies.

example, Britain and France have both been keen privatisers, yet they have had right-wing and socialist governments, respectively. Throughout the 1980s, Germany had a right-wing government, but only engaged in privatisation after reunification when it inherited thousands of former East German state-owned companies. Certainly in much of Europe (particularly the UK, France and Italy) there was a strong sense that social ownership had failed to deliver. Technological change meant that some industries lost their market power and so the justification for state ownership was lost as markets became globalised domestic industries began to face competition. It was also feared that, under state ownership, enterprises would not have access to the financial or capital resources which would allow them to take advantage of the advances in technology. A further pressure was the development of the Single European Market, which placed restrictions on the level of state aid to domestic industry. Wright (1994) discusses these issues, paying particular attention to the differences in scope, ambition and motivation between the privatisation programmes within Western Europe.

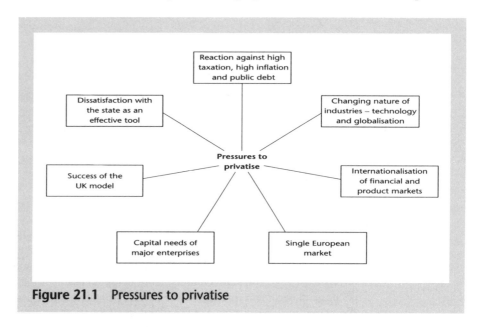

**Figure 21.1    Pressures to privatise**

## 21.2  Public or private ownership?

In this section, we will examine first the main efficiency issues associated with the debate of public or private ownership. We will then consider some of the more normative issues, including the political motivations which have been used to justify one form of ownership rather than another.

### Market power and efficiency

**Pareto efficiency**

Where best use is being made of available resources, $P = MC$

When firms have monopoly power, prices rise above marginal cost, $P > MC$, so the top-level condition for **Pareto efficiency** is no longer satisfied. Under monopoly, production will be lower and prices higher (see Figure 21.2); the shaded area reflects the loss of efficiency associated with a monopoly. However, there is another source of inefficiency which occurs outside of the competitive environment: firms may be under less pressure to control their costs. This is known as **X-inefficiency**. It is

**X-inefficiency**

Costs are higher due to the absence of competition or poor internal structure

therefore possible that two otherwise identical firms can have quite different costs because of internal management. X-inefficiency measures the gap between actual costs and the lowest possible costs. Figure 21.2 illustrates the existence of X-inefficiency under a monopoly; marginal costs rise from MC to MC'. These two sources of inefficiency have led to opposing policy outcomes: concern with the first has led to nationalisation and with the second to privatisation.

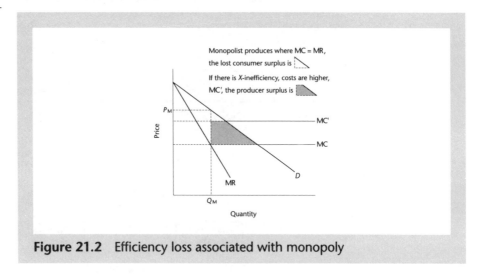

**Figure 21.2** Efficiency loss associated with monopoly

## Why do governments nationalise?

### Increasing returns to scale

Where there are increasing returns to scale, production cannot take place in a competitive environment. Instead we would expect to see the development of monopoly power, which as we saw in Figure 21.2, results in a loss of consumer surplus. **Natural monopolies** represent the extreme case, where only a sole supplier is desirable/viable because a single firm can produce a given level of output at a lower cost. Were the government to require efficiency, through marginal cost pricing, natural monopolies would make losses. However, under state ownership, the profit motive no longer dominates. The objectives of a state-owned enterprise will include low costs, low prices, universal access and high employment. Once a company is no longer constrained by profit maximisation and the government bears the cost of any losses, it is possible to impose marginal cost pricing. Therefore, nationalisation was seen as a way of preventing monopoly abuse in such cases.

**Natural monopoly**

Where a single supplier is the most efficient market structure

However, monopolies can also arise under constant or diminishing returns to scale due to anti-competitive behaviour and it is by no means clear that all monopolies should be taken into state ownership. In Table 21.1, we outline the implications of the competitive environment for government. Where a natural monopoly exists, competition is neither feasible nor desirable and regulation, perhaps through nationalisation, is needed. If monopoly occurs for other reasons, the response of government should be to encourage competition, where appropriate, and anti-monopoly regulation through competition policy.

In the UK, many state-owned industries were either single suppliers or dominant monopolies. But only the utilities, where the high fixed costs associated with the networks yielded increasing returns to scale, could be described as natural monopolies.

**Table 21.1**

|  |  | Is competition desirable? | |
|---|---|---|---|
|  |  | Yes | No |
| Is competition feasible? | Yes | **Competitive environment** No need for regulation | **Cream-skimming** Issue of sustainability. Should entry be encouraged? |
|  | No | **Monopoly abuse** Regulatory measures to protect against predatory behaviour | **Severe natural monopoly** Anti-monopoly regulation is the only check on firm's behaviour |

Source: Kay and Vickers, Figure 1, 1988

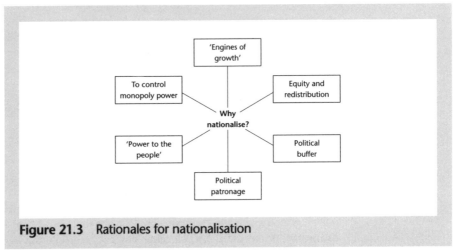

**Figure 21.3**   Rationales for nationalisation

Therefore dealing with market power is only one of many arguments used to justify social ownership (see Figure 21.3). We discuss some of the other main arguments below.

## Economic arguments

### Equity

Under private ownership, it will not always be considered economically viable to connect some consumers to the utility networks, perhaps because of low-income levels or rural location. There may also be little incentive for a private operator to run regular and reliable transport services in all areas of the country. Such issues would not constrain a state-owned enterprise, since universal access would be a goal under public ownership.[2] Greater equity may also be achieved through the pricing policies; for example, there is a single price for sending a letter within the UK, regardless of the very different costs associated with delivery. The same was true of telephone services (local calls are all charged at the same rate regardless of location, likewise

---

[2] Under state ownership, most homes receive the benefits of electricity and water services, although mainline gas has not always been available in rural areas and in the 1950s and 1960s many homes were not connected to the telephone network. Protection in terms of access to the network for those in rural or remote areas is explicitly made in the objectives of the telecommunications and water watchdogs, OFTEL and OFWAT (see Chapter 22).

national and international calls) and energy supply. State ownership gave protection, in terms of price and service provision, to those living in rural and remote areas.

### Employment

Under public ownership, employment levels can be higher because the firm is no longer constrained by the profit motive. This is justified on the grounds that it contributes towards the goal of full employment. A large element of the political consensus which existed for much of the post-war period was government responsibility for the pursuit of full employment. Until the late 1970s, management of the economy took account of this responsibility. Whilst the goal of full employment certainly influenced the development of macroeconomic policy, the policy areas where it had greatest impact were industrial and regional policies. Table 21.4 illustrates the high levels of employment in many of the nationalised industries.

### Macroeconomic policies

Public ownership not only enabled governments to pursue full employment and greater equality; industries were often managed to help governments achieve macroeconomic targets such as inflation. However, greater government intervention created difficulties for the enterprises by adding some confusion to their objectives. This was particularly evident during the 1970s when prices and incomes policies were used to control inflation. The public sector was one area in the economy where the government could impose these policies.

## Political arguments

### Political pressures

Socialists believe that capitalists are greedy and exploitative and that labour can only be protected though common ownership of the means of production. Portugal probably provides the best example outside of the former Communist economies of this more overtly political motive for nationalisation. An extensive nationalisation programme followed the 1974 revolution which saw the overthrow of the dictator Salazar. The public sector was given constitutional protection as 'an irreversible victory of the working class'. Other left-of-centre groups, such as the Liberals under David Lloyd George, also believe that state ownership provides the only means by which minimum standards and universal access to a service can be ensured.

There are other political pressures which explain the trend for nationalisation. State ownership can increase the political power of the government, simply because of the potential for political patronage. It is the government, or more likely a Minister of State, who makes appointments to positions within state-owned enterprises and this certainly extends the sphere of influence. Whilst political patronage may be used to further an individual's career, it may also be used to achieve political stability. As an owner of a public enterprise, the government can broker deals with trade unions or any other interest groups. Here the government is using public enterprise as a political buffer. This was often the justification for nationalisation within European countries, such as Belgium, which have religious divides. When a nationalised industry is used in this way, it is virtually impossible for the management to pursue long-term objectives.

### National security

Most nationalisations in the UK and Western Europe took place in the 1940s and 1950s, as part of the reconstruction of devastated economies. The coal, steel and transport industries were viewed as 'Engines of growth', and thus regarded as essential for the regeneration of the economy in the post-war period. Under government ownership, it was argued that these industries could be managed in a way to lead to widespread economic growth and prosperity.

The experience of the war years also served to emphasise the value to the economy and to the country of the coal, steel and railways industries. In times of national crisis, it seemed much more appropriate that these core industries should be owned by the state and that private enterprise should not be in a position to make excessive profits. Also of importance were the country's defence industries; companies such as the aircraft company Short Brothers and the aircraft components company Harland were taken into state ownership to protect the nation's defensive capabilities. In France, there was an additional motive. Several firms (including Renault) were nationalised as punishment to their owners who had been collaborators during the war.

## Why do governments privatise?

### X-inefficiency

It is argued that high prices, lack of profitability and poor service are the inevitable outcome of public ownership, where the state-owned industries are isolated from competitive pressures. Large organisations can become inefficient when they are too bureaucratic or have a poor internal structure, leading to higher costs (see Figure 21.3). Non-profit-maximising organisations can be more prone to X-inefficiency, for example, if the objectives of agents are to maximise influence or to build empires. This is one source of government failure discussed in Chapter 9. Privatisation is seen as one solution to the problem of X-inefficiency.

It seems that, in the case of natural monopolies, governments face a trade-off between the cost of monopoly abuse under private ownership and X-inefficiency under public ownership (the relationship between ownership and efficiency is examined below). Whilst public ownership provided governments with one method of dealing with monopoly abuse, it had led to X-inefficiency. Privatisation may eliminate the X-inefficiency, but the drawback was the degree of market power held by many of the nationalised industries. It is for this reason that regulation of post-privatisation activities may be required (this is discussed in Chapter 22).

There was a general sense that in the UK, the state-owned enterprises were extremely inefficient and too remote from market pressures. Employment levels and costs were high, and the management did not seem responsive to the demands and concerns of the consumer. Thus, a problem of X-inefficiency existed. When recalling a discussion concerning the corporate logo for British Telecom, Cecil Parkinson, the Secretary of State for Trade and Industry at the time of privatisation in 1984, referred to the joke that the logo should represent several telecom vans parked at the side of the road in the mid-afternoon waiting to go home rather than attend another job. This joke certainly had some resonance, not only in the case of the telecommunications industry.

Privatisation was, as shown in Figure 21.4, motivated not only by concerns of efficiency, but also financial and ideological arguments.

### Public finances

A major motive for privatisation was to reduce public borrowing. However, the transfer of assets meant that, whereas previously profits made by these firms

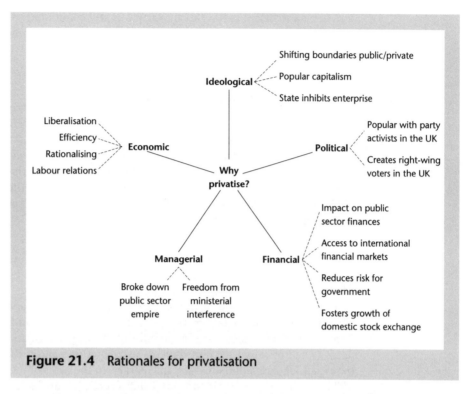

**Figure 21.4** Rationales for privatisation

contributed to government revenue, they would now accrue to private-sector share-holders, although this was of little concern, notably where profits were low or the firm was making a loss. In the UK, the Public Sector Borrowing Requirement (PSBR) was a key strand of the Conservative government's 'medium term financial strategy'. The proceeds from privatisation, which were quite large, particularly in the second half of the 1980s when the utilities were privatised, helped the government to reduce public borrowing.

## Political motives

*Free market ideology*
Virtually all government intervention was seen as unwelcome. The state was blamed for blunting incentives and preventing entrepreneurship.

*Share-owning democracy*
It is also argued that the nation's economic performance would be enhanced if employees and consumers were also shareholders. By extending share ownership and in particular by encouraging employees to become shareholders of the company within which they were employed, more people would have a stake in industry. The anticipated effect of this was greater corporate pride, as well as added incentives for efficiency and labour productivity. Also, people were being given a choice. They were no longer *de facto* shareholders through the process of social ownership, but investors who exercised the choice to invest.

*Political gain*
A further political benefit is that those who benefited from the sales became loyal supporters. In the UK, privatisation was very popular with Conservative Party

activists, particularly as the Labour Party was still committed to renationalisation at the selling price and had no intention of compensating shareholders for the post-privatisation gain in share value.

## 21.3 Ownership, incentives and efficiency

It has been argued that the problems of X-inefficiency can be overcome through private ownership. In fact, we shall see that the change in ownership may improve the set of tools to overcome agency or delegation problems that are available to a firm. But, without increasing the degree of competition within the industry, little progress towards economic efficiency will be made. Merely changing the nature of ownership may not deliver benefits.

### Competition

Whilst some socially owned enterprises were operating in industries where competition existed, many, including the utilities, were statutory monopolies. The transfer of ownership from the public to the private sector does not on its own change the competitive environment. In the absence of existing competition, the government needs to address any legal impediments to competition and consider whether incentives exist for competitors to enter the market. In the cases of the utilities, the extent of their market power, both horizontal and vertical, is a major barrier to entry. Hence, the structure of the industry at the time of privatisation is a key consideration (see Chapter 22 for further discussion). Martin and Parker (1997) in their extensive analysis of the relationship between ownership and efficiency suggest that the outcomes under private/public ownership and the extremes of market conditions can be ranked as follows: A > B > C > D.

|  | Monopoly | Competition |
| --- | --- | --- |
| Public ownership | D | B |
| Private ownership | C | A |

*Agency problems*

**Agency problems**

Associated with delegation, where the objectives of the parties involved diverge and it is not possible to monitor actions perfectly

In Chapter 6, we discussed the **agency problems** that can arise when the Principal (P) delegates a task to an Agent (A). Since P cannot perfectly monitor the actions of A, it is unlikely that P's objective is maximised. The extent to which it is possible to overcome agency problems will reflect the ease with which we can define and measure the goals of the Principal (see Figure 21.5). Where the Principal has a simple goal, this can be used to measure performance and encourage appropriate actions on the part of the Agent. In the case of an employment relationship between the Principal and the Agent, the career structure will also be relevant. If the Agent's job is insecure, perhaps future employment is dependent upon present performance, or where the possibility of promotion exists, it may be easier to overcome the agency problems. Alternatively, in a situation where employment is certain (a job for life) or the career structure is flat, the Principal has fewer tools. Here, the Principal may need to rely on the Agent sharing some of the Principal's objectives. Let us now consider the link between ownership and agency problems.

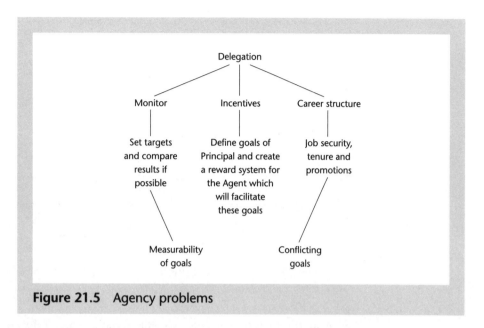

**Figure 21.5** Agency problems

*Private sector*

The goal or objective of private-sector firms is typically to maximise profit. Therefore, in the private sector the problems of delegation can be overcome when pay is related to profits or stock options are offered. But similar solutions to agency problems are not readily found in the public sector. This view is contested. The first objection is that these solutions are rarely effective. At issue is that the schemes are not sensitive enough to individual effort and that there are many workers and organisations who are unwilling to take up such schemes. Also, trade unions have been very sceptical, suggesting that asymmetries of information concerning the firm's performance may lead to exploitation of the workers. Second, it is argued that efficiency and improved performance are brought about from staff development through training, better internal communications and developing cooperative decision-making. Finally, private-sector managers may have more discretion than their public-sector counterparts to pursue their own objectives, such as salary maximisation. This suggests that some agency problems may be more acute in the private sector.

*Public sector*

The agency problems within state-owned enterprise are usually more complex than those in the private sector. Within the private sector, the management itself is only answerable to the shareholders and the employment relationship involves the management and the employees. The relationship is not always this simple in the public sector, where there is a more complex chain of P–A relationships (see Figure 21.6).

In addition, publicly owned enterprises may have a variety of goals, such as low costs, full employment and greater equity. Not only does the Principal's objective include a number of goals but the importance or emphasis attached to each may change over time. Thus it may be difficult to overcome agency problems in the public sector. However, there are further concerns, the first being that the goals may not be mutually consistent. For example, if a publicly owned enterprise is pursuing full employment, it cannot at the same time be minimising costs. Equally, the pursuit of low prices and high quality may be contradictory goals. Second, it may be difficult to

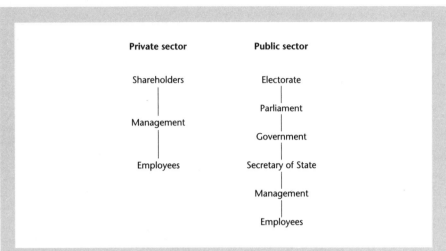

**Figure 21.6** Private and public sector chains of command

measure the goals of a socially owned enterprise. Should the enterprise simply aim to maximise the size of its workforce, attempt to minimise total, marginal or average costs, or charge lower and lower prices? How can distributional goals be measured and then incorporated within a socially owned industry? A third concern, raised in the public choice literature, is the motives of the public officials. Are they really as Herbert Morrison, one of the architects of nationalisation, hoped 'high custodians of the public interest' or are they self-interested? Do they perhaps compensate for relatively poor salaries with a quiet life, or seek to maximise the size of their budget? Experience suggests that even if managers in the public sector seek to maximise their budget, there is no evidence that they have been successful in doing so. Finally, job security is a key issue. Since managers are employed by the shareholders, poor managerial performance will result in replacement of the incumbent management. Employment in the public sector was typically very secure, which could lead in some circumstances to complacency and low productivity. This was certainly a concern in the managed economies in the former Soviet bloc. However, perhaps in contrast to the private sector, public-sector employees often share the objectives of their employers and may be very committed to the public-service ethos.

To summarise, although theory suggests that it may be easier to overcome agency problems in the private sector, in practice very few private-sector employers use profit-related pay. Figures from the British Institute of Management revealed that by the early 1990s, only 36% of management held shares in their companies (although other incentives such as promotion may be used more effectively in the private sector). Instead, performance targets are regularly set in both the private and the public sector, aiming to improve efficiency. For example, sales targets, the number of contacts made and production targets are all commonly used in the private sector, while the public sector may set goals such as raising literacy and numeracy rates and reducing the length of waiting lists, although many are critical of the meaning and value of some of the targets set in the areas of education and health. Also, although levels of effort do enter individuals' utility functions with a negative sign, other factors such as professional pride and satisfaction associated with a job well done or peer-group recognition add to utility. This suggests that agency problems may be overstated.

### Fear of takeover

A low stock-market valuation makes the organisation vulnerable to takeover. Raider firms can buy shares at a price below their potential value, replace the management and benefit from improved subsequent performance. Since public-sector firms are not floated on the Stock Exchange, their management is not subject to the same pressure.

To understand the dynamics at work, let us assume that current profits $\pi_L$ are lower than potential profits $\pi_H$; a raider firm would offer $b$, $\pi_L < b < \pi_H$. However, other factors may be relevant. If the share ownership is diverse, individual shareholders may attempt to free-ride by not selling their shares. If they assume that the raider bid will be successful, they have an incentive to hold onto their shares. If all shareholders rationalise their actions in this way, none will sell up and the raider bid will fail.

In fact, the capital market can only act as an effective constraint on management if there is close to full information and minimal transaction costs. If the costs of making a bid are $t$, then the gap between potential profits and the bid price must be large enough to ensure gains to the raider firm ($\pi_H - b > t$). Inertia, along with the transaction costs of trading shares, may mean that funds are not moved, even when a higher return could be earned elsewhere.

Institutional differences may also influence the effectiveness of the capital markets in ensuring managerial efficiency. If there is a maximum shareholding, for example, or limits are placed on the level of foreign ownership, a raider may not be able to purchase sufficient shares to take over control of the firm. Alternatively, if the government retains a sizeable share in privatised companies, although it may improve accountability, it also removes the pressures towards efficiency created by the capital market. Another aspect is the ability of managers to protect themselves against the possibility of unwanted takeovers through 'golden parachutes'. If the management has already negotiated a generous compensation scheme in the event of redundancy, the attractiveness of replacing them may not be as great.

This is not to say that takeovers will not occur. Empirical evidence on the relationship between takeovers and profitability is mixed. Studies by Singh (1975) and Firth (1979) found small differences in profitability and financial performance between firms that have been taken over and those which have not. Singh also found that larger firms were much less likely to be taken over. This certainly casts doubt on the effectiveness of this mechanism for ensuring managerial efficiency, particularly in large industries, such as the utilities. More recent evidence from Franks and Harris (1989) suggests that firms involved in takeover bids do have improved financial performance, but that this may simply be a signal of increased market share. They also find that the increase in the share value of the firm which is taken over tends to be short-lived. This raises some concern about the effect of the capital market on the strategies pursued by private firms. The fear of takeover may lead to short-termism. Given the knowledge that the investment that might be needed for growth and innovations may diminish current profits and the share value, managers may seek to ensure their own employment and maximise short-run rather than long-run profits.

### Threat of bankruptcy

Firms borrowing in the private sector compete for finance and so are subject to pressure to make cost-effective investment schemes. Failure to do this could lead to bankruptcy. In the public sector, firms borrow from the government with no threat of bankruptcy. There may be some limited competition for finance with other socially owned enterprises, but, unlike the private finance market, the government will not just finance the most profitable investment schemes. The criteria used to judge public-sector investment will often differ from those used in the private sector, as we saw in Chapter 7. Typically in its cost–benefit analysis, the government will apply a social rate of return which is lower than the private rate of return, and take account of externalities and intergenerational effects. As a consequence, there is no expectation that a public-sector project will break even or make profits within the lifetime of normal private-sector projects.

There are limits to the likely impact of a competitive credit market upon the performance of a privatised, once state-owned, industry. It is unlikely to transform the industry. One reason is that government would be unwilling to allow important industries to go into bankruptcy, particularly since in the past this was a justification for state involvement; the threat of bankruptcy is not a reality.

To summarise, in this section we have discussed a number of arguments which suggest that, under private ownership, firms are likely to be more efficient because they have better incentive structures. Not only do the goals of private-sector firms and the career structures of those employed make it easier to implement payment systems which overcome agency problems, but also the financial environment within the private sector is also more likely to ensure efficient management and more profitable investment. However, we have also seen that many of the pressures (the threat of takeover or bankruptcy) are unlikely to bear heavily on privatised utilities and that whilst in theory agency problems could be overcome by using profit or share options, these are rarely used in the private sector. Performance is assessed in both the public and the private sector, although the criteria used may often be different. For example, it may be appropriate to compare the financial profitability of some public-sector investment with those made in the private sector, but not so in other cases.

## 21.4 The privatisation process in the UK

In the introduction, attention was drawn to the magnitude of the privatisation process in the UK. The value of assets transferred from the public to the private sector between 1979 and 1996/7 is estimated at £60 billion. From Table 21.2, we see that in the first Thatcher administration, 1979–83, the annual value of privatisation was relatively low at round £0.5–1 billion. The privatisations in these years were generally partial sales and included sales of shares in several oil companies (BP, Britoil and Enterprise Oil), Cable and Wireless and council housing (this is not represented in Table 21.2 because the sales were not in large tranches, although they were sizeable; over half a million council homes were sold between 1979 and 1983). These were sales of assets into competitive markets. During the mid-1980s, the second and third Thatcher administrations, the privatisation programme was much more ambitious and the annual revenue raised considerably greater, around £5 billion. These privatisations included BT, the utility companies (gas, electricity and water). British Rail was privatised under the Major government. These were all monopolies and required considerable regulation. The government did incur costs with each privatisation: advertising and employing banks to allocate the shares. These costs also rose with the size of the companies being privatised.

At the time of each privatisation, the government passed an Act of Parliament. The Acts outlined the intention to privatise, established an industry regulator or watchdog, and granted the licences to operate within an industry. Regulation is discussed in Chapter 22. Here we focus on how the change in ownership occurred and whether the programme achieved the stated objectives.

The main choices facing the government concerning the method of privatisation are summarised in Figure 21.7. The first choice relates to the post-privatisation structure of the company being privatised: should it retain its monopoly status or be split up? A company which maintains its monopoly status is likely to be a more attractive investment because it will achieve high profits post-privatisation but this raises concerns over efficiency. The incumbent management are likely to prefer this option too. However, a government which is keen to improve efficiency and to introduce competition would restructure where possible. The second choice relates to the method of sale of the assets. In making this choice the government is likely to have the following concerns: the revenue raised, the number of new shareholders that are created and the distribution of the new shares; it is important to remember that privatisation results in a transfer of an asset which is commonly owned to a much smaller number of private owners. If the government wishes to maximise revenue, then it should engage in an bidding process and sell the company to the buyer offering the highest price. This is likely to result in a small number of owners of the privatised company and would be the least equitable outcome. If instead the government is interested in achieving the most equitable outcome and maximising

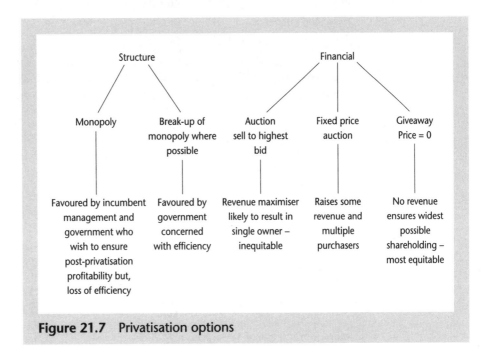

**Figure 21.7** Privatisation options

the number of new shareholders, it should give away the shares, although this will not raise revenue. A third option is to fix the price and then sell the shares as widely as possible, although this will result in a loss in equity. This is the option largely taken by the UK government.

**Table 21.2**

| Company | Date | Proceeds £ million | Expenses £ million | Expenses % of proceeds |
|---|---|---|---|---|
| BP | Nov. 79 | 290 | – | – |
| British Aerospace | Feb. 81 | 149 | 6 | 3.8 |
| Cable and Wireless | Nov. 81 | 224 | 7 | 3.1 |
| Amersham International | Feb. 82 | 63 | 3 | 4.6 |
| Britoil | Nov. 82 | 548 | 17 | 3.2 |
| Associated British Ports | Feb. 83 | 22 | 2 | 11.2 |
| BP | Sept. 83 | 565 | – | – |
| Cable and Wireless | Dec. 83 | 224 | – | – |
| Enterprise Oil | July 84 | 393 | 11 | 2.8 |
| Associated British Ports | April 84 | 52 | – | – |
| Jaguar | Aug. 84 | 294 | – | – |
| British Telecom | Dec. 84 | 3,920 | 263 | 6.8 |
| British Aerospace | May 85 | 550 | – | – |
| Britoil | Aug. 85 | 450 | – | – |
| Cable and Wireless | Dec. 85 | 600 | – | – |
| TSB | Oct. 86 | 1,360 | – | – |
| British Gas | Dec. 86 | 5,600 | 360 | 6.4 |
| British Airways | Feb. 87 | 900 | 42 | 4.7 |
| Rolls-Royce | May 87 | 1,360 | 29 | – |
| BAA | July 87 | 1,280 | 43 | 3.4* |
| BP | Oct. 87 | 7,200 | – | – |
| British Steel | Dec. 88 | 2,500 | 46 | 1.8 |
| 10 Water authorities | Nov. 89 | 5,400 | 131 | 2.5 |
| 12 Electricity companies | Nov. 90 | 5,180 | 191 | 2.4 |
| National Power/Powergen | July 91 | 2,100 | 79 | 2.7 |
| Scottish Power | March 91 | 2,900 | 98 | 2.8 |
| Trust Ports | 1992 | – | – | – |
| Coal industry | 1995 | – | – | – |
| Railways | 1995–7 | – | – | – |
| Nuclear energy | 1996 | – | – | – |

\* Excluding £53.9m cost of bonus share.    – not available
Source: Jackson and Price, Tables 2.2 and 2.7, 1994

## Floating shares

**Flotation**

Process of selling shares in a company

The method typically used was a general **flotation**, where bids for the number of shares were invited at an announced price. Since one aim of privatisation was to encourage wider share ownership, priority was given to smaller bids and employees were given special treatment. One difficulty with this approach was how the sale price was reached. This was the first time that many of these assets were being floated, many were monopolists, so there was no existing share price nor the price of a similar organisation that could be used as a guideline. Many argued that prices were far too low, thus reducing the value of the sale to the government.[3] It was even suggested that the prices were deliberately set low in order to ensure the success of the programme. In Table 21.3, there is some evidence to support the claim that shares were underpriced. We can see the percentage gains made by shareholders on the first day of trading. Gains were particularly great in the case of BT, the first major privatisation.

Another concern is the impact of privatisation on the distribution of income and wealth. At each privatisation, assets that had been communally held were transferred into the hands of the few who could buy them. Vickers and Yarrow (1988) refer to Samuel Brittan writing in the *Financial Times*, who argued that rather than selling BT and British Gas, the government should have given every adult a share in each. Such a scheme would sidestep the need to arrive at a share price and would ensure that post-privatisation each person would retain the same share in these assets. Of course under the Brittan scheme, privatisation would raise a lower revenue.

Alternatives to this method of flotation include share tenders or bids, the advantage being that the shares would be sold at a rate close to the value placed on the assets by the market. However, it is likely that the buyers would be exclusively institutional investors, a disadvantage in the eyes of the government, given their desire to develop popular capitalism. Also, there is no assurance that the offers would be close to the true value. Vickers and Yarrow (1988) quote from the 'Lex' column in the *Financial Times*, 16 February 1987, 'Naturally the funds name the lowest price that does not beggar belief and frequently get away with it'. Probably the most reliable method would be to sell the assets in smaller tranches. Although there would still be difficulties associated with setting the initial selling price, once sold, a market value would be established which could be used as a benchmark price for later sales. Table 21.2 shows that this is the method used in the cases of BP and Cable and Wireless.

## The golden share

**Golden share**

Where government retains the majority shareholding

The **golden share** is where the government retains a sizeable shareholding in the privatised industry. The desire to hold a golden share is often explained in terms of the politics of national identity, i.e. ensuring that the asset cannot fall under foreign control. There are other arguments; for example, some agency problems can be overcome when there is a single large shareholder or the regulation of a privatised industry is easier if the government retains a substantial shareholding. Currently the government holds a 'golden share' in eighteen of the privatised firms in the UK. In some industries, such as BP, the government has sold its remaining shareholding.

---

[3] This is the conclusion of the National Audit Commission. They argue that the government should have made provisions to 'claw-back' some of the post-privatisation gains in value. In their report on the sale of the railway rolling stock, they found that many of the companies which bought the rolling stock from the government were resold at a substantial profit within six months of privatisation.

**Table 21.3**

| Company | Sale price (p) | Opening price | % Gain |
|---|---|---|---|
| British Gas | 50 | 62.5 | 25 |
| British Telecom | 50 | 93.0 | 86 |
| TSB | 50 | 85.5 | 71 |
| British Airways | 65 | 109.0 | 68 |
| Rolls-Royce | 85 | 147.0 | 73 |
| BAA | 100 | 146.0 | 46 |
| *Water Companies* | | | |
| Anglian Water | 100 | 140.0 | 40 |
| Northumbrian Water | 100 | 168.0 | 68 |
| Severn Water | 100 | 135.0 | 35 |
| Southern Water | 100 | 141.0 | 41 |
| Thames Water | 100 | 140.0 | 40 |
| Welsh Water | 100 | 138.0 | 38 |
| Wessex Water | 100 | 148.0 | 48 |
| Yorkshire Water | 100 | 143.0 | 43 |
| *Electricity Companies* | | | |
| Eastern Electricity | 100 | 147.0 | 47 |
| East Midland Electricity | 100 | 164.0 | 64 |
| London Electricity | 100 | 151.0 | 51 |
| Manweb | 100 | 176.0 | 76 |
| Midland Electricity | 100 | 157.0 | 57 |
| Northern Electricity | 100 | 155.0 | 55 |
| Norweb | 100 | 153.0 | 53 |
| Southern Electricity | 100 | 153.0 | 53 |
| South Wales Electricity | 100 | 163.0 | 63 |
| South West Electricity | 100 | 158.0 | 58 |
| Yorkshire Electricity | 100 | 170.0 | 70 |
| *Electricity Generation Companies* | | | |
| National Power | 100 | 119.0 | 19 |
| PowerGen | 100 | 126.0 | 26 |
| Scottish Power/Hydro-electric | 100 | 120.0 | 20 |

Source: Jackson and Price, Table 2.6, 1994

## Franchising and contracting-out

These schemes offer an alternative to the sale of shares in public enterprises, while still transferring the responsibility for supplying the good or service from the public to the private sector. Under a franchise, the government sells to a private company the right to supply a market. For example, the UK government sells to private companies the rights to run commercial television stations. The market is still regulated. In the case of television, there are quality controls on programmes and regulations governing the timing and length of news broadcasts. Under a franchise, licencing rights are usually granted to the highest bidder, although the government may dismiss excessively high bids on the grounds that they are over-optimistic or unrealistic.[4] Contracting-out or tendering has typically been used by local authorities in the areas of catering, cleaning and refuse collection. Here local government pays the private company to perform a service, and private firms compete to offer the best price. The contract is usually awarded to the company that offers the lowest price, although again some quality constraints may be stipulated.

Contracting-out or tendering has a direct effect on public-sector employment. Once the department or authority decides to contract out a service, those already employed cease to be public-sector employees and are often required to apply for the same jobs with the private employer. In many cases, this change of status is accompanied by changes in the employment package as a whole, affecting working times, holiday entitlements and fringe benefits.

To summarise, in the UK there is evidence that the shares in privatised industries were underpriced, so the method chosen to float the shares in the privatised companies did not maximise revenue for the government. However, we argued that a government concerned with equity would not wish to maximise privatisation proceeds, it would instead ensure that all households retained a shareholding in the privatised companies, just as they 'owned' the nationalised company. But this did not happen either. The shares were underpriced and sold to a small number of households, representing poor value for money for the state and a transfer in wealth from the many to the few. Finally, most of the companies sold were monopolies, so the UK government missed an opportunity to ensure a more efficient outcome.

## 21.5 The impact of privatisation in the UK

Privatisation has had a number of consequences for the role of the state within the economy and the performance of industries (see Figure 21.8). Our main interest will lie in the impact of the change in ownership upon efficiency.

### Social ownership and efficiency

There are problems in comparing the performance of public- and private-sector industries. Thus it is important to take a range of measures: profits, total factor productivity and labour productivity. We would expect profits to be higher in the private sector, since privately owned companies are profit maximisers, but this measure alone does not provide conclusive evidence that the private sector is more efficient than the public sector. A further problem is in the type of comparisons made, for example, whether it is possible to assess the efficiency of a nationalised industry when it is also a monopoly and there is no meaningful comparison to be made in the private sector.

---

[4] In the case of TV franchises, the companies, particularly those new to broadcasting, may overestimate the likely advertising revenue.

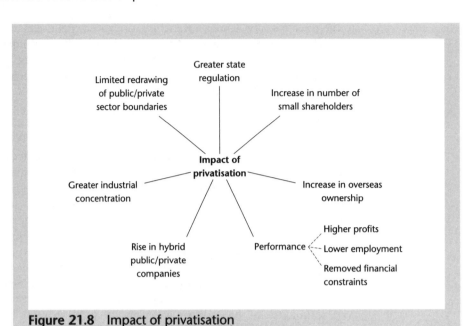

**Figure 21.8** Impact of privatisation

In the UK, nationalised industries were given a set of objectives: impose marginal cost pricing, break even and make a reasonable return on investment. These objectives were set out and financial regulation was tightened over the 1960s and 1970s in a series of White Papers. However, the White Papers did not prioritise the objectives of a socially owned enterprise, nor did they seek to limit ministerial or political interference. Instead, the White Papers attempted to replicate the conditions of a competitive financial market. In 1961, financial targets and rates of return on new investment were introduced, but there was no discussion of how to meet these objectives. Therefore, the industries could either meet the targets by improving efficiency and reducing costs or they could increase prices or use cross-subsidisation. Some of these issues were addressed in the 1967 White Paper, where goals were set for marginal cost pricing and cross-subsidisation was discouraged. The financial targets were set more precisely, for firms rather than industries, and a required rate of return of 8% was set on new investment. Problems remained because of the difficulties associated with monitoring, measuring and enforcing these targets. Also, nothing was done to reduce ministerial interference. In the 1978 White Paper, the importance of marginal cost pricing was reduced, the required rate of return was reduced to 5% and external financing limits (which restricted net indebtedness to government) were introduced.

The following performance table is taken from Vickers and Yarrow (1988). At the time of the election of Margaret Thatcher, the nationalised industries were major employers (see Table 21.4). Comparing the performance of these industries in the years before and after her election, we also see that productivity did improve; both total factor productivity and labour productivity rose. In the period leading up to privatisation, employment fell in many of the nationalised industries. Under the Chairmanship of Lord King in 1979–80, BA cut its workforce by one-third and this accounted for approximately 25% of the redundancies made in the London area in that year.

**Table 21.4**

| | Employment (thousands) 1978–9 | Output per head % per annum | | Total factor productivity % per annum | |
|---|---|---|---|---|---|
| | | 1968–78 | 1978–85 | 1968–78 | 1978–85 |
| British Rail | 243 | 0.8 | 3.9 | – | 2.8 |
| British Steel | 190 | –0.2 | 12.6 | –2.5 | 2.9 |
| Post Office | 411 | –1.3 | 2.3 | – | 1.9 |
| British Telecom | – | 8.2 | 5.8 | 5.2 | 0.5 |
| British Coal | 300 | –0.7 | 4.4 | –1.4 | 0.0 |
| Electricity | 160 | 5.3 | 3.9 | 0.7 | 1.4 |
| British Gas | 102 | 8.5 | 3.8 | – | 1.2 |
| National Bus | 64 | –0.5 | 2.1 | –1.4 | 0.1 |
| British Airways | 58 | 6.4 | 6.6 | 5.5 | 4.8 |
| UK manufacturing | – | 2.7 | 3.0 | 1.7 | – |

– Not available.
Source: Vickers and Yarrow, Tables 5.3 and 5.7, 1988

Vickers and Yarrow (1988) also show that profitability of the nationalised industries was low when compared to the private sector. The level of debt was high, although this was falling over the 1970s and by 1985 there was actually a surplus. This surplus may have arisen from reduction in wasteful investment (investment fell slightly in the late 1970s and in the early 1980s)and productivity gains. Wright (1994) argues that, across Europe, the performance of the public sector since the early 1980s has shown that it is possible to transform their performances. Nationalised industries, notably the steel and coal industries, were restructured and reduced their labour force. Moreover, productivity growth in many nationalised industries has exceeded that of the private sector. These improvements may in part be due to impending privatisation or the credible threat of privatisation.

## Privatisation and efficiency

The more specific question of whether the performance of the privatised industries has improved after privatisation is very important. Parker (1994) considers the issue of ownership status and performance in the UK, posing the question, did performance change as expected? In most cases, Parker finds that performance has moved in the direction suggested by theory. However, Martin and Parker (1997) in their extensive survey of studies of efficiency, including international studies and studies of the UK privatised industries, find no conclusive evidence that one form of ownership is more efficient than the other. An international study conducted by the World Bank in 1993 (Golal and Shirley, 1993) compared the performance of three privatised industries in four different countries. The authors found that in eleven cases privatisation resulted in increases in wealth. But, they conclude that the change in ownership only produces superior outcome if it occurs in conjunction with increased competition and close regulation.

## Privatisation and market structure

The Conservative governments were aware of the importance of introducing competition into the privatised industries. Kay *et al.* (1986) cite two speeches made by John Moore, Financial Secretary to the Treasury, as evidence of this: 'Our main objective is to promote competition and improve efficiency' (November 1983) and 'The long-term success of the privatisation programme will stand or fall by the extent to which it maximises competition' (July 1985).

As noted above, the early privatisations were of companies that operated in competitive markets. This was not changed by privatisation. Market structure was a much more important issue in the cases of the utility companies, since they were natural monopolies. Both BT and British Gas were privatised as single enterprises, but there was some restructuring of the electricity, water and rail industries. In fact, the government avoided restructuring as a sweetener to the incumbent management. It was essential that the scheme received support from within, since the same group of managers would run the privatised industries.

In the case of BT, only one competitor (Mercury) was given a licence to operate in the telecommunications industry. This duopoly, in which BT was the dominant partner controlling over 90% of the market, was brought to an end by the White Paper in 1991. Since then many operators have been allowed to enter the market, taking advantage of the technological revolution in the industry, offering phone services using cables, radio waves, satellites and electricity cables. In this case, at the time of privatisation in 1984, BT had a natural monopoly advantage created by its ownership of the network of telephone lines. However, as technology has advanced, alternatives to the BT lines have become available and BT has lost its natural monopoly. The gas industry remains dominated by British Gas. At the point of regulation, British Gas was the sole supplier. The legislation changed in 1990 to allow other suppliers into the market. By September 1997 there were fifteen suppliers operating in parts of the south-west and south-east of the UK.

By the time that the remaining utility industries were privatised, the government was more confident of the success of the process itself, but it was forced to respond to criticism that earlier privatisations had simply transferred monopoly power from the public sector to large private companies. Both the electricity and water industries were restructured to create regional or area supply companies and separate generation companies in the case of electricity. By establishing regional companies, the government also made yardstick competition and regulation possible. British Rail was also restructured; the natural monopoly element is owned by a single company, Railtrack, but passenger services are franchised out.[5]

A further concern is that the activities of some of the privatised companies have led to a strengthening of their market position. For example, shortly after privatisation BA bought its major UK competitor and BT enhanced its vertical integration with the purchase of a manufacturer of telephone exchange systems and has sought to strengthen its global position through merger with a US telecommunications company.[6] These developments raise questions about the regulation of privatised companies. Not only have industry watchdogs been established to perform this function,

---

[5] There are distinct groups of franchisees: local services, intercity services and open access, all discussed further in Chapter 22.

[6] There have also been mergers between regional water companies and between regional water and electricity companies. All were subject to Monopolies and Mergers Commission (MMC) investigations.

but the activities of the post-privatisation companies are also subject to national and sometimes European competition authorities. These issues are discussed in Chapter 22.

## Other effects

### Privatisation and popular capitalism

To assess the success of the privatisation programmes in achieving popular capitalism, it is necessary to consider how many shareholders retain shares and after privatisation for how long. Table 21.5 shows that most shareholders of privatised companies sold their shares within a year of purchase. The results seem to support the view that many shareholders took advantage of privatisations as a means of making a quick but large return on a small investment (see Table 21.3 for the premiums on share prices and % gains made on the opening day of trading). Evidence from the 1990 General Household Survey also indicates that privatisation did not result in widespread share ownership. After the privatisation programmes of the 1980s, only 6% of unskilled manual workers (compared with 43% of professionals) and 7% of council tenants (compared with 53% of home owners) were shareholders. Home ownership is another indicator of popular capitalism. This increased throughout the 1980s; by the early 1990s more than 70% of homes were owner occupied. Much of this has occurred due to the policy of selling council houses to tenants. Overall, whilst there was some growth in popular capitalism, privatisation has resulted in a transfer of assets towards the middle classes and contributed towards a widening of the distribution of income and wealth.

**Table 21.5**

| Company | % of original shareholders holding shares a year after privatisation |
| --- | --- |
| Amersham International | 13.2 |
| British Telecom | 73.6 |
| BAA | 48.7 |
| British Gas | 70.6 |
| British Airways | 38.2 |
| Jaguar | 43.3 |
| Associated British Ports | 34.4 |
| Enterprise Oil | 103.3 |
| Rolls-Royce | 46.2 |
| 12 electricity companies | 40 |
| Scottish Power | 67 |

Source: Jackson and Price, Table 2.5, 1994

### Increase in overseas ownership

Several of the regional water and electricity boards are owned by the French company Lyonnaise des Eaux, S.A. This pattern is not only in the direction of overseas ownership in the UK. UK companies, most notably BT, also own shares in overseas utilities.

### Changes in corporate culture

Privatisation has meant that the firms are no longer constrained by the statutes of nationalised companies. It has given the firms the freedom to expand their markets and take advantage of globalisation in both product and finance markets. In many instances, the privatised firms have also diversified their activities. Water companies now have interests in the leisure industry and the electricity industry is developing telecommunications technology. The companies now attempt to sell themselves not only nationally through advertising, but also using their images as major international operators. In the process, companies have been transformed from ailing nationalised companies to world leaders. While this is a source of national pride, there is public unease associated with the market power and the accompanying profits of these companies, some fear and scepticism created by their diversifications and most particularly the salaries paid to their directors.

### Privatisation of welfare

**Privatising welfare**

Where measures have been taken to encourage individuals to provide for themselves, rather than relying upon the state

In the UK, governments have pursued policies which have been described as **privatising welfare**, but welfare provision has not been privatised in the same sense as BT or BA. The responsibility for social security and social policy has not been transferred to the private sector; the government remains the major provider. However, over the last twenty years its monopoly status has been challenged and a more pluralist system of welfare provision now exists; the private and voluntary sectors are increasingly involved. Evidence for this can be found in the increasing numbers covered by private health insurance and private pensions. However, the private sector has shown an unwillingness to offer comprehensive coverage, tending only to 'cream-skim', particularly in the areas of health where the cost of private insurance is extremely costly for the chronically or seriously ill and the elderly. The response of the voluntary sector has also been circumspect. The voluntary sector tends to represent interest groups and is often community-based. It has been reluctant to extend its services. In addition it has not been ready to enter into arrangements whereby its activities are subject to close state scrutiny or to become dependent upon the state for funds.

Whilst extending the nature of the providers of welfare services has increased choice, and in the case of community projects brought a closer link between the providers and recipients, there are some concerns. The first relates to the problems of the extent of geographic coverage. Provision may be extensive in large urban areas, but patchy in rural ones. The second is that such a system leaves a residual role for government, e.g. in education, health, housing and personal services, which is likely to be concentrated on the unprofitable and unattractive services for the poor, thus establishing a two-tier welfare system, which would take the UK much closer to the US model.

The proposal that people should be given the option to transfer out of SERPS[7] into private pensions was more successful, both in terms of the participation of the private sector and the numbers who chose to opt out.[8] There was a double incentive to opt out of SERPS: tax benefits were offered to those who opted out and the value of SERPS was reduced.

---

[7] SERPS is the State Earnings-Related Pension Scheme and this is discussed in more detail in Chapter 18.
[8] Associated with this, however, has been the problem of mis-selling pensions. This is briefly discussed in Chapter 22.

Other examples of privatisation within the welfare system include competitive tendering within the NHS and local authority services, especially cleaning, catering and refuse, and the establishment of quasi-markets in the areas of health and education (see Chapters 19 and 20). Perhaps the biggest change has occurred in the area of local authority housing. The Conservative government not only extended the 'Right to buy' for council tenants, but it also introduced legislation which gave tenants the right to transfer management of housing estates from local authorities to housing associations.

## 21.6 Conclusion

Privatisation has had a number of consequences for the role of the state within the economy and the performance of the industries involved. The state is no longer an owner of the means of production; it is instead a regulator of the activities of the newly privatised companies. This role as a regulator is particularly important in the cases of the utilities, where the company is a natural monopolist. The exact scope of regulation is discussed in Chapter 22, but our discussion in this chapter has shown that privatisation has not so much reduced the role of the state in the economy, rather has redefined it.

## Summary

- Privatisation world-wide between 1985 and 1993 has resulted in a transfer of assets from the public to the private sector worth approximately $328 billion.

- The UK has played a pioneering role. Between 1979 and 1996, the value of privatisation in the UK was close to £60 billion.

- Economic efficiency is one of a number of motives for privatisation. Others are ideological (shareholder democracy) or political (reducing government debt).

- The form of the privatisation process is itself a compromise between achieving these goals, ensuring that potential investors will purchase shares, and obtaining the support of the incumbent management.

- The privatisation of natural monopolies raises the important issue of a new regulatory role for government.

- Privatisation has certainly resulted in much more profitable enterprises. Without the introduction of competition, it is not clear that efficiency gains would have been made.

## Questions

1. What (a) according to positive economics and (b) according to normative economics, would be the main reasons for social ownership?

2. What (a) according to positive economics and (b) according to normative economics, would be the main reasons for privatisation?

3. Are agency problems easier to overcome in the private sector?

4. Critically assess the likely effect of a competitive financial market on the behaviour of private firms.

5. When a government is privatising, what are the main options for floating shares? Which should the government choose?

6. What are the main effects of privatisation?

## Further reading

Vickers and Yarrow (1988) provide a more detailed account of the privatisation debate and include chapters on each of the main industries that have been privatised. Jackson and Price (1994) give a more recent assessment of the impact of privatisation and include discussions of issues such as deregulation, franchising and privatisations in Eastern Europe and developing economies. Wright (1994) gives a useful account of the political economy of privatisation in Western Europe.

## References

Adam, C., Cavendish, W. and Mistry, P.S. (1992) *Adjusting Privatisation*, London: Heinemann Educational Books.

Beesley, M. E. (1992) *Privatization, Regulation and Deregulation*, London: Routledge (in association with the Institute of Economic Affairs).

Bishop, M., Kay, J. and Mayer, C. (eds) (1994) *Privatization and Economic Performance*, London: Oxford University Press.

Galal, A. and Shirley, M. (1993) 'Does privatisation deliver? Highlights from a World Bank conference', World Bank, Washington, DC.

HM Treasury (1967) 'Nationalised Industries: A review of Economic and Financial Objectives', Cmnd 3437, London: HMSO.

HM Treasury (1978) 'Nationalised Industries', Cmnd 7131, London: HMSO.

Firth, M. (1979) 'The profitability of takeovers and mergers', *Economic Journal* 89, 316–28.

Franks, J.R. and Harris, R.S. (1989) 'The role of the MMC in merger policy: costs and alternatives', *Oxford Review of Economic Policy* 2(4), 58–78.

Jackson, P. and Price, C. (eds) (1994) *Privatisation and Regulation: A Review of the Issues*, London: Longman.

Kay, J. and Vickers, J. (1988) 'Regulatory reform in Britain', *Economic Policy*, October, 7, 285–351.

Kay, J., Mayer, C. and Thompson, D. (eds) (1986) *Privatisation and Regulation: The UK Experience*, Oxford: Oxford University Press.

Martin, S. and Parker, D. (1997) *The Impact of Privatisation: Ownership and Corporate Performance in the UK*, London: Routledge.

OECD (1993) *Trends and Policies in Privatisation*, Paris: OECD.

OECD (1995) *Mass Privatisation*, Paris: OECD.

OECD (1997) *Privatisation of Utilities and Infrastructure*, Paris: OECD.

Parker, D. (1994) 'Nationalisation, privatisation, and agency status within government: testing for the importance of ownership', in P.M. Jackson, and C.M. Price (eds) *Privatisation and Regulation: A Review of the Issues*, London: Longman.

Singh (1975) 'Takeovers, economic natural selection and the theory of the firm: evidence from the post-war UK experience', *Economic Journal* 85.

Vickers, J. and Yarrow, G. (1988) *Privatization: An Economic Analysis*, London: MIT Press.

Wright, V. (1994) 'Industrial privatization in Western Europe: pressures, problems and paradoxes', in V. Wright (ed.) *Privatisation in Western Europe*, London: Pinter.

# CHAPTER 22

# Regulation and Competition Policy

## Key concepts

| competition | choice | monopoly abuse | regulatory capture |
|---|---|---|---|
| quality | market power | rate of return | yardstick |
| information | RPI–X | | competition |

## 22.1 Introduction

Governments all over the world have engaged in privatisation programmes. The factors that motivated this transfer of assets varied across countries, but all governments confront a similar problem once the firms become privately owned: what control mechanisms are needed to be put in place to protect consumers? The precise mechanisms depends on the extent of market failure, reflecting both the nature of the industry and the degree of market power wielded by the privatised company. Where the firm has considerable market power, regulation of the price and industry structure will be of primary concern. However, in industries where there are health and safety considerations, regulation to ensure high quality will be essential. In all cases, governments will want to avoid the failings ascribed to state-owned enterprise. Thus regulation should in particular ensure that there are appropriate incentives for efficiency and cost reduction.

The focus of this chapter will be on regulation in the UK. Since privatisation in the UK has encompassed a greater range of industries and enterprises than in most other countries, the regulatory challenge has been varied and demanding. Regulation is not only an issue for privatised companies, however; the activities of all commercial enterprises may require regulation, and competition policy comprises a significant part of any government's industrial policy. The principle underpinning UK competition policy is that the activities of a monopolist should not act against the public interest, raising the difficult issue of what exactly constitutes the public interest. Another key question concerns the definition of monopoly activity.

This chapter examines the general arguments for regulation, before focusing more specifically on why and how the privatised industries are regulated. The recent history of regulation of privatised utilities is considered and an assessment made of government policy in this area.

## 22.2 Theory of regulation

Regulation is a means of overcoming market failure. Our attention will be directed toward the regulation of the most recently privatised industries, since these generate the most significant regulatory problems. Regulation, in the form of competition policy, is also applied to industries and firms which have always been in private ownership.

### Market power

Where firms exercise significant market power, the regulator needs to consider the extent to which competition is both feasible and desirable (see Table 21.2). Kay and Vickers (1988) distinguish between such cases and draw the following guidelines: regulation is not necessary in competitive markets; where competition is desirable but not feasible, regulate in order to encourage competition; where competition is feasible but not desirable, regulate entry; and finally, heavily regulate the uncompetitive areas where competition is neither desirable nor feasible.

At the time of privatisation, most firms had monopoly power but were not natural monopolies (for example steel and coal), so competition was both feasible and desirable. In these cases, entry should be encouraged and if this occurred, there would be no need for regulation. However, when industries are natural monopolies, competition would be wasteful. The utility industries (gas, electricity and water) and the railways are all examples of situations where the **networks** confer natural monopoly status and where competition is limited by the need to negotiate satisfactory access to the network. In these cases, it is essential to regulate the activities of the privatised monopoly. Less stringent regulation may be needed in industries where advances in technology have challenged the natural monopoly status and facilitated competition. In the case of telecommunications, the monopoly status of British Telecom was created by the phone network system. The experience of Mercury bears testimony to the difficulties that competitors faced in negotiating satisfactory access to the network. However, technological change has created alternatives to the traditional technology and undermined the monopoly of the phone network. Phone and TV cable systems, radio waves for mobile phones, satellite for international calls, and even electricity cables are all alternative telecommunications technologies. Similarly, terrestrial television depended on the Hertz system, where frequencies were limited to four stations. With the development of satellite dishes and cable systems many more channels can be broadcast. Advances in technology mean that greater competition now exists in both telecommunications and television industries.

A second concern relates to the post-privatisation activities of firms. Should the privatised firms seek to extend their market power through mergers or takeovers, the competition authorities may need to intervene. Within the UK, the domestic competition bodies, the **Monopolies and Mergers Commission (MMC)** and the **Office of Fair Trading (OFT)**, have the responsibility for enforcing competition. They monitor and perhaps regulate against any proposed merger or takeover activity undertaken by the privatised firms. Where markets are international, the responsibility

### Network

The means through which the service is provided; wires or cables in the case of telecommunications or electricity, pipelines in the case of gas or water, and railway lines

### MMC and OFT

Monopoly and Mergers Commission and Office of Fair Trading, the main UK competition authorities

**DG IV**

The Directorate-
General within
the European
Commission
responsible for
enforcing EU
competition
policy

for enforcing competition is shared with international competition authorities. In the cases where Europe is considered to be the relevant market, **DG IV**, the Directorate-General within the European Commission responsible for enforcing European Union competition policy, will become involved. Where European companies operate in the USA, US anti-trust law may also be invoked.

Quite soon after privatisation, both British Airways (BA) and BT sought to consolidate their market position. BA increased its dominant position in air transport through the takeover of its main UK rival, British Caledonian (BCal). BT extended its vertical market power by the acquisition of MITEL, a manufacturer of telephone exchange equipment. Both takeovers were subject to MMC investigations. The MMC recommended that BA should give up some of its landing slots at London airports, but that no action should take place in the case involving BT. European competition law was also invoked in the case of the BA/BCal merger, since the merger established BA as a dominant force in the European and world markets. As a result, BA was required to give up more landing slots. More recently, most major European airlines have made deals with US domestic carriers in order to extend their cross Atlantic services; BA has made an arrangement with US Air. BA's proposed merger with American Airlines was examined by DG IV and BA has again been compelled to give up landing slots in London, but the issue is yet to be resolved by the regulatory authorities in the USA.

A further concern is the potential for anti-competitive behaviour by the incumbent. The position of a new entrant to the market is very insecure, since it needs to establish a reputation, so new competitors may need to be protected from predatory behaviour by the incumbent. This was highlighted by the activities of BA in relation to its rival Virgin Airlines.[1] In this case, some of the measures undertaken by BA were illegal; Virgin was protected under US anti-trust legislation.

## Externalities

In the utility industries and in the case of the railway industry, there are positive externalities associated with the network. Taking the telecommunications industry as an example, it is clear that the marginal benefit of connection to the network is greater when the coverage of the network is more extensive. The benefit of having a phone rises as more of your friends and acquaintances are on the same network. A monopolist may charge prices which take this into account. A role for the regulator arises when competition is introduced. A competitor would be at a disadvantage if it operated on its own network, not only because of the high fixed costs, but also if its network coverage was less extensive. Continuing with the telecommunications example, a switch to a competitor of BT would be less attractive if you were only able to phone a subset of your friends and acquaintances. If competitors share the network, the regulator will oversee the price charged by the monopolist to competitors for access to the network.

**Cream-
skimming**

Where firms only
enter the most
profitable
sections of the
market

The social benefit associated with facilities such as public phone boxes is also an important consideration. At the time of privatisation, BT was required to maintain this public service. Since privatisation there are indications that **cream-skimming** in the provision of call boxes has taken place. Competitors have targeted the highly profitable sections of this market, for example providing call boxes in busy airports and stations, but not along country roads. The regulator may decide that it is

---

[1] This is discussed in Gregory (1996).

necessary to protect the incumbent industry from this type of competition, particularly where it is only the profits in one area of activity which allow the firm to offer the same service in other areas. In the case of BT, it may be that the profits associated with the call phones in busy cities, airports and stations subsidise the losses associated with providing call boxes in remote areas.

Regulation may also be required on grounds of equity. As discussed in Chapter 21, private companies do not always have the incentives to provide a universal service. The regulators ensure that universal access rights are protected, regardless of location. This includes a commitment to offer a service to rural communities, even when it is not profitable to do this. The preservation of rural services is stated explicitly in the mission statements of both OFTEL and OFWAT, regulatory bodies for the telecommunications and water industries, respectively.

Negative externalities may also exist. Examples include the potential for pollution associated with the water and electricity industries. The regulators, in conjunction with the Department of the Environment, Transport and the Regions, monitor the activities of the privatised industries which have an impact on the environment. This is particularly important in the water industry, where the regulators ensure that the water companies meet international standards on drinking water and safe effluent disposal.

**BOX 22.1**

## Health and safety: the case of railways

After the Clapham Junction rail crash in 1988, an investigation considered the costs and benefits of full implementation of an Automatic Warning System (AWS) which would alert the driver, thus preventing the train from passing through a red signal. At the time, it was argued that the system was too expensive to implement on all trains, although AWS has been fitted on many new trains. In the rail crash involving the Swansea to London train at Southall in London in September 1997, a passenger train which was fitted with AWS passed through a red light and collided with a freight train. Early investigations into the crash suggest that it was known when the train left Swansea that the AWS was not functioning. The Health and Safety Executive announced in October 1997 that some railway companies were using an 'overly liberal interpretation of the rules' regarding AWS. In response to this, the Health and Safety Executive has ordered all railway companies to take trains out of service immediately if they have this type of fault.

### Asymmetric information

In many of the privatised industries there are also safety issues, see Box 22.1. A further responsibility of the regulators is to protect the consumer against firms exploiting their informational advantages. In many areas, the service provider has superior information to that held by the consumer (see Chapter 6). This is a significant problem in the provision of healthcare and, to a lesser extent, education (see Chapters 19 and 20). The problems created by asymmetric information exist in many private-sector companies, including the privatised companies. Two examples which involve privatised companies are: misleading advertising campaigns for BT services and incorrect ticket information at railway stations.[2] In both cases, the industry regulators intervened.

In the private sector, the recent controversies associated with the mis-selling of pensions illustrate the advantages of regulation in the area of financial services. It is estimated that more than half a million people were mis-sold pensions; most of these cases involved members of occupational pensions schemes who were advised to opt out and invest in much less valuable personal pension schemes. The matter is subject to a long-standing review undertaken by the pension providers and the new Labour government has placed pressure on them to speed up their enquiries and offer compensation to the people involved. In early summer 1997, a 'list of shame' was published. This was a list of companies with a particularly poor record in mis-selling or those making slow progress towards compensating those involved. Fines were later imposed by the financial regulators on companies which have made insufficient progress towards compensating those who were mis-sold pensions.[3] Between January and October 1997, the Personal Investment Authority (PIA) and the Investment Management Regulatory Organisation (IMRO) imposed fines of roughly £2 million on 49 companies associated with mis-selling. This includes a fine of £450,000 on Friends Provident and £150,000 on Midland Bank. The Securities and Investment Board (SIB) has also issued a severe warning to the Prudential, one of the largest pensions providers.[4] The Prudential has 70,000 mis-selling cases, more than any other company, and it is the only pensions provider which is regulated by SIB rather than PIA or IMRO.

## 22.3 Regulation and privatisation

There are two stages at which regulatory issues need to be addressed where privatisation is concerned. The first is the regulation established at the point of privatisation. This is determined by the government and is established through discussion between the government and the management of the nationalised industry. The second is post-privatisation regulation, which is conducted by the industry watchdog and is the result of bargaining processes between the regulator and the management of the recently privatised industry. A key question concerns the length of time that should elapse between the two stages. We have already emphasised that technological change may alter the environment in which the utility industry operates. Where there is rapid technological change (e.g. telecommunications), the regulators need to be able to respond very quickly. This suggests that a more immediate adjustment in post-privatisation regulation is appropriate. In cases where technology adjusts very slowly (e.g. water), a longer time period between privatisation and post-privatisation regulation can elapse.

Finally, we should note that regulation is a costly exercise. The tighter the regulatory requirements, the greater the expense. In the UK, the regulatory approach was

---

[2] There is limited competition on some railway routes; as the competing trains do not always take the same route, the service offered differs both in terms of price and journey length. A survey conducted by the Consumers' Association published in *Which?* found that when investigators asked for the cheapest ticket at ticket offices, they were usually given the price of the more expensive but more direct former BR route.

[3] The current system of financial regulation is conducted by nine bodies and is jointly overseen by the Bank of England, the Treasury and the Department for Trade and Industry. In May 1997, the Chancellor of the Exchequer announced an overhaul of the system. Financial regulation will be the responsibility of a single body, popularly referred to as 'SuperSIB', overseen by the Treasury.

[4] SIB can only publicly criticise companies; it has no power to fine, unlike PIA and IMRO, who, as we saw above, have already imposed fines.

that of light-handed regulation. This was partly motivated by cost, but also the ideological position that state intervention inhibits free enterprise.

## Structure

**Vertical integration**

This increases the market power of a firm because they control all stages of production from raw materials through to supply of the finished product

The structure of an industry is an important feature in determining the extent or nature of the regulation required. Figure 22.1 illustrates three forms of industry structure: Case A is a **vertically integrated** monopoly which has a monopoly in both market 1 and market 2; Case B is a vertically separated monopoly which has a monopoly in market 1 and where its network is used by competitors to serve market 2; and Case C is a vertically integrated monopoly with some liberalisation, where the firm has a monopoly in the first market but because the market is liberalised, it faces some competition in the second market. Prices need to be regulated in any industry which is supplied by the monopolist, in order to protect the consumers. In Cases A and C the monopolists supply both markets, so prices in both markets need to be regulated; in case B the monopolist only supplies market 1, so only the prices in market 1 need to be regulated. In addition, where the market is either vertically separate or liberalised, access to the network must also be regulated in order to protect the other firms in the industry. Therefore, in both cases B and C, where other firms need access to the network to supply the second market, the network access price charged by the monopolist must be regulated.

In the case of natural monopolies, it is important to consider what aspects of their activities might be unsuitable for competition. Usually, the natural monopoly element is the network and the problem for the regulators resides in the integrated nature of the industries. In these cases, it is necessary either to separate the utility vertically or to liberalise the industry, as in Cases B and C in Figure 22.1. In practical

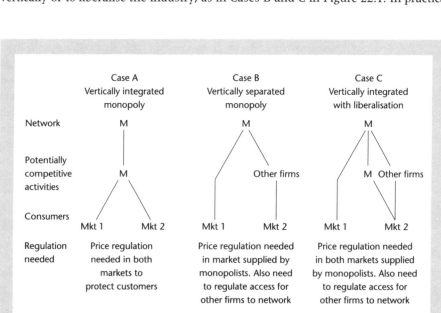

**Figure 22.1** Market structure and the nature of regulation required
(Source: Adapted from Armstrong, Cowan and Vickers, 1994, Figures 1.1, 1.2 and 1.3, where M is a monopolist)

terms, this may prove difficult, because a successful privatisation needs investor interest and the transition to private ownership is facilitated if it also has the support of the incumbent management. It is questionable whether the incumbent management would find these changes to the structure acceptable, since the position of the company is diminished and potential investors may be deterred from taking an interest in an industry which is no longer able to command monopoly profits. These considerations influenced the structure of British Telecom and British Gas on privatisation (see below).

## Prices

In most cases of privatisation, it has not been considered appropriate to regulate all prices, only prices in areas where there is no competition are regulated (see Figure 22.1). In industries with multiple tariffs, it is too costly to regulate each and every price, so the average of a 'basket' of prices is regulated. However, in industries where a single tariff applies, such as the gas industry, regulation can be applied to a single price and average revenue is regulated. Price regulation should not impose excessive burdens on the privatised companies. Price constraints should only be applied where the costs of production are under the firm's own control. In most price regulation, allowance is made for cost pass through of costs beyond the control of the utility company. Examples in the UK include the cost pass through of extraction costs for British Gas, and the costs of safety and quality regulation for the water industries (see below).

## Investment

One of the criticisms of social ownership related to the poor performance of the nationalised industries was costs were too high and productivity too low. One explanation put forward was the absence of appropriate incentives to encourage cost-reducing investment. In the absence of competition (as we saw in Chapter 21), the main pressures on the firm to improve performance come from the financial markets. As these pressures may not be sufficient to ensure productive efficiency, the regulatory regime must incorporate incentives for firms to reduce costs.

## Quality

Regulators may be required to ensure that certain standards, in terms of quality of good or service, are respected. There are several reasons for this. First, a high-quality product or service may be in conflict with the goal of low prices; second, in the absence of competition, pressure on firms to provide a high-quality product is absent. Finally, there are some areas where firms are legally obliged to provide a high-quality good, for example drinking water. Regulation must ensure that these standards are met.

## Regulatory failure

Just as the effectiveness of socially owned enterprises was constrained by multiple objectives, so regulators may be faced with too many goals. The possible conflict between price regulation and quality assurance has already been noted. Conflict may also result between public-service goals and profitability, as was the case with 'cream-skimming' in the provision of call boxes in the telecommunications industry.

Asymmetry of information between the regulators and the firm may also limit the effectiveness of the regulator. This problem is particularly acute when the privatised industry is also a monopoly, because the regulator is dependent upon the firm for information. Such problems may be overcome by using yardstick competition, where the regulator compares the performance of the firm with that of other relevant companies.

A final concern is that the interests of the regulator may become too closely linked with those of the firm (see Box 2.2). This is known as **regulatory capture**. There is little evidence of regulatory capture. One possible explanation for this is that the position and performance of the regulator are under public scrutiny. As we shall see, the gradual toughening of the stance of the regulators suggests that they are at least in part motivated by the desire to be seen to be doing a good job. This is particularly evident in the case of the rail regulator, John Swift QC; his early performance attracted severe criticism, but he has more recently adopted a much tougher line. In his evidence to the Commons Select Committee, the electricity regulator, Professor Stephen Littlechild, suggested that a tougher combined energy regulator should be established. It is expected that this will be established, since deregulation in the gas and electricity markets means that many companies now supply both markets.

**Regulatory capture**

Where a firm which is being regulated is able to influence the decisions taken by the regulator

---

**BOX 22.2**

## Regulatory failure: the case of the food industry

One problem is that the Ministry for Agriculture, Fisheries and Food (MAFF), which represents the interests of the food industry, is also the regulator for food standards. There is a clear conflict of interests, since producers cannot always be relied upon to ensure consumer protection. Public confidence in the food industry has been further eroded by the series of health scares associated with BSE and *E. coli*. These relate more to health and safety in the production and supply of food, meat in particular. The new Labour government has committed itself to establishing an independent Food Standards Agency which would assume the responsibility for regulating standards from MAFF.

---

## 22.4 Regulatory bodies

Each of the privatisation acts established an industry regulator, who in conjunction with the minister from the relevant government department, oversees the activities of the newly privatised company. As we have already mentioned, in addition to this, the privatised company is subject to domestic and European regulations and competition laws.

### Industry watchdogs

There are five industry-specific regulatory bodies, OFTEL, OFGAS, OFFER, OFWAT and ORR. The Director General (or chief regulators) work alongside the Department of Trade and Industry, the Department of the Environment, Transport and the Regions, and the Health and Safety Executive. The privatisation Acts set out the main duties and responsibilities of each regulatory body. The following descriptions in Box 22.3 are taken from the regulators' own publications.

In each case, the regulators are required to monitor the number of firms operating in the industry by controlling the issue of licences. The regulators are required to protect the consumer against the abuse of monopoly power through the regulation of prices and the quality of service. Where competition is introduced, the regulators must ensure the financial security of the service providers. On grounds of equity, the regulator also protects the rights of access of citizens in rural areas and limits discrimination on grounds of ability to pay.[5] In order to overcome some of the asymmetries in information, the regulators encourage the development of good practice and dissemination of information. Finally, the regulators are required by law to take account of externalities and protection of the environment.

The regulators of the utilities may request that the MMC modify the licences granted in the regulated utilities. They may also refer monopolies and anticompetitive practices within their industry to the MMC. Finally, the privatised utilities can be referred to the MMC by the usual processes described below.

---

**BOX 22.3**

## Examples of the responsibilities of regulatory bodies

### OFTEL – Office of Telecommunications

Functions:

- to ensure that the licensees comply with their licence conditions;
- to advise the Secretary of State for Trade and Industry (President of the Board of Trade) on telecommunications matters and the granting of new licences;
- to obtain information and arrange for publication where this would help users;
- to consider complaints and enquiries made about telecommunications or apparatus.

The Director General of OFTEL is charged with:

- ensuring that telecommunications services are provided in the UK to meet all reasonable demands for them (this includes emergency services, public call boxes, directory information services and services in rural areas);
- ensuring that those providing services are able to finance them;
- promoting the interests of the consumer;
- maintaining and promoting effective competition;
- ensuring that those providing services are doing so efficiently;
- promoting research and development.

### OFWAT – Office of Water Services

Functions:

- to set price limits;
- to check that the prices charged are fair and reflect the cost of supplying the service;

---

[5] For example, energy companies were forced by the regulators to abandon payment schemes which gave discounts to customers who prepaid their bills on the grounds that low-income households would be unlikely to be able to afford such schemes.

- to ensure that the companies improve standards through investment and greater efficiency;
- to protect customers: give company codes of practice; ensure that companies offer reasonably priced and customer-friendly water metering schemes; and check that companies are meeting responsibilities, such as reducing the number of houses flooded from sewers;
- to force companies to offer compensation if they fail to achieve the standards set in the Guaranteed Standards Scheme.

The Director General of OFWAT is charged with ensuring that:

- the functions of a water and sewerage company are properly carried out in all areas of England and Wales;
- companies can finance their function, in particular by securing a reasonable rate of return on their capital;
- no undue preference is shown between customers, that there is no undue discrimination in the way in which companies fix and recover charges and that rural customers are protected.

### ORR – Office of the Rail Regulator

Functions:

- the issue, modification and enforcement of licences to operate trains, networks, stations and light maintenance depots;
- the enforcement of domestic competition law with the provision of railways services;
- the approval of agreements for access by operators of railway assets to track, stations and light maintenance depots;
- customer protection and promotion of passengers' interests.

The Rail Regulator is charged with the responsibility of carrying out these functions in a way which will:

- protect the interest of users of railway services, including disabled people;
- promote the use and development of the national railway network for freight and passengers;
- promote efficiency, economy, competition and through-ticketing;
- minimise the regulatory burden;
- ensure commercial certainty and security;
- protect persons from dangers arising from the operations of railways with advice from the Health and Safety Executive;
- consider the environmental effect of railway services;
- consider the financial position of the Franchising Director and holders of licences.

## UK competition policy

The Secretary of State for Trade and Industry has the ultimate responsibility for competition policy in the UK. She or he can refer cases of monopoly abuse or restrictive practice to the MMC, although referrals are typically made by the Director General of Fair Trading, and decides on the appropriate action based on recommendations from the MMC. Main competition authorities in the UK are discussed in Box 22.4. Referrals are made if a monopoly is thought to exist. Broadly speaking, under the Fair Trading Act (FTA) there are two different kinds of monopoly situations:

- *scale*: when an individual or a single company, or companies within the same group, account for at least 25% of the supply or acquisition of a particular good or service; and

- *complex*: when individuals or companies, which together account for at least 25% of the supply or acquisition of particular goods or services, follow a course of conduct, by agreement or not, that prevents, restricts or distorts competition.

---

**BOX 22.4**

## The main competition authorities in the UK

### OFT – Office of Fair Trading
The Director General of Fair Trading (DGFT) has a general responsibility for keeping competition under review. The DGFT may refer monopolies and anti-competitive practices to the MMC for investigation. The DGFT also oversees the monitoring of the operation of any undertakings given or orders made following an adverse MMC report on a monopoly, merger or an anti-competitive practice.

### DTI – Department of Trade and Industry
The Secretary of State for Trade and Industry may refer mergers and monopolies to the MMC. She or he is also responsible for deciding what action should be taken following an adverse MMC report on a monopoly, merger or an anti-competitive practice.

### MMC – Monopolies and Mergers Commission
The MMC investigates and reports on matters referred to it relating to mergers, monopolies and anti-competitive practices, the regulation of utilities and the performance of public-sector bodies. It has no power to initiate inquiries or to choose which inquiries it undertakes.

---

In its investigations, the MMC is not concerned with establishing whether or not the firm has market power (therefore it does not presume that monopoly is bad), but whether the firm uses its market power to act against the public interest. The public interest is considered to consist in the following:

- maintaining and promoting competition in the UK;
- promoting the interests of consumers;
- promoting, through competition, the development of new products and the reduction of costs;
- maintaining and promoting the balanced distribution of industry and employment; and
- maintaining and promoting competitive activity in overseas markets by companies in the UK.

If the MMC makes an adverse finding, it can make recommendations to remedy or prevent the adverse effects which it has identified. The final decision on what action should be taken is made by the Secretary of State for Trade and Industry. In the case of a merger report, for example, the MMC could recommend that the merger should not be allowed to take place. If it has already taken place, the MMC could recommend disposal in the form of partial sales of its business or of other assets. After the BA/BCal merger, the new company was forced by the MMC to give up a substantial number of its valuable landing slots at London airports.

Since the privatisation of the utility industries, there have been four types of references about privatised industries made to the MMC. The first three types were references made by the industry watchdogs (OFTEL, OFWAT and the CAA), while the fourth was made by the Secretary of State. In each case, we have given the titles of MMC reports:

- Licence modification references (which may involve changes to charging conditions), as in *Telephone Number Portability* (1995) and *Scottish Hydro-Electric* (1995).
- Water price determination references, as in *South West Water Services Ltd* (1995) and *Portsmouth Water plc* (1995).
- Airport references, as in *BAA plc* (1996).
- Water merger references, as in the case of *Lyonnaise des Eaux SA and Northumbrian Water Group plc* (1995).

In addition, the following types of references were made by both the industry regulator and the Secretary of State, under the Fair Trading Act:

- Monopoly references, for example *Gas* (1993) and *Classified Directory Advertising Services* (1996).
- Merger references, for example *PowerGen plc/Midlands Electricity plc* and *National Power plc/Southern Electricity plc* (1996).
- Anti-competitive practices.

### European competition policy

The main EC competition law of relevance to the operation of domestic competition policy is contained in Articles 85 and 86 of the Treaty of Rome and the regulation on the control of mergers. Article 85(1) prohibits all agreements and concerted practices which may affect trade between Member States and which have as their object or effect the prevention, restriction or distortion of competition within the common market. Article 86 prohibits any undertaking from abusing a dominant position which it enjoys insofar as it may affect trade between Member States. Although it is not the MMC's function to determine whether an agreement or practice is contrary to Article 85 or 86, where relevant it takes account of EC law in the course of an investigation

## 22.5 Regulation of privatised industries in practice

At the time of the first major UK privatisation, BT in 1984, the US system of regulation was the only model of utility regulation in current use. The main remit of the US regulators is to control prices and has only recently been extended to include encouraging competition. This contrasts with the position in the UK where, according to the Littlechild Report (1983), a regulatory system should satisfy as many as possible of the following objectives: to protect the consumers from potential monopoly abuse; encourage efficiency and innovation; minimise the burden and cost of regulation; promote competition; and safeguard the prospects of the privatised firm.

The whole style and approach of regulation in the UK is very different to that practised in the USA. The US system is based on a judicial process; the activities of the regulators are open and legally binding. Since large volumes of evidence need to be considered, the deliberations tend to be protracted, and the process is expensive and time-consuming. The procedure ends with the submission of an open and transparent judgement. Thus the regulators are clearly accountable. In the UK, the regulatory bodies are established as expert commissions. The deliberations and bargaining processes are conducted in private. Though this certainly allows the regulators more discretion, they are also less accountable. The only checks on the activities of the UK regulators come from the government or the possibility that the utility will themselves request an MMC referral.

The UK system was initially designed to be much cheaper than that in the USA. Over time, the remit of the regulators has been extended and regulation has become tighter, so it is not, as originally envisaged, regulation with a 'light hand'. Opinion is divided on the relative merits of the US and UK systems. Beesley and Littlechild (1992) praise the flexibility and speed of decision-making with the UK system, whereas Majone (1994) emphasises the professionalism and accountability of the US system. An additional difference is in the form of regulation. In the USA, the utilities are regulated by rate of return regulation. This was one of five options considered by Littlechild, but ultimately rejected in favour of price cap regulation in the form RPI – X. Both methods of regulation are discussed below.

## Structure

The structure of the industry at privatisation is determined by the first stage of regulation and is the result of a negotiation between the government and the incumbent management, who it is assumed would prefer to retain its vertically integrated monopoly status. The structures of the privatised utilities are summarised in Table 22.1. BT and British Gas were privatised as single enterprises, whereas electricity and water saw regional boards restructured into regional companies for supply. The electricity industry was also separated into three parts: generation, distribution and services. Limited competition was allowed in some markets at the point of privatisation. BT faced some competition in the supply of telephone equipment and in the area of long-distance phone calls. There were no competitors in the gas industry. Three companies were created in the electricity generation industry. Although there were regional companies in the distribution of electricity and water, they cannot be considered to be competitors, but are regional monopolies.[6]

Since privatisation, greater competition has been encouraged. In the telecommunications industry this has been reasonably successful, helped by technological change and the recent MMC ruling *Telephone Number Portability 1995*.[7] There has also

---

[6] However, the Observer column in the *Financial Times*, 10 October 1997, gave the example of Anglia Water poaching a customer from Essex and Suffolk Water.

[7] Movement between the competing telephone call suppliers has been facilitated by recent MMC ruling that the telephone number is the property of the individual and not BT, so the phone number is now portable between suppliers.

been a rush of competition in the supply of gas in several regions, but not yet on a national scale.[8] It was proposed that competition in electricity supply should start in March 1998. British Gas have already announced their intention to enter the electricity supply industry.

A completely different approach was taken to regulating the structure of the railways. In the case of British Rail (BR), the network element was sold as a single separate enterprise, Railtrack. The providers of passenger rail services pay access fees to Railtrack for use of the tracks. In a move similar to the restructuring of the US telecommunications industry, passenger rail services were divided into groups of activities: local services which fall under the responsibility of regional train operators, and long-distance services which are provided by intercity operators. A further departure from earlier privatisations was in the way in which the companies providing rail passenger services were established. The government offered franchises for operating passenger rail services, rather than establishing companies from within the existing operation. Franchises are awarded after a competitive bidding process to provide a service (discussed in Chapter 21). In the case of rail, the franchises are usually awarded for a seven-year period and the franchisees are subject to price and quality of service regulation. The access fee paid to Railtrack is also regulated. In addition, some direct competition has been introduced. Examples include several operators on the extremely profitable London Victoria to Gatwick Airport route; and some intercity services from London. Ticket sales and information are the responsibility of the train operators. Some concern has been raised about 'cream-skimming' by operators on open-access franchise routes such as London Victoria to Gatwick Airport.

The separation of the rail industry in this manner has led to safety concerns. The first of these relates to the responsibility for signalling. In circumstances where companies compete for franchises and several operators use the same track, it is not clear that there are sufficient safety regulations in place to prevent collisions between trains from different operators. These concerns resurfaced after the train crash at Southall in London in September 1997. A further safety concern relates to the condition of the rolling stock. It is not clear that there are sufficient incentives for the franchisees to invest. This is partly a consequence of the length of time for which the franchise is awarded and also because the franchisees will seek to make a profit. For example, when a fault was discovered in the links between carriages, one rail operator locked the interconnecting carriages rather than replace the faulty carriages; this led to industrial action being taken by the drivers.

Finally, the new structure makes it more difficult to plan for an integrated transport policy. For the railways to offer a viable alternative to road transport, both for individuals and companies, it must offer a fast and reliable service. Given the increasing levels of road congestion, rail travel is frequently quicker, but there are concerns over the quality of service (see below). One reason why companies use road freight is the size of the road network. As the rail network is much less extensive, a mechanism is needed to off-load freight from rail to road. Some supermarket chains have experimented with containers that can be transferred from a train to a lorry without cranes. This is only a viable alternative if Railtrack invests in more rail sidings.

---

[8] OFGAS are introducing competition in three phases: phase one, April 1996, which was restricted to customers in Devon, Cornwall and Somerset. Twelve new companies entered the market, all of them undercutting British Gas. Phase two, February 1997, extended competition to also include customers in Avon, Dorset, Sussex and Kent. Phase three, started in February 1998, will extend competition in regional tranches.

**Table 22.1**

|  | British Telecom | British Gas | BAA |
|---|---|---|---|
| Regulated | Inland calls, line rentals, leased lines and (since 1991) international calls, 57% of activities in 1984 70% in 1994 | Supply to small users, 63% of activities | Airport charges in London airports, 37% of activities |
| Unregulated | Apparatus supply, mobile services and VANS* | Supply to large users | Car parking, catering and duty-free shopping |
| Structure | Competition in supply of equipment and UK long-distance calls. Duopoly on calls ended in 1991 | No change at privatisation. Competition introduced in 3 phases† | No change |
| Regulatory lag | Initially 5 years, now 4 years, next review 2001 | 5 years, next review 2001 | 5 years, next review 1998 |

|  | Water | Electricity supply | British Rail |
|---|---|---|---|
| Regulated | Water and sewerage charges, trade effluent and infrastructure charge, 95% of activities | All transmission, distribution and REC customers, 95% of activities | Ticket prices, network access charge |
| Unregulated | All other activities | All other activities |  |
| Structure | Regional water authorities. National Rivers Authority to oversee rivers and pollution control | Separate companies for generation, distribution and other services. Regional distribution companies and four generation companies. Competition within regions established in 1998 | Infrastructure owned by Railtrack. Passenger services provided by franchised passenger rail service companies. Four groups of franchisees: regional, intercity, Network SE, open-access passenger operations |
| Regulatory lag | Next review 1999 | Transmission, 3 years, now 4 years next review 2001. Supply 4 years, next review 1998 | 7 years, next review 1999 |

* VANs – Value-Added Network Services – voice mail/e-mail/databases
† 3 phases in SW England in 1996, SE England in 1997, across the UK in 1998
Source: Armstrong, Cowan, and Vickers, Table 6.1, 1994, and material from regulatory bodies

## Prices

### *Rate of return – regulation system used in the USA*

In the USA under a system of rate of return regulation, the profits of the firm are restricted to a given proportion of capital. A major limitation of this is that, as firms pursue higher profits, over-capitalisation occurs. This is known as the Averch–Johnson effect (see Armstrong *et al.*, 1994; Beesley and Littlechild, 1992; Vickers and Yarrow, 1988 for further details). This system is particularly costly because a utility must request the permission of the regulator before it can change prices. Before a decision can be given, the regulator must audit the firm's accounts and then determine an appropriate return on capital.

### *RPI – X – regulation system used in the UK*

RPI – X has been chosen as the formula for price control and is seen as providing incentives for cost reduction. X is set by the regulators for a given period of time (usually 4–5 years) and represents the potential for efficiency gains associated with managerial efficiency, internal efficiency and technological advances. Each year, prices must decline by X% in real terms. Under this system, the firm retains flexibility over pricing because the formula usually applies to a basket of prices, which cannot on average rise above RPI – X. Profits will rise if the rate at which firms can achieve cost reductions exceeds X. In the case of the water companies, prices are regulated by RPI + K. This accepts that price rises are needed to finance the high levels of investment to improve quality. A similar justification is given for X = 0 in the case of the railways. It has been suggested that this formula should be adapted to allow for Y, a measure of the quality of service, for example RPI – X – Y. This has not occurred, mainly because of the difficulties of arriving at a single measure of quality.

The RPI – X system satisfies most of the Littlechild criteria. The fact that it is a direct control on price ensures that the regulator targets monopoly abuse. As the rate of X is set for a fixed period, the firms have an incentive to improve their own performance during the regulatory period, as this will further reduce costs and increase profits. Once X is set, the formula is easy to apply, thus reducing the cost of regulation. Finally, incentives remain for competitors to enter the market, because the formula only applies to prices in the areas where there is no competition.

However, some problems can arise as a result of the length of the regulatory period. The first is that, if the regulatory periods are too short or regulatory reviews are held too often, short-termism on the part of the utility industries is encouraged and RPI – X becomes a form of rate of return regulation. Similar problems may emerge if the length of the regulatory period is uncertain or there is a fear that the regulator may interfere between the appointed times. If the regulatory period is too long, utilities make excessive profits. Finally, there may be a problem if the utilities believe that past behaviour may influence future values of X. This could lead to strategic decisions being taken which are unlikely to be consistent with productive efficiency.

Beesley and Littlechild (1992) conclude that RPI – X may be most appropriate in an industry which is gradually becoming more competitive, and rate of return where competition is non-existent or limited. Price (1994) suggests that once the problems described above, associated with the length of the regulatory period and uncertainty, are taken into account, the early optimism associated with RPI – X may have been misplaced.

## Yardstick competition

**Yardstick competition**

Where the regulator is able to compare the performance of similar companies

In our earlier discussion of regulatory failure, attention was drawn to the problem of limited information that the regulator may have at her or his disposal when regulating a monopoly. One option is to introduce **yardstick competition** in order to allow a comparison in performance. This was much heralded in the cases of the water and electricity companies. It was hoped that the regulator could use the additional information gathered from all of the regional companies to inform the choice of X and to compare performance. However, yardstick competition is not formally built into the regulatory process. It has a more informal role.

Details of price regulation are shown for each of the major utilities in Table 22.2. In the case of BT, a basket of prices is regulated because the company charges multiple tariffs (daytime, evening and weekend rates on local, inland long-distance and international calls). Where a single rate is charged (BG, BAA and electricity), the approach is to regulate price via the annual average revenue. Post-privatisation regulation has become tougher; the values of X set at each subsequent regulatory review are higher than those set at the point of privatisation. In the case of BT, for example, X has risen from 3 in 1984 to 7.5 in 1993. This is a consequence of the technological changes identified earlier, which have produced cheaper international calls. In several cases the value of X has been reset within the given regulatory lag. Again BT provides an example. This suggests that there may be some grounds for the concerns, identified earlier, that frequency and uncertainty associated with the length of the regulatory lag can undermine the RPI – X process. It also illustrates the difficulty of a forward-looking regulatory system, where the regulator has to predict the rate of cost reduction and technological advance. If the rate of technical progress is faster than expected, the regulator may be forced to intervene and correct the value of X, even though this may create uncertainties.

The cost pass through reflects the supply costs in the gas and electricity industries and safety requirements for BAA and in the water industries. The rail service providers receive a government subsidy. Together with their ability to increase prices at the rate of inflation, this is intended to ensure investment in the rolling stock. However, many commentators believe that the short length of the franchises, seven years, will not provide sufficient incentives for long-term investment.

As the toughening of the regulatory structure suggests, the privatised utilities have made significant profits. The size of these profits has led the new Labour government to impose a Windfall Profits Tax (discussed in Chapter 10). The tax was imposed at a rate of 20% on the excess profits, which have an estimated value of £50 billion.

## Quality

The regulations on quality of service in the privatised industries are summarised in Table 22.3. Quality requirements are not included in the price cap formula, but are separately identified. There are two reasons for this: first there are difficulties associated with finding a single measure for quality and second, the price cap formula would not incorporate a mechanism by which the firm is forced to compensate consumers for poor-quality service. BT, BG and the electricity companies have service standards which outline response times to fault reports, etc., and compensation for failing to achieve these response times.

Regulation of quality in the water industry is more complex, since the provision of water and its quality are included along with response times to reported faults. In the

**Table 22.2**

|  | British Telecom | British Gas | BAA |
| --- | --- | --- | --- |
| Price index | Tariff basket | Average revenue per therm | Average revenue per passenger |
| Values of X or K | X = 3.00 (1984–89)<br>X = 4.50 (1989–91)<br>X = 6.25 (1991–93)<br>X = 7.50 (1993–97) | X = 2 (1987–92)<br>X = 5 (1992–94)<br>X = 4 (1994–97)<br>X = 4 (1997–2001) | X = 1 (1987–92)<br>X = 8, 8, 4, 2, 1, 1 (1992–97) |
| Price structure | X = 6–12 (1997–2001)<br>RPI + 2 for rentals<br>RPI + 0 for all other prices<br>RPI + 0 on median users bill | X = 0 cap on fixed charge for less than 5000 therms | Same cap for Heathrow and Gatwick |
| Cost pass through | None | All gas supply costs (1987–92) GPU –1 (1992–) energy efficiency factor | 75% of extra security costs (1987–92), 95% of extra security costs (1992–) |

|  | Water | Electricity supply | British Rail |
| --- | --- | --- | --- |
| Price index | Tariff basket | Average revenue per KWh | Tariff basket |
| Values of X or K | K varies by firm, average is +5.4 (1989–94) | X = 0 (1990–94)<br>X = 2 (1994–98) | X = 0 (1993–99) |
| Price structure | 1.4 (1995–99) | | |
| Cost pass through | Cost of new environmental and quality regulations | Cost of power purchase, transmission and distribution, fossil fuel levy | |

Source: Armstrong *et al.*, Table 6.1, 1994 and material from regulatory bodies

summer of 1996 after a year of particularly low rainfall, some water companies were forced to limit water consumption. This typically took the form of hosepipe bans, but extreme measures were needed in Yorkshire, where households were forced to use water standpipes rather than taps in their houses. Compensation is not offered in the case of hosepipe bans, as these are frequently applied in hot summers, but Yorkshire Water did compensate households for the disruptions to their water supply. The water shortages created by low rainfall are often exacerbated by the problem of water leakage from the pipelines; it is estimated that on average 25% of water is lost through leakages. There is considerable variation between the water companies in

**Table 22.3**

|  | British Telecom | British Gas | BAA |
| --- | --- | --- | --- |
| Quality regulation | Fixed compensation for delays in repairs and connections. Contractual liability | Compensation scheme | |
|  | Water | Electricity supply | British Rail |
| Quality regulation | EC and UK standards for drinking water and bathing beaches. Levels of service monitored. Reduce water leakage. Compensation scheme | Fixed penalties for performance failures (capacity element in pool price promotes supply security) | Passenger Charter, compensation for excessively late trains. Penalties imposed on rail operators for poor sales information |

Source: Armstrong *et al.*, Table 6.1, 1994

their leakage rates. Companies operating in areas of the country with low rainfall typically have lower leakage rates. OFWAT has now imposed targets for the water companies to reduce their rates of water leakage.

In the rail industry, ticketing sales and enquiries are still managed by the rail operators. It has been argued that these companies do not have the appropriate incentives to give accurate and impartial advice, since this can result in selling tickets for a rival operator. In a survey run by the Consumers' Association, published in *Which?*, it was reported that significant inaccuracies were found in the advice given. In response, the rail regulator, John Swift QC, announced in January 1997 a programme of action for improvement. The regulator clarified the retailing requirements as 'Providing accurate information and advice on journey and ticket options – irrespective of which company provides the train service – to allow passengers to make an informed choice; and providing the means to purchase the product which best meets their needs.' To assess whether the companies improved their performance, it was also announced that the regulator would duplicate the *Which?* research, using 'mystery shoppers'. In June, a general warning was issued to operators failing to meet the standards; in July, the regulator identified a sliding scale of penalties with largest fines for those failing to meet the targets by the greatest amount. In September and October 1997, fines were imposed on companies failing to meet the target of answering at least 90% of telephone enquiries. Over the year, improvements in the service offered to customers were made: in April only 51% of calls were answered; the figures for later months were May 65%, June 55%, July 71%, August 82%, September 85% and October 88%.

In addition, the Rail Regulator reported in October 1997 that the quality of service has declined. Trains run by thirty-one of the sixty route groups were less reliable than at the same time in 1996 and trains run by forty-five of the sixty route groups were less punctual. Two (Connex South Central and Regional Railways North West) rail operators who reduced the size of their workforce subsequently found themselves to be short of drivers and unable to offer a full service, and were fined by the Rail Regulator. Others (Great Western Trains and Virgin Trains) have very poor records in providing punctual rail services.

## 22.6 Conclusion

The key to effective regulation is that where viable, competition should be encouraged. In the case of the utilities which are natural monopolies, this involves a separation of the vertically integrated monopoly. One possibility is to separate the company into the network element, the production process and supply and a deregulation of the separate markets. As we have seen, whilst BT and BG were privatised as vertically integrated monopolies, the structure of the electricity, water and rail companies was changed on privatisation. It has taken time for competition to be established, but some form of competition now exists in telecommunications, gas supply, electricity generation and passenger rail services. The pressure of real or potential competition results in falling prices and as competition evolves, consumer choice is widened. Prices have also been controlled by RPI – X regulation, which has gradually become tougher. With the exception of the water and rail companies, this has resulted in real price reductions. Quality is separately regulated. The regulator specifies standards and the compensation to consumers that should be offered if the company fails to meet these standards.

There is therefore a paradox inherent in the regulation of privatised firms. One of the motives for privatisation was to reduce the role of government in the economy. In fact, although the government has relinquished ownership, it has become more involved in the regulation of their activities.

## Summary

- Regulation aims to control for market failure.
- Most attention has been given to the regulation of the natural monopolies, where the network and the vertical integration of the utilities has made it more difficult to introduce competition.
- Prices have been regulated by the price cap formula RPI – X. The regulators have increased the value for X; this is particularly noticeable in the cases of British Telecom and British Gas.
- Quality is regulated separately. Standards are set and compensation is offered where the firm fails to meet these standards.
- Limited competition has now been established in the telecommunications, gas and rail industries and will soon be introduced in the electricity industry.
- There is no evidence of regulatory capture. The actions of the regulators suggest that they are imposing tougher conditions.
- In the years since privatisation, it is generally accepted that the utilities made excess profits in the region of £50 billion. This was the justification of the Windfall Tax and the introduction of tougher regulation.

# Questions

1. Is monopoly power the only reason to regulate a privatised company?
2. Can competition be introduced in a market where there is a natural monopoly?
3. How do asymmetries in information affect the ability of regulators to regulate a privatised company?
4. To what extent does technical progress in the industry being regulated affect the job of the regulator?
5. What are the advantages of the RPI – X formula for price regulation?
6. Why do the regulators need to regulate quality?

# Further reading

For a more theoretical treatment of regulation see Armstrong *et al.* (1994) or Braeutigam (1989). There is a special issue of *Oxford Review of Economic Policy* (1997) devoted to regulation and the introduction of competition into regulated industries. See Majone (1994) for a discussion contrasting in the UK and the US approach to the regulation of utilities.

The following are useful websites:
**OFTEL – Office of Telecommunications**  http://www.oftel.gov.uk/
**OFGAS – Office of Gas Supply**  http://www.ofgas.gov.uk/
**OFFER – Office of Electricity Regulation**  http://www.open.gov.uk/offer/offerhm.htm
**OFWAT – Office of Water Services**  http://open.gov.uk/ofwat/
**ORR – Office of the Rail Regulator**  http://www.rail-reg.gov.uk/
**OFT – Office of Fair Trading** http://www.oft.gov.uk/
**DTI – Department of Trade and Industry** http://www.dti.gov.uk
**MMC – Monopolies and Mergers Commission** http://www.open.gov.uk/mmc/mmchome.htm
**European Competition Law**  http://europa.eu.int

# References

Armstrong, M., Cowan, S. and Vickers, J. (1994) *Regulatory Reform: Economic Analysis and British Experience*, London: MIT Press.

Beesley, M.E. and Littlechild, S.C. (1992) 'The regulation of privatised monopolies in the United Kingdom', in M.E. Beesley, *Privatisation, Regulation and Deregulation*, London: Routledge (in association with Institute for Economic Affairs), 55–80.

Braeutigam, R.R. (1989) 'Optimal policies for natural monopolies', in R. Schmalensee and R.D. Willig, *Handbook of Industrial Organisation, Volume II*, Amsterdam, Oxford: Elsevier Science Publishers, 1289–1346.

*The Financial Times*, 10 October 1997.

Gregory, M. (1996) *Dirty tricks: inside story of BAs secret war against Richard Branson's Virgin Atlantic*, London: Warner.

Kay, J. and Vickers, J. (1988) 'Regulatory reform in Britain', *Economic Policy*, October, 7, 285–351.

Littlechild Report (1983) *Regulation of British Telecommunications' Profitability*, London: Department of Industry.

Majone, G. (1994), 'Paradoxes of privatization and deregulation', *Journal of European Public Policy* 1(1), 53–69.

*Oxford Review of Economic Policy* (1997) *Competition in Regulated Industries*, Spring, Vol. 13, No. 1.

Price, C.M. (1994) 'Economic regulation of privatised monopolies', in P.M. Jackson and C.M. Price (eds) *Privatisation and Regulation: A Review of the Issues*, London: Longman, pp. 77–98.

Vickers, J. and Yarrow, G. (1988) *Privatisation: an Economic Analysis*, London: MIT Press.

# The Environment

## Key concepts

| | | |
|---|---|---|
| sustainability | intergenerational equity | global commons |
| anthropocentrism | tradable permits | natural capital |
| side-payments | | |

## 23.1 Introduction

The environment has marched steadily up the league table of issues mentioned when polls are conducted to find voters' current worries, with acid rain, ozone depletion, polluted water, recycling, noise, lead in petrol, genetic modification of food, nuclear power, disappearing rain forests, biodiversity and global warming all forming part of a long list of concerns. The main factors which give rise to environmental market failures are external effects and public goods. Yet, unlike goods such as health or education, where the failings of the market are perhaps not so clear cut, government spending on the environment is small in most OECD countries. Most of the impact of government intervention arises through tax and subsidy distortions to the pricing system and in particular through laws and regulations.

Complicating the analysis of environmental issues are three important ingredients:

● Public bads, such as the risks from nuclear power or the loss of biodiversity, are marked by uncertainty over the science involved and the economic consequences. This means we may never know that actions taken to reduce a problem represent a worthwhile *ex post* investment. Intervening represents investing in buying insurance and it is in this light that you should think of actions taken to limit, for instance, global warming.

● Environmental public bads, such as global warming and acid rain, cross national boundaries. The absence of supranational governments will limit what is feasible, since no country will wish to accept agreements which make it worse off than the absence of agreement.

● The third complicating factor arises out of attitudes to the environment, which, like healthcare, is often viewed as not being an economic good at all and hence not susceptible to economic analysis. Views of this kind have implications both for normative analysis and also for the positive analysis of policy.

Our goal in this chapter is not to survey the gamut of environmental problems, but to build on the foundations provided by the chapters on externalities and cost–benefit analysis, which are particularly relevant here. We focus on three themes: the equity issue as it applies to environmental problems; the role of market-based instruments, such as road pricing and tradable emissions permits, and problems which cross international boundaries, such as global warming.

# 23.2  Equity and the environment

Building roads through unspoilt wilderness or areas of great natural beauty is contentious. Often it seems the planners who propose such roads have omitted from their calculations the value of the wilderness itself. But it would be naive to suppose that everyone would accept a policy in which economic benefits were weighed against environmental costs. Some people do not accept that we can buy and sell nature in this way, arguing that the natural world has rights or that animals should enter the social welfare function. In order to understand the economics of environmental policy, we therefore have to consider some of the ethical issues raised by environmental problems.

### Discounting the future

If we use 5% as the real discount rate, then the UK's GDP 200 years in the future is worth about the same as a new family saloon car today. To put it another way, at this discount rate, given a choice between the family saloon now or the UK's GDP in 200 years' time we should opt for the car. As the example demonstrates, standard discount rates mean that little weight is given to the well-being of our descendants in choices involving current sacrifice. Yet, for many of the most serious environmental problems, the major costs will not arise for generations. The burden of dealing with nuclear waste will be felt hundreds of years into the future; the consequences of the depleted ozone layer will last long into the next century; global warming may affect lives in perpetuity. Standard discount rates would therefore lead us to place only a low weight on future environmental costs. The key argument is therefore whether it is morally acceptable to take the market discount rate (or a rate derived from the market rate) and employ it in issues such as global warming.

To examine this issue, consider an immortal Crusoe who knows his or her own rate of time preference and also knows the rate at which capital will become more productive in the future, as inventions increase the ability to exploit capital. Crusoe chooses an optimal consumption and production plan; there seems no reason to reject the discount rate implicit in this optimal plan, unless we reject also the principle of consumer sovereignty. Now suppose that Crusoe lives for only the normal span, to be replaced by another Crusoe and another afterwards and so on. Each Crusoe, while living, plans his or her lifetime of consumption and production without regard to the well-being of future descendants. At the end of their life, some resources may be left to succeeding generations, but the amount will only be coincidentally optimal. It is as if the living Crusoe is asked to divide up a cake. Any left will be available to future generations, but there is no particular reason why the size of the slice left by Crusoe will be fair.

In practice, intergenerational altruism exists; parents do care about their children. But the links to future generations are much weaker than the links between adjacent generations, making caring about the distant future something of a public good and thereby underprovided. Moreover, the fact that one generation does care about the next does not necessarily mean that the division of the cake chosen by the living is fair to the unborn. To see this, suppose that the living maximise $U + \lambda V$ where $U$ is the well-being of the living, $V$ is the well-being of the unborn with $\lambda$ as the weight the living attach to their welfare by the living. If the living set $\lambda = 0$, many people would view this as unjust, but the argument is hardly changed if instead of $\lambda = 0$, we have for instance, $\lambda = 0.001$. Thus the weight attached by the living to future generations might not be optimal, even if it is positive. There is therefore no strong reason to accept the rate of time preference for a living generation as the discount rate which should govern the division between generations.

We still have to suggest a figure for the discount rate. The thrust of the arguments made above suggests that a rate of zero is the fairest way of preserving intergenerational equity. Unfortunately zero is unworkable; sums added up across an infinite number of generations do not converge and this gives us no practical way of choosing between different consumption streams in many cases. Economists such as Cline (1992) have therefore tended to use low but positive rates in their assessment of long-term issues such as global warming. He uses a rate of 1.5%, but even this small figure means that the well-being of people born 200 years in the future is given less than one-tenth the weight of those already alive.

## Environmental values

Do animals have rights? Is the natural world sacrosanct? Do we have duties to the world? The environment raises all sorts of questions about the adequacy of using traditional social welfare functions to examine policy issues. The number of criticisms of the utilitarian tradition is immense, as is the variety of alternatives on offer. Below we offer some organisation of the options.

Possible views on the environment

|  | Consequentialist | Deontological |
|---|---|---|
| Anthropocentric | Welfarism, Rawls | Rights, e.g. Nozick |
| Non-anthropocentric | Benthamite, Singer | Animal rights, Deep Ecology |

**Anthropo-centrism**

The belief that things, such as the natural world, only have value if they are valued by specific human individuals

First, utilitarianism and its extended family may be criticised because, for a utilitarian objects and animals are not valued in themselves, but only if they are valued by human beings. So a dog, for instance, or a butterfly, would have no welfare weighting unless a human valued them. This perspective is known as **anthropocentrism**. Yet many believe that animals should count, whether or not they enter human utility functions. For instance, Singer favours including sentient animals in the welfare function, meaning that chimpanzees would count, whereas bacteria would not (for instance). And, in the original formulation of utilitarianism, Jeremy Bentham included animals, since he saw that they could suffer pain and enjoy pleasure. Other authors reject consumer sovereignty. For instance, Klaasen and Opschoor (1991) conclude that 'Environment is a "merit good", not merely to be determined by the aggregation of individual . . . willingness to pay at any point in time' (p. 110).

As we saw in Chapter 3, we may also differentiate between views where what matters is the outcome (consequentialist) and those where it is the process itself which is valued (deontological). Arguing that the natural world has rights is an example of the deontological perspective. A four-way classification is therefore possible.

Different value systems will have different implications for the economics of the environment. For instance, the welfarist tradition underlies the standard cost–benefit analysis approach. With amendments to include gains and losses for animals, the Benthamite approach would also accept the cost–benefit methodology.[1] However, someone who believes that future generations have a right to an unspoilt view, for instance, would not accept a CBA of a proposal which ruined the view, since this would involve trading that right for money (or some other gain). They might though accept a cost-effectiveness exercise, designed to find the best way of preserving the view.

Ethical principles have implications both for what is right for society and for the positive question of what policies will be actually pursued. A particular example is that of Kantian ethics, the belief that an individual should choose acts on the assumption that all other individuals choose the same act. For the Kantian faced by the Prisoner's dilemma, cooperation should be chosen, since the moral choice is between the (cheat, cheat) outcome and the (cooperate, cooperate) option. In the case of international public goods such as combating global warming, the Kantian lobbyist may therefore push the country towards unilateral action.[2]

One of the problems of the deontological approach is that rights often clash. When this occurs, it does not mean that some form of cost–benefit analysis should step in as arbiter. Someone who believes that the landowner has a right to do whatsoever he or she wishes to do with their own land disagrees fundamentally with someone who believes that the fauna and flora on that land have rights to existence, but both individuals agree in their rejection of the economist's consequentialist methods of project appraisal. While this sounds bleak, some recent research by Nick Hanley and Jennifer Milne, summarised in Table 23.1, suggests that, for many individuals, attachment to rights is fungible: if the price is high enough, then people are willing to abandon a strictly deontological viewpoint. If this is true, it means that the useful domain of cost–benefit analysis may be greater than might be supposed.

**Table 23.1**  Trading rights for money

| Scenario | Percentage saying 'Yes' |
| --- | --- |
| Do wildlife and landscape have the right to be protected? | 99 |
| Even if this costs jobs/money? | 49 |
| If the cost was 10% of your income? | 38 |
| If the cost was 25% of your income? | 19 |

Source: Hanley and Milne, Table 1, 1996

[1] Though developing appropriate methods for measuring welfare gains and losses for animals might pose something of a challenge.

[2] As we shall see below in section 23.6, several European countries have recently adopted carbon taxes in cases where standard theory would not have predicted it.

## Sustainability

Of all the buzz words which have invaded discussion of the environment, **sustainability** is the most popular as well as one of the least clear.[3] Activities are said to be unsustainable if by doing them, we threaten the ability of future generations to carry out the same activity. Thus sustainability is an extra constraint on economic activity. The form of this constraint varies from author to author. It can be:

- a non-decreasing level of consumption,
- a non-decreasing level of well-being,
- a non-decreasing capital stock,
- a non-decreasing natural capital stock(s).

The first two represent constraints on the standard of living of our descendants. The first is more practical but the second is more general and fits with notions of economic welfare. The third option, the desire for a non-decreasing capital stock, can also be seen as a constraint aimed at preventing current generations from seizing the income of the future. However, it provides no clear-cut route to the protection of the natural world. For instance, cutting down trees would not be sustainable if the wood were then burnt for fuel, but it would be if the trees were turned into long-lived furniture.

*Natural capital*, the basis of the fourth sustainability rule, is the element of the natural world from which we ultimately derive value. It includes all living things, as well as parts of the non-living world such as the ozone layer and oil reserves. How binding is such a sustainability constraint? It depends on the level of aggregation. If we viewed each blade of grass as unique, then a natural capital constraint would inhibit us from mowing the lawn, let alone chopping trees for paper or furniture. On the other hand, if we valued each part of the natural world at its price and then summed to form an aggregate of natural capital, then the constraint would seem little stronger than the total capital sustainability constraint.

Perhaps the prime justification for advocating sustainability in these forms is as a means to an end. We have already seen that those living today may undervalue those not yet born when making decisions which will have consequences for the future. Within the welfarist framework, the appropriate response is to place a value on the unborn in the social welfare function, and typically we would expect people born in the future to have the same weighting as those alive today. If this is the case, then there is little reason for having an extra constraint which keeps the standard of living from declining. However, it is all too easy to ignore future generations in making policy decisions. Perhaps therefore, the sustainability constraint represents a practical way of incorporating their views into the decision-making when they would be undervalued in a social welfare function constructed by the living.

**Sustainability**

The idea that economic activity by one generation should not endanger the living standards or natural world of future generations

## 23.3 Market-based instruments and environmental policy

We begin this section by setting out the institutional framework within which policy is conducted, before examining the role of economic thinking in environmental policy.

---

[3] As Robert Solow says, 'It is very hard to be against sustainability. In fact, the less you know about it, the better it seems', p. 179 (Dorfman and Dorfman, 1993).

## Environmental policy

In the UK, the main body with responsibility for the environment is the recently established Environmental Protection Agency (EPA), created in 1996 out of the National Rivers Authority, Her Majesty's Inspectorate of Pollution, the Waste Regulatory Authorities and the sections of the Department of the Environment dealing with contaminated land and waste. Many of the functions of the agency are inherited from its predecessors, but the 1995 Environment Act responsible for its creation also required the Agency to 'discharge its functions to protect or enhance the environment, taken as a whole, so as to make the contribution that Ministers periodically consider appropriate towards achieving sustainable development' (Environmental Agency, 1996, p. 116). In practical terms, the Agency's main responsibilities include the setting and enforcement of water quality standards for rivers, estuaries and the shoreline, control of hazardous discharges from factories and other polluters, the monitoring and enforcing of waste management regulations, as well as a wider role in the provision of information on the quality of the UK environment.

The Agency is by no means the only vehicle for environmental policy. Policies pursued by government departments, such as the Department for Transport, may have as great an effect on the environment. Moreover, many Green activists argue that consumer attitudes and beliefs are the keys to reducing pressures on the environment and therefore that all government departments have a role to play. Increasingly, environmental policy is also set in conjunction with the European Union (EU). Although no environmental policies were embodied in the Treaty of Rome, the founding treaty for the then European Economic Community, since 1973 successive agreements between Member States have led to the creation of an environmental policy, which was further extended by articles in the Single European Act and the Treaty on European Union (the Maastricht Treaty). Decisions are made by qualified majority voting in the Council of Ministers, except when fiscal, energy policy or land use issues are at stake, when the unanimity rule may be invoked.[4] Broadly speaking, the EU has three kinds of environmental policies: directives to limit the levels of environmental hazards; coordination and information-dispersal policies, such as the establishment of the European Environmental Agency in Copenhagen, which is responsible for gathering and sharing data and scientific knowledge; and negotiation of international treaties with non-EU States. Directorate-General XI is the part of the European Commission responsible for environmental policy. Its Fifth Environmental Action Programme, which sets goals for the years 1992–2000, marks a sea change in EU policy in its raised awareness of the value of economic instruments for dealing with environmental policies and its determination to see environmental considerations influence other areas of EU policy, particularly agriculture and transport.

## Regulation

There are two main ways where economic considerations could enter into environmental policy: setting targets (allocative efficiency), and designing means of meeting targets (cost and technical efficiency). For instance, in deciding on the acceptable level of a pollutant allowed to enter a river, the EPA could investigate the costs and benefits of setting different discharge levels. The Agency could also choose between the various means available for meeting a target: setting uniform discharge

---

[4] See Chapter 24 for more on the institutions of the European Union.

allowances, setting a price for discharges or using tradable permits. Ideally, these two aspects would be integrated; the Agency would find the means for minimising the cost of reaching a given target and then choose an optimal target level.

Economic thinking is commonly absent in the formulation and execution of actual environmental policy (see Hahn, 1989, for instance or Hanley et al., 1990, who, in their survey of UK policy makers, found that cost-effectiveness was low on the agenda). Targets are not usually set on the basis of an explicit cost–benefit analysis and, compared to the use of instruments such as taxation and tradable permits, regulations or direct controls are a much more common means of achieving pollution goals. The introduction of the Landfill Tax (a tax on waste dumped into landfill sites) in September 1996 represents one of the few tax-based environmental instruments introduced into the UK. Table 23.2 lists some other mechanisms around the OECD. What is notable about this table and its source (OECD, 1994) is how few market-based instruments are employed and how limited is their impact. Moreover, Opschoor and Vos (1989) argue that because their level falls well below the marginal abatement cost, the prime role of pollution charges is typically to raise revenue rather than alter behaviour.

Now, Chapter 5 did show that direct controls may sometimes be preferable to pricing mechanisms. Yet when costs of meeting pollution targets vary amongst firms or when marginal benefit curves are flat compared to marginal costs, there are significant gains from abandoning rigid controls of the kind commonly encountered. Moreover, using the pricing mechanism also provides greater incentives for cost-saving innovation, as Figure 23.1 shows. The figure, based on Milliman and Prince (1989), shows two marginal abatement lines for a single firm, its current line (old) and a lower schedule (new), which could be achieved through investment. With a fixed emission control of $e^f$, the incentive to invest is given by the area $e^u ab$, the savings in abatement costs from the new technology. However, with a tax of $t$, that produces the same level of emissions with the old technology, the firm's optimal abatement with the new equipment is $e^n$. The abatement costs of meeting this are $e^n e^u c$ and the tax paid will be $te^n$, compared to a tax of $te^f$ and abatement costs of $e^f e^u b$, giving net benefits from innovation of $bce^u$ which are clearly higher than $e^u ab$. Overall therefore, the gains from investment in emissions-reducing technology are higher with taxes than with regulations.

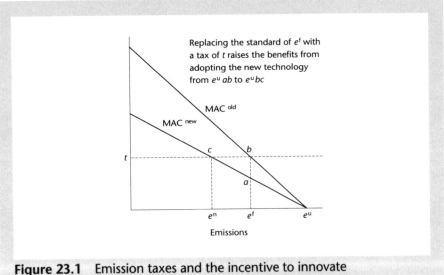

Replacing the standard of $e^f$ with a tax of $t$ raises the benefits from adopting the new technology from $e^u\, ab$ to $e^u bc$

MAC old

MAC new

$t$

$c$  $b$

$a$

$e^n$  $e^f$  $e^u$

Emissions

**Figure 23.1**   Emission taxes and the incentive to innovate

**Table 23.2** Market-based environment incentives in OECD countries

| | % Tax in petrol price | Unleaded fuel discount (% of excise duty on leaded) | Deposit–refund systems | Waste disposal and management |
|---|---|---|---|---|
| Australia | 48.4 | No | – | Management charge on solid and liquid commercial waste |
| Austria | 58.5 | 13.4 | BA, BOT, fridges, fluorescent bulbs | Contaminated sites clean-up charge levied on hazardous and household waste per tonne |
| Belgium | 65.2 | 14.1 | BOT | Waste dumping charges, charges on import/export and transit of waste |
| Canada | 42.7 | 10.5 | BOT | – |
| Denmark | 73.0 | No | BA, BO, CB | Per tonne waste charge |
| Finland | 52.4 | No | CB | Charges for oil, water, nuclear and hazardous waste |
| France | 74.6 | 12.2 | – | Waste oil charge |
| Germany | 65.0 | 10.8 | BOT | Charges on domestic and hazardous waste per tonne |
| Greece | 55.8 | – | – | – |
| Ireland | 69.1 | 8.9 | – | Waste disposal charge |
| Italy | 75.9 | 6.7 | – | – |
| Japan | 47.1 | No | – | – |
| Netherlands | 65.3 | 5.7 | BOT | Domestic refuse charge |
| New Zealand | 47.0 | – | – | - |
| Norway | 62.7 | 16.5 | Car wrecks, BOT | Waste oil charge |
| Portugal | 65.0 | 10.6 | – | – |
| Spain | 64.3 | – | – | – |
| Sweden | 59.1 | 11.5 | BOT, cans | Waste charges |
| UK | 63.6 | 13.3 | – | Landfill tax |
| USA | 29.3 | No | Drink containers | Superfund (for cleaning up polluted sites) excise tax on hazardous chemicals |

The absence of an entry may mean that (i) the country concerned did not respond to that query or (ii) it has no measures in that category or (iii) measures in that category are dealt with at a sub-Federal level of government. BA = batteries, BOT = bottles, CB = car batteries
Source: OECD, 1994

So, given the advantages of instruments such as taxes or tradable permits, why is the economic approach not widely employed? There are four potential reasons:

- The rejection of the economic approach brought about by the belief that it is wrong to trade off economic costs against animal or natural world rights, or that it is wrong for firms and individuals to profit out of pollution, irrespective of the gain to the environment. For instance, Kelman (1981) in a survey of US environmental lobbyists, found that 68% believed that pollution taxes debase the idea of environmental quality.

- Government failure in the form of capture of the body or bodies responsible for environmental policy.

- Naive over-optimism about the advantages of market-based methods on the part of economists. Seskin *et al.* (1983) show that a uniform tax on point-source emissions of $NO_2$ in the Chicago area of the USA would lead to higher costs compared to the existing system of uniform design requirements for similar sources, because of the imperfect mixing of $NO_2$ over the city and the differing abatement cost schedules for emitters.

- Conversely, the failure of non-economists to appreciate the value of the market-based approach (Beckerman, 1975).

We have already considered the first of these reasons in section 23.2. We now explore the second reason which has wider implications for all forms of regulation, before using the example of tradable permits to address the final two points.

## Regulatory capture

In a widely quoted paper, Buchanan and Tullock (1975) argue that established firms will prefer direct controls on output over taxes. The argument is illustrated by Figure 23.2. The left-hand diagram shows the cost curves for an individual firm; the right-hand diagram depicts the industry. The optimum output ($Q^*$) is below the competitive equilibrium, perhaps because of a negative environmental externality and the government must choose between a tax and output restrictions as means of reaching the optimum. With a perfectly elastic long-run supply curve ($S^E$) the optimal tax is $t$, which would mean fewer firms in the industry, but with each remaining firm producing at an output of $q^0$. Alternatively, the government could simply limit the output of firms already in the industry. Suppose that the individual firm is restricted to an output of $q^1 = Q^*/N$ where $N$ is the original number of firms in the industry. The equilibrium price is then the same, $p^1$, but now the firms make positive profits (the price is above the AC curve), as indicated by the shaded area. In fact the price could go higher; since entry is effectively barred by the output restrictions, the existing firms are under no threat from potential competitors. It is therefore easier to maintain implicit collusion, which could force prices higher and lower output below $Q^*$. In short, with taxes, the existing firms face the possibility of exit from the industry, but with regulated output they make positive profits from the restrictions and remove the threat of potential entrants. Given this choice, they are therefore likely to press the regulator to adopt the output option rather than taxes. For the regulator, faced with a choice between being actively opposed by the threatened industry or actively encouraged, the decision may be easy.

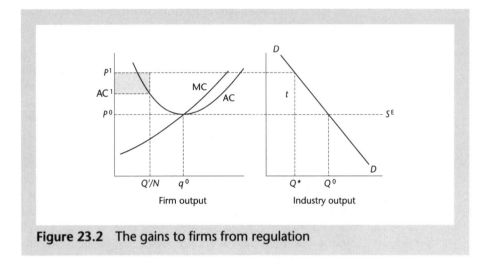

**Figure 23.2** The gains to firms from regulation

A second argument relates to the prices versus quantities debate outlined in Chapter 5. Recall the major conclusion: prices are more desirable as an instrument of control under conditions of uncertainty, when marginal costs are steep compared to marginal benefits. This result was based upon maximising the expected sum of aggregate producer and consumer surpluses. However, total surplus is the sum of many individual components. Public choice theory tells us that different groups are more likely to invest in an attempt to secure a particular policy when the benefits to them are large compared to the costs. The outcome of this investment in policy shaping is that the regulator will maximise a sum of expected surpluses, weighted according to the efforts of the various interest groups. If those with steep marginal benefit (i.e. demand) curves are over-weighted,[5] then the outcome is more likely to be quantity rather than price regulation. The positive theory of regulation therefore does not predict that taxes and tradable permits will be favoured over regulations and as we shall now see, there are further impediments to the use of market mechanisms.

## Tradable permits

**Tradable permit**

Permission to emit a fixed amount of pollutant which may then be traded

We have already met the idea of **tradable permits** in Chapter 5, where it was shown that, if abatement costs differ between firms, creating a market for pollution permits can in theory lead to the costs of controlling pollution being minimised. To be effective, there are a number of practical issues which have to be confronted by tradable permit schemes. Hahn (1989) argues that it is partly economists' failure to take note of these issues that has slowed the application of tradable permits.

For instance, discharges into a small river may do much greater damage to the environment than the same discharge into the open sea, where it can disperse. The price of the permit should therefore reflect the damage done, the pollution rather than the level of emissions. One way this can be done is through 'transfer coefficients', tables which convert a discharge of one unit at site *x* into equivalent

---

[5] For instance, environmental lobby groups may have inelastic demand for the good in question.

units of pollution at site y. If the damage done by a discharge when emitted by polluter A is calculated as twice what it will be for B, then the size of the permit is effectively halved when it is transferred to A from B (Montgomery, 1972). The problem with this fix is that it is potentially complex and the more complex the system, the less likely it is that firms will trade permits. Hahn (1989) offers the case of the Fox River system of tradable permits in the USA where the restrictions placed on trades (including the fact that companies were not allowed to exchange permits simply because it was cost saving) led to only one trade in seven years, despite the large gains from trading predicted prior to the introduction of the system.

There may also be a temporal relationship between emission and pollution. For instance, salmon travelling up an estuary are most at risk during the summer when the water is at its warmest, which, combined with low river flow, means that the dissolved oxygen vital to their survival is at its lowest level (Hanley *et al.*, 1990). Some dissolved pollutants remove further oxygen from the river, implying that allowed emission levels should be lower in summer compared to winter. Underlying this point is the assumption that permits allow units of emission per time period. Again the permit system must either be complicated in order to prevent environmental degradation, compared to the no-trade situation, or represent a compromise between environmental costs and economic benefits.

Firms given tradable permits are effectively handed a valuable capital asset. The initial allocation therefore affects the distribution of gains from the project and therefore the acceptability of the system to the participating firms. **Grandfathering**, whereby the initial endowment matches (or is proportional to) previously permitted discharge levels, means that no existing firm will lose from the permit system, provided no charge is levied for the permits. Alternatively, auctioning off the permits will maximise the reward to the regulatory authority and ensure that the least cost allocation of emissions should be achieved immediately. In a survey of Forth Estuary firms in the UK, Munro *et al.* (1995) found that one reason firms would be reluctant to sell permits was uncertainty over what would happen to their future property rights, once the scheme was reviewed. Selling a permit might lead to lower allocations in future, raising the reservation price for sellers.

Once the system is in operation, how do the firms buy or sell permits? If trades occur sequentially and bilaterally, rather than simultaneously and multilaterally, the gains from trading may be exhausted before the abatement cost-minimising allocation is reached. In a simulation by Atkinson and Tietenberg (1991) of a permit market where firms were picked to trade at random and then paired off with the partner for whom the gains from mutual trade were largest, on average only 48% of the potential for cost savings were achieved. A second impediment may arise from the small number of firms involved in many permit systems. Hahn (1984) argues that if firms exploit their monopoly power when setting the price of their permits, then as with any such market, exchange will be below its efficient level. This ignores the fact that, with small numbers, uniform pricing will not be optimal; the setting is almost perfect for the Coase Theorem to work and the gains from trade to be exhausted (Munro *et al.*, 1995). Nevertheless, as Misiolek and Elder (1989) argue, market power may be exercised in a different way, by existing firms using their permits as barriers to entry in a manner similar to the Buchanan and Tullock (1975) argument discussed above.

It is not surprising therefore that, as Hahn (1989) reports, the number of real-world tradable permit schemes and their performance have fallen well short of theorists' hopes.[6] In this section we have seen suggestions why: the creation of real

---

**Grandfathering**

A process of allocating tradable permits according to who previously had the right to emit pollutants

market mechanisms is not a simple manner and their introduction may be resisted by powerful forces.

## 23.4 Roads and the environment

One of the most serious threats to environmental quality arises from road transport. As the following quote suggests, this is very much a twentieth-century phenomenon:

> About half-way on their journey they crossed a main road running due east and west – the old road from London to Land's End. They paused and looked up and down it for a moment, and remarked upon the desolation which had come over this once lively thoroughfare . . . (Ch 2 of Part Third, *Jude the Obscure*, 1896).

In the late nineteenth century, when the country was criss-crossed by a rail network, the final decline of road transport seemed inevitable. Today's transport issues are slightly different and, as with tradable permits, illustrate some of the difficulties of adapting simple economic theory to a complex world.

The main costs of road use are: private user costs, such as petrol and engine wear; road damage; noise and pollution; congestion and accidents. The last four are all external costs and therefore tend to lead to excessive road use. The costs of the roads themselves include land loss, their construction costs and their scenic and biological impact on the neighbouring environment. In addition, because of the sub-optimal pricing of roads, there are additional costs from excessive urban sprawl. The appraisal of road projects in the UK does not attempt to quantify most of these costs.

### CoBA – the UK's official road appraisal method

Cost–benefit analysis principles lie behind CoBA, in that an attempt is made to compare some of the costs of a new road with some of the benefits. Costs are equated with the construction costs and loss of agricultural, industrial or housing land. Benefits are composed of two parts: the time saved (about 60% of benefits) and the lives and accidents saved (about 40% of benefits). The value of a life saved is set at around £0.5 million, following work by Professor Jones-Lee and colleagues, using the contingent valuation method (see Chapter 7), while the value of time employed is set at around 0.4 of the average hourly wage. Time is valued relative to wages, because, for individuals using roads for work purposes, marginal productivity theory states that in a competitive industry the marginal value of an extra hour's production equals the real wage. For individuals using roads for leisure purposes, the theory of the consumer states that individuals will wish to supply labour up to the point where the marginal benefit of an extra hour's leisure equals the lost income from that hour (i.e. the real wage). In practice, many individuals are constrained in the hours they can work, or do not work at all and this provides justification for some of the essentially arbitrary reduction of the value of time to 0.4 of average wages.

It is clear that although CoBA will provide a systematic ranking of all proposed projects, the method is a fairly crude one which will distort the resources devoted to

---

[6] Cost savings have still been substantial though, with the *Financial Times* (1 March 1995) reporting that the newly introduced system of tradable permits for sulphur dioxide emissions in the USA had already generated savings of over $2 billion.

road-building away from the efficient level. What is less apparent is whether it leads to under- or overinvestment in roads.

### Factors biasing road-building upwards

- With a few exceptions, roads are not priced in the UK, leading to excessive demand and therefore an overestimate of the benefits of new roads.
- The government requires new rail projects to pass a profitability test (not a cost–benefit test), leading to underinvestment relative to roads. With privatisation of the railways, this bias is likely to increase.
- Omission of pollution impact, which is considerable, as Table 23.3 illustrates.

Although emissions are declining for most pollutants, they are rising for carbon monoxide, created largely by road transport.

- Although the road appraisal is supposed to take into account the impact of a new road on the natural world, no attempt is made to quantify the lost value. New roads take land, but the damage they do to wilderness is disproportionate to the land-take. A highway which splits a wood in two, for instance, may make both fragments too small to support the species which previously lived there; a view may be ruined by the line of a motorway.

**Table 23.3**   Pollution and transport in Europe

| Pollutant | % of total emissions from transport |
| --- | --- |
| Nitrogen oxides | 51 |
| Carbon monoxide | 81 |
| Carbon dioxide | 40 |
| Sulphur oxides | 3 |
| Particulates | 8 |
| Hydrocarbons | 45 |

Source: Button, Table 2, 1990

### Factors biasing road-building downwards

- Road projects are not automatically built if they pass the CoBA test. In practice, the government limits the funds available for road schemes, meaning that the marginal road scheme often has a benefit : cost ratio of close to 2.0.
- New roads tend to divert traffic away from built-up areas. This lowers noise and pollution for urban dwellers, transferring it to the countryside where fewer people live. Thus although the total *quantity* of these external effects might rise, the economic impact is reduced.

## Estimates of congestion costs

The argument that current UK policy leads to overinvestment in roads depends in part on the sub-optimality of a zero price for road use. The case for a positive road price depends on the degree of congestion, as Figure 23.3 shows. An individual will use a road if the private marginal cost (PMC) outweighs the marginal benefit (MB). So the outcome with unrestricted access will be at $q^E$. Joining a stream of traffic slows everyone else down, so the social marginal cost (SMC) of road use lies above the private marginal cost. The optimum level of road use is therefore at $q^A$, where the marginal benefit equals social marginal cost and a lower level than the equilibrium with unrestricted access. The welfare loss associated with excessive use is the shaded area AEB and the optimal road **congestion charge** is $t$. Some attempts have been made to estimate these external costs, most notably by Newbery (1990); see Table 23.4, which provides figures for marginal congestion costs, and thus omits any other external costs created by road use. Casual observation suggests that road congestion is far worse in large cities than in small towns and varies over the course of the day and this is confirmed by Newbery's estimates of the optimal road prices.

These marginal costs of congestion dwarf other elements of road costs. Optimal pricing would actually raise income (the final line of Table 23.4) about equal to the current take from fuel taxation, meaning that achieving efficient pricing of road congestion could be revenue-neutral. Despite this apparently attractive feature, road pricing schemes are limited to a few cities such as Oslo and to a few trials, such as in Cambridge and Hong Kong, but interest in pricing is increasing as the technology for road pricing becomes more available and the costs of clogged roads ever more apparent. In the UK, for instance, the government has proposed pilot schemes in Leicester, Edinburgh and Bristol.

**Congestion charge**

Taxes designed to cut road congestion by charging road users according to the congestion they create

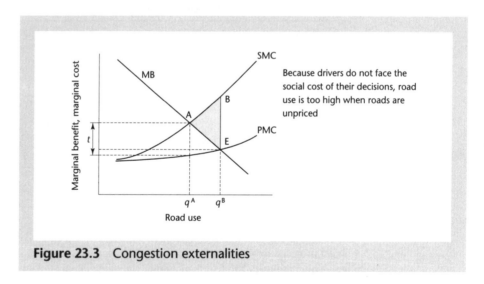

**Figure 23.3** Congestion externalities

## 23.5 Transboundary pollution and the global commons

**Transboundary pollution**

Pollutants which cross national boundaries

When sulphur dioxide is emitted from the power stations of the UK or Germany, it creates **transboundary pollution**, in the form of acid rain over Scandinavia. If the UK and Germany cut back on sulphur dioxide emissions then, amongst others, the Scandinavian countries benefit, but the gains from reducing greenhouse gas emissions will be felt across the planet, making the atmospheric temperature a global common. The line between simple transboundary pollution and a global common is not always clear. It is easier and perhaps more accurate to think of a range of cases,

**Table 23.4** Marginal time costs of congestion, Great Britain, 1990

| Road type/time | Marginal costs of congestion (pence/ PCUkm) |
|---|---|
| Urban central peak | 36.37 |
| Urban central off-peak | 29.23 |
| Non-central peak | 15.86 |
| Non-central off-peak | 8.74 |
| Small town peak | 6.89 |
| Small town off-peak | 4.20 |
| Motorway | 0.26 |
| Other trunk and principal | 0.19 |
| Other urban | 0.08 |
| Rural dual carriageway | 0.07 |
| Other rural | 0.05 |
| Weighted average (1) | 3.40 |
| Total passenger car units km/year (2) | 375 billion |
| (1) * (2) | £12,750 million |

Source: Newbery, Table 2, 1990

spanning the simple case where one nation's emissions affect the quality of life in a single, neighbouring country and the other extreme, where all the actions of all the nations on the planet affect well-being in all the other nations via a universal public good, such as the size of the ozone layer, global warming or biodiversity. Even if all nations are affected, it is important to remember that the costs and benefits of improvement to these public goods will rarely be evenly distributed. We begin this section with a discussion of some of the extra obstacles to obtaining a Pareto-efficient outcome when pollution spills across borders, before illustrating the issues with the important case of global warming.

## The problems

The key problem with transboundary pollution is enforcement. When property rights to purely domestic goods have been assigned, then the courts can intervene if these rights are violated. If Bill has the right to a smoke-free environment and Ann smokes, then Bill can sue and the court will enforce his property rights. International equivalents do not exist. Fundamentally therefore, the public good nature of the commons encourages free riding and preference falsification, which limit the scope for international agreement.

Chapter 4 argued that sometimes public goods are privately provided, albeit usually at less than optimal levels. The same may be true for improvements to the global commons, as Figure 23.4 illustrates. The lower downward-sloping curve, $MB_1$, shows the marginal benefits from abating greenhouse gas emissions for a single country. The upper curve, $MB_G$, shows the global marginal benefits if $N$ identical countries all reduce emissions; it is the $N$ individual marginal abatement schedules, summed vertically. A single country, considering only the welfare of its citizens and taking other countries' emissions as given, will set emissions at the level where the marginal cost of abatement equals its own marginal benefits, or $Q_1$, but the cooperative outcome and optimum is at $Q^*$. Each country prefers $Q^*$ to $Q_1$, but this is not a Nash equilibrium. In other words, if other countries set abatement at $Q^*$, the country's welfare would be optimised by setting its abatement at $Q_1$. The welfare cost of the non-cooperative outcome is given by the shaded area on the diagram and this depends on a number of factors. If the slope of the individual marginal benefit curve is $b$, and $c$ is the slope of the marginal cost curve, then an increase in $c$ lowers the welfare loss, as does a rise in $b$. Meanwhile, if the number of countries rises, then this raises the welfare loss. In short, provided large numbers of countries are involved, marginal abatement costs are shallow ($c$ small) and the gains from abatement do not diminish rapidly ($b$ small), then the welfare losses from non-cooperation will be relatively large.

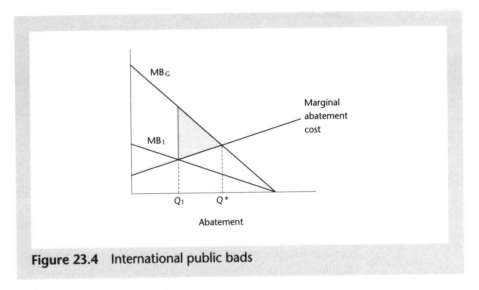

**Figure 23.4**  **International public bads**

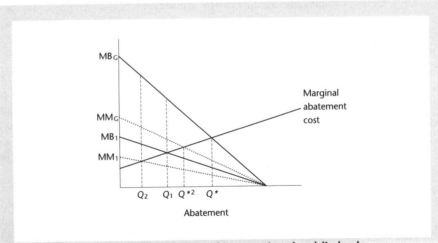

**Figure 23.5**  **The median voter and international public bads**

Treaties, though, are written, signed and adhered to, which suggests that countries do have some powers over other nations. Of course, a country may sign a treaty to cut pollution because it has already determined to reduce emissions unilaterally (Barrett, 1990, argues that this is largely the case), but even leaving this aside, there are means of persuading nations to agree, including: moral opprobrium if they do not sign; the threat of trade wars; consumer boycotts and the withdrawal of cooperation in other areas of activity. Now, agreements can be enforced without a central authority, provided that the numbers involved are small, interaction is repeated indefinitely and discount rates are low enough. Neighbouring countries with common interests and significant trade volumes may satisfy these conditions and it is this which enables some transboundary pollution problems to be ameliorated through self-enforcing agreements.

After the collapse of communism and the withdrawal of cheap oil supplies from what was the Soviet Union, many of the countries of eastern Europe were forced to increase their reliance on nuclear power, often produced in poorly designed plants with limited safety features. The increased threat of a nuclear accident was an external cost, not only for the citizens of eastern Europe, but also for their neighbours in the West. The countries of the EU therefore paid for some of the costs of improving the safety features of the reactors and helped invest in alternative power sources. Examples of such *side-payments* between countries are rare (though see Barrett, 1990, for some examples), but attaining Pareto efficiency might require it, just as in the examples of Chapter 5, reaching the efficient level of smoke required the owner of the property right to be compensated for sacrificing some of those rights. One reason why payments in cash between countries are rare is the scope for preference falsification that they offer. Payments in kind, such as for the nuclear power expertise given to eastern Europe, or the transfer of technology, offer one way of limiting the gains from lying about preferences, but as with the case of unilateral investment, the outcome is unlikely to be Pareto-efficient.

We have so far assumed that a nation pursues the policy which maximises its welfare, but of course, public choice theory predicts that foreign policy will be determined by interplay between the efforts of domestic interest groups and other political agents. Non-altruistic living voters, for instance, will tend to reject policies which impose costs in the short term for benefits mainly accruing to future generations.

## 23.6 Global warming

The problem of climate change exemplifies the issues discussed so far in this chapter: the science is uncertain and is likely to remain so; much of the debate concerns the ethical treatment of future generations; effective policy requires successful coordination between nations with competing interests, and while there is a role for market-based instruments such as carbon taxes and tradable permits, they are also viewed with much mistrust by many of the actors involved.

With so much at stake, it is no surprise that the facts and forecasts associated with global warming are so controversial. What is not in doubt is the theory of the greenhouse effect, the source of global warming. Light and other electromagnetic radiation reach the earth from the sun, but the fact that the planet is colder than the source of the energy means that the energy is re-radiated at longer wavelengths. The water vapour in the atmosphere, together with the greenhouse gases (carbon dioxide, methane, CFCs, nitrous oxide and ozone),[7] allow most of the incoming energy past, but absorb a significant proportion of the radiation leaving the earth's surface, so warming up the atmosphere and hence the planet. Without this effect, the earth would have a surface temperature 33°C below its current average of 15°C. It has been accepted since the late nineteenth century that an increase in the concentration of greenhouse gases in the atmosphere should lead to a rise in temperatures and the fact that carbon dioxide levels are rising and have risen, about 20% since pre-industrial times, is also not disputed.

What is far less clear is the prognosis for the future. Models of climate change are used to forecast the impact of the current rises in greenhouse gases, but they have so far overestimated the change in temperature, predicting a rise of 0.8°C, nearly double what has actually happened. Possible explanations for this discrepancy include a longer than anticipated time-lag between rises in greenhouse gases and global temperatures, the effects of pollution (which tends to lower temperatures), the ozone-stripping consequences of CFCs and the incorrect specification of the climate models employed in the forecasts. Whatever the reason, the Intergovernmental Panel on Climate Change (IPCC) has downgraded its forecast for the average temperature rise from 3.5–4°C to 2.5°C following a doubling of pre-industrial greenhouse gas levels.

This doubling is expected to occur around the year 2025 and most models of the warming process have confined themselves to a limited time period (up to 2100 is typical), but on current trends there is no reason to suppose that greenhouse gas concentrations will not continue to grow for 200–300 years, until equilibrium is attained between the extra carbon dioxide being added to the atmosphere and that absorbed by the deep oceans and other 'sinks'. The rise would not be the same across the globe; most models predict higher than average warming in temperate and polar zones and in the Northern Hemisphere. Table 23.5 provides illustrative predicted changes for 2075 in average summer daily maximum temperatures for some major cities around the world.

Caution must be observed in interpreting such a table: it is based upon a sixteen-fold rise in $CO_2$-equivalent gases in the atmosphere; global climate models are unable to predict at the accuracy of an individual city and the calculations are based upon the robustness of the physical relationships used for predicting the effects of $CO_2$-equivalent doubling. Nevertheless it does give a glimpse of the possible impacts of global warming on our major cities.

Just as with the science, uncertainty surrounds the economic effects of global warming. The costs of warming separate into two categories: the temporary costs of adaptation to the new higher temperatures and the long-run equilibrium costs. Included in the latter are costs from reduced crop and forest yields, from species loss, coastal incursion, air-conditioning, weather-related illnesses, reduced amenity, raised hurricane and storm damage, restrictions to water supply, drought and air pollution. For some countries and for some ranges of global warming, some of these items might represent benefits rather than costs. For instance, most residents of northern Europe would appreciate hotter summers; the northward shift in the limit to feasible agriculture in Canada and Russia may raise crop production there and raised carbon dioxide concentrations also increase plant yields.

---

[7] The gases differ in their ability to trap outgoing radiation and hence in their global warming capabilities. It is usual therefore to talk in terms of '$CO_2$-equivalents' and so, in what follows, a 'doubling of greenhouse gas concentrations' means a doubling in terms of their $CO_2$-equivalents.

**Table 23.5** Predicted rises in summer temperature

| City | Average summer daily maximum temperature | | | City | Average summer daily maximum temperature | | |
|------|---------|------|------|------|---------|------|------|
| | current | 2275 | Gain | | current | 2275 | Gain |
| Amsterdam | 21 | 26.1 | 5.1 | Vienna | 24 | 32.1 | 8.1 |
| Athens | 32 | 43.1 | 11.1 | Toronto | 26 | 37.0 | 11.0 |
| Berlin | 29 | 39.8 | 10.8 | New York | 29 | 39.8 | 10.8 |
| Brussels | 23 | 28.3 | 5.3 | San Francisco | 22 | 32.6 | 10.6 |
| Copenhagen | 22 | 30.4 | 8.4 | Tokyo | 28 | 31.0 | 3.0 |
| Dublin | 19 | 27.6 | 8.6 | Seoul | 29 | 37.1 | 8.1 |
| Edinburgh | 18 | 26.5 | 8.5 | Singapore | 31 | 33.8 | 2.8 |
| Helsinki | 22 | 29.9 | 7.9 | Sydney | 26 | 25.6 | –0.4 |
| Lisbon | 26 | 37.0 | 11.0 | Sao Paulo | 27 | 27.2 | 0.2 |
| London | 23 | 31.0 | 8.0 | Johannesburg | 26 | 28.3 | 2.3 |
| Madrid | 31 | 41.5 | 10.5 | New Delhi | 36 | 41.1 | 5.1 |
| Paris | 24 | 32.6 | 8.6 | Lagos | 28 | 28.3 | 0.3 |
| Rome | 31 | 39.3 | 8.3 | Riyadh | 42 | 52.6 | 10.6 |
| Stockholm | 21 | 29.3 | 8.3 | | | | |

Source: Cline, Table 2.3, 1992, p. 70

The measures which could be used to limit global warming range from the bizarre (giant mirrors in space to reflect back the sun's rays) to the mundane (wear more woollies in winter). They include measures changing land-use such as restrictions on logging and the encouragement of afforestation, as well as economic measures, such as introducing a **carbon tax**. It is widely but not universally accepted that there is something of a 'free lunch' in the initial reduction of carbon dioxide emissions, because turning fuel subsidies (where they exist) into fuel taxes and raising fuel taxes where they are already positive would reduce the burden of taxation on other goods, the so-called 'double dividend', which arises because the MCPF is higher for other taxes, particularly those on labour, than it is for taxes on carbon. There are also many energy-saving devices where the benefits of adoption would outweigh the costs, even ignoring global warming issues (see Cline, 1992, who estimates that the first 20% of reductions in emissions can be achieved costlessly).

**Carbon tax**

Taxes on goods in proportion to their contribution to greenhouse gas emissions

## Costs and benefits

Most discussion of the consequences of cutting greenhouse gas emissions has focused on the costs of such a policy rather than the benefits; some estimates of the costs of global warming have been made, notably by Nordhaus (1991), whose low figures of 0.5–2% of world GDP have been widely criticised. Cline (1992), for instance, notes that Nordhaus's figures rest on no population growth, no growth except through technical change (hence static greenhouse gas emissions) and the low proportion of GDP taken up by sectors of the US economy sensitive to global warming. However, a significant reduction in the supply of agricultural products, for instance, would lead to the large rises in prices omitted from Nordhaus's work. Overall typical estimates of the cost of a doubling of atmospheric carbon dioxide lie in the range 1–2% of GDP per annum, although for some fast-growing developing nations, the figures are much higher. Figures for China, for instance, are closer to 5% of GDP (Bruce *et al.*, 1996, p. 205).

Estimates of the cost of cutting emissions beyond the 'free-lunch' point are sensitive to a number of factors. Obviously, the cost depends on when emissions are cut and by how much. The centrepiece of international coordination on global warming is the Global Convention on Climate Change, agreed in Rio de Janeiro in 1992, committing signatories to stabilising greenhouse gas emissions at 1990 levels by 2000 (see Box 23.1 below for the Kyoto Protocol, an update to the agreement). Many countries (e.g. Germany) have gone beyond this and agreed to a 20% cut in emissions by 2005 (again relative to 1990),[8] so most modellers have concentrated on these bench marks, but the present value of the cost is sensitive to the discount rate employed and is also increasing in the anticipated rate of growth of energy use, which in turn is an increasing function of GDP per capita and the rate of population growth, among other factors. The cost will also rise if the price of alternative technologies ('backstop technologies') is high or if the ability of firms and consumers to substitute away from energy and carbon-intensive lifestyles is limited. Models must embody assumptions about all these parameters and then grind out predictions for a hundred years or so. It is not surprising therefore that they differ so much, even when some attempt is made to standardise assumptions. For instance, despite an attempt at standardisation in which growth rates and the backstop technology were agreed (amongst several other key variables), twelve US models produced estimates of the carbon tax required to stabilise carbon dioxide emissions at 1990 levels by 2000 ('stabilisation') varying from $20 per tonne of $CO_2$ to $150 per tonne at a cost of between 0.2 and 0.7% of GDP. Cutting carbon dioxide by 20% by 2010 ('20% cut') produced a loss of between 0.9 and 1.7% of GDP per annum and taxes of anywhere between $50 and $330 (Bruce *et al.*, 1996). Meanwhile, on a larger scale, in a five-region model of the world economy with a growth rate of 2% and an exogenous rate of increase of energy efficiency of between 0.5 and 2% (the number varying according to region), Manne and Richels (1991) estimate that coal prices have to rise by between 5 and 8 times as part of a programme designed to cut carbon dioxide emissions by 20% in the year 2020 and keep them at that level until 2100. Comparing these figures to the costs of global warming, we can see that the range covers cases where 'do nothing' is the optimal action, to the other extreme where swift and strong limits on greenhouse gas emissions are imperative and this encapsulates the dilemmas posed by global warming.

Any instrument will have distributional as well as efficiency implications, as Table 23.6 shows, comparing the impact on British and German households of the once-proposed EU carbon/energy tax. Losers from such a tax could be expected to object to it, as could individuals with egalitarian principles, if the tax is regressive. In fact, in Britain the tax would be regressive, with the largest burden falling on the poorest households, compared to Germany where the burden of the tax is spread more evenly across the income distribution. The difference arises largely because of the much higher proportion of income spent on fuel by low-income households in the UK.

---

[8] Even if greenhouse gases remain at this level, global warming will continue. For instance, the IPCC recommends a 60% cut in emissions compared to 1990, not simply stabilisation (IPCC, 1990).

**BOX 23.1**

## Global warming and the Kyoto Protocol

In December 1997, the parties to the UN Framework Convention on Climate Change met in Kyoto, Japan to update the original Rio convention, and draw up a new agreement on greenhouse gas emissions for the new millennium. The main features of the agreement were:

- Binding emissions targets for developed nations: 8% below 1990 emissions levels for the EU, 7% for the USA, 6% for Japan, no change for Russia, 10% rise for Australia. The emissions targets include all six major greenhouse gases.
- A five-year budget period for emissions targets. The first period will be 2008–2012.
- Activities that absorb carbon, such as planting trees, will be offset against emissions targets.
- Emissions trading will be allowed. Rules and guidelines for verification, reporting, and accountability will be discussed at the next meeting of the Parties in Buenos Aires in November 1998.
- Countries with emissions targets may get credit towards their targets through project-based emission reductions in other such countries.
- 'Clean Development Mechanism' (CDM). With the CDM, developed countries will be able to use certified emissions reductions from project activities in developing countries to contribute to their compliance with greenhouse gas reduction targets.
- To enter into force, the Protocol must be ratified by at least fifty-five countries, accounting for at least 55% of the total 1990 carbon dioxide emissions of developed countries. By July 1998, forty-three countries, including all those in the EU, Canada, Australia and New Zealand, had ratified the Protocol, though the largest emitter of greenhouse gases, the USA, had not.

The Protocol illustrates some of the difficulties of making binding agreements between sovereign nations and has been widely criticised for being too lax on greenhouse gas emissions. Since gas emission in Russia and the Ukraine has crashed alongside economic activity, in the wake of the end of communism, the Protocol actually allows emissions in developed nations to *grow* over the target period, bringing the idea of tradable permits into disrepute. Nations can simply purchase the permits unused by countries of the former Soviet Union. Meanwhile, fast-growing countries, such as China, successfully fought off efforts to place caps on their emissions growth.

**Table 23.6** The distributional effects of a European Union carbon tax for two Member States

| | Payment as % of household expenditure, by quartile | | | | |
| | First 25% | Second 25% | Third 25% | Richest 25% | All |
|---|---|---|---|---|---|
| Germany | 1.01 | 0.94 | 0.87 | 0.77 | 0.86 |
| UK | 2.10 | 1.45 | 1.16 | 0.92 | 1.19 |

Source: Smith, Table 6.3, p. 83, 1995

**BOX 23.2**

## Carbon tax pioneers

Within Europe, Finland, Norway, Denmark, Sweden and The Netherlands have all begun taxing fuels on the basis of their carbon content. This is not the optimal form of taxation to combat global warming, since, for instance, it provides no incentive for fuel users to limit carbon dioxide emission through absorption. Moreover, in most cases the impact on fuel prices will be too small to have a significant impact on carbon use. Finland's tax of FMk 24.50 per tonne of carbon, for instance, increases leaded petrol prices by 7%,[9] while the Norwegian tax pushes petrol up by NKr 0.60 per litre and the Swedish tax, which raises petrol prices by SKr 0.58 per litre, is accompanied by cuts in other energy taxes and a variety of exemptions (OECD, 1994).

Nevertheless, these countries have gone much further than most others, in a situation where the simple Prisoner's dilemma model of international cooperation would not predict any unilateral actions. One reason lies in the negative costs of abatement for small reductions in carbon dioxide emissions. UNEP (1994) estimates that, for Denmark, the marginal abatement cost for reducing emissions through conversion to natural gas is −$222 per tonne and −$70 for heat conservation in houses, while Bovenberg (1993) justifies The Netherlands' policies in a similar way.

Public choice theorists would combine this with the gains to committed environmental pressure groups as a reason for the new taxes. As we saw in Chapter 9, a policy is more likely to be passed if the costs are spread across many individuals and the benefits are concentrated. Svendsen (1993) argues that this was the case in Denmark where in 1993 a carbon tax of $8 per tonne of $CO_2$ was instituted after successful lobbying by environmental groups. Nevertheless there was opposition from power generators in particular and the original suggested tax of $16 per tonne was first reduced and then accompanied by rebates to affected firms which lowered the expected net tax yield from $200 million per annum to $50 million.

Another argument why countries might go it alone arises from the theory of reciprocity (Sugden, 1984). A pioneer in carbon taxes might anticipate that other countries would respond in kind, gradually leading to the world-wide implementation of a tax. However, the costs of misreading other countries' intentions may be severe. Martin Hoel (1991), shows that unilateral action by one country may be counterproductive, since other countries may see this as an invitation not to cut back (i.e. the predicted behaviour in standard public good models) and this may lead to higher total greenhouse gas emissions, compared to the situation with no unilateral action. Finally, as we saw in section 23.2, Kantian ethics, rather than reciprocity, may also lead to unilateral action.

One unsurprising point of consensus does emerge: for a given emissions target, carbon taxes impose substantially lower burdens compared to taxes on fuel or energy use. For instance, Barker *et al.* (1994) show that UK road fuel prices would need to rise by only 5% if a carbon tax was used to meet the Rio target, compared to 22% if the government's chosen programme of road fuel duty and VAT increases is pursued.

---

[9] As a comparison, according to Ingham and Ulph (1991), UK oil prices would have to rise by between 57 and 128% in order to meet the Rio targets.

The case of greenhouse gas emissions shows how decisions must often be made under conditions of extreme uncertainty. Action to combat potential warming relies on upgrading the weighting given to the interests of future generations; it needs agreement between sovereign states and to be efficient it requires tax-based policies rather than simple regulations. As we have seen in this chapter there are good public choice reasons why agreements between states may founder, why future generations may receive little weighting in the political process, and why regulation may be favoured over taxes. However, as Box 23.2 suggests, some countries have begun to make tentative moves towards the efficient taxation of carbon emissions.

## 23.7 Conclusion

Perhaps more than any area of the economy, there is a clear link between the abstract ideas of market failure and the principles which should underlie environmental policy. Nevertheless, it is only recently that policy makers have begun to incorporate economic thinking into the design of environmental policies. Much of this is tentative; permit schemes are hedged around with restrictions, and taxes are often set at a level too low to have a significant impact on behaviour. We have seen in this chapter that there are a number of reasons why, amongst them ignorance, interest group behaviour and over-simplification by economists.

## Summary

- The relationship between the concept of market failure and the problems of the economy is probably nowhere clearer than in the case of environmental goods such as pollution.

- Many of the most serious environmental problems cross international boundaries, which causes major difficulties for cooperation. Nevertheless international cooperation and unilateral action can be found in most spheres of the environment.

- Most economists have a particular approach to valuation which is not universally shared. This clash is particularly sharp in the case of the environment, where many individuals, interest groups and governments have stated beliefs which are hostile to trade-offs between the environment and other sources of value.

- The economic approach to ameliorating environmental problems is not widely favoured. Instead, direct controls and regulations are more common than taxes and tradable permits. As environmental regulations become tighter, however, increasing interest has been shown in market-based approaches.

- Many environmental costs lie in the future. Public choice theory predicts that the interest of the living will be put before the interests of future generations.

## Questions

1. It is sometimes argued that even if there is no consensus over the use of cost–benefit analysis, cost-effectiveness is a goal that can draw on wide support. What range of ethical beliefs are compatible with cost-effectiveness as a goal?

2. Explain the problems involved with (a) using a zero discount rate and (b) having as a sustainability constraint the requirement that the stock of natural capital does not fall.

3. How would you implement a road-pricing programme for a city?

4. (a) What market failures are addressed by the use of deposit and refund systems (as used on glass bottles, for instance)? (b) When are deposit/refund systems superior to a tax on waste disposal?

5. Countries sign international agreements (and stick to them) even when simple game theory says they will not. Why?

6. What is the case for non-tradable permits?

## Further reading

General treatments of environmental economics include the texts by Hanley et al. (1996) and Bateman et al. (1996), while cost–benefit issues are tackled in Hanley and Spash (1993). The ethics of discounting are examined in Broome (1992) or Spash (1993) in the journal Environmental Ethics, which is a sensible starting point for more general discussions of this fast-growing area. Hahn (1989) provides the benefits of his own experience in examining why non-economists are often slow to spot the value of economists' ideas; the issue is also covered in Hanley et al. (1990), while Tietenberg (1990) is a good overview of the general theory of permits. Barrett (1990) is a useful discussion of the economics of international agreements and Newbery (1990) is a survey of his important work on road pricing.

A summary of thinking on the impact of climate change is Bruce et al. (1996), which is comprehensive, but at times suffers under the weight of its multiple authorship. Most of the writers in this volume are sympathetic to the view that global warming is an impending catastrophe. A more sceptical line is taken by Nordhaus (1991). A survey of the use of market mechanisms such as environmental taxation can be found in OECD (1994), with a more detailed comparison of the UK and Germany in Smith (1995). The homepage for the UN Framework Convention on Climate Change is http://www.unfccc.de/ and has the full text of the Kyoto Protocol.

## References

Atkinson, S. and Tietenberg, T. (1991) 'Market failure in incentive based regulations: the case of emissions trading', Journal of Environmental Economics and Management 21, 17–31.

Ayres, R.U. and Walter, J. (1991) 'The Greenhouse Effect: damages, costs and abatement', Environmental and Resource Economics 1(3), 237–70.

Barker, T., Baylis, S. and Bryden, C. (1994) 'Achieving the Rio target: $CO_2$ abatement through fiscal policy in the UK', Fiscal Studies 15(3), 1–18.

Barrett, S. (1990) 'The problem of global environmental protection', Oxford Review of Economic Policy 6(1), 68–82.

Barrett, S. (1994) 'Self enforcing international environmental agreements', Oxford Economic Papers 46, 878–94.

Bateman, I., Pearce, D. and Turner, K. (1996) Environmental Economics, Hemel Hempstead: Prentice Hall.

Beckerman, W. (1975) Pricing for Pollution, London: Institute for Economic Affairs.

Bovenberg, A. (1993) 'Policy instruments for curbing carbon dioxide emissions: the case of the Netherlands', *Environmental and Resource Economics* 3(3), 233–44.

Broome, J. (1992) *Counting the Cost of Global Warming*, Cambridge: White Horse Press.

Bruce, J.P., Lee Hoesung, and Haites, E.F. (1996) *Climate Change 1995: Economic and Social Dimensions of Climate Change*, Cambridge: Cambridge University Press.

Buchanan, J.M. and Tullock, G. (1975) 'Polluters' profits and political response: direct controls versus taxes', *American Economic Review* 65(1), 139–47.

Button, K. (1990) Environmental externalities and transport policy', *Oxford Review of Economic Policy* 6(2), 61–75.

Cline, W. (1991) 'The scientific basis for the Greenhouse Effect', *Economic Journal* 101, 909–14.

Cline, W. (1992) *The Economics of Global Warming*, Washington: Institute for International Economics.

Dorfman, R. and Dorfman, N.C. (1993) *Economics of the Environment*, 3rd edn, London: Norton.

Environmental Agency (1996) *The Environment – A Snapshot*, London: HMSO.

Hahn, R. (1984) 'Market power and transferable property rights', *Quarterly Journal of Economics* 99, 753–65.

Hahn, R. (1989) 'Economists' prescriptions for environmental problems', *Journal of Economic Perspectives* 3, 95–114.

Hanley, N. and Milne, J. (1996) 'Ethical beliefs and behaviour in contingent valuation surveys' Journal of Environmental Planning and Management, 39(2), 255–272.

Hanley, N. and Spash, C.L. (1993) *Cost–Benefit Analysis and the Environment*, Aldershot: Edward Elgar.

Hanley, N., Moffatt, I. and Hallet, S. (1990) 'Why is more notice not taken of economists' prescriptions for the control of pollution?', *Environment and Planning A* 22, 1421–39.

Hanley, N., Shogren, J. and White, B. (1996) *Environmental Economics*, London: Macmillan.

Hoel, M. (1991) 'Global environmental problems: the effects of unilateral actions taken by one country', *Journal of Environmental Economics and Management* 20, 55–70.

Ingham, A. and Ulph, A. (1991) 'Market-based instruments for reducing $CO_2$ emissions – the case of UK manufacturing', *Energy Policy* 19, 135–48.

IPCC (1990) *Scientific Assessment of Climate Change*, Geneva: United Nations Environmental Programme.

Kelman, S. (1981) 'Economists and the environmental policy muddle', *Public Interest* 64, 106–23.

Klaasen, G. and Opschoor, J. (1991) 'Economics of sustainability or the sustainability of economics', *Ecological Economics* 4, 93–116.

Manne, A.S. and Richels, R.G. (1991) 'Buying greenhouse insurance', *Energy Policy* 19(6), 543–52.

Milliman, S.R. and Prince, R. (1989) 'Firm incentives to promote technological change in pollution control', *Journal of Environmental Economics and Management* 17, 247–65.

Montgomery, W. (1972) 'Markets in licenses and efficient pollution control programmes', *Journal of Economic Theory* 5, 395–418.

Munro, A., Hanley, N., Faichney, R. and Shortle, J. (1995) *Impediments to Trade in Permit Markets*, Stirling: University of Stirling.

Newbery, D. (1990) 'Pricing and congestion: economic principles relevant to pricing roads', *Oxford Review of Economic Policy* 6(2), 22–38.

Nordhaus, W. (1991) 'To slow or not to slow: the economics of the greenhouse effect', *Economic Journal* 101, 920–38.

OECD (1994) *Managing the Environment: The Role of Economic Instruments*, Paris: OECD.

Opschoor, J. and Vos, H. (eds.) (1989) *Economic Instruments for Environmental Protection*, Paris: OECD.

Seskin, E.P., Andersen, R.J. and Reid, R.O. (1983) 'An empirical analysis of economic strategies for controlling air pollution', *Journal of Environmental Economics and Management* 10, 112–24.

Smith, S. (1995) *"Green" Taxes and Charges: Policy and Practice in Britain and Germany*, London: Institute for Fiscal Studies.

Solow, R. (1993) 'The economics of sustainability or the sustainability of economics', in R. Dorfman and N.C. Dorfman, *Economics of the Environment*, 3rd edn, London: Norton.

Spash, C.L. (1993) 'Economics, ethics and long-term environmental damages', *Environmental Ethics* 15(2), 117–32.

Sugden, R. (1984) 'Reciprocity: the supply of public goods through voluntary contributions', *Economic Journal* 94, 772–87.

Svendsen, G.T. (1993) *The Danish $CO_2$ Tax and Emissions Trading*, Aarhus: University of Aarhus.

Tietenberg, T. (1990) 'Economic instruments for environmental protection', *Oxford Review of Economic Policy* 6(1), 17–33.

UNEP (1994) *Greenhouse Gas Abatement Costing Studies, Phase Two Report, Part 1: Main Report and Part 2: Country Studies*, UNEP Collaborating Centre on Energy and Environment, Risø National Laboratory, Denmark.

# CHAPTER 24

# Federal Issues and the European Union

## Key concepts

| | | |
|---|---|---|
| subsidiarity | asymmetric information | fiscal tiers |
| spillovers | harmonisation | tax competition |
| Federalism | Tiebout hypothesis | |

## 24.1 Introduction

**Assignment problem**

The issue of which functions should be assigned to which tier of government

The principal concern of this chapter is the **assignment problem**, the question of which of the functions of government should be placed in the hands of local or regional government and which should be executed by a central or federal authority. This issue has played a central part in the politics of Europe in the last decade or so, while in many nations, including Spain, the UK and Italy, movements advocating regional autonomy have come to play a major role in political decision-making. We shall concentrate on some underlying economic principles, using the European Union (EU) as an example of the dilemmas to be faced, but it is worthwhile noting our limits here: as countries such as the UK, the former Soviet Union, Yugoslavia, Canada and the EU itself demonstrate, much of the emotive debate over sovereignty and autonomy cannot be placed within a narrow economic framework.

## 24.2 Why have layers of government?

We begin with a basic question: What is the economic case for having different layers of government?

### Why have higher levels of government?

Imagine a region populated by small and identical communities. There are three main arguments why these communities might wish to pool their sovereignty and form a higher level of government which reigns over all of them.

### Economies of scale in government

The broadly fixed costs of foreign embassies, tax collection and the civil service may be shared by pooling sovereignty. Meanwhile, demand for some goods, such as judicial judgements, is intermittent. If localities share one judiciary they can share the costs of a permanent justice system.

### Spillovers

**Spillovers**

External effects (including pecuniary externalities) between jurisdictions

The second argument is familiar from the discussion of the provision of international public goods in the previous chapter and arises because, for many games, the Nash equilibrium is not Pareto efficient. If one town provides a free swimming pool, individuals in a neighbouring town may elect to free-ride (or free-swim) rather than pay for their own pool there are spillover effects. If the first town anticipates this and decides not to build its own pool, because its citizens would not enjoy a congested pool, then the result may not be provision of the public good.[1]

Therefore, as long as costs (or benefits) from one region spill over into another, and these costs are not considered when one region makes its decisions, then there is scope for deviation from the optimal and therefore a role for higher level government. The welfare gain from centralisation depends on two factors: (1) the gap between the optimal value of $x$ and its non-cooperative level and (2) the curvature of the benefit function. If, for instance, the optimal value of $x$ chosen by one community is highly sensitive to the optimal value of $x$ chosen by the other, then the gap described in (1) is likely to be large. However, if the benefit function is fairly flat, the resulting loss of welfare may be minor.[2]

If the provision of service $x$ by one community raises the incentive for an adjacent community to increase $x$ itself, then the services of the two communities are *strategic complements* and the level of $x$ chosen by the communities acting separately will tend to be above the optimum. Conversely, if as with the swimming pool, the incentive to provide $x$ is lowered by the provision of $x$ by other communities, then the services are **strategic substitutes** and the level of $x$ chosen by the communities acting in isolation will tend to be too low.

**Strategic substitutes**

Strategies where the marginal gain from increasing one player's strategy decreases if the level of the other player's strategy rises

Public goods, such as defence and other non-excluded goods such as free healthcare and social protection expenditure, are therefore strategic substitutes, as are taxes on capital and corporations, both of which tend to be mobile and attracted to low-tax communities. Meanwhile, inward investment subsidies, infrastructure and education spending (provided labour is immobile) are strategic complements. Note the dependence on the degree of mobility of the item in question or, in the case of non-excluded services, of the potential users.

### The indirect spillovers case

A useful distinction can be made between policies where the spillovers are large enough in themselves to justify provision by a central government and those

---

[1] Thus in this, and many other cases, the argument for higher level government follows closely that for the provision of public goods and in general. See Chapter 4 and sections on transboundary pollution in Chapter 23.

[2] For instance, within The Netherlands, a large deviation from the highest point in the country will not mean a significant drop in height, but on Everest, even a small change in coordinates can mean a difference to one's altitude.

functions where the case for centralisation is indirect. Suppose that two policies are interrelated in the sense that the optimal value of one depends on the optimal value for another. However, viewed individually, it is only desirable to centralise one. If, though, responsibility for this policy is transferred to a central authority, this typically raises the gains from coordination of the second policy area. For instance, if countries or regions are restricted in their ability to engage in competitive subsidy of inward investment, they may switch to subsidising alternatives such as training or education, which then creates arguments for the central control of training subsidies. As we shall see below, many of the arguments for centralisation in the European Union seem to be of this kind.

### Coordination

Suppose two adjacent communities, Trumpton and Camberwick Green, have connecting road systems; each can legislate in favour of driving on the right or driving on the left. If they both agree 'left' or they both agree 'right' drivers will be able to move safely between the towns, but if they choose different sides of the road, drivers will have to cross over between the towns, inevitably causing confusion and accidents. The payoffs are therefore as shown.

|  |  | Trumpton | |
|---|---|---|---|
|  |  | Left | Right |
| Camberwick Green | Left | 1,1 | 0,0 |
|  | Right | 0,0 | 1,1 |

Obviously either (Left, Left) or (Right, Right) would be preferred by each community, yet if they each choose separately, there is no guarantee that (Left, Right) will not be chosen. A higher level government could simply choose one side of the road and both communities would be happy. Areas where coordination brings gains include legal and trading systems, product and safety regulation and transport systems.

These three arguments are not overwhelming: adjacent communities can harmonise through agreement without the need for an overarching authority and, as we saw in Chapter 4, public goods may be supplied by voluntary action at the Pareto-efficient level, provided the numbers of players are small, relationships are repeated and all players are patient, conditions which can characterise adjacent communities. The Eurovision Song Contest, for instance, is not provided by any European government, but through agreement and cooperation. More importantly (perhaps), so are UEFA, NATO and the World Trade Organisation (WTO).

## Why have local government?

Let us now imagine the opposite end of the spectrum: one overarching state. Why might there be Pareto gains from splitting up that state into smaller units?

### Local information

The essential argument focuses on the knowledge available at the local level about the costs and benefits of local public goods, that is, non-rival goods, the enjoyment of which can be denied to people living outside a particular area (see Oates, 1972).

Suppose a national government has to set the level of a local public good, such as the fire service. Without local information it sets a uniform level, shown as $QN$ in Figure 24.1, which is where the average of the two communities' marginal benefit curves cuts the marginal cost line. If the communities are not identical, as is the case in Figure 24.1, then each would wish to deviate from this point; in other words both lose from uniform provision. Left to its own devices, Trumpton would set public good provision at $Q^T$, with $Q^C$ as the corresponding level for Camberwick Green. The total cost of the uniform national policy is therefore the shaded area in the diagram, divided between ABC for Trumpton and BDE for Camberwick Green, against which must be weighed any savings from centralising administration.[3]

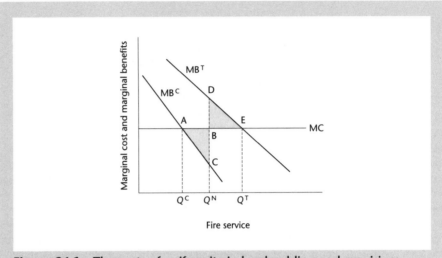

**Figure 24.1** The costs of uniformity in local public good provision

**Tiebout
Theorem**

States that Pareto efficiency in local public good provision can come about through the mobility of citizens between competing jurisdictions

The **Tiebout Theorem** provides an extreme example of the potential value of local control. Within its framework, agents vote with their feet to choose a local community on the basis of its local public good provision, just like consumers opting between different suppliers in the competitive market for a private good. If the conditions of the theorem are met, then the outcome is Pareto-efficient, which is a remarkable result, since it obviates the need for the kind of preference revelation mechanisms discussed in Chapter 4. There we saw that naive methods of preference elicitation could lead to under- or overprovision of public goods, while sophisticated mechanisms, such as the Clarke tax, were probably too complex to be practical. For local public goods, the Tiebout Theorem offers an apparently simple means of solving the preference revelation problem, so it is worthwhile exploring its underlying assumptions in a little more detail.

The main assumptions of the basic Tiebout model are: (1) costless mobility for all citizens; (2) full information about the choices on offer; (3) the number of communities is greater than the number of citizen types and each has a fixed provision of the local public good, the costs of which are split equally between all local residents; (4) returns to scale are not present or, at least, exhausted at low levels of provision;

---

[3] Note the no-spillovers assumption implicit in this diagram, i.e. that the provision of fire protection changes in Trumpton does not alter the marginal benefits to providing the same good in neighbouring Camberwick Green (and vice versa).

(5) citizens' incomes are independent of where they reside, and (6) no spillovers. Under these conditions, consumers sort themselves into homogeneous communities where every member shares the same preferences for the public good.

Unfortunately, these assumptions *are* extreme. Typically, moving between communities is not costless; information is not complete. Meanwhile, if there is more than one public good, then the number of communities has to be extremely large and this requirement can clash with assumption (4). For instance, if there are 100 different preferred levels of fire services provision and 100 levels of leisure facility provision, then there must be at least 10,000 communities if all types of preference are to be served. Incomes often do depend on location: lifeguards typically earn more in Majorca than in Madrid and finally as we have noted, the benefits of local public goods often do spill over into neighbouring communities.

The Tiebout Theorem is therefore best classified alongside the Ricardian Equivalence Theorem (see Chapter 12) and the Fundamental Theorems (see Chapter 2) as a proposition which does not claim to be true, but rather sets out the kind of conditions which would have to be fulfilled if it were to be true. It thereby provides us with a guide to how the real world differs from the perfect model.

### Public choice

A second kind of reason for local control is based more on public choice foundations, but is related to the ideas of the Tiebout Theorem. Bureaucrats and politicians have private information about the costs of providing public goods. If there are multiple units producing the same public good, then voters can compare the performance of their community with others with similar characteristics and use this to temper the rent seeking ambitions of their public servants. The value of this yardstick competition will be felt particularly if politicians aim to maximise revenue (the 'Leviathan' hypothesis), as is argued by Brennan and Buchanan (1980). In their model, the ability of citizens to vote with their feet limits the ability of politicians to raise taxes and so more decentralised political systems should have lower expenditure. While intuitively appealing, in two comparisons, of forty-three countries and of the US states, respectively, Oates (1985) found no evidence of a link between the degree of decentralisation and public sector size. Against this, Zax's (1989) study is amongst a number of those which do find a positive link between centralisation and public sector size, especially within the USA.

### Small is beautiful

Smaller communities may give individuals a greater sense of autonomy and of community. These kinds of argument can be compelling for some people, even if they do not necessarily fit into a simple economic framework. They may also nurture the voluntary provision of the kind of public goods (e.g. 'neighbourliness'), which are not usually produced through the formal mechanisms of the state.

## Why have multilevel government?

In practice, most countries have several tiers of government. In Britain, there are at least two tiers for all citizens and three for some (UK, county and town in England; UK, country and region or city in Scotland and Wales); in France and Germany four tiers of government are the norm. Part of the argument in favour of such a mix is that the optimal decision level differs between public goods. Defence issues are unsuitable items for local agendas, because of the spillovers; swimming pool provision is best left to local decision-makers. However, a moment's thought suggests that each area of government activity probably has a different optimal level. Moreover, optimal government regions might not form a simple hierarchy, with higher levels of government including all lower levels under their domain. Folkestone and Calais, for instance, might find it beneficial to share a jurisdiction to cover Channel Tunnel issues, but Calais would presumably want to be under French jurisdiction when it comes to making a decision about the appropriate side of the road to drive on, just as Folkestone would want to stay with the rest of Britain.

Economies of scope in government provide the main argument against this kind of patchwork of jurisdictions. Given only a limited number of tiers of government, the question of which tier will deal with what function is known as the *assignment problem*, mentioned in the introduction. Grouping functions together means that no single activity is provided at its optimal level; instead there is a trade-off between internalising spillovers and responding to local information. Added into the equation is the issue of separability between activities, whether, in other words, the optimal level of one activity depends on the level of another activity. This is a question which we will return to in section 24.4.

These arguments about the appropriate design of government are relatively simple, but they mask a fundamental issue about where power should truly lie. For instance, a national government may make decisions at a national level, but use local information about demand for local public goods to institute the decentralised outcome depicted in Figure 24.1. Thus there is local differentiation, but no true political decentralisation.[4] Similarly, as we noted in this section, through negotiation local governments may reach agreement between themselves about the provision of a good with strong spillover effects. Thus in theory the same level of provision of national and local public goods could be achieved through three different means: one higher tier of government; two sovereign communities; or two tiers of government, with one function assigned to each tier.[5] In practice, we might wonder if this conclusion is justified. Perhaps there is something missing from our discussion that means these three different forms of government will not lead to the same outcome. Questions of this type are also faced by economists interested in vertical relationships between firms; questions, for instance, about why firms make some components in-house and buy in others. One important lesson seems to be that issues of this kind are better studied in a framework which allows for the fact that in the real world it is not always possible for two parties to make a binding contract over all aspects of a deal or, more fundamentally, to cover all contingencies. Thus contracts are *incomplete*. In the context of relationships between independent communities (or, say, countries in the EU), if binding contracts are not enforceable for some variables (say the regulation of job markets) then this may increase the argument for the creation of a central government.

Paul Seabright (1996) offers a reason for decentralisation, based on public choice considerations, which provides an example of incomplete contracts reasoning at work. In his model, voters have no direct power over public good provision; instead their elected politicians choose between serving their own goals and serving the

---

[4] In practice, perhaps because of the economies of scale reasons discussed above, the functions of local government are often a mixture of the administration of national policies and locally determined policies.
[5] In the latter case, the two lower level communities may still have to coordinate provision of local public good production if there are complementarities between it and the national public good.

electorate. The greater the extent that the electorate is sacrificed, the greater the probability that the government will not be re-elected at the end of its term, a possibility it wishes to avoid. Public good provision can be locally differentiated by a central government or governments can be local, in which case each local council can decide upon its own public good provision. Spillovers make centralisation of power desirable, but an opposing force for local control is created by the increase in accountability associated with local government. In other words, a national government can only be dethroned by a national vote against it. Meanwhile, local voters control the fate of a local government, which will therefore tend to be more sensitive to its voters' wishes. As in standard models, larger spillovers push the argument in favour of centralised government, but one interesting conclusion from the model arises out of politicians' desire to be re-elected. If the costs of not being re-elected are higher for national politicians than for their local equivalents, then this improves the case for central control. Alternatively, if it is local politicians who most fear loss of office, then local control is more likely to be optimal.

Other arguments stress the constitutional importance of uniformity at the national level, even if the information on local preferences is available. If taxes are set at the national level, then a larger region could effect a hidden transfer from a smaller region by voting in local public good provision rules which favour its own region. Uniformity of local public good provision is then the price to be paid to avoid discrimination.

Arguments of this kind are relatively new in public economics and consequently underdeveloped (though see also Tirole, 1994). They are likely to receive more attention in the future, particularly in the EU, with its perennial questions about the appropriate assignment of powers. Nevertheless, the trade-off between internalising spillovers and fine-tuning policies to local preferences always seems to be fundamental to the discussion in one way or another. On this basis, Musgrave and Musgrave (1984) have proposed the following rules for assignment of taxes between authorities:[6]

1. Progressive, redistributive taxation should be the responsibility of the central authority, given the relative mobility of labour.
2. More generally, the centre should have responsibility for all taxes on mobile goods and factors, such as capital.
3. Local taxes should be based on immobile factors, such as land or on user fees for local services.
4. For equity reasons, the centre should also assume responsibility for the taxation of assets which are distributed unevenly, such as natural resources.

These assignment rules were formalised in an American context and may not, for instance, be applicable for the EU, where the low mobility of labour between Member States provides one reason for confining redistributive policies to a lower level of government.

## Federal and unitary governments

Before moving on, it is worth pointing out the obvious: the assignment problem and the issue of what levels of government to have do not take place in an institutional

---

[6] Note that there need be no match between the assignment of expenditure and taxation functions, so that transfers between one level of government and another may be necessary. Moreover these transfers may be formalised in a constitution, so that the central authority becomes an effective machine for administering and collecting taxes, but has little or no responsibility for spending them.

vacuum. Many states, such as the USA, Germany, Australia and Canada are explicitly federal in nature, while others, such as the UK (for the time being) and France, are unitary. In a unitary state, the central government may decide on how many lower tiers of government it wishes to have, on the geographical split between jurisdictions and on which powers it wishes to decentralise. Typically, in a **federal state**, the central government is constrained: it cannot alter the boundaries of its constituent states, except with their agreement; the states may, in theory, secede from the federation and some functions are assigned to the states.

**Federal state**

A country in which the physical boundaries and responsibilities of tiers of goverment are constitutionally fixed

Some indication of the importance of institutional context is provided by Table 24.1 Part of the variation shown in this table is due to the same economic forces acting in barely comparable environments: many states in Germany or the USA have populations higher than Austria or Switzerland; some provinces and states in the three largest countries could swallow whole the three European countries, but even between apparently similar countries, significant differences remain. Australian expenditure, for instance, is far more centralised than Canadian.

**Table 24.1** Percentage division of expenditure between central government, state and local levels in six federal countries

| | Australia (1988) | | Austria (1989) | | Canada (1989) | | Switzerland (1984) | | USA (1988) | | Germany (1987) | | Average | | |
|---|---|---|---|---|---|---|---|---|---|---|---|---|---|---|---|
| | C | S | C | S | C | S | C | S | C | S | C | S | C | S | L |
| General public services, public order | 43 | 46 | 76 | 24 | 42 | 36 | 25 | 42 | 45 | 18 | 30 | 47 | 37 | 38 | 25 |
| Defence | 100 | 0 | 100 | 0 | 100 | 0 | 86 | 0 | 100 | 0 | 100 | 0 | 97 | 1 | 1 |
| Education | 10 | 90 | 68 | 32 | 4 | 31 | 7 | 57 | 4 | 25 | 2 | 75 | 5 | 56 | 39 |
| Health | 42 | 57 | 79 | 21 | 3 | 90 | 46 | 31 | 50 | 35 | 73 | 12 | 43 | 45 | 12 |
| Social security, welfare, housing | 86 | 9 | 91 | 9 | 65 | 29 | 80 | 7 | 75 | 15 | 72 | 12 | 75 | 14 | 11 |
| Recreation, culture, religious affairs | 29 | 38 | 59 | 41 | 19 | 24 | 6 | 30 | 15 | 13 | 3 | 27 | 14 | 26 | 59 |
| Total | 53 | 42 | 84 | 16 | 42 | 40 | 48 | 28 | 59 | 18 | 61 | 22 | 52 | 30 | 18 |

C = central government; S = state government; L = local government. L values can be inferred from C and S values for individual countries, noting that Austria has only two tiers. The average omits Austria. 'Total' includes two other areas of expenditure: economic affairs and 'other'.
Source: Adapted from Costello, Table 1, 1993a

Apart from defence, which is almost totally controlled at the national level, and education, where almost all expenditure takes place at state and local level, other areas of expenditure show a wide variation. Health is mainly centrally administered in Germany, but devolved almost entirely to the provincial level in Canada. The bulk of social security expenditure is nationally organised, but Canada is again an outlier, while the bulk of recreation spending is locally administered, except in Australia, where responsibility is split evenly between three tiers of government.

## Assignment in the UK

In the UK, the unitary nature of the state has enabled an enormous amount of change to take place in the shape of local government and the functions assigned to it (see Appendix 1 of Byrne, 1994, for a summary). The current structure, which is about to change once more with the creation of assemblies in Northern Ireland, Scotland and Wales, involves twenty-two single-tier authorities in Wales and twenty-nine in Scotland. In England the situation is more complex. Within London, metropolitan areas such as Birmingham and across much of the remainder of England, local government is in the form of a single tier which handles all locally provided services. However, in a number of counties, such as Norfolk, there are two tiers: a county council, below which are usually several district councils.

**Table 24.2**   The assignment of expenditure functions in the UK

| Local | | National | United Kingdom |
|---|---|---|---|
| District | County | England<br>Northern Ireland<br>Scotland<br>Wales | |
| • Refuse collection<br>• Environmental health<br>• Housing<br>• Local tax collection | • Planning, strategic and transport<br>• Education and libraries<br>• Refuse disposal<br>• Roads<br>• Personal social services<br>• Consumer protection<br>• Fire and police services | • Health<br>• Higher education<br>• Transport<br>• Legal system<br>• Inward investment and economic development<br>• Agriculture and the environment<br>• Housing policy<br>• Local government | • The UK constitution<br>• Foreign policy<br>• Relations with Europe<br>• Defence and national security<br>• Macroeconomic policy<br>• Common markets for UK goods and services<br>• Employment legislation<br>• Social security<br>• Most transport safety and regulation<br>• Broadcasting regulation |

Notes: (1) Unitary councils combine the functions listed under 'local'; (2) the listing anticipates that the enacted constitutional changes for Northern Ireland, Scotland and Wales will be implemented by 2001 as planned; it omits the regional assemblies proposed for England; (3) it is not exhaustive and in many areas functions overlap between tiers to a significant degree; (4) in London most local functions are assigned to the boroughs, but a London-wide authority (to be replaced by an executive mayor) has some responsibilities, for example public transport, fire and police services; (5) in Northern Ireland, the 26 district councils are not responsible for education, fire and police services, housing and highways (see HMSO, 1996).

In broad terms, the assignment pattern displayed in Table 24.2 follows that seen in the federal countries of Table 24.1; generally, too, higher levels of government are responsible for goods with higher spillover effects. However, there are some anomalies; inward investment promotion, for instance, is a good with strong strategic complementarities that is nevertheless largely under the control of national assemblies rather than the federal parliament as a whole. Moreover, in the UK local diversity is restricted in practice, first by the controlling effects of central government policy and second, by the limited tax-gathering powers of lower tiers of government. A typical district or county, for instance, receives around 80% of its income from central government (Byrne, 1994), while revenue allocation for Wales, Northern Ireland and Scotland as a whole is closely tied to the Treasury's allocation for England through a series of formulae.[7]

## 24.3 The European Union

The European Union (EU) provides a case study in the economics of federalism. For its own citizens, it is also an important element of government in its own right (see Box 24.1).

---

**BOX 24.1**

### The European Union – A snapshot

Established by the six founding countries (Belgium, France, West Germany, Italy, Luxembourg and The Netherlands) in 1957, it was later expanded with the accession of Denmark, Ireland and the United Kingdom (1973), Greece (1981), Spain and Portugal (1986) and Austria, Finland and Sweden (1993). Major constitutional changes have built on the Treaty of Rome, the founding agreement, and include the Single European Act (SEA) of 1986, the Maastricht Treaty (Treaty on European Union, 1993) and the Amsterdam Treaty (1997). The Treaty on Economic Union (TEU) sets out the main objectives of the Members, notably:

> The Community shall have as its task, by establishing a common market and an economic union to promote throughout the Community a harmonious and balanced development of economic activities, sustainable and non-inflationary growth respecting the environment, a high degree of convergence of economic performance, a high level of employment and social protection, the raising of the standard of living and quality of life and economic and social cohesion and solidarity among Member States (TEU, 2)

The *main* institutions of the EU are:

1. **The European Commission** is headed by the President of the EU with twenty commissioners, nominated by Member States (two each from the five most populated countries, one each from the smaller), and is both the bureaucracy but also the initiator of legislation and the mediator between Member States, as well as the organ responsible for seeing that legislation is enforced and the representative of the EU in external negotiations (e.g. over world trade).

---

[7] Though these formulae will continue to apply post-devolution, the Scottish Parliament alone will have the ability to change the standard rate of income tax in Scotland within 3% of the UK rate.

2. **The Council of Ministers**, comprising the ministers of each Member State, which initiates and agrees legislation, by the unanimity rule in some areas, but increasingly by qualified majority voting (see below). In addition, under the TEU, the **European Council** which meets for a summit twice a year and consists of the President of the EU, the heads of Member State governments (except France, from which the President attends), and foreign ministers has become a formal organ of government, responsible for laying down strategy, but leaving formal decisions to the Council of Ministers.

3. **The European Parliament (EP)** is directly elected by citizens in the Member States and traditionally the weakest leg of the decision-making process; it has authority to amend some legislation, 'co-decision-making' powers in some areas and oversees the actions of the Commission and the Council of Ministers, as well as more draconian powers, which it has never used, including the ability to sack the entire Commission.

4. **The European Court of Justice** (ECJ) and the Court of Auditors are the supreme court and the auditing authority of the EU, respectively. In areas of conflict the ECJ has precedence over national courts, as community law has precedence over national law.

**Qualified Majority Voting (QMV)** In most instances (including fisheries, agriculture, the internal market, environment issues and transport), the Council decides by QMV. At least 62 votes must be cast in favour for a proposal to be carried, but if the proposer is not the Commission then at least 10 Member States must vote in favour as well. Member States have weights as follows:

| | |
|---|---|
| Germany, France, Italy and the United Kingdom | 10 votes |
| Spain | 8 votes |
| Belgium, Greece and The Netherlands | 5 votes |
| Austria and Sweden | 4 votes |
| Ireland, Denmark and Finland | 3 votes |
| Luxembourg | 2 votes |
| Total | 87 votes |

This box provides the minimum necessary for an understanding of the remainder of the chapter, but we also suggest the reader consults the EU's website, Europa, or one of the wide number of good texts on the EU, such as El Agraa (1994), Hitiris (1994) or Artis and Lee (1994), for a fuller picture.

As far as the economic theory of federalism goes, there are at least three main ways in which the EU differs from a typical federal nation. First, the small budget of the EU (see below) means that the union is heavily constrained in its ability to effect substantial income changes across Europe. As we saw in Chapter 5 and again in our discussion of transboundary pollution in Chapter 23, the achievement of an optimal level of a policy variable often means one agent compensating another. If Ann owns the right to smoke, then Bill must compensate her to get her agreement to reduce her smoking. In a true federal system, the feasible limit on income transfers between regions is large enough to enable such an efficient bargain to be achieved. If such transfers are constrained, then also constrained is the ability to achieve Paretian gains from coordinating policies.

Second, and perhaps underlying the first point, many individuals within the EU feel a much weaker concern with the welfare of citizens in other parts of the union compared to citizens in their own country. There is no consensus for large income transfers across the EU, from Germany to Greece for instance, in the same way that there often is a consensus for transfers within a country.

Third, the cohesion of national legal systems and the coordination of much of tax policy by national governments limit within-country tax avoidance and tax evasion. However, the sharing of tax and income information between countries in the EU is still at a relatively primitive stage, making it easier to avoid taxes or even evade them by switching transactions between countries (see Box 24.2 for two examples).

These three factors are matters of degree, not kind; the EU shares many of the features of the federal nations. What in particular makes it more than an intergovernmental conference is the increasing use of qualified majority voting in place of the unanimity rule.

## Budget

Budget-setting procedures have changed with the growth of the EU, but the Council of Ministers, the Commission and the Parliament all play a part (see Artis and Lee, 1994, for details), under the principle of co-decision making. Table 24.3 provides a snapshot of the EU's budget, showing the main areas of expenditure:

1. **The Common Agricultural Policy** – takes up the lion's share of expenditure, although its role has diminished in the last ten years.

2. **Structural operations** – include payments to the EU's structural and cohesion funds, designed to aid development in the poorer or more marginal areas of the community and to cushion the undesirable aspects of other policies.

3. **Internal policies** – include expenditure on research support, the environment, trans-European networks and education.

4. **External action** – means such things as aid to developing countries and eastern Europe.

The principal sources of income for the EU are:

1. **Agricultural duties** – including the tax on sugar production.

2. **Customs Duties** – which, in calculations of the net contribution to the budget, are typically assigned to the country in which the goods are landed. This gives rise to the 'Rotterdam effect' whereby Dutch contributions to the EU budget appear excessive.

3. **VAT** – traditionally the largest source of revenue, though in decline. Member States must pay a proportion of their *potential* VAT revenue from a commonly defined base, which can be no larger than 55% of GNP for States with average per-capita income above 90% of the EU's average figure, and no larger than 50% for the remaining States. There is a cap on VAT revenue of 1.4% of its potential yield, declining to 1% by 1999.

4. **The Fourth Resource** – a proportionate levy on the GNP of Member States, capped at 1.2% of GNP in 1996, rising to 1.24% in 1997. This last form of income allows Member States to raise their contributory revenue in any way they see fit, removing some of the pressure to harmonise VAT systems.

**Table 24.3** The budget of the European Union (ECU million)

|  | 1996 | 1997 (forecast) |
|---|---|---|
| **Expenditure** |  |  |
| Common Agricultural Policy | 40828.0 | 41805.0 |
| Structural Operations | 29131.0 | 31477.0 |
| Internal Policies | 5337.0 | 5603.0 |
| External Action | 5264.0 | 5622.0 |
| Administration | 4191.0 | 4352.0 |
| Reserves | 1152.0 | 1158.0 |
| Compensation | 701.0 | 212.0 |
| **Income** |  |  |
| Agricultural duties | 808.8 | 873.4 |
| Sugar and Isoglucose Levies | 1210.4 | 1366.0 |
| Customs Duties (net of collection costs) | 11560.1 | 11979.2 |
| VAT own Resources | 35595.8 | 34587.8 |
| GNP-based own Resources | 21084.4 | 32947.2 |
| Balance of VAT and GNP-based from previous years | 833.7 | – |
| Budget Balance from previous year | 9215.2 | – |
| Other | 720.0 | 612.0 |
| Total | 81028.0 | 82365.6 |

Note: At the time of writing 1.5 ECU = £1
Source: Eurostat, 1997

The picture which emerges from this table is the limited extent of EU expenditure and income compared to its Member States. With a population of 340 million, six times that of the UK, EU government expenditure is only one-quarter of the annual UK budget. Now, the impact of a government is not measured by the size of its expenditure; laws and regulations may have an impact out of all proportion to their budgetary cost. Nevertheless, the low figure for the EU budget (less than 2% of EU GDP) and the fact that nearly one-half of that is taken up with the Common Agricultural Policy, means that it has only a limited ability to execute compensatory income transfers and certainly does not for instance have the budget required to engage in meaningful Keynesian demand. However, for the poorer, smaller nations of the EU, such as Portugal, Ireland and Greece, transfers from the EU can be significant, making up to 5% of GDP.

## 24.4 The assignment problem in the European Union

We have already encountered most of the issues relevant for an economic appraisal of what functions should be assigned to the EU and which should remain with Members States and noted the ways in which the EU differs from a nation state. Broadly

**Subsidiary**

A principle which states that the functions of government should be assigned to the lowest possible tier compatible with the internalisation of spillover effects

speaking the EU policy of **subsidiarity** conforms to these principles, since it advocates assigning only those decisions to the centre which cannot be made adequately at the national level. However, while the framework is clear, the details of the argument make it much less apparent which functions should be assigned to Brussels and which to Member States. We illustrate the arguments in two ways: first in Table 24.4, we list some of the objectives for the EU agreed by Member States in the 1993 Maastricht Treaty. Alongside each we suggest a justification for centralisation, based on the arguments of section 24.2. Second, in the remainder of the section we examine the particular issue of tax harmonisation.

**Table 24.4**   EU objectives and the economic case for their centralisation

| Objective | Economic justification for centralisation |
| --- | --- |
| (a)  Trade liberalisation within the EU | (The original economic goal of the community); to avoid the harmful effects of trade barriers |
| (c)  A single market, based on the four freedoms, goods, services, persons and capital | Necessary for (a) |
| (d)  Measures on the entry and movement of people from outside the EU | Local policies not feasible given (c) |
| (g)  A system of competition policy in the single market | Desirable once (c) in place |
| (h)  Harmonising the laws of Member States to the extent required for operating the common market | Necessary for (c) and therefore (a) |
| (i)  A social policy, comprising the European Social Fund | Side-payments necessary to lubricate achievement of (a) and (c) |
| (j)  Strengthening economic and social cohesion | Side-payments necessary to lubricate achievement of (a) and (c), plus to avoid 'social dumping' – the competitive lowering of national levels of social protection |
| (k)  An environmental policy | Spillovers between nations, e.g. acid rain, pollution of shared river basins |
| (l)  Strengthening the competitiveness of Community industry | Unclear |
| (m) Promoting research and technological development | Economies of scale, perhaps |
| (n)  Encouragement for establishing and developing trans-European networks | Coordination |
| (o)  A contribution to a high level of health protection | Unclear |
| (s)  A contribution to strengthen consumer protection | Unclear |

Note: the letters are those of the TEU, section 3

As can be seen from the table, particularly goals (c–j), the case for centralisation is largely an indirect one, arising from the original case for an economic community or from measures taken to support its achievement. Only (k), (m) and (n) have clearly separate justifications, while for some of the goals, such as health protection, it is hard to provide any reason for centralisation and this accords with the pattern of health expenditure across federal nations, depicted in Table 24.1.

## Tax competition, harmonisation and coordination

**Tax competition**

The tendency for countries to undercut each others' tax rates on internationally mobile goods, such as capital

**Tax competition** describes a situation in which communities compete for footloose factors of production, particularly capital, by lowering tax rates. Tax harmonisation occurs when a central government limits the allowable range for a tax levied by lower tiers of government. In the EU, the minimum standard VAT rate is now 15% with existing exemptions respected, but further extensions discouraged. Tax coordination refers to a more general situation where the Member States of the union seek to agree on tax rates. Unlike tax harmonisation, where some rates fall as others rise, all taxes may rise (or fall) with coordination.

The four freedoms (goods, services, people and capital) embodied in the 1986 Single European Act (SEA) are a classic instance of a case where attempts to coordinate policy in one arena have implications for the desirability of coordination in other policy-making areas. First, lowering the barriers to the free flow of goods and factors makes these items more mobile (see Box 24.2). This increases the incentive for Member States to engage in tax competition. Second, higher mobility generally means higher administrative costs and this is particularly true when greater cooperation between national tax authorities is required.

**Destination principle**

When goods are taxed at rates applicable in the country where they are consumed

In particular, the removal of cross-border controls raises the cost of collection of taxes based on the **destination principle**, that is, goods are taxed on the basis of where they are consumed, rather than where they are produced (the **origin principle**). VAT collection provides a good example of the problem, because its effective enforcement requires a chain of paper passing between each step in the production process. Each link charges VAT on the unfinished good, but provided the good is sold on, each link is able to claim back any VAT paid to earlier links, which gives them an incentive to cooperate in the procedure. Under the destination principle, exports are VAT free, so that the good enters the receiving country free of tax, but with the fresh documents necessary to create a new VAT chain. When border controls are removed, exporters are unable to claim back VAT paid, while tax authorities in the new country are unable to trace the movement of goods which they would like to tax.

**Origin principle**

When goods are taxed on the basis of where they were produced

If this is not acceptable, then there are two main options:

(A) Stick to the destination principle, but now have a central clearing house, which enables the chain to continue across countries.

(B) Move to the origin principle for taxation.

The EU advocates a version of option (A). Its current proposals involve a common system of paperwork. If country A exports a good worth 100 and adds on 10% VAT, but the rate of VAT in country B is 20%, then the differential is added once the good moves countries. Country A then must pay the original 10% to country B via the clearing house, once the fiscal year's tally has been made. This is a highly bureaucratic option; it does not remove the problem of cross-border shopping (see Box 24.2), since personal shoppers are not registered for VAT and it means that countries will face considerable uncertainties over their final VAT receipts.

## BOX 24.2

# Tax-gathering problems created by mobility

*Germany and capital flight*

Not only has Germany the highest rate of corporation tax amongst G7 countries, but in many recent years its level exceeded that of the next highest by 10% (Weichenrieder, 1996). As a result, Germany has seen tax revenue ebb away in three main ways. First, German companies have used transfer pricing to report profits in foreign subsidies abroad rather than at home. So, in 1988, BMW reported 88% of its profits at home, but by 1992, the proportion had collapsed to 5%. Second, companies have taken advantage of loopholes in Germany's double taxation treaties with other countries, and established passive investment vehicles in the USA, Benelux countries and Ireland designed to siphon off tax liabilities. As an example, in 1987 Ireland cut its corporation tax to 10% on foreign-owned subsidiaries creating purely financial investments in the country, provided at least 'some' jobs were created as a result in the financial centre of Dublin. In 1990, German firms owned DM1.9 billion worth of assets in Ireland, but by 1992 this had rocketed to DM12.9 billion. Third, foreign firms investing in Germany have debt-financed their operations, thereby opting to repatriate the net earnings from their investments as interest repayments and so paying corporation tax at their home rates. In 1990/1, 60% of foreign investment into Germany was loan-financed, compared to only 25% of investment by German firms abroad.

The German response to this has met with mixed success. In 1994, the corporation tax rate was cut to 44% and in the same year, attempts were made to limit excessive loan financing of inward investment, by treating 'loans' to highly geared subsidiaries as equity. The tax code has been altered in other ways, so that German firms investing abroad face tax on their subsidiaries' profits if more than 50% of those profits are earned from financial assets. German investment in Ireland slumped, but it is still substantially higher than pre-1987.

*Britain and alcohol*

In Germany it is the mobility of capital which has created problems for the tax authorities; in Britain it is the mobility of shoppers, crossing the Channel in the wake of the SEA, to take advantage of the lower duty rates on alcohol in France and Belgium. The scale of savings is substantial. On 1 January 1993, rates of duty on beer and wine were as follows:

|         | Duty on beer (Ecu/ hectolitre) | Duty on wine (Ecu/ hectolitre) |
|---------|------------|------------|
| UK      | 54.6       | 165.89     |
| Ireland | 92.4       | 271.88     |
| France  | 2.5        | 3.30       |
| Belgium | 14.6       | 36.28      |

In an effort to reduce border controls, the SEA sanctioned unlimited imports of goods between Member States for personal use. Faced with ambiguity over the exact interpretation of the last phrase, UK Customs and Excise suggest a figure of 120 litres of wine or beer as upper limits on what constitutes personal use. Such a figure would, for instance, allow savings of over £100 on the purchase of wine in Calais rather than Dover and Britons have rushed to take advantage of the opportunities. For 1993, Customs and Excise estimate a loss of £200 million duty.

Subsequently, the UK government has been lobbied hard for lower duties on alcohol by domestic producers, who argue that such a move would restore the lost revenue. This is unlikely to be case: perhaps only one-quarter of the population are in a position to profit from personal importation, so that, while any cut in tax rates might make the drink shoppers return to their local supermarket, the gains would be wiped out by the intramarginal loss of tax revenue from the captive three-quarters of the nation.

Alternative (B) has traditionally been viewed as equally flawed, since it is argued that moving to an origin principle would distort prices. The basic problem is illustrated using the following example of Germany and Portugal. Suppose that the Germans export machinery worth 100 DM to Portugal and Portugal exports 10,000 Escudos worth of shoes to Germany. The exchange rate is 1 DM = 100 Escudos and the VAT rates are 10% (Portugal) and 20% (Germany). Under the destination principle the price of machinery in Germany is 120 DM, the same as the price of shoes. In Portugal, the price of shoes is also equal to the price of machinery, at 11,000 Escudos, so there are no price distortions.

Now consider a switch to the origin principle. It appears that shoes in Germany fall in price to 110 DM, while machinery in Portugal rises in price, to 12,000 Escudos, changing the equilibria of the two economies. This implies an imbalance in trade, however, and so if there are no other countries in the world and the exchange rate is flexible, then the rate will change to 1 DM = 110/1.2 Escudos restoring the original equilibrium. At this rate, the price of shoes in Germany is now 10,000 × 1.1 × 1.2/110 = 120 DM; meanwhile, the price of machinery in Portugal becomes 100 × 1.2 × 110/1.2 = 11,000 Escudos. Trade is in balance, government revenues are unchanged and there is no difference in the real economy at all between the two systems of taxation (Shibata, 1967).

More recently, Lockwood *et al.* (1994, 1995) have argued that this result is more general than at first appears. It requires (a) a uniform national rate of taxation; (b) no holding of foreign assets (such as currency or shares) by domestic residents and that (c) at least either the exchange rate or the real wage to be flexible. But it is generalisable to any number of goods, to any market structure (oligopolistic, competitive, etc.) and to markets with transport costs. They argue that though conditions (a), (b) and (c) are not met completely in practice, the gains from reduced bureaucracy and lower rates of cross-border shopping are substantial enough for the origin principle to be the superior option.

There is one proviso: under most versions of the origin principle, exports to third countries face no tax, just as under the destination principle. This does mean that relative prices under origin and destination regimes will be different. Only if the origin principle is also applied to exported goods is the real economy identical under the two regimes. They therefore advocate a switch to origin taxation, with no exemption for exports.[8]

---

[8] However, it is worth pointing out that with European Monetary Union, assumption (c) is less likely to hold, weakening the arguments of the origin principle.

### Tax competition

The story so far has assumed that countries maintain existing tax rates. However, if the destination principle is maintained or prices are sticky, then greater integration gives countries higher incentives to engage in tax competition, that is, cutting taxes to attract revenue from abroad. Provided tax rates are significant, the incentive to cut tax rates is larger for smaller countries. This is because a cut in a tax rate on a mobile commodity will raise welfare in the domestic country, but (usually) lower revenue on existing, domestic sources, creating a cost in terms of lower expenditure on public goods or higher tax rates on other goods. But the lower rate will attract more of the mobile commodity into the country. For a small country the extra revenue attracted from larger neighbours will outweigh the domestic revenue lost. For a large country, with smaller neighbours, the balance will be reversed.

Tax competition is therefore more of a problem between large and small countries than it is between two equal-sized nations. Apart from doing nothing, there are three main ways of responding to it:

1. **Impediments**. As we saw in Box 24.2, it may be possible to reduce outflows of capital and shoppers by placing restrictions on personal imports or requiring firms to make active investments abroad if they are to avoid double taxation. However, there is still an incentive for countries to induce flows into the country as the Irish government's tax rules indicate and if the impediments to free movement are too large they can undo the original benefits of liberalisation.

2. **Harmonisation**. Lower bounds on tax rates can limit tax competition, while still preserving some element of autonomy for the countries involved. The EU has pressed for greater harmonisation in a number of areas with mixed success. Standard VAT rates are bounded below by 15%, while duty on wine, for instance, has a lower limit of 0%.

3. **Centralisation/standardisation**. In the limit harmonisation of tax rates leads to a single rate, which may be set by a central authority. We have seen in Chapter 11 that optimal tax rates depend on such factors as the degree of inequality aversion and the elasticity of demand. Since these factors vary between nations, there is a prima facie case for differentiation of tax rates between countries in general. However, as the VAT example discussed above illustrates, there are a number of savings on administrative costs which would accrue from a single EU tax rate. This suggests that once harmonised rates become close, full standardisation becomes desirable.

## 24.5 Conclusion

This chapter has concentrated on the issue of assignment, extending the theory of public goods encountered in Chapter 4 to a multijurisdictional world. We have seen that though the economic principles involved are often straightforward, the actual pattern of assignment that we observe has arisen as a result of the interaction of a number of forces, which often extend far wider than the narrow considerations of economic efficiency. The evolution of the European Union provides a good example; it was not created primarily to internalise economic spillovers, but as a political edifice to minimise the possibility of another pan-European war.

## Summary

- Spillovers provide the main case for centralising government powers.

- Local variation in tastes and costs makes local control more desirable, but the argument is undermined if a central authority can obtain the same information.

- The Tiebout Theorem provides conditions under which voting with the feet reveals individual valuations of local public goods and yields a Pareto-efficient outcome.

- Centralisation of some functions might be appropriate even if the direct case is limited, provided that these functions interact strongly with activities which have been centralised.

- Generally, taxes on mobile factors should be controlled by the central authority rather than local government, for which taxes on immobile goods such as property are more appropriate.

- Since people are mobile, it is usually argued that taxation for income-redistributive purposes should be centrally organised.

- The EU budget is small compared to that of most Member States. Largely missing from its functions are defence and income redistribution.

- Much of the argument for centralisation of activities in the EU is an indirect one, arising from goals such as the removal of internal barriers to trade and factor movement.

- Removal of borders makes taxes based on the destination principle harder to collect. Options include centralising their collection or moving to the origin principle, in which case goods sold for export should then be taxed at the same rate as goods not leaving the union.

## Questions

1. What tier of government should the following functions be assigned to: (a) social security expenditure, (b) bathing water quality and (c) company taxation? Do your answers depend on how other functions are assigned?

2. How should the size of a country change the argument over assignment, where size means (a) population and (b) geographical area?

3. How do improvements in information technology alter the balance of the arguments in the assignment problem?

4. 'Since voting with the feet leads to an efficient outcome, geographical mobility should be encouraged.' Discuss.

5. 'Models of benevolent government are unable to provide a convincing case against centralisation of all state functions. Therefore any justification for decentralisation must have public choice foundations.' Is this true?

6. Explain how the case for the origin principle in taxation changes (a) once border controls are removed and (b) after monetary union.

# Further reading

Classic texts on fiscal federalism include Tiebout (1956) and Oates (1972), with Brennan and Buchanan (1980) for the argument in favour of decentralisation as a constraint on the leviathan. Bewley (1981) is an advanced critique of the Tiebout thesis. Recent surveys of the theory of club goods (closely related to local public goods) can be found in Cornes and Sandler (1986) and Mueller (1989). King (1984) is a detailed text on the economics of fiscal tiers, while Costello (1993a, 1993b) are up-to-date surveys of the assignment problem set in the context of the EU. Sinn (1994) makes the case for greater coordination in many areas of EU policy. Smith (1993) and Keen (1994) are good sources on tax harmonisation issues and provide convenient entry points into the large literature on the subject.

The Website for the European Union is: **http://europa.eu.int/**. More information about the ongoing process of devolution in the UK can be found by accessing the Northern Ireland, Scottish and Welsh Offices through **http://www.open.gov.uk/**.

# References

Artis, M.J. and Lee, N. (eds) (1994) *The Economics of the European Union*, Oxford: Oxford University Press.

Bewley, T. (1981) 'A critique of Tiebout's theory of local expenditures', *Econometrica* 49, 713–40.

Brennan, G. and Buchanan, J. (1980) *The Power to Tax: Analytical Foundations of a Fiscal Constitution*, Cambridge: Cambridge University Press.

Byrne, T. (1994) *Local Government In Britain*, 6th edn, Harmondsworth: Penguin.

Cornes, R. and Sandler, T. (1986) *The Theory of Externalities, Public Goods and Club Goods*, Cambridge: Cambridge University Press.

Costello, D. (1993a) 'Fiscal federalism in theory and practice', *European Economy: Reports and Studies, No. 5*, Commission of the European Communities, 1–52.

Costello, D. (1993b) 'Public finances in federal and unitary states', *European Economy: Reports and Studies, No. 5*, Commission of the European Communities 53–112.

Crawford, I. and Tanner, S. (1995) 'Bringing it all back home: alcohol taxation and cross-border shopping', *Fiscal Studies* 16(2), 94–114.

El Agraa, A.M. (ed.) (1994) *The Economics of the European Community*, Hemel Hempstead: Philip Allan.

Eurostat (1997) *Europe in Figures*, Luxembourg: Eurostat.

Hitiris, T. (1994) *European Community Economics*, London: Harvester Wheatsheaf.

HMSO (1996) *Local Government*, London: HMSO.

Keen, M. (1994) 'The welfare economics of tax coordination in the European Community', *Fiscal Studies* 14(2), 15–36.

King, D. (1984) *Fiscal Tiers: The Economics of Multi-Level Government*, London: George Allen Unwin.

Lockwood, B., de Meza, D. and Myles, G. (1994) 'When are origin and destination tax regimes equivalent?', *International Journal of Public Finance* 1, 5–24.

Lockwood, B., de Meza, D. and Myles, G. (1995) 'On the European Union VAT proposals: the superiority of origin over destination taxation', *Fiscal Studies* 16(1), 1–18.

Mueller, D.C. (1989) *Public Choice II*, Cambridge: Cambridge University Press.

Musgrave, P. and Musgrave, N. (1984) *Public Finance in Theory and Practice*, New York: McGraw-Hill.

Oates, W.E. (1972) *Fiscal Federalism*, New York: Harcourt Brace and Jovanovich.

Oates, W. (1985) 'Searching for the Leviathan: an empirical study', *American Economic Review*, 75, No. 4, 748–57.

Seabright, P. (1996) 'Accountability and decentralisation in government: an incomplete contracts model', *European Economic Review* 40, 61–89.

Shibata, H. (1967) 'The theory of economic unions: a comparative analysis of customs unions, free trade areas and tax unions', in C. Shoup (ed.) *Fiscal Harmonisation in Common Markets*, Columbia: Columbia University Press, 145–67.

Sinn, H.W. (1994) 'How much Europe? Subsidiarity, centralization and fiscal competition', *Scottish Journal of Political Economy* 41(1), 85–107.

Smith, S. (1993) 'Subsidiarity and the coordination of indirect taxes in the European Community', *Oxford Review of Economic Policy* 9, 67–93.

Tiebout, C.M. (1956) 'A pure theory of local expenditure', *Journal of Political Economy* 64, 416–24.

Tirole, J. (1994) 'On the internal organisation of government', *Oxford Economic Papers* 46, 1–29.

Weichenrieder, A. (1996) 'Fighting international tax avoidance: the case of Germany', *Fiscal Studies* 17(1), 37–59.

Zax, F.S. (1989) 'Is there a Leviathan in your neighbourhood?', *American Economic Review* 79 No. 3, 560–7.

# Author Index

# Subject Index

# Planning and Enabling Learning
## in the

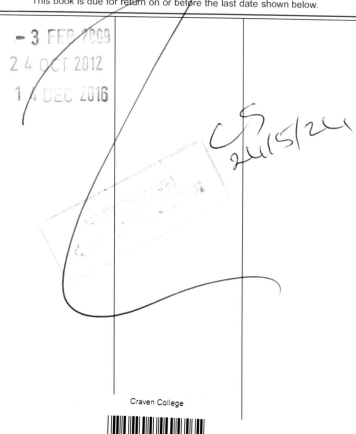